BY BIRTH OR CONSENT

Published for the OMOHUNDRO INSTITUTE OF

EARLY AMERICAN HISTORY AND CULTURE, *Williamsburg, Virginia,*

by the UNIVERSITY OF NORTH CAROLINA PRESS,

Chapel Hill and London

HOLLY BREWER

BY BIRTH OR CONSENT

CHILDREN, LAW, *and the* ANGLO-AMERICAN

REVOLUTION IN AUTHORITY

The Omohundro Institute of Early American History and Culture
is sponsored jointly by the College of William and Mary and the
Colonial Williamsburg Foundation. On November 15, 1996, the Institute
adopted the present name in honor of a bequest from
Malvern H. Omohundro, Jr.

Set in Scala types by Keystone Typesetting, Inc.
Manufactured in the United States of America

Library of Congress Cataloging-in-Publication Data
Brewer, Holly, 1964–
By birth or consent : children, law, and the Anglo-American revolution
in authority / Holly Brewer.
p. cm.
Includes bibliographical references and index.
ISBN-13: 978-0-8078-2950-9 (cloth : alk. paper)
ISBN-10: 0-8078-2950-1 (cloth: alk. paper)
ISBN-13: 978-0-8078-5832-5 (pbk. : alk. paper)
ISBN-10: 0-8078-5832-3 (pbk. : alk. paper)
1. Minors—England—History. 2. Children—Legal status, laws, etc.—
England—History. 3. Capacity (Law)—England—History. 4. Consent
(Law)—England—History. 5. Children—England—Social conditions.
I. Omohundro Institute of Early American History & Culture. II. Title.
KD735.B74 2005
346.4201'35—dc22   2004019071

The paper in this book meets the guidelines for permanence and
durability of the Committee on Production Guidelines for Book Longevity
of the Council on Library Resources.

This volume received indirect support from an unrestricted book
publications grant awarded to the Institute by the L. J. Skaggs and
Mary C. Skaggs Foundation of Oakland, California.

09 08 07 06 05   5 4 3 2 1
10 09 08 07 06   5 4 3 2 1

To my mother,
Gwendolyn Cleo Whitehead Brewer,
who first brought me into the
eighteenth century

"I shall desire, that the learned Reader will not conceive
any Opinion against any part of this painful and large Volume,
until he shall have advisedly read over the whole, and diligently searched
out, and well considered of the several Authorities, Proofs and Reasons
which we have cited and set down for Warrant and Confirmation
of our Opinions throughout this whole work."
Sir Edward Coke, *The First Part of the Institutes of the Laws of England*
(1628)

"Thus we are *born Free*, as we are born Rational; not that we
have actually the Exercise of either: Age that brings one, brings with
it the other too. And thus we see how *natural Freedom and Subjection to
Parents* may consist together, and are both founded on the same
Principle. A *Child* is *Free* . . . by his Father's Understanding,
which is to govern him, till he hath it of his own."
"To turn him loose to an unrestrain'd Liberty, before he has
Reason to guide him, is not the allowing him the priviledge of his Nature,
to be free; but to thrust him out amongst Brutes, and abandon him to a
state as wretched, and as much beneath that of a Man, as theirs. This is
that which puts the *Authority* into the *Parents* hands to govern the
Minority of their Children."
John Locke, *Two Treatises of Government* (1689)

"As far as I can judge from the experiments which have been
made, to give liberty to, or rather, to abandon persons whose habits
have been formed in slavery is like abandoning children."
Thomas Jefferson, January 26, 1788/9

ACKNOWLEDGMENTS

This project has been more than a decade in the making, and I owe many debts, of inspiration and aid, to more people than I can count and probably more than I will remember to acknowledge here.

The faculty I had the good fortune to work with at the University of California at Los Angeles were wonderful: from Gary Nash and Daniel Howe, who shaped my perspective and questions in very different ways, to Joyce Appleby, who influenced my intellectual development (particularly my fascination with political theory) more than she will ever know. John Brewer first encouraged me to use the law as a way to measure changing attitudes, and his seminars were always a delight because of his quirky insights about historical methods. Richard Ashcraft, Perry Anderson, and especially Carole Pateman guided me through early modern English political theory. My adviser, Ruth Bloch, has been beyond measure wonderful and supportive as I ventured the first tentative steps that broke new ground and challenged assumptions. Her subtle mind and careful reading not only helped to shape the book manuscript in its early phases but remain a continuing inspiration to me. I also want to thank the members of the Early American Thesis Seminar (EATS) at UCLA, who gave helpful comments over more than four years.

Some scholars who have commented on papers I gave at conferences, and on my work more generally, gave important feedback that really helped to shape the book. Three I want to mention in particular are Michael Grossberg, J. R. Pole, and Jan Lewis, whose comments on the book manuscript were especially thorough and rich. Chris Tomlins and Bruce Mann gave wonderful feedback on my "Age of Reason?" essay that appeared in their edited volume *The Many Legalities of Early America* (Chapel Hill, N.C., 2001) (parts of which appear in Chapters 5 and 7 in different form) that helped to shape the subtlety of my legal interpretation.

Several of my colleagues have read and commented on parts of the manuscript as I struggled for just the right expressions and flow, including David Zonderman and Ross Bassett. David Gilmartin deserves especial thanks (for being endlessly patient about titles). Members of the Triangle Early American History Seminar have also helped shape the final book, especially Don Higginbotham, Peter Wood, Bob Calhoon, John Nelson, and Jennie Lamonte.

I am grateful for a fellowship from the National Endowment for the Humanities, which provided essential support for the (backbreaking) portions of this book on children's criminal responsibility. That chapter would have been thin indeed without their support; I now regard it as one the most important sections of the book. The Littleton-Griswold Fund of the American Historical Association supported one of my early trips in graduate school, providing help at a critical time. I also received important support from North Carolina State University (via a leave, summer stipend, and research support). UCLA and the William Andrews Clark Memorial Library and the Center for Seventeenth- and Eighteenth-Century Studies provided essential fellowship support while I was in graduate school there that helped me to complete the research and writing of my dissertation.

The staffs at various libraries and archives have helped immeasurably. I would particularly like to thank the staff at the Library of Virginia (formerly the Virginia State Archives), most of all Brent Tarter, who was very kind to a young graduate student. The Chester County Archives in Pennsylvania was a very nice place to work. I also did some very pleasant work at the Massachusetts Archives. The staff at the Law Libraries at UCLA (which has a remarkable collection) were very helpful, as were the law library staffs at the University of North Carolina, Chapel Hill, and Duke University, who were patient with me as I requested books and cases that were long out of date and that no one else ever wants to see. The British Library and the Institute for Historical Research in London have been homes away from home for me at various points in my research. The newly refurbished Public Record Office was helpful as well. The regular libraries at the Research Triangle universities have been patient with my endless book requests. I especially wish to thank the staff at North Carolina State's "Tripsaver" office, which has indeed saved me numerous trips by getting books from other libraries quickly and efficiently. Thanks to George Stevenson at the North Carolina Archives for his small discoveries and to Bill Owens for his great help with the index.

My editors at the Omohundro Institute of Early American History and Culture have been remarkable for their perseverance and close attention to detail. Gil Kelly, with his careful reading and copy editing, has helped to give the book its final polish and flow. If anything is still wrong (a misspelled word or an awkward sentence), it is a miracle (and I take full responsibility). Fredrika J. Teute's invaluable advice and deep reading pushed me to give this book the depth and breadth that it now encompasses. Her fifty pages of substantive comments on the book manuscript are the highest compliment a scholar could give.

My family deserves the most appreciation. Thanks to Roland Stephen, for being patient with all my abstract academic speculations, even before breakfast, for his wonderful meals, and for his love and support. Thanks to my

Mom, Gwendolyn Cleo Whitehead Brewer, a now-retired Professor of Restoration Drama, for making the seventeenth and eighteenth centuries real to me from my earliest memories, by dragging me to plays and to lectures when I was young on "latitudinarianism" and Blackstone's influence on eighteenth-century Indian jurisprudence as if it were normal. (And I guess I should thank the Clark Library, which sponsored those lectures!) Last, I want to thank Isabella and Everett for teaching me what it means for a parent to love a child.

CONTENTS

BY BIRTH OR CONSENT

LIMITING AND DEVELOPING
INDIVIDUAL CONSENT

CHILDREN AND ANGLO-AMERICAN
REVOLUTIONARY IDEOLOGY

*"Men are as Fearfull to be under the imputation
of a reformer of the Law, as they would [to] be of the
name of knave or fool, or hypocrite."*
Sir Matthew Hale, "Considerations touching the
Amendment or Alteration of Lawes" (ca. 1660–1664)

*"Pur ceo que cest prescription est encounter reason
ceo est voyd [Littleton]. This contaies one of the Maximes
of the Common Law, viz. that all customes and prescriptions
that be against reason, are voyd."*
Sir Edward Coke, The First Part of the Institutes of
the Laws of England (Coke upon Littleton) (1629)

In sixteenth-century England, children over age seven were of "ripe age" to marry (under seven they could contract only "espousals," or betrothals). Four-year-olds could make wills to give away their goods and chattels. Children of any age could bind themselves into apprenticeships. Eight-year-olds could be hanged for arson or any other felony. Teenagers were routinely elected to Parliament. Children who owned sufficient property could vote. And custody as we know it did not exist. These norms applied not only in England but in Virginia as it was founded during the seventeenth century. Although modified by Massachusetts and Pennsylvania at their founding, those norms changed even more in England over the next two centuries, a change accelerated in America by the Revolution. Still, laws that accepted children's consent, and even in some cases their broader authority, had not changed completely in England or its former colonies by the early nineteenth century. In Pennsylvania in 1811, two-year-old Phoebe Stuart still placed her mark at the bottom of an apprenticeship contract, indicating that she consented to her indenture.

But in the seventeenth and eighteenth centuries a fundamental shift occurred in the legal assumptions about childhood, adulthood, and responsibility. This book tells that story. It explains why children consented then and what that consent meant, but mostly it explains why that consent began to seem absurd. This is not a story of consensus; it is a story of struggle. Political theorists, ministers, judges, legislators and lawyers, ordinary men and women, and even children themselves fought over the meaning of consent. They did so because major questions of political power and the fundamental ordering of society hinged on the meaning of consent. The competing meanings of consent could rebalance the scales of justice.

Questions about children and authority permeated the political and religious debates of early modern Britain and its colonies. During the late sixteenth century, children became a metaphor for obedience and submission to church and kingdom, wherein subjects were commanded to obey their religious and temporal superiors just as children should obey their parents. On some level this image transcended metaphor, became, in its pervasiveness, a structure through which many people understood their world. This equation was enforced through catechisms, almost universally taught to all Christian children. In this vision of the world, children should revere and obey not only their parents but all social superiors, as a duty enjoined by God. In this vision, likewise, most adults also had the status of perpetual children, at least in their relations with those above them in the hierarchy. Children as such were thus not clearly distinguished from most adults. They owed obedience, not to all adults, but to their parents and to social superiors regardless of age.[1]

This ideology grew in strength as a consequence of the Reformation, yet the Reformation also set in motion the forces that would undermine it. The reformers' challenge would become sharpest (in the Anglo-American world, at least) in the religious and political ferment of seventeenth-century Britain. Instead of accepting that most subjects were political children, many political reformers of seventeenth-century England distinguished children's political identities from adults', emphasizing experience and reason as requirements for the exercise of political power. Their distinctions grew out of attempts to justify a form of government based on consent. But who should consent to a government, and under what circumstances? Children became the main example of the group for whom consent should not apply. The separate space allocated to children—indeed, the extension of that space—reveals the ten-

1. England was not unique among European countries in the centrality of this imagery about children, yet the focus here on England reflects the degree to which it directly influenced its colonies. Other, non-English scholars will be cited and discussed as they were by contemporaries—as they shaped England and its colonies, both their laws and ideas.

sions within modern political theory. To explore this theoretical space is to encounter the underlying inequalities within a theory of equality.

Children and childhood held a central place in seventeenth- and eighteenth-century political thought. The word itself, in its various forms (child, children, infant), was omnipresent in the political debates, as other names differentiated from "men" were not (such as women, blacks and Indians, slaves and servants). This word was so critical because the debates over authority had deep roots in the Reformation. One side invoked biblical injunctions about children's obligation to parents to justify monarchical authority. The other side did not challenge this obligation, but emphasized that it ended when a child became an adult: adults could reason and consent to authority, whereas children could not. Adult subjects, therefore, should be able to consent to their government. The seventeenth-century political theorists writing about consent who were most influential on the radicals and reformers of the next century—James Harrington, Algernon Sidney, and John Locke—argued that all humans possessed the capacity to reason, which could enable them to make responsible political decisions. They differed over whether reason needed to be cultivated in order to grow well (that is, whether formal education was necessary) and over how easily it could be corrupted. For most political theorists of these two centuries, the character of the government each advocated rested heavily on his or her assumptions about who could exercise reason. Those lacking reason, like children, became unable to consent. They became unable to make most legal decisions that affected themselves or others.

Other scholars have recognized that children were important to the political debates leading up to the American Revolution, but they have usually treated the place of children as only a metaphor. (They have seen these debates as not really about children themselves, but only about authority.) A few have explored the meaning of this debate for real children but have dealt only with the positive aspects of children's position after the Revolution: sons were free from their father's authority after they became adults, and education encouraged that eventual liberty and independence. Other studies have argued that children, like white males, gained liberty as a result of a new leniency by parents and their own rebellions. But did the ideology of the Revolution bring freedom to children in the same way it brought freedom to men?[2]

2. On children as metaphor: see Gordon S. Wood, *The Radicalism of the American Revolution* (New York, 1992), 146–168; Jay Fliegelman, *Prodigals and Pilgrims: The American Revolution against Patriarchal Authority* (Cambridge, 1982); Melvin Yazawa, *From Colonies to Commonwealth: Familial Ideology and the Beginnings of the American Republic*

I argue that children—as children—were explicitly excluded from equality in Revolutionary reforms and the ideology underpinning them. Their exclusion from the right to choose is explicit in early-nineteenth-century custody law, which built on John Locke's theory of human development. His emphasis on human understanding, broadly associated with the eighteenth-century Enlightenment, denies the authority of the young to make decisions, even over their own lives, until they have attained full use of their reason. They need to learn to reason to obtain training for future consent. However, they cannot actually consent.

This emphasis on an age of reason was new. Under patriarchal political theory, obligations did not end or begin at a particular age: obligations depended upon status relationships, upon one's rank in society. Although rank could be partly shaped by youth, it was not the primary determinant. The primary determinant was birthright. In the emerging consent-based political ideology, age played the role that birth status had formerly played in power allocation: the new political theory by definition disqualified those under specific ages from exercising public and even private consent. Only in opposition to patriarchal theory did this age-circumscribed, yet more complete kind of dependence for children take form. Those who opposed patriarchal arguments for absolute monarchy acknowledged the necessity of obedience, but said it applied to children only during their "minority." Adult males, in particular, should have equality, freedom, and the ability to consent to their government; children in their "minority" should not. By creating these distinctions, they set the stage for modern distinctions between public and private (or family) law.[3]

(Baltimore, 1985); Winthrop D. Jordan, "Familial Politics: Thomas Paine and the Killing of the King, 1776," *Journal of American History*, LX (1973–1974), 294–308; Jack P. Greene, "An Uneasy Connection: An Analysis of the Preconditions of the American Revolution," in Stephen G. Kurtz and James H. Hutson, eds., *Essays on the American Revolution* (Chapel Hill, N.C., 1973), 32–80; Edwin G. Burrows and Michael Wallace, "The American Revolution: The Ideology and Psychology of National Liberation," *Perspectives in American History*, VI (1972), 167–306. Nathan Tarcov, *Locke's Education for Liberty* (Chicago, 1984), focuses more narrowly on John Locke's political philosophy and the role of education in creating the citizen who can participate in government. On gaining liberty, see Robert Bremner, ed., *Children and Youth in America: A Documentary History*, I, 1600–1865 (Cambridge, Mass., 1970), part 2, esp. 131–132.

3. The best book on patriarchalism is Gordon J. Schochet, *Patriarchalism in Political Thought: The Authoritarian Family and Political Speculation and Attitudes, Especially in Seventeenth-Century England* (Oxford, 1975). Wood, in *Radicalism of the American Revolution*, uses the term "patriarchal absolutism" (147), but I prefer "patriarchalism," because patriarchal theory was not always absolute. Also see J. P. Sommerville, *Politics and*

Political theory connected closely with legal practice. In English society from the sixteenth through the eighteenth centuries, children of high status often held positions of political and legal power. In American society after the Revolution, to the extent that the Revolutionaries consciously adopted what they would call republican or whig political ideas, children became the group most clearly excluded from both political and personal power. (In continuing slavery, a birth status, the Revolutionaries either did not apply the new principles or twisted them, as I discuss in the conclusion.) This paradigm shift, from authority based on birthright to authority based on reasoned consent, reconstituted the nature and legitimacy of power. The implications of this reconfiguration of power can be fully understood only by focusing on the child whose status drew so much attention.

When ten-year-old William York murdered his five-year-old fellow apprentice (because she "foul[ed]" the bed they shared) in 1748, he caused a furor. By English law, he should have been executed, even "though the taking away the Life of a Boy of Ten Years old may savour of Cruelty." But, fortunately for him, his case occurred at a crossroads in the history of justice. His execution was delayed at every court session for nine years (while he was held in jail). Finally, the king pardoned him on condition that he join the navy. The continual delays in his execution reveal a profound underlying shift. His case helped to define a transition in standards for authority and responsibility, standards that applied not simply to children but to all members of society.[4]

Status to Contract: From Primogeniture to Consent

The prominence of children in the political debates of these two centuries illuminates the struggle over the basis of political authority: inherited right versus the consent of the people. At the beginning of the seventeenth century, primogeniture—whereby land and power usually descended from father to eldest son—was the primary basis for authority in England. By the end of the eighteenth century, differing methods for the transfer of power hung in a precarious balance in England but had tilted in favor of consent as a conse-

Ideology in England, 1603–1640 (London, 1986), chap. 1; J. P. Allen, *A History of Political Thought in the Sixteenth Century* (London, 1928), 135; Susan Dwyer Amussen, *An Ordered Society: Gender and Class in Early Modern England* (Oxford, 1988), chap. 2. "Patriarchalism" also has a different and more specific meaning than the broad term "patriarchy." "Patriarchy," as used by Gerda Lerner, for example, refers to men's power over women, a system of organizing society that has dominated Western consciousness for the last several millennia (*The Creation of Patriarchy* [New York, 1986], 8–9, 238–239).

4. Sir Michael Foster, *A Report of Some Proceedings on the Commission of Oyer and Terminer and Goal Delivery . . .* (Oxford, 1762), 70–73.

quence of the Revolution in England's renegade colonies. Legal scholars, beginning with Sir Henry Maine in 1861, have characterized this transition from "status to contract" as central to the way the law defined individual relations. "The rights and duties, capacities and incapacities of the individual are no longer being fixed by law as a consequence of his membership of a class; but those former incidents of status are coming more and more to depend for their nature and existence upon the will of the parties affected by them." In English medieval law, "What a man had largely determined what he was." By the late eighteenth century, however, English and, particularly, American law began to emphasize contractual relations instead of status. Contractual relations, including consent to government, rose to a prominence in determining the basis of both political authority and legal relations between adults. A hierarchical system based on status, where people have "grades of legal capacity," began to give way to one where all people were legal equals, free to define their relations with others by means of contracts.[5]

J. R. Pole and Gordon S. Wood see this legal transition from status to contract as the core of the political transition introduced by the American Revolution. Pole argues that after the Revolution this transition was striking. "Status was formally abolished, and contract installed as a governing principle in the Constitution itself." Wood shows how the emphasis on political contracts affected status-based authority by decreasing the deference toward public officials and by increasing the use of contracts to specify legal relations. Both see this shift as creating a society that promised legal equality to all and granted it to many via the gradual expansion of the suffrage and a decline in deference.[6]

Did this transformation in political ideology and legal practice create such a society? Not for everyone. Children were excluded, along with other groups who would be compared to them. Maine himself, along with most commentators on his legal theory since, acknowledged that elements of status remained within the common law and that some members of the community were not legal equals. In the early nineteenth century, the legally unequal

5. R. H. Graveson, *Status in the Common Law* (London, 1953), 7, 34; Manfred Rehbinder, "Status, Contract, and the Welfare State," *Stanford Law Review*, XXIII (1970–1971), 951. Sir Henry Sumner Maine saw this transformation as relatively complete in mid-nineteenth-century Britain: *Ancient Law: Its Connection with the Early History of Society and Its Relation to Modern Ideas* (1861), new ed. (London, 1930), 180–181. P. S. Atiyah, in *The Rise and Fall of Freedom of Contract* (Oxford, 1979), has expanded on this argument about contractual relations. Also see Bruce H. Mann, *Neighbors and Strangers: Law and Community in Early Connecticut* (Chapel Hill, N.C., 1987).

6. J. R. Pole, *The Pursuit of Equality in American History*, rev. ed. (Berkeley, Calif., 1993), xiv; Wood, *Radicalism of the American Revolution*, esp. 162–166.

included married women, slaves, and laborers. But children were the only group completely excluded from equality.

> The apparent exceptions [to the shift from status to contract] are exceptions of that stamp which illustrate the rule. The child before years of discretion, the orphan under guardianship, the adjudged lunatic, have all their capacities and incapacities regulated by the Law of Persons. But why? The reason is differently expressed in the conventional language of different systems, but in substance it is stated to the same effect by all. The great majority of Jurists are constant to the principle that the classes of persons just mentioned *are subject to extrinsic control* on the single ground that they *do not possess the faculty of forming a judgment* on their own interests; in other words, that they are wanting in the first essential of an engagement by Contract.[7]

Maine excluded children from this broad shift from status to contract with an argument similar to John Locke's: children cannot make contracts, because they lack the ability to form their own judgments; therefore, they cannot be included as equals. He implied that the distinct legal status of childhood was one of the few remnants of the older system.[8]

However, the exclusion of children on the basis of their inability to form judgments was not a residue of a past order. Children remained, as it were, born to a particular status—but a very different one. Their status was determined by their age, which rendered them unable to form contracts, not by their place in the social order or their inheritance of property and title. The legal incapacities of children as a distinct category can be traced to the seventeenth and eighteenth centuries. Although it is undeniable that very young

7. Maine, *Ancient Law*, 181 (my emphasis). On slavery, see, particularly, Philip J. Schwarz, *Twice Condemned: Slaves and the Criminal Laws of Virginia, 1705–1865* (Baton Rouge, La., 1988). On the legal status of women, see Carole Pateman, *The Sexual Contract* (Stanford, Calif., 1988); Susan Staves, *Married Women's Separate Property in England, 1660–1833* (Cambridge, Mass., 1990); Marylynn Salmon, *Women and the Law of Property in Early America* (Chapel Hill, N.C., 1986); Nancy Isenberg, *Sex and Citizenship in Antebellum America* (Chapel Hill, N.C., 1998); Linda K. Kerber, *No Constitutional Right to Be Ladies: Women and the Obligations of Citizenship* (New York, 1998). On laborers, see Karen Orren, *Belated Feudalism: Labor, the Law, and Liberal Development in the United States* (Cambridge, 1991); Christopher L. Tomlins, *Law, Labor, and Ideology in the Early American Republic* (Cambridge, 1993), 244–246.

8. Martha Minow, in a thought-provoking analysis of this legal transition, has pointed out that, however this shift happened, it left in its wake "a residual category of legal statuses where the shift had failed to occur." *Making All the Difference: Inclusion, Exclusion, and American Law* (Ithaca, N.Y., 1990), 126.

children, especially, did have some limits on their legal abilitites before the seventeenth century, childhood itself was redefined as a consequence of the shift in political legitimacy during the seventeenth and eighteenth centuries. This shift began during the Reformation but became more focused in England during its two revolutions in the seventeenth century. Changes were gradually implemented by common lawyers influenced by these revolutions and by the Enlightenment and were taken even further in North America as a consequence of the American Revolution.

The roots of change lie in the struggle for political authority in seventeenth-century England, a struggle intertwined with religious authority. Birth into a certain church, a certain status, or a certain religious and political hierarchy was contrasted to choosing a church, to choosing a king or a country. One should not inherit the obligation of obedience, whether to minister, lord, or king. Privileging choice, however, required answers to other questions: Who can choose, and under what circumstances? If everyone, even a one-year-old, then is consent rendered meaningless? Implicit in consent was the ability to dissent, but when? If consent is presumed at birth or soon after, such as with an infant baptized into church membership or the child born a subject of a kingdom, can that person change her or his mind after attaining an age of reason and understanding? Be charged with heresy or treason for trying? Thus the political debate was framed by the questions raised by the Reformation: of who has authority and on what basis, about how truth can be known and who knows it.

The concept of an "age of reason" became critical for determining who could give meaningful consent. Although classical authors such as Aristotle and earlier Christian authors such as Thomas Aquinas had referred to an "age of reason," seventeenth-century Continental Protestant natural law theorists such as Hugo Grotius and Samuel von Pufendorf as well as English Dissenting thinkers developed this concept, granting it much greater weight: they defined it, puzzled over its meaning, marked its boundaries, made the concept of reason itself central to their emerging religious and legal systems of thought. The changing status of childhood was a consequence of this emphasis on an age of reason, which arose as part of the new basis for political legitimacy. In turn, this stress on an age of reason created a limit to consent, shaping the application of these new political ideas to the larger society. This limitation on consent became a powerful weapon in the hands of those who sought to limit the radical implications of equality within the new ideology, either to maintain older exclusions or to create new ones.

I began this study with a question about how policy toward children changed as a result of the American Revolution: did a new ideology affect the legal status of children? I examined laws and local court records in three representative counties for the 1750s, 1780s, and 1810s: Plymouth, Massachusetts; Frederick, Virginia; and Chester, Pennsylvania. But I became increasingly frustrated trying to understand the full meaning and context of the fragments of cases I was seeing. Broadening my scope and poring over legal guides and laws, I realized that the dramatic changes did not encompass solely the Revolution: they had started earlier and followed a surprisingly clear pattern. The resulting research comprehends court cases and records from as early as the 1560s and as late as the mid-nineteenth century, from English assize courts through Coke's reports and the Virginia superior courts, from debates about baptism through children's literature and high political theory.

One of the issues with which I struggled hardest was moderating and refining my conclusions to fit my evidence. I could have made my conclusions more speculative, but I chose instead to do more research and compile more evidence to figure out whether the changes that the legal guides and laws indicated had a basis in fact. If both legal guidelines and practice supported each other in the earlier period—guidelines that are now completely outside the bounds of acceptability—that would establish the change in norms. I have made the guides to the law central to my analysis, focusing on where and how they were used, and backed them up with examples of practice. Practice was difficult to track for the earlier period. The problem is self-defined: Because children were not as clearly distinguished from adults and age was not as important, children and age were only rarely mentioned in the court cases. Thus the cases were difficult to find. Despite this difficulty, I have now put together a comprehensive map of change.

Although I do not have the whole of the change delimited, I am able to show a real shift in the boundaries of acceptability. To give only a few examples: We would not now elect a thirteen-year-old to the House of Representatives (and certainly not have him give a keynote speech on an important bill at fourteen). We would not accept a will signed by a four-year-old. We would not permit a fourteen-year-old, regardless of wealth, to judge (as a juror) someone's guilt or innocence. We would not hang an eight-year-old for arson. We would not permit an eight-year-old to legally marry. We would not allow a five-year-old to bind himself to labor—and force him to abide by his agreement until he reached twenty-four. Yet the laws and legal guides and judges found these practices acceptable in sixteenth- and seventeenth-century England and Virginia. My study does not show prevalence, which is nearly impossible to discern, or the details of struggles over these questions in every decade or every county or every colony. Instead, it sketches the big picture— establishing that assumptions were very different from our own and that we, whether social or political historians, should not take our own norms for granted.

British colonial judges all referred extensively to English legal treatises and English court cases in reaching their own decisions, and they continued to do so after the Revolution. While in Massachusetts colony they did so less and in Virginia more, all three colonies had judges who made frequent references to English decisions and English legal treatises—so much so that this study has had to address broad changes in English law. Thus most chapters trace legal developments within both English law and treatises in parallel with developments in the colonies. English practice sometimes provided the only unifying ground between the colonies even after they became states. Simply put, with regard to the law, the colonial and even new Republic sources constantly interacted with the English ones.[9] This acknowledgment of the constant interaction with English law even after the American Revolution does not deny that colonies developed their own legal traditions. The various interpretations that each colony placed on the common law, or what each chose to adopt or reject, provided the fodder for disagreements in the early decades of the nineteenth century, even as federal statutes and courts sought to exert a unifying influence.[10]

This reliance on English common law—on precedent—is complicated by the critical fact that many collections of the common law were written by men who actually sought to shape the common law, who were active re-

9. This general observation is not new. See, particularly, David H. Flaherty, "An Introduction to Early American Legal History," in Flaherty, ed., *Essays in the History of Early American Law* (Chapel Hill, N.C., 1969), 3–40; William E. Nelson, *Americanization of the Common Law: The Impact of Legal Change on Massachusetts Society, 1760–1830* (Cambridge, Mass., 1975), 8–10.

10. For a complete discussion of the legal treatises most commonly used and available in these three colonies/states, see the Appendix. I have generally adopted the notation used by English and American lawyers when referring to collections of printed reports of cases and of English laws. These notations are much more condensed than the normal citations that historians use. When referring to groups of cases, they are almost indispensable. An English law such as 5 Eliz. I, c. 4, for example, would mean that the law was passed in the fifth year of the reign of Elizabeth I (1562 or 1563) and was the fourth law passed. If an "s" follows, it refers to the section, or paragraph, from which a particular cite derives. Collected reports of decisions on cases are usually cited under the name of the author of the report, though, after the Revolution, sometimes by state or federal government. A typical cite might be 10 U.S. 226, meaning that this case appears in volume X of the records of the United States Supreme Court, page 226. Many earlier (and non-U.S.) references are more difficult to decipher; *A Uniform System of Citation* is the place to start. Guidelines for legal citations are outlined in *The Chicago Manual of Style.*

formers. Thus each treatise and court decision provides not only a glimpse into the past but also might well have been shaping that past. Sir Edward Coke, Sir Matthew Hale, and Sir William Blackstone, the three most frequently cited legal compilers of the seventeenth and eighteenth centuries, all actively molded the common law: partly to make it conform to reason and partly to turn it into a coherent system. Their compilations of the common law would be taken by most later scholars as precedent. In incorporating some of the epistemological changes of the seventeenth and eighteenth centuries into the common law, these men helped to create the common law as we know it today.

American judges and lawyers did not accept these compilations blindly. The story, like real history and real life, is neither a simple one-way street nor a straight one. Instead, we have many routes, often curvy and with hills and sea voyages, whereby influence traveled in both directions. That acknowledged, the law itself did traverse some distance, not only physically but ideologically, in content and shape. Some would call this distance simply a refinement of the law of contract. Others might call it the road from feudalism to enlightenment. Both explanations oversimplify the actual course. To understand the course, we must first understand the lay of the land; we must acknowledge the mapmakers and their ideological setting. The three revolutions in England and America profoundly affected the common law even, and especially, as it fissured into slightly different courses in the wake of the American Revolution.

The organization of the material in this study seeks to balance chronology with analysis. It begins with the centrality of real children to political power in the seventeenth century, explaining how children's status entered the debates over the basis of authority. Chapter 2 discusses the debates themselves and how they grew out of the Reformation, with its contrary emphases on free consent and the authority of parents. Infant baptism serves as a window into the debates about political consent as they were forming in the seventeenth century. Chapter 3 pursues the dispute between inherited right and government based on consent, with children as the focus, into political theory more explicitly, explaining the conceptual and actual links between the earlier religious discussions and democratic-republican political theory.

The remainder of the book focuses on practical questions of children's legal identity and how children's status was responding to the religious and political debates. It examines every way in which a person had to consent or give voice, whether children could participate and at what ages, and how the rules were changing. Chapter 4 traces these debates to the legal status of children vis-à-vis citizenship, jury service, and militia service. Chapter 5 addresses their changing ability to be witnesses in courts and the consequences of their legal silencing. It also examines legal reform and legal reformers within the common law and how these reforms were linked to the shifts in ideology sketched earlier. Chapter 6 examines children's liability for crime, focusing on intent, which is closely linked to consent. Chapter 7 takes on the paired issues of children's ability to form legal contracts and the rise of parental custody. Chapter 8 carries through the discussion of custody and consent revealed in changing norms for children's consent to marriage.

The conclusion examines how historians have often tried to explain away the evidence that children had legal identities before the eighteenth century. These norms are so different from our own that we tend to assume, especially when faced with only a small piece of the puzzle, that it must be an error in the record. It then addresses questions about the connections between social history and legal history to argue that social history, using legal records, cannot be done reliably without an understanding of the law itself. It finally examines the implications of this study for understanding democratic-republican theory and for the ways that inequality and exclusion could be—and were—justified within it.

By naturalizing the position of children, we not only distort the past but make it impossible to understand the debates over authority during this period and the transformations in social order and ideology for all of society. Unless we pay attention to those who are unequal in this theory of equality, to those who cannot consent in this theory of consent, we cannot see what the theory really meant, in the abstract and as it shaped the logic of the laws. We cannot understand how people could manipulate this theory to create a new structure of privilege, one that could be twisted to justify even slavery. The construction of consent, grounded in an ideology of reason, deeply affected norms in a supposedly unchanging legal system. With its abstract principles, it projected an ahistorical system of values that cover and obscure historical struggles over power. If we cannot see these connections, we lose the ability to justify or understand many modern norms.

What this book now does is connect religious and political ideology—via legal manuals and judges' decisions—to practice. It takes abstract ideas about justice and authority and shows how they shaped the lives of real people, especially children. It makes their dilemmas come to life. It has relevance to many questions that are hotly debated today. Its most significant contribution is to trace how the concept of meaningful consent became central to the law and to what we would call democracy. Without meaningful consent, that is, consent that is neither forced nor overtly influenced, democracy has nothing to stand on. In order for democracy to exist in any form, meaningful consent had to become central to the law. What this meant, however, was far from clear. It had to be hammered out and was often disputed. What this meant is what this book is all about.

A Note on Terminology

Terms such as "puritan," "democratic," "patriarchal," and "republican" had various frangible meanings in their own times and still do in ours. In many ways such terms are defined not only by the people included in each group but also by which characteristics we emphasize in describing them. Such terms are tools of analysis, and were even in their own time. Their meanings are, not innate, but contingent on who is using them, for what purpose, and in what context. While other authors clearly may describe the characteristics of these groups somewhat differently, I have defined these words in order to recapture how contemporaries would have used them and to better delineate the major political and intellectual alignments of these two centuries.

Both "republican" and "democratic" are terms that can describe that body of political writers in seventeenth-century England who sought to justify authority based on consent and opposed authority based on inherited right. Both, however, are problematic in various ways, partly because they have been given somewhat different meanings by historians: "republican," for example, has usually been defined as those who support a mixed form of government (or a distribution of power) between king, aristocracy, and commons (monarchy, oligarchy, democracy). But to associate "republican" only with those who supported balance of power is too narrow. Those thinkers from the seventeenth century who became so popular in America before and during the Revolution did not all support distribution of power (at least not as the main point of their works). To the extent that any of them supported monarchy, it had to be based upon the consent of the people, not inherited right (for example, a limited monarch whose power is circumscribed by his covenant with the people). Their main point was less about the form of government than the justification for authority itself.

The word "democratic" (or "democraticall," as they would say) also carries modern connotations (it can be confused with today's ideas about democracy or even Democrats). Yet it seems to have been the more popular term in the seventeenth century. John Aubrey, whose *Brief Lives* described so many of the major seventeenth-century figures and who knew, among others, James Harrington personally, began his description of him as follows: "His genius lay chiefly towards the politiques and democraticall government." Sidney made clear throughout his magnum opus that he supported "democracy." Many of these thinkers who favored consent and opposed inherited right spoke positively about the term in the seventeenth century and allied it closely—indeed, intertwined it—with the "consent" of the people. The term "democracy" could have a much narrower meaning (it could deny all representative authority, so people had to consent directly to all laws), at least as some Puritans used it. Still, it seems a more appropriate term to describe those who favored government based on consent, since it was associated closely with ideas about contract. Indeed, although "republican" became a more common term during the American Revolution (and "democratic" more likely to be seen in a negative light), it continued to be associated with the consent of the people.[11]

Although the term "republican" was more popular with the leaders of the American Revolution, the larger point is that there are strong continuities in ideas between the "democraticall" thinkers of the seventeenth century and "republican" revolutionaries. ("Republican," in the eighteenth century, was often used to mean simply a government based upon the consent of the people.) Throughout, as I use these terms, they mean all of those thinkers who were arrayed on one side during this period so as to capture the main issue they had in common: their contention that authority should originate in reason and consent.

In suggesting that historians have defined these terms too narrowly and in refocusing on the issue of consent, I create different alignments. Historians have used the term "republican"—particularly "classical republican"—to describe one strand of revisionist thought that they distinguish from "liberalism" and from which they exclude Locke. Although this may reflect late-eighteenth-century (or nineteenth- or twentieth-century) debates, singling out Locke as not "republican" is ahistorical for the seventeenth and most of the eighteenth centuries. Locke's, Sidney's, and Harrington's arguments about political legitimacy shared much more with each other than they did with patriarchal theorists. They not only shared their ideas but acted on them together. Sidney and Locke probably were involved in the Rye House Plot of 1683 to assassinate Charles II and his brother, the future James II. John Trenchard (who wrote *Cato's Letters* with Thomas Gordon) was involved in the same plot. (Trenchard was arrested but freed for lack of evidence, Sidney was found guilty of treason and had his head chopped off, and Locke fled to Holland, where he stayed until the Glorious Revolution, six years later.) Gordon and Trenchard cite "the eminent Locke" repeatedly. Harrington, Sidney, and Anthony Ashley Cooper (later the first earl of Shaftesbury and Locke's patron) were on Interregnum committees together. Indeed, had Harrington still been alive, he might have participated in the Rye House Plot as well.

11. John Aubrey, *Brief Lives*, ed. Oliver Lawson Dick (Ann Arbor, Mich., 1957), 124; B. Katharine Brown, "A Note on the Puritan Concept of Democracy and Aristocracy," *Mississippi Valley Historical Review*, XLI (1954–1955), 105–112.

The aging Sidney certainly seems an unlikely revolutionary. Neither Bernard Bailyn nor Gordon Wood, who have considered republican ideology, leaves out Locke. The seventeenth century witnessed a fundamental argument between two camps, and the artificial exclusion of Locke draws attention away from this real division.[12]

While issues such as balance of power and the use of history (upon which other studies have focused) were being debated, they did not demarcate the main political divisions of that century. Harrington, Sidney, Locke, and, later, Gordon and Trenchard substantially agreed in their cause: they were fighting on a common front against patriarchal and absolutist ideology. This study focuses on that battle. The differences between Locke and Harrington pale next to their similarities when seen in light of the alternative justifications of power. They were not arguing with each other—they were arguing against those they would have called papists or absolutists (those who justify inherited authority, obedience without question). Defining these groups as "liberal" and "republican" in the seventeenth century creates a schism that, simply put, was not there. Only when their ideas were predominant—in the last decade of the eighteenth century—would these divisions emerge.[13]

12. J. G. A. Pocock, especially, has claimed that a dichotomy exists between Algernon Sidney and James Harrington, on the one hand, and John Locke, on the other, and he describes the "founding fathers" in America as torn between two opposing schools of thought, "Lockean Liberalism" and "Classical Republicanism." This difference, however, has been drawn too rigidly, because it rests partly on an overemphasis on the place of "liberty" in Locke's thought and a corresponding underemphasis on the place of liberty, equality, and consent in "Classical Republican" thought. See *The Machiavellian Moment: Florentine Political Thought and the Atlantic Republican Tradition* (Princeton, N.J., 1975); *Three British Revolutions: 1641, 1688, 1776* (Princeton, N.J., 1980). Many scholars have pointed out that Locke's thought is not as distinct from that of classical republicanism as it has sometimes been portrayed and that classical republicanism itself has been so attractive because it was so protean. For an overview of the literature, see Daniel T. Rodgers, "Republicanism: The Career of a Concept," *JAH*, LXXIX (1992–1993), 11–38; Alan Craig Houston, *Algernon Sidney and the Republican Heritage in England and America* (Princeton, N.J., 1991), 8, 225. See also Isaac Kramnick, *Republicanism and Bourgeois Radicalism: Political Ideology in Late Eighteenth-Century England and America* (Ithaca, N.Y., 1990); Shelley Burtt, *Virtue Transformed: Political Argument in England, 1688–1740* (Cambridge, 1992); Joyce Appleby's essays in *Liberalism and Republicanism in the Historical Imagination* (Cambridge, Mass., 1992). Bernard Bailyn, although credited with being one of the authors of the republican synthesis, did not separate Locke's thought as different from the other authors'. See Bailyn, *The Ideological Origins of the American Revolution* (Cambridge, Mass., 1967).

13. Differences between Harrington, Gordon and Trenchard, Sidney, and Locke undoubtedly exist, particularly on the issue of public virtue. Although Harrington and

Many of the same issues that surround the term "republican" or "democratic" also surround the terms "patriarchal." When used here to describe political thinkers, three elements must characterize their vision of political authority: they compare the power of a king to that of a father; they at least implicitly reject consent as a basis for authority; and they support the hereditary authority of the king. That said, not all political thinkers in the seventeenth century fall neatly into these two categories. Many thinkers, including lawyers and judges, straddled both ideologies: many Puritans, in particular, retained important strands of patriarchal thought.

Supporting consent, however, did not necessarily equate with how we think of government based on consent—without coercion. The most important exceptions to the somewhat artifical way I have drawn the lines here are Thomas Hobbes and, to varying degrees, earlier natural law theorists such as Hugo Grotius and Francisco Suárez: they agreed that government should be based on consent. But they held force and influence to be allowable elements of that consent. In other words: if you say yes because I force you to, you still consent. Your consent (even superficial), your mark or seal on the paper, your agreement, was what mattered.[14]

The group of writers that I cluster into the democratic-republican camp was reacting not only against patriarchalism but against the authoritarian definition of consent that permitted force. Crafting a new meaning for consent—and the ways that this meaning for consent became fundamental to the law—is what this book is about. Only by writing force and influence out of the equation could they create the basis for a different political order.

Gordon and Trenchard put more value on it, Locke had more to say about virtue and restraint than most scholars acknowledge. It is critical not to neglect those facets of Locke's thinking (he was not advocating unrestrained liberty). If we shift the debate away from public virtue (or *virtù*) versus rights and focus on their use of consent, the common ground for this body of thinkers becomes much more obvious. Their differences become magnified over time, when their body of ideas came to dominate.

14. Thomas Hobbes, *Leviathan*, ed. Richard Tuck (Cambridge, 1996), chap. 14; Richard Tuck, *Naural Rights Theories: Their Origin and Development* (Cambridge, 1979), 3, 56–57, 71–73. On Hobbes, see also Chapter 3, below.

CHAPTER I

CHILDREN, INHERITED POWER, AND PATRIARCHAL IDEOLOGY

*"By this means it comes to pass that many a child, by
succeeding a king, hath the right of a father over many a grey-headed
multitude, and hath the title of pater patriae."*
Sir Robert Filmer, Patriarcha *(1680)*

*" 'Tis not to be imagined, that a company of men
should so far degenerate from their own nature,
which is reason, to give up themselves and their posterity,
with all their concernments in the world, to depend
upon the will of a child."*
Algernon Sidney, Discourses concerning Government
([1681–1683], 1698)

After his election to the House of Burgesses for Elizabeth City, Virginia, "Mr." Willis Wilson, eighteen years old, traveled to Jamestown to attend the session of April 1692. The voters had chosen him to hold his father's former seat, but the Committee of Elections and Privileges objected. After some debate, the full house refused to accept him as a burgess, he "appearing to this house to be under the Age of one and Twenty years." Elizabeth City then held another vote, electing William Armistead in Willis's place. A year later, when the governor dissolved the Burgesses and called for a new election, the voters again returned Willis. Now Captain Willis Wilson (an appointed militia officer), he was still only nineteen. This time the Burgesses accepted him without comment. Indeed, the fuss over his first election was unprecedented. In 1688 Daniel Parke was elected for James City (replacing his father-in-law, Philip Ludwell, whom the governor had promoted to the Council). At eighteen, Parke was the same age Wilson would be in 1692, but no burgess challenged his right to sit. In 1699 the Burgesses went further than simply rejecting a particular member on the basis of his age. They passed a law making the elections of all those under age twenty-one void. Anyone could challenge such an election, whether inside or outside the House.[1]

1. H. R. McIlwaine, ed., *Journals of the House of Burgesses of Virginia, 1659/60–1693* (Richmond, Va., 1914), 381–382, 394, 412. Wilson was born in 1673, according to his

Concern about electing persons under age twenty-one did not arise from local Virginia politics. Virginia's 1699 law mirrored one passed by Parliament in 1696. The concerns were transatlantic and deeply rooted in the ideological arguments that underlay England's two seventeenth-century revolutions. The challenge to Wilson was a symptom of a much larger contest over the basis of authority in England and its colonies during the seventeenth and eighteenth centuries. To challenge Wilson was to raise questions about birthright and the transmission of authority from father to son (explicit in this case). The roots of this challenge to birthright reached into the Reformation. The Reformation, however, had more than one impact on the debates about authority in England and its colonies: it could also encourage, ironically, blind obedience. These countervailing pressures fed a struggle over legitimate authority in England and America during the seventeenth and eighteenth centuries.[2]

In early-seventeenth-century England, authority was perceived to originate in three ways: by election, by succession, or by conquest. Arguments for authority by conquest had few strong adherents: conquest set a dangerous precedent, and morally it had weak persuasive force. Although some political power in England was determined by election, Parliament being the most notable example, much power—much authority—was determined by succession, by inheritance, by birth. The source of authority shaped the degree to which obedience could be justified. "Tyrants and wicked governours may be remooved by the whole state, as Athens and Rome were delivered from their cruell governours: but this must be understood of such kingdomes where the kingdome goeth by election; as in Polonia, and Venice: for from whom kings receive their authoritie, by them they may be constrained to keepe within their bounds: but where kingdomes goe by succession, the reason is otherwise." By this logic, subjects could not replace their ruler in kingdoms where the monarch inherited his crown, such as England.[3]

The Reformation challenged the norm of birthright by emphasizing the responsibility to choose religious membership, which implied that political identity might also be chosen (the subject of the next chapter). At the same time, it provided a way to strengthen obedience to authority: Reformation

---

gravestone in St. John's churchyard in Hampton, Virginia. Given that the new year had begun a week before the 1692 session started, he almost certainly was eighteen. For Parke, see 297 (Apr. 28, 1688), and below.

2. 7 and 8 Will. II, c. 25, s. 7; William Waller Hening, ed., *The Statutes at Large: Being a Collection of All the Laws of Virginia* . . . (rpt. Charlottesville, Va., 1969), III, 174–175 (1699).

3. Andrew Willet, *An Harmonie upon the First Booke of Samuel* . . . (Cambridge, 1607), 294–295.

theology emphasized the authority of fathers especially. Equating the authority of kings with that of fathers could provide a basis for absolute authority. Only in the face of challenges to the norm of authority by birthright in the wake of the Reformation did political authority become so closely aligned with fatherly authority.

Equating the authority of a king or pope with that of a father was not completely new to the Reformation. Elements of this kind of patriarchal thinking existed within medieval Catholic theology, though it was invoked more to justify the spiritual power of the pope and his ministers than the temporal power of kings. The title "Pope" derived from a Greek word for "father." The laity addressed priests, bishops, and other Catholic Church authorities as "father." The description of the king as a temporal "father" of his people was a direct analogy to the spiritual "father" God and his spiritual earthly representatives in the church. This analogy strengthened the church's authority.[4]

Medieval principles of political authority, however, did not rest on this analogy. Instead, the main justifications for the power of the monarch rested on his divine sanction (as conveyed by a pope) and on the principle that the king owned all of the land of the country and thus had dominion over it and all those who lived upon it. The king's "dominium" gave him lordship, both of the land and the people. His authority was conveyed (as was obligation) by birth. A child should be baptized a member of the church just as the child was born a member of the kingdom—if the parents were Christians and subjects. While political authority descended via primogeniture, obligation was inherited by all children from their parents. Everyone was born to a particular status in a hierarchy such that Christ's kingdom on earth was an imperfect parallel of the hierarchies in heaven.[5]

The central analogy that equated a king's authority with that of a father became more important in the wake of the Reformation as a result of its new emphasis on the Ten Commandments, particularly the fifth. Medieval theology emphasized the seven deadly sins, which did not contain the same injunctions about authority as the Ten Commandments. (Although Aquinas and a few other medieval theologians supported teaching the Ten Commandments to parishioners, their influence was limited.) Notably, Jean Bodin, the

4. Ernst H. Kantorowicz, *The King's Two Bodies: A Study in Mediaeval Political Theology* (Princeton, N.J., 1957), 8, 18–19. *Pappas* is "father" in Greek. In Old English, "pope" was *papa*, as it still is in Italian. See *Oxford English Dictionary*, s.v. "papa."

5. This sketch simplifies a complex debate. On this topic, see Francis Oakley, "Christian Obedience and Authority, 1520–1550," 159–192, J. H. Burns, "Scholasticism: Survival and Revival," 132–155, esp. 140–146, both in Burns, ed., *The Cambridge History of Political Thought, 1450–1700* (Cambridge, 1991); Ewart Lewis, *Medieval Political Ideas* (London, 1954), chaps. 2, 3, 88–92.

originator of patriarchal political theory in sixteenth-century France, who strongly influenced English political theorists such as Robert Filmer, was one of the early promulgators of the Ten Commandments.[6]

The Reformation in England introduced a national program of religious instruction that taught that obedience to superiors was divinely enjoined, a duty parallel to and part of obedience to parents, one of the Ten Commandments given by God himself. While the fifth commandment in the Bible itself only instructs readers, "Honour thy father and mother," every Tudor and Stuart rendition of it linked obedience to parents with obedience to political authority. The standard catechism (from the Anglican prayer book of 1549) instructed children and adults to recite their duties toward others: "To love, honour, and succour my father and mother. To honour and obey the kyng and his ministers. To submitte my selfe to all my governours, teachers, spirituall pastours and maisters. To ordre my selfe lowly and reverentelye to all my betters."[7] The basic catechism that all Anglicans memorized, therefore, equated parental power with legitimate government, and all children were supposed to be catechized. A law passed in Virginia in 1632, for example, required every minister to instruct the children of his parish every Sunday. The same law required the children, in turn, to memorize the commandments, and their parents, masters, and mistresses to send them to church "upon pain of censure by the county court." Similar laws existed in England. Literally millions of copies of catechisms would be published there over the next two centuries. Other catechisms, similar in form, remained in manuscript and were taught and repeated orally. This spiritual "milk for babes," as some of the catechisms were called, formed one of the first conscious ways by which children learned norms of obedience to authority. English popular culture was thus shaping political ideology via religion. This political ideology, which

6. John Bossy, "Moral Arithmetic: Seven Sins into Ten Commandments," in Edmund Leites, ed., *Conscience and Casuistry in Early Modern Europe* (Cambridge, 1988), 214–234.

7. [Thomas Cramner], *Boke of Common Prayer, and Administracion of the Sacramentes and Other Rites and Ceremonies in the Churche of Englande* (London, 1649), reprinted in F. E. Brightman, ed., *The English Rite . . .* , 2d ed. (London, 1921), II, 784–785. (The 1652 and later official versions are similar.) After 1661, apparently in an attempt partially to accommodate Dissenters, the phrase "his ministers" was changed to "and all that are put in authority under him." Brightman collates the texts of 1549, 1552, 1604, and 1661. Before 1549 the laity was expected to have only a "general familiarity" with the Decalogue. See Margaret Aston, *England's Iconoclasts* (Oxford, 1988), 344–354, as cited by Ian Green, *The Christian's ABC: Catechisms and Catechizing in England, c. 1530–1740* (Oxford, 1996), 13–20, 422; and Bossy, "Moral Arithmetic," in Leites, ed., *Conscience and Casuistry,* 214–234. The prayer book catechism of 1549 was the first official English catechism.

would be labeled "patriarchal," pervaded English religious instruction of the late sixteenth and early seventeenth centuries.[8]

These catechisms contained not only the Decalogue but also the other fundamentals of Christian belief that their hundreds of authors held to be most important. Particularly, they all addressed church membership and how one might obtain salvation. These discussions, in which baptism played a central part, also raised questions about authority, in some cases asserting a different type of authority, one based on consent. The awesome publishing record of these texts shows the significance of these issues and illustrates the close connection between religious and political ideology in England during this period, reinforced by the explicit connection between church and state. The primers both emerged from and gave rise to a body of political ideology and to more systematic thinkers, who would in turn change the shape of the debate. The religious turmoil spawned by the Reformation would fundamentally test ideas about authority: Should children obey parents? Servants obey masters? Subjects obey kings? How much obedience should inferiors give to their superiors?

Thus, largely because it was so central to Anglican indoctrination about authority, and certainly also because it fitted so easily with the English allocation of power, the political ideology dominant during the founding of the first English colonies in the early seventeenth century was patriarchalism. This theory combined claims for monarchical and religious authority in order to emphasize how the status to which one was born determined one's place in society. Patriarchal theory compared the king's power over his people to a father's power over his children. "The king towards his people is rightly compared to a father of children, and the people must behave dutifully towards their king," wrote the future James I in 1598 in *The True Lawe of Free Monarchies*, his major work on political principles. The people do not consent to the king's government. Rather, the king's right is based only on his being "their heritable overlord, and so by birth . . . comes to his crown . . . [as] the nearest and lawful heir" of the previous monarch. No matter how "wicked"

8. Hening, ed., *Statutes at Large*, I, 181–182 (1632); Sadie Bell, *The Church, the State, and Education in Virginia* (1930; rpt. New York, 1969), 99; Green, *Christian's ABC*, chaps. 3, 4. Green counts 1,043 discrete versions of the catechism published between the 1530s and the end of the 1730s. Many of these went through numerous editions. Each edition was of 1,250–1,500 copies before 1620, and 2,000 or so copies by the 1630s. The official versions of catechisms alone (usually modifications of the prayer book) were published at a rate of 20,000–100,000 per decade between the 1560s and 1630s. William Perkins's unofficial work, to use another example, went through at least thirty editions between 1592 and 1642. See Green, *Christian's ABC*, 45–67.

any king's actions, he was king by the will of God, and it should be left to God to judge his actions, not to the people.[9]

These three elements—the equation of the king's authority with paternal power, the transference of that right via inheritance (primogeniture), and the appointment by God's will (so that the king should be accountable to God alone)—were central to this system of thought. Both a father's power and a king's power arose from birth: the king gained his right by inheritance through primogeniture, the father through progeniture. Originally, according to this theory, monarchical right had been paternal, but then the father bequeathed the power to rule over his children to his eldest son; all his other children inherited the duty of obedience. After many generations, the kin connections became invisible. To neither father nor king could a child consent; a child's allegiance was due from birth. As Sir Robert Filmer wrote:

> It is true, all kings be not the natural parents of their subjects, yet they all either are, or are to be reputed as the next heirs to those progenitors who were at first the natural parents of the whole people, and in their right succeed to the exercise of supreme jurisdiction. And such heirs are not only lords of their own children, but also of their brethren, and all others that were subject to their fathers. . . . By this means it comes to pass that many a child, by succeeding a king, hath the right of a father over many a grey-headed multitude, and hath the title of *pater patriae*.

But there was a built-in contradiction within this theory: while patriarchal power relied on the principle of paternal authority, it was really about lordship. It gave the king or lord primary authority over lesser men's children.[10]

Patriarchal ideas were espoused by James I and his son Charles I, by most Anglican ministers both explicitly and through the catechisms that were the staple of their religious instruction, and by members of the nobility such as Filmer. Two ministers who wrote formal treatises were Robert Sibthorp, vicar of Brackley, and Roger Maynwaring, royal chaplain, both in the 1620s. Filmer, who would become the main formal exponent of these theories by the 1640s, when he published several concisely argued pamphlets, emphasized, like Sibthorp and Maynwaring, the absolute power that these principles granted to the king. His absolutism was part of a broad move by the

9. James I, *The True Lawe of Free Monarchies* . . . (Edinburgh, 1598), rpt. in. David Wootton, ed., *Divine Right and Democracy: An Anthology of Political Writing in Stuart England* (Harmondsworth, 1986), 99, 105.

10. Robert Filmer, *Patriarcha; or, The Natural Power of Kings* (London, 1680), in Johann P. Sommerville, ed., *Patriarcha and Other Writings* (Cambridge, 1991), 12.

Stuarts and Royalists to justify increasing the powers of the monarch. Indeed, in his efforts to grant absolute power to the king, Filmer gave more power to fathers than the laws then granted them, as Filmer's critics pointed out. Both the responsibilities and the privileges of the king were the same as those of a "political father." "If we compare the natural duties of a father with those of a king, we find them to be all one. . . . As the father over one family, so the king, as father over many families, extends his care to preserve, feed, clothe, instruct, and defend the whole commonwealth."[11]

Primogeniture formed the basis for status relationships in both ideology and practice during this period. Primogeniture dictated that property, authority, and status descend from father to the "nearest and lawful heir," usually to the eldest son or, in the absence of a son, to the daughter(s). Primogeniture was the primary means of gaining landed property and an aristocratic or even monarchical title—and thus political power. Between the thirteenth century and 1540, most aristocratic titles and landed property descended via primogeniture in England, and after that date, with slight disruption, both continued to descend so until the early twentieth century.[12]

Filmer acknowledged the ultimate irony of this equation between obedience to fathers and that due kings whose authority derived from primogeni-

11. J. P. Sommerville, *Politics and Ideology in England, 1603–1640* (London, 1986), 29–34, 127–131; Filmer, *Patriarcha*, in Sommerville, ed., *Patriarcha*, 12. This was Filmer's main treatise, written in the 1630s and 1640s but not published until after his death in 1653. His ideas circulated earlier (usually anonymously) in various forms: *Of the Blasphemie against the Holy Ghost* . . . (London, 1647); *The Free-holder's Grand Inquest* . . . (London, 1648); *The Anarchy of a Limited or Mixed Monarchy* . . . (London, 1648); *The Necessity of the Absolute Power of All Kings* . . . (London, 1648); *Observations concerning the Originall of Government* (London, 1652); *Observations upon Aristotles Politiques touching Forms of Government*, including his *Directions for Obedience to Governours in Dangerous and Doubtfull Times* (London, 1652). In 1679 all of these works then published, with the exception of his *Necessity of the Absolute Power of Kings*, were reprinted. In 1680, the last was republished as *The Power of Kings*.

12. Frederick Pollock and Frederic William Maitland, *The History of English Law before the Time of Edward I*, 2d ed. (Cambridge, 1968), II, 363. Although some titles could be "bought" from the king initially (technically, they could be granted by the king in exchange for numerous favors in recognition of somehow noble "blood"), they then descended via primogeniture. James I and Charles II, especially, dramatically expanded the number of members of the House of Lords during the seventeenth century, as a way of consolidating their influence and money. See J. V. Beckett and Clyve Jones, "Introduction: The Peerage and the House of Lords in the Seventeenth and Eighteenth Centuries," in Jones, ed., *A Pillar of the Constitution: The House of Lords in British Politics, 1603–1784* (London, 1989), 1–19.

ture: primogeniture could produce "fathers of their country"—kings—who were children. Power could thus be granted to the very young. "It comes to pass that many a child, by succeeding a king, hath the right of a father over many a grey-headed multitude, and hath the title of *pater patriae* [father of the country]." Patriarchalism thus did not justify the power of older people, but justified inherited authority. A son who was young could, and often did, inherit a kingdom with the power to rule over many older subjects. Filmer's philosophy was echoed in English law and practice through the eighteenth century. According to the legal treatises of Sir Matthew Hale, writing in the late seventeenth century, and even of William Blackstone, writing in the mid-eighteenth, the king could never be limited in his legal capacities, even when nine months old. "The king in his politic capacity is always of full age." The king was always king, and his power came regardless of his age, though he could seek the advice of councillors or a protector. Filmer offered an argument based on status. The king gained his position through primogeniture, not by demonstration of his abilities or his judgment.[13]

Shakespeare's *Richard III* (1597) described the fears and hopes of the populace about young kings. Three citizens discuss Edward V's recent accession to power at age twelve:

> *Third Citizen:* Woe to that land that's govern'd by a child.
> *Second Citizen:* In him there is a hope of government
>   Which, in his nonage, council under him,
>   And, in his full and ripen'd years, himself,
>   No doubt, shall then, and till then, govern well.
> *First Citizen:* So stood the state when Henry the Sixth
>   was crown'd in Paris but at nine months old.
> *Third Citizen:* Stood the state so? no, no, good friends, God wot;
>   For then this land was famously enrich'd
>   With politic grave counsel; then the king
>   Had virtuous uncles to protect his grace.

(2.3.11–21)

13. Filmer, *Patriarcha*, in Sommerville, ed., *Patriarcha*, 10; Matthew Hale, *The Prerogatives of the King* (1640s–1660s?), ed. D. E. C. Yale, Selden Society, Publications, XCII (London, 1976), 93, 99. Also see William Blackstone, *Commentaries on the Laws of England* (Oxford, 1765–1769), I, 241. Blackstone wrote, "Neither can the king in judgment of law, as king, ever be a minor or under age." Kantorowicz, in *The King's Two Bodies,* traces the origins of this idea of the king's authority regardless of his age to the Tudor period (one would assume to the reign of Edward VI, who inherited the throne at nine, or even to Henry VIII, inheriting the throne at seventeen). Yet young kings clearly had significant power earlier.

Although Third Citizen casts doubt on the ability of the new king to reign wisely, by referring to Solomon's injunction, "Woe to the land that's govern'd by a child," the others reassure him, at least temporarily, by arguing that the young king, with good counsel, "shall then, and till then, govern well."[14] Third Citizen's reminder that the person who would provide counsel for the new king, Edward V, would be his uncle the duke of Gloucester, however, leaves the citizens worried. In Shakespeare's play, the citizens had cause to be concerned: Gloucester would murder his nephew Edward and ascend to the throne himself as Richard III. Although this passage warns that evil men like Richard III can gain positions of power by usurping control over a child and then murdering him, it confirms the ability of children to inherit and to rule. It also gives a sense of the frequency with which it happened.

That young kings often came to power would have been acknowledged in England and America. For example, the commonplace book of a young law student, Henry Wells, from Worcester, Massachusetts, about 1770, listed all the kings and queens of England, their years of birth, and their years of accession. He listed ten kings of England who were under the age of twenty-one when they ascended the throne.[15]

Although the young king usually had a protector or councillors, they were technically only councillors: Shakespeare, for example, referred to "council under him" guiding the young king. Edward VI's "protector," his maternal uncle the duke of Somerset, was imprisoned in 1549 for acting without Edward's authority when Edward had been eleven. As Edward expressed it in his own words, Somerset's crime was "following his own opinion, and doing it all by his own authority, etc." instead of Edward's. The king himself was the one who had the honor, who participated in the ceremonies and rituals of power and made the formal decisions. Henry VI inherited the throne at the age of nine months, as Shakespeare acknowledged. At the age of only one year Henry VI was appearing at public functions and took his place in Parlia-

14. This is almost a direct quote from Eccl. 10:16. Algernon Sidney also quoted this passage, citing Solomon, as "Woe unto the kingdom whose king is a child." *Discourses concerning Government* (1698), ed. Thomas G. West (Indianapolis, Ind., 1990), 119.

15. Kings under twenty-one from the commonplace book of Henry Wells, Worcester, Mass., ca. 1770, Harvard Law Library, MS 5250.

	King	Age	Accession		King	Age	Accession
1	Henry II	20	1154	6	Edward IV	19	1460
2	Henry III	9	1216	7	Edward V	12	1483
3	Edward III	15	1327	8	Henry VIII	17	1509
4	Richard II	11	1377	9	Edward VI	9	1546
5	Henry VI	1	1422	10	Charles II	18	1648

ment. He was knighted in May 1426 at age four and crowned in November 1429 when only seven. He was also heir to the monarchy of France and was crowned there in December 1431 at the age of ten.[16]

Young children among the nobility often inherited property and power as well, partly because of shorter life spans. One study of fifteenth-century England found that 50 percent of sons inherited their titles and property from their fathers when they were twenty or younger. Although many young nobles had guardians to manage their lands, like the councillors to the king, these guardians had limited authority over the land and the person of the heir. These boys (and sometimes girls) would inherit their title immediately. Of the many thousands of nobility who inherited their titles while very young, two poets illustrate the policy: John Wilmot, the second earl of Rochester, succeeded to his father's earldom at the age of ten in 1658; and George Gordon, sixth Lord Byron, inherited his granduncle's title at age ten in 1798. The accession to a title made such boys eligible for a seat in the House of Lords if the title bore that privilege and the king issued a writ calling them to attend. Indeed, at least before the English Civil War, it was routine to call both the lord *and* his eldest son who would inherit the title to the House of Lords, a practice that would have made for many youthful members.[17]

Inheriting land could also make boys eligible to stand for the House of Commons, including many future peers whose fathers were still alive. While one had to have inherited a title (for the House of Lords) or fulfilled a property qualification (for the House of Commons), one's age was largely irrelevant. Indeed, many teenagers were elected to the Commons in the seventeenth century. Between 1660 and 1690 alone, forty-three boys under age twenty-one gained seats in the Commons. Christopher Monck, for example, won the by-election for Devon at age thirteen in 1667. He was immediately assigned

16. W. K. Jordan, ed., *The Chronicle and Political Papers of King Edward VI* (Ithaca, N.Y., 1966), as cited by Jennifer Loach, *Edward VI*, ed. George Bernard and Penry Williams (New Haven, Conn., 1999), 91. Edward VI participated in political decisions and left many political writings in his own hand from his reign, between his ascension to the throne at age nine and his death at fifteen.

17. Joel T. Rosenthal, *Patriarchy and Families of Privilege in Fifteenth-Century England* (Philadelphia, 1991), 38, and table, 34. His study of inheritance of titles was based on postmortem "inquisitions" in Yorkshire, Nottinghamshire, Lancashire and chancery court records for the region. Girls also inherited property and titles, but only if they had no brothers. On serving in the Lords, see Elizabeth Read Foster, *The House of Lords, 1603–1649: Structure, Procedure, and the Nature of Its Business* (Chapel Hill, N.C., 1983), 13, 15. In some cases minor sons were not called, and the issue was clearly disputed, even during the early seventeenth century.

to committees and at the age of fourteen gave a critical floor speech in which he argued for the impeachment of the first earl of Clarendon. The voters of Monmouth chose Charles Somerset for their representative in 1677, when he was only sixteen. Ralph Grey became a member for Berwick upon Tweed at age seventeen in 1679, and Peter Legh for the "family borough" in 1685 at age fifteen. This pattern was not new to the seventeenth century: in 1572 the borough of Wigan elected Richard Molyneux II to Parliament when he was only twelve years old.[18]

The election of these young men reflected their status. Christopher Monck, for example, was also the earl of Torrington and at age sixteen succeeded his father as duke of Albemarle. He had entered Gray's Inn to study the law at age eight, was appointed captain of His Majesty's Foot Guards at age twelve and commissioner for assessment at Devon at age thirteen, was made knight of the Garter at age sixteen, and married the daughter of the duke of Newcastle, Elizabeth Cavendish (heir to twenty thousand pounds), in the same year. Charles Somerset, Lord Herbert of Raglan, was the godson of Charles II. Of the forty-three teenagers elected to Parliament between 1660 and 1690, twenty-four, or more than half, were the sons of peers. The election of these young men to Parliament was consistent with patriarchal theory; their election rested on their birth status.[19]

Their election reflected not only their own but also their families' influence over the voters in those boroughs in a period when all votes were viva voce, when particular families controlled even who stood for elections. Some of those many sons who inherited properties and titles at young ages were chosen to run for Parliament in order to retain control over the seats their fathers had held. They were either the prominent landowners in their borough or chosen by that landowner. Indeed, the election of teenagers seemed most frequent in cases of patronage, where noble families or powerful political appointees had control over who would stand for election. In 1621, for example, Thomas Wriothesley, the fifteen-year-old son of the earl of Southampton, was elected from Callington, in Cornwall, by the patronage of the earl of Pembroke. Even after the passage of the 1696 law that prohibited "infants under 21" from standing for a seat in Parliament, some constituen-

18. 7 and 8 Will. III, c. 25, An Act for the Further Regulating Elections. The 1696 law did not apply to the House of Lords. See Basil Duke Henning, ed., *The House of Commons, 1660–1690* (London, 1983), I, 1–3, II, 443–444, 533, 727–728, III, 73–74, 453–454. Also see Keith Thomas, "Age and Authority in Early Modern England," British Academy, *Proceedings*, LXII (1976), 213.

19. Henning, ed., *House of Commons, 1660–1690*, I, 2.

cies continued to elect teenagers (particularly constituencies dominated by powerful families).[20]

Virginians followed the English model of sometimes electing elite young members to its lower house on the basis of their status. Thus, Daniel Parke's election to the House of Burgesses in April 1688 at the age of eighteen reflected his connections. Daniel was the only son of a wealthy and prominent father of the same name, who had also served as a burgess and had died when Daniel was only nine or ten in 1679. At age fifteen, in 1685, Daniel married Jane Ludwell, who possessed, according to a contemporary account, a "great fortune." Philip Ludwell, her father, was Daniel's guardian and had married the widow of Governor Berkeley, in whose mansion at Green Spring she had grown up. Philip Ludwell was extremely powerful in Virginia politics during the 1680s; it was he, in fact, who apparently helped to secure Daniel's election in 1688. Both Daniel Parke and Willis Wilson thus fit the picture of teenage males elected to Parliament during the seventeenth century: significant wealth, high status, powerful patron, previous membership of father, often early inheritance.[21]

Many appointed offices could also be held by children, as is clear in the case of Christopher Monck, above, who became an army captain at age twelve and a commissioner for assessment at age thirteen. The official rule was that one should be at least eleven to be appointed to positions at court or a ministry. Military officers were supposed to be at least sixteen after 1677 for the navy and after 1711 for the army, but younger officers were appointed throughout the eighteenth century. Other offices, such as justice of the peace, king's attorney, or sheriff, had no age limitations. Sir John Randolph, for example, was appointed king's attorney in the county courts of Charles City, Henrico, and Prince George in Virginia at age eighteen. Children could inherit offices such as "Steward, or Ward of the Fleet," through the nineteenth century in England.[22]

20. John K. Gruenfelder, *Influence in Early Stuart Elections, 1604–1640* (Columbus, Ohio, 1981), 129; Thomas, "Age and Authority," British Academy, *Proceedings*, LXII (1976), 231.

21. Edward W. Greenfield, "Some New Aspects of the Life of Daniel Parke," *VMHB*, LIV (1946), 306–315. The fragmentary nature of birth dates for Virginians during this period means that we will never know the precise number of burgesses who were teenagers. Edward Digges, who was elected to the House of Burgesses in 1734, might have been under twenty-one, since his father was born in 1692 (forty-two years earlier). But his date of birth cannot be determined.

22. On appointive offices, see, for example, Hening, ed., *Statutes at Large*, III, 250–251 (1705), where the law prevents blacks and Indians from holding office and requires a three-year residency in a county but says nothing about age. Also see *The Infants Lawyer;*

That young men exercised power illuminates the irony within patriarchal ideology wherein children were the model of obedience and subordination: as Filmer noted, many a young man ruled over a "grey-headed multitude." In part this apparent contradiction arose because patriarchal theory was a sixteenth- and seventeenth-century patchwork, put together in response to the challenge of the Reformation in order to rationalize an earlier system. This irony would help spawn the debates over the theory and practice of hereditary status. Patriarchal theory saw children's obedience as a filial duty that did not end with age; it did not differentiate between children and adults. This duty might end with the father's death—with succession and inheritance— but, for most of society, it did not. Younger siblings were supposed to owe the obedience they owed to their father to his replacement, their eldest male sibling. Subjects of a king owed their allegiance to his heir. Therefore, although parent-child relations were at the core of patriarchal theory, it was not really about children: the purpose of this ideology was to reify status relationships.

One of the most repeated arguments against primogeniture as a rule for the allocation of property and power was the fact that children, sometimes infants of a year or two, might come to positions of great power. The possibility that the king could be a child enabled a sharp critique of inherited right as justified by patriarchal ideology. In the 1680s Sidney, for example, condemned the rules of primogeniture, since they made "women and children . . . patriarchs; and the next in blood, without any regard to age, sex, or other qualities of the mind or body, . . . the fathers of as many nations as fall under their power. We are not to examine whether he or she be young or old, virtuous or vicious, sober minded or stark mad; the right and power is the same in all." One hundred years later, Thomas Paine condemned hereditary government because it "puts children over men, and the conceits of nonage over wisdom and experience." The brunt of their criticism centered on the figure of the child king (partly since monarchy was purely hereditary and the institution remained unreformed).[23]

---

or, The Law (Both Ancient and Modern) Relating to Infants (London, 1697), 15: "He at 11 years of age may be Grantee of an Office . . . and as an Infant may have an Office by Discent as to be Steward, or Warden of the Fleet, etc., so he may by grant." On Randolph, see Dictionary of American Biography, s.v. "Randolph, Sir John." On naval and army commissions, see Eric Robson, "Purchase and Promotion in the British Army in the Eighteenth Century," History, XXXVI (1951), 69–70; Charles M. Clode, The Military Forces of the Crown (London, 1869), I, 383, II, 91, 609–610; Thomas, "Age and Authority," British Academy, Proceedings, LXII (1976), 213 n. 5.

23. Sidney, Discourses concerning Government, ed. West, 6; Thomas Paine, The Rights of Man (1791–1792), rpt. in Michael Foot and Isaac Kramnick, eds., Thomas Paine Reader (Harmandsworth, 1987), 274. Also see, for example, Common Sense (1776), rpt. in

The arguments against "Beard-less Politicians" appeared first and most strongly among the Puritans, in both England and New England. In 1621 they introduced legislation to bar those under twenty-one from Parliament, but the bill did not pass the Commons. The fragmentary notes on the debate say simply, "Mr. Weston Moved to have added to the bill [on reforming elections] that no man may be chosen under xxi yeares of Age, that he may not dispose of the Countryes estate before he can dispose of his owne." Puritans in Massachusetts passed the first such legislation in 1641, limiting both the ability to vote and to be elected to "Freemen" to the age of "twenty and one years." During the Interregnum in 1653, the Barebones Parliament, under the influence of Oliver Cromwell and largely Puritan, required that members of Parliament be twenty-one. With the restoration of Charles II, a newly elected, pro-Royalist Parliament repealed this exclusion, as it did all of the Interregnum legislation.[24]

Likewise, Virginia followed England's pattern nearly exactly during the Interregnum. With Puritans temporarily in control in Virginia (by aid of Commonwealth warships and commissioners and enforced loyalty oaths to the new "common wealth"), the Virginia assembly passed the same law, virtually word for word, in 1655. The English law reads: "That the persons who shall be elected to serve in Parliament shall be such (and no other than such) as are persons of known Integrity, fearing God, and of Good Conversation, and being of the Age of twenty-one years." The Virginia law: "That the persons who shall be elected to serve in the Assembly shall be such and no other then such as are persons of knowne integrity and of good conversation and of the age of one and twenty yeares." These issues of integrity and "good conversation" were Puritan, and Virginia was simply copying this Rump Parliament legislation. As in England, a restored, Royalist Virginia assembly "utterly abrogated and repealed" this law as one of the "alterations of the lawes" during the "late unhappy distractions" that encouraged "deviations from his majesties obedience." That Virginians repealed this law is

_____

Thomas Paine Reader, 77: "Another evil which attends hereditary succession is, that the throne is subject to be possessed by a minor at any age."

24. Wallace Notestein, Frances Helen Relf, and Hartley Simpson, eds., Commons Debates, 1621 (New Haven, Conn., 1935), II, 460, IV, 446, V, 221, VI, 205. Edward Coke, among others, clearly supported this bill reforming elections, which was offered again, with even less support, in 1626. See William B. Bidwell and Maija Jansson, eds., Proceedings in Parliament, 1626 (New Haven, Conn., 1992), II, 25. On the Puritan legislation, see entries under "Age" and "Elections" (esp. item 4) in The Laws and Liberties of Massachusetts (San Marino, Calif., 1998) (facsimile of Cambridge, Mass., 1648), 1–21. On the Barebones Parliament, see C. H. Firth and R. S. Rait, eds., Acts and Ordinances of the Interregnum, 1642–1660 (London, 1911), II, 817 (Dec. 16, 1653).

almost more interesting than the English repeal at the Restoration. In England, Parliament repealed all laws passed during the Commonwealth, whereas in Virginia the assembly did so only selectively: in Virginia, therefore, repealing this guideline for electing burgesses was a conscious, judicious action.[25]

Between the Civil War and the Glorious Revolution, age became more of a republican or Whig issue and less associated with Puritans or Dissenters. During the reign of Charles II, the election of minors was controversial partly because Sir Edward Coke had tried to effect the reform (which he had supported as a member of Parliament in 1621) via common law fiat in the fourth volume of his *Institutes of the Laws of England*. The pamphlet wars of the 1680s and the Glorious Revolution of 1688 led to substantial reforms in age restrictions on who could serve in both houses of Parliament. After 1685, members of the House of Lords who were under age twenty-one were supposed to hold only observation privileges, not voting rights (they could attend but could not speak). And after 1696 the election of minors to the House of Commons was officially void.[26]

25. On the control of Puritans in Virginia and loyalty oaths to the Commonwealth, see Thomas J. Wertenbaker, *Virginia under the Stuarts, 1607–1668* (Princeton, N.J., 1914), 103; Hening, ed., *Statutes at Large*, I, 363–364, 371 (1652). For the laws themselves, see Firth and Rait, eds., *Acts and Ordinances of the Interregnum*, II, 817 (Dec. 16, 1653); Hening, *Statutes at Large*, I, 411–412 (March 1655). For the repeal of the laws with the Restoration in Virginia, see Hening, ed., *Statutes at Large*, II, iii–iv: "These revised laws were compiled from those previously enacted, with such alterations as rendered them consistent with the monarchical government then re-established." For the texts of the laws, see II, 41–43, 82. Virginia's 1653 law requiring burgesses to be twenty-one appeared only in manuscript. Because the House of Burgesses published all laws in force, that 1653 law was one of those repealed.

26. On Coke, see Chapter 7. For the 1685 standing order in the House of Lords, see John Hatsell, *Precedents of Proceedings in the House of Commons* (London, 1796), II, 11. Because the right to sit in the House of Lords depended on the king's pleasure (on his issuing a writ calling for their attendance), in some individual cases before 1685 it is clear that young lords were not called to attend the House of Lords until they were over twenty-one. The issue was contested especially after 1660 (and the restoration of the House of Lords itself, along with the monarchy). Indeed, the fact that this reform precedes the Glorious Revolution, that it came in the midst of the turmoil of the 1680s, indicates the contention surrounding it. Especially in the period before the Civil War, the House of Lords seems to have been more like a privy council to the monarch, who called those with whom he (or she) wanted to consult (Foster, *The House of Lords, 1603–1649*, 13–16). Charles II issued writs for minors to attend the House of Lords at least twice in 1667 (the earls of Mulgrave and Rochester, both nineteen or twenty), cases that we know about because the House of Lords took it upon itself to refuse them admission,

These reforms during Cromwell's reign and just before and after the Glorious Revolution were passed in the face of a flood of pamphlets that argued for even higher age limitations than twenty-one on those who could be elected. Harrington suggested thirty in *Oceana* (1656). Gerrard Winstanley, a Leveller pamphleteer, suggested forty as the minimum age of service for high public office. The Parliamentarian William Prynne, who argued so fiercely against the corruption of the English bishops and against Archbishop Laud in particular in the 1630s and 1640s that he had his ears cut off twice (first the ears and then the stumps) and his face branded, wrote a pamphlet entitled *Minors No Senators* in 1646.[27]

The Royalist Arise Evans, in *A Rule From Heaven* (1659), urged that both king and members of Parliament should be over fifty, apparently not understanding that this reform was incompatible with succession by primogeniture. (By this rule, kings could not die until at least age seventy, presuming that they had fathered a living child in their teens.) It was rarer for Royalists to take this stand, but not exceptional: James I had urged, in a royal proclamation, that electors not choose "young and inexperienced men" for the Commons, and sometimes refused to issue writs to younger men to serve in the Lords. Both men illustrate how this issue could partially cut across political camps.[28]

Henry Care, a popular and persuasive Whig pamphleteer in the critical decade of the Glorious Revolution, argued that maturity was necessary for elected members of Parliament. His *English Liberties; or, The Freeborn Subject's Inheritance*, published in 1680 and reprinted many times in England and North America, fulminated against the practice of electing "young Green Persons." Minors, he claimed, did not have reason and could more easily be corrupted.

> Be resolved (against all Temptations) to choose *no minors:* What, will you be content with *sucking Statesmen?* and *Beard-less Politicians?* . . . then expect, for well you deserve to be lasht with *Scorpions:* Can you Judge them fit to dispose of your Liberties, Lives Estates and Religion, who cannot legally dispose of their own Estates or themselves? What security can they give you, that they will not give away *yours and you,* whose Bond in the eye

---

apparently afraid that admitting them would compromise its integrity. Andrew Swatland, *The House of Lords in the Reign of Charles II* (Cambridge, 1996), 33–34.

27. George H. Sabine, ed., *The Works of Gerrard Winstanley* (Ithaca, N.Y., 1941), 515, 543, 551, 577, 596, and cited by Thomas, "Age and Authority," British Academy, *Proceedings,* LXII (1976), 229.

28. James F. Larkin and Paul L. Hughes, *Stuart Royal Proclamations* (Oxford, 1973–), I, 494.

of the Law will not be taken for 40 s[hillings]? but sure your own experience of what such *young Green persons* have been and done in former Parliaments, hath I hope learned you sufficient wisdom, not to chuse the like again.[29]

Do not elect minors, because they cannot make wise decisions. In making this argument, Care exaggerated the legal disqualifications of those under twenty-one.

William Penn played an important role in these debates, publishing pamphlets that urged electors to choose representatives carefully, appealing to their reason and conscience. He made the governorship of Pennsylvania inheritable via primogeniture. He did, however, set up provisions in case the governor were under twenty-one that provided real power to a regent, significantly beyond that given a protector of a king. So, although Penn did not abandon the idea of inherited right based on primogeniture, he did respond to one of the chief objections to it.[30]

England's monarchy, meanwhile, remained unreformed. Influential Whig political writers of the early eighteenth century, even after the reforms in the Lords and the Commons, continued to express alarm at the idea of young kings in power—the last and most problematic of the three main arenas of formal political power in early-eighteenth-century England where a child could rule. Thomas Gordon and John Trenchard, in their popular *Cato's Letters,* argued that a king who was a child was a horrifying proposition: by definition he would be inexperienced, unlearned, and probably amoral. They described a young king who refused to obey his "governor," or tutor. They argued that, if a king gained power while young, it would be difficult for him to be properly instructed in right or wrong, as children needed to be instructed. For Gordon and Trenchard, unrestrained power in a prince's hands would corrupt his character and lead him to tyranny.

I have been told of a Prince, who, while yet under age, being reproved by his Governor for doing things ill or indecent, used to answer *Je suis Roy, I am King;* as if this Quality had altered the Nature of Things, and he himself had been better than other Men, while he acted worse. . . . What then, Sir? . . . By Nature you are no better than your people.[31]

29. [Henry Care], *English Liberties; or, The Free-born Subject's Inheritance* . . . [London, 1680?], 103.

30. Staughton George, Benjamin M. Nead, and Thomas McCamant, comps., *Charter to William Penn, and the Laws of the Province of Pennsylvania* . . . (Harrisburg, Pa., 1879), 98.

31. [John Trenchard and Thomas Gordon], *Cato's Letters; or, Essays on Liberty, Civil and*

Here Gordon and Trenchard sought to undermine the argument based on status. A king was no better than his people. While young and untaught, he should not have too much power to act "ill or indecent." A king who had not learned reason needed a governor and not unlicensed political authority. But no laws appeared in eighteenth-century England, during its long period of peace and stability, to limit the authority of young kings (perhaps because none in fact ascended the throne).

After the American Revolution, reformers introduced much higher age restrictions for elected office than had existed in England or in any of its colonies. The American Constitution imposed even higher age qualifications than twenty-one: twenty-five for serving in the House of Representatives, thirty for the Senate, thirty-five for the presidency. These restrictions did not come without debate. Notes taken by James Madison give insight into the controversy over age restrictions at the Constitutional Convention. Generally, the delegates agreed that the opinions of even a twenty-one-year-old "were too crude and erroneous to merit an influence on public measures" and that a young man should be better educated via experience before he should be able to obtain a position of such importance. The dominant view was summarized by George Mason of Virginia:

> Col. [George] Mason: . . . thought it absurd that a man to day should not be permitted by the law to make a bargain for himself, and tomorrow should be authorized to manage the affairs of a great nation. . . . He would if inter-rogated be obliged to declare that his political opinions at the age of 21. were too crude and erroneous to merit an influence on public measures. It had been said that Congress had proved a good school for our young men. It might be so for any thing he knew but if it were, he chose that they should bear the expence of their own education.[32]

Mason almost echoed Henry Care: if one cannot make "bargains," that is, personal contracts, one should not be able to hold elected office and consent to political contracts. Both Care and Mason exaggerated children's legal disabilities to make their point. In fact, children could make a variety of legal contracts, although this right too was changing during the eighteenth

---

Religious, and Other Important Subjects, 3d ed. (London, 1733), II, 89. Also see Daniel Defoe, *Six Distinguishing Characters of a Parliament-Man* (London, 1700), one of which characteristics, he argued, should be advanced age.

32. Wilbourn E. Benton, ed., *1787: Drafting the U.S. Constitution* (College Station, Tex., 1986), I, 242. Mason's and Wilson's remarks are taken from James Madison's notes.

century, as the following chapters will trace. Indeed, Mason probably read Care's *English Liberties*. Mason, like Care, used the question of children's legal abilities to underline a point about education and understanding. Even at twenty-one, claimed Mason, a person is likely to hold "crude and erroneous" ideas.

James Wilson of Philadelphia responded to Mason by arguing that reason did not necessarily correlate with age. Yet both agreed that certain qualifications were necessary.

> Mr. Wilson was against abridging the rights of election in any shape. It was the same thing whether this were done by disqualifying the objects of choice, or the persons chusing. . . . There was no more reason for incapacitating *youth* than *age,* where the requisite qualifications were found. Many instances might be mentioned of signal services rendered in high stations to the public before the age of 25; The present Mr. Pitt and Lord Bolingbroke were striking instances.

Wilson thus argued against having an age qualification, implying that age did not determine wisdom, but his ideas were overruled in the final debate.

The *Federalist Papers* themselves did not comment explicitly on this debate, but James Madison supported the essence of Mason's speech. In Federalist No. 62, on the Senate, Madison wrote:

> The qualifications proposed for senators . . . consist in a more advanced age, and a longer period of citizenship. . . . The propriety of these distinctions is explained by the nature of the senatorial trust; which requiring greater extent of information and stability of character, requires at the same time that the senator should have reached a period in life most likely to supply these advantages.

Madison did not describe those under thirty as having "erroneous" ideas, as did Mason. But his linking of "advanced age" with "extent of information and stability of character" shows that he thought that age would bring broad experiences and greater control over passions. Indeed, Madison elaborated on this point in Federalist No. 63. Still referring explicitly to the purpose of the Senate and the qualifications of the senators, he asked: "[When the people go astray] how salutary will be the interference of some temperate and respectable body of citizens, in order to check the misguided career, and suspend the blow meditated by the people against themselves, until reason, justice and truth can regain their authority over the public mind." In the Virginia ratifying convention (1788), the delegates agreed to such age limitations for elected office: "We find no qualifications required except those of age and residence, which create a certainty of their judgment being matured, and of being attached to their state."[33]

The American Constitution not only attacked primogeniture indirectly by limiting the ages of those who could hold national office; it disallowed all hereditary offices. All political offices must thereafter be appointive or elective. This might seem to be a minor, or even an obvious stance, given that America had no hereditary aristocracy, no titled nobility. Of course, it did have some nobility before the Revolution—major propertyholders such as Lords Baltimore and Fairfax, Penn, and others who had titles in England. But the property of most of these titled, major landholders was confiscated on the grounds of treason (loyalty to England) during the Revolution itself. So almost no one with an English title retained land in America.[34]

But could not some new titles have been created as a reward for service or based on wealth, as Napoleon would do after the French Revolution? (Napoleon even created "senatoriates," an imperial nobility inspired by ancient Rome.) Hereditary titles could also have become a reward (or source of income and loyalty), following the practice of James I and Charles II in England during the previous century. The English system of government, upon which the Constitutional Convention was modeling its own, had two preserves where power was based on inherited right: the monarchy and the House of Lords. And in some areas of the country, particularly Virginia, South Carolina, and New York, a substantial inherited quasi aristocracy with vast estates (upheld by primogeniture) had been growing and developing. These landowners could have served as the basis of a new aristocracy had the members of the convention and the populace who were to approve the Constitution been so inclined. In a letter to her husband in 1774 Abigail Adams wrote of the elite in Virginia: "Are not the Gentery Lords and the common people vassals?" Or what about commencing a hereditary aristocracy with those who had been officers in the Continental army? (The Society of the Cincinnati, which was meeting at the same time as the convention in Philadelphia, proposed to limit its membership to this group and its descendants via primogeniture.) These persons could have formed the Senate. Of course, the founding fathers did none of these things. The Constitutional Convention rejected all proposals to endow inherited right with continued legitimacy. What was it in the ideas about

33. Jacob E. Cooke, ed., *The Federalist* (Middletown, Conn., 1961), 415, 425; George Nicholas, as quoted in David Robinson, comp., *Debates and Other Proceedings of the Convention of Virginia* ... (1788), 2d ed. (Richmond, Va., 1805), 18.

34. Fairfax was one of the few who did not lose his claim, in his case, to the Northern Neck in Virginia. His case was disputed, however, for years after the Revolution and finally resolved only by the Supreme Court in 1816.

political legitimacy that dominated the Revolution, that existed among the founding fathers who were members of the elite themselves, that caused them to make such a break with the English past?[35]

Indeed, the Revolution was a more successful echo of the English Civil War of more than a century before, at least of the radical, heady period of the late 1640s: demolishing the monarchy and the House of Lords, enshrining the House of Commons, celebrating the idea that government should be based on the consent of the governed. The differences between the two, certainly in context, are more striking than their similarities. Yet what eerie parallels, at least in initial ideological approach! And why did the one collapse inward upon itself, becoming, in the end, its own antithesis, with a new hereditary monarchy in the person of Oliver Cromwell and no true consent? Cromwell's son Richard then proved no fit king—or protector—and Charles II was restored to the throne. The American Revolutionaries had the benefit of hindsight. But what strains and patterns of thinking, ideologically, connected the two revolutions? Why did Puritans play such an important role in these reforms in the seventeenth century? And why did many Americans come to be attached to the same ideas?

In the years after the Revolution, the Americans challenged inherited right with one further reform, which the English did not implement until the twentieth century, a reform that also measured the limits of their radicalism. They abolished entail, the legal system that enforced primogeniture and governed the transfer of most estates (and titles in England). Even reformers during the English Civil War had not abolished entail, although the Interregnum commission on legal reform of 1652–1653 questioned it.[36]

35. Beckett and Jones, "The Peerage and the House of Lords," in Jones, ed., *A Pillar of the Constitution*, 4–7; Louis Bergeron, *France under Napoleon*, trans. R. R. Palmer (Princeton, N.J., 1981), 62–70; Martyn Lyons, *Napoleon Bonaparte and the Legacy of the French Revolution* (New York, 1994), esp. 173; Georges Lefebvre, *Napoleon: From 18 Brumaire to Tilsit, 1799–1807*, trans. Henry F. Stockhold (New York, 1969), 184; L. H. Butterfield, Marc Friedlaender, and Mary-Jo Kline, eds., *The Book of Abigail and John: Selected Letters of the Adams Family, 1762–1784* (Cambridge, Mass., 1975), 112, 120.

36. Mary Cotterell, "Interregnum Law Reform: The Hale Commission of 1652," *English Historical Review*, LXXXIII (1968), 696–697, 701; Donald Veall, *The Popular Movement for Law Reform, 1640–1660* (Oxford, 1970); Firth and Rait, eds., *Acts and Ordinances of the Interregnum*, II, 587; Stuart E. Prall, *The Agitation for Law Reform during the Puritan Revolution, 1640–1660* (The Hague, 1966), 61–62; Joan Thirsk, "The European Debate on Customs of Inheritance, 1500–1700," in Jack Goody, Joan Thirsk, and E. P. Thompson, eds., *Family and Inheritance: Rural Society in Western Europe, 1200–1800* (Cambridge, 1976), 190. Objections stemmed not only from concerns about equality but from fraud in conveyances.

Entail, seen by eighteenth-century lawyers as feudal rules for the inheritance of power that enforced primogeniture, was much more common in colonial Anglo-America, especially in the South, than most historians have assumed. It had a powerful grip on a large portion of the land in tidewater Virginia. Entail, in lay terms, was a process by which some ancestor wrote in a will, "I leave this to my son and to *the heirs of his body* after him." This coded legal passage then prohibited the man who inherited the property from choosing to whom the property would descend: it automatically followed general rules of primogeniture and went to his eldest son or, if he had no son, to his daughters; if he had no daughter, to his brother; and on and on forever. (The property could descend to daughters, so long as the entail did not specify male heirs.) Primogeniture also described the system of inheritance in Virginia, throughout much of the South, and in England where a person who possessed nonentailed real property died intestate. Primogeniture and entail were part of English common law.[37]

Dissenter colonies, including Massachusetts and Pennsylvania, provided less legal support for entail, especially during the seventeenth century, and testators in these colonies invoked it less frequently. Massachusetts and most New England colonies had never used primogeniture to govern intestates, and entail was uncommon from the seventeenth century. Pennsylvania, although it allowed entail, probably never had a high proportion of testators who used it: fewer than 4 percent of Bucks County wills made between 1685 and 1756, for example, contained entail provisions. Even allowing that the 4 percent is an undercount and that over the eighty-year period from 1685 to 1765 (assuming four generations) 15 percent of property might have been entailed, entail was used much less frequently than in Virginia, where in the tidewater about three-quarters of all property was entailed by the time of the Revolution. When a landowner died intestate, Massachusetts divided the property among the male children but gave a double share to the eldest. Here, as in many instances that affected the legal status of children, the Dissenter colonies took a different path than both England and the southern colonies. Seventeenth-century and early-eighteenth-century fathers in Massachusetts and Pennsylvania had greater testamentary power than fathers in Virginia who possessed entailed property, and thus more real power over their children, at least before the Revolution.[38]

37. Holly Brewer, "Entailing Aristocracy in Colonial Virginia: 'Ancient Feudal Restraints' and Revolutionary Reform," *William and Mary Quarterly*, 3d Ser., LIV (1997), 307–346.

38. See Carole Shammas, Marylynn Salmon, and Michael Dahlin, *Inheritance in America: From Colonial Times to the Present* (New Brunswick, N.J., 1987), 34, and esp.

Those American states that had followed primogeniture and entail reacted against it years after the Revolution, for a variety of reasons, but especially because it had been the central pillar of birthright and aristocracy. They no longer felt that inherited right should be the reason for one brother's having power over his siblings, they accepted at least in part the arguments about equality, and they wanted to control children longer and to prevent them from gaining power while young. For example, the changes Jefferson proposed and Virginia legislators accepted abolished both systems (entail and general primogeniture). Estates were to be divided among all children (females as well as males) when a propertyholder died intestate. A testator had discretion over the disposal of his or her estate and the education of the children. This change generally increased the father's power over his children, since women rarely owned property separately when married, and even as widows often did not have more than a "life interest" in an estate (that is, they had no power over to whom the estate would go). Jefferson described a father's lack of beneficiary control under entail as a problem in the preamble to his bill to abolish it. Entail did "injury to the morals of youth, by rendering them independent of and disobedient to their parents." Jefferson regarded these reforms as the cornerstones of "the foundation . . . for a government truly Republican." They were doubly so: not only did they increase equality of opportunity for the younger generation, but they increased fathers' powers over their children by increasing paternal control over inheritance. Most of all, however, they challenged the power of a hereditary aristocracy. They shifted power, inasmuch as it was associated with land ownership itself, away from inherited right. They did not do so completely, however. Jefferson, like most post-Revolutionary leaders, did not seek to redistribute property among *all* people: the reforms still left the property with the family.[39]

---

table 32-3. Massachusetts, Connecticut, New Hampshire, Rhode Island, Pennsylvania, and Delaware all gave the eldest son a double share of the estate relative to the other sons in the absence of a will. New York, New Jersey, Maryland, Virginia, and North and South Carolina gave all real estate to the eldest son, although personal estate was usually subject to a more equitable division. For an excellent study of the practical effects of paternal control over wills and the power it gave to fathers over their children in Massachusetts, see Philip J. Greven, Jr., *Four Generations: Population, Land, and Family in Colonial Andover, Massachusetts* (Ithaca, N.Y., 1970).

39. Hening, ed., *Statutes at Large*, IX, 226. See bills 20 and 21 of the revisal of the laws, in Julian Boyd et al., eds., *The Papers of Thomas Jefferson* (Princeton, N.J., 1950–), II, 391–392, 394. Also see bill 60, where it is directed that "any father, even if he be not twenty one years old, may, by deed, or last will and testament, either of them being executed in presence of two creditable witnesses, grant or devise the custody and tuition of his child, which had never been married, although it be not born during any part of the infancy of

One last issue, a critical one, is who could vote. Most scholars who have examined suffrage have simply assumed that children could not.[40] Yet all evidence indicates that, if they met the requirements (usually property ownership), they could vote by age twelve. To acknowledge their votes is to chart a sea change in what it means to vote. Whether one was a "freeholder" or "freeman" might allow one to vote (although precise rules varied by borough). The terms could refer to males as young as twelve and did not explicitly refer to those over twenty-one, since most guardianships of land ended at age fourteen before the early eighteenth century. (Elite guardianships of land, those in knight's service, lasted longer.) Peter Legh, for example, discussed above, born in 1669, was made a freeman of Preston in 1682 (at age twelve) and a freeman of Liverpool in 1686 (at age sixteen), the year after he was elected to Parliament. During the Middle Ages, the laws rarely excluded children on the basis of age. When they did so, the ages were much lower, and different boroughs varied in what age or competency was relevant to legal maturity. Instead of age, the main qualifications rested on property ownership.[41]

---

such child, to whomsoever he will" (II, 485). Jefferson, "Autobiography," in Andrew A. Lipscomb, ed., *The Writings of Thomas Jefferson*, I (Washington, D.C., 1903), 73.

40. Inattention to age-based restrictions on suffrage is surprising, since so many historians have written about suffrage. Yet scholars have paid little attention to changes in age qualifications. When they have noticed age-based changes, they have explained them away, much as did William Blackstone in his contemporary discussion of eighteenth-century English voting requirements. Blackstone acknowledged that Parliament passed the first law that explicitly prohibited those under twenty-one from voting in 1696, yet in his effort to make the common law seem consistent he made no attempt to discover prior practice and implied that the 1696 law had ratified earlier policy. Albert Edward McKinley's classic study of suffrage noted that the first age restrictions on suffrage in Virginia appeared in 1699, but he misrepresented the text of the law when he claimed that it showed that such restrictions on those under twenty-one had existed earlier. John K. Gruenfelder's study of English elections has pointed simply to "confusion . . . over just who could vote" even within boroughs. See Blackstone, *Commentaries*, I, 157–158; McKinley, *The Suffrage Franchise in the Thirteen English Colonies in America* (Philadelphia, 1905), 35. The text of the 1699 law, however, merely introduces the requirement without much explanation. Gruenfelder, *Influence in Early Stuart Elections*, 13; Derek Hirst, *The Representative of the People? Voters and Voting in England under the Early Stuarts* (Cambridge, 1975), 29–40, 43, 104, 113, 115–116.

41. On the variations in medieval competency, see Mary Bateson, ed., *Borough Customs*, II, Selden Society, Publications, XXI (London, 1906), esp. 157–160. "Full age" requirements ranged from being able to tell a good penny from a bad, to measuring cloth or counting money. Age requirements ranged from twelve upward for a variety of types of legal activities, with variations between boroughs. On Peter Legh, see Henning, ed., *House of Commons*, II, 727.

The basic requirement for voting in England during the seventeenth century was an annual income of at least forty shillings, although different counties and boroughs in England displayed dramatic variation in their suffrage requirements. In some, suffrage rights were inherited and belonged to a "self-perpetuating oligarchy." John Cannon describes four classes of voting requirements for boroughs: freeholder boroughs, scot and lot boroughs, burgage boroughs, and corporation boroughs. Freeholder boroughs set requirements that related to the value of the property, and scot and lot boroughs related suffrage to the payment of taxes. The last two both made suffrage hereditary: burgage boroughs attached suffrage to a particular piece of property, whereas in the corporation boroughs suffrage rights were personally inherited. Voting rights, in short, were usually attached to property ownership, not to age; they seemed to follow the same pattern of inherited right as, for example, the House of Lords, although they were obviously far less exclusive.[42]

The same law of 1696 that excluded them from serving in Parliament also barred those under twenty-one from voting for members. Before 1696, there was no requirement that electors be over twenty-one. During the Leveller debates in the 1640s at the end of the Civil War, John Wildman had demanded that those who elected the members of the House of Commons should be "all the free-born at the age of twenty-one years and upwards." Virginia followed England in 1699, in an act that used almost exactly the same language as its English counterpart: both acts not only excluded those under twenty-one from the suffrage and from elective office, but they also tried to limit corruption in voting, for instance, by excluding the treating of voters with food and drink before elections as an unjust form of influence. These were parallel attempts to limit the role of influence in elections, whether via children or drunk adults.[43]

Massachusetts and Pennsylvania introduced age qualifications for voting earlier than England or Virginia: Massachusetts in 1634 at twenty years, but raised to twenty-one in 1641 and to twenty-four for non–church members in 1664, and Pennsylvania at twenty-one in its "Laws Agreed upon in England,"

42. R. K. Webb, *Modern England: From the Eighteenth Century to the Present*, 2d ed. (New York, 1980), 52. On borough and county variations, see Mark A. Kishlansky, *Parliamentary Selection: Social and Political Choice in Early Modern England* (Cambridge, 1986), 13, 15, 19; John Cannon, *Parliamentary Reform: 1640–1832* (Cambridge, 1973), 29.

43. John Wildman, "The Case of the Army Truly Stated" (1647), in A. S. P. Woodhouse, ed., *Puritanism and Liberty: Being the Army Debates (1647–9)* . . . (Chicago, 1951), 433; 7 and 8 Will. III, c. 25. For Virginia, see McKinley, *The Suffrage Franchise*, 35; Hening, ed., *Statutes at Large*, III, 172–175.

written in 1682.[44] Massachusetts permitted non–church members to vote only after intense pressure from Charles II, and then attached this higher age (and a higher property requirement). William Penn's "Frame of Government" was directly indebted to the controversies of the early 1680s. Algernon Sidney helped to draft it, and Penn himself was the author of two political tracts on the rights and responsibilities of electors, published in 1679 and 1687. In one, *England's Great Interest in the Choice of This New Parliament* (1689), he encouraged the electors to choose only *"Sincere Protestants."* Those who were not *"Sincere Protestants"* would support the *"Papal Interest,* which indeed is a Combination against good *Sense, Reason* and *Conscience,* and to introduce a blind Obedience without (if not against) Conviction. And that Principle which introduces Implicit Faith and Blind Obedience in *Religion,* will also introduce Implicit Faith and Blind Obedience in *Government."* Penn's equation of "good *Sense, Reason,* and *Conscience"* with the responsibilities of electors and his condemnation of blind obedience in religion, which leads to passive assent to government, illuminate the connection between Dissenters and consensual politics. The ties between Sidney and Penn as well as Penn's own expressions in these political tracts are consistent with Penn's introduction of age requirements.[45]

A century later, the argument that children should not vote was central to the broader debate about suffrage. In the constitutional debates over suffrage qualifications, Gouverneur Morris of Pennsylvania reflected on why the

44. McKinley, *The Suffrage Franchise,* 309, 277; George, Nead, and McCamant, comps., *Charter to William Penn, and the Laws of the Province of Pennsylvania,* 102, par. 34, "Qualifications of electors"; Nathaniel B. Shurtleff, ed., *Records of the Governor and Company of the Massachusetts Bay in New England* (Boston, 1853–1854), I, 115. The age of electors was raised to twenty-one in Massachusetts in 1641; see *The General Laws and Liberties of the Massachusetts Colony* (Cambridge, Mass., 1672), 1. On pressure from Charles I, see Perry Miller, *The New England Mind: From Colony to Province* (Cambridge, Mass., 1953), 127. Even in New England, consensus was not necessarily reached at once on this issue. John Demos notes that, in the early years of Plymouth Colony, freemanship might well have come "before the age of twenty-one" and gives an example of a "puzzling" notation in the colony records from 1667. Demos, *A Little Commonwealth: Family Life in Plymouth Colony* (New York, 1970), 148.

45. On Sidney's contribution to William Penn's "Frame of Government," see Alan Craig Houston, *Algernon Sidney and the Republican Heritage in England and America* (Princeton, N.J., 1991), 232–233; Peter Karsten, "Who Was 'Colonel Sidney'?: A Note on the Meaning of the October 13, 1681, Penn-Sidney Letter," *Pennsylvania Magazine of History and Biography,* XCI (1967), 193–198. The tracts published by William Penn were *England's Great Interest in the Choice of This New Parliament, Dedicated to All Her Freeholders and Electors* [London, 1679] and *Advice to Freeholders and Other Electors of Members to Serve in Parliament . . .* (London, 1687). The quote is from *England's Great Interest,* 4.

states prevented children from voting in order to make larger arguments about other groups. "Children do not vote. Why? Because they want prudence, because they have no will of their own. The ignorant and the dependent can be as little trusted with the public interest." Morris was here using the exclusion of children from the suffrage as a basis for excluding others. Yet he was also making a larger, very strong argument that children could not consent, that their consent was in fact irrelevant, since "they have no will of their own" and were dependent. This argument makes some sense in a world where all votes were oral, before observers who would include one's father, landlord, or employer. John Adams made exactly the same argument in a letter arguing for the denial of the vote to all who were dependent, particularly poor men. "Children . . . have as good Judgment, and as independent Minds as those Men who are wholly destitute of Property." Children, like poor men and women, servants, and slaves, were dependent on those who fed, clothed, and employed them. Thus, for Adams, their votes could be swayed. He thought them incapable of making independent, rational decisions and of voting.[46]

Indeed, although all states settled on the age of twenty-one as appropriate for voting privileges, this settlement was not a given. George Mason, during the Virginia constitutional convention in 1776, had proposed that the suffrage be limited to those over twenty-four with property or to the fathers of three or more children. Also in 1776, Major John Cartwright, a radical in England, proposed lowering the voting age there to eighteen, when "a man is a sufficient judge between palpable right and wrong," and suggested that militia rolls then could be used as voting lists.[47]

Adams's and Morris's justification for excluding those "wholly destitute of property" from the vote was the strongest justification of property qualifications for suffrage, which reflected the ambiguities in republican political theory, the tension between equality and dependence. It described poor adult males as "dependent" and compared them explicitly to children. The arguments comparing poor men to children thrived in the late seventeenth and

46. Benton, ed., *1787: Drafting the U.S. Constitution*, I, 228, 229 (also see Hamilton's *Federalist* no. 79: "A power over a man's subsistence amounts to a power over his will" [Cooke, ed., *Federalist*, 531]); Adams to James Sullivan, May 26, 1776, in Robert J. Taylor et al., eds., *Papers of John Adams* (Cambridge, Mass., 1977–), IV, 208–213.

47. Julian A. C. Chandler, *The History of Suffrage in Virginia* (Baltimore, 1901), 16; John Cartwright, *The Legislative Rights of the Commonalty Vindicated; or, Take Your Choice!* . . . , 2d ed. (London, 1777), 147–148, cited in Thomas, "Age and Authority," British Academy, *Proceedings*, LXII (1976), 232. Thomas sees Cartwright as exceptional. Thomas, however, did not notice the debate over age-based suffrage qualifications described above.

early eighteenth centuries, an outgrowth of the same political theories that led to the introduction of age requirements and provided the justification for the American Revolution. This description of those without property as without "good judgment" enabled older status codes to be justified in new ways.

But these new connections were fragile. Outside of justificaton for the authority over children, consent-based political theory had a powerful egalitarian message that undermined the older status-based distinctions. Breaking the connection between the "dependence" of those who did not own property and their inability to make "good judgments" and have "independent minds" meant allowing them citizenship rights. Property requirements were removed in Pennsylvania during the Revolution, but not in Massachusetts until 1821 and not in Virginia until 1850. Thus, as the many refused to accept the fragile connection between property, independence, and reason during the late eighteenth and early nineteenth centuries (and the secret ballot gave them more independence), ancient property restrictions on the franchise disappeared. Yet even as poor men ceased to be compared to children, other groups, such as women, native Americans, and African Americans, became more likely to be compared to children in their ability to make informed and independent judgments.[48]

The transition from primogeniture and patronage to consent as the fundamental principle underlying legitimate authority is clear. But why exclude children so pointedly? Focusing on children illuminates the meaning of consent and the contest over that meaning. It casts in sharp relief the emergence and construction of that body of ideas clustered around equality and consent. Indeed, in arguing for government based on consent versus government based on inherited right, children were at the center of the controversy.

48. Alexander Keyssar, *The Right to Vote: The Contested History of Democracy in the United States* (New York, 2000). There is a well-established literature on property qualifications for voting in the various states. See, among others, J. R. Pole, *Political Representation in England and the Origins of the American Republic* (Berkeley, Calif., 1971); Donald S. Lutz, *Popular Consent and Popular Control: Whig Political Theory in the Early State Constitutions* (Baton Rouge, La., 1980); Willi Paul Adams, *The First American Constitutions: Republican Ideology and the Making of the State Constitutions in the Revolutionary Era*, trans. Rita Kimber and Robert Kimber (Chapel Hill, N.C., 1980); McKinley, *The Suffrage Franchise*; Chandler, *The History of Suffrage in Virginia*; Chilton Williamson, *American Suffrage: From Property to Democracy, 1760–1860* (Princeton, N.J., 1960); Marchette Chute, *The First Liberty: A History of the Right to Vote in America, 1619–1850* (New York, 1969); Rosemarie Zagarri, *The Politics of Size: Representation in the United States, 1776–1850* (Ithaca, N.Y., 1987); John Phillip Reid, *The Concept of Representation in the Age of the American Revolution* (Chicago, 1989).

CHAPTER 2

"BORNE THAT PRINCES SUBJECTS"? OR "CHRISTIANITY IS NO MANS BIRTH RIGHT"?

THE RELIGIOUS DEBATE OVER INHERITED RIGHT AND CONSENT TO MEMBERSHIP

"Verely·I saye unto you: whosoever doth not receyve the kyngdom of God, as a little childe: he shall not entre therein . . . doubte ye not therfore, but earnestlye believe, that he will lykewyse favourably receive these presente infantes . . . that he will . . . make them partakers of his everlasting kingdome."
Ritual of Baptism, Book of Common Prayer *(1549)*

"A church then I take to be a voluntary society of men, joining themselves together of their own accord. . . . . . . Nobody is born a member of any church; otherwise the religion of parents would descend unto children, by the same right of inheritance as their temporal estates, and every one would hold his faith by the same tenure he does his lands; than which nothing can be imagined more absurd."
John Locke, An Essay on Toleration *(1689)*

Ann Greenough died at age five, but luckily, or so Cotton Mather hoped, not before converting. She "gave astonishing Discoveries of a Regard unto GOD and CHRIST, and her own Soul." "She would put strange *questions* about Eternal Things, and make *answers* her self that were extreamly pertinent." Indeed, her faith and understanding were such that she was "willing to die." Told and retold in one of the only books for children published during the early eighteenth century, her story helped to frame the most difficult dilemma of the Reformation. If faith requires active understanding, then are not children doomed to hell if they die young? Perhaps their parents or others can promise or bind them to the faith, thus protecting them; but, if not, they must be urged to convert as young as possible. "How do you know," the preface to her story queried, "but that you may be the next Child that may die?" *A Token for Children,* which recounted the conversions and deaths of Ann and many other children, was part of a debate over the terms of consent, one that crossed and recrossed the narrow divide between the religious and the political. Like the stories of the heretics burned alive under Queen Mary in the 1550s, her story would help to shape the meaning and conditions of consent, contributing directly and indirectly to the debates over political authority.[1]

Consent played a controversial role in the English political order in the seventeenth century. While some pointed to consent as the basis of authority, others, like Robert Filmer in his effort to justify absolutism, discounted all consensual elements in the English political tradition. The latter must have been purposeful: Parliament had, after all, been functioning on some level since the thirteenth century, and the king had granted most colonies some degree of self-government by means of representative assemblies even during the early seventeenth century, when Filmer was writing. Such representation, however, was not completely inconsistent with Filmer's theory. The king called Parliament rarely and could dismiss it at his pleasure. Filmer insisted that Parliament was called by the king in order to give him advice that was not binding. Thus Filmer dismissed the idea that Parliament embodied the consent of the people.[2]

Such a Parliament whose members (of both houses) were substantial property owners could be seen, as it was in the late Middle Ages, as a division of lordship rather than the representation of those below. Even voters were defined as those who owned property.[3] Property ownership granted "dominium," a power equated on some level with God's. Dominium referred "above all . . . to the power of God," but it also justified status relationships within society. Literally translated, it meant both lordship and property ownership. The transfer of land was also a transfer of power, ideologically as well as

1. James Janeway, *A Token for Children . . . to Which Is Added,* [Cotton Mather,] *A Token for the Children of New England* (Boston, 1728), ix, 97 (Mather's example 4).

2. Robert Filmer, *The Freeholder's Grand Inquest* (London, 1648), rpt. in Johann P. Sommerville, ed., *Patriarcha and Other Writings* (Cambridge, 1991), 69–130, esp. 69–80; this is the main point of the pamphlet.

3. A 1429 statute established a forty-shilling freehold as the basis for voting right. While great variation existed among boroughs as to actual rules, in some cases that law remained in effect and, with inflation, meant a gradual increase in suffrage. The 1614 and 1628 parliaments—Puritan parliaments—tried to expand the idea of who could vote toward "inhabitants" and to disconnect the right from property ownership. By 1641, as Derek Hirst shows, twenty-six boroughs dissociated property ownership from voting (*The Representative of the People? Voters and Voting in England under the Early Stuarts* [Cambridge, 1975], 99). Also see J. H. Plumb, "The Growth of the Electorate in England from 1600–1715," *Past and Present*, no. 45 (November 1969), 90–116, esp. 108–109; Richard Ashcraft, *Revolutionary Politics and Locke's "Two Treatises of Government"* (Princeton, N.J., 1986), 145, 151–153.

legally, and those who owned land were lords over those who lived on it. Not only was the concept of dominium "crucial for thinking about temporal as well as spiritual authority" in sixteenth-century England, but it provided the language for struggles over political legitimacy in late-medieval Europe. Thus the sixteenth-century English lawyer and political theorist Sir John Fortescue referred to "dominium politicum et regale" as the idea that the king must share his authority with others who owned a share of lordship, or substantial amounts of property. "Conciliarists," from the thirteenth century on, had used this concept of dominium to question and eventually challenge the authority of the pope within the Catholic Church on the same grounds by which Fortescue challenged the absolute authority of the king. The influential fifteenth-century French theologian Jean Gerson, a leading figure of the conciliarist movement, argued for the divisibility of dominium within the Catholic Church and expanded his discussion to include royal power as well as papal power. He contended that the king could forfeit his power (if he abused it) to those who had a lesser share of the dominium, who could then consent to another ruler. But these concepts of sharing power invoked consent under conditions circumscribed by birthright. Dominium arose, like kingship itself, from inherited authority. Those who could "consent" to the new monarchy were born to that privilege. These principles thus stayed within the justification of authority via inherited right.[4]

Of course, not everyone in the early seventeenth century agreed with Filmer's views about Parliament. But even supporters of the claims of Parliament could not deny that only a small minority of the nation actually voted and that elections were hardly an exercise in free choice. The consent of the electors was not what we would call "informed consent" or independent consent: elections were fraught with what we would now label corruption. Voting was oral; thus everyone knew how a person voted, and large landowners could influence the choices of those who lived nearby. Their methods included treating people before elections, threatening them, buying goods from them and paying them for services, changing the election places at the last minute, controlling the sheriff who took the votes, and determining who could stand for election. Still, even if many of these voters' votes were bought, they did consent to the election of a member of Parliament for their borough or county. And in some regions voters seemed to resist the control of elites and to take this responsibility seriously.[5] The point is that most voters were

4. J. H. Burns, *Lordship, Kingship, and Empire: The Idea of Monarchy, 1400–1525* (Oxford, 1992), esp. chap. 2, 35–39, 59, 152.

5. John K. Gruenfelder, *Influence in Early Stuart Elections, 1604–1640* (Columbus, Ohio, 1981), contains numerous examples of all of the above.

not making "independent" judgments, and the boundaries and meaning of their consent were carefully circumscribed. Neither was such consent for a member of Parliament a regular and predictable exercise. Parliament might be elected only once in a person's lifetime, or it might be called and dismissed repeatedly at the king's pleasure. Therefore, the idea that a member of Parliament should be responsible to his constituents was fragile, at best.

The principle that consent should play more of a role was boosted by the Reformation. Luther's and Calvin's claims for a priesthood of all believers, who should interpret the Bible for themselves and, joining together, assent to their own leaders had radical implications of religious equality. This threat was recognized by Elizabeth I and seemed to underlie her refusal to accept radical Protestant revisions, even in the face of her obvious alienation from Catholicism. As head of the church, she valued its episcopal, top-down framework. Elizabeth's archbishop John Whitgift wrote that, if individual congregations could choose their ministers and control church membership as the reformers desired, each minister would become "king and pope in his own parish," and the minister would be elevated above even "the prince herself." Indeed, Filmer, like Jean Bodin, who inspired him, sought to justify absolute power for the king in part as a reaction against the threat to monarchical authority posed by the Reformation.[6]

Dissent and Consent

The debate over the just basis of authority was fundamentally transformed by the Reformation. First, the Reformation made patriarchal arguments much more important. The arguments arose both as an outgrowth from it, as in the great weight that both Luther and Calvin placed on paternal authority, and as a response to it, as in the writings of Bodin in France. Second, the Reformation brought to the fore questions of church membership and, by extension, political membership, a debate as much about religious authority as about simple group identity. This debate about church membership raised questions about consent. It also raised questions about just religious authority. Last, the Reformation emphasized the role of the understanding in acquiring faith (as can be seen by the use of the catechism itself and the substitution of vernacular for Latin in religious services) at the same time as it deemphasized visual images. In answering questions about consent to church mem-

6. Elizabeth chose Whitgift as her archbishop in 1583. E. Brooks Holifield, *The Covenant Sealed: The Development of Puritan Sacramental Theology in Old and New England, 1570–1720* (New Haven, Conn., 1974), 38.

bership, this concern with human understanding and its stages of development proved crucial.

Political thought in England did not expose the fault lines in the philosophical justification for monarchical power opened by the Reformation until about 1642, during the English Civil War, for reasons undoubtedly connected to restrictions on what could be published and punishments for sedition. Puritans in England and America initiated this radical phase. They offered an alternative to patriarchalism and dominium as justifications for political power: the consent of the governed.[7] The Dissenters' consent-based arguments inspired democratic-republican political thought. Their arguments for political authority were extensions of their arguments about religious authority and about the role of the individual conscience in making decisions, particularly about faith and church membership. Thus some of the debates over authority happened within religious boundaries more than political, but they had political implications.

Although other scholars have described the weight placed on consent in Puritan political writings, they have paid little attention to what qualified a person to consent or the terms of that consent.[8] Yet the meaning of consent was worked out first in the religious writings, particularly those about baptism and about conscience. The central religious dilemma that was to overlap into political debates was whether membership and leadership should arise from inheritance or from choice. What and who determined the ability to choose church membership? Protestants did not completely separate themselves from the "inherited" right to church membership, but it was one of the central questions of the seventeenth century, if the number of books published on this subject and the sheer volume of pages devoted to it are any guide.

While all Protestants agreed that God's grace was essential to salvation, they disagreed over the extent to which persons could choose to be saved and what they needed to know or do to achieve salvation. Some argued that conversion could be as simple as seeing the light of God. But many argued that only through understanding could a person exercise the choice necessary for conversion and faith: conversion could not be solely an emotional experience,

7. Corrinne Comstock Weston and Janelle Renfrow Greenberg, *Subjects and Sovereigns: The Grand Controversy over Legal Sovereignty in Stuart England* (Cambridge, 1981).

8. See Edmund S. Morgan, ed., *Puritan Political Ideas, 1558–1794* (Indianapolis, Ind., 1965), among others. T. H. Breen, *The Character of the Good Ruler: Puritan Political Ideas in New England, 1630–1730* (New Haven, Conn., 1970), points out that John Wise, Benjamin Franklin, and Jonathan Mayhew urged voters that voting for good rulers was "a matter of conscience" and that in urging this they carried on the Puritan "political traditions" (xix).

because emotions were too wayward and unreliable. The role of the understanding led to a dilemma: What happened when individuals had no understanding, no experience, and could not reason? In short, what about children? The disputes over infant baptism—so fierce that they led to the splintering of Protestant sects, the publishing of literally hundreds of pamphlets, and the making of martyrs—reveal the centrality of this question to the Reformation. Attitudes toward those who were not members—toleration—and the ability to dissent, to separate from membership, were an integral part of the larger issue of membership. These issues were even more important in England as a result of how political and religious power were intertwined: was membership in "Christ's Kingdom" to be determined in the same way as in Elizabeth I's or Charles I's kingdom? Who was to receive authority in these kingdoms, and on what basis? Could Elizabeth I inherit authority over Christ's kingdom as well as over England itself?

The question of infant baptism became crucial because it had determined the creation and retention of church membership for the Catholic Church. The Catholic Church defined heresy, a crime punishable by burning at the stake, as having religious beliefs that differed from those of the Catholic Church after being baptized as an infant. One of the most popular books of the sixteenth and seventeenth centuries recounted the histories of those martyred during the Reformation and Counter Reformation in England. This book, John Foxe's *Book of Martyrs,* repeatedly illustrates the Protestant conundrum. Thomas Causton, for example, was christened and baptized as an infant within the Catholic Church and upon "coming to the age of discretion, that is to say, to the age of fourteen years, didst not dislike or misallow that faith, that religion, or promise then used and approved." A few years later he became Protestant. Godparents had promised on his behalf while he was a baby, yet that was enough—combined with his failure to reject the promise immediately upon turning fourteen—to make him a full member of the Catholic Church. Since he then disagreed with Catholic religious ideas, he was guilty of heresy, of breaking the promise he made in his baptism. He was thus burned alive by Queen Mary in 1555. Yet obviously Causton had not made what we would call an "informed decision" about his baptism. *He* had made no decision at all.[9]

9. Case of Thomas Causton, in John Foxe, *Book of Martyrs* . . . (1563; rpt. New York, 1965), VI, 729–737. Foxe also gave numerous examples of people burned for preaching against infant baptism. *Book of Martyrs,* first published in English as *Actes and Monuments* in 1563, was much expanded in 1570 and republished seven more times by 1684. On its popularity and context, see William Haller, *Foxe's Book of Martyrs and the Elect Nation* (London, 1963). "The stories told in Foxe's book became . . . an essential part of

Just so did birthright determine membership in the Catholic Church. Aquinas, following Augustine, raised concerns about the Catholic Church's position yet ultimately upheld it.

> It seems that infants should not be baptized for the intention of receiving the sacrament is required of the one to be baptized, as was said above. Infants cannot have such an intention since they do not have the use of free will. . . .
>
> Moreover, baptism is the *sacrament of faith,* as was stated above. But infants do not have faith *which requires an act of the will of those who believe,* as Augustine says. . . .
>
> Moreover, I *Peter* states that *baptism saves men not as a removal of dirt from the body, but as the examination of a good conscience towards God.* But infants have neither good nor bad conscience since they do not have the use of reason. Nor can they be suitably examined since they do not have sufficient understanding. Therefore, infants should not be baptized.

If "infants" do not have reason, they cannot believe and therefore cannot be baptized, Aquinas summarized. But Aquinas then responded to this position: "On the other hand . . . the apostles, *approved of infants receiving baptism.*" Aquinas went on to conclude that "the act of those who bring them for baptism," or the intentions and consciences of those who bring the child, provide the belief for them and promise for their future belief. "Just as the infant when he is baptized believes not of himself but through others, so he is not questioned himself but through others, and these profess the faith of the Church on behalf of the child who is joined to the same by the *sacrament of faith.*" While this form of baptism is not ideal, it is necessary. Since "by birth they incurred damnation through Adam," they were doomed to hell if left unbaptized. Babies need baptism for their spiritual survival in the same way they need mother's milk for their physical survival; they naturally long for both: "[1 Peter:] Like newborn babes long for milk, that by it you may grow up into salvation." Baptism both "takes away past sins" and helps to shield the child from future sins. Infants of church members should be baptized as soon as possible after birth, by which they are "incorporated in Christ as his members."[10]

------

that familiar code of reference and expression which no one sharing in the life of that dynamic age could do without" (15). David D. Hall likewise remarks on the popularity of the *Book of Martyrs* in New England, in *Worlds of Wonder, Days of Judgment: Popular Religious Belief in Early New England* (New York, 1989), 45, 50–51.

10. Thomas Aquinas, *Summa Theologiae* (London, 1975), 3a.68.5, 9–10, also 3a.68.3: "If it is a question of infants who are to be baptized, their baptism should not be delayed."

The Catholic Church retained this stance even after the Reformation; the Council of Trent repudiated all Protestant arguments against infant baptism. It held that baptism creates membership, via God's grace, in the Catholic Church. While baptism does not automatically follow birth—and certainly some children of Catholic parents died before receiving it—it was supposed to follow as soon as possible. It was thus, in a real sense, a birthright. Baptism was also christening. During the resurgence of Catholicism under Queen Mary, for example, Protestant heretics were discovered when they failed to immediately baptize their children. When, three weeks after his son was born, Thomas Hawkes had not yet baptized him, authorities investigated him: "Sir, this man hath a child which hath lain three weeks unchristened (as I have letters to show); who refuseth to have it baptized, as it is now used in the church." Hawkes was burned alive for his failure to renounce his heresies and baptize his son.[11]

Protestants claimed that their baptism as infants by the Catholic Church had not made them indubitably members. Rather, they held, their repentance and conversion as adults determined their church membership. When Protestants dissociated themselves from the Catholic Church and formed new groups, they did so on the basis of choice as exercised by God and the individual. That religious experience marked the boundary between membership in one group versus another and was marked in physical terms by baptism. But in doing so they questioned the sacramental character of baptism: did baptism itself really transmit God's grace? Most Protestants equivocated on how much choice was actually exercised by the individual as opposed to God in making this transition, yet held that there must be repentance and understanding and commitment in the person who made that choice, or else it meant nothing. Yet, if those qualities were required of the person before baptism, where did that leave the infant who died at less than a year old, who had no chance of learning about or expressing her or his faith? Was this child doomed to hell?

John Calvin offered two solutions to this dilemma, largely followed and elaborated on by many Puritans, both in England and in America. "Assuredly baptism were not in the least suitable to them were their salvation not already included in the promise. 'I will be a God unto thee, and to thy seed after thee.' For they do not become the sons of God through baptism; but because, they

---

11. Foxe, *Book of Martyrs*, VII, 98–99. A good background treatment of the Catholic position on baptism is Jaroslav Pelikan, *The Christian Position: A History of the Development of Doctrine*, I, *The Emergence of the Catholic Tradition (100–600)* (Chicago, 1971), chap. 1.

are heirs of adoption, in virtue of the promise, therefore the Church admits them to baptism." Calvin cited the Old Testament covenant God made with Abraham that allowed Abraham to promise to God on behalf of himself and his children; so, by comparison, could fathers promise for their children in a new covenant. But Calvin argued that baptism was merely a seal of the covenant, not a sacrament, and did not determine whether a child would be saved (thus the covenant promise of the father would operate even if a child died before baptism). When pressed about the inability of children themselves to make such a commitment, Calvin responded that they are "baptized into future repentance and faith . . . the seed of each of these is latent in them."[12]

> This whole thing, if I mistake not, may be clearly and briefly stated in the following position: that persons of adult age, who embrace the faith of Christ, having been hitherto aliens from the covenant, are not to receive the sign of baptism except upon the profession of faith and repentance which alone open to them an entrance to the fellowship of the covenant: but the infant children of Christian parents, since they are received by God into the inheritance of the covenant as soon as they are born, are also to be received in baptism.[13]

Thus Calvin held that, because of God's covenant with Abraham, the children of parents who had professed faith and repentance could be baptized. But was this merely the same position taken by the Catholics, one that did not require learning or understanding to become a church member, one that still emphasized the heredity of membership? What did "sign of baptism" mean? Did baptism still transmit God's grace? If the ritual itself was not necessary for the salvation of those who died too soon after birth, was it necessary at all? Did all children born in the covenant (whose parents were truly in the covenant and had received God's grace) then receive God's grace and remission of the sins of Adam (along with a somehow reduced propensity to commit sins)? What happened if such a child did not become a good church member?

These questions would haunt the Reformation over the next two centuries; they would splinter the Protestant movement itself. In the passage above, Calvin was responding to one of the fiercest debates of his day with groups

12. Lewis Bevens Schenck, *The Presbyterian Doctrine of Children in the Covenant: An Historical Study of the Significance of Infant Baptism in the Presbyterian Church in America* (New Haven, Conn., 1940), 9, citing John Calvin's tract of 1544, and 19, citing *Institutes of the Christian Religion* (1559), book 4, chaps. 16, 20.

13. Schenck, *Children in the Covenant*, 23, citing Calvin, *Institutes*, book 4, chaps. 16, 24.

that came to be labeled Anabaptists. Ulrich Zwingli, also influential on the English and Scottish reformers, ultimately took a similar stance, but not without first accepting and then rejecting the idea that baptism should only follow a profession of faith. "That error also seduced me some years ago, so that I thought it was much better that one should not baptize children until they should have attained to proper age."[14]

Few open objections to infant baptism were published in England before 1640, undoubtedly because of both fear of punishment (two ministers who published objections against baptism and other sacraments as administered by the Anglican Church in the 1590s were executed, for example) and tight restrictions on the presses. The few English books printed bear a Holland pressmark.[15] The issue was clearly very important, however, and a range of opinions about the meaning of baptism appeared among the hundreds of catechisms published between the 1530s and 1630s, where it occupied dispro- portional space. But, with the English Civil War, the floodgates opened, and hundreds of books on infant baptism poured out of English presses. Thou- sands of other books, including catechisms, addressed the disputes surround- ing infant baptism. Disagreements over these issues account for the origins of Baptists and Quakers, to name just two sects. Infant baptism was debated fiercely between the 1630s and 1660s in New England, which was involved directly in the English debate, with theologians such as John Davenport, John Cotton, and Richard Mather responding to English antipaedobaptists such as John Tombes, who in turn addressed one of his writings specifically to the "Elders of the Churches of Christ in New England. . . . Understanding that there is some disquiet in your churches about Paedobaptisme."[16]

14. Schenck, *Children in the Covenant*, 24, citing Ulrich Zwingli, "Vom touf, vom wider touf, und vom kindertouf [Of baptism, of antibaptism, and of child baptism]," in *Werke*, II, part 1 (Zurich, 1830), 245.

15. John Smyth repudiated infant baptism in *The Character of the Beast* . . . [Mid- dleburg, 1609]; he actually led a group of Separatists to Amsterdam to settle. Henry Barrow and John Greenwood were executed in 1593. See Holifield, *The Covenant Sealed*, 65–66. Also see, for example, John Davenport, *A Just Complaint against an Unjust Doer* . . . (Amsterdam, 1634) and *An Apologeticall Reply to a Booke Called an Answer* (Rotterdam, 1636); William Best, *The Churches Plea for Her Right* . . . (Amsterdam, 1635). Davenport, while admitting the ability to baptize a child if one parent had experienced saving grace, objected against "promiscuous baptism" (*An Apologeticall Reply*, 132–140).

16. Ian Green, *The Christian's ABC: Catechisms and Catechizing in England, c. 1530– 1740* (Oxford, 1996), 527 ("The weight of interpretation placed on the simple act of sprinkling water on a child's head was a heavy one"); John Tombes, *An Apology, or Plea, for the Two Treatises* . . . (London, 1646), 13, published with *Two Treatises and An Appendix*

The dilemma of the reformers over church membership was captured by John Cotton in 1647.

> Satan . . . now pleadeth no other arguments [against children's baptism] in these stirring times of Reformation than may be urged from a maine Principle of Purity and Reformation, to wit, "that no duty of Gods worship, nor any ordinance of religion is to be administered in the church but such as hath just warrant from the word of God." And by urging this argument against the Baptisme of children, Satan transformeth himselfe into an Angell of Light. . . . And so he hopeth to prevaile, either with those men who doe believe the lawful and holy use of childrens baptisme to renounce that principle, and so to renounce also all Reformation brought in by it: or else, (if they stick by that principle) then to renounce the baptisme of children.[17]

Cotton believed that children left unbaptized were more likely to be Satan's subjects. To prevent their baptism, Satan garbed himself in God's language of faith and repentance: If the Reformation was committed to the idea that only those who had "just warrant from the word of God" could become church members, then admitting children who could not understand God's word was a contradiction. Including them without any expectation that they understood their commitment and God's grace seemed to undermine the Reformation itself and lead back to Catholicism. By attributing these arguments to a Satan clothed as "an angell of light," Cotton both acknowledged their power and sought to refute them.

New England ministers who objected to the baptism of infants included Roger Williams, John Norcott, and Henry Dunster, who resigned as first president of Harvard College over this issue in 1654. John Tombes, one of the most prolific authors to oppose infant baptism in England, expressed their main objection succinctly: "If we once admit men to baptism without their own personal profession, we shall be utterly confounded." Ignorance would grow apace, and no one would struggle to seek the truth. "He that shall heare you preach, that the children of believers are in the Covenant of grace, and that they that are in the Covenant of grace cannot fall away, may be apt to conceive himselfe within the Covenant of grace without repentance and faith,

---

to Them concerning Infant Baptism (London, 1646). Tombes also named John Cotton as one of his opponents in his 1654 pamphlet, Anti-paedobaptism; or, The Second Part of the Full Review of the Dispute concerning Infant-Baptism (London, 1654).

17. John Cotton, The Grounds and Ends of the Baptisme of Children of the Faithfull . . . (London, 1647), 3.

and that he shall be saved without obedience, and so lay a ground-work for *Antinomianisme,* and consequently Libertinisme."[18]

New England Puritan orthodoxy, as it formed, tried to walk a balance between two chasms. The leading ministers wanted neither the inclusive vision of the Church of England nor to exclude infant baptism altogether. They feared the latter would tread a path toward anarchy. As a formal act of the Massacusetts General Court declared in 1644, "Since the first rising of the Anabaptists, about one hundred years since, they have been the incendiaries of the commonwealths." By challenging the authority of ministers, Anabaptists threatened to undermine good order. "Divers of this kind have since our coming into New England appeared amongst ourselves, some whereof . . . denied the ordinance of magistracy." Many of them also opposed war with the Indians, calling it a violation of the Ten Commandments. As a consequence of the threats they posed to order, all those who denied infant baptism could be banished.[19]

Despite this threat, infant baptism was the major concern of every synod (or formal attempt to define religious doctrine) called in New England during the seventeenth century.[20] The call for the synod of 1646, for example, which took the form of a bill passed by both houses of deputies and magistrates, made this purpose clear:

> Some differences of opinion and practice of one church from another do already appeare amongst us, and others (if not timely prevented) are like speedily to ensue, and this not onely in lesser things, but even in pointes of no small consequence and very materiall, to instance in no more but only those about baptisme, and the persons to be received thereto, in which one particular the apprehensions of many persons in the country are knowne not a little to differ; for whereas in most churches the ministers do [baptize]

18. Williston Walker, ed., *The Creeds and Platforms of Congregationalism* (New York, 1893), esp. 169; John Tombes, *Felo de Se . . .* (London, 1659), 34; Tombes, *Anti-paedo-baptism,* 53.

19. This act of the General Court, dated November 13, 1644, is cited in Isaac Backus, *A History of New England, with Particular Reference to the . . . Baptists* (1777–1796), 2d ed., ed. David Weston (1871; New York, 1969), I, 126.

20. This point is also made by Stephen Foster, *The Long Argument: English Puritanism and the Shaping of New England Culture, 1570–1700* (Chapel Hill, N.C., 1991), chap. 5; and Holifield, *The Covenant Sealed,* chap. 3; but neither fully explains why. While drawing attention to the centrality of baptism, Foster is puzzled by why they had "so extraordinary a contest over so limited and necessary an adjustment" (188). Also see Michael Watts, *The Dissenters: From the Reformation to the French Revolution* (Oxford, 1978), esp. chaps. 1–4; J. F. McGregor, "The Baptists: Fount of All Heresy," in McGregor and B. Reay, eds., *Radical Religion in the English Revolution* (Oxford, 1986), 41.

onely such children whose nearest parents, one or both of them, are setled members, in full communion with one or other of these churches . . . [some baptize grandchildren, some think there should be even] more liberty and latitude . . . on the other side there be some amongst us who do thinke that whatever be the state of the parents, baptisme ought not to be dispensed to any infants whatsoever.

Infant baptism, the only issue to be addressed at any length in this call for the synod, was "of no small consequence and very materiall."[21]

The 1648 synod adopted the majority practice and conformed with Calvin's position: "The matter of a visible church are *Saints* by calling. By Saints wee understand, Such, as have not only attained the knowledge of the principles of Religion, and are free from gros and open scandals, but also do together with the profession of their faith and Repentence, walk in blameles obedience to the word. . . . The children of such, who are also holy." It elaborated further on the conversion experience that would admit members to the church: All church members must have *"Repentance* from sin, and *faith* in Jesus Christ" as shown by a "personall and publick *confession.*" Although it did allow the children of those who had this experience to be "also holy," this holiness was clearly temporary, lasting only during childhood:

The like tryall is to be required from such members of the church, as were born in the same, or received their membership, and were baptized in their infancy, or minority, by vertue of the covenant of their parents, when being grown up [u]nto years of discretion, they shall desire to be made partakers of the Lords supper. . . .

Yet these church-members that were so born, or received in their childhood, before they are capable of being made partakers of full communion, have many priviledges which others (not church-members) have not: they are in covenant with God . . . are in a more hopefull way of attayning regenerating grace.[22]

The children of persons who had repentance and faith were permitted to be baptized and held to be members of the covenant and church members (or at least of the "outward covenant"). However, such children had not attained "regenerating grace" and could not do so until they reached "years of discretion." This 1648 synod thus set out a theory of partial membership for children, one that granted infant baptism some measure of the sacramental power attributed to it by the Catholic Church to erase the sins of Adam and to

21. Walker, ed., *Creeds and Platforms,* 169–170.
22. Ibid., 205–206, 222–224.

limit the propensity of future sins. At the same time, it equivocated: "a more hopefull way of attayning regenerating grace" is a murky promise, at best.

This synod implicitly rejected the extension of membership to the next generation, born to those who had only this partial membership; only the children of those who had a calling themselves could transmit the privilege of baptism. Such, in fact, was the majority opinion in 1648. Both Richard Mather and Thomas Hooker, for example, took similar stances. In his summary of New England practice and belief in 1643, *Church-Government and Church-Covenant Discussed,* Mather answered with an unequivocal no to the seventh question about whether ancestors beyond their parents could qualify a child for baptism.

> Such Children whose Father and Mother were neither of them Believers, and sanctified, are counted by the Apostle (as it seemes to us) not faederally holy, but uncleane, what ever their other Ancestors have been. 1. *Cor.* 7.14. And therefore we Baptise them not. If you can give us a sufficient Answer, to take us off from that Scripture, 1. *Cor.* 7. which seemes to limit this faederall sanctity or holynesse to the Children whose next Parents one or both were Believers, we should gladly hearken to you therein; but for the present, as we believe we speake, and practise. . . . And if we should goe one degree beyond the next Parents, we see not but we may goe two, and if two, why not 3, 4, 20, 100, or 1,000? For where will you stop? And if we shall admit all Children to Baptisme, whose Ancestors within a thousand Generations have been Believers, as some would have us, we might by this Reason Baptise the Children of *Turkes,* and of all the *Indians* and *Barbarians* in the Country; for there is none of them but they have had some Believing Ancestors within lesse than a 1000. Generations, it being farre from so much since *Noah* and his Sonnes came forth out of the Arke.[23]

Mather here held that extending the privilege of the covenant to more than the children of those who had experienced conversion would negate the necessity of belief for membership. He distinguished the partial membership of baptism from the full membership of communion. Only those with sufficient knowledge and faith can undergo conversion and accept communion, for "without knowledge men cannot well Examine themselves and discerne the Lords body, as Church Members ought to doe when they come to the Lords Table." How old they have to be before they can experience conversion

23. [Richard Mather], *Church-Government and Church-Covenant Discussed, in an Answer of the Elders of the Severall Churches in New-England to Two and Thirty Questions, Sent over to Them by Divers Ministers in England to Declare Their Judgements Therein* (London, 1643), 1, 22.

(and emerge from the protective, temporary grace of their baptism) he refused to state exactly, "as having of our selves hitherto had no occasion to search into those Questions; onely this we thinke, that one certaine rule cannot be given for all, whereby to determine how long they are under age, but according as God gives experience and maturity of naturall understanding, and spirituall; which he gives sooner to some then unto others." Thomas Hooker took the same position in 1648. It is ironic that Hooker and Mather linked baptism so strongly to an inherited right, at least for one generation, more strongly than did Catholic doctrine, which allowed baptism for any child so long as the parents permitted it and godparents promised for them (whether Turk or heathen).[24]

John Cotton was the only prominent minister in New England during the 1630s and 1640s to argue that the grandchild of a converted member could be baptized. In 1630 he urged that all subjects of England had the right to baptize their children. He renounced his own opinion in 1636, on the grounds that parents must make a particular covenant with a church in order to have their descendants baptized within it: "I [would] rather make a plaister bigger than the sore, than that it should be pleaded against my practise after my departure." Yet, despite this narrowing, he interpreted the covenant as granting a kind of inherited right, though a conditional inherited right. So long as the parents kept God's ordinances, "you shall keep a constant entail of

24. Aquinas, *Summa Theologiae*, 3a.68.10–11; [Mather], *Church-Government*, 22–23. Apparently in a first draft, however, Mather had stated, "Such as are borne in the ch[urch] as members, though yet they be not found fitt for the Lords Supper, yet if they be not culpable of such scandalls in Conversation as do justly deserve ch[urch] Censures, it seemeth to us, when they are marryed and have children, those their children may be recd to Baptisme" (Walker, ed., *Creeds and Platforms*, 224, citing the MS at the American Antiquarian Society). Thomas Hooker stated that all agreed that "such who are come to ripenesse of yeers, and are rightly received" are "members" of the "true visible Church of Christ." But what of those who have not "come to ripenesse of yeers"? They may be baptized, he argues, and he disagrees with the Anabaptists, who would "wholly exclude [them] from partaking of baptisme, untill they come to yeers of discretion, when they make actuall profession of their faith." But should the children of "godly parents" who are not actually in "church fellowship" be admitted? He answers with an unequivocal no. *"Conclusion* I. Children as Children have not right unto Baptisme, for then all children of all Nations, sects and sorts of men should be made partakers of it." *"Conclusion* II. It belongs not to any Predecessors, either neerer or further off removed from the next Parents . . . to give right of this priviledge to their Children; when I say Predecessors neerer or further off, I include and comprehend all, beside the next parent, Grand-father, [etc.] . . . it doth not belong to any of them." *A Survey of the Summe of Church-Discipline, Wherein, the Way of the Churches of New-England Is Warranted out of the Word* . . . (London, 1648), part 3, 12–13, and esp. 9–18.

the covenant to you." Just as land could be entailed on a particular family in perpetuity, so could church membership be "perpetual."[25]

Cotton was deeply troubled by the issue of baptism. He devoted an entire book to the debate in 1647, *The Grounds and Ends of the Baptisme of Children of the Faithfull*. He structured his argument as a debate between Silvester, who doubts that infants should receive baptism at all, and Silvanus, who justifies it. Silvester's position captures beautifully the logic of the antipaedobaptists, although Silvanus (representing Cotton himself) wins the argument. But he does so only by presenting justifications for conversion much more liberal than those of Hooker, Mather, or Calvin.

> *Silvester*. It is very doubtful to me, neither hath the scripture revealed it, that such as dye Infants are in a state of salvation, for without the hearing of the word, no faith, and without faith no salvation.
>
> *Silvanus*. See what uncomfortable and desperate conclusions these ways of error drive men unto; Jacob while he was in his mothers womb was in a state of election. Rom. 9.11.13. . . . What though children do not receive faith by hearing of the gospel, as the nations of the Gentiles do . . . yet as children can see the light, and be taken with it, and turn their eyes to it: so the Lord can shine into the dark hearts of children, and give them faith to see his light, and to be taken and affected with it, though they never heard of it by the hearing of the eare.
>
> *Silvester*. What the Lord can doe in inlightening Infants, is a secret known to himself; the Lord can even of stones raise up children unto Abraham, math. 3.9. In which sense children may also be said to be capable of the spirit; to wit, as well as stones. But if children should be said to be capable of the spirit, so as to comply with the spirit in hearing, receiving and believeing the spirits testimony, and so to be capable of regeneration, faith and repentance, this I deny: and to affirm this to be the way to bring persons to the faith by working so upon them by his Spirit in their infancy, argueth from ignorance of the true nature and work of grace, as the gospel holdeth forth.
>
> *Silvanus*. There is a middle way between these two, in which God can and does convey the spirit of Grace unto infants: for neither are infants so

25. John Cotton, *A Sermon Delivered at Salem, 1636*, in Larzer Ziff, ed., *John Cotton on the Churches of New England* (Cambridge, Mass., 1968), 43. On Cotton and his influence on this question, see Edmund S. Morgan, *Visible Saints: The History of a Puritan Idea* (New York, 1963), 98–100. Also see George Phillips, *A Reply to a Confutation of Some Grounds for Infants Baptisme . . . .* (London, 1645). Phillips, pastor of the church at Watertown, Massachusetts, argued that God's covenant was with a people and lasts forever.

incapable as stones (for stones must first have a reasonable soul conveyed into them, before they can be capable of the spirit of grace, whereas infants have a reasonable soule already:) Neither yet are infants so capable of complying (as you call it) with the spirit, as to heare, believe, and repent, yet nevertheless [they are capable of receiving the spirit].[26]

Thus while Silvester compared the understanding and faith of children to the abilities of stones, Silvanus alleged that even infants, inasmuch as they can turn their heads toward the light, can receive "faith to see the light." This debate thus centered on the meaning of faith itself. Does faith presuppose understanding, or knowledge of God's word? Does conversion have to be understood? Remembered? Can one distinguish between degrees of faith? Or is faith as simple as turning toward the light as a baby might do? Silvester's argument that children are as "capable of the spirit . . . as stones" is damning.

That the debate over infant baptism was above all about the meaning of faith was dictated by the biblical passage that dominated the discussion between Silvester and Silvanus and, indeed, the larger debate.

> *Silvester.* The Scripture in Math. 28.19. Being well considered, and rightly understood, would stop mens mouths forever, from having a word to say for the baptizing of infants. This blessed commission of Christ to his apostles; was chiefly for us Gentiles, saying "All power is given to me both in heaven and earth, Goe ye therefore and teach all nations, baptizing them in the name of the father, Sonne, and holy Ghost," etc. . . . So that here teaching goeth before baptizing, and presupposeth understanding and faith in that which is taught.[27]

Silvester argued that baptism should be preceded by "understanding" because Christ had set teaching before baptizing. Silvanus, of course, since he spoke for Cotton, persuaded Silvester (after 196 pages) that he must be wrong. But the grounds of faith that Cotton offered, which implied that conversion was not necessary to salvation or that conversion was as simple as "turning towards the light," hardly provided the final word.

In 1657, and more decisively in 1662, the next two synods in Boston accepted the idea that grandparents' conversions could provide surety enough to allow the baptism of their grandchildren, and indeed to "their seed unto *a thousand generations*" so long as the parents do "in the least degree shew themselves to be *lovers of God, and keepers of his* Covenant and *Commandments.*" This acceptance of an inherited right to membership in the covenant

26. Cotton, *Grounds and Ends,* 12–13.
27. Ibid., 20–21.

became known as the Half-Way Covenant.[28] It was the logical extension of the argument from Abraham's seed, but it was one step farther away from the conversion experience—and one step closer to the Anglican and Catholic position of an established and perpetual church, a move the synod made despite, in the words of the church at Roxbury, a "ffeare it might . . . bring in time the Corruption of Old England which we ffled ffrom." John Oxenbridge, in 1673, cautioned even more pointedly: the Half-Way Covenant, with its baptism of grandchildren of the faithful, would lead to corruption such that it will "turn your Churches into Parishes, and your Ministers into Priests and Prelates, I cannot think the Lord will ever endure it." The churches were extending membership so far via infant baptism that a conversion experience might no longer be necessary or likely. They were thus privileging inheritance over choice.[29]

But the ministers who agreed to these principles (the Half-Way Covenant) also hedged their agreement carefully. They emphasized earlier distinctions between the "visible" church (that can be seen on earth and into which these children were baptized) and the invisible church (those true members whom only God can recognize), and they separated the partial membership of such baptized children from the complete membership of those who had a conver-

---

28. Walker, ed., *Creeds and Platforms*, 296 (1657), 303–304 (1662). The 1657 synod made clear the disagreement and difficulty surrounding this issue: "In case they [the children of covenanters] understand the grounds of Religion, are not scandalous, and solemnly own the Covenant in their own persons, wherein they give up both themselves and their children unto the Lord, and desire Baptism for them, we (with due reverence to any Godly Learned that may dissent) see not sufficient cause to deny Baptism unto their children." The 1662 synod made the difficulty even plainer: "Hence when he [God] takes any into Covenant with himself, he will not only be *their God*, but *the God of their seed after them in their generations*. . . . The Mercy and Grace of the Covenant is extended to the faithful and their seed unto *a thousand generations*, if the successive parents do but in the least degree shew themselves to be *lovers of God, and keepers of his* Covenant and *commandments*. . . . Hence we dare not (with the Antipaedobaptist) exclude the *Infant-children of the faithful* from the *Covenant*, or from *membership* in the visible church, and consequently not from *Baptism* the Seal thereof. Neither dare we exclude the same children from Membership . . . when they are *grown up*, while they so walk and act, as to keep their standing in the Covenant. . . . God owns them still, and they doe in some measure own him: God rejects them not, and therefore neither may we; and consequently *their children* are not to be rejected." But after this acceptance of the inheritablity of the right to baptism, the synod left room that it was in error: "How hard it is to finde and keep the right middle way of Truth in these things."

29. Walker, ed., *Creeds and Platforms*, 255; Foster, *Long Argument*, 203, citing J[ohn] O[xenbridge], *New England Freemen Warned and Warned* . . . (Cambridge, Mass., 1673), 19.

sion experience and fully accepted communion. The logic behind the first seemed to be that, if God would distinguish true church members in the end anyway, why not admit more and let him judge? This certainly fitted with the wishes of many congregants. Many mothers, particularly, seemed to think that baptism would make their child more likely to be saved. The second distinction (between partial and full membership) strove to retain the importance of the conversion experience. They were thus creating two levels of membership.[30]

Yet, despite these careful hedges, the truth remained that accepting church members who did not have conversion experiences but had only been baptized as infants threatened (for them) the meaning of church membership itself. Thus the synod tried to get the parents to maintain the promise of their baptism by "owning the covenant" of their ancestors, an attempt that would accelerate in the 1680s under the leadership of Increase Mather and his son Cotton Mather (the grandson of Richard Mather and John Cotton).[31] Despite this effort, the fears of those who had objected to infant baptism in the 1650s appeared to be coming to pass by 1680, as the covenant fell on generations farther removed from the original. The baptism of infants diminished the need for conversion as an adult. This compromise thus conceded considerable ground toward the heritability of church membership.[32]

Debate about the baptism of the infant grandchildren of the converted occurred in England during the Interregnum. The 1647 Westminster Confession of Faith and the Savoy Declaration of Faith eleven years later were similar in most respects. But Savoy shifted ground substantially on the question of baptism. The Westminster Confession stated, "Not onely those that do

30. Anne S. Brown and David D. Hall, "Family Strategies and Religious Practice: Baptism and the Lord's Supper in Early New England," in Hall, ed., *Lived Religion in America: Toward a History of Practice* (Princeton, N.J., 1997), 41–68.

31. Foster, *Long Argument*, 212–228. It is in light of the dispute over baptism itself that the calls for renewing the covenant by Increase and Cotton Mather (and other ministers) at the end of the seventeenth century make sense. Increase Mather, who initially disapproved of the baptizing of the second generation, changed his mind, publishing *The First Principles of New England, concerning the Subject of Baptisme and Communion of Churches* (Cambridge, Mass., 1675), wherein he claimed that all of the founding generation had supported the baptism of the second generation from the beginning (10–11). Also see Walker, ed., *Creeds and Platforms*, 252.

32. The call for the 1679–1680 synod expressed its concern that "many of the Rising Generation are not mindfull of that which their Baptism doth engage them unto, *viz.* to use utmost endeavours that they may be fit for, and so partake in, all the holy Ordinances of the Lord Jesus," as among the "Evils that have provoked the Lord to bring his Judgements on New-England." Walker, ed., *Creeds and Platforms*, 426, 428.

actually profess faith in, and obedience unto Christ, but also the Infants of one or both believing parents are to be baptized." Savoy, however, added "and those onely," thus changing a question mark into a definitive no. The New England ministers adopted the Savoy Declaration virtually intact in their Reforming Synod of 1679–1680 but left out "and those onely," which limited the baptism of infants to the children of the converted. Thus Puritans in New England moved toward the Anglican position, stressing inheritable status within the church over choice, but did so uncomfortably.[33]

Yet many church members in New England in the late seventeenth century still refused to baptize their children, let alone their grandchildren. Many churches still refused to accept the Half-Way Covenant as well. Infant baptism itself, in short, was still debated and would become a major issue—if not the major issue—during the two great awakenings.[34] Solomon Stoddard provided a dissonant voice to the consensus of the late-seventeenth-century synods, allowing that infant baptism entitled a person to full membership. Half a century later, Stoddard's grandson Jonathan Edwards would initially accept his grandfather's broad-mindedness, but ultimately break with the extension of the privileges of baptism to the grandchildren of believers, and openly disagree with the Half-Way Covenant, raising doubts even about the baptism of infants of visible church members. Instead, his stress on the role of the affections rather than reason in conversion allowed younger persons access to conversion. He reveals, for example, how Phoebe Bartlett converted at age four. His stance may be related to his increasingly restrictive view of church membership and his attempt, ultimately, to limit both communion and baptism to the converted and their immediate children. Edwards did thus emphasize choice, but more his than his communicants'; especially toward the end of his career in Northampton, he sought to deny the validity of conversion experiences, to deny, in other words, the choice of his parishioners, and to be the final arbiter of membership himself. His flock would certainly have agreed that the question of choice could be a double-edged sword.[35]

33. Ibid., 398, 438–439.

34. On debate, see ibid., 433–434, from synod of 1679–1680, reference to "Disputes respecting the Subject of Baptism"; also see Foster, *Long Argument*, esp. 201–237. Hall, in *Worlds of Wonder*, 153–155, suggests that more lay church members than ministers would have wanted to follow the Half-Way Covenant because they were concerned about their children's salvation. Foster, in *Long Argument*, claims, "By 1668 many churches and even some of the magistrates had lost interest in persecuting church members who scrupled over infant baptism and refused to present their newborn children for the sacrament" (177).

35. David D. Hall, introduction, in Jonathan Edwards, *Ecclesiastical Writings*, The Works of Jonathan Edwards, XII (New Haven, Conn., 1994). Edwards did not completely

Outside New England, the situation was more diffuse. The Anglican Church continued to baptize all infants, so long as some "God-parent" would promise for them, and this was the practice in colonies where the Anglican Church predominated. Such groups as Quakers and Baptists (including anti-paedobaptists) renounced the baptism of infants altogether: the Quakers on the grounds that infants were not innately sinful (so the cleansing of baptism was unnecessary) and the Baptists on the grounds that only those who had faith and repentance, who had been taught, could justifiably be baptized. George Fox, the founder of Quakerism, condemned Anglican baptism in particular as an invented ritual that could not be justified by Scripture and was, in fact, absurd: "Concerning your sprinkling of infants, and your fonts, and your signing them with the sign of the cross, and your gossips and God-Fathers and God-Mothers, etc. These things you cannot prove in all the scriptures of the Old and New Testaments." Fox then went through the Scriptures, commenting particularly on Genesis, where God named Adam: "And you do not read, that there was any God-fathers and God-mothers then." After many more such paragraphs of scriptural commentary that all end with the same sentence, Fox concluded, "Then be not angry with us, that we follow not you in these things." Fox acknowledged the importance of the "baptism of Christ" but interpreted this in a universal way: his baptism cleansed all people of original sin. Consequently, all persons are born with "Christ, which doth enlighten every man which cometh into the world."[36]

The term "discretion" that the Puritans focused on was not new to the seventeenth century. The Catholic authorities under Queen Mary used it in the sixteenth-century inquisitions of the Marian Martyrs; Thomas Causton, for example, had not expressed his disaffection with the Catholic Church by fourteen, which his trial record specified as the age of discretion. But the focus on this term in the seventeenth century gave it a new meaning and weight. According to Catholic doctrine, active assent at age fourteen was not necessary: only active dissent during that window of opportunity could break the connection. The ability to partake of the Lord's Supper, to ingest of the Body of Christ, was linked to confirmation, which tended to be very young. Although

---

ignore reason. For the narrative of Bartlett, see Edwards, *A Faithful Narrative of the Surprising Work of God* . . . (London, 1737). My thanks to Ruth Bloch for this reference.

36. G[eorge] Fox, *Concerning the True Baptism and the False* [London, 1676], esp. 4–6; G[eorge] F[ox], *A Catechisme for Children, That They May Come to Learne of Christ, the Light, the Truth, the Way* . . . (London, 1658), 1, 10: "Now Christ is he that makes alive, and quickens from the trespasses which the first Adam is in, and destroys death, and the power of it, who doth enlighten every man that cometh into the world."

the Catholic Church had distinguished between the two sacraments of baptism and confirmation during the Middle Ages, with baptism creating membership and confirmation imparting increased grace, confirmation did not involve voluntary consent. Like baptism, it was often performed shortly after birth. Two synods in England in the thirteenth century, for example, differed over whether confirmation had to be administered within one year after birth or within three years. Under age one or three (and confirmation was an act, like baptism, for which the parents were held responsible) was obviously a recommendation that did not expect an answer or commitment from the child. Confirmation could occur at any time from just after baptism (even at less than one year of age) to seven: usually it was supposed to immediately follow baptism. Some theologians held that the child should be able to recite the vows (so should be at least three or so), others that the "age of reason" (seven) should be reached before confirmation. But confirmation and even first communion were much less important than the ritual of baptism, since baptism indubitably created membership. Confirmation became a much more important ritual within the Catholic Church in response to the Reformation's concerns about understanding and faith.[37]

The prayer book used by the Anglican Church between 1549 and 1660 encouraged rituals of baptism and confirmation similar to those of the Catholic Church but addressed a few of the Puritan concerns. It contained instructions for baptizing only infants (a procedure in which the godparents vouched for the infant), and it portrayed baptism itself as a sacrament that saved the child and cleansed it of sin. At the same time, it required both that all children memorize the catechism before being confirmed by a bishop and that confirmation precede taking the sacrament of the Lord's Supper. It was also in English, and it raised a few doubts about the permanence of baptism.

In 1660, as part of the Restoration settlement, Charles II agreed to revising the Anglican prayer book to accommodate some Puritan concerns about baptism. His promise, however, proved to be a kind of bait and switch. The 1662 Act of Uniformity evicted all ministers from their posts who refused to agree that infants could be baptized and that they were undoubtedly saved by that sacrament. His actions, which led to thousands of dismissals, reveal the centrality of this issue to Anglican doctrine but also the level of dissent.

The revised prayer book changed a few words so that infant baptism did not imply certain salvation. For example: where the earlier ceremony had

37. *The Catholic Encyclopedia* (New York, 1907–1912), s.v. "Confirmation"; *Dictionary of the Middle Ages*, s.v. "Confirmation"; *The Oxford Dictionary of the Christian Church*, s.vv. "Baptism," "Confirmation," "Sacraments." Also see William J. Levada, "Reflections on the Age of Confirmation," *Theological Studies*, LVII (1996), 302–312.

stated, "It is certayn by goddes worde, that children being Baptised (yf they depart out of this lyfe in their infancye) are undoubtedly saved," the new version stated, "It is certain by Gods word that children which are baptized dyeing before they commit actuall sin, are undoubtedly saved." It made several other changes that Puritans had sought. Passages where the priest consecrated the baptismal water and many references to divine unction and the sacramental character of baptism were deleted. The revisers added (for the first time) a procedure for adult baptism that was similar to a profession of faith advocated by Puritans and Presbyterians (one without godparents). There was also an expectation that some would be much older when confirmed (the word "person" was substituted for "child" in the post-1660 confirmation ceremony).[38]

The revision established that baptism created a temporary rather than a permanent membership: it added that the godparents promised to be the child's "surities" only until "he come of age to take it upon himself." And it made clearer, throughout, that the godparents' promise was theirs and not the child's. Thus the earlier version addressed the godparent as if he or she were actually the child: "Doest thou forsake the devill and all his woorkes? Answere: I forsake them." The revised version read, "Dost thou in the name of this child, renounce the devil and all his works?" The changes assumed that some of those who came for baptism and confirmation would be "of riper years" and more would be demanded of them than being able to recite the catechism for confirmation. They slightly undercut the sacramental character of the baptismal service, and they made confirmation more important by linking it to permanant membership. But the revision retained infant baptism in the form of the godparents' promising for the child, and confirmation could still be obtained upon recitation of the catechism. Baptism still created membership (and was normally expected to occur in infancy), though it was a less permanent one.[39]

Both versions of the prayer book associated confirmation loosely with "discretion." The 1549 version claimed that, when children came to "yeres of discrecion," they "maye then themselves with their owne mouthe and with their owne consent, openly before the churche, ratifie and confesse the same" as their godparents had previously promised for them. Only the earlier version noted that during this period of life (presumably twelve for girls and fourteen for boys, the age associated with the term "discretion" in the canon law for marriage) children "begyn to be in daunger to fall into sinne." Confirmation

38. F. E. Brightman, ed., The English Rite . . . , 2d ed. (London, 1921), II, 728–729, 746–747, 778–779. Also see 795, where "child" can be interchanged with "servant."
39. Ibid., 734–735, 761–777.

should wait until then, and baptism was sufficient for salvation if children died before that time (a statement that responded to concerns from laity that confirmation should happen earlier, as Catholic practice had encouraged).[40]

This emphasis on their "owne consent" and awaiting "discretion," or until puberty, was a Protestant innovation. Indeed, the assocation of the word "discretion" with full church membership was very much a consequence of Protestantism. The 1660 version used "years of discretion" to demarcate whether the infant or the adult baptismal ceremony should be performed. The 1660 version of the confirmation ceremony also stated in its title that it was intended only for those who "are baptized and come to years of discretion."[41]

Indeed, in this respect the Anglican procedure clearly grew out of Reformation concerns and continued to be influenced by them. Puritans in England such as Richard Baxter agreed with Calvin and those in New England that the status of the parents as consciously covenanted members gave their children the right to be baptized. These children still had to choose to be church members, however, once they had reached an "age of discretion." Hooker also suggested an "age of discretion," as did the 1662 synod.[42]

What, however, was the age of discretion, and what qualities characterized discretion? Richard Mather stated in 1643 that New England ministers had not considered the issue deeply yet, but that the age must vary, depending on a person's "experience, maturity of natural understanding, and spiritual" awareness. John Cotton indicated that babies could have some form of conversion.[43] The 1657 synod addressed the question directly and at length, especially in the second and third questions:

> Quest. 2. *Whether all children of whatever years or condition be so, as, 1. Absent children never brought to the Church. 2. Born before their Parents Covenanting. 3. Incorrigible of seven, ten, or twelve years old. 4. Such as desire not to be admitted with their parents, of such an age.*
>
> Ans. Onely such children as are in their minority, covenant with their

40. Ibid., 776–778.

41. Ibid., 777–793.

42. David Ingersoll Naglee, *From Font to Faith: John Wesley on Infant Baptism and the Nurture of Children* (New York, 1987), 78–81; Perry Miller, *The New England Mind: From Colony to Province* (Cambridge, Mass., 1953), 96–104. Also see John Robinson, "Of Children and Their Education" (1628), in Philip J. Greven, Jr., ed., *Child-Rearing Concepts, 1628–1861* (Itasca, Ill., 1973), 10. "And as we judge of the plant or graft, by the stock whence it was taken, till it be grown able to bring proper fruit, and that the tree be known by the fruit; so do we of children by their parents, till coming to years of discretion they choose their own way."

43. [Mather], *Church-Government*, 22; Cotton, *Grounds and Ends*, 12–13.

Parents. . . . We do not hereby exclude such as being defective in their intellectuals, are as children in respect of their incapacity. . . . 2. Children in their minority, though absent, covenant in their Parents. . . . 3. Children born before their Parents covenanting, yet if in their minority when their Parents enter into covenant, do covenant with them. . . . 4. There is no sufficient reason (at least ordinarily) to conclude a child of seven, ten, or twelve years old to be incorrigible.

The synod neatly evaded stating the exact age or capabilities of those who must covenant for themselves (or how long the parents' covenant lasted). While it clearly linked those abilities to the "intellectual" capacity of the individual, it refused to be any more specific.

Quest. 3. *Till what age shall they enter into Covenant with their Parents, whether sixteen, 21, or 60?*

Ans. As long as in respect of age or capacity they cannot according to ordinary account, be supposed able to act in a matter of this nature for themselves, . . . much is to be left unto the discretion of Officers and Churches in this case."[44]

The synod of 1662 was more explicit: "They that are come to years of discretion, so as to *have knowledge and understanding*, fit to act in a matter of that nature, are to covenant by their own personal act, *Neh.* 10. 28, 29. *Isa.* 44 5." In practice, ministers in New England rarely accepted conversions of those under fourteen, indicating they thought that to be the age of discretion, in accord with the Marian inquisitions.[45]

Yet Cotton Mather's *Token for the Children of New-England*, which followed the pattern of James Janeway's *Token for Children* with its stories of children's early conversions and deaths in England (and was printed with it), encouraged much younger conversion. Ann Greenough, who "had an unspeakable Delight in Catechizing," died at age five. Children were as old as fourteen (two children) when they converted, while others were eleven (two children), "little," and six. Janeway recounted children who converted at such ages as two, four, five, seven, and eight. Jonathan Edwards published a pamphlet on the conversion of four-year-old Phoebe Bartlett. These ministers sought to

---

44. Walker, ed., *Creeds and Platforms*, 293. The synod entitled its results *A Disputation concerning Church-Members and Their Children in Answer to 21 Questions*. The first question and answer asserted that the children of "confederate" parents had the right to be baptized—so infant baptism itself was still an issue.

45. Walker, ed., *Creeds and Platforms*, 324; Ross W. Beales, Jr., "In Search of the Historical Child: Miniature Adulthood and Youth in Colonial New England," *American Quarterly*, XXVII (1975), 379–398, esp. 387–390.

reemphasize the importance of the conversion experience for church membership. By making conversion possible for the very young, they made infant baptism less important. In the early eighteenth century, John Wesley, the founder of Methodism, placed the age of discretion for religious matters at six or seven but claimed it differed for each child. Generally, those such as John Cotton and Jonathan Edwards who emphasized the emotional rather than the rational aspects of the conversion experience tended to allow lower ages for that conversion. But the lowest age of conversion remained disputed.[46]

The critical point is this: whereas the Catholic Church had used the term "discretion" in a limited way before the Reformation, the earlier vows, made on behalf of the child, were considered binding except for this window of opportunity when that membership was voidable. It was invoked for marriage ceremonies, for example, when it signified the age after which a child could no longer reject a marriage he or she had agreed to while younger, and for the last age at which a child could renounce a baptism. The Protestant movement placed much more stress on discretion, plumbed its meaning, dissected it, measured it, and weighed it. The Protestants cared so much about it because at this age membership either became possible (if one rejected infant baptism) or became void and had to be actively renewed (if one accepted a covenantal position). The Catholic Church and, to a great degree, the Anglican Church had designated this as an age when membership was only voidable. The importance of the distinction cannot be overstated. It is thus clear why the age of discretion became of much greater interest to the Protestants: either the children could just become members (and so be saved), or the promise for children then expired and they had to renew the covenant, their membership, in their own voice. In working out the meaning of discretion, Protestants elaborated on the meanings of reason and understanding and conscience. What does "owne consent" mean? When is it valid?

The battle between the main contenders for and against infant baptism in the 1640s captures the close connections between this debate over church membership and the debate over political membership. It appeared during the Interregnum when there were no restrictions on publishing pamphlets

---

46. Janeway, *A Token for Children . . . to Which Is Added,* [Cotton Mather,] *A Token for the Children of New England,* 97 (Mather's example 4), 87–108 (Mather's stories), and 1, 10, 11, 44, 47 (Janeway's stories); Beales, "In Search of the Historical Child," *American Quarterly,* XXVII (1975), 384. Beales also gives some citations from pamphlets that were part of the debate over infant baptism, such as those by John Cotton, in an effort to prove that Puritans had concepts of maturity, yet does not give the context of these citations. Naglee, *From Font to Faith,* 212.

on baptism. Stephen Marshall, a moderate Presbyterian who sought to compromise on these issues to retain a national church, justified an Anglican position on baptism as a birthright. He gave this sermon in Westminster Abbey by official appointment of the House of Commons in 1644.

> As it is in *other* Kingdoms, Corporations, and Families, the children of all Subjects borne in a Kingdome, are borne that Princes Subjects; where the Father is a *Free* man, the childe is not born a *slave;* where any are *bought* to be *servants,* their children born in their Masters house, are born his *servants.* Thus it is by the Laws of almost all Nations, and thus hath the Lord ordained, it shall be in his kingdome and family; the *children* follow the Covenant-condition of their *Parents,* if he take a Father into Covenant, he takes the Children in with him, if hee reject the Parents out of Covenant, the children are cast out with them.

For Marshall, as for the Church of England, a child inherits the status of the parent as a church member just as a child inherits the status of the father as a subject, freeman, slave, or servant. Marshall pointedly did not distinguish himself from the "Orthodox Church [the Anglican]": his point was to argue for infant baptism as a possibility (except for "Indians" and "Turks"). He did focus on the easiest case, the children of professed believers.[47]

Marshall's arguments of 1644 and Cotton's of 1630 accept the Anglican position that all children born to English parents were granted the right to baptism and membership in the church, just as they were born subjects. (Cotton was then still arguing that Puritans in New England should be part of the Anglican Church.) Marshall was a key compromise player in the religious disputes of the 1640s, appointed by the House of Lords in 1641, for example, to reconcile Presbyterians to the Anglican Church. While he distinguished himself, as the 1640s progressed, from the Anglican Church's episcopal hierarchy, he adhered to much of the Anglican orthodoxy.[48]

Like Marshall, Thomas Blake, an influential Puritan in England, argued that church membership was a hereditary status:

> The *priviledges* or *burdens,* which in Family or Nation are hereditary, they are conveyed from parents to posterity, from Ancestors to their Issue: As is the father, so is the child, as respecting these particulars: The child of a Free-man with St. *Paul* is *free borne:* The child of a *Noble man* is *noble:* The

47. Stephen Marshall, *A Sermon of the Baptizing of Infants: Preached in the Abbey-Church at Westminster, at the Morning Lecture, Appointed by the Honorable House of Commons* (London, 1644), 7, 8, 14–15. Also quoted in [John Tombes], *An Examen of the Sermon . . . about Infant-Baptism . . .* (London, 1645), 54.
48. *Dictionary of National Biography,* s.v. "Marshall, Stephen."

child of a *bond-man* (where servants were wholy their Masters to dispose) is a *bond-man* likewise. So the child of a *Turke* is a *Turke;* The child of a *Pagan* is a *Pagan;* The child of a *Jew* is a *Jew;* The child of a *Christian* is a *Christian:* As by vertue of the grand *Charter* of heaven among the people of God, this priviledge doth *descend:* So it is of the nature of those things that are *descendable.*[49]

"As is the father, so is the child." While Blake elsewhere was careful to note that these rules of baptism identified only the "outward" church, his attachment to these norms indicates an inclusive, hereditary, and hierarchical vision.

John Tombes, a self-described "antipaedobaptist," took the lead in arguing against this position. Tombe's response to these arguments was twofold: it is wrong to "imagine the Church of God to be like Civill corporations," and "Christianity is no mans birth right" but comes only by "free election of grace, and according to Gods appointment." Baptism should be a matter of election and choice, not inheritance: *"In the confession of baptism, every ones free choice is shewed. . . .* None were to be baptized, but such as shewed their own free choice by confession."[50]

Tombes's position on infant baptism was similar to that of John Locke's forty years later, in his *Essay on Toleration.*

A church then I take to be a voluntary society of men, joining themselves together of their own accord. . . .

. . . Nobody is born a member of any church; otherwise the religion of parents would descend unto children, by the same right of inheritance as their temporal estates, and every one would hold his faith by the same tenure he does his lands; than which nothing can be imagined more absurd.[51]

Thus Locke emphasized choice for religious membership, differentiating it pointedly from inheritance. The critical point for Locke, as for Tombes, was that religion should not be inherited. When Locke stated that a church was a "voluntary society," he agreed with the Puritans in New England—and Locke was raised a Dissenter, so his stand in this respect is no surprise. That position was critical and uncontested among all Dissenters, Puritans included.

49. Thomas Blake, *The Birth-Privilege; or, Covenant-Holinesse of Beleevers and Their Issue . . .* (London, 1644), 6 (also quoted by Tombes).

50. [Tombes], *Examen,* 50; Tombes, *Apology for the Two Treatises,* 87, discussing the decision of the council of Neocaesarea.

51. Locke, *Essay on Toleration* (1685), in *The Works of John Locke,* 9th ed. (1794; rpt. London, 1997), V, 13.

But in the end Locke differed with Calvinist, covenental theology on the inheritability of the right to baptism. He spent the last years of his life commenting on Paul's Epistle to the Romans, wherein lay the critical tracts on baptism. His notes on the covenant of grace read:

> He who, by baptism, is incorporated into the kingdom of Christ, and owns him for his sovereign, and himself under the law and rule of the gospel, ceases not to be a christian, though he offend against the precepts of the gospel, till he denies Christ to be his king and lord. . . . God . . . has, since the fall, erected two kingdoms in this world, the one of the jews, immediately under himself; another of christians under his Son Jesus Christ, for that farther and more glorious end, of attaining eternal life, which prerogative and privilege, of eternal life, does not belong to the society in general, nor is the benefit granted nationally, to the whole body of the people of either of these kingdoms of God; but personally, to such of them, who perform the conditions required in the terms of each covenant.[52]

Locke here denied the covenantal principle that a people can inherit the covenant of grace their fathers or grandfathers had made; membership in "the kingdom of Christ" belongs only to those who "personally" make the commitment. Or, as he said above, "Nobody is born a member of any church." Locke's position was largely consistent with and probably profoundly influential upon his political ideology. His claim that baptism created entrance into the "kingdom of Christ" reinforced the parallels between political and religious membership.

While he separated himself partially from the mainstream Puritan position that allowed an incomplete membership for children of church members, his stance owed much to the Puritan stress upon conversion. In some ways the Puritan position is closer to Locke's position in his political theory, in which children are temporarily subjects and then can choose whether to remain subjects after they gain reason.[53]

But Locke and all Baptists, and to a lesser degree many Puritans, were separating themselves from the Anglican position. In maintaining that all

52. Locke, *Works*, VII, 306–307 (Rom. 6:15)

53. Also see John Locke, *The Reasonableness of Christianity* . . . (1695), ed. I. T. Ramsey (Stanford, Calif., 1958), 44–45, 55, 74. I have not found anywhere in Locke's writings that he explicitly condemned the baptizing of infants. This may be connected to the fact that, after 1662, expressing such a thought was an explicit violation of the Act of Uniformity, one that branded that person as a Dissenter and could lead to confiscation of property and loss of the right to vote, hold office, and many other civil rights. While the Act of Toleration (1689) restored a few of those rights, it still did not allow Dissenters to vote and hold public office. Locke did most of his writing before the Act of Toleration.

children could be baptized and that baptism was the gateway to membership, Anglicans and Catholics created a church for which conversion, and therefore choice, was not a real issue, a church for which assent and membership were assumed. One had to actively dissociate oneself—to dissent—in order to not be a member. For the English government, the question of allowing persons to dissent remained critical in the late seventeenth century. Should Dissenters lose their political voice? Should they lose their property? Should they be punished with stronger, corporal, or even capital penalties, as earlier monarchs had encouraged?

These were real questions that hinged on the same issues of heresy that the Catholic Church had defined. They had an added punch in England, however, where the king was the head of the church, where Christ's kingdom and the English kingdom had similar boundaries, where religion had played such an important role in the English Civil War and would play it again in the Glorious Revolution. In short, toleration and inclusive baptism, questions of church membership and choice, assumed new critical importance when religion and politics were so closely intertwined. Richard Baxter's *Judgment of Non-Conformists of the Interest of Reason* (1676) shows the close connection between the development of reason and political as well as religious choice. "All Protestants disclaim that inhumane, atheistical assertion, that in Religion, *Inferiours* must believe all that their *Superiours* assert, and do all that they shall command . . . without using their own *Reason* to discern . . . whether it be agreeable, or contrary to the Laws of God."[54]

Reason, Understanding, and Conscience

This emphasis on the role of the understanding and reason in faith led to intense discussions about what both terms meant. Likewise, one other word, "conscience," was often invoked as a measure of both. Conscience was central to the disputes about church membership: most Baptists contended, for example, that, until capable of exercising conscience, a person could not choose to become a member of a church and, therefore, could not be baptized. But conscience had its own literature as well, called casuistry, which went beyond issues of church membership. Once one became a church member, conscience was supposed to guide one's behavior. Did most people have a conscience that, through understanding, could control personal actions? Dissenters and even most Anglicans argued that people did not need a

54. [Richard Baxter], *The Judgment of Non-Conformists of the Interest of Reason in Matters of Religion* . . . (London, 1676), 18.

confessor; they needed only to consult themselves. The basic laws of morality and of nature could be understood by all persons and needed to be thought through by all.

Three questions from these debates over baptism and conscience would lay the groundwork for the revolutionary arguments over who had reason and judgment enough to exercise religious and political choice. First, what role did understanding play in discovering the moral laws of nature and in exercising the conscience? Second, did everyone have the ability to reason and to employ conscience? Third, what was the role of experience versus formal education in enabling all people to use their reason?[55]

These religious disputes over baptism and casuistry led to a change in the definition of reason and understanding during the seventeenth century: from reason as the recognition of the correct ordering of the universe to reason as a process, as conscious actions. The earlier definition of reason conformed with a conception that the universe was ordered as a great chain of being. As explored by Arthur O. Lovejoy and others, the medieval world was hierarchical, with people and animals, angels and devils, positioned along a great chain of being, with God at the top. Part of this hierarchy was based on the intellectual superiority of humans over animals: humans had a higher place because God had endowed them with reason, defined as the "perception of the natural or right order." The seventeenth century transformed the meaning of reason, "from substance to procedure, from found to constructed orders," based on religious and, increasingly, scientific investigations about the nature of truth.[56]

New methods for each individual to use reason characterized this transformation in its meaning. These methods formed the core of "the attempt to build an intermediate level of knowledge, short of absolute certainty but above the level of mere opinion," embracing many different disciplines in the late seventeenth century, from religion to science to law. Religious authors, particularly, sought methods for knowing probable truth in the shadow of uncertainty cast by the Reformation. The scientific method developed by Francis Bacon, Isaac Newton, and others also sought to discover the rules of the natural world via analytical reasoning deeply rooted in experience. They sought the rules of the universe, "natural law," by means of scientific hypoth-

55. Perry Miller, *The New England Mind: The Seventeenth Century* (Cambridge, Mass., 1939), chaps. 5, 6.

56. Arthur O. Lovejoy, *The Great Chain of Being: The Study of the History of an Idea* (Cambridge, Mass., 1948); Charles Taylor, *Sources of the Self: The Making of the Modern Identity* (Cambridge, Mass., 1989), 121.

eses, observation, and experiment. Techniques for ascertaining truth, which moved toward a methodology of probability based on observation, rather than "absolute certainty" based on syllogistic logic, reshaped many disciplines. These new strategies transformed evidence law in the seventeenth and eighteenth centuries, for example, by changing its epistemological basis. Under the older canon law, simple rules of evidence, such as "two witnesses," would prove guilt. The new rules placed much more weight on the quality, verifiability, and reasonableness of the witnesses' testimony.[57]

The central contributors to the debates over casuistry were the sixteenth-century French theologian Petrus Ramus, William Perkins, the most influential English Puritan of the Elizabethan era to remain within the established church, and William Ames, whose influence in New England, in particular, was immense. All three were frequently cited and read by Puritans in Old and New England. Ramus, in particular, provided a link between experience and simple but clear rules of logic and led the way to the new understanding of the term "reason," seeking to break down the barriers between logic and experience. In focusing on practical observation in determining probable laws of nature, Ramus gave primacy to the senses and individual reasoning. His breakdown of the rules of observational logic into invention, judgment, and method would contribute to Locke's description of the process of human understanding. Perkins and Ames emphasized observational logic but connected it more explicitly to shaping the individual conscience and enabling the conscience to control action.[58]

Hooker's *Of the Laws of Ecclesiastical Polity*, which would influence many of the political theorists of the seventeenth century, invoked reason in terms

57. Barbara Shapiro, *Beyond "Reasonable Doubt" and "Probable Cause": Historical Perspectives on the Anglo-American Law of Evidence* (Berkeley, Calif., 1991), 7, 13–14, 187–188; Gerard Reedy, *The Bible and Reason: Anglicans and Scripture in Late Seventeenth-Century England* (Philadelphia, 1985); Miller, *The New England Mind*, both *The Seventeenth Century* and *From Colony to Province;* Henry G. Van Leeuwen, *The Problem of Certainty in English Thought, 1630–1690* (The Hague, 1963); Richard S. Westfall, *Science and Religion in Seventeenth-Century England* (New Haven, Conn., 1958).

58. Miller, *The New England Mind: The Seventeenth Century*, 116, 132. "The fundamental fact concerning the intellectual life of New Englanders is that they ranged themselves definitely under the banner of the Ramists." Miller emphasizes a somewhat different change in the meaning of reason, although he too notes that the origins and nature of the "reason" is a subject of considerable debate. Also see Norman Fiering, *Moral Philosophy at Seventeenth-Century Harvard: A Discipline in Transition* (Chapel Hill, N.C., 1981), 23, 28. Barbara J. Shapiro also sees Ramus as a central figure (*Probability and Certainty in Seventeenth-Century England: A Study of the Relationships between Natural Science, Religion, History, Law, and Literature* [Princeton, N.J., 1983], 6, 8).

similar to Perkins's definition of conscience, as "determining and setting down what is good to be done." Education and experience were necessary for the full development of reason, virtue, and the ability to discriminate between good and evil. Yet, ultimately, Hooker's definition of reason differed from Perkins's in equating reason with the existing order. It was embodied, for example, in customary law, and all could agree upon its identity. It was not something that individuals constructed for themselves. Hooker was therefore a transitional figure in his use of the term "reason."[59]

Patriarchal thinkers such as Samuel Parker attacked the new definitions of reason, seeing in them an attempt to legitimate religious nonconformity and to undermine government. Parker's *Discourse of Ecclesiastical Polity* (1669) denied the ability to dissent itself. Parker not only challenged the Dissenters' arguments about the origins of government, which directly challenged monarchical power, but even their " 'definition of conscience,' their belief in 'reason,' their assumptions about morality, revelation, natural law, their epistemological distinction between faith and knowledge, [and] their philosophical arguments concerning 'will' and 'understanding.' " Why did Parker, in his conservative defense of the powers of the king, which invoked the patriarchal analogy, find it necessary to attack such abstract concepts as the Dissenters' arguments about conscience, human reason, and will and understanding? John Owen, in one of the first responses to Parker, saw that Parker deemed "mere dissent" a threat. He sought to demolish the grounds for religious dissent, even if it led only to thought and not action. Dissent based on each person's understanding and conscience was dangerous particularly as it translated into control over the will or actions. Those who set up their own system of moral laws challenged both the authority of the king and the established system of laws. Richard Baxter, in response to Parker, explicitly asserted the right of the Christian to determine *"true reason"* and to act upon it. "The more the Understanding of a Christian discerneth the *Evidences, and true Reasons* of all things in Religion," the stronger his or her faith. A Chris-

59. Robert Eccleshall, *Order and Reason in Politics: Theories of Absolute and Limited Monarchy in Early Modern England* (Oxford, 1978), 137; Richard Hooker, *Of the Laws of Ecclesiastical Polity: Preface, Book I, Book VIII* (1593, 1648), ed. Arthur Stephen McGrade (Cambridge, 1989), 66–86, 188 (book 8). On the one hand Hooker drew deeply on Aquinas and therefore on Aristotle. He sympathized with the Catholic and high Anglican position on baptism, and he argued against Separatists. On the other hand, Hooker was deeply influenced by Calvin and was sympathetic with resistance theory. On his sympathy with the Anglican position on baptism, see Holifield, *The Covenant Sealed,* 35. Otherwise, see J. P. Somerville, *Politics and Ideology In England, 1603–1640* (London, 1986), 11.

tian must behave "as a Rational free Agent, whose *will* must be guided by the light of his Understanding."[60]

The Puritans did not offer a theory of human development that depended solely on the gaining of reason or argue that reason alone had complete control over the will. But in their discussions about religious truth and who had the ability to experience conversion and become full church members, the understanding and reason were critical to the exercise of conscience and judgment. Revelation, piety, and divine grace also played important roles in the discovery of truth, although the balance was matter for dispute. Reason and piety were not always or even usually perceived as opposites; certainly, most Puritans upheld both. Reason was often seen as a mystical quality, containing part of God's grace. Various ministers and ordinary church members weighed the balance between the two differently, and popular religious culture, especially, placed more weight on piety. While Anglo-Christian philosophy contained a tension between reason and piety as means for knowing truth, most agreed that understanding was necessary in order to exercise conscience, to understand moral law, or to cast a judgment. And they held the exercise of public authority, in particular, to be the province of judgment, of conscience exercised under the guidance of God, which necessitated the use of the understanding and reason. The ability to consent to political authorities, likewise, was a power limited to those who could give "reasoned" consent, who could offer a wise, virtuous, or reasonable interpretation of the Bible, and who were fit to offer explicit guidance in the framing and administration of laws. Yet what level of reason was sufficient was disputed.[61]

60. Quoting Ashcraft, *Revolutionary Politics*, 43, 44; [Richard Baxter], *The Judgment of Non-Conformists of the Interest of Reason*, 14, and *The Judgment of Non-Conformists about the Difference between Grace and Morality* ([London], 1676), 7.

61. With respect to the Dissenters who responded to Parker, several wrote tracts against Socinianism, arguing explicitly that certain Christian truths were revealed and "mysterious." See Ashcraft, *Revolutionary Politics*, 59. Several historians have explored the roles of piety and emotion among the early Puritans. See Fiering, *Moral Philosophy;* Harry S. Stout, *The New England Soul: Preaching and Religious Culture in Colonial New England* (New York, 1986); Philip F. Gura, *A Glimpse of Sion's Glory: Puritan Radicalism in New England, 1620–1660* (Middletown, Conn., 1984); Robert Middlekauff, *The Mathers: Three Generations of Puritan Intellectuals, 1596–1728* (New York, 1971), particularly the section on Cotton Mather; Charles E. Hambrick-Stowe, *The Practice of Piety: Puritan Devotional Disciplines in Seventeenth-Century New England* (Chapel Hill, N.C., 1982); Charles Lloyd Cohen, *God's Caress: The Psychology of Puritan Religious Experience* (New York, 1986).

These men who made the most radical political arguments for consent in the early years of the English Civil War extended those religious beliefs to construct arguments for political inclusion, although they still disagreed about the boundaries of that inclusion. Thus as William Walwyn wrote in 1643: All the information "either for the enlightning of our understandings, or the peace of our mindes" was so clearly stated in the Bible "that the meanest capacity is fully capable of a right understanding thereof." This confidence in the ability to interpret the Bible extended to the ability to understand political principles. To whom that freedom of judgment could be granted, however, was a subject of sharp debate, centered upon who had understanding and judgment and defining what these terms meant. So, while Walwyn presumed even "the meanest capacity" to be "fully capable," other Levellers argued that, while all might have the potential to perceive their freedoms, they could not necessarily do so. Overton wrote in frustration in 1646: "The poore deceived people are even (in a manner) bestiallized in their understanding, become so stupid, and grosly ignorant of themselves . . . and as bruits they'l live and die for want of knowledge, being void of the use of Reason for want of capacitie to discern, whereof, and how far God by nature hath made them free." So, too, Maximilian Petty asserted that, although all men should be able to vote, "apprentices, or servants, or those that take alms" should be exceptions because "they depend upon the will of other men and should be afraid to displease" them, such that their reason might be swayed by those upon whom they depend. Gerrard Winstanley emphasized age and experience in granting political authority. Thus even some Levellers questioned how broadly the principle of equality would apply and limited equality by defining who had reason and who did not.[62]

Likewise, most Puritans limited equality and the ability to consent by connecting both to the understanding. Indeed, they granted parental control over children until their understanding had developed "by slow degrees." Their emphasis on the development of the understanding prior to full church membership parallels Enlightenment ideas about education.

It is common to distinguish sharply between Puritan ideas about child rearing and those of the Enlightenment as typified by John Locke: Puritans sought to break children's wills while Locke sought to shape them; Puritans

62. [William Walwyn], *The Power of Love* (London, 1643), 7; Overton in Brian Manning, "The Levellers and Religion," in McGregor and Reay, eds., *Radical Religion in the English Revolution*, 85, 89, and G. E. Aylmer, "The Religion of Gerrard Winstanley," 91–119; A. S. P. Woodhouse, *Puritanism and Liberty: Being the Army Debates (1647–9)* . . . (Chicago, 1951), 83.

saw children as innately evil while Locke saw them as a blank slate. But these distinctions are too sharp and rest on a variety of misperceptions. The phrase "breaking the will" was both relatively uncommon and is often misunderstood. Most Puritan child-rearing manuals, in fact, encouraged development of self-control over the will and eventual self-mastery, not the permanent dependence of children implied in "breaking the will," which Puritans sought, more simply, to discipline. Most Puritans did to some degree believe that infants were depraved, that as inheritors of original sin they had an "evill will."[63]

Yet the doctrine of the covenant saw the children of godly parents as within God's covenant and by baptism cleansed, at least in part, of Adam's original sin. Consider John Cotton's catechism of 1646, for example, *Milk for Babes Drawn out of the Breasts of Both Testaments*. It begins

> Q: Are you then born a sinner?
> A: I was conceived in sinne, and born in iniquity.
> Q. What is your birth-sinne?
> A. ADAMS Sinne imputed to me, and a corrupt Nature dwelling in me.

But the covenant lifts that burden of sin via baptism:

> Q: What are the seales of the Covenant now in the dayes of the gospel?
> A: Baptism and the Lords Supper.
> Q: What is done for you in Baptism?
> A: In baptisme, the washing with water is a signe and seale of my washing with the blood and spirit of Christ, and thereby of my ingrafting into Christ: of the pardon and clensing of my sinnes: of my rising out of Affliction: and also of my resurrection from the dead at the last day.[64]

Richard Mather, in another popular catechism, agreed about the role of baptism: it was the "seale of the covenant between God and his people" and gave "union with Christ and forgivenesse of sinnes." Increase Mather claimed that God would "infallably make them [children baptized into the covenant] the

---

63. See especially Philip J. Greven, Jr., *The Protestant Temperament: Patterns of Child-Rearing, Religious Experience, and the Self in Early America* (Chicago, 1977), 32–43; John Demos, *A Little Commonwealth: Family Life in Plymouth Colony* (New York, 1970), 128–144; Edmund S. Morgan, *The Puritan Family: Religion and Domestic Relations in Seventeenth-Century New England*, rev. ed. (New York, 1956), 90–93. C. John Sommerville, in *The Discovery of Childhood in Puritan England* (Athens, Ga., 1992), challenges the contention that all Puritans assumed children to be sinful (12, 94–95).

64. John Cotton, *Milk for Babes Drawn out of the Breasts of Both Testaments, Chiefly for the Spirituall Nourishment of Boston Babes in Either England: But May Be of Like Use for Any Children* (London, 1646), 1–2, 11–12.

offer of his covenant [of grace]." God "cast the line of Election . . . through the loyns of Godly parents." Baptism, Mather asserted, grants some measure of God's grace, a future promise of God's grace, or union with Christ.[65]

For Mather as for many Puritans, baptism offered a conditional entrance into the covenant of grace, but the child needed proper cultivation in order to fulfill that promise. Baptism itself both washed away Adam's sins and gave some aid against committing future sins. If Adam's actual sin is relieved by one's birth within the covenant, then the propensity to sin is lessened, but the capacity does not disappear. As the New England primer said in its alphabetical catechism under *A*, "In Adam's fall so sinned we all." Though Puritans still feared that children could be overcome by sin, they moderated this fear by the premise that birth within the covenant and the guidance of parents could help those children to control negative inclinations. That propensity to sin was lodged in the will, which was controlled by the passions. What parents had to do was educate their children so that their understanding could control their passions and permit only good passions to result in actions.[66]

Passions could be good but were often bad. In league with the will, they could overrule the understanding, even in adults. "By reason of this commanding power, the Will is the first cause of unadvisednese, and blameworthy error in the understanding," wrote William Ames, expressing a common argument. William Perkins differentiated between two faculties of the soul: the will and the understanding. "Will" itself was another word for inclinations or desires or wants. It was the "facultie whereby we doe will or nill anything, that is choose or refuse it," and he allied it with the affections.

65. Richard Mather, *A Catechisme; or, The Grounds and Principles of Christian Religion* . . . (London, 1650), 91; Hall, introduction, in Edwards, *Ecclesiastical Writings*, 25–26, citing Increase Mather, *Pray for the Rising Generation* . . . , 2d ed. (Boston, 1679), 25, 26.

66. This interpretation agrees with that put forward by Morgan in *The Puritan Family*, 91–95, except that Morgan sees less debate on whether children born within the covenant had evil wills. Greven's portrayal of Puritans as wholly negative about the sins of children I find highly problematic. Most of the passages cited by Greven on children's sinfulness, for example, are from such eighteenth-century reformers as Jonathan Edwards, John Wesley, and Samuel Davies, who had doubts about infant baptism and thus did not believe that children could be redeemed by the covenant promise. He quotes several nineteenth-century evangelicals, but none of the mainstream Puritans of the seventeenth century. He also exaggerates the physical brutality toward children. See Greven, *Protestant Temperament*, 28–43. Linda A. Pollock, *Forgotten Children: Parent-Child Relations from 1500 to 1900* (Cambridge, 1983), surveyed almost five hundred diaries and autobiographies (including many by Puritans in England and America) to conclude that most parents exercised little physical violence toward their children in the seventeenth and eighteenth centuries.

Conscience, which uses reason, he allied with the understanding. Placed on a higher level, conscience is the part of the mind that determines "this may be done, this may not be done; this was well done, this was ill done." Conscience, then, obviously involves choice, but choice of a different caliber from the simple choice exercised by the will. Conscience involves understanding, reason, determination, and judgment. Understanding informed the conscience and allowed a reasoned control over the will.[67]

Once a child had gained enough understanding to have a developed conscience, that child would then be able to control her own will or curb her own passions. So Cotton Mather encouraged parents to develop their children's understanding, because "every Grace enters into the Soul through the Understanding." Susanna Wesley (mother of John) advised, "In order to form the minds of children, the first thing to be done is to conquer their will. . . . When this is thoroughly done, then a child is capable of being governed by the reason and piety of its parents till its own understanding comes to maturity." So the repression of the will of children is only a temporary measure, enabling the parent to guide the child until she develops her understanding, after which the child can control her own will. Yet "to inform the understanding is a work of time, and must with children proceed by slow degrees."[68]

But the affections were far from always bad; they played a critical role in piety and in perceiving God's grace. The will could be most influenced by God's divinity. Therefore neither the affections nor the will was to be completely restrained (nor did Puritans think they could be). Rather, the child should be taught to distinguish positive inclinations from negative ones. The will could (or even should) be more inclined to goodness but could be controlled by the bad. An image invoked by both Luther and Calvin (taken from Augustine) portrayed the will as a horse upon which either God or Satan could ride. John Leverett (later the president of Harvard) explained how the will should be taught. The will is queen of the mind and ultimately controls actions. But she acts wisely upon the advice of the intellect, who is "the first

67. Fiering, *Moral Philosophy*, chap. 3, esp. 122–125; William Perkins, *A Discourse of Conscience*, 2d ed. (1608), in Thomas F. Merrill, ed., *William Perkins, 1558–1602: English Puritanist: His Pioneer Works on Casuistry: "A Discourse of Conscience" and "The Whole Treatise of Cases of Conscience"* (The Hague, 1966), 5, 6.

68. Quoted by Morgan, *The Puritan Family*, 89, from Cotton Mather, *Cares about Nurseries: Two Brief Discourses* (Boston, 1702), 34. Morgan summarizes Mather: "In order to be saved, men had to understand the doctrines of Christianity, and since children were born without understanding they had to be taught" (89–90). Susanna Wesley, "On the Education of Her Family" (1732), in Greven, ed., *Child-Rearing Concepts*, 47–48.

of the will's privy advisors." God's grace (as conferred partially via baptism and more fully via conversion) is also critical to enabling the will to follow the good.[69]

In part because they saw children as governed more by their wills and passions than by reason and piety, Puritans and other Dissenters distinguished them from adults in the ability to experience conversion and thus to consent to both church membership and public authority. Indeed, by separating the authority of the state from that of parents, Puritans and other Dissenters generally agreed that consent was necessary for adults but not for children, a distinction that many republican political theorists would later emphasize in justifying consent-based political power. Calvin claimed that the father of the family was God's minister, and emphasized fatherly authority, but his invocation of paternal power lent limited support to patriarchal ideology, because he distinguished between state power and familial power, as did many Puritans. John Winthrop referred to the family as a little commonwealth, for example, but declared that political government should be based on consent and that familial government should not.[70]

Hooker also separated the powers of parents sharply from the powers of the state.

> To fathers within their private families Nature hath given a supreme power. . . . Howbeit over a whole grand multitude having no such dependency upon any one, and consisting of so many families as every politic

69. Fiering, *Moral Philosophy*, 129, 117.

70. Morgan, ed., *Puritan Political Ideas*, introduction. On Calvin, see Michael Walzer, *The Revolution of the Saints: A Study in the Origins of Radical Politics* (Cambridge, Mass., 1965). "The Calvinist saints, however, required a recognition that all subjects were knowledgeable and active citizens rather than naive political children, that government was not a household, the state not an extended family, and the king not a loving father" (14).

On Winthrop: John Winthrop, "A Declaration in Defense of an Order of Court Made in May, 1637," in Morgan, ed., *Puritan Political Ideas*, 145–146: "1. No common weale can be founded but by free consent." "7. A family is a little common wealth, and a common wealth a greate family. Now as a family is not bound to entertaine all comers, no not every good man (otherwise than by way of hospitality) no more is a common wealth." The separation of familial authority from state authority in Puritan thought is in fact extremely complicated. Through the eighteenth century, some ministers continued to equate the two (and at the same time challenge the king's authority). See, for example, Jonathan Mayhew's sermon, *The Snare Broken* . . . (Boston, 1766), in Ellis Sandoz, ed., *Political Sermons of the American Founding Era, 1730–1805* (Indianapolis, Ind., 1991), 252–253. Others followed more in Calvin's or Winthrop's path.

society in the world doth, impossible it is that any should have complete lawful power, but by consent of men, or immediate appointment of God.

While he emphasized that the authority of a government must originate in consent, Hooker excluded children from being able to consent even to the authority of their parents.[71]

Yet Puritans did not always separate the power of parents from that of the state: indeed, in some ways, the equation between the two was reinforced by the Reformation. The new questions of church membership and church authority forced a defining and redefining of the meaning of consent, of inherited right, and of the connections between fatherly power and these other justifications for authority. Many Commonwealth tracts published by Puritan authorities used the same analogy employed in Anglican catechisms to inculcate obedience to superiors, although, of course, without the king at the top. Robert Ram's *Countrymans Catechisme* (1655), for example, listed those to whom all subjects owed obedience by the fifth commandment as "1. Our naturall Parentes, Fathers and Mothers in the flesh. 2. Our Civil Parents, Magistrates, Governours, and all in Authority, [and] 3. Our spiritual Parents, Pastors, Ministers, and Teachers." The Anglican Richard Allestree's *Whole Duty of Man* (1659) likewise listed the "several sorts of Parents" for whom the fifth commandment enjoined obedience: "the Civil, the Spiritual, the Natural." This equation of parental and patriarchal authority continued to appear in Nonconformist catechisms and sermons, including those in New England, where it bolstered political authority during the seventeenth and eighteenth centuries. As others who have studied the impact of the Reformation in Germany and England have argued, Protestants often increased paternal power.[72]

71. Quoted by Eccleshall, *Order and Reason in Politics*, 139, from Hooker, *Of the Laws of Ecclesiastical Polity*, book 1.

72. Gordon Schochet, *Patriarchalism in Political Thought: The Authoritarian Family and Political Speculation and Attitudes, Especially in Seventeenth-Century England* (Oxford, 1975), 78–81 (quoting Ram and Allestree); Walzer, *The Revolution of the Saints*, 183–198.

One example of the equation of parental and patriarchal authority is a sermon by Charles Chauncy, D.D., *Civil Magistrates Must Be Just . . .* (Boston, 1747), in Sandoz, ed., *Political Sermons*, 169: "And as your Excellency is our common father, we repair to you as the friend and patron of all that is dear and valuable to us; depending that you will employ your time, your thought, your authority, your influence and best endeavours, to ease our burdens, to lead us out of the labyrinths we have run into, and to make us a happy and prosperous people." Or see 173–174, where he addresses his "civil fathers" and "my honoured fathers in the government": "You are, my fathers, accountable to that God whose throne is in the heavens, in common with other men."

On the Reformation generally, see Steven Ozment, *When Fathers Ruled: Family Life in Reformation Europe* (Cambridge, Mass., 1983). Walzer, *Revolution of the Saints*, has come

Quaker catechisms varied dramatically from both Anglican and most Puritan catechisms, placing much more emphasis on Christ's injunction to "love thy neighbour as thyself" than on the Old Testament commandments. George Fox addressed the Ten Commandments in one brief paragraph of a catechism of more than forty pages. That lonely paragraph dwelt on the principle, "Love thy neighbour," which he interpreted as the underlying meaning of all Ten Commandments. "As thou loves the light, thou loves God who is light and thou loves thy neighbour who is enlightened with the same light . . . and this brings to love God with all thy minde, and all thy soul, and thy Neighbor as thy self, and so the Law [the Ten Commandments] is fulfilled in one word." Fox mentioned some of the other commandments, such as "not to covet, not to doe any murther, not to steal not to commit adultery," but he ignored the fifth commandment, about obedience to parents. Whether he did so because of how that commandment was invoked in most catechisms to inculcate obedience to superiors, or whether he did not want to emphasize parental authority itself, is open to question. Whatever his reason, Quaker theology, emphasizing how each soul is born enlightened by Christ, tended toward a radical egalitarianism, one that saw even children as equal. Quakers believed that children were innately good and did not need harsh discipline. Parents' roles were to help their children see their own inner light.[73]

The debates over baptism both grew out of and raised questions over individuals versus community. The Catholic doctrine of inclusive baptism, by making it automatic, granted an embracing community based on God's grace, especially among kin. Among Christians, all were baptized. It cast a wide net of membership. By emphasizing individual choice, the Protestants introduced a differentiating category, which cast sharp boundaries within communities and even families. When groups such as the Puritans in New England broke off to start their own communities, they came face-to-face with these boundaries, which threatened to close their own children and grandchildren off from them. In consequence, they compromised on the question of choice and moved toward inheritable, permanent status, without rejecting the conversion experience as essential for full membership. Their emphasis

---

to much the same conclusion: Puritan ideology in some ways accentuated paternal power (49).

73. F[ox], *Catechisme for Children*, 34–35; Barry Levy, *Quakers and the American Family: British Settlement in the Delaware Valley* (New York, 1988), esp. 76–77. Generally, Quakers advocated gentler child-rearing methods than the Puritans. See also J. William Frost, *The Quaker Family in Colonial America: A Portrait of the Society of Friends* (New York, 1973). This fits with the irrelevance of baptism to them. On Quakers' position against baptism, see Geoffrey F. Nuttall, *The Holy Spirit in Puritan Faith and Experience* (Oxford, 1946).

on choice had important implications for power. Corporatist membership along the lines of Catholic or Anglican gave control to those at the top of each church's hierarchy; the New England congregational model, where parishioners chose their minister, could sharply limit ministerial control (and certainly hierarchical control). Still, the body of those allowed to choose a minister was restricted to adults and usually to men. And if a minister stayed in power for a considerable period of time, he could influence who became members of the local church, and thereby limit who could choose to dismiss him. Did the Catholic model of membership give more influence to the young because of their greater sacramental inclusion as recipients of God's grace? Perhaps. At the same time, however, it more explicitly supported other types of hierarchy. The Quaker model compromised between the Catholic and most other Protestant stances: it both rejected hierachy and rejected a sharp discontinuity between childhood and adulthood. It was more radically egalitarian. It thus neither pointedly demanded conversion (as did the Puritan model) nor assumed belief (as did the Catholic model).

The Puritans and other radical Protestants, by stressing individual, active choice to church membership, engaged a debate over what the ability to consent means, one that involved many Catholics as well, especially during the Counter Reformation. They linked that ability to a process of reasoning that was systematic and experiential. The principles that the ability to consent depends on having reason and that reason itself is a process translated directly into the political arena. The various Dissenting groups, including the Puritans in New England and the Quakers in Pennsylvania, anchored their arguments that government should be based on consent on the potential of all persons to consent to church membership. However much conversion depended on God's grace, it depended also on having a conscience that grew out of the understanding and was based on experience; it depended on the ability to reason. Conscience enabled the making of judgments, which in turn allowed control over human will and enabled reasonable consent. Acknowledging these links not only helps to delineate the origins of modern political theory but also to understand why the Puritans passed some of the first legal reforms with respect to the status of children. That reason came only with experience and that reason was important for the exercise of conscience implied that children could not consent or give judgment. Thus Puritans in New England and in England during the Interregnum under Cromwell passed some of the first laws that raised legal age limits and expanded parental power. They likewise helped to shape the principles that would underlie democracy.

CHAPTER 3

THE DILEMMAS OF GOVERNMENT BY CONSENT
AND THE PROBLEM OF CHILDREN
FORCE, INFLUENCE, IMPLIED CONSENT,
AND INHERITED OBLIGATION

*"Dominion is acquired two wayes; By Generation, and by
Conquest. The right of Dominion by Generation, is that, which
the Parent hath over his Children; and is called* PATERNALL.
*And is not so derived from the Generation, as if therfore the
Parent had Dominion over his Child because he begat him;
but from the Childs Consent, either expresse, or by other
sufficient arguments declared.*

* * *

*He that hath the Dominion over the Child, hath Dominion also
over the Children of the Child; and over their Childrens Children.
For he that hath Dominion over the person of a man, hath
Dominion over all that is his."*
Thomas Hobbes, Leviathan *(1651)*

"Thus we are born Free, *as we are born Rational; not that we
have actually the Exercise of either: Age that brings one, brings
with it the other too. And thus we see how* natural Freedom *and
Subjection to Parents* may consist together, and are both
founded on the same Principle. A Child *is Free by . . .
his Father's Understanding, which is to govern him,
till he hath it of his own."*
John Locke, Two Treatises of Government *(1698)*

Dissenters and Consent

Dissenters were the core opponents of patriarchal ideology during the seventeenth century: radical religious ideology about choosing church membership and interpreting the Bible for themselves pushed them toward an ideology that emphasized choice in political allegiance. Indeed, the most influential political theorists, especially in their impact on later thinkers, were religious radicals, supporting consent instead of inherited right. The Levellers were some of the first to make these connections. Most democratic political theorists of seventeenth- and early-eighteenth-century England, including John Milton, Algernon Sidney, Locke, and Thomas Gordon and John Trenchard, were Dissenters and heavily involved, in plots and plans and on battlefields and parliamentary committees, in efforts to limit both "popery" and "arbitrary government."

John Locke and Algernon Sidney, among the philosophers most cited by the American Revolutionaries, were from Dissenting backgrounds; their political treatises were in direct response to Robert Filmer and emerged from the religious debates and religious wars of seventeenth-century England. John Locke's father, for example, fought with Cromwell in the Civil War. Sidney and the first earl of Shaftesbury, Locke's mentor, likewise both fought on the side of Parliament. Both were also members of Cromwell's commission to revise England's code of laws in 1652–1653.[1] Locke, Shaftesbury, Sidney, John Trenchard (part author of *Cato's Letters*), and many other Dissenters were probably all involved in the Rye House Plot of 1683, the insurrection that was to begin with the assassination of both Charles II and his Catholic brother and heir, James, duke of York. They sought to prevent James II's assuming the throne at his brother's death, objecting to his Catholicism, which they thought would lead to absolutism politically. In the wake of the plot's failure, Locke fled to Holland, not returning to England until the Glorious Revolution had succeeded. John Trenchard was imprisoned but finally released for lack of evidence, and Sidney was executed for treason. At Sidney's trial, the crown read passages from the manuscript of his "Discourses concerning Government" to prove his antipathy for monarchy. Locke wrote his *Two Treatises of Government* and revised it during this period. As soon as Trenchard was freed, he fled to Holland, where he joined Locke.[2]

1. Richard Ashcraft, *Revolutionary Politics and Locke's "Two Treatises of Government"* (Princeton, N.J., 1986), esp. 178–181; *Several Draft Acts Heretofore Prepared by Persons to Consider the Inconvenience, Delay, Charge, and Irregularity in the Proceedings of the Law* (1653), in *Somers Tracts*, VI (London, 1809), 177. Page 1 of the pamphlet lists the members of the commission.

2. Christopher Hill, *The World Turned Upside Down: Radical Ideas during the English Revolution* (New York, 1972), and *Puritanism and Revolution: Studies in the Interpretation of the English Revolution of the Seventeenth Century* (London, 1958); Ashcraft, *Revolutionary Politics*. Melinda Zook, "Violence, Martyrdom, and Radical Politics: Rethinking the Glorious Revolution," in Howard Nenner, ed., *Politics and Political Imagination in Later Stuart Britain* (Rochester, N.Y., 1997), 75–95, argues that, of the one hundred Whigs most involved in radical politics in the 1680s, virtually all were Dissenters, although "several" were Anglicans (92).

Samuel Rawson Gardiner first coined the term "Puritan Revolution" in his *History of the Great Civil War, 1641–1649*, new ed., 4 vols. (London, 1893) and his *History of the Commonwealth and the Protectorate*, 3 vols. in 4 (London, 1894–1903). A very fine survey of the historiography about the role of religion in causing this conflict (and of the

These seventeenth-century political writers as well as many who followed them in the eighteenth century emphasized consent as critical to political legitimacy. Locke and Sidney, especially, attacked primogeniture as a means of transferring political power. Those who inherited a kingdom were not the best rulers, they argued. Birth was no way to determine who had sufficient wisdom, virtue, and reason to rule—those who ruled should be determined by the people. Even James Harrington, who most strongly supported a balance of power between different bodies of government, opposed inheritance as the basis for power. He sought to replace a House of Lords and a monarch determined by birth with a "senate" and "sole legislator" determined by choice. All three branches of government should be elected.[3]

Locke and Sidney were not alone in their attack on patriarchalism or in connecting primogeniture and arbitrary government with Catholicism. Many of the political tracts published during the late 1670s and early 1680s concentrated on the problems with "the succession" or allocating a kingdom by primogeniture. Their very titles connected Catholicism, inherited right, and arbitrary power: *Account of the Growth of Popery and Arbitrary Government* (Andrew Marvell), *Vox Patriae; or, The Resentments and Indignation of the Free-Born Subjects of England against Popery* (anon.), *Three Great Questions concerning the Succession and the Dangers of Popery* (anon.). The possibility of a Catholic king recalled the last explicitly Catholic monarch—who had prosecuted her Protestant subjects for heresy. As one scholar noted, after reading hundreds of tracts, "The reign of Bloody Mary was repeatedly invoked. . . . [Readers] were advised to 'read the book of Martyrs, if these things so easily slip your mind.'" In debates in the House of Commons during the early 1680s some made the references explicit. Once a Catholic king assumes control: "We are heretics, they will burn us, and damn us." Many members feared that a Catholic king would seek to exercise absolute power by imposing control with an army rather than trying to govern through Parliament. The fear of what a Catholic king might do built on intertwining concerns: that the king would be the head of the Anglican Church with ability to shape doctrine and punish religious crimes, the historic prosecution of heretics by Queen

---

competing arguments for a causation) can be found in Norah Carlin, *The Causes of the English Civil War* (Oxford, 1999), chaps. 3, 6.

3. James Harrington, *The Commonwealth of Oceana* (1656), in J. G. A. Pocock, ed., *The Political Works of James Harrington* (Cambridge, 1977), 231–237, 358 (and see discussion below); Pocock, *The Machiavellian Moment: Florentine Political Thought and the Atlantic Republican Tradition* (Princeton, N.J., 1975), esp. 385–394. Pocock is trying to link Harrington's ideas to earlier and later ideas of "ancient consitution." Certainly, there are some similar ideas about balance. But Harrington's stand against inherited right marks a critical difference.

Mary, and the top-down structure (and apparent lack of consent within) the Catholic Church. The last, particularly, suggested that, if the future king James II held to those religious principles, he would also adhere to absolutist principles in the political arena.[4]

Not everyone who adopted ideas about government based on consent came from a Dissenting background, nor did all of those who were Dissenters oppose hereditary right. Consent and hereditary authority were sometimes combined, as in the writings of Thomas Hobbes, who devised a theory of government based on consent that permitted a hereditary, absolute monarchy. In his *Leviathan* (1651) "dominion" could be "acquired two wayes: By Generation, and by Conquest." If by conquest, then men "for fear of death, or bonds, do authorise all the actions of that Man, or Assembly, that hath their lives and liberty in his Power." Force could coerce consent, and, once granted, that consent was irrevocable. "Covenants entred into by fear, in the condition of meer Nature, are obligatory." Likewise, in governments "by Generation," the parents' authority arose from the consent of the child, "either espresse, or by other sufficient arguments declared." Like conquerors, parents could bind their children to perpetual obedience. Therefore, once a father swore allegiance to a king, his bond permanently bound his children and his children's children, and so on in perpetuity (regardless of their age or competence). Hobbes further argued that consent did not have to be explicit and that the bond of parents was descendible to their children. "He that hath the Dominion over the Child, hath Dominion also over the Children of the Child; and over their Childrens Children."[5]

In many ways the law of mid-seventeenth-century England allowed the coerced consent outlined by Hobbes, including the consent of children, that might be obtained by parents through force. The representative government that we would consider democracy is thus not characterized solely by the principle of consent. Any consent-based system of government faces questions, questions that we assume have fixed answers because they have become

---

4. See Ashcraft, *Revolutionary Politics,* chap. 5, esp. 202, 204; John Miller, *Popery and Politics in England, 1660–1688* (Cambridge, 1973).

5. Thomas Hobbes, *Leviathan,* ed. Richard Tuck (Cambridge, 1996), chap. 14 (p. 97), chap. 20 (pp. 138–141), chap. 22 (p. 154). For Hobbes, the reigning king can choose his heir (he need not follow primogeniture), but the people are still bound to the new king (see chaps. 20, 21). In this Hobbes was following other natural law theorists such as Francisco Suárez and John Selden (and to a lesser degree Hugo Grotius), who also considered force legitimate to the making of binding contracts. On this issue, see particularly Richard Tuck, *Natural Rights Theories: Their Origin and Development* (Cambridge, 1979), 3, 56, 70, 97, for example. Tuck's evidence about Grotius's condoning force and slavery does not seem as strong.

so embedded in modern understandings of consent. But these questions had different answers then. Can consent be coerced? If not, what constitutes coercion? Can one revoke one's consent—if so, under what conditions? Is the consent of the father inheritable? If not, what binds children when young? Does consent have to be explicit? Or can it be tacit (you live here, under this system, therefore you agree to it)? What rights, if any, can a person not give away, or alien?

John Locke was the most comprehensive and influential writer to answer these questions in a way that crafted a different, narrower meaning of consent. In doing so, he focused on the consent of children. Separating paternal authority from political authority, he argued that all people are created equal and that government should be based on consent, not on inherited right via primogeniture. Parental authority, however, did not arise from consent, and parents could not bind their children in perpetuity. The entire first treatise was an explicit, point-by-point response to Filmer, but it was also, less explicitly, a response to Hobbes. Locke assailed questions of hereditary status and obligation at length.

In his "Second Treatise," Locke shifted away from criticizing Filmer and primogeniture and began to formulate an alternative origin for government based on the consent of the people. People should be able to consent, he argued, because most subjects are not children, as Filmer contended, but can reason for themselves. He distinguished adults who could reason from children who could not. *"Children* I confess, are not born in this full state of *Equality,* though they are born to it. Their Parents have a sort of Rule and Jurisdiction over them."* Locke referred to children as "weak and helpless, without Knowledge or Understanding." The parents' task was to "govern the Actions of their yet ignorant Nonage, till Reason shall take its place." "Though I have said above," he began, *"That all Men by Nature are equal,* I cannot be supposed to understand all sorts of *Equality: Age* or *Virtue* may give Men a just Precedency."

Thus we are *born Free,* as we are born Rational; not that we have actually the Exercise of either: Age that brings one, brings with it the other too. And thus we see how *natural Freedom and Subjection to Parents* may consist together, and are both founded on the same Principle. A *Child* is *Free* by . . . his Father's Understanding, which is to govern him, till he hath it of his own. The *Freedom of a Man at years of discretion,* and the *Subjection* of a child *to* his *Parents,* whilst yet short of that Age, are so consistent, and so distinguishable.[6]

6. John Locke, *Two Treatises of Government,* ed. Peter Laslett (Cambridge, 1988), 304–305, 308 ("Second Treatise," chap. 6, pars. 55, 56, 58).

Thus for Locke, until children attained reason, an "age of discretion," they should be dependent on their parents and subject to their will. His argument here was an elaboration of his earlier *Essay concerning Human Understanding* and led into one further, more practical treatise on the exercise of reason: how to cultivate it through education. Both these other treatises described the lengthy process a child undergoes in order to develop the ability to reason, what Locke called "reflection," or the ability to "abstract" generalizations from particular observations, which he held were essential to the exercise of freedom and consent.[7]

This power belongs to parents in particular because the child is dependent on them. "This *power* so little belongs to the *Father* by any peculiar right of Nature, but only as he is Guardian of his Children, that when he quits his Care of them, he loses his power over them, which goes along with their Nourishment and Education, to which it is inseparably annexed." Not only did Locke place limits on the powers of parents, but he linked the physical dependence of children to their mental dependence. He made this link even more explicit: "When he comes to the Estate that made his *Father a Freeman,* the *Son is a Freeman* too." "Estate" could mean both "state" as in "condition of independence" and "estate" as in property. Still, Locke was tentative about this equation between mental and physical dependency. He undercut that link when he acknowledged: "If the Father die, and fail to substitute a Deputy in this Trust, if he hath not provided a Tutor to govern his Son during his Minority, during his want of Understanding, the Law takes care to do it; some other must govern him, and be a Will to him, till he hath *attained to a state of Freedom,* and his Understanding be fit to take the Government of his Will." Locke clearly accentuated reason, or mental independence, as critical to freedom, but he correlated this mental independence only weakly with physical independence, or property ownership.[8]

Thus while Locke, as most scholars have emphasized, advocated equality and made consent the basis of legitimate authority, he also excluded some from having a political voice because they did not have reason. He thereby upheld elements of patriarchal ideology, particularly the power of parents over children. Yet Locke limited parental authority much more than Filmer, since Filmer held that the father had the power of life and death over his children, whereas Locke held that only the state had that power. For Locke, that parental authority arose neither from "any peculiar right of nature" nor

7. John Locke, *Some Thoughts concerning Education* (1693), ed. John W. Yolton and Jean S. Yolton (Oxford, 1989).

8. Locke, *Two Treatises,* ed. Laslett, 306–307, 310 ("Second Treatise," chap. 6, pars. 58, 59, 65).

from the consent of the child, even implicit, but from mental dependence (their lack of reason) and their physical dependence on their parents for sustenance. His justifications for parental authority circumscribed parental power. Just as commitments made by children during this period of minority cannot bind them, parental commitments made for them during this period are likewise temporary and end when they mature and can reason for themselves. Obligation cannot be hereditary.

On this same principle, Locke's *Two Treatises of Government* criticized hereditary status, particularly hereditary slavery. Although he allowed slavery as punishment for a crime such as starting an "unjust" war, slavery could never be inherited by children.

> I say, this concerns not their Children, who are in their Minority. For since a Father hath not, in himself, a Power over the Life or Liberty of his Child; no act of his can possibly forfeit it: So that the Children, whatever may have happenened to the Fathers, are Free-Men, and the Absolute Power of the *Conqueror* reaches no farther than the Persons of the Men, that were subdued by him, and dies with them; and should he Govern them as Slaves, subjected to his Absolute, Arbitrary Power, he *has no* such *Right of Dominion over their Children*. He can have no Power over them, but by their own consent, whatever he may drive them to say, or do; and he has no lawful Authority, whilst Force, and not Choice, compels them to submission.[9]

Locke's distinction between "force" and "choice" was central to his theory, as was being born equal. Such children cannot be forced to agree; if they are, consent is not binding on them. Consent that is forced is the opposite of real choice. Locke clearly meant that such children could not "consent" to give their father's master any power over them until they had reason (and then would not).

Locke's speculations about human reason preceded his political writing by more than a decade, and he would return to them afterward. His initial thoughts on *An Essay concerning Human Understanding* were apparently prepared in 1670–1671 and grew out of a study group that met to discuss religious issues.

> Were it fit to trouble thee with the history of this *Essay*, I should tell thee, that five or six friends, meeting in my chamber and discoursing on a subject very remote from this [apparently toleration], found themselves quickly at a stand by the difficulties that arose on every side. After we had awhile puzzled ourselves, without coming any nearer a resolution of those

9. Ibid., 393 ("Second Treatise," chap. 16, "Of Conquest," pars. 188, 189).

doubts which perplexed us, it came into my thoughts that we took a wrong course; and that before we set ourselves upon enquiries of this nature it was necessary to examine our own abilities, and see what objects our understandings were or were not fitted to deal with.

For the next thirty years Locke examined how humans develop and exercise their abilities, particularly their "understandings."[10]

Locke was not the only one to make these connections. The religious debates over baptism and church membership generally had political implications, and many of the writings about casuistry were clearly deeply influential on Locke's concepts of the will and understanding. Whole chapters of his *Essay* concern how true liberty, for example, consists in granting the understanding control over the will—and in limiting the authority of the passions over the will.[11] The question for him, as for many who debated consent and church membership, was what enabled a person to give consent: what gave a person the abilities to make that choice? Like the mainstream Protestants, particularly the Puritans and early Baptists, Locke emphasized reason and understanding. Locke asked in the last book of the *Essay*: "What need is there of *reason*? Very much: both for the enlargement of our knowledge, and regulating our assent." His whole purpose in writing was to "inquire into the original, certainty, and extent of human knowledge, together with the grounds and degrees of *belief, opinion,* and *assent*." He sought to "search out the bounds between opinion and knowledge; and examine by what measures, in things whereof we have no certain knowledge, we ought to regulate our assent and moderate our persuasion." In other words, his whole purpose in analyzing human understanding was to analyze how humans can give "assent." His description of faith—"In truth it is nothing else but an assent founded on the highest reason"—reveals most clearly the origin of his thirty-year obsession with the human understanding, with reason, and with

10. John Locke, *An Essay concerning Human Understanding* (1690), ed. Alexander Campbell Fraser (New York, 1959), epistle to the reader, I, 9; Ashcraft, *Revolutionary Politics*, esp. 106–109. Ashcraft links the essay's origins, pretty persuasively, to the debate surrounding Samuel Parker's *Discourse of Ecclesiastical Polity*. Fraser points to James Tyrrell's marginal notation in his copy of the *Essay*. Tyrrell, the author of *Patriarcha Non Monarcha* and a member of the group, wrote that they were discussing "principles of morality and revealed religion"—not a very specific point, certainly, but helpful in pointing attention toward its context, at least in part, in religious discussion. See *Essay,* I, xvii.

11. Locke, *Essay concerning Human Understanding*, ed. Fraser, book 2, chap. 21, "Of Power" (I, 308–374). These same debates undoubtedly influenced Hobbes, who in turn influenced Locke's ideas about sensation.

assent. He emphasized reason over revelation: the latter he put into the category of the unknowable. He equated real faith with assent that is based on reason: this should be the grounding of church membership.[12]

This essay, so often regarded as separate from his political works, was in fact critical to his political theory. He proffered a theory of how humans gain reason and provided a model of the stages in human development. Beginning with a theory of sensations, he argued that young children first began to develop "ideas" and finally came to "compare" and contrast these ideas, ultimately acquiring the full use of their understanding, which education could facilitate. It is here that he extended his religious ideas to the political realm in order to develop the concept of reason. Consider, for example, one of his many descriptions of how children acquire reason.

> When children have, by repeated sensations, got ideas fixed in their memories, they begin by degrees to learn the use of signs. And when they have got the skill to apply the organs of speech to the framing of articulate sounds, they begin to make use of words, to signify their ideas to others. . . .
>
> The use of words then being to stand as outward marks of our internal ideas. . . . the mind makes the particular ideas received from particular objects to become general. . . . This is called ABSTRACTION, whereby ideas taken from particular beings become general representatives of all of the same kind. . . .
>
> These, I think, are the first faculties and operations of the mind, which it makes use of in understanding . . . [they are] simple ideas.

He went on to describe more "complex" processes and ideas, such as place, duration, and infinity, all of which, he theorized, proceed from experience and come through time to children as they get older; over time, he argued, the human mind gains greater abilities to compare, relate, and contextualize.[13]

For Locke, most people attain reason with experience. He attacked traditional learning, particularly as embodied in medieval scholasticism.

> God has been more bountiful to mankind than so. He has given them a mind that can reason, without being instructed in methods of syllogizing: the understanding is not taught to reason by these rules; it has a native faculty to perceive the coherence or incoherence of its ideas, and can range them right . . . I say not this any way to lessen Aristotle. . . . But yet I think,

12. Ibid., introduction, book 4, chap. 16, par. 14, chap. 17, par. 2 (I, 26–27, II, 384, 386–387).

13. Ibid., book 2, chap. 11, pars. 8, 9, 14 (I, 206–207, 210).

without any diminution to him, I may truly say, that they are not the only nor the best way of reasoning, for the leading of those into truth who are willing to find it.[14]

Locke distinguished between four types of argument that people use to persuade others. In some cases, people cite powerful or well-respected authorities, whom others are intimidated by or afraid to disagree with. Or they might begin with a proof (that cannot be proven). Or they might ridicule the consequences of their opponents' arguments. Last, they might draw on the "foundations of knowledge and probability." "This alone, of all the four, brings true instruction with it, and advances us in our way to knowledge. . . . [Truth] must come from proofs and arguments, and light coming from the nature of things themselves, and not from my shamefacedness, ignorance or error." Locke gave experience a crucial role in developing each person's understanding; but, once attained, he made reason a nearly universal quality. "Reason, therefore . . . I take to be the discovery of the certainty or probability of such propositions or truths which the mind arrives at by deduction made from such ideas, which it has got by the use of its natural faculties; viz. by sensation or reflection." He did grant, however, at the end of his treatise, that some men hold erroneous opinions because they are led there by faulty reasoning: "This is evident, that there is a difference in men's understandings, apprehensions, and reasonings, to so great a latitude, that one may, without doing injury to mankind, affirm, that there is a greater distance between some men and others in this respect, than between some men and some beasts."[15]

However, Locke did not argue that any group of people lacked reason, except children (and, briefly, madmen and idiots): Experience brings reason to all. His use of the masculine gender at many points in his analysis ("mankind," "men") might be interpreted as excluding women, but that was not his intent. He at no point distinguished women as not being able to reason, and he gave examples of women who, based on their experience, used their reason well. Thus in his section on reason, he discussed the misperception that only scholastic education teaches reason:

Tell a country gentle-woman that the wind is south-west, and the weather lowering, and like to rain, and she will easily understand it is not safe for her to go abroad thin clad in such a day, after a fever: she clearly sees the probable connexion of all these, viz. south-west wind, and clouds, rain, wetting, taking cold, relapse, and danger of death, without tying them

14. Ibid., book 4, chap. 17, par. 4 (II, 391–392).
15. Ibid., book 4, chap. 17, pars. 19–22, chap. 20, pars. 1–2, 5 (II, 410–412, 416, 446).

together in those artificial and cumbersome fetters of several syllogisms, that clog and hinder the mind.

In short, his argument was that a "country gentle-woman" has greater understanding than a learned clergyman versed in syllogisms.[16]

Because of the clarity and depth with which Locke laid out these arguments about human reason, his treatise became deeply influential during the next century. It helped to shape the Enlightenment: it helped to define the Age of Reason itself. In eighteenth-century North America, students were more likely to be familiar with his *Essay concerning Human Understanding* and *Some Thoughts concerning Education* than with his treatises on government.[17] Any careful reading of them in conjunction, or even a reading of "The Second Treatise of Government" that highlights the status of children, illustrates that, for Locke, liberty and equality come only with control over the passions and the exercise of reason. Locke's writings formed the strongest philosophical argument for the formal education of children in eighteenth-century England and North America. *Some Thoughts concerning Education* and *An Essay concerning Human Understanding,* in particular, led to the appearance in England and North America of a literature, the first of its kind, directed specifically toward children. Isaac Watts's songs and instruction manuals for children, which first appeared in 1715, were heavily influenced by Locke. John Newbery, among the first to publish an extensive collection of children's literature, advertised that he was answering Locke's call for books tailored for children. He began publishing in 1744, and many of these books were republished in America, especially after the Revolution.[18]

Locke's vision of education was to teach virtue and reason; in many ways the two goals overlapped. He rejected the old rules for "reasoning" by syllogism. Instead, Locke sought to use experience to help teach the laws of nature and the abilities to abstract, synthesize, compare, and reflect that he laid out in his *Essay concerning Human Understanding*. He then sought to teach children to follow the guidelines of that reason rather than their passions. Education leads to virtue by teaching a child to suppress simple self-interest. "The great Principle and Foundation of all vertue and Worth, is placed in this, That

16. Ibid., book 4, chap. 17, par. 4 (II, 392).

17. See David Lundberg and Henry F. May, "The Enlightened Reader in America," *American Quarterly,* XXVIII (1976), 273.

18. John Newbery, *A Little Pretty Pocket-Book* (1744), republished by Isaiah Thomas (Worcester, Mass., 1787), introduction, 10, 12; Samuel F. Pickering, Jr., *John Locke and Children's Books in Eighteenth-Century England* (Knoxville, Tenn., 1981), esp. 11–17, and app. B; Sydney Roscoe, *John Newbery and His Successors, 1740–1814: A Bibliography* (Wormley, 1973).

a Man is able to *deny himself* his own Desires, cross his own Inclinations, and purely follow what Reason directs as best, tho' the appetite lean the other way." Locke was building on older religious disputes concerning conscience: only with the development of reason and understanding, William Perkins had argued, could humans have a conscience to direct them that would inform them of the meaning of virtue, of good and bad.[19]

Locke was not alone in isolating children from political authority. Harrington would have agreed with Locke on the essential point about basing a just government on the consent of those who have reason: "The liberty of a man consists in the empire of his reason." "They that govern should govern according to reason." In Harrington's *Commonwealth of Oceana* the ones who make decisions are the wise, and those who vote for these "Fathers" are those men above the age of thirty who have "paternal power" and wisdom. In a way Harrington sought to compromise between Filmer's emphasis on fatherly power and an authority based on consent: those who should elect and be elected should be wise but also be "fathers" (he suggested that the senate should be addressed as "your fatherhoods"!) and bear fatherly authority. Thus Harrington did not separate parental power from state power, as did Locke and Sidney, but he did link the just exercise of power to those who had the most reason.[20]

Writing at the same time as John Locke, Algernon Sidney's *Discourses concerning Government* emphasized "virtue" and "wisdom" more than "reason." Yet he attacked Filmer's ideas at precisely the same points as did Locke:

19. Locke, *Some Thoughts concerning Education*, ed. Yolton and Yolton, par. 33 (p. 103). In many ways, what Pocock described as *virtue* in republican writings is similar to education in Locke's writings. One strand of public virtue in classical republican theory, according to Pocock, meant the gaining of independent, rational thought and control over the passions, a self-control that was the same goal of Locke's education. This is not to argue that Locke and Harrington, for example, had the same ultimate vision of the common good. The social ends of education emphasized self-sacrifice for the public weal more in Harrington's discussion. Shelley Burtt, *Virtue Transformed: Political Argument in England, 1688–1740* (Cambridge, 1992), discusses the different meanings of civic virtue in early-eighteenth-century England. See also Ruth H. Bloch, "The Gendered Meanings of Virtue in Revolutionary America," in *Signs: Journal of Women in Culture and Society*, XIII (1987–1988), 37–58; James T. Kloppenberg, "The Virtues of Liberalism: Christianity, Republicanism, and Ethics in Early American Political Discourse," *Journal of American History*, LXXIV (1987–1988), 9–33.

20. Pocock, *Machiavellian Moment*, 424; Harrington, *Commonwealth of Oceana*, in Pocock, ed., *Political Works*, 162, 170, 212–213, 349, also 358, where Lord Archon, the founder of the mythical kingdom of Oceana, has his tombstone inscribed with "pater patriae."

he objected to primogeniture as a system for the allocation of power and to his link between familial and state power. For Sidney, the merit of experience, wisdom, and virtue, not birth, should advance men to leadership. The fact that children, who lacked wisdom and experience and could more easily be corrupted, could be advanced to leadership was the best proof of the problems with a monarchical, feudal system, as opposed to a "Republican" system. Sidney began simply by describing Filmer's theories:

> [Primogeniture is the] *Royal Charter* granted to kings by God. They all have an equal right to it; women and children are patriarchs; and the next in blood, without any regard to age, sex, or other qualities of the mind or body, are fathers of as many nations as fall under their power. We are not to examine, whether he or she be young or old, virtuous or vicious, sober minded or stark mad; the right and power is the same in all.[21]

Although the lack of age and reason was not the only characteristic that Sidney mocked in Filmer's claim that kings were patriarchs (clearly Sidney held that a woman could pose as much danger as a child), it was the crux.[22]

Other Whig, or country, political writers from about 1680 onward similarly emphasized that those who had liberty and those who could consent to their government were those who had reason. Henry St. John, Lord Bolingbroke, for example, in the many-times-republished *Freeholder's Political Cate-*

21. Algernon Sidney, *Discourses concerning Government,* ed. Thomas G. West (Indianapolis, Ind., 1990), 6–7. Locke's criticism of primogeniture is subtle but persistent. Consider, for example, how he challenges the rules of primogeniture as not logical enough to support the whole structure of Filmer's argument about paternal power. "I go on then to ask whether in the inheriting of this *Paternal Power,* this *Supreme Fatherhood,* the Grand-Son by a Daughter, hath a Right before a Nephew by a Brother? Whether the Grand-Son by the Eldest Son, being an Infant, before the Younger Son a Man and able?" Locke, *Two Treatises,* ed. Laslett, 230–231 ("First Treatise," chap. 11, par. 123).

Sidney, a member of the Long Parliament who had participated in the Civil War, was executed in 1683 for treason, largely because of his *Discourses concerning Government.* His writings were popular in eighteenth-century America, where he was considered a martyr for liberty. See Alan Craig Houston, *Algernon Sidney and the Republican Heritage in England and America* (Princeton, N.J., 1991), esp. chap. 6.

22. For other explicit references to a child-king who lacks reason, a situation that Sidney regards as neither "reasonable nor just," see Sidney, *Discourses,* ed. West, 81, 119, 248, 279–280, 299, 300–301, 389, 390, 392, 393, 400, 404, 464, 532–534, 549, 552. Sidney acknowledged that a particularly wise child might not be the worst choice for king. Citing Solomon's dictum that *"a wise child is better than an old and foolish king"* (Eccl. 4:13), he argued that power should not simply be based on the right of the eldest— but it should be based on who is the worthiest (38).

chism, begins the catechism thus: "Who are you? I am T. M. a freeholder of Great Britain. . . . I am governed by laws, to which I give my consent. . . . Liberty is the natural right of every human creature; he is born to the exercise of it as soon as he has attain'd to that of his Reason." And not before.[23]

John Trenchard and Thomas Gordon's *Independent Whig* elaborated the principles of government based on consent and connected it to a reform of the Anglican Church. They exalted reason, understanding, and independent judgment. "Here, in England, why are we free, why Protestants, but because we are guided by Reason, and judge for ourselves?" In a section entitled "Of Reason," they argue that the ability to reason, which grows out of the senses, allows the mind to form judgments, to measure, to compare, and to choose.

> It distinguishes subjects from slaves, and shews the lovliness of liberty, and the vileness of vassalage: It shows that, as to political privileges, all men are born equal, and consequently, that he who is no better than others, can have no right to command others, who are as good as himself, unless for the ends of their own interests and safety, they confer that right upon him during their good pleasure, or his good behavior.

Thus for Trenchard and Gordon, reason is a light from God, "a ray or impulse of the divinity" that leads to independent judgment and choice. "All men are born equal," and only the consent of the whole allows one person to rule over the others. Only reason allows people to see beyond what they are told. "Credulity and implicit belief are equally dangerous in Government as in Religion: They have made the world slaves, and they keep it so." Liberty, equality, consent, and reason are on the one side; on the other are vassalage, slavery, credulity, and implicit belief.[24]

Not all thinkers who championed consent or who criticized Filmer elaborated on the meaning of consent. Benjamin Hoadly attacked primogeniture and emphasized equality—but only cautiously advocated government based on consent, did not examine the meaning of consent, and discussed children only in the context of primogeniture and their duty to resist an abusive father. Others, like John Somers, advocated consent and equality and attacked primogeniture in strong, clear language:

> There being no Natural or Divine Law for any one form of Government, or that one Person rather than another should have the Sovereign Adminis-

23. [Henry St. John, Lord Bolingbroke], *The Freeholder's Political Catechism* (London, 1733), 3–4.

24. John Trenchard and Thomas Gordon, *The Independent Whig; or, A Defense of Primitive Christianity, and of Our Ecclesiastical Establishment* . . . , 6th ed. (London, 1732), 39, 221, 216–218.

tration of Affairs, or have Power over many Thousand different Families, who are by nature all equal, being of the same rank, promiscuously born to the same advantages of nature, and to the use of the same common faculties, therefore Mankind is at Liberty to chuse what form of government they like best.

"Where human institutions give it not, the first Born has no Right at all above his brethren." If people are equal, then no one has naturally the right to rule over any other. The only rightful rule must be based on the choice of the governed. Somers's brief pamphlet, however, never went beyond this type of assertion. He never probed the meaning of consent; he thus addressed the issue of children only briefly, to argue that they had a right to resist their father and to distinguish a king's power from a father's.[25]

Although Locke developed arguments concerning human understanding and linked them into a theory of consensual government in greater depth than most others, he was not alone in sketching out the principles of that theory. All those who advocated government based on consent did at least mention the question of authority over children, sometimes almost as an aside. In part, it was a question of when someone was writing: the arguments about consent became deeper over time. Locke was building on many Civil War thinkers, including, for example, John Milton, who delineated Locke's basic ideas about the origin of government and was one of the earliest and most influential advocates of government based on consent in seventeenth-century England. Milton argued that "no man who knows ought, can be so stupid to deny that all men naturally were borne free" (at least until Adam's fall from grace). The right to resist unjust rulers resides in "the root and source of all liberty, to dispose and oeconomize in the Land which God hath giv'n them, as Maisters of Family in their own house and free inheritance." The implication is that those without "free inheritance," who are not fathers of families, do not have such liberties. A king is a "deputy" of the people, not their "Lord" or "Master," but a father is "maister" of his family.[26]

Although Milton did not use the term "reason" to describe those who

25. John Somers, *The Judgment of Whole Kingdoms* . . . , also called *Vox Populi, Vox Dei* (London, 1709) (rpt. in the colonies in four editions in the 1770s: Philadelphia [1773]; Newport, R.I., Boston, and New York [1774]); Benjamin Hoadly, *The Original and Institution of Civil Government. Discuss'd, Viz. I. An Examination of the Patriarchal Scheme of Government; II. A Defense of Mr. Hooker's Judgment* . . . , 2d ed. (London, 1710), i, vi, 1–2, 5, 6, 8–12, 14, 22, 27, 101–102, 111, 131, 133–134, 135–138; Hoadly, *The Measures of Submission to the Civil Magistrate Consider'd* . . . (London, 1708), vii, xi–xii, 6, 10, 70–71, 86–87, 92–95, 97.

26. John Milton, *The Tenure of Kings and Magistrates* . . . (London, 1649), 8–9, 41.

should exercise political power, he stated that those whom the people chose as leaders should have "eminence of wisdom and integritie." Thus not all thinkers elaborated and developed these points as carefully as did Locke, but, for virtually all of those who advocated government based on consent, these arguments and assumptions were part of their thought. Some emphasized parts of this argument more than others, but we can generalize from them as follows: authority should not be based on inheritance (particularly not on primogeniture), because all are equal; authority should be based on consent (of all? of men? of masters of families? of property owners?); the power of fathers is different from the authority of kings.

The most significant difference between these authors was the degree to which they rejected property ownership as the basis for consent: the degree to which, in other words, they rejected the older concept of dominium as the logic for consent. All of them rejected property ownership somewhat because of their emphasis on equality. Harrington linked consent to property owner-ship most explicitly but advocated a wide dispersal of property. The implica-tions of Locke's and Sidney's extended attacks on primogeniture were to undermine primogeniture as a basis of transferring private inheritance as well—but they did not criticize the inheritance of property itself (a father should share his bequest among his children). In some ways their ideas were radical, aimed as they were at the lower classes, but they also needed support from the lower gentry and the aristocracy to make their revolution succeed. These two groups, of course, worried about the threat that equality posed to property ownership. Locke and Sidney, therefore, tried to address those fears by arguing that equality and government based on consent need not under-mine all property claims. However, they never explicitly supported the idea that a person must own property in order to vote.[27]

While these authors overtly advocated equality as prerequisite for gov-ernments based on consent, some of them suggested that the ability to con-sent should be linked to property ownership. What other space did they leave for inequality? Were women explicitly excluded and designated as un-

27. Pocock, *Machiavellian Moment*, 387; Ashcraft, *Revolutionary Politics*, 249–285. Ashcraft makes a powerful case against C. B. Macpherson's equation of the Levellers with Locke to contend that both had an agenda of excluding laboring men from voting (*The Political Theory of Possessive Individualism: Hobbes to Locke* [London, 1962], esp. chap. 3). Ashcraft's analysis should affect the arguments of those who have relied on Macpherson's interpretation, including Pocock, in *Machiavellian Moment* (who uses Macpherson's interpretation to challenge the radicalism of the Levellers) and Edmund S. Morgan, *American Slavery, American Freedom: The Ordeal of Colonial Virginia* (New York, 1975), esp. 322–325, who portrays Locke as justifying forced labor and, by exten-sion, slavery.

equal? By implication they were, in passages that use the male noun, such as "all men are created equal." Sidney, particularly, goes out of his way to criticize women who gain positions of power, and Harrington specifically excluded them, along with children and servants.[28] Yet women were not usually specifically excluded from the ability to consent by these seventeenth- and early-eighteenth-century theorists who justified consent (indeed, Locke actually responds to Filmer by pointing out that the fifth commandment states, "Honor thy father and *mother*"). In fact, in a weird way, Locke allowed a woman to consent to government—by consenting to her husband's government when she agrees to marry him, and then he consents for her to political government. This inclusion of women within the rubric of consent but somehow outside political consent is awkward at best. And his point is briefly made. A few of these writers also mention slavery and servitude and vassalage, but rarely to justify them: they are almost always condemning such institutions. The only consistent justification of inequality in these writings is the inequality of those who do not, or cannot, exercise reason.[29]

Because of this focus on reason in the political ideology of consent, children had a very different place within it than within the status-based patriarchal theory. While they had an important niche within patriarchal theory, children were not uniquely disadvantaged. They owed their obedience and allegiance to their social superiors and to their father because of natural filial bonds. Authority descended by the rules of primogeniture, which frequently bestowed great power on the very young. Consent-based political theory, on the other hand, particularly as elaborated by Locke, emphasized the reason of those who consent, distinguishing children as those who could not have reason. It gave explanations, beyond their natural filial obligation, for parents' power (indeed, for children's inability to make decisions about their own lives and about public, political life in their society): they were physically dependent upon their parents and mentally lacking in understanding. It related the two awkwardly: physical dependence can create mental dependence, since those upon whom a person is dependent can sway their judg-

28. Sidney uses biblical references to support his argument that women should not be kings: "That law of nature would overthrow its own work, and make those to be the heads of nations, which cannot be the heads of private families; for as the Apostle says, 'The woman is not the head of the man, but the man is the head of the woman' [Eph. 5:23]" (Sidney, *Discourses*, ed. West, 59–61). See also James Harrington, *The Rota; or, A Model of a Free State or Equal Commonwealth*, in Pocock, ed., *Political Works*, 809: "Let the whole inhabitants (except women, children and servants)" form the popular assembly.

29. Carole Pateman, *The Sexual Contract* (Stanford, Calif., 1988); Linda K. Kerber, *Women of the Republic: Intellect and Ideology in Revolutionary America* (Chapel Hill, N.C., 1980), 15–18.

ment. But the mental development was most central: a person needed the ability to exercise reason, and age was to serve as a preliminary marker.

I have tried to illustrate how Protestant thought overlapped with ideas about consent. Many Whigs—who were radical Protestants—allied Catholicism with inherited right and arbitrary government. The very concept of consent was forged in the debates during the seventeenth century over church membership, which included questions of church leadership and toleration. It was a much bigger issue for them than for us, as illustrated by the numerous tracts about baptism, far more than in any other century. The close parallels between Locke's and Sidney's ideas about the exercise of consent, the exercise of the understanding, and their exclusion of children were no accident. Not only were they influenced by each other, but their ideas were also shaped by these debates over church membership: Who can join a church? Can one dissent? What does consent mean? Does one inherit the irrevocable obligations and privileges of a subject at the same time and in the same way that one inherits the obligations and privileges of church membership? Or should one be able to choose, at least at some point in one's life?

While some historical examples were fodder for these thinkers, the examples did not inspire their theories of government. Obviously, the Italian city-states, as well as ancient Greece and Rome, provided evidence that these were not simply abstract arguments. But why seek out these historical examples? I would contend that the need to find historical examples of republics grew out of these political ideas about consent that were spawned by the Reformation. Even Harrington, who invoked historical examples most explicitly, wrote that he had "ransacked 'the *Archives of ancient prudence'* in search of evidence and arguments with which 'to vindicate the reason of popular government.' "[30]

Such selective reading of historical evidence makes the picture especially complicated, because the desire to use historical examples as political arguments of course distorted the reading of history. Later historians relied on these findings, such that the distortions became embedded in the very fabric of historiography. English history, in particular, furnished seventeenth-century theorists with two models of its past: one, antedating the Norman Conquest, provided an example of "ancient liberties," and an "ancient constitution." The other, feudalism, accompanied the conquest. Others saw English liberties as persisting longer but constantly under threat. Feudalism as a

30. Paul A. Rahe, *Republics Ancient and Modern: Classical Republicanism and the American Revolution* (Chapel Hill, N.C., 1992), 409, quoting James Harrington's *Oceana*, ed. S. B. Liljegren (Heidelberg, 1924), 59; Pocock, ed., *The Political Works of James Harrington*, 390, and *The Prerogative of Popular Government* (1658).

term first came into use during the seventeenth century. Some of those who discovered it (when looking through old laws and records) clearly thought that, by labeling it as foreign and by appealing to a past as it existed before 1066, they could describe the real English system that should be operating and the real liberties that Englishmen should have. That past, of ancient liberties and ancient constitution, became part of the political mythology of England.

Feudalism, meanwhile, became linked with all of those characteristics of the English system of government that many of the reformers sought to dispense with: particularly, primogeniture as a system for the allocation of power, an absolute monarchy, and a status-based society generally. Some of those who offered the first descriptions of feudalism and ancient liberties, were, like Harrington, radical Protestants involved already in revolution (most of the discussion of feudalism actually occurred during and after the English Civil War). They were, in short, inventing a past in order to justify a future. The system of government and laws that they identified as feudalism has been debunked by modern historians: such a utopia, or to some a dystopia, never existed in a pure form. But the particular laws that they flagged as the extant remnants of feudalism, such as primogeniture, really did exist. And their identification of these laws as "feudal"—and their link to monarchy and aristocracy—would influence legal scholars and political thinkers over the next few centuries. The other utopia, or dystopia, of "ancient constitution" and "ancient liberties" did not exist in pure form before either the Roman Conquest or the Norman Conquest (as Harrington and William Penn contended); if it did, it lies beyond our historical record. What is critical to recognize is the way the political theorists from both camps in the seventeenth century invoked the past in order to present a model for the present and future. In so doing, they fictionalized the past.[31]

Feudalism thus became a political tool, one used by both sides. Robert Brady and Henry Spelman used their theory of feudalism to argue that Parliament originated in the king's desire for advice, that thus its power was limited. Brady also argued that all land had once belonged to the king and that this ownership gave him political authority over his tenants. Harrington, on the other hand, described feudalism in order to unmesh it from ancient liberties, then identified the ancient liberties in order to claim that those were England's real past, which must be returned to. Feudalism in its pure form

31. J. G. A. Pocock, *The Ancient Constitution and the Feudal Law: A Study of English Thought in the Seventeenth Century* (Cambridge, 1987); Susan Reynolds, *Fiefs and Vassals: The Medieval Evidence Reinterpreted* (Oxford, 1994), esp. chaps. 1, 8.

was nearly always equated, by both sides, with the absolute power of the king, with the power of a landed aristocracy, and often with Catholicism as well.[32]

While historical arguments buttressed arguments about consent and about monarchy, then, and undoubtedly helped to shape opinion, they were not the main force shaping the debate. One must ask why debaters sought historical precedent. Is it really historical precedent if one has to return to A.D. 50, before the Roman Conquest (about which few records remained)? Those who saw feudalism as an ideal and invoked a more recent past were on firmer ground with their historical precedent. But they were defending an institution that was under attack from Reformation ideology. Their search through history was also an effort to respond. Undoubtedly, real issues such as Charles I's monetary policies, his refusal to call Parliament, even the rise of a new trading empire and merchants, helped to fuel these fires. But the radical Protestants in the seventeenth century formed the strongest opposition to monarchy, aristocracy, and the arguments that buttressed them. They sought historical precedents to argue for norms they wanted for other reasons that grew out of their religious ideas about choice and understanding.

One might suppose that radical Protestants would always propose a theocracy, and that would be the only way to link religious ideology with political ideology. Some did. But these Whig theorists of the late seventeenth century did not simply say that religious membership created political membership. Instead, they transliterated the arguments, dropping much of their explicitly religious content (although many biblical references remained throughout). But the substance of their arguments about consent was not derived from biblical precedent or simply from Aristotle (or Polybius) or other ancient thinkers or even from ideas about ancient liberties. What was most powerful about their arguments was that they took the logic of one set of debates and extended it to another. In that sense they were not drawing on the past: they were trying to create a future.[33]

This is also not to argue that Locke's and Sidney's arguments won the day in 1689. Locke, for example, arguably thought that the revolutionary settlement was much too conservative, that the aristocracy had kept too much power.[34] The older patriarchal arguments still retained many adherents and

32. Pocock, *Ancient Constitution and the Feudal Law*, 122. "The feudal interpretation of parliamentary history was to be used many times in the future [after Spelman was writing in the 1620s] to check the claims of the lower house."

33. I am not the only one to make this point about the source of their arguments. On differences between ancient ideas about republics and those of the seventeenth-century thinkers, see especially Rahe, *Republics Ancient and Modern*.

34. See Ashcraft, *Revolutionary Politics*, postscript.

would retain them throughout the eighteenth century. Benjamin Hoadly would write in 1705, "It has been a common thing, in later ages, to reduce, as we say, the Duty of Subjects to the injunctions laid upon Children; and so of all inferiors to superiors." The persistence of the patriarchal doctrine was undoubtedly due in part to the continuing use of the catechism and the long version of the fifth commandment by the Anglican Church. Thus in 1771, Dr. John Gordon stated unequivocally that most subjects were and "must ever in a great degree be . . . mere children; and pay of course a due submission to the authority of their political Fathers." Debate over the validity of ideas about government based on consent would continue through the eighteenth century: Locke, Sidney, Harrington, and other republican thinkers were widely criticized.[35] The aristocracy and larger property owners would in some ways gain power over the course of the eighteenth century, and primogeniture and entail remained powerful forces in England. Ideas about balance of power— as put forward by Charles I in *His Majesty's Answer to the Nineteen Propositions of Both Houses of Parliament* in 1642—continued to undergird both king and aristocracy throughout the eighteenth century. Locke wisely refused to attach his name to his *Two Treatises,* even in the immediate wake of the Glorious Revolution. Had he tried to publish it in 1683, when he wrote it, he might well have been executed like Sidney. Sidney's *Discourses concerning Government* appeared in print for the first time in 1698 when only fifteen years previously he had been beheaded for its contents.[36]

35. Hoadly, *Original and Institution of Civil Government,* 8–9; John Gordon, *The Causes and Consequences of Evil Speaking against Government,* quoted in J. C. D. Clark, *English Society, 1688–1832: Ideology, Social Structure, and Political Practice during the Ancien Regime* (Cambridge, 1985), 214. Clark maintains, "Patriarchal doctrine, then, was sustained after 1688 not so much by the polemical needs of a dynastic regime as by the continued domination of society by the Anglican Church, on the one hand, and, on the other, by the aristocracy and gentry" (82, 214, 224, 293).

36. The percentage of adult male voters shrank consistently over the eighteenth century. See John Cannon, *Parliamentary Reform: 1640–1832* (Cambridge, 1973), 6–7; J. H. Plumb, "The Growth of the Electorate in England from 1660–1675," *Past and Present,* no. 45 (November 1969), 90–116; Pocock, *Machiavellian Moment,* 361. Pocock refers to Charles I as presenting balance of power arguments for the first time, calling it a "disastrous tactical error in royalist polemic" and pointing out that Charles repudiated these ideas of balance later on. He tries to contend that this is really a republican argument. I would contend, however, that it is at most a compromise position with republican arguments because it still gave great authority to a hereditary aristocracy and monarchy. Even Pocock notes that the king's *Answer* was aimed at the aristocracy. Its authors (speaking for the king) were "placing themselves in a position to appeal to the Lords against the Commons" (363). James M. Blythe, *Ideal Government and the Mixed Constitution in the Middle Ages* (Princeton, N.J., 1992), contends that these ideas about

The Glorious Revolution did mark a shift in the balance of power and in the balance of opinion. The ideas of Locke, in particular, would be incorporated and reined in and critiqued by a host of other thinkers that we have come to associate with the Enlightenment. And the religious discourse on baptism and church membership continued to lend support to, indeed, to imbricate itself with, the ideas of political consent. The Glorious Revolution also marked the introduction of some of the legal reforms with regard to children advocated by political theorists such as Locke and Sidney. Some of these reforms with regard to the status of children restrained the privileges of primogeniture and the worst excesses of patriarchalism; they were, in effect, a response to the concerns raised by Locke and Sidney and other radical Whig pamphleteers of the 1680s such as Henry Care. Primogeniture had meant in some cases granting authority to the very young. Changes that accompanied the English Civil War, the Glorious Revolution, and finally the American Revolution placed sharp limits upon their political authority.

American Republicans

English colonists in North America, embedded in English political culture, were familiar with many of these writings. Indeed, as surveys of their libraries and booksellers' catalogs and publishing records make clear, many colonial leaders owned these books and pamphlets. Those Americans who published their own treatises cited these authors repeatedly, Locke most of all, in the two decades before the Revolution. But Locke's and Milton's and Sidney's and Harrington's ideas also influenced later thinkers read by American colonists; Thomas Gordon and John Trenchard drew deeply on Locke, in particular, as did Rousseau, Montesquieu, Blackstone, and many others. Indeed, Locke's influence was felt in realms beyond the political. His ideas on education led to the emergence of children's literature. His *Essay concerning Human Understanding* helped to define the Enlightenment itself. The colonists were familiar with both sides of the argument about consent and authority: they themselves inculcated the versions of the fifth commandment that equated obedience to fathers with obedience to kings. Principles of authority were still contested in eighteenth-century England, and the colonists were part of the debate. Whigs in North America echoed many of the same arguments against status first raised by the English "Democraticall" republicans, including the attack on primogeniture.[37]

---

balance of power existed during the Middle Ages, at least among some thinkers, especially after Thomas Aquinas brought Aristotle's *Politics* to scholarly attention.

37. Donald S. Lutz, "The Relative Influence of European Writers on Late Eighteenth-

Thomas Paine's *Common Sense*, the most popular and powerful pamphlet of the American Revolution (it sold more copies, most in 1776, than any other book except the Bible in eighteenth-century North America and was probably heard by most white men in coffeehouses and alehouses, even if not read by them), had three parts to his call for revolution. The first criticized England's hereditary monarchy, the second contended that America was mature enough to be independent from her "mother country," and the third laid out a new form of government for America based on relatively direct consent. The first two parts of his argument, especially, drew on the English republican ideas about children and consent. Paine criticized monarchy on the grounds that qualifications for government in a monarchy derived solely from birthright. It was likely that the person to inherit would lack wisdom, reason, and the ability to represent the interests of the people. Not only could hereditary succession produce foolish kings, but "the throne is subject to be possessed by a minor at any age." He objected to two of the three branches of the English government—aristocracy and monarchy—on the basis of their origins in inherited right rather than consent.[38]

Not only is hereditary succession an unreliable method of determining a leader, but the very principle, which assumes that subjects inherit obedience just as kings inherit authority, is deeply flawed. "Though they might say 'We choose you for our head,' they would not, without manifest injustice to their

----

Century American Political Thought," *American Political Science Review*, LXXVIII (1984), 189–197. In a sample of 916 pamphlets and books between 1760 and 1805, Locke was cited (either by name or by quoting a passage from his work) in 11 percent of items in the 1760s and in 7 percent in the 1770s. Only Montesquieu comes close, with 8 percent and 7 percent, respectively. Also see Lundberg and May, "The Enlightened Reader in America," *American Quarterly*, XXVIII (1976), 262–293; Bernard Bailyn, *The Ideological Origins of the American Revolution* (Cambridge, Mass., 1967), 26–40, 59; Thomas L. Pangle, *The Spirit of Modern Republicanism: The Moral Vision of the American Founders and the Philosophy of Locke* (Chicago, 1988) 124–127; John Dunn, "The Politics of Locke in England and America in the Eighteenth Century," in John W. Yolton, ed., *John Locke: Problems and Perspectives: A Collection of New Essays* (Cambridge, 1969), 45–80; Oscar Handlin, "Learned Books and Revolutionary Action, 1776," *Harvard Library Bulletin*, XXXIV (1986), 362–379; Houston, *Algernon Sidney*.

Such a thinker as Hobbes, whom political theorists now see as very important, was cited only with disdain (Bailyn, *Ideological Origins*, 28). Even in his own times, Hobbes had appealed neither to patriarchalists nor republicans—although he supported an absolute monarchy, his religious ideas alarmed most other patriarchalists, especially among the Anglican clergy. See C. B. Macpherson, introduction, in Thomas Hobbes, *Leviathan* (London, 1985), 23.

38. Thomas Paine, *Common Sense* (1776), in Michael Foot and Isaac Kramnick, eds., *Thomas Paine Reader* (London, 1787).

children, say 'that your children and your children's children shall reign over *ours* forever.'" Parents could not bind their children to permanent obedience. (The choice of words is so similar that Paine might be responding directly to Hobbes.) Likewise, he emphasized in part 2 the principle that a time comes for independence, that the control of England had been only a temporary "guardianship" until the colonies "came of age." Since "the late rapid progress of the continent to maturity," independence, therefore, should come soon and naturally. His underlying point was that, if father or mother could bind their children, they could do so only until they came "of age." The colonies, like the colonists' children, were not bound by inherited obligation. Paine's words responded to Hobbes and, while more radical than Locke's (Paine's reference to William the Conqueror as "a French bastard landing with an armed banditti," for example, went far beyond Locke's careful critique), picked up some of Locke's main points. "Bastard," of course, is a word that in and of itself challenges legitimate succession: William could have been anyone's child.[39]

As this brief examination of *Common Sense* suggests, in the decade leading up to the Revolution, children became central to the political debate. This was in part because the political debate drew so deeply on the earlier English and American religious controversy: both John Adams (in his "Dissertation on the Canon and the Feudal Law") and Paine condemn "popery," which had become a byword for patriarchalism (whether justified or not). "For monarchy in every instance is the Popery of government." Still, the political had become more separate from the religious than it had been in the seventeenth century.[40]

Some of the questions raised by Locke during the Glorious Revolution about succession, authority, maturity, and consent had been raised earlier by Puritans in New England, and colonists had also referred to Locke's ideas on government in sermons and books on education and politics. Authors such as Isaac Watts popularized Locke's theory of knowledge in the form of songs and instruction manuals for children. Watts's books of children's hymns, stories, and instruction manuals went through many editions in New England in the early part of the eighteenth century. During the decade before the Revolution, however, the colonists began to cite political theory more extensively, including Locke's as well as all of the texts discussed above.[41]

39. Ibid., 75, 87, 89.

40. Ibid., 75, 76. Comparing popery to feudalism is the whole point of John Adams's 1765 essay "A Dissertation on the Canon and the Feudal Law."

41. Pickering, *John Locke and Children's Books*, 17–19; Alice M. Baldwin, *The New England Clergy and the American Revolution* (1928; New York, 1965), 8, 66–67, 129, 139,

A published sermon by Elisha Williams in 1744, for example, paraphrased, summarized, and quoted sections of Locke's "Second Treatise." Williams, a Congregational minister in Boston, in *The Essential Rights of Protestants*, touched on exactly the points of Locke's political philosophy highlighted above: Locke's separation of state power from parental power and his justification of parental power on the basis of children's dependence and lack of reason. Most of the following passage is directly from Locke:

> Altho' true it is that children are not born in this full state of equality, yet they are born to it. Their parents have a sort of rule and jurisdiction over them when they come into the world, and for some time after . . . and govern the actions of their yet ignorant nonage, 'till reason shall take its place and ease them of that trouble. . . . And whilst he is in a state wherein he has no understanding of his own to direct his will, he is not to have any will of his own to follow: He that understands for him must will for him too. . . . For the freedom of man and liberty of acting according to his own will (without being subject to the will of another) is grounded on his having reason, which is able to instruct him in that law he is to govern himself by. . . . So that we are born free as we are born rational. Not that we have actually the exercise of either as soon as born; age that brings one, brings the other too.[42]

Liberty is not given to men at their birth. "For the freedom of man and liberty of acting according to his own will . . . is grounded upon his having reason." In other words, in order for a person to be able to choose effectively, his reason and understanding, or his conscience, must direct his will. Only with age, which brings reason, does a person actually gain the freedom to make choices, both personal and political.

176; Perry Miller, "The Moral and Psychological Roots of American Resistance," in Jack P. Greene, ed., *The Reinterpretation of the American Revolution, 1763–1789* (New York, 1968), 258–274.

   Watts: Isaac Watts, *Logick; or, The Right Use of Reason in the Enquiry after Truth, with a Variety of Rules to Guard against Error, in the Affairs of Religion and Human Life* . . . (London, 1725). The entire book is a condensed version of Locke's *Essay concerning Human Understanding*. Consider even the first two chapter headings, "Of the Nature of Ideas" and "Of the Objects of Perception." See especially p. 2: "Now the design of Logick is to teach us the right Use of our Reason, and the Improvement of it in our selves and others."

   42. Elisha Williams, *The Essential Rights and Liberties of Protestants: A Seasonable Plea for the Liberty of Conscience, and the Right of Private Judgment, in Matters of Religion, without Any Controul from Human Authority* . . . (Boston, 1744), in Ellis Sandoz, ed., *Political Sermons of the American Founding Era, 1730–1805* (Indianapolis, Ind., 1991), 56.

Still, Williams appears to have been somewhat unusual. Jonathan Mayhew, another New England minister whom historians have cited as an early Whig, actually wrote within a patriarchal paradigm in 1750 in his most famous sermon, *A Discourse concerning Unlimited Submission and Non-Resistance to the Higher Powers*. Rather than giving consent (or the lack thereof) as the basis for rebellion, he argued that parents and government do not have unlimited authority.

> But who supposes that the Apostle ever intended to teach that children, servants, and wives should, in all cases whatever, obey their parents, masters, and husbands respectively, never making any opposition to their will even although they should require them to break the commandments of God or should causelessly make an attempt upon their lives?

So too did Charles Chauncy stay within the patriarchal compass when he reminded the political leaders of Massachusetts in 1747: "You are, my fathers, accountable to that God whose throne is in the heavens, in common with other men." On the one hand, the colony's leaders were political parents who deserved respect; on the other, they recognized limits to what they could legitimately do.[43]

This link between dissent and consent can be overemphasized, yet in some ways it is clear that there were overlapping intellectual roots, if only because of the religious context of the two English revolutions of the seventeenth century. Indeed, many of the most fervent Tories and patriarchalists in North America in the years preceding the American Revolution were Anglican ministers. They included Samuel Seabury (who wrote under the pseudonym A. W. Farmer), Thomas Bradbury Chandler, and Jonathan Boucher. Since the British monarch was the head of the Anglican Church, perhaps the imagery of patriarchalism (calling, as it did, on the temporal "fatherhood" of the king, a "fatherhood" that related closely to the spiritual "fathers" of the church) had more power for them. Thus religious boundaries, while not distinctly drawn, still helped to sway individual ministers toward one side or

43. Jonathan Mayhew, *A Discourse concerning Unlimited Submission and Non-Resistance to the Higher Powers* . . . (Boston, 1750), in Bernard Bailyn, ed., *Pamphlets of the American Revolution, 1750–1776* (Cambridge, Mass., 1965), 224; Charles Chauncy, *Civil Magistrates Must Be Just* . . . (Boston, 1747), in Sandoz, ed., *Political Sermons*, 174.

Such also was the argument of John Dickinson against British policy in 1765. "Thus [the colonists'] hearts, glowing with every sentiment of duty and affection towards their mother country and expecting, not unreasonably perhaps, some mark of tenderness in return," "have received unmerited blows from a beloved parent." *The Late Regulations respecting the British Colonies Considered* . . . (Philadelphia, 1765), in Bailyn, ed., *Pamphlets*, 690.

the other. As others have noted, Tories as well as some Whigs made patriarchal arguments frequently during the years before the American Revolution, and some patriarchal assumptions continued to be embedded within post-Revolutionary thought. Even Paine, though skeptical, did not completely dismiss the patriarchal analogy. He contended that, even if it applied, it would justify rebellion as well, since there should be limits on the powers of parents.

> But Britain is the parent country, say some. Then the more shame upon her conduct. Even brutes do not devour their young, nor savages make war upon their families; wherefore the assertion, if true, turns to her reproach; but it happens not to be true, or only partly so.

This aspect of patriarchalism, the comparison of the appropriate behavior of parents toward their children to the just behavior of the state toward its subject, of Britain toward her colonies, did not vanish. Its legacy can be seen in modern usage of the term "Founding Fathers" and in references to George Washington as the "father" of the country.[44]

What is most illuminating about the continuing presence of these patriarchal arguments during the 1760s and 1770s, however, is how Tories and even initially moderate Whigs such as James Otis used them to counteract arguments for the consent of the governed. Some pamphleteers subscribed to the Lockean distinction between children and adults and compared the Whigs to children who did not have the ability to reason. Others undercut the issue of consent by asking whether everyone could consent and, if not, whether any could. In raising these questions, they forced a debate on who should be able to consent to government, on what basis, and under what circumstances.

44. Paine, *Common Sense,* in Foot and Kramnick, eds., *Thomas Paine Reader,* 81. Only one-third of Anglican ministers in Virginia and Maryland supported the Revolution. On patriarchalism and the Anglican Church: Jon Butler, *Awash in a Sea of Faith: Christianizing the American People* (Cambridge, Mass., 1990), 202. Also see James E. Bradley, *Religion, Revolution, and English Radicalism: Nonconformity in Eighteenth-Century Politics and Society* (Cambridge, 1990), 158: "The majority of English pro-Americans were Anglicans, not Dissenters, and yet the Dissenters provided both the dominant ideology of opposition and the bulk of charismatic leadership for the pro-American agitation."

On patriarchalism, see Gordon S. Wood, *The Radicalism of the American Revolution* (New York, 1992); Melvin Yazawa, *From Colonies to Commonwealth: Familial Ideology and the Beginnings of the American Republic* (Baltimore, 1985); Winthrop D. Jordan, "Familial Politics: Thomas Paine and the Killing of the King, 1776," *JAH,* XL (1973–1974), 294–308; Edwin G. Burrows and Michael Wallace, "The American Revolution: The Ideology and Psychology of National Liberation," *Perspectives in American History,* VI (1972), 167–306.

The struggle over the comparison of the subject to the child and the state to the family was a struggle over the grounds for political authority. At its center lay a vision of the helpless infant, dependent on others. By separating familial power from state power, Locke and other republicans denied the dependence of the reasoning adult. At the same time, his sharp delineation of the two roles emphasized the distinct nature of childhood. The rhetoric of virtual representation grows out of this distinction. The concept of "virtual representation" meant that, although Parliament did not actually represent— was not elected by—*all* subjects of Great Britain, it *virtually* represented them, since the members of Parliament acted to protect all subjects and speak for them. The Whigs did not argue that all people should actually choose representatives, but they opposed the idea that Parliament represented all Britons if American colonists had no voice. The Revolutionaries opposed, therefore, virtual representation where it excluded geographical regions. The Whigs and Federalists, even the Jeffersonian Republicans, did not dismiss the concept in the wake of the Revolution, as it applied to others. Once they raised the challenge to virtual representation, however, the Whigs opened a Pandora's box, and the door to other kinds of issues about valid representation. Some challenged, and it was often Tories, the demarcating of who could consent and who should not.[45]

In short, a debate that began with a challenge to parliamentary representation based on geographic issues expanded into an explicit debate about who could consent, which ended up compromising newer ideas with older orders. Bernard Bailyn called the concern over representation the "first serious intellectual problem to come between England and the colonies." Two American pamphlets of 1764 over separate issues of taxation stress the central Whig point: laws are valid only when they have been made with the consent of the subjects. Richard Bland's *Colonel Dismounted,* published in Williamsburg, Virginia, asserted, "Under an English government all men are born free [and] are only subject to laws made with their own consent, and cannot be deprived of the benefit of these laws without a transgression of them." Thomas Fitch's *Reasons Why the British Colonies, in America, Should Not Be Charged with Internal Taxes,* against the Sugar Act, began by asserting: "The English are a

45. Joan R. Gundersen makes the same general comment in an essay that primarily confronts the question of women's citizenship: "By 1760 colonial political thought rejected the argument that the colonies were virtually represented in parliament, that they shared a community of interests with England. Thus leaders of the resistance to English taxes developed theories of direct representation. However, these leaders continued to apply theories of virtual representation to colonial legislatures and to families." "Independence, Citizenship, and the American Revolution," *Signs,* XIII (1987– 1988), 63.

free people. Their freedom consists principally if not wholly in this general privilege, that 'NO LAWS CAN BE MADE OR ABROGATED WITHOUT THEIR CONSENT BY THEIR REPRESENTATIVES IN PARLIAMENT.'"[46]

Most republican thought justified political power on the basis of the consent of reasonable, deliberative citizens. "THE PEOPLE, I say, are the only *competent* judges of *their own welfare,*" wrote Josiah Quincy, Jr., in response to the Boston Port bill in 1774. "If at this period of public affairs, we do not think, deliberate, and determine *like men*—men of minds to conceive, hearts to feel, and virtue *to act*—what are we to do?—to gaze upon our bondage?" Clearly Quincy did not believe that the ability to "think, deliberate, and determine" was antithetical to having "hearts to feel." In a casual way, Quincy linked a more affectionate vision of the origins of human virtue with one based on the ability to reason. Quincy stressed the faculty of intelligence as critical to rightful political action. "The faculty of intelligence may be considered as the first gift of GOD. . . . Believe me (my countrymen) the labor of examining for ourselves . . . must be submitted to; there is no other alternative: and unless we weigh and consider what we examine, little benefit will result from research." This introspection by men, in Quincy's case explicitly only freeholders, should form the basis of political consent and political decision making.[47]

John Adams's "Dissertation on the Canon and the Feudal Law," a piece emblematic of the earlier, more radical stage in his political thought, also allied the important and necessary consent of the "the people" with their understanding.

> And Liberty cannot be preserved without a general knowledge among the people, who have a right, from the frame of their nature, to knowledge, as their great Creator, who does nothing in vain, has given them understandings and a desire to know; but besides this they have a right, an indisput-

46. Bailyn, *Ideological Origins*, 161. Also see Gordon S. Wood, *The Creation of the American Republic, 1776–1787* (Chapel Hill, N.C., 1969), chap. 5; John Phillip Reid, *Constitutional History of the American Revolution: The Authority of Rights* (Madison, Wis., 1986), 16, 230. Reid quotes James Duane in 1774: "If the Subject is bound by a Law to which he does to assent, either personally or by his Representative, he is no longer free but under an arbitrary power, which may oppress or ruin him at pleasure."

Richard Bland, *The Colonel Dismounted . . .* (Williamsburg, Va., 1764), and Thomas Fitch, *Reasons Why the British Colonies, in America, Should Not Be Charged with Internal Taxes . . .* (New Haven, Conn., 1764), in Bailyn, ed., *Pamphlets*, 319–320, 386, 393. Fitch acknowledges that all do not directly consent.

47. Josiah Quincy, Jr., *Observations on the Act of Parliament Commonly Called the Boston-Port Bill, with Thoughts on Civil Society and Standing Armies* (Boston, 1774), 3, 27, 30.

able, unalienable, indefeatable, divine right to that most dreaded and en-
vied kind of knowledge, I mean of the characters and conduct of their
rulers. . . . The people have a right to revoke the authority that they themselves have deputed.

We have been afraid to think.

His emphasis on each individual's understanding, on each person's ability to
make a judgment about independence, and ultimately his encouragement of
each individual to "think" was a grand inclusive vision, reminiscent of William Walwyn and the most radical of the Levellers. Yet precisely the emphasis on understanding, on judgment, and on thinking would later result in
Adams's much more restrictive analysis of who had, for example, the ability to
exercise suffrage. Indeed, seeds of his later opinions are apparent in his
careful separation of state power from familial power: the former is based
on consent, the latter not. Because government authority is not comparable to parental authority, because the former is based on consent, "Is not
there something extremely fallacious, in the common place images of mother
country and children colonies?"[48]

The conservative challenges to the concept of consent to government that
centered on exactly who should be included have not been fully explored.
Some Tories used this issue to question or even ridicule consent-based arguments for governmental legitimacy. Tory objections to the pamphlets that
urged "no taxation without representation" queried: If one accepted the basic
notion, where did one stop? Should every human consent to every governmental act? What constituted representation? They pointed out that suffrage,
in England as in North America, was far from universal—so was it therefore
illegal to tax anyone who could not vote? Thomas Bradbury Chandler's *American Querist* (1774) asked, "Whether the *English* constitution does not make the
king and parliament the representatives of all the people within the kingdom,
whether they be actual electors or non-electors?" His *Friendly Address to All
Reasonable Americans* of the same year elaborated on the same point. "There
are many people in England, who are natives of the country, that do not
consent to acts of parliament which can make a *nominal* consent, but *not a
real* one." Daniel Dulany had settled on the same middling ground in his
popular pamphlet *Considerations on the Propriety of Imposing Taxes in the
British Colonies* (1765). "The electors, who are inseparably connected in their
interests with the nonelectors, may be justly deemed to be the representatives

48. [John Adams], "A Dissertation on the Canon and the Feudal Law," in *The True
Sentiments of America . . .* (London, 1768), 127–128, 132, 136.

of the nonelectors at the same time they exercise their personal privilege in their right of election, and the members chosen, therefore, the representatives of both." Thus he lumped children and adults into the category of nonelectors who would be represented on some level by others who could interpret their wishes and needs better than they.[49]

An anonymous Tory in *The Triumph of the Whigs* explicitly attacked the argument that all should consent to their own government, even if through representatives: according to the Whigs, "Every man, woman, boy, girl, child, infant, cow, horse, hog, dog, and cat who *now* live, or ever *did* live, or ever *shall* live in this province are fully, freely, and sufficiently represented in this present glorious and august Provincial Congress." In attempting to undermine the legitimacy of consent-based arguments, he referred to children in four different ways and to animals in five. With these references to the consent of children and animals he implied that adult men might have no more reason than an animal or a young child. Yet this Tory also raised the most important question about consent-based arguments and pushed the Whigs to define the boundaries of legitimacy. The question of who was qualified to consent was a real issue, not just a rhetorical strategy.[50]

James Otis raised similar questions about who should consent and under what circumstances in his popular pamphlet *The Rights of the British Colonies Asserted and Proved*, which went through three American editions. He claimed that "highfliers and others" posed these questions and thus they were not his own, yet he did not attempt to resolve them.

---

49. A North-American [Thomas B. Chandler], *The American Querist; or, Some Questions Proposed relative to the Present Disputes Between Great Britain and Her American Colonies* (New York, 1774), 21, query 62. Chandler also elaborated here the philosophical question that arises when those who vote against a tax or law are in the minority: must they still pay the tax even if they have not consented?

[Thomas Bradbury Chandler], *A Friendly Address to All Reasonable Americans, on the Subject of Our Political Confusions: In Which the Necessary Consequences of Violently Opposing the King's Troops, and of a General Non-Importation Are Fairly Stated* ([New York, Boston?], 1774), 11. See also Martin Howard, Jr., who argued that not all men vote and not all areas in England are represented, yet that Parliament speaks for all England. [Howard], *A Letter from a Gentleman at Halifax, to His Friend in Rhode-Island, Containing Remarks upon a Pamphlet, Entitled, The Rights of Colonies Examined* (Newport, R.I., 1765), in Bailyn, ed., *Pamphlets*, 537.

[Daniel Dulany], *Considerations on the Propriety of Imposing Taxes in the British Colonies* ... ([Annapolis, Md.], 1765), in Bailyn, ed., *Pamphlets*, 612.

50. Quotation in Bailyn, *Ideological Origins*, 170. The full title of this pamphlet was *The Triumph of the Whigs; or, T'Other Congress Convened* (New York, 1775).

Who acted for infants and women, or who appointed guardians for them? Had these guardians power to bind both infants and women during life and their posterity after them? . . . Is not every man born as free by nature as his father? Has he not the same natural right to think and act and contract for himself? . . . Are not women born as free as men?

Otis's broad point is clear: why should only men at some arbitrary age begin to exercise consent, while others cannot? Otis never attempted to justify a contractual basis for government, even though he opposed British policy. Rather, he maintained that most humans are always dependent.

We come into the world forlorn and helpless; and if left alone and to ourselves at any one period of our lives, we should soon die in want, despair, or distraction. So kind is that hand . . . which feeds the rich and the poor, the blind and the naked, and provides for the safety of infants by the principle of parental love, and for that of men by government!

So although Otis began to distance himself from the questions he had asked by maintaining, for example, that "it is left to every man as he comes of age to choose *what* society he will continue to belong to," the questions posed above are clearly his own questions as well: who should consent and under what circumstances? He ultimately advocated a loose form of virtual representation that would have allowed the colonists themselves, as a body, some representation in Parliament but that would not have allowed the bulk of the population to vote. For Otis (although on some level a Whig, at least initially), most men remained political children who needed a guiding hand. In claiming that the bulk of the people were helpless and dependent he drew a narrow boundary around who had the right to consent and who did not.[51]

Mary V. V.'s *Dialogue between a Southern Delegate and His Spouse, on His Return from the Grand Continental Congress* also criticized the concept of consent by asking where the line demarcating who can consent should be drawn. She explicitly criticized the idea that all males should participate in government, then withdrew to a status-based argument that people should be born to positions of power just as they are destined for specific professions. How are men different from women and children in their knowledge of the arcane subject of politics? The humor of the following passage depends on the audience's equating children, women, and ordinary men and laughing at the idea of any of them making political decisions.

51. See James Otis, *The Rights of the British Colonies Asserted and Proved* (Boston, 1764), in Bailyn, ed., *Pamphlets*, 419–420, 422–423, 425.

Husband: Mind thy Household-Affairs, teach thy Children to read,
　And never, Dear, with Politics, trouble thy Head.
Wife: Good Lord! how magnanimous! I fear Child thou'rt drunk,
　Dost thy think thyself, Deary, a Cromwel or Monck?

　.　.　.　.　.　.　.　.　.　.　.　.　.

Because Men are Males, are they all Politicians?
Why then I presume they're Divines and Physicians,
And born all with Talents every Station to fill,
Noble Proofs you've given! no doubt, of your Skill:
Wou'd! instead of Delegates, they'd sent Delegates Wives;
Heavens! we cou'dn't have bungled it so for our Lives
If you had even consulted the Boys of a School,
Believe me, Love, you cou'd not have played so the Fool.[52]

After the husband ordered the wife not to bother with politics, she admonished him that his rightful place was also not to meddle and that he had committed high treason. She offered an argument based on status: not all men are born politicians any more than they all are born to be bricklayers or "Physicians"—women and children are as suitable to play politics. Politics takes a particular talent that not all have. She herself did not advocate consent; but, to the extent it is an issue, why are men the only ones who should consent?

Besides attacking the notion of consent by raising the issue of exactly who should be able to consent, many pamphlets satirized the republican emphasis on coming of age by portraying the American colonies and their representatives to the Continental Congress as spoiled young children who had not attained maturity. Consider, for example, Bob Jingle's versification of the statements of *The Association of the Delegates at Congress.*

For Nature's Law is clear and plain,
That PARENTS *should their* BRATS *maintain.*[53]

Another anonymous Tory pamphlet of 1775 versified, not the statements, but the actions of the Continental Congress, describing them as those of spoiled young children who are "fond premature to play the man." It also relied on

52. Mary V. V., *A Dialogue between a Southern Delegate and His Spouse, on His Return from the Grand Continental Congress: A Fragment Inscribed to the Married Ladies of America* ([New York], 1774).

53. Bob Jingle, *The Association, etc. of the Delegates of the Colonies, at the Grand Congress, Held at Philadelphia, Sept. 1, 1774, Versified, and Adapted to Music, Calculated for Grave and Gay Dispositions; with a Short Introduction* ([New York], 1774).

older status-based arguments: people are born for government, they do not grow into it. The authority of the state is similar to the authority of the family, and the "ign'rant Multitude" are incapable of making any contribution to their own government aside from disruptive (and punishable) rabble-rousing.

> The harmless, ign'rant Multitude
>
> . . . .
>
> Wanton, and bold, in Pride of Youth
> Deaf to Remonstrance, blind to Truth
> Fond premature, to play the Man
>
> . . . .
>
> The gen'ral Tenor of it runs,
> That Father's shan't controul their Sons,
>
> . . . .
>
> Enjoy the dear, delusive Instant,
> While Masters, Fathers, all are distant.

Yet, while the author upheld older norms of leadership, he also ironically incorporated elements with which Filmer might well have disagreed—that is, the emphasis on maturity, and maturity of the reason in particular. But the patriots had been misled to think

> That Boys were all by Nature free,
> and College Laws, rank Slavery.
>
> . . . .
>
> Some of the Lads, perchance have Sense,
> Talents, and Wit, and Eloquence:
> But want Experience, Practice, Knowledge.

The implication is that, if the members of the Continental Congress had been "Men" instead of "Boys" or even "Babes" in the development of their wisdom, they might have just grounds for seeking independence or remonstrance against unjust treatment. Still, this argument is also one of status. The patriots, claim this Tory, are "form'd for the Oar, the Sledge, the Saw" and not for "Government and Law." The author of *The Patriots of North-America* drew on a variety of sources to justify authority: claims to status, the identity of familial and governmental power, and the lack of wisdom and knowledge of the members of the Continental Congress, a condition that makes them comparable to "Babes" or "Boys."[54]

54. *The Patriots of North-America: A Sketch, with Explanatory Notes* (New York, 1775), 6–14.

Both Tories and Whigs modified the power behind the patriarchal analogy with an argument that, since the colonies had matured to adulthood, they deserved different treatment. One Tory pamphleteer, Samuel Seabury, argued that the colonies should stand on a different footing with mother Britain now that they had reached "manhood." Earlier, when the colonies were in their "infancy and childhood," arbitrary government was tolerable.

> [The colonies] are arrived to that mature state of manhood which requires a different, and more exact policy of ruling, than was necessary in their infancy and childhood. They want, and are entitled to, a fixed determinate constitution of their own. . . . which shall mark out the line of British supremacy, and colonial dependence.[55]

Thus Seabury attempted to balance the two paradigms. He ultimately argued that state power rested on parental power and that children were dependent upon and owed allegiance to their parents regardless of their own age. Yet he qualified the latter point with a bow in the direction of the republican emphasis on how the child's attainment of "manhood" altered the relation between parent and child. Paine also sought to defuse the patriarchal argument for legitimacy with a similar claim that, if England were the mother country, now that the colonies had reached adulthood they should be set free. The dependent status of the colonies should have been "no more than a temporary expedient, or a kind of government by guardianship, which can last no longer than til the colonies come of age."[56]

The questions raised before the Revolution about where the lines of political participation should be drawn initiated debates that echoed through legislative assemblies across the new nation. As Chapter 1 briefly showed, children provided the standard by which competence could be measured for voting. Gouverneur Morris applied his argument for excluding children from voting to urge that others should not vote on the same grounds. "Children do not vote. Why? Because they want prudence, because they have no will of their own. The ignorant and the dependent can be as little trusted with the public interest."[57]

John Adams also emphasized that only those who are independent should be able to consent.

---

55. A. W. Farmer [Samuel Seabury], A View of the Controversy between Great-Britain and Her Colonies . . . (New York, 1774), 19.

56. Paine, Common Sense, in Foot and Kramnick, eds., Thomas Paine Reader, 89.

57. Morris is cited in Wilbourn E. Benton, ed., 1787: Drafting the U.S. Constitution (College Station, Tex., 1986), II, 228.

It is certain in Theory, that the only moral Foundation of Government is the Consent of the People. But to what an Extent Shall We carry this Principle? . . .

. . . Children have not Judgment or Will of their own. True. But will not these Reasons apply to others? Is it not equally true, that Men in general in every Society, who are wholly destitute of Property, are also too little acquainted with public Affairs to form a Right Judgment, and too dependent upon other Men to have a Will of their own?

Equality is not meant to apply to all, he argued. "You must fix upon some period in life, when the understanding and will of men in general, is fit to be trusted by the public." Thus those who had not reached a certain "period of life" did not have a fit understanding or will, and should be excluded. All those who were physically dependent on others could be influenced by those who fed, clothed, and employed them. Physical dependency could undermine reason and "right judgment."[58]

The emphasis on reason in granting authority to a just government is repeated in political writings in the American colonies during the American Revolution and afterward. Madison in Federalist No. 49 wrote, "It is the reason of the public alone that ought to controul and regulate the government." Hamilton in Federalist No. 79 related physical dependence to mental dependence: "A power over a man's subsistence amounts to a power over his will." Tom Paine's *Rights of Man* (1791–1792) used the terms "mental manhood" and "gigantic manliness" when referring to men's ability to reason and to understand and the necessity of those faculties to a republican government. Jefferson's 1800 inaugural address modified the legitimacy granted to majority rule when he argued, "Though the will of the majority is in all cases to prevail, that will, to be rightful, must be reasonable." Although Madison and Jefferson described the general character of government, they were also, by implication, commenting on the qualifications of the electors. Where these men differed was not on the significance of reason; on that, they agreed. They differed in their conclusions about who had reason.[59]

58. John Adams to James Sullivan, May 26, 1776, in Robert J. Taylor et al., eds., *Papers of John Adams,* IV (Cambridge, Mass., 1979), 208–213.

59. Shannon C. Stimson, *The American Revolution in the Law: Anglo-American Jurisprudence before John Marshall* (Princeton, N.J., 1990), 101; Jacob E. Cooke, ed., *The Federalist* (Middletown, Conn., 1961), 343, 531; Andrew A. Lipscomb, ed., *The Writings of Thomas Jefferson* (Washington, D.C., 1903–1904), III, 318; Paine, *Rights of Man,* in Foot and Kramnick, eds., *Thomas Paine Reader,* 257, 278. "Government in a well-constituted republic, requires no belief from man beyond what his reason can give. He sees the *rationale* of the whole system. its origin and its operation; and as it is best supported

Like Locke and Sidney, Jefferson believed that a person needed to be able to exercise reason in order to be a participatory citizen. This is a simple statement. Yet it hid layers of assumptions and created, by definition, two tiers of equality, which defined children, in particular, as nonreasonable. That participation in government demanded the exercise of reason was the key theoretical formulation underpinning Jefferson's plan for public education and his statute on religious toleration. His belief also affected a range of public policies that defined and limited children's participation. Jefferson still advocated equality; the fact that there were differences in who could participate did not mean that "equality" was merely a "fiction." Rather, "equality" needs to be understood within the context of this emphasis on reason. Equality was clearly an important element of republican thought and the basis for many legal reforms.

Like other republican authors, Jefferson implied that all humans possessed free will and were equal in that freedom as soon as they had been created. "All Men are created equal," he wrote in the Declaration of Independence. "They are endowed by their Creator with certain unalienable Rights; that among these are Life, Liberty, and the Pursuit of Happiness." In his manuscript for "A Summary View," published in July 1774, he wrote similarly, "The god who gave us life, gave us liberty at the *same time:* the hand of force may destroy, but cannot disjoin them." In the original published version of his "Bill for Establishing Religious Freedom," Jefferson wrote that he (and the Virginia legislature) were "well aware . . . that *Almighty God hath created the mind free,* and manifested his supreme will that free it shall remain by making it altogether insusceptible of restraint."[60]

However, a closer examination reveals what kind of limits he set on that equality and that freedom. The clause that follows "Life, Liberty, and the Pursuit of Happiness" in the Declaration of Independence is, "To secure these Rights, Governments are instituted among Men, deriving their just Powers from the Consent of the Governed." Did Jefferson believe that all should consent? The restrictions on voting that Jefferson proposed in his draft of the Virginia constitution, written in the same year, reveal that he did not. In the same vein, while Jefferson promoted the independence of adult males, he regarded the independence of children as dangerous, since they did not have the reason and the will to make decisions: independence would spoil

---

when best understood, the human faculties [or reason and understanding] act with boldness, and acquire, under this form of government, a gigantic manliness."

60. Julian P. Boyd et al., eds., *The Papers of Thomas Jefferson* (Princeton, N.J., 1950–), I, 135 (emphasis added), II, 545 (most of this passage was cut in the version of the bill finally passed).

them. "To render a child independant of it's parents," Jefferson wrote on the question of leaving money to grandchildren, "is to ruin it's education, it's morals, it's reputation and it's fortune."[61]

Public Education and the Cultivation of Reason

The growth of public education in the years after the Revolution was remarkable. This educational program reflected not only the desire to create properly educated citizens but assumptions about how children differed from adults in their political and personal capabilities.[62] While disciplining children and teaching them obedience can be antidemocratic, everything depends on what is taught and for what purpose. There was virtually no strand of republican thought in the late eighteenth century that saw the separate status of children as actually antiegalitarian; rather, it was training for a future equality. The arguments put forward by Thomas Jefferson, Noah Webster, and Benjamin Rush for public education drew directly on John Locke's thought: in order to become independent adults, children need to learn self-discipline and obedience. Until they gain reason, they should respect and obey those who cared for them. Most significantly, Locke taught that some formal education was critical to developing the understanding, to creating the reasonable adult who could make an informed political decision and thus earn the right of citizenship.[63]

61. "Jefferson's Third Draft of the Virginia Constitution, 1776," ibid., I, 358. Jefferson restricted the suffrage to "male persons of full age and sane mind" who had one-quarter acre in a town or twenty-five acres of land in the country or who had paid taxes for two years. The implications of "reasonability" and property restrictions will be more fully discussed below.

On children: Jefferson to Robert Pigott, June 3, 1788, ibid., XIII, 235.

62. See, particularly, Lawrence A. Cremin, *American Education: The Colonial Experience, 1607–1783* (New York, 1970), and *American Education: The National Experience, 1783–1876* (New York, 1980); Ellwood P. Cubberley, *Public Education in the United States: A Study and Interpretation of American Educational History,* rev. ed. (Boston, 1934), esp. chap. 4. Cremin's thorough and careful survey of American education concludes that parents transferred many of their responsibilities for educating children to the state government, a transfer concentrated in the decade following the American Revolution. Cubberley attributes the growth of public education to the theory and practice of democracy.

63. Peter S. Onuf has suggested that many of the tracts that encouraged public education in the new Republic were actually profoundly antidemocratic: they encouraged obedience to the state and reflected doubts about the natural virtue and intelligence of the common people. Onuf separates Noah Webster and Benjamin Rush from such reformers as Thomas Jefferson, who, he argues, supported public education merely to teach the common people how to evade tyranny. "State Politics and Republican Virtue: Religion, Education, and Morality in Early American Federalism," in Paul Finkelman

Noah Webster echoed Locke's *Essay concerning Human Understanding* almost exactly in "On the Education of Youth in America," arguing for public education: "Our senses are the avenues of knowledge. . . . The most natural course of education is that which employs, first the senses or powers of the body or those faculties of the mind which first acquire strength, and then proceeds to those studies which depend on the power of comparing and combining ideas." Webster described why public education was necessary to a republic: through education citizens develop the use of their reason and learn "the principles of virtue and of liberty [that] inspire them with just and liberal ideas of government and with an inviolable attachment to their own country."

> It is observed by the great Montesquieu *[The Spirit of Laws]* that "the laws of education ought to be relative to the principles of the government."
>
> In despotic governments the people should have little or no education, except what tends to inspire them with servile fear. Information is fatal to despotism.
>
> In monarchies education should be partial and adapted to the rank of each class of citizens. But "in a republican government," says the same writer, "the whole power of education is required." Here every class of people should *know* and *love* the laws. This knowledge should be diffused by means of schools and newspapers, and an attachment to the laws may be formed by early impressions upon the mind.

Thus while discipline (which Webster certainly encourages, although by the term "absolute" he meant "unswerving," not "all-powerful") might seem on the face of it to be the opposite of liberty, discipline and the education of youth are critical for learning the ability to be free, according to republican theory. As Locke had said, *"Children . . . are not born in this full state of Equality, though they are born to it."* A republic has a better chance of survival where its citizens are sufficiently reasonable that they will not be corrupted or intimidated by tyrants. The time to shape citizens is in their youth.[64]

Benjamin Rush made the argument about discipline and good citizenry even more sharply, inserting the age of twenty-one as when youth should begin to exercise their own wills. "I am satisfied that the most useful citizens have been formed from those youth who have never known or felt their own

and Stephen E. Gottlieb, eds., *Toward a Usable Past: Liberty under State Constitutions* (Athens, Ga., 1991), 91–116.

64. Noah Webster, "On the Education of Youth in America" (1787–1788, 1790), in Frederick Rudolph, ed., *Essays on Education in the Early Republic* (Cambridge, Mass., 1965), 45, 51, 65–66.

wills till they were one and twenty years of age, and I have often thought that society owes a great deal of its order and happiness to the deficiencies of parental government being supplied by those habits of obedience and subordination which are contracted at schools." Once they are past twenty-one, however, male youths, at least, should be able to vote and exercise their own judgment, though Rush suggested that they prove their ability to read and write before exercising the suffrage. Still, compared to Locke, Webster, or Jefferson, Rush placed more restrictions on even the adult citizen, who continued to have very strong obligations to the community, which should outweigh his own desires when they collided. "Let our pupil be taught that he does not belong to himself, but that he is public property."[65]

Simeon Doggett, a New England minister, in his *Discourse on Education* (1797) referred to the emerging consensus about child development when encouraging public education. Children need a thoughtful and careful education to nourish their reflective and moral powers, to enable them to be good citizens.

> All these intellectual, active, and moral powers and capacities . . . are under the influence of . . . IMITATION and HABIT, . . . and hence, by the powerful hand of a well-directed education, and due attention, may be vastly heightened and improved; or, by neglect and vicious indulgence depressed, enervated, if not finally destroyed.

This education is critical to citizenship: it enables a republic. Otherwise republics tend toward aristocracies or monarchies.

> The throne of tyranny is founded on ignorance. . . . Let general information and a just knowledge of the rights of man be diffused through the great bulk of the people in any nation, and it will not be in the power of all the combined despots on earth to enslave them.[66]

Thomas Jefferson promoted public education as both a tool to empower the people to exercise their authority and a means to create new leaders who could challenge an aristocracy of birth. It would "enlighten" the people and help

65. Benjamin Rush, *A Plan for the Establishment of Public Schools and the Diffusion of Knowledge in Pennsylvania* . . . (1786), ibid., 13, 14, 16. "In a republic where all votes for public officers are given by *ballot*, should not a knowledge of reading and writing be considered as essential qualifications for an elector? And when a man who is of a doubtful character offers his vote, would it not be more consistent with sound policy and wise government to oblige him to read a few verses in the Bible to prove his qualifications than simply to compel him to kiss the *outside* of it?"

66. Simeon Doggett, *A Discourse on Education, Delivered at the Dedication and Opening of Bristol Academy, the 18th Day of July, A.D. 1796* (1797), ibid., 154, 156.

them to use their reason. In 1786, with regard to the far-reaching changes he recommended for the legal code of Virginia, he wrote: "I think by far the most important bill in our whole code is that for the diffusion of knowledge among the people. No other sure foundation can be devised for the preservation of freedom, and happiness." Education was also a prerequisite for "rightful" informed consent, as Jefferson elaborated in January 1787, in a letter responding to news of Shays's Rebellion in Massachusetts. Instead of endorsing the military force that was in fact used, Jefferson warned, "To punish [the] errors [of the people] would be to repress the only safeguard of the public liberty." He told Edward Carrington not to "be too severe upon their errors but *reclaim them by enlightening them.*" Education would help to filter out a "natural aristocracy" of "virtue and talents" that would challenge hereditary aristocracy. Via his education proposal, he wrote John Adams in 1813, "Worth and genius would thus have been sought out from every condition of life, and compleatly prepared by education for defeating the competition of wealth and birth for public trusts." Thus, unlike John Adams and Gouverneur Morris, who sought to exclude the unenlightened, Jefferson's solution was to educate them. Public education, in more ways than one, would provide a bulwark against "an artificial aristocray founded on wealth and birth."[67]

Democratic-republican political theory, then, contextualized liberty and equality and connected them to a theory of human development, one that depended on education to reach full fruition. Locke and Paine distinguished themselves from patriarchalism by emphasizing that consent was the only legitimate source of authority. But, in and of itself, consent could be seen as meaningless if it could be coerced or parents could bind their descendants in perpetuity. Locke's writings on human development, which grew out of the religious debates of the seventeenth century, helped to lay the basis for a theory of meaningful consent, one that took as its basis a fundamental difference between adults and children in their ability to reason and, therefore, to consent.

By the late eighteenth century, Locke's theories of child development that concentrated on the gaining of reason had inspired many other thinkers, many of whom partially disagreed with the emphasis on only reason, including Francis Hutcheson, David Hartley, Lord Kames, Thomas Reid, and Jean-Jacques Rousseau. In concert with the earlier political theorists and many religious reformers, they helped to create a new definition of childhood, wherein

67. Jefferson to Edward Carrington, Jan. 16, 1787, in Boyd et al., eds, *Papers of Jefferson*, XI, 49; Jefferson to Adams, Oct. 28, 1813, in Lester J. Cappon, ed., *The Adams-Jefferson Letters: The Complete Correspondence between Thomas Jefferson and Abigail and John Adams* (Chapel Hill, N.C., 1959), 387–392.

the child was defined in opposition to the rational adult. The implications of separating common human attributes into a "childhood" of irrationality, playfulness, dependence, and innocence from an "adulthood" characterized by rationality and responsibility can be seen in the Romantic reaction to the Enlightenment during the early nineteenth century. Romantic writers maintained the same distinctions between childhood and adulthood as those of the Enlightenment, but reversed the characteristics that should be most honored, idealizing the qualities associated with childhood instead of adulthood.

One interesting aspect of the shift in political legitimacy, from birthright to meaningful consent, is how many legislators sought to justify older political structures in new terms and so to retain them. For example, dominium, the medieval concept that linked both lordship and power to those who own property, continued to be justified in two ways. First, some justified property ownership as giving an interest and investment in the community; second, some, such as Morris and Adams, justified the exclusion of non–property-owning males by comparing them with children in their dependence and their inability to reason. Therefore, in spite of the Revolutionary transformation in the basis for political legitimacy, political practices of exclusion could be continued and expanded.[68]

While equality was usually allied with reason and independence in much of the political thought of the late eighteenth century, these concepts were separable as well. There was more than one possible reading of the Revolutionary rhetoric. Some stressed, for example, radical equality more than the necessity of reason. Thus "children" themselves did not necessarily follow the advice to deny their wills, and accept their inequality. The chapters that follow, however, while they give examples of children who rebel, generally chronicle the construction and consolidation of age limits with respect to personal and political participation. This process relied upon the link between reason, understanding, and equality and drew upon political philosophy.[69]

68. George Mason, for example, argued that property ownership gave people more of an interest in the political and social order. So, too, did some members of the Massachusetts Constitutional Convention of 1780, at least for the senate. See J. R. Pole, *Political Representation in England and the Origins of the American Republic* (Berkeley, Calif., 1971), 138, 195–196.

69. James C. Scott notes that "the public transcript is an indifferent guide to the opinion of subordinates," in *Domination and the Arts of Reistance: Hidden Transcripts* (New Haven, Conn., 1990), 3. The language of authority will not necessarily be accepted by the weak, and, especially in situations where they have no fear of those in power overhearing them, they may articulate "a social space in which offstage dissent to the official transcript of power relations may be voiced."

CHAPTER 4

SUBJECTS OR CITIZENS?

INHERITED RIGHT VERSUS REASON, MERIT, AND VIRTUE

"Anye man being the Queenes Subject . . . within the age of sixtie
yeares . . . [shall have] a long Bow . . . everie man childe in his
house betweene seaven yeres and seaventeene of age a Bow and
two Shaftes, and for everie such being above seventeene yeares,
a Bowe and foure Shaftes."
William Lambarde, Eirenarcha; or,
Of the Office of Justices of Peace *(London, 1581)*

"Infants under fourteen years,
may not be jurors in any case whatsoever."
George Webb, Office and Authority of a Justice of Peace
(Williamsburg, Va., 1736)

On July 6, 1776, Joseph Plumb Martin sat staring at the "enlisting orders" in front of him, hesitant to sign. His grandfather, with whom he lived, refused to agree to his joining up, as Joseph was only fifteen. "I took up the pen, loaded it with the fatal charge, made several mimic imitations of writing my name, but took especial care not to touch the paper with the pen." Then someone jostled him from behind, "which caused the pen to make a woeful scratch upon the paper. 'O, he has enlisted,' said he. 'He has made his mark; he is fast [bound] enough now.'" Thinking the deed done, Martin then signed his name "fairly upon the indentures." At age fifteen, in the wake of the Declaration of Independence, he thus became a soldier in the Continental army. He had wanted to enlist since April 1775 but, then two years shy of the minimum age for the militia in Massachusetts, had not done so "for fear of being refused." Even after he had signed the indenture, his grandfather might have challenged it. But the recruiting officer sought only Joseph's own consent, and no one asked his age. Indeed, his consent was not only valid but slightly pushed.[1]

---

1. Joseph Plumb Martin, *Private Yankee Doodle: Being a Narative of Some of the Adventures, Dangers, and Sufferings of a Revolutionary Soldier,* ed. George F. Scheer (Boston, 1962), 7–9, 16–17.

Although he might have been obliged, as a subject, to enter the militia in another six months, even that was a choice of sorts in the midst of that war. Whose subject? When is one bound to obedience and obligation to a kingdom? While the recruiting officer might have pushed his hand, he did not hit him over the head and drag him aboard ship, as British navy press-gangs sometimes had done in previous decades. What does consent mean, and when is it binding? Which matters more: form (the mark on the paper), or the intention behind it? These questions swirled around such legal acts and obligations as that signed by Martin in 1776. Two centuries earlier, even less attention than this would have been paid to his age, or to parents' or grandparents' consent. Generally the move was toward emphasizing that only intention and competency can create binding consent, but, as even this one scene makes clear, the issue of consent was hardly black and white. Influence and force could take guises: when is any consent perfectly uninfluenced? Another question swirls around his story as well: when were the laws about competency enforced, and when waived? Recruiting officers clearly had an incentive to look the other way, but would town officials likewise have turned their heads if he had tried to vote?[2]

For Robert Filmer, any child born to a father who owed obedience to a king would in turn owe obedience to the same king and his heirs in perpetuity. The laws defined English subjects as those born within the realm, including its colonies. Birth created subjects and obligation. This was the message reinforced by catechisms. John Locke agreed within limits: a father's obligation could in some cases bind the child, but only temporarily. When children attained understanding, then they could choose their own allegiance. If one focuses merely on childhood, their arguments were similar, but only superficially. The dilemma here is whether one should be bound by the laws of the realm even if one does not consent explicitly. It is also whether one should have to serve a king (or government) in any civil capacity.

To be a "subject" implies that one has no choice over one's allegiance. Yet even in Elizabethan England one did have choice, of a sort. One could refuse to take the oath of allegiance. But refusing to take the oath of supremacy, if asked twice, could make one guilty of treason, a crime punished with the

2. For an entertaining review of some of the strategies that recruiting officers employed to gain potential recruits' "consent," see George Farquahar's 1706 play, *The Recruiting Officer*. On the Royal Navy's impressment, see J. R. Hutchinson, *The Press Gang: Afloat and Ashore* (London, 1913), esp. 10–17, 83–85, 174–175, 194–195; Jesse Lemisch, "Jack Tar in the Streets: Merchant Seamen in the Politics of Revolutionary America," *William and Mary Quarterly*, 3d Ser., XXV (1968), 371–401.

grisliest of deaths (drawing and quartering). "Refusing Oath of Supremacy upon Second tender Treason. . . . Absolving Subjects from Obedience, or reconciling them to Obedience of *Rome* [converting to Catholicism], Treason . . . Priest coming into *England,* not submitting in two days, Treason. The like for Englishmen in Forreign Seminaries." Failing to acknowledge one's monarch was not the only way to get convicted of treason: converting to Catholicism, likewise, was regarded as changing one's political allegiance, which was treason. Birth in England, in short, made one a subject, and any attempt to change one's status was defined as a heinous crime. Defining treason as a crime with such penalties was, of course, an attempt to intimidate, to coerce consent. As this treason statute makes clear, forced consent was legitimate under Elizabethan law. One could not choose one's allegiance in any open way.[3]

Those who justified authority via the inheritance of power through nobility and landed wealth and those who justified it via the consent of the governed disagreed over whether one could choose one's allegiance. This debate dramatically affected legal definitions of the subject and the citizen—indeed the very origins of the "citizen" in Anglo-America can be attributed to the victory of the latter. The shift in assumptions about the exercise of any level of political authority was dramatic during these two centuries. The ultimate victors were those who argued that members of a nation were not subjects: were not children who had to obey political fathers who inherited their right and power. Instead, they argued, full members of a nation were "citizens" who had various rights to the exercise of political power—at the least, they should be able to consent to those in authority over them, and not be punished for not retaining allegiance.

To rationalize why those who did not consent should be under political authority, democratic-republican theorists in seventeenth-century England kept one aspect of earlier patriarchal political theories: the power of parents over children. They gave that power, however, a new justification: dependence and lack of reason. Thus in some ways they extended patriarchal power. They excluded children from the privileges of citizenship and, increasingly, from some of its obligations, emphasizing that only those who had discretion, who could reason, could be bound to obedience. They did so in order to distinguish between consent that was coerced and influenced, and consent that was free.

This chapter will focus on three obligations/privileges of subjects and citizens: allegiance, military service, and jury service. The rights and duties of subjects and military service were more universal (although both tended to

---

3. [Matthew Hale], *Pleas of the Crown; or, A Brief but Full Account of Whatsoever Can Be Found Relating to That Subject* (London, 1678), 20–21.

focus more on males); jury service, however, had a property requirement. In a way, subjects had no minimum age. But, in prosecutions for treason, the minimum age was probably eight, the age at which one assumed criminal responsibility (an issue we will return to in Chapter 6). For all three issues, then, an age limit existed of seven or eight or twelve for military obligation and oath taking, of fourteen for jury service. Attaching the property requirement to jury service marked it as a privilege. In placing so much weight on reason and holding that children do not have it, the political writers of the eighteenth century developed new categories of those who could exercise the rights and obligations of subjects and citizens, definitions that increasingly rested on age (and higher age) as opposed to property and that began to coalesce around one age in particular by the late eighteenth century: twenty-one.[4]

Citizenship in its modern sense, as a right that can be officially chosen, or "volitional allegiance," was a product of the Revolutionary era in America. In sixteenth- and seventeenth-century English law, subjectship was perpetual and generally determined by birth (a combination of place of birth and status of parents). To attempt to change one's allegiance could open one to charges of treason. Clear parallels exist between the debate over church membership in the seventeenth century and over citizenship in the era of the Revolution, between heresy and treason. To what extent should birth determine allegiance? Should people be able to choose their allegiance?[5]

The violation of loyalty oaths could lead to prosecution for treason, as had happened since the Middle Ages. Loyalty oaths were usually demanded only of subjects whose allegiance was questionable. In Anglo-Saxon England and through much of the medieval period, youths could be asked to swear an oath of allegiance at twelve.[6] According to Sir Thomas Littleton's late-fifteenth-century treatise *Tenures,* one had to pay homage and fealty (in the form of an

---

4. Twenty-one was the outside boundary for exercise of political authority during the medieval period, when an age had been mentioned. A knight's son had to swear fealty to the king for knight's service, for example, by the age of twenty-one at the latest. However, having twenty-one as the outside age is very different from having it as the earliest limitation. Other boys and most girls reached an age of majority when younger, depending on the type of land they held; the norm, in fact, seemed to be fourteen. These issues are discussed in detail in Chapter 7. Also see T. E. James, "The Age of Majority," *American Journal of Legal History,* IV (1960), 29 n. 34.

5. James H. Kettner, *The Development of American Citizenship, 1608–1870* (Chapel Hill, N.C., 1978), esp. chap. 7.

6. J. G. Bellamy, *The Law of Treason in England in the Later Middle Ages* (Cambridge, 1970), gives two examples where breaking a loyalty oath provided the justification for a prosecution for treason (54, 198). They involved two Scottish noblemen (1347) and the duke of York (1459).

oath) to one's lord when one inherited the obligation and the land. He mentioned no lower age limit. In 1628, when Sir Edward Coke commented on these practices, he acknowledged that most of the legal authorities thought children bound to give oaths of homage when they inherited the tenancy. One can easily imagine a child performing the following ceremony:

His Lord shall sit, and the Tenant shall kneel before him on both his Knees, and hold his Hands jointly together between the Hands of his Lord, and shall say thus: I become your Man from this Day forward of Life and Limb, and of earthly Worship, and unto you shall be true and faithful, and bear to you Faith for the Tenements that I claim to hold of you; (saving the Faith that I owe unto our Sovereign Lord the King).

Coke debated the question of age, noting that opinion varied in his own time but that in many instances children were required to give homage. By the early seventeenth century, loyalty oaths were required for all religious recusants (those who did not attend church) who were eighteen or older.[7]

Loyalty oaths could make aliens into subjects in many colonies during the seventeenth century and were used in a similar way for Protestant aliens, in particular, in Britain during the eighteenth. In Virginia during the seventeenth century oaths specified no age but were required of "all such persons" who arrived on ships. Perhaps very young children were excluded, but the law made no explicit exception. In fact, as we shall see, this fitted a pattern in Virginia.[8]

In the new United States, people began to use the term "citizen" instead of the older term "subject" to describe membership in the nation. Subjects owed allegiance to a king from birth; citizens owed allegiance to a nation as a conscious choice. During the Revolution itself, in declaring their independence and starting a new country, many colonists renounced their former membership and entered into a new political body, thus indicating, in principle at least, their attachment to the issue of choice. But citizenship retained many ambiguities after the Revolution. It was not clear that even the Revolution-

7. Keith Thomas, "Age and Authority in Early Modern England," British Academy, *Proceedings*, LXII (1976), 223 (citing 3 Jac. I, c. 4, s. 8 [1606]; the protestation of 1642; the engagement of 1650; the oath of allegiance to George I [1 Geo. I, st. 2, c. 13.] and the Test oath of 1723 [10 Geo. I, c. 4.]); Edw[ard] Coke, *The First Part of the Institutes of the Laws of England; or, A Commentary upon Littleton* . . . (1628), 11th ed. (London, 1719), 64a–65b.

8. Kettner, *American Citizenship*, esp. 70–103. The law that mandated the administration of these oaths, dated February 1631/2, did not specify age (or gender) limits. It merely said that "all such persons" on the ships shall take the "oathes of supremacy, and allegeance." William Waller Hening, ed., *The Statutes at Large: Being a Collection of All the Laws of Virginia* . . . (rpt. Charlottesville, Va., 1969), I, 66.

aries would let persons renounce their new state and national citizenship. They continued to use the older standard, birth, as the measure of basic citizenship but never clarified it by statute. Children were allocated their father's choice of allegiance until they came of age to choose for themselves, and excluded from choosing their own citizenship. Nor was their tacit consent—consent to a government that lawyers and judges presumed to arise from their continuing to reside in a certain state—considered adequate to grant them citizenship in a state. What was new in rules of subjectship-citizenship were thus three elements: the focus of allegiance, questions about perpetuity, and choice linked to age. The latter two issues reveal the limits on the new choice. From the very beginning, citizenship was not equally accessible or deniable to all in the eyes of the law.

During and after the Revolution, the new state governments demanded loyalty oaths of those who chose to stay, but such oaths were not required of women or slaves or the young. The age limits for those who had to take loyalty oaths during the Revolutionary war varied among different states, indicating that they disagreed about who could make that choice. Pennsylvania required in 1777 that all "male white inhabitants of this state . . . above the age of eighteen" had to swear (or affirm, for Quakers) allegiance. In the same year, Virginia required oaths of allegiance from "all free born male inhabitants of this state, above the age of sixteen years." Age specifications for loyalty oaths ranged between sixteen and twenty-one. These new state uses of loyalty oaths and of age, gender, and race restrictions correlated with their requirements for military service. Indeed, Pennsylvania's age limit of eighteen and Virginia's of sixteen corresponded to the age at which a male could join the military. Yet these oaths also determined who could *make* that choice, and that choice was important. The decisions these young men made would determine whether their land could be confiscated and whether they were liable to prosecution for treason.[9]

Married women fell into a similar, ambiguous category of those not entitled to choose their citizenship during the Revolutionary period. They were assumed to exercise choice by choosing a husband, who would choose citizenship for them. In *Martin v Massachusetts* (1805), the plaintiff argued successfully that a son should be able to regain his mother's property, which had been confiscated after the Revolution because of her choice to leave the state of Massachusetts. The plaintiff argued that his mother had no right to make a

9. James T. Mitchell and Henry Flanders, comps., *The Statutes at Large of Pennsylvania, from 1682 to 1801* (Harrisburg, 1896–1911), IX, 111; Hening, ed., *Statutes at Large*, IX, 281; Claude Halstead Van Tyne, *The Loyalists in the American Revolution* (New York, 1902), 132.

choice about citizenship, since she was a married woman, or feme covert. George Blake argued for the plaintiff, James Martin: "Upon the strict principles of law, a *feme covert* is not a member; has no *political relation* to the *state* any more than an alien. . . . The legislature intended to exclude femes-covert and infants from the operation of the [loyalty] act; otherwise the word inhabitant would have been used alone, and not coupled with the word member."[10]

After the Revolution, the federal government passed laws that associated the ability to choose citizenship with twenty-one. But it retained ambiguities. A law of 1790 granted aliens the ability to gain citizenship after a two-year residence. However, for those under twenty-one, their father chose for them. Birth in the new states also granted citizenship to the young without their consent, continuing English practice. Yet it was not clear that such youth could renounce citizenship. In *United States v Isaac Williams,* Chief Justice Oliver Ellsworth held that Williams could not renounce his United States citizenship without first obtaining permission from the United States. "All the members of the civil community are bound to each other by compact. . . . One of the parties to this compact cannot absolve it by his own act." In effect, this decision reiterated earlier English ideas of perpetual allegiance. Yet not everyone agreed with this continuation of perpetuity, particularly because it denied choice to young men even after they came of age to choose. An anonymous contributor to the *Aurora* (Philadelphia) described the decision as "manifestly unjust" because "birth-duty of allegiance is a fraud upon infancy." "It is the adult only who can decide what country best suits his interest, but the chains of slavery are fastened upon him while he is incapable of resisting."[11]

Jefferson speculated at length on this question soon after the Revolution, clearly fascinated by it. He finally decided that all were citizens who either were born within the territory of "this commonwealth" or migrated to it and swore allegiance, including "all infants [children under twenty-one] wheresoever born, whose father, if living, or otherwise, whose mother was, a citizen at the time of their birth" or whose parent migrated to Virginia. He thus argued that the parent determined the citizenship of the child—and the child could not choose it until coming of age (although Jefferson did think that children who migrated of their own accord might be considered citizens). He

10. Linda K. Kerber, "The Paradox of Women's Citizenship in the Early Republic: The Case of *Martin vs. Massachusetts,* 1805," *American Historical Review,* XCVII (1992), 349–378, esp. 369.

11. "Trial of Isaac Williams . . . ," in Francis Wharton, ed., *State Trials of the United States during the Administrations of Washington and Adams* (1849; rpt. New York, 1970), 652–658; Kettner, *American Citizenship,* 236, 271–273.

continued this logic in his reflections on who could inherit property in Britain, a right restricted to British subjects. An adult citizen of the United States could not inherit property from a relative in Britain, because the American citizen would be an alien in Britain. Children, however, could inherit British property even while living in America if born in Britain or its colonies before Independence, because they would not be of age to choose their citizenship or to owe "allegiance" to another state, and so could still be classified as a "natural subject" of Britain. The youth could make that choice, then, upon reaching majority. In Jefferson's reflections, one can see Locke's influence.[12]

In 1801, a United States circuit court extended the logic laid out by Jefferson. In the case of *Hollingsworth v Duane*, the jury followed the judge's direction in finding that Duane, who had been born in New York in 1760 but had lived for most of his life in England, was not a citizen, since he had not chosen to migrate to the United States immediately after he turned twenty-one in 1781. Instead, he remained in England until 1795. Therefore, he had not chosen to be an American citizen when he came of age to decide, which the judge gave as twenty-one. Early-nineteenth-century Supreme Court decisions upheld this verdict. A child under twenty-one was held not able to make a choice and so had the citizenship of his father, but he retained the "right of disaffirmation, in a reasonable time after the termination of his minority." Court decisions and states themselves continued to differ over whether a person actually had to take a loyalty oath in order to become a citizen during the Revolution or whether all inhabitants were made citizens by tacit consent.[13]

12. Julian P. Boyd et al., eds., *The Papers of Thomas Jefferson* (Princeton, N.J., 1950–), II, 477, and "Notes on British and American Alienage" (1783), VI, 433–434. This article may be misdated by the editors, who guessed at 1783, because it must have occurred after peace with England. Yet this same argument is expressed in a letter to John Adams dated Feb. 7, 1786, IX, 259. This letter makes it clear that Jefferson differed from others on the question of whether adult American citizens could inherit English property.

"Qu. 2. The father a British subject; the son in America, adult, and within the description of an American citizen, according to their laws. Can the son inherit?"

"He owes allegiance to the states. He is an alien then and cannot inherit."

"Qu. 3 The father is a British subject. The son as in Qu. 2. but an infant. Can he inherit?"

"[Yes, so long as the child is] born within the King's obedience."

13. *Hollingsworth v Duane*, 12 Fed. Cas. 356 (U.S.C.C. Pa. 1801); Justice Smith Thompon for the majority in *Inglis v Trustees*, 28 U.S. (3 Pet.) 99, 126 (1830). In Massachusetts in 1812, for example, it was held that all inhabitants transferred their allegiance with the Declaration of Independence. In other states, such as Virginia and North Carolina, it was held that they were assumed not to be citizens unless they took a loyalty oath or

Military Service

The ability to serve one's country as a soldier was an obligation of subjects in political writings from the sixteenth century on, and the citizen-soldier held a central place in the classical republican thought of Machiavelli, Harrington, and the "neo-Harringtonian" Andrew Fletcher. According to these thinkers, only if citizens were also soldiers, and the only soldiers, could political tyranny be avoided: military service was critical to virtuous citizenship. Yet equating citizenship with military service was not the distinct preserve of the "classical Republicans." The principle is implicit, for example, in Locke's justification of rebellion after "a long train of abuses," in the section on the right to bear arms in the Bill of Rights, and elsewhere through the seventeenth and eighteenth centuries.[14]

In the early modern period, the age for military obligation was young. The age limit for militia service in Elizabethan England was seven. Any "man childe" of seven or above should be ready to defend the kingdom, with "a Bow and two Shaftes," according to the Elizabethan law. Every man under sixty "being the Queenes Subject" should have a longbow, and "everie man childe in his house betweene seaven yeres and seaventeene of age a Bow and two Shaftes, and for everie such being above seventeene yeares, a Bowe and foure Shaftes."[15]

A significant change in age requirements for military service occurred between the late seventeenth and the late eighteenth centuries. In England, many teenagers were given commissions in the army and navy or knighted during the seventeenth century. From 1677, navy cadets were supposed to be at least sixteen, as were army officers after 1711. As Keith Thomas claims, however, "The evasion of these age-limits in the eighteenth century is notorious." Neither statute was enforced before the reign of George III, and even then "exceptions were made." The minimum age of general military service in the infantry also increased from fifteen in the thirteenth century to sixteen in the sixteenth century and eighteen in George II's mid-eighteenth-century militia. But, even during the eighteenth century, poor boys age ten or above could be "apprenticed" to the navy. And it is not clear that the press-gangs

---

remained in the state. Kettner, *American Citizenship,* 192–198; *Ainslie v Martin,* 9 Mass. 454 (1813); *McIlvaine v Coxe,* 8 U.S. (4 Cranch) 209 (1808); *Shanks v Dupont,* 28 U.S. (3 Pet.) 241 (1830).

14. See J. G. A. Pocock, *The Machiavellian Moment: Florentine Political Thought and the Atlantic Republican Tradition* (Princeton, N.J., 1975), esp. 199–200, 428–430.

15. William Lambarde, *Eirenarcha; or, Of the Office of the Justices of Peace* (London, 1581), 378.

that roamed the streets of eighteenth century port towns paid particular attention to the ages of the persons they forcibly recruited.[16]

In Massachusetts and Pennsylvania the initial laws passed in the seventeenth century gave sixteen as the age at which one had to attend militia exercises, but Virginia specified no age for service until 1705. The age remained sixteen in Massachusetts until 1792, when the United States government mandated that it should be eighteen.[17]

Virginia's legal revision was more complicated, illustrating a continuing tension between those whom the House of Burgesses considered of sufficient age to bear arms and the need for more soldiers, which compelled a broadening of the age requirements. But it also reflected, unlike the other colonies but like England, property requirements. Before 1705 militia service in Virginia fell first on "ALL persons" except "negroes" and then on "every man able to beare armes," with no lower age limit. The exemption of blacks, in a society where they were clearly already of the lowest rank (in 1640), shows that military service, for Virginians, was not universal. (It was not merely an obligation, of course: those who bore arms could also pose a threat.)[18]

By 1705, Virginia had set the first age restrictions on militia duty at sixteen. During the eighteenth century, the age requirements would seesaw dramatically. In 1723 the age requirement was lifted to twenty-one, it dropped to eighteen at the beginning of the Seven Years' War in 1755, and it dropped again to sixteen in 1775 at the beginning of the Revolutionary war. Afterward, in 1784, the legislature raised the minimum age for service to eighteen, which was confirmed by the federal law of 1792. Although the Virginia legislature preferred older soldiers, it lowered the qualifications when it wanted more. Its minimum age to fight thus fluctuated wildly: from none in the seventeenth century to as high as twenty-one in the eighteenth.[19]

In Pennsylvania, the age requirements are more puzzling, yet they followed a similar pattern. The minimum age for the militia was sixteen until the eve of the Revolutionary war in 1776, when it was raised to eighteen, exactly when Pennsylvania needed more soldiers. Pennsylvania was also the

16. Thomas, "Age and Authority in Early Modern England," British Academy, *Proceedings*, LXII (1976), 213, 223 n. 7, 231.

17. *The General Laws and Liberties of the Massachusetts Colony: Revised and Re-Printed* (Cambridge, Mass., 1672), 109; *The Acts and Resolves, Public and Private, of the Province of the Massachusetts Bay* . . . (1775–1776) (Boston, 1869–1922), V, 445; *The Public and General Laws of the Commonwealth of Massachusetts* . . . (1810) (Boston, 1816), IV, 118.

18. Hening, ed., *Statutes at Large*, I, 226 (1639/40), 525 (1658/9).

19. Ibid., III, 355 (1705), IV, 118 (1723), V, 16 (1738), VI, 531 (1755), VII, 93 (1757), IX, 27 (1775), XI, 476 (1784), XII, 10 (1785). Also see below, note 22.

only state to require parental consent (1755) for those under twenty-one who wished to enter the militia at the beginning of the Seven Years' War, a requirement still in force during the Revolutionary war.[20] Although the Pennsylvania legislature provided no rationale, the pattern of change suggests one. In raising the age of entry into military service as well as increasing parental restrictions, the Quakers, who forswore violence and formed a significant part of the electorate, provided parents with a means to prevent younger men from doing something they might regret, delaying their free entry into military service until the legislators deemed they had reached an age to make their own decisions.

The gradual rise in the age of military service from sixteen to eighteen in all three colonies over the course of the eighteenth century gains significance in light of the concurrent changes in age requirements for other areas of citizenship. This development can be explained only partly as the response to military need. Thus Pennsylvania raised the age of service to eighteen at the beginning of the Revolutionary war. Although the evidence is only circumstantial, the most plausible explanation for this shift is a different definition of who could best follow orders, who could best make a decision about the side on which to fight, who should be able to swear an oath of fealty, and who could be trusted or even expected to fight for his country. Taken together, these amounted to a definition of who could be a reasonable, participating citizen.

The right to vote was sometimes connected with military service. The initial draft of the Pennsylvania Constitution of 1776 gave the vote to anyone who served in the militia and paid taxes, a provision that would have opened the door to youths between eighteen and twenty-one. But a later draft dropped the military requirement and substituted residency and the age of twenty-one. Jefferson also suggested correlating militia service with voting rights, as did the "citizens" of Frederick County, Virginia, in 1815, who argued that "every man who pays taxes, or serves in the Militia" should have a "voice in the National and state Legislature" in order to "comport with our Republican doctrine."[21] Although military service does not illustrate the simple tran-

20. Staughton George, Benjamin M. Nead, and Thomas McCamant, eds., *Charter to William Penn, and the Laws of the Province of Pennsylvania* . . . (1676) (Harrisburg, 1879), 39; Mitchell and Flanders, comps., *The Statutes at Large of Pennsylvania*, V, 200 (1755–1756), IX, 77 (1776–1777).

21. Marchette Chute, *The First Liberty: A History of the Right to Vote in America* (New York, 1969), 199–200; J. R. Pole, *Political Representation in England and the Origins of the American Republic* (Berkeley, Calif., 1971), 301. For an example of Maryland militiamen who did not meet property requirements but demanded the right to vote, see Chilton

sition between property ownership and age qualifications that suffrage did, for example, property qualifications were clearly essential to becoming an officer. Virginia also had property restrictions for militia service soon after Bacon's Rebellion of 1676.[22]

In all three states, by 1792, the minimum age for militia service was eighteen, but the minimum age to vote was twenty-one. Although voting privileges might logically be related to militia service, the two conformed for neither age nor property requirements. Clearly, although both voting and military service were considered part of citizenship, the requirements for voting were higher. To use John Adams's words, these higher requirements indicate that "good judgement" and an "independent mind" were more important for those who voted than for those who served as soldiers. Yet the long-term rise in age requirements for military service suggests that the increased importance of reason affected even the qualifications of those who defended their country.

Jury Service

Unlike military service, for which the recruiting net was widely cast, jury service was esteemed a privilege, to be reserved for the propertied. Serving on a jury was important to the enforcement of criminal laws, arguably more important even than voting, which also had an official property requirement and underwent a similar transition. Gradually, in both England and North America, jury service became an obligation determined less by property and more by age. The focus on higher age to judge the actions of one's fellow citizens was a clear outgrowth of two phases of political turmoil in England and North America: the Glorious Revolution and the Revolutionary war. Demands in England to limit the voice of those who were most corruptible (because they had inadequate reason) resulted most dramatically in the restriction in the late seventeenth century of jury service to those above the age of twenty-one.

During the medieval period the qualifying age for jurors was twelve. Before the Norman Conquest every free man over twelve was a member of the

---

Williamson, *American Suffrage: From Property to Democracy, 1760–1860* (Princeton, N.J., 1960), 35, 108–109.

22. William L. Shea, *The Virginia Militia in the Seventeenth Century* (Baton Rouge, La., 1983), esp. 138. Shea compares Virginia militia service to the English pattern. He notes increasing property restrictions on militia service in seventeenth-century Virginia, such that Virginia's militia began more to resemble England's. It included specific restrictions on slaves, most servants, and poorer freemen.

local hundred, that is, the local legislative body, the pool from which juries were drawn through the seventeenth century. A medieval scholar cites only one example where age was an explicit local restriction for jury service: age twelve at Wycombe in 1275.[23]

The requirements for jury service, in both property and age, went up and down in an ideological seesaw during the seventeenth century. Indeed, the association of the Restoration of 1660 (and monarchical ideology) with higher property requirements, and of the two English revolutions (and republican ideology) with lower property requirements but higher age limits fits almost too well. Before the end of the seventeenth century, Parliament's only qualifications for jury service were based on property ownership. In the actual composition of English juries, members "ranked well upon the national scale of wealth, and they exercised a tangible power over the lives of their own communities."[24] Property qualifications for jury service increased several times between 1584 and 1692, starting at four pounds, although the gradually falling value of money might have made these changes insignifi-

23. Theodore F. T. Plucknett, *A Concise History of the Common Law*, 4th ed. (London, 1948), 86; John Marshall Mitnick, "From Neighbor-Witness to Judge of Proofs: The Transformation of the English Civil Juror," *American Journal of Legal History*, XXXII (1988), 204; Mary Bateson, ed., *Borough Customs*, II, Selden Society, Publications, XXI (London, 1906), 158. The text reads "quod quam cito habeat plus quam xij. annos potest," or "as soon as he has turned the age of 12."

For the best discussion of the broad evolution of the jury trial in England, see Thomas Andrew Green, *Verdict according to Conscience: Perspectives on the English Criminal Trial Jury, 1200–1800* (Chicago, 1985).

24. P. G. Lawson, "Lawless Juries? The Composition and Behavior of Hertfordshire Juries, 1573–1624," in J. S. Cockburn and Thomas A. Green, eds., *Twelve Good Men and True: The Criminal Trial Jury in England, 1200–1800* (Princeton, N.J., 1988), 117–157, esp. 121. Also see J. M. Beattie, "London Trial Juries in the 1690's," 214–253.

Several studies of England regarding the question of who jurors were have all focused on class and ignored age. The one exception (in studies of jurors prior to the 1694 reform) is Lawson, who notes merely that sixteenth-century jurors had to be "adult," but the two sources that mention age exclude only "infants" under "14," a very different age than would be required of later jurors, and not necessarily "adult" in our modern sense (121). He cites Lambarde, *Eirenarcha*; Michael Dalton, *Officium Vicecomitum: The Office and Authoritie of Sherifs . . .* (London, 1623); [Hale], *Pleas of the Crown*. The first two (quoted from below) mention age; Hale does not.

For an excellent collection of studies on jury membership, see Cockburn and Green, eds., *Twelve Good Men*. Also see J. S. Morrill, *The Cheshire Grand Jury, 1625–1659: A Social and Administrative Study* (Leicester, 1976). Morrill does note that the selection of grand jurymen appeared to be limited to those who had actually inherited the freehold (so sons were eligible when their fathers died). The grand jury, however, was usually more elite than those called for routine jury service (see 48 n. 10).

cant. Still, the dates of the changes (in 1664, just after the Restoration, the requirement was raised to twenty pounds, and dropped to ten pounds only in 1692, just after the Glorious Revolution) indicate the links between the Restoration and higher property requirements.[25]

Meanwhile, during the Interregnum, the commission appointed by Parliament to revise English laws in 1652, headed by Sir Matthew Hale, recommended that, in addition to owning property, all jurors should be older than twenty-five, able to read, and "of good understanding." Although that attempt at reform was unsuccessful, the Glorious Revolution of 1688 led to age qualifications for jury service. Whereas earlier sheriffs were to make lists of potential jurors from those who had "sufficient estates," by 1695 they were additionally directed to include only those between the ages of twenty-one and seventy.[26]

While this was the first appearance in statutory law of any age requirement, common law, as laid out in English and American guides to justices of the peace, had set fourteen as the minimum age for jury service. These guides provided virtually the only legal training for justices of the peace in seventeenth- and eighteenth-century America.[27] No formal legal training, in fact, was even available in North America before the late eighteenth century. Thus these guides, even though mostly published in England, proved influ-

25. These general property requirements (of four pounds, twenty pounds, and ten pounds) had variations in Wales and some rural areas. This property could be in the form of "freehold or copyhold lands or tenements . . . or in rents, or in all or any of the said lands, tenements or rents, in fee-simple, fee-tail, or for the life of themselves, or some other person." 27 Eliz. I, c. 6, s. 1; 16 and 17 Car. II, c. 3, s. 1; 4 Wm. and Mar., c. 24, s. 16.

26. "Several Draughts of Acts Heretofore Prepared by Persons to Consider of the Inconvenience, Delay, Charge, and Irregularity in the Proceedings of the Law" [London, 1653], in Walter Scott, ed., *The Somers Collection of Tracts: A Collection of Scarce and Valuable Tracts, on the Most Interesting and Entertaining Subjects: But Chiefly Such as They Relate to the History and Constitution of These Kingdoms . . .* 2d ed. (London, 1811), VI, 218; 7 and 8 Will. III, c. 32. The upper age limit perhaps suggests that old age represented a return of childhood and its incompetence. Sir Edward Coke had sponsored legislation in Parliament in 1621 that would have sought to ensure that jury members be "sufficient . . . in estate and understanding." For his speeches in support of this legislation, see Wallace Notestein, Frances Helen Relf, and Hartley Simpson, eds., *Commons Debates, 1621* (New Haven, Conn., 1935), II, 300–301, III, 21, IV, 237, V, 337; also see Stephen D. White, *Sir Edward Coke and "The Grievances of the Commonwealth," 1621–1628* (Chapel Hill, N.C., 1979), 55.

27. See Appendix A, below. Also see Norma Landau, *The Justices of the Peace, 1679–1760* (Berkeley, Calif., 1984). Although Landau's book covers English justices, the scenario is helpful.

ential in America. In William Lambarde's popular *Eirenarcha; or, Of the Office of Justices of Peace* (1581), "Women, infants under foureteene yeres of age, Aliens, and such as bee within orders of the Ministerie or Cleargie, cannot be empanelled amongst others." *Tryals per Pais; or, The Law of England concerning Juries by Nisi Prius* exempted "Clerks, Tenants in ancient Demesne, Ministers of the Forest (out of the Forest), Coroners, Infants under the age of fourteen years, Officers of the Sheriff, [and] sick decrepit Men." Michael Dalton's *Officium Vicecomitum: The Office and Authoritie of Sherifs* also explicitly excluded any "enfant under fourteene yeares of age." The latter two books were popular in the colonies, and many copies have been found in colonial law libraries.[28]

In 1736, George Webb, a justice of the peace for New Kent County, Virginia, wrote and published Virginia's first local guide, in which he mixed Virginia statutes with English common law. He specified the same guidelines, with the addition of Virginia's own property requirements. The chief reasons for excluding persons from jury service were insufficient wealth or age. Webb's *Office and Authority of a Justice of Peace* did not incorporate the 1695 English requirement for sheriffs to make lists of those from twenty-one to seventy. The *only* age requirement it gave was that "infants under fourteen years, may not be jurors in any case whatsoever." The property requirement for Virginia jurors was relatively high, however: one hundred pounds for jurors on superior courts and fifty pounds for jurors on county courts.[29]

During the eighteenth century, Pennsylvania guides to the justices of the peace retained the older customary age restriction of fourteen alongside the new requirement for sheriffs. Reprinted three times between 1722 and 1750, *Conductor Generalis; or, The Office, Duty, and Authority of Justices of the Peace* listed the same guidelines in all three editions: that "Infants under 14 years of

28. Lambarde, *Eirenarcha*, 304–305; [Giles Duncombe], *Tryals per Pais; or, The Law of England concerning Juries by Nisi Prius . . . ,* 4th ed. (London, 1702), 75; Dalton, *Officium Vicecomitum: The Office and Authoritie of Sherifs,* 121. For the popularity of these books, see Herbert A. Johnson, *Imported Eighteenth-Century Law Treatises in American Libraries, 1700–1799* (Knoxville, Tenn., 1978), 17, 19; and Appendix A, below.

29. George Webb, *The Office and Authority of a Justice of Peace, and Also the Duty of Sheriffs, Coroners, Churchwardens, Surveiors of Highways, Constables, and Officers of Militia . . .* (Williamsburg, Va., 1736), 196. His guide lists both the exemption from jury service of those under fourteen (along with convicts, apothecaries, clergy, and others) and the Virginia property requirements, so he clearly attempts to integrate common law with Virginia statutes. The initial Virginia laws on jurors (1645) directed that they should be "the most able men of the county." In 1699 the high property requirements were added. Hening, ed., *Statutes at Large,* I, 303, III, 175–176, reiterated IV, 404 (1734), V, 524–525 (1748).

age are excepted from serving on jurie" but that constables were to submit lists during *"Michaelmas* Sessions" of "all persons qualified to serve on Juries between the Age of 21 and 70 Years." Pennsylvania laws themselves said nothing of age, but directed that jurors should be "freemen," defined as all those who owned land and all who paid "scot and lot" (taxes).[30]

Early Massachusetts laws had much the same jural limitations as Pennsylvania: they initially restricted jury service to freemen. (Since Massachusetts had no guides for justices of the peace, those clues to practice are missing.) In 1670 Massachusetts added an age requirement of twenty-four for jury service for those who lived in towns, along with a high property requirement, of eighty pounds. This reform echoed the Interregnum attempt in England in 1653 to raise the age to twenty-five, about which the Massachusetts legislators would probably have known. Apparently because of adverse reaction, the legislature overturned this law in 1680/1. When Massachusetts introduced a new, lower property requirement for jurors in 1692 of forty shillings per annum or personal estate worth fifty pounds, the new law contained no age requirement.[31] Thus the one attempt to place high age restrictions, after its

30. *Conductor Generalis; or, The Office, Duty, and Authority of Justices of the Peace* . . . (Philadelphia, 1722), 58, 141–143 (reprinted 1749, 1750). For the listing requirement, this guide cites the appropriate English statute exactly. The dictum that those under fourteen cannot serve on juries appears in a longer list of those who cannot serve. "All Aliens, Apothecaries, Physitians, Clergy-Men, persons Indicted and attainted for any Crime, Conspirators, non Compos mentis, Infants under 14 years of Age, are excepted from serving on Jurie, by 6 and 7 *William* 3, 1 *Anne.*" Oddly, the statutes to which this refers except only apothecaries (because they are so sorely missed if they are not performing their job). It seems clear that the other exclusions must be customary.

On freemen: George, Nead, and McCamant, comps., *Charter to William Penn, and the Laws of the Province of Pennsylvania,* 99, 117, 129. The definition of freemen is from the "Laws agreed upon in England." The definition of who should be on a jury was among the first laws passed in Pennsylvania in 1682.

31. No guides for any local officers were published until the 1768 appearance of *The County and Town Officer; or, An Abridgment of the Laws of the Province of the Massachusetts-Bay, relative to County and Town Officers* (Boston, 1768), a guide that consisted mostly of Massachusetts laws. Thus, unlike the Virginia and Pennsylvania guides, which contained mostly common law, it provides few clues outside the laws themselves as to legal practice. See William Brigham, ed., *The Compact with the Charter and Laws of the Colony of New Plymouth: Together with the Charter of the Council at Plymouth* . . . (1623) (Boston, 1836), 42; *The General Laws and Liberties of the Massachusetts Colony* (1672), republished in *The Colonial Laws of Massachusetts* (Boston, 1890), 86; *The Acts and Resolves, Public and Private, of the Province of the Massachusetts Bay* (1692), I, 74. The 1670 law also required that jurors have a developed conscience: they were to take an oath of fidelity and be "of honest and good conversation." When this law was overturned by the Mas-

initial rejection, was not retried until after the American Revolution. It is possible that those who met the property qualification (males who married young and were given property by their father or males whose father had died) served on juries regardless of their age.[32]

Just after the Revolutionary war Massachusetts and Virginia limited jury service to those over age twenty-one. There are two potential explanations for the appearance of age restrictions in the decade after the Revolution. First, if these states dropped property requirements, children in general might suddenly be qualified. In fact, property or gender requirements for jury service were not suddenly dropped in any of these states. Massachusetts and Virginia merely added age requirements to the other qualifications: Massachusetts linked jury service to the ability to be an elector, for which one had to be twenty-one years old and own property, in 1784; Virginia kept its high property qualifications and added the age qualification of twenty-one in 1792.[33]

The second explanation, the only one that makes sense, was that principles about who was qualified to be a juror were shifting. The year 1784 marked the first time a minimum age of twenty-one became required for jury service in any of these three colonies/states. Virginia's change in age exclusions from fourteen to twenty-one in 1792 illuminates this shift particularly well. In 1803, St. George Tucker's Virginia version of Blackstone's *Commentaries* emphasized, as earlier guides to justices of the peace had not, that those chosen for jurors should "be men above the suspicion of improper bias, or corruption; men whose understandings may be presumed to be above the common level."[34]

Pennsylvania made two changes in juror qualifications in the years during and after the Revolution that correlate with the changes in Virginia and went

---

sachusetts General Court in 1680/1, it was specified that the "inhabitants of every town . . . may choose any of their Towne for constables, select Men or Jurors, althoe not rated as expressed in the said law." *The Colonial Laws of Massachusetts*, 148, 352.

32. To know how many boys between fourteen and twenty-one would have been freeholders, or had sufficient income to qualify them for jury service (or indeed, had been chosen for juries), one would need to discover the ages (which were not listed) of grand jurors and the petit jurors for individual cases.

33. *The Laws of the Commonwealth of Massachusetts . . . 1780 to . . . 1807* (Boston, 1807), I, 186 (June 26, 1784). In Virginia jurors should be selected from all those "freeholders and inhabitants in their towns, qualified to vote in the election of Representatives." Samuel Shepherd, ed., *The Statutes at Large of Virginia, from October Session 1792, to December Session 1806, Inclusive* (1835; rpt. New York, 1970), I, 19 (October 1792).

34. St. George Tucker, *Blackstone's Commentaries: With Notes of Reference, to the Constitution and Laws, of the Federal Government of the United States; and of the Commonwealth of Virginia* (Philadelphia, 1803), IV, 64–65 ("Of the Trial by Jury in Virginia").

even further in emphasizing that jurors should be impartial and independent. In 1782, Pennsylvania legislators gave a very broad qualification by linking jury service to the payment of taxes, a provision that qualified all those over eighteen who owned property, but they emphasized that jurors should be "sober and judicious persons." Sheriffs had to swear that they would use their "utmost diligence to prevent any man from being summoned or returned . . . for a juror who . . . will be influenced . . . by hatred, malice, or ill-will, fear, favor or affection or by any partiality whatever." An 1805 law directed that jurors should be "sober and judicious persons" selected from the list of "taxable citizens." Aside from being "sober and judicious," having the status of "taxable citizens" was the initial qualification. Theoretically, women or youths as young as eighteen could have been selected if they met the property requirements for taxation.[35]

Other studies on the role and function of the jury during the seventeenth and eighteenth centuries help to explain the shifting concerns about juror qualification. Jurors ceased to be required to be from the vicinity of the crime at the same time as they began to be required to make judgments on *only* what they heard in the court. During the Middle Ages and through the sixteenth century, legal guides held not only that jurors could be witnesses to a particular crime but that jurors could reach verdicts on the basis of information obtained outside the courtroom, such as their personal knowledge of the accused and secondhand information they might have heard. Even if all jurors did not actually have knowledge of the crime, what matters here is the conception of the jury's role and its instructions. Dalton's influential *Officium Vicecomitum* of 1623 specified that only those who are "next neighbors, and which have best knowledge of the truth" should be empaneled on juries. This description of jurors was very different from that used almost two centuries later, which stressed jurors' rational objectivity.[36] Only in the mid-eighteenth century did legal guides direct juries to base their judgments solely on the evidence presented to them in court and begin to eliminate the requirement that jurors come from the vicinity of the crime. These changes show a movement away from the kind of character witness that would be given by a neighbor and toward evaluations based on analytic reasoning or proofs. Legal

35. Mitchell and Flanders, comps., *The Statutes at Large of Pennsylvania*, XI, 487 (1782), XVII, 1011 (1805).

36. Dalton, *Officium Vicecomitum: The Office and Authoritie of Sherifs*, 120b; Mitnick, "Transformation of the English Civil Juror," *American Journal of Legal History*, XXXII (1988), 201–235. In an earlier study, John H. Langbein suggested that, by the sixteenth century, jurors did not have outside knowledge of the crimes they tried, but he offers inconclusive evidence ("The Origins of Public Prosecution at Common Law," *American Journal of Legal History*, XVII [1973], 314–315).

guides began to require that jurors come from other localities than where the crime was committed—a reversal of former rules. Instead of acting as character witnesses, they were required to base their verdicts only on facts they learned during the trial. Such requirements reflect the new concern with abstract reason instead of personal encounters in forming verdicts.

The new expectations of jurors grew out of the Enlightenment emphasis on abstract reason and rule-based analysis in the reaching of verdicts. The now commonplace instruction to juries, that they adjudge guilt beyond a "reasonable doubt" or "moral certainty," appeared only in the late seventeenth century. These instructions conform to the reigning epistemological formulations of the late seventeenth and early eighteenth centuries. These formulations originated in Protestant moral thought and in political thought. There is a close correlation between the language of instructions to juries and conceptual phrases used by John Locke, Samuel von Pufendorf, Jeremy Taylor, David Hartley, Isaac Watts, and Thomas Reid, among others. Before the seventeenth century there were no formal instructions to juries. But, beginning in the late seventeenth century, jurors in some cases were encouraged to have a "satisfied conscience," and Whig political writers from Henry Care to Sir John Hawkes encouraged juries to use their "understanding and reasoning." By the late eighteenth century, the phrase "reasonable doubt" had become common in instructions to juries, a term based on the equation of juries with "reasonable men." Likewise, "laws of evidence" began to be rigorously formulated in the early eighteenth century. The appearance of "laws of evidence," which describe what kinds of evidence are acceptable in a trial, including what kinds of testimony and the qualifications for witnesses, shows a profound interest in what constitutes proof and how human reason should operate.[37]

The very creation of a supreme court in America after the Revolution, with authority over all verdicts reached by juries in lower courts, indicates the new weight placed on public, abstract reason. The supreme court ensured a space of "public reason"; it was a high court that was above democracy. Both the transfer from a jury (or legislature) to a supreme court as a final deliberative body, on the grounds that it had a greater ability to exercise reason, and age requirements of twenty-one for juries restrained democracy. Arguments of using only the most "reasonable" people could be and were used to exclude people from civil participation. While both were justified as restraints on the

37. See Barbara J. Shapiro, "To a Moral Certainty: Theories of Knowledge and Anglo-American Juries, 1600–1850," *Hastings Law Journal*, XXXVIII (1986), 153–193, esp. 162, 165, 175. Also see Shapiro, *"Beyond Reasonable Doubt" and "Probable Cause": Historical Perspectives on the Anglo-American Law of Evidence* (Berkeley, Calif., 1991).

less rational—restraints that created a more stable system with less room for influence and corruption—much depended on how they defined corruption, influence, and, indeed, reason. They assumed that the "reason" of judges was above their political interests and ideologies and thus could move beyond the reach of corruption and influence. In sacrificing the democracy of the many for the greater reason of the few, they were creating a system that rested significantly on these judges' integrity.[38]

Instructions to English and American juries changed during the seventeenth and eighteenth centuries to emphasize the importance of abstract reasoning, which was held to be impossible for children to attain. This shift in the expected role of jurors went hand in hand with an increase in the minimum age for jury service from fourteen to twenty-one. Parliament made the first change in 1694 just after the Glorious Revolution (although it seems to have been somewhat weakly enforced). Age restrictions of twenty-one on juries were not incorporated fully in America until after the Revolution. Certainly they were not explicit even in Massachusetts, the only place they might have applied, until after the Revolution. The age at which a person had to take loyalty oaths increased from twelve to various ages between sixteen and twenty-one, and citizenship itself became a privilege confined to adults. Minimum ages for military obligations increased from age seven in sixteenth-century England to sixteen in early Massachusetts and Pennsylvania (with no minimum age in seventeenth-century Virginia) to eighteen in the wake of the Revolution. Even during the eighteenth century, the lower age limit increased from sixteen to eighteen in all three colonies/states.

Legislators, legal treatise writers, and judges did not make these changes in a vacuum, without justification. The authors of various legal tracts and notes from political debates reveal the logic behind them. They are linked to broad epistemological changes critical to early modern political theory, changes that placed much more weight on the role of reason in decision making and that specifically described children as irrational.

Age became a key demarcator of legal equality. Why age requirements and not literacy tests such as those suggested by Benjamin Rush, for example, were used to measure an individual's reason and understanding might be explained by expediency. Perhaps its appeal lay in part in its assignation of a specific number and thus an appearance of scientific certainty to the develop-

38. Shannon C. Stimson, *The American Revolution in the Law: Anglo-American Jurisprudence before John Marshall* (Princeton, N.J., 1990), 9, 147–148.

ment of the understanding. Regardless, age became the main measure of the ability to reason and cast judgment.[39]

Age thus began to assume a central role in determining the exercise of public obligations and rights, replacing, as it did so, ideas both of perpetual obligation by birth and of rights associated with property ownership. Legislators and jurists proposed these changes in response to a shift in arguments about political legitimacy, a shift that began in England and North America with religious radicals. To identify these relocations of political authority is to understand how the movement from feudalism to a modern political order introduced different patterns of exclusion. Most of all it is to understand how choice began to challenge birthright, whether to obligation or to privilege. To some degree all these changes directly challenged the idea of inherited obligation and inherited right: the obligation of citizenship itself should come from choice, not from birth. Yet even for responsibilities such as military service, consent was supposed to be conditional upon the attainment of reason.

39. Patricia Cline Cohen links the increasing use of quantification to the scientific revolution, commerce, and "certain ideas associated with the fostering of democracy, especially the notion that rationality in the greatest possible number of people was desirable." She shows the many ways in which numbers began to be used in eighteenth-century America, but notes, "No one was yet suggesting quantitative measures of intelligence; that was left for an elite intelligentsia of a later age" (*A Calculating People: The Spread of Numeracy in Early America* [Chicago, 1982], 45, 149). While no scientific measurements of brain size were conducted until the mid-nineteenth century, and no I.Q. tests were conducted until the early twentieth century, age *is* a quantitative measure of intelligence. See above, Chapter 3, n. 65, on Benjamin Rush.

CHAPTER 5
"TO STOP THE MOUTHS" OF CHILDREN
REASON AND THE COMMON LAW

*"Whereupon the childe was brought before the Bench, and stoode
upon the Table betweene the Bench and the Jury. Where after
that the foresaid [judge] had opened some part of this foule
offence, the childe was asked diverse of the former questions: to
which she answered as before."*
The Horrible Murther of a Young Boy of Three Yeres of Age
(London, 1606)

*"In Cases of foul Facts done in secret, where the Child is the Party
injured, the repelling their Evidence entirely is, in some Measure,
denying them the Protection of the Law."*
Francis Buller, An Introduction to the Law relative to
Trials at Nisi Prius *(London, 1772)*

In 1784, twelve-year-old Susannah Brown was not allowed to testify against
the man who raped her, because the Virginia judges thought her too young.
These same judges, however, deemed her old enough to consent to marry the
same man. Why such inconsistency? The answer is embedded in the tension
within the common law between custom (or precedent) and reason (or abstract ideas about justice). Norms about what was reasonable or just, with
respect to age limits for both marriage and witness testimony, would undergo
a fundamental transition during the seventeenth and eighteenth centuries.
This transition followed a winding and sometimes contradictory course, but
one that explains the process and logic of change within the common law. It
also reveals how the common law could be contested on questions of principle. In short, the common law was changing in England and America in
response to some of the same forces and ideologies that led to the American
Revolution. Such seemingly private rules defining the status and abilities of
children related intimately to the very public ideology of revolution. How old
did one have to be, or what attributes did one have to have, to have a legal
voice? Susannah Brown was caught in the middle of these changes.

The case of Susannah Brown reveals how limiting a person's ability to
testify created situations where, despite corroborating evidence, judges might

find an assaulter not guilty. In a three-page letter, her father begged the Virginia legislature in 1784 to punish her rapist, to dissolve her forced marriage, and to prevent similar situations in the future by fixing the loopholes that had permitted it to occur. Technically, Peter Hopwood, Susannah's assaulter and new "pretended husband," had violated the law. Yet the justices refused to let the twelve-year-old girl testify, and without her testimony there was insufficient evidence to convict him.

Susannah was eleven years old when her father and some neighbors hired a "stranger . . . but wearing the semblance of great piety" as a schoolmaster to teach their children. "Soon after she went to school, Hopwood treated her with severity, gave [her] difficult tasks and confined her to the house while the other scholars went to play, under pretense that she had not done her tasks." For a variety of reasons, her father wrote, "long before the year [for which Hopwood had been hired] expired, [he] became dissatisfied with him," but Hopwood refused to resign his one-year contract. In June 1783, while still her schoolmaster and only days after Susannah had turned twelve (and could legally consent to marriage), Hopwood raped her while her parents were away. "After having perpetrated the crime he informed her if it ever came to the knowledge of her parents they would treat her with cruelty and contempt, and make her a waiting maid to her sister and if she did not marry him he would publish her to the world as a prostitute that would be despised by everybody and that the Deavil would get her when she died." Six months later, when Susannah was still only twelve, Hopwood finally persuaded her, under threats that he would "publish her to the world as a prostitute," to go with him to be married. The fact that Hopwood committed the rape and initiated the pressure to marry just days after Susannah turned twelve suggests that he was familiar with the law. Since Hopwood was poor and Susannah would inherit money and land from her father, it was a profitable arrangement for him.

When Brown discovered the marriage, he questioned his daughter closely, and she told him her side of the story. Brown immediately had Hopwood imprisoned for rape. The evidence for the rape consisted of Susannah's story, the fact that the key to Susannah's room was missing for some days before her parents left to go away and was later "accidentally" discovered in Hopwood's possession, that Hopwood had forced Susannah to return from her cousins, where her parents had sent her to sleep while they were gone,

> that she returned with tears in her eyes, that he prevented another of her
> female cousins from coming to sleep with her, that he ordered the servant
> woman who usually slept in her room with her to sleep in another room.
> That she was seen in the morning bathed in tears and refused to give an

account of her distress. That she uniformly spoke of him with the utmost detestation. That she had been heard to exclaim "No creature knows what the villain has done to me. He has done enough to make me hate him forever." . . . It was further proved that Hopwood had said he had lain with her.

Despite this evidence, however, "a majority of the magistrates [of the Frederick County court] were of the opinion, that the said Susannah ought not to be examined as a witness. Consequently he was acquitted of the rape there being no positive proof."[1]

Only three witnesses can be positively identified from the official court records, and they include Peter Hopwood (the defendant), David Brown (Susannah's father), and Michael Ireton (a "material witness" for Hopwood). Although the judges acquitted Hopwood of the rape, they referred Hopwood to a grand jury, which was to investigate whether he should be indicted under "4 and 5 Ph. and Mary [the 1558 abduction statute] for carrying away the said Susannah from her father without consent." Three months later, the grand jury decided not to indict Hopwood, a puzzling verdict since Hopwood was unequivocally guilty of abduction, having married a twelve-year-old heiress without her father's consent. Perhaps the grand jury was unwilling that he risk the punishment, which was either five years imprisonment or death. It might have thought the punishment out of proportion to the crime, especially since the justices had invoked the English statute of 1558 rather than their own, milder 1696 statute on clandestine marriages, which specified only that the wife would forfeit her inheritance during her coverture (thus depriving the husband of access to her property).[2] The very existence of the different Virginia law hints that the Virginians had not, in 1696, been following the English law terribly closely. Yet the judges' invocation of the English law in 1784 shows that they valued the English law more highly than the century-old Virginia statute. Their choice suggests a continuing reverence for English law in the new American states even after the Revolution.[3]

1. Frederick County, Virginia (FCV), Legislative Petitions, May 29, 1784.
2. FCV Order Books (OB) and Minute Books (MB) (1782–1786), 200–203 (Feb. 5–7, 1784), 244 (May 5, 1784); William Waller Hening, ed., *The Statutes at Large: Being a Collection of All the Laws of Virginia* . . . (rpt. Charlottesville, Va., 1969), III, 150–151 (1696); George Webb, *Office and Authority of a Justice of Peace* . . . (Williamsburg, Va., 1736), cites three laws: 4 and 5 P. and M., c. 8; 39 Eliz. I, c. 9; and the 1696 Virginia law; see 262–263, 219, respectively.
3. They might also have thought the Virginia law merely unnecessary, since Susannah's father presumably had control over his property and could disinherit his daughter

The grand jury's failure to indict Brown on either the abduction or the rape was undoubtedly connected to the judges' decision not to let Susannah testify, a decision that also built on English precedent, albeit more recent. There were two possibilities for why the "majority of magistrates" thought that Susannah "ought not to be examined as a witness": first, a wife under some circumstances could not testify against her husband; second, Susannah was too young. But none of the legal guides, either Virginia or English, barred a wife from testifying against her husband in this situation. George Webb's *Office and Authority of a Justice of Peace,* published in Virginia in 1736, a standard reference for these judges, claimed that, although in general a wife could not give testimony against her husband, "yet a wife who is an heiress, taken away, and by Threats, prevailed upon to marry the Man, shall be good Evidence against him; and if convicted upon her evidence, he shall be hang'd." Such was exactly Susannah's situation. Webb referred explicitly to the statute of 1558 whereby it was illegal to take away any heiress under sixteen without her own and her father's consent. Yet, on the question of age, Webb implied that those under fourteen were not able to testify. "Any person above the age of fourteen years, and not disabled by law, may be a witness."[4]

Blackstone, whose *Commentaries on the Laws of England* was widely read in America after 1770, generally agreed, although he was more sympathetic to hearing the testimony of those under age fourteen. Like Webb, he emphasized that any limits on a woman's testifying against her husband should be ignored in cases where the husband harmed his wife, especially where he forced her into marriage.

> But where the offence is directly against the person of the wife, this rule has been usually dispensed with . . . in case a woman be forcibly taken away, and married, she may be a witness against such her husband, in order to convict him of felony. For in this case she can with no propriety be reckoned his wife; because a main ingredient, her consent, was wanting to the contract: and also there is another maxim of law, that *no man shall take advantage of his own wrong;* which the ravisher here would do, if by forcibly marrying a woman, he could prevent her from being a witness, who is perhaps the only witness, to that very fact.[5]

---

under the same terms if he chose. The statute was probably necessary only when the property was entailed or the girl was the next beneficiary by a will already implemented or when the daughter had already inherited.

4. Webb, *Justice of Peace,* 136, 262.

5. William Blackstone, *Commentaries on the Laws of England* (London, 1765–1769), I, 431 (emphasis added).

In a later volume Blackstone expanded on this point, stating that it is "absurd, that the offender should thus take advantage of his own wrong, and that the very act of marriage, which is a principal ingredient of his crime, should (by a forced construction of law) be made use of to stop the mouth of the most material witness against him." It was volume IV, with its forceful language, that the Virginia judges probably used. Both Blackstone and Webb thus agreed that wives should be able to testify against husbands when coerced into marriage, especially with a rape involved.[6]

Blackstone held that all witnesses who "have the use of their reason" should be permitted to testify and that the jury should "have an opportunity of observing the quality, age, education, understanding, behaviour, and inclinations of the witness" in determining their credibility. He made a partial exception to his guidelines about the reason of witnesses for rape cases, which he coupled with a caution against believing young children.

> Infants of any age are to be heard; and, if they have any idea of an oath, to be also sworn: it being found by experience that infants of very tender years often give the clearest and truest testimony. But . . . whether the child be sworn or not, it is to be wished, in order to render her evidence credible, that there should be some concurrent testimony, of time, place and circumstances, in order to make out the fact; and that the conviction should not be grounded singly on the unsupported accusation of an infant under years of discretion [under fourteen].[7]

Blackstone's doubts would still have permitted twelve-year-old Susannah to testify. Therefore, Webb's general objection to the testimony of those under age fourteen, as the only general objection that fitted her situation, makes it the most likely explanation for the judges' exclusion of Susannah's voice. Webb's treatise probably provided their primary legal resource, since it was published in Virginia and Webb had been a Virginia justice of the peace.

But why the disagreement between Webb and Blackstone? Regardless of the judges' precise motives, this case, with the disagreement among legal commentators, provides an example of a broad phenomenon. By the late eighteenth century, there were significant loopholes in laws for the protection of children: there was some doubt whether they could testify, and, even when they could, their word was not to be measured against an adult's with-

---

6. Ibid., IV, 209. The edition of Blackstone's *Commentaries* published in Philadelphia in 1771–1772 was a reprint of the first London edition (1765–1769). It listed eight subscribers from Frederick County.

7. Ibid., III, 370, 374, IV, 214.

out, as even Blackstone urged, "concurrent testimony." These doubts and exceptions increased dramatically from the seventeenth to the nineteenth century, spreading from England to its colonies in North America. Beginning with Sir Matthew Hale in the late seventeenth century, legal scholars argued that those without "discretion" should be neither believed nor even heard. To fully understand the influence of these arguments, we must first look at the testimony itself.

Case Evidence of Children's Testimony

Children's ability to testify was fundamental to how well the justice system could protect them. But did they testify in the earlier period? Court records of the seventeenth and, to a great degree, the eighteenth century are usually silent about age. To determine whether children testified and the age of witnesses, I focused on the small body of cases where age was explicitly an issue. Throughout the early modern period, children technically had access to the same protections from assault as other persons (except that parents and masters were permitted to "chastise" them). The one violent crime for which children received special protection was rape: girls under the age of ten were presumed unable to consent to sexual intercourse, and men proven to have had sex with them could be found guilty of what we now call statutory rape. While the common law defined rape as sexual intercourse with a woman without her consent, only a statute (18 Eliz. I, c. 7, of 1575) defined intercourse as rape even when the girl consented. The very definition of this crime shows that the members of Parliament and Elizabeth I presumed that girls of nine and younger could not "consent" to sex. Since young girls were singled out, the cases of statutory rape provide an avenue to explore changing attitudes toward child witnesses. Other cases where a child testified or was purposely excluded are illuminating as well.

During the early seventeenth century, young children in both England and America often testified, apparently without even the doubts of their veracity later offered by Blackstone. A published English case from 1606, for example, reveals that two people were convicted of murder on the basis of testimony by an eight-year-old about events she had witnessed when she was four. *The Horrible Murther of a Young Boy of Three Yeres of Age, Whose Sister Had Her Tongue Cut Out* describes the prosecution of Annis Dell, an innkeeper, and her son for murder. The evidence included the testimony of a tailor, who saw a girl and boy led into a tavern, the body of the boy, and the testimony of the girl. According to her testimony, in 1602 the Dells killed her brother, cut out her tongue so she could not describe what they had done, and left her in a forest many miles away. She wandered and begged for four years until she happened again upon the tavern, where she began babbling and attracted a crowd. Seemingly miraculously, she could talk (the Dells must have left part of her tongue). Authorities were summoned, and a trial ensued.

> Whereupon the childe was brought before the Bench, and stoode upon the Table betweene the Bench and the Jury. Where after that the foresaid knight [judge] had opened some part of this foule offence, the childe was asked diverse of the former questions: to which she answered as before. The taylor likewise was there, who tolde unto the Jurie what he had seene. Then the Jurie was willed to goe togither. . . . The Jurie staid not long before they returned with their verdite guiltie.[8]

Judges and jury accepted the memories of an eight-year-old about an event that had happened when she was four. Without her testimony Annis Dell and her son would not have been convicted and hanged.

Other cases from both England and America support that young children appeared as witnesses. While ages are infrequently specified in the court records, their scarcity is itself a clue to their relative unimportance.[9] A deposition in 1643 from Accomack County, Virginia, for example, includes unproblematically the testimony of a "boy" named William Allinson. He was "sworne and examined in open Court" about whether Goodwife Trevellor murdered her apprentice girl, Elizabeth Bibby. Some evidence in the trials of witches from Salem in 1692 came from girls, such as Abigail Williams (age eleven). Part of the testimony from these girls was given indirectly through parents or other adults, providing what modern lawyers would call "hearsay" evidence. Children's testimony was not restricted to witchcraft. Six-year-old Henry Simpson gave the crucial evidence against his mother's rapist in Massachusetts in 1650. A study of rape cases in seventeenth-century court records of Massachusetts found twelve depositions by girls under the age of twelve, the majority of them under ten. In another case, in 1680, Mehitabel Avis, a girl who we know was "under ten years old" because William Nelson was indicted for that crime, testified to the sexual assault. Her testimony,

8. *The Horrible Murther of a Young Boy of Three Yeres of Age, Whose Sister Had Her Tongue Cut out* . . . (London, 1606).

9. Some regions seemed to be more concerned about the ages of witnesses. One such was Essex County, Massachusetts, in whose courtroom young Mehitabel Davis testified (see below). The court records of Norwich, England, which John H. Langbein has examined, show a similar concern during the early seventeenth century (*Prosecuting Crime in the Renaissance: England, Germany, France* [Cambridge, Mass., 1974], 85–90).

coupled with his confession and the testimony of a third person, was the basis for a guilty verdict.[10]

The first moves toward excluding the testimony of children came from England and then slowly and intermittently affected American decisions. Some judges in England during the late seventeenth century began to question whether children should be heard. The initital focus was on whether those testifying understood the nature of an oath. Cases where a judge questioned whether a particular child could be a witness and then admitted the testimony involved witnesses aged seventeen (1679), fifteen (1680), thirteen (1684), "under twelve" (1710), and under ten (1698).[11] About 1700, the highest courts began to disqualify some children. In a trial at the Old Bailey in 1704 (of a man who had allegedly committed rapes upon two young girls) the testimony of a ten-year-old girl was admitted while the testimony of a six-year-old was not. The sole authority cited in this case was Hale's *Pleas of the Crown* (1678). In 1726, a seven-year-old was prevented from testifying in what became an often cited precedent. Her case had first been heard when she was six but had been dismissed because "Lord Chief Baron Gilbert refused to admit the child as evidence against [the defendant]." After she turned seven, the case was tried again, and her ability to be a witness was debated at length.

10. Susie M. Ames, ed., *County Court Records of Accomack-Northampton, Virginia, 1640–1645* (Charlottesville, Va., 1973), 271. It is possible that Allinson was called a "boy" because he was a servant *(Oxford English Dictionary)*. The usage in this instance is somewhat ambiguous, since Goodwife Trevellor "bidd the boy carry the child into the Creeke."

On Salem, see Paul Boyer and Stephen Nissenbaum, *Salem Possessed: The Social Origins of Witchcraft* (Cambridge, Mass., 1974), 2–3, 6, 210–211.

On rape cases, see Catharine S. Baker, "Rape in Seventeenth Century Massachusetts," paper delivered at the Third Berkshire Conference on the History of Women, Bryn Mawr, Pa., 1976, 6.

On Avis, see George Francis Dow, ed., *Records and Files of the Quarterly Courts of Essex County, Massachusetts* (Salem, Mass., 1911–1921), VIII (1680–1682), 15. Mary Beth Norton remarked on several cases where children were witnesses in *Founding Mothers and Fathers: Gendered Power and the Forming of American Society* (New York, 1996), including the six-year-old boy (353–354).

11. T. B. Howell, ed., *Cobbett's Complete Collection of State Trials, and Proceedings for High Treason and Other Crimes and Misdemeanors from the Earliest Period to the Present Time* (London, 1809–1828) (State Trials): *Rex v Atkins* (1679), VII, 231–250; *Rex v Giles* (1680), VII, 1130–1160; *Rex v Braddon and Speke* (1684), IX, 1127–1331. *The English Reports* (Edinburgh, London, 1900–1932) (Eng. Rep.): *Young v Slaughterford*, 88 Eng. Rep. 1007 (11 Mod. 229) (1710). The 1698 Old Bailey case was not formally reported, but was cited by later decisions.

The judges concluded, "A child of six or seven years of age, in point of reason and understanding, ought to be considered as a lunatick or a madman."[12]

In 1759, a judge admitted the testimony of a ten-year-old girl after considerable debate, and her rapist was executed. Her testimony was supported by the fact that both she and her mother's seventeen-year-old apprentice, her rapist, had gonorrhea. The report of this case is more descriptive than most, containing the judge's questions and the girl's responses. Before admitting her testimony, he made clear that she "understood the nature of an oath."

> *Judge:* You are going to swear upon the bible; do you know what is the consequence of taking an oath if you speak falsely?
> *Child:* I shall go to the naughty man?
> *Judge:* What do you mean by going to the naughty man?
> *Child:* Going to the devil.
> *Judge:* Suppose you should speak the truth?
> *Child:* I shall go to God Almighty.[13]

Based on this example, one innovative judge in England in 1795 postponed a trial until the next court session while the young victim was "instructed in the mean time by a clergyman in the principles of her duty, and the nature and obligation of an oath." By the time her case was heard, she knew how to answer questions about an oath, her testimony was accepted, and her attacker convicted and then executed.[14]

In 1757, a Pennsylvania case of "assault with intent to ravish" listed ten-year-old Mary Good as a witness, apparently without controversy. The court did not seem to consider her age important, since it appeared only in the loose papers and not in the dockets, or basic minutes, of the cases that came before the court. In Chester County, Pennsylvania, the records of 1750–1820 rarely listed age, at least with respect to rape and other felony cases. Pennsylvanians thus did not alter their rules about children's testimony until very late—a pattern that will become understandable below.[15]

12. *Rex v Travers,* 93 Eng. Rep. 793–794 (2 Strange 700–701) (1726).

13. J. M. Beattie, *Crime and the Courts in England, 1660–1800* (Oxford, 1986), 129 n. 121.

14. The citation to this case is rather strange. It was never itself reported and is discussed only in a footnote to *Rex v White,* 168 Eng. Rep. 317 (1 Leach 430) (1786). Although no case name was given there, it was heard in the Gloucester Assizes by Justice Rooke, about 1795, and cited by, among others, J[oseph] Chitty, *A Practical Treatise on the Criminal Law* . . . (London, 1816); and Matthew Bacon, *A New Abridgment of the Law,* 1st American ed., 6th London ed. (Philadelphia, 1813), II, 577. Later cases in turn cited these compilations.

15. See Chester County, Pennsylvania (CCP) Quarter Sessions Dockets (QSD), May

In New England, by 1790, even people who did not use the courts regularly were increasingly aware that children's testimony in criminal cases might be unacceptable. In New Hampshire in that year, for example, Abigail Bailey wrote in her diary that she could not initiate a prosecution of incest against her husband (who had violently raped their teenage daughter in front of the younger children), because the daughter in question was too frightened to testify (she was then sixteen) and the eldest of the children who had witnessed the scene was "too young to be a legal witness," although "old enough to tell the truth."[16] The fact that Abigail Bailey was conscious of the rules about legal witnesses shows how new attitudes toward children's testimony could permeate popular understandings of legal relationships, defining what came before the court even before judges decided whether an individual child could testify.

By the early nineteenth century, most criminal court decisions in America set fourteen as the minimum age for witness testimony in criminal cases. Depositions taken for murder inquests in Virginia, for example, specified that the witness was of "full age," that is, over twenty-one. Six-year-old Nancy Geer was not allowed to testify in an 1820 rape trial in Virginia. The judges of the General Court did not even consider her inability to be a witness disputable; they relied on English precedents, referring to such manuals as Joseph Chitty's *Practical Treatise on the Criminal Law*.[17] Judges retained the ability to make exceptions at their discretion if the child could prove extraordinary understanding or grasped the nature of an oath. In 1806, a Tennessee judge barred a ten-year-old boy from testifying about the murder of his father because "upon examination, it appeared that he had not any sense of the obligation of an oath, nor of any of the consequences of swearing falsely." One of the key issues in allowing the testimony of younger children was

---

1757, 287, and the loose papers, filed chronologically by year and then alphabetically by defendant (in this case, Denning); *Conductor Generalis; or, The Office, Duty, and Authority of Justices of the Peace* . . . (Philadelphia, 1722), 79 (reprinted in 1749 and 1750).

16. Ann Taves, ed., *Religion and Domestic Violence in Early New England: The Memoirs of Abigail Abbot Bailey* (Bloomington, Ind., 1989), 87. Although Abigail Bailey does not describe the rape of her daughter in detail, she had long been convinced of incest but unable to prove it legally.

17. For example, see the case against "Negro Flora," 1808, FCV, "Inquests on Dead Bodies" file. All three witnesses, at the beginning of their depositions, are specified as "of full age."

On Nancy Geer: *Commonwealth v John Bennet*, 235–240, in William Brockenbrough, comp., *Virginia Cases; or, Decisions of the General Court of Virginia . . . 1815 [to] . . . 1826* (Richmond, Va., 1826), vol. II of *A Collection of Cases Decided by the General Court of Virginia* (4 Va. Cases).

similar to the question above: whether the child "understood the nature of an oath." In an 1810 New Jersey case, a boy was actually over fourteen years old but appeared to the judge to be younger. The Superior Court upheld the judge's decision to exclude him, even though the boy provided proof of his age. It ruled that "his capacity as a witness was a proper subject of discretion in the justice." The justices reinforced this decision two years later when they upheld a decision to exclude the testimony of a thirteen-year-old boy because the judge questioned the boy's "capacity and understanding."[18]

Some state superior courts held that juries, not judges, should make the final decision but that judges should instruct the juries to carefully consider the qualifications of the witness. In an 1813 Massachusetts case, an eight-year-old was allowed to testify after "the court put sundry questions to him, in order to ascertain the measure of his understanding and moral sense, to most of which he gave rational and pertinent answers." However, while allowing the jury to judge the boy's credibility, the judge cautioned the jury, "The credit of the witness, which is greatly impaired by his age, is to be judged of by the jury from the manner of his testifying, and other circumstances." The judge's decision to permit such testimony drew on many English authorities, including several of the cases discussed above. In general, however, by the mid-nineteenth century, fourteen years of age for witnesses would become the "prima facie" or "good and sufficient" rule to which some judges allowed occasional exceptions.[19]

These rules of evidence, however, seemed to be changing fastest with regard to felonies. Older norms that permitted children to testify in civil cases had not changed in Virginia, for example, even by 1820. Ann Weaks, at the same age of twelve as Susannah Brown, was able to testify against her master for ill-treatment only a year later in the same Virginia courtroom, most probably because apprenticeship abuse cases were not technically criminal.[20] Thomas Hargis complained about mistreatment at age ten in 1754, as

18. *Van Pelt v Van Pelt*, 3 N.J.L. 236 (1810). For later cases on children and oaths, see *State v Morea*, 2 Ala. 275 (1841); *Flanagin v State*, 25 Ark. 92 (1867); *Warner v State*, 25 Ark. 447 (1867); *Johnson v State*, 61 Ga. 35 (1878); *Moore v State*, 79 Ga. 498, 5 S.E. 51 (1887); *State v Mary Doherty*, 1 Tenn. (2 Overt.) 475 (1806); *Anonymous*, 3 N.J.L. 487. Sometimes those under age fourteen were allowed to testify, to their detriment. Twelve-year-old James Guild was convicted of murder—based on his own confession—and hanged in New Jersey in 1828. See *State v James Guild*, 10 N.J.L. 163 (1828).

19. *Commonwealth v Ezra Hutchinson*, 10 Mass. 225 (1813); *The American Digest: A Complete Digest of All Reported American Cases from the Earliest Times to 1896*, Century edition (St. Paul, Minn., 1897–1904), L, 114.

20. FCV MB, 1782–1786, 357 (June 1785) for binding and 372 (August 1785) for

did William Finnichan at age eight in 1757, although his mother initiated the complaint on his behalf. By the 1810s, some apprentices appeared in the courtroom only via a "next friend," as did William Majors, age twenty. Still, William Majors's example was not the rule, even in the 1810s: Jesse Majors complained at age twelve and Kesia Vass (a black girl) at age nine.[21]

Legal and Historical Assumptions

Modern legal scholars have assumed that children have always been excluded from courtrooms. The only two who have treated this issue seriously did so in the context of broad surveys of legal history and evidence law. W. S. Holdsworth's encyclopedic early-twentieth-century history of the common law concluded: "Infants below a certain age were, like insane persons, absolutely incapable because they 'wanted discretion.' It would seem that Coke put this age at fourteen." John Henry Wigmore, on whom Holdsworth drew, portrayed children's ability to testify as increasing during the eighteenth century, arguing that judges moved from a simple age-based equation to one inquiring more closely into each child's competence.[22]

---

complaint. Her complaint was held to be valid, and she was transferred to another master. Age is easily identifiable in these cases because a child's age determined the length of his or her service.

21. FCV OB, Hargis, III, 375 (February 1751), for binding record, which gives his age, and VI, 134 (November 1754), for his complaint. The Finnichan case spans many entries in the order books, but see esp. IV, 378 (February 1753), which records his apprenticeship and age (he was then almost four), and VII, 222 (April 1757), which records the complaint and court action.

Majors: FCV MB III, 252 (February 1811), for binding; III, 299 (June 1811), for initial transfer; and V, 252 (June 1819), for complaint in question. The initial complaint of 1811 was also made on his behalf by an adult. Jesse Majors was bound at age five, III, 252 (February 1811), and complained at age twelve, V, 44, and V, 47 (February and March 1818). Kesia Vass complained at age nine and was transferred over a year later. See III, 353 (January 1812), IV, 196 (October 1815), and IV, 372 (December 1816).

22. W. S. Holdsworth, *A History of English Law*, IX (Boston, 1926), 188; John Henry Wigmore, *A Treatise on the Anglo-American System of Evidence in Trials at Common Law, Including the Statutes and Judicial Decisions of All Jurisdictions of the United States and Canada*, III (Boston, 1923), 867–868.

No historians have really examined the exclusion of children from the courtroom. J. M. Beattie, Barbara J. Shapiro, and William E. Nelson have commented on the issue of children's testimony during this period, but only briefly in the context of broader issues. Beattie, *Crime and the Courts;* Shapiro, *"Beyond Reasonable Doubt" and "Probable Cause": Historical Perspectives on the Anglo-American Law of Evidence* (Berkeley, Calif., 1991), 187–

Wigmore assumed that early-eighteenth-century attitudes typified those of the century before. But they did not. It was only during the late seventeenth century that the rule that children should not testify was introduced—for the first time. The eighteenth century was one of debate over when that line should be drawn. In his study of criminal cases in English courts between 1660 and 1800, J. M. Beattie acknowledged the disparate opinions: "There was clearly some confusion in the eighteenth century about the validity of children's evidence." Wigmore cited only one source that antedated Hale's *Pleas of the Crown* (1678): Coke's *Institutes* (1628). In citing Coke, he was following several earlier jurists who had sought "common law" precedents for the exclusion of children.[23] Although the passage Wigmore cited in Coke's *Institutes* did limit the testimony of those without "discretion," it concerned only who could witness a deed, not who could bear witness in a criminal prosecution. Coke disqualified witnesses to deeds who were "parties interested" on the grounds that they were not reliable guarantors of a land sale, but such interested parties were not prevented from testifying in criminal cases. (A criminal courtroom would be empty if anyone with a stake in the outcome were prevented from testifying.) Coke did address criminal prosecu-

---

189; William E. Nelson, *Americanization of the Common Law: The Impact of Legal Change on Massachusetts Society, 1760–1830* (Cambridge, Mass., 1975).

23. Beattie, *Crime and the Courts,* 128 n. 121; Wigmore, *System of Evidence,* III, 867–868.

The volume Wigmore cited, vol. I of the *Institutes,* discussed the holding and transfer of property. He placed no explicit exclusions on children.

And it appeareth by the antient Authors and Authorities of the Law; that before the Statute of 12. E. 2. ca. 2. Processe should be awarded against the witnesses named in the deed, testes in carta nominatos. . . . But the delay therein was so great, and sometimes (though rarely) by exceptions against those witnesses, which being found true, they were not to be sworne at all . . . (1) as if the witnesses were infamous, for example, if he be attainted of a false verdict, or of a conspiracie at the suite of the King, or convicted of perjury, of a Premunire, or of forgerie . . . , or convict of felony, or by judgement lost his eares, or stood upon the pillorie or tumbrell, or beene stigmaticus branded, or the like. . . . or if the witnesse be an infidell, or if non sane memory, or not of discretion, or a partie interested, or the like.

His use of the term "discretion" does imply that some witnesses could be excluded who did not have discretion and understanding, so presumably children could be excluded by this rule, at least from being witnesses to deeds. Edw[ard] Coke, *The First Part of the Institutes of the Lawes of England . . . ,* 2d ed. (London, 1629), 6. (This volume is sometimes called *Coke upon Littleton* and will be so referred to hereafter.) The first to find this passage from Coke was Thomas Wood, *An Institute of the Laws of England; or, The Laws of England in Their Natural Order, according to Common Use,* 6th ed. (London, 1738), 598.

tions in his third volume, but prescribed no qualifications for witnesses. Since Coke made clear that different rules applied to different types of legal procedure, the extension of Coke's comment from witnesses to deeds to testimony in criminal trials is a stretch at best.[24]

Although Coke's contemporaries and predecessors said little on this question, they allowed children's testimony, even against parents. A range of late-sixteenth-century treatises such as William Stanford's *Les plees del coron* (1567), William Lambarde's *Eirenarcha; or, Of the Office of the Justices of Peace* (1581), and Richard Crompton's *L'office et aucthoritie de justices de peace* (1584) placed no age limits on who could be a witness. Such books were standard references for judges and those accused of crimes, and many editions with similar contents appeared in the sixteenth and seventeenth centuries. Dalton's popular *Countrey Justice* (1618), published a decade before Coke's *Institutes*, gave examples of children testifying: in one case children testified against their mother for witchcraft, and in the other the testimonies of a nine-year-old and a fourteen-year-old were heard in open court "upon their oaths."[25]

Hale's popular *Pleas of the Crown* (published posthumously in 1678) contained the first age limits on witness testimony. With respect to capital cases, including felony and treason, where the life of the accused was at stake, he recommended that, while the testimony of those between nine and thirteen should be "allowed in some cases," normally witnesses should have reached the age of fourteen.[26] In another popular treatise, *The History and Analysis of the Common Law of England* (1713), he suggested that juries should consider "the very Quality, Carriage, Age, Condition, Education, and Place of Commorance [residence] of Witnesses." His general discussion of "infancy" and age, in this treatise, ironically entitled *Historia Placitorum Coronae: History of Pleas of the Crown*, which was itself new to a legal treatise, tried to uncover some sort of "natural law." In doing so, he drew somewhat on Catholic

24. The only place where Coke addressed the issue of witnesses was with respect to cases of high treason, where "it is most necessary to have substantial proof." Following a law of Queen Elizabeth's, he states that there must be "two lawful witnesses." *The Third Part of the Institutes of the Laws of England* . . . (London, 1644), 24–26.

The only reference Coke makes about witnesses in courts of common law is in his fourth volume on procedures in different courts, where he states that witness testimony must be "viva voce," that is, not by deposition but live, that witnesses should take an oath before testifying, and must not perjure themselves. *The Fourth Part of the Institutes of the Laws of England: Concerning the Jurisdiction of Courts* (London, 1760), 279.

25. Michael Dalton, *The Countrey Justice* (1618; rpt. Amsterdam, 1975), 261.

26. [Matthew Hale], *Pleas of the Crown; or, A Brief, But Full Account of Whatsoever Can Be Found Relating to That Subject* (London, 1678), 224.

ecclesiastical law and deeply on Roman law. Indeed, he devoted more effort in *History of Pleas of the Crown* to discussing Roman law than English, especially Justinian's *Institutes*.[27]

In justifying his extensive discussion of Roman civil law in this "history" of English criminal law, he acknowledged that, while English laws are "binding by their own authority; yet it must be confessed, the civil laws are very wise and well composed laws, and such as have been found out and settled by wise princes and law-givers . . . and therefore may be of great use to be known." Although Roman laws were not English precedent ("Neither I, nor any else may lay any weight or stress upon them"), he chose to "here particularly mention them." He then based his conclusions about the legal status of children in England on them as well as on a few scattered and unpublished English decisions, none of which related specifically to witnesses.[28]

The most remarkable aspect about Hale's writings on this subject is that Hale had permitted, without a question, eleven-year-old Elizabeth Pacey to testify in a witchcraft trial over which he had presided in 1664. Her nine-year-old sister, Deborah, did not testify only because she was too sick to come to the court. Instead, Deborah's father testified, giving what modern lawyers would call hearsay evidence about the contents of Deborah's visions. Hale thus developed his arguments against children's testimony only during the last few years of his life.[29]

Treatises on evidence law quickly incorporated Hale's guidelines as though they had always been common law; indeed, they treated them as custom. The first treatise that dealt solely with evidence law, William Nelson's *Law of Evidence*, appeared in England in 1717 and was found in many lawyers' libraries in the colonies throughout the century. It said little about the ability of witnesses except that "infants of the age of twenty are good witnesses." Yet he gave an example, when making a separate point, of a man sentenced to be hanged for the abduction of a fourteen-year-old girl based on her testimony. By the second edition of Sir Geoffrey Gilbert's *Law of Evidence* (1760), the arguments for excluding children under age fourteen had been greatly ex-

27. Matthew Hale, *Historia Placitorum Coronae: The History of the Pleas of the Crown* (1736), 2d ed. (London, 1778), I, 16–29; Hale, *The History of the Common Law of England*, 3d ed. (1739), ed. Charles M. Gray (Chicago, 1971), 164. In his introduction to this volume, Gray acknowledges the place of this work "as a document of the complex intellectual transformation of the seventeenth century. The magnitude of that transformation in science and philosophy, religion and political theory, is well recognized" (xiii).

28. Hale, *Historia Placitorum Coronae*, I, 16–29, II, 276–284.

29. *A Tryal of Witches at the Assizes Held at Bury St. Edmonds for the County of Suffolk, on the Tenth Day of March, 1664* . . . (London, 1682). The notes from this trial were taken by someone who attended it but were published for the first time only after Hale's death.

panded. Children should be barred for "want of skill and discernment," because they lack "common knowledge," and because they "are perfectly incapable of any Sense of Truth." After making his point about the age of fourteen very precisely, Gilbert backtracked to acknowledge, "There is no Time fix'd wherein they are to be excluded from evidence, but the Reason and Sense of their Evidence is to appear from the Questions propounded to them, and their answers to them." Gilbert cited no fewer than ten authorities in justifying their exclusion: three references to writings of Hale, three to cases tried after the publication of Hale's text, one to Justinian's *Institutes* (discussed by Hale), one to Nelson's *Law of Evidence,* one to Giles Duncombe's *Tryals per Pais* (1702) (which cited only Hale), and one to William Hawkins's *Treatise of the Pleas of the Crown* (1716) (drawing on Hale). Gilbert's earliest citation of an English authority is Hale. Hale's modifications had had a snowball effect: Gilbert's ten authorities for his opinion that those without "Reason and Sense" should not be able to testify led back to Hale.[30]

Hale's text, however, did not provide the final word; instead, it initiated a debate. Long after the publication of his *Pleas of the Crown,* some texts ignored his exclusion of children's testimony while others modified it. *The Infants Lawyer* (1697) placed no limits on children's testimony and even held that children under age twenty-one could be punished for perjury "if Infant judicially perjure himself in point of Age, or otherwise," indicating not only that those under age twenty-one testified but that they could be held responsible for the truth of their testimony. Dalton's views, which permitted the testimony of children, were cited instead of Hale's by the early- and mid-eighteenth-century Pennsylvania guides for justices of the peace. William Blackstone equivocated: they should be heard but not necessarily believed. Yet Hale was the only precedent cited by Blackstone in his discussion of

---

30. [William Nelson], *The Law of Evidence: Wherein All the Cases That Have Yet Been Printed in Any of Our Law Books or Tryals . . . Are Collected . . .* (London, 1717), 7, 36–37. The testimony was by Lucy Ramsey, whose age of fourteen is specified because she was an heiress who had been "forcibly tak[en] away" and married informally with an exchange of promises. Her new husband was hanged. Sir Matthew Hale was the judge in this case. *Case of Brown,* 84 Eng. Rep. 671 (3 Keb. 193) (1673).

On Gilbert, see [Sir Geoffrey Gilbert], *The Law of Evidence,* 2d ed. (London, 1760), 146–147; [Giles Duncombe], *Tryals per Pais in Capital Matters; or, Some Brief and Useful Observations Relating to Such Tryals* (London, 1702), 23–24; William Hawkins, *A Summary of the Crown-Law . . .* (London, 1728), I, 425–426.

Perhaps part of the reason Gilbert supported the exclusion of children's testimony was that he was profoundly influenced by Locke's epistemology. Gilbert was also the author of *An Abstract of Mr. Locke's Essay on Human Understanding* (noted by Shapiro, "*Beyond Reasonable Doubt,*" 26).

whether children could be witnesses. Later editions of Blackstone, such as that of 1800 (after Blackstone's death, edited by others), went further in silencing children: they removed the passages suggesting children might be heard without taking an oath; they also excluded the secondhand testimony that a child might have told an adult as "hearsay" evidence and thus invalid.[31]

While Francis Buller's *Introduction to the Law relative to Trials at Nisi Prius* of 1772 cited Hale as well as two early-eighteenth-century cases to claim that "a Child under the Age of ten shall in no Case be admitted," Buller acknowledged that this limitation did cause problems in the prosecution of crimes against children. He carefully encouraged the court to be more lenient toward children's testimony than Hale had suggested in cases where children were the victims of crimes, particularly of "foul facts done in secret."

> Doubtless the Court will more readily admit such a Child in the Case of a personal Injury (such as Rape) than on a question between other Parties; and perhaps, in such Case, would even admit the Infant to be examined without Oath; for certainly there is much more Reason for the Court to hear the Relation of the Child, than to receive it at second-hand from those that heard it say so. In Cases of foul Facts done in secret, where the Child is the Party injured, the repelling their Evidence entirely is, in some Measure, denying them the Protection of the Law; yet the Levity and want of Experience in Children, is undoubtedly a Circumstance which goes greatly to their Credit.

Thus Buller undercut somewhat the strength of Hale's arguments, although he cited them dutifully and presented them as the standard opinion. Chitty's *Practical Treatise on the Criminal Law* (1816), cited in the 1820 Virginia statutory rape case, explicitly critiqued Hale. Hale, the author claimed, had thought:

31. *The Infants Lawyer; or, The Law (Both Ancient and Modern) Relating to Infants, Setting Forth Their Priviledges, Their Several Ages for Divers Purposes . . .* (London, 1697), 68. For the prevalence of this book in the colonies during the eighteenth century, see Herbert A. Johnson, *Imported Eighteenth-Century Law Treatises in American Libraries* (Knoxville, Tenn., 1978), 31. Johnson found three copies of this guide in the twenty-two libraries of eighteenth-century lawyers he surveyed.

On Dalton's views: Dalton, *The Countrey Justice*, 366; *Conductor Generalis* (1722), 79.

On Blackstone: Blackstone, *Commentaries* (1765–1769), IV, 214. The 1800 London edition deleted Blackstone's partial qualification to Hale by deleting his reference to "infants of any age." See the discussion of Susannah Brown's case, above, and note 7, for Blackstone's original wording.

If under nine or ten, they cannot be sworn. . . . But, in modern times, more rational principles have been admitted to prevail. The admissibility of testimony now depends not on the age, but on the understanding of the witness. Children of any age who comprehend the nature of an oath, and are capable of feeling the obligations it imposes, may be admitted to give evidence.

Actually, since Hale had emphasized the "discretion" of the child and had given age as a guideline to discretion, Hale would not have disagreed markedly. However, Chitty's perspective did allow the testimony of younger witnesses in certain cases.[32]

Most eighteenth-century legal guides followed Hale. As shown in the discussion of Susannah Brown's case, Webb's Virginia *Office and Authoritie of a Justice of Peace* (1736) offered fourteen as the guideline for the age at which a person could testify. Richard Burn's *Justice of the Peace,* which went through dozens of editions during the eighteenth century (and was popular in the colonies), cited Hale and Hawkins to conclude that infants without "discretion" could be prevented from testifying. Thomas Wood's *Institute of the Laws* (1738) excluded those "without discretion" from giving evidence in courtrooms. Two popular and influential guides in early-nineteenth-century Virginia, William Waller Hening's *New Virginia Justice* (1795) (for justices of the peace) and St. George Tucker's edition of Blackstone's *Commentaries* (1803) (which added Virginia laws), both cited Hale as their earliest source for excluding the testimony of children. The first American edition of Matthew Bacon's popular *New Abridgment of the Law* (1813) began the discussion of "who may be witnesses" by excluding those without "sufficient discretion" or "a right sense of the sanctity of an oath" but allowed that in some cases "infants [under fourteen] . . . may be witnesses." His first citation was also Hale.[33]

32. Francis Buller, *An Introduction to the Law relative to Trials at Nisi Prius* (London, 1772), 288–289; Chitty, *Practical Treatise on the Criminal Law,* III, 814–815, and also see I, 590–591; *Commonwealth v John Bennet,* in Brockenbrough, comp., *Virginia Cases,* 238. In the margin of the volume of Buller I examined, the controversy aroused on this point is revealed in the marginalia by an English lawyer in 1831. "There is now no determinate age, for the admission or rejection of a child's evidence. Three days ago, a child under six was a witness against Bishop and Williams for murder." This anonymous lawyer also cited Blackstone's *Commentaries,* presumably an early or unaltered edition of Blackstone. The volume with these marginalia resides in the UCLA law library.

33. Richard Burn, *The Justice of the Peace, and Parish Officer,* 8th ed. (London, 1764), I, 342. Burn did suggest that "an infant of tender years may be examined without oath, where the exigence of the case requires it; which possibly, being fortified with concur-

Whereas earlier treatises advocated the hearing of all evidence, even of young children against their parents, the broad historical trend was away from this simple acceptance and toward hearing their evidence but discounting it, and then toward excluding the evidence of those under ten or even under fourteen. This transition was especially pronounced in criminal trials. Hale intended his initial restrictions on children's testimony to apply to felonies. Such cases as that involving Susannah Brown, where the defendant's punishment could be death if convicted of the rape, were among the first to explicitly apply the guidelines on children's testimony. This initial exclusion quickly extended to other cases.[34]

Why did Hale introduce such changes? Partly, he was caught in the midst of long-term transformations in procedures in English courtrooms, particularly in the respective roles of witnesses and juries. Only during the fifteenth century did witnesses first start to be used in English courtrooms. Throughout the sixteenth and seventeenth centuries, the roles of jurors and of witnesses overlapped. Before the early seventeenth century, there were virtually no guidelines about who could be witnesses. But these "transformations" were not predestined to follow a particular path. Hale and common law reformers like him shaped the rules for who could be witnesses and how witness testimony should be evaluated at the same time as they shaped evidence law. They did so in conformity with transformations in English epistemology during the seventeenth and eighteenth centuries that drew on Puritan theology.

During the Interregnum, Hale was openly Puritan and consciously connected his religious ideals with an agenda of legal reform. Hale headed a Commonwealth commission to revise England's entire legal code. His suggestions for reform included establishing a high minimum age for marriage

---

rent evidences, may be of some weight; especially in cases of rape, buggery, and such crimes as are practiced upon children."

Wood: Thomas Wood, *An Institute of the Laws of England . . .* , 6th ed. (London, 1738), 598. Wood was the first to seek a precedent that antedated Hale.

Hening: William Waller Hening, *The New Virginia Justice: Comprising the Office and Authority of a Justice of the Peace . . .* (Richmond, 1795), 177–178, 356–357, 453; and also see later editions: *The New Virginia Justice*, 4th ed. (Richmond, 1825), 549–551. Hening focused on the decision of Lord Chief Justice Robert Raymond in 1726, which reversed a 1698 Old Bailey decision. In the earlier case, "Ward chief baron admitted one to be a witness who was under the age of ten years, as the child had been examined about the nature of an oath and had given a reasonable account of it. But Raymond chief justice" reversed the earlier decision.

Bacon: Bacon, *New Abridgment*, II, 576–577.

34. *Rex v Travers*, 93 Eng. Rep. 793 (2 Strange 700) (1726).

(fourteen for girls, sixteen for boys) and raising the minimum age for jury service from fourteen to twenty-five. After the Interregnum, he continued to be sympathetic with Dissenters; his close friends included such activists as the Nonconformist Richard Baxter (who in turn influenced Locke).[35] Dissenters in the seventeenth century advocated not only political reform in England and its colonies but also legal reform. They sought to redistribute authority by making laws available for everyone to read, understand, and judge just as they had done with the Bible. The significance of Coke's writing his *Institutes* in English, for example, must not be underestimated. He acknowledged that having the law written in English made it accessible and comprehensible to more people. The call for legal treatises in English paralleled the demands for religious services and reading the Bible in English. Laws written in English would also be a main concern of the Levellers. Yet there was a tension in that goal: it could lead to anarchy by encouraging people to think they might make law as well. To prevent the unfit from misunderstanding and misforming law, Hale (among many others) sought to limit legal access for those whom he deemed unable to properly exercise their understanding. He did so not only in theory, in elaborating Coke's concept of an acquired ability to exercise legal reason, but in practice.[36]

That Hale himself was deeply involved in these epistemological debates is revealed especially in his religious writings, which explored how humans acquired knowledge, religious as well as legal. His theory of knowledge was similar to but preceded Locke's. Hale focused on the importance of reason in

35. Mary Cotterell, "Interregnum Law Reform: the Hale Commission of 1652," *English Historical Review*, LXXXIII (1968), 689–704; C. H. Firth and R. S. Rait, eds., *Acts and Ordinances of the Interregnum, 1642–1660* (London, 1911), II, 715–718.

On John Locke's involvement in these epistemological debates, see Richard Ashcraft, *Revolutionary Politics and Locke's "Two Treatises of Government"* (Princeton, N.J., 1986), esp. chaps. 1, 2.

36. *Coke upon Littleton*, I, preface. He argues, however, that he does not want to dispense with all of the French and Latin phrases, since they are "Vocables of Art, so apt and significant to expresse the true sense of the Laws, and are so woven into the laws themselves, as it is in a manner impossible to change them."

On the concerns of Levellers, see, among others, Barbara J. Shapiro, "Law Reform in Seventeenth Century England," *American Journal of Legal History*, XIX (1975), 290.

On limiting legal access: Charles Gray, "Reason, Authority, and Imagination: The Jurisprudence of Sir Edward Coke," in Perez Zagorin, ed., *Culture and Politics from Puritanism to the Enlightenment* (Berkeley, Calif., 1980), 25–66, esp. 30–32. For Hale's perspective, see 53 n. 20. "Hale . . . developed this argument for lawyers especially strongly—very much in the context of asserting that the reason of lawyers is distinctive, as the best reason for particular purposes is always the trained reason of a special craft or profession."

separating humans from animals and of "wisdom" in separating each human being from any other. "The great *preheminence* that Man hath over Beasts is his *Reason,* and the great preheminence that one man hath over another is *Wisdom;* Though all men have ordinarily the priviledge of Reason, yet all men have not the habit of Wisdom." It was critical that children learn to read, because it enabled them not simply to "understand what others have written, [but also] to know what they knew and wrote, thereby improving their knowledge and understanding." Hale's theory of knowledge placed human understanding at its center, relying on time and sensory perception to improve that understanding via both "artificial" and "natural" sources; the development of the human understanding came only with age. Only with age, then, could one have sufficient understanding to testify.[37]

More important almost than why he introduced such changes is why the legal treatise writers who followed him accepted his changes so uncritically. His extensive knowledge and writing in the law and his position as chief justice of England between 1671 and 1675 certainly gave him credibility. But the manner in which he made the reforms, the way in which he declared them to be custom, made them difficult to recognize as changes. And, after 1660, Hale was careful not to label himself a reformer, conscious that to do so after the Restoration would give him a bad name. In an essay not published until after his death, Hale emphasized that judges should make reforms where they could, "without troubling a Parliament": if they did so, "truly this would go a very great way in the reformation of things amiss in the law." Legal changes should be made by judges, who understood better than legislators the consequences of reforms, and then only warily. "The business of amendment or alteration of lawes is a choice and tender business, neither wholly to be omitted when the necessity requires, and yet very cautiously and warily to be undertaken." Yet such revisions were necessary at intervals. Therefore, instead of merely reporting the law, he reformed it. In the decades and centuries after Hale, the many legal treatise writers who quoted Hale's judgments assumed he spoke not merely for natural law but for the "ancient common law."[38]

---

37. [Matthew Hale], *Contemplations Moral and Divine* (London, 1676), 17, 486–487; Hale, *A Discourse of the Knowledge of God, and of Our Selves: I, By the Light of Nature; II, By the Sacred Scriptures* (London, 1688), 2–4. *Contemplations* was his only work published while he was alive; according to the preface, it was published without his consent.

38. Sir Matthew Hale, "Considerations touching the Amendment or Alteration of Lawes," in Francis Hargrave, ed., *A Collection of Tracts relative to the Law of England, from Manuscripts* (Dublin, 1787), I, 253, 266–267, 272–273. "I think good and wise men may and ought to make some prudent essay even in this great business [reforming laws], and

Not only children's direct testimony but also their indirect testimony began to be excluded on the grounds that it was hearsay evidence. Consider, for example, Chitty's *Practical Treatise on the Criminal Law*.

> It was once thought that where the party immediately injured was an infant of tender years, the parents of the child might be admitted to state the account he had given of the transaction immediately after it had taken place, and that the infant might be examined though not sworn; but both these ideas are now rejected; and it is fully established that if the infant is of competent discretion, he may be sworn, however young; and, if not, no evidence whatever can be given respecting his assertions.[39]

Banishing children from courtrooms formed one part of the development of evidence law during the seventeenth and eighteenth centuries in England. As Barbara Shapiro has shown, the formation of evidence law in the eighteenth century was influenced profoundly by the epistemological theories of John Locke, in particular, but also, by the late eighteenth century, by those of David Hartley, Thomas Reid, and others. While Reid is linked to the Scottish Common Sense school, both he and Hartley elaborated on Locke's theories of human development, which in turn were ladled from the Dissenting cauldron that Locke and Hale helped to stir. As the discussion of Hale's ideas illustrates, however, evidence law was not a simplistic outgrowth of Dissenting epistemology: that epistemology led him to try to find an underlying natural law by searching for grand symmetries in different legal traditions. Relying for his precedents in part on Roman civil law and even canon law, he sought to formulate an underlying "natural law" compatible with his developing epistemology. This "natural law" led him to raise ages and shift standards of proof.[40]

------

with very good success both to their own reputation and the publick benefit" (266). Laws need to be reformed not only because they "are subject to corruption and putrefaction," but also because some parts of the law are simply not beneficial or do not fit changes in society. "There are some things, that are really and truly parts of the law, as necessary to be reformed as the errors and abuse of it" (268–269).

39. Chitty, *Practical Treatise on the Criminal Law*, I, 590–591.

40. Shapiro, *"Beyond Reasonable Doubt,"* 25–26, 196. On witnesses, see esp. 187–189. Also see William Twining, "Evidence and Legal Theory," in Twining, ed., *Legal Theory and Common Law* (Oxford, 1986), 62–80, esp. 70: "In short, nearly all Anglo-American writers [on evidence law] seem by and large to have adopted, either explicitly or by implication, a particular ontology, epistemology and theory of logic. All of these are closely identified with a particular philosophical tradition, that is English empiricism, as exemplified by Locke, Bentham and John Stuart Mill."

On Roman and Catholic law, see Shapiro, *"Beyond Reasonable Doubt,"* 187–188.

The new attitude toward human nature and the development of the human understanding that grew out of these debates was neither immediately nor universally accepted, whether in England or its colonies. Individual judges and jury members had some latitude in deciding which witnesses to hear and believe, within somewhat flexible guidelines. What, precisely, did "understand the nature of an oath" or "have sufficient understanding" mean? Virginia was the most careful and thorough in following the English pattern. Massachusetts initiated a somewhat democratic version of these guidelines: the jury, not the judges, should decide on the validity of witness testimony. Still, the jury was forewarned to treat children's testimony with skepticism. Apparently because judges in Pennsylvania used a guide for justices of the peace that ignored Hale's guidelines, Pennsylvania continued to hear children's testimony at least until the Revolution. This continued use of the earlier guide might have been a conscious decision, related to Quaker belief that an inner light from God dwelt in all persons from birth, even children. Because of this inner light, they believed that the understanding of children did not need to be cultivated to the same degree and that children could speak as truly as adults.

Before leaving evidence law altogether, a few observations are in order. Hale was central not only to excluding children's evidence but also to excluding hearsay evidence, wives' testimony against their husbands (to a point that alarmed Blackstone in his discussion of Hale on this issue), husbands' testimony against their wives, and one's evidence against oneself. His strictures, though debated during the eighteenth century, formed the foundations of evidence law by the early nineteenth century. The logic for excluding all of these voices centered on the reliability of their testimony, as is clearest in his arguments against both children's testimony and hearsay evidence.[41]

These principles were applied also (not, it seems, on Hale's recommendation, although his logic might be forced in this direction) to excluding the testimony of non-Christians in Virginia, who began to be described as unable to take an oath and therefore unable to give reliable testimony. The Virginia House of Burgesses in 1705 barred "popish recusants convict [that is, Catholics who would not attend Anglican services], negroes, mulattoes and Indian servants, and others, not being christians" from testifying in any trials, modifying the law to allow "negroes, mulattoes, or Indians" to testify in the capital trials of fellow slaves in 1748. The explanation in 1748 was that, because these peoples were not Christian, their evidence was therefore "corrupt and pre-

---

These Roman and canon law texts, apparently, first excluded minors under fourteen from testifying in civil cases and those under age twenty in criminal cases.

41. Hale, *Historia*, I, 43, 48, II, 276–284; Blackstone, *Commentaries*, I, 269.

carious." The restriction of their testimony in 1705 was actually preceded by common law limits on children's testimony (which undoubtedly circulated before they were officially published in Virginia in 1736 as part of Webb's *Office and Authoritie of a Justice of Peace*). The author behind the 1705 law was almost certainly William Fitzhugh (at work on a grand revision of the law before he died in 1701), who had a large legal library.[42] The 1705 law on its surface focused on the reliability of the evidence of "negroes, mulattoes, and Indians." Although the justification for children's exclusion was slightly different—they did not understand the nature of an oath (or vow)—it was clearly related. But opening that question of the reliability of children's evidence and of the necessity of an oath (a point made by Coke) opened the larger question as well.

Whether the common lawyers purposely sought to increase the power of adults at the expense of children in barring their testimony is debatable. But that was its effect. Likewise, excluding slaves from testifying usually denied them, as well, the protection of the laws. The 1705 law was important to maintaining the legal superiority of whites: it prevented slaves from accusing masters or other whites of crimes. An enslaved woman, for example, would be unable to testify against a white man if he raped her. If one cannot testify, one is legally silenced. The logic behind the guidelines excluding children's testimony was more focused on the question of reason than that behind the law excluding slaves' testimony. In applying the logic to other groups, in this case to non-Christians and people of other races, the burgesses were consolidating inequality of a very different sort. Ultimately, on the question of children and power, patriarchal theory and consent-based theory might superficially come together: both saw obedience to superiors as important. But they gave it a very different basis. The former would concentrate on the naturalness of inequality; the latter, on the importance of reason. Fitzhugh falls more into the former category: inferiors should not testify against superiors. Yet the later burgesses did not hesitate to also invoke the logic of the law about reason and reliability to justify excluding the testimony of slaves.

Over the course of two centuries, these debates about reason and authority helped to alter practical and omnipresent rules about such mundane but critical issues as who could testify in a court of law. Throughout this period children were protected by the same rules that protected adults. But a shift in attitude toward children's credibility as witnesses meant that the standard laws did not protect them as well as they had protected them before, and

42. Hening, ed., *Statutes at Large*, III, 298, VI, 107; Richard Beale Davis, ed., *William Fitzhugh and His Chesapeake World, 1676–1701: The Fitzhugh Letters and Other Documents* (Chapel Hill, N.C., 1963), 33–34.

certainly not as well as they protected adults. This shift, whose real effects were deeply entrenched only by the beginning of the nineteenth century, ultimately underlies the movements for the special protection of children. Excluding the testimony of young children as well as hearsay testimony from them (through others) meant that laws that had protected them from sexual or physical assault often could not be enforced. Their voices were legally silenced. As Francis Buller acknowledged in 1772, "In Cases of foul Facts done in secret, where the Child is the Party injured, the repelling their Evidence entirely is, in some Measure, denying them the Protection of the Law."[43]

Reason and Custom in the Common Law

Coke, Hale, and Blackstone were the most important of the common law reformers, not only because they tried more to shape the law but because their authority was so great that they largely succeeded. Each openly acknowledged that he sought to make the law conform to "reason"; each ignored precedents that did not fit with his revision and reduction of the common law. While they sometimes justified reform on a theoretical level, they rarely acknowledged their alterations as new, always camouflaging them as precedent.

Coke and Hale, particularly, have to be seen in light of the religious and political conflicts in England in the seventeenth century. Both sought to reform the law in ways that attempted to limit corruption and to regularize and clarify procedure. Both sided with what could be termed the Puritan, or Nonconformist faction, in Parliament. In serving as members of Parliament multiple times, both actively sought to revise legal procedure. Both, however, asserted that judges could and should revise and regularize the common law without reference to Parliament.

As one Coke scholar has acknowledged, "All historians agree that Coke used earlier legal sources in ways that now seem blatantly inaccurate and anachronistic." Coke sought to "reshape the law through his legal decisions and writings." He sought to make decisions and to lay down rules that were "reasonable." The fact that the legal treatise writers who followed Coke and

43. Buller, *Trials at Nisi Prius*, 288–289. For a good discussion of the increasing protection of children, see Joseph M. Hawes, *The Children's Rights Movement: A History of Advocacy and Protection* (Boston, 1991).
Of course, even in the earlier period, crimes against very young children would always have been more difficult to prosecute, since below age one or two they literally could not speak, and slightly older children would not have known the law, so could not make a direct appeal for its protections.

Hale cited them merely as compilers of the common law has led to a variety of distortions. As Stephen White has commented pointedly with regard to this naive idealization of Coke's work, "Nothing could be more misleading than to characterize Coke as an obdurate defender of the legal status quo." Yet that is what many lawyers in the eighteenth century did.[44]

While Coke clearly had multiple agendas, by the end of his life when he was composing the *Institutes* he had a particular set of goals, which grew out of his Puritan-influenced faith. Educated in Norwich, that sixteenth-century center of Puritanism and haven for Huguenot refugees, he sought to apply Reformation ideas about access to the Bible and religious services in the vernacular—not to the religion itself, but to the law. Defensive about publishing his treatise on the laws in English, he justified it on the grounds that it would make them more accessible and comprehensible, so that more people could follow them.

> This part wee have (and not without president [precedent]) published in English, for that they are an introduction to the knowledge of the nationall Lawes of the Realme; a work necessarie, and yet heeretofore not undertaken by any, albeit in all other professions there are the like. We have left our Author [Littleton, upon whom Coke is commenting, wrote in law French] to speake his owne language, and have translated him into English, to the end that any of the Nobilitie, or Gentrie of this Realme, or of any other estate, or profession whatsoever, that will be pleased to read him and these Institutes, may understand the language wherein they are written.
>
> I cannot conjecture that the generall communicating of these lawes in the English tongue can worke any inconvenience, but introduce great profit, seeing that . . . Ignorance of the Law excuseth not.

Coke's treatise, the first translation into English of "the nationall Lawes of the Realme," a work "heeretofore not undertaken by any," was to prove very influential.[45]

Coke did not create a wholly new legal system. But his molding a largely shapeless mass of varying precedents into a recognizable and coherent form

44. Stephen White, *Sir Edward Coke and "The Grievances of the Commonwealth," 1621–1628* (Chapel Hill, N.C., 1979), 14, 16, 46, 80. Also see J. G. A. Pocock, *The Ancient Constitution and the Feudal Law: A Study of English Historical Thought in the Seventeenth Century* (Cambridge, 1987), 268–269. "Coke's habit of citing as maxims what it is hard to find so cited before was not altogether as outrageous as it might appear. The ongoing reason of the courts contained custom but was not limited to it; it need not cite custom, but might do so whenever it saw fit."

45. *Coke upon Littleton*, preface, and see note 36, above.

gave it a particular shape—one inspired by his religious and political beliefs and by his own experiences. As one scholar rather tactfully put it, "Hostile contemporaries were aware, and legal historians cannot help becoming so, that accuracy was sometimes the loser [in Coke's attempts to create a coherent synthesis]; Coke's power to shape the law under color of reporting it was to exceed his expectations." His *Reports,* which appeared in eleven volumes between 1600 and 1615, were among the first published reports of cases and were almost more influential than his *Institutes.* He was preceded in this only by Edmund Plowden; earlier reports had all been in manuscript. In both his *Reports* and his *Institutes* he consciously reflected on his standards and purposes in making certain generalizations and decisions and even occasionally warned his readers not to trust other reports as much as his own.[46]

Hale was arguably more of a reformer, albeit not as radical as some of the other members of Parliament during the Interregnum. Although he seemed at heart to be a Puritan, he did not oppose monarchy in principle. His entire history is one of moderation during a period of bitter struggle. During the Civil War he stayed in London rather than joining the king at Oxford, but he did not actively support Parliament either. He was friends with John Selden, who, though attached to ideas of government based on consent, tended much more toward allowing force and implied consent. Early on, Hale might have sympathized with the king as Selden did, but his support was never more than lukewarm. One historian has suggested that his defense of Royalists on treason charges illustrates his true loyalties. Yet Hale took the "covenant" promising allegiance to the new state, apparently without qualm. Seemingly disillusioned with the Interregnum experiment, which ended with Oliver Cromwell's son's inheriting the protectorship, a clear return to monarchical principle, Hale resigned his judgeship. Hale did support the return of the king, but he voted in the Restoration Parliament to extract more concessions from Charles II before allowing his return. He was cautious in word and deed not to openly offend. He left his land entailed on his sons, a provision that fitted more with ideas about hereditary monarchy, but did not allow them their inheritance until age twenty-five, much later than the norm at that time. He explicitly defended the prerogatives of the king, although within limits.[47]

46. Gray, "The Jurisprudence of Sir Edward Coke," in Zagorin, ed., *Culture and Politics from Puritanism to the Enlightenment,* 27. Gray cites the prefaces to vols. III, V, VII, and X of his *Reports,* as well as *Coke upon Littleton,* 370a, and *Fourth Part of Institutes,* 17.

47. Edmund Heward, *Matthew Hale* (London, 1972), 15–16, 21, 56, 68 (esp.), 112 (on his will entailing property); and see also Alan Cromartie, *Sir Matthew Hale, 1609–1676: Law, Religion, and Natural Philosophy* (Cambridge, 1995), 44, 63, 88, 189–190.

Yet he was good friends with such Nonconformists as Richard Baxter, at whose house he might have attended religious services. He also wrote several religious tracts. Hale dressed himself in notably plain and dark clothes, which drew remark and identified him to contemporaries as a Puritan. During the 1660s he refused to enforce the religious laws against Puritans, Baptists, and other Dissenters. He himself drafted a revised version of the Act of Uniformity that would have allowed much greater latitude in forms and places of worship. He believed, clearly, in liberty of conscience and was sympathetic even to Quakers (with whom he disagreed) and to the Baptist John Bunyan. He sought to limit the authority of the House of Lords after the Restoration. A Puritan throughout his life, in his youth he was more radical and emphasized God's grace in his thinking. Toward the end of his life he saw God's grace as acting solely though human understanding. He stressed that reason and understanding were critical to faith and to the exercise of good actions. This latter perspective was most in conformity with the position he took on age.[48]

Acknowledging their links to radical Protestantism should not imply that either Hale or Coke thought that the common law should be replaced with biblical law, or even strictly with natural law. Both, rather, argued that the law should be continually considered and revised to conform with reason. Hale did write a treatise on natural law (still unpublished), which bears many similarities to John Locke's *Two Treatises of Government*. Others of his published works indicate a fascination with discovering a universal law.[49]

Hale's moderate stance, along with his ability to both justify and conceal his changes, made him one of the most effective and influential legal reformers. Thus he was both head of the parliamentary commission to revise and reconsider England's whole code of laws in 1652–1653 and, later, chief

---

(Hale accepted, as did Grotius [and contract law in his own time, as we shall see], that force could be used to obtain consent to contracts [Cromartie, *Sir Matthew Hale*, 48].) While Cromartie claims that Hale was "intellectually a royalist" (3), the point is not whether Hale expressed any support for monarchy, but how much, under what circumstances, and how that power was supposed to be balanced with Parliament. Heward identifies Hale as a Puritan, but a moderate one.

48. Cromartie, *Sir Matthew Hale*, chaps. 9, 10, esp. 170–171. Also see Heward, *Matthew Hale*, 49–50, where Hale was upset at some Anabaptists for disturbing a Church of England service on the grounds that "it was intolerable for men who pretended so highly for liberty of conscience to go and disturb others."

49. Hale, "Alteration of Lawes," in Hargrave, ed., *Collection of Tracts*, I, 258–259; D. E. C. Yale, *Hale as a Legal Historian* (London, 1976), 12. (Hale cites BM. Harl. MS 7159, copied in 1696.) Cromartie, *Sir Matthew Hale*, excerpts some quotes in his chapter 6.

justice under Charles II.[50] Charles's choice of experienced judges was constrained, undoubtedly, by the long Interregnum, when many persons unsympathetic with his views had held judgeships. Yet Hale's moderation put him in the unusual position of being prominent in both Commonwealth and monarchy. By 1660, realizing his delicate position, he had grown more circumspect about how reforms should be accomplished and what reforms should be attempted. He was careful not to label himself a reformer and to hide his changes as custom.

> Exemplary miscarriages, in the late times, of such as have undertaken reformation both in matters civil and ecclesiastical, hath brought a disrepute upon the undertaking of any reformation in either: so that the very name of reformation and a reformer begins to be a stile or name of contempt and obloquy; so that men are as fearfull to be under the imputation of a reformer of the law, as they would be of the name of knave or fool, or hypocrite.

Yet he urged judges to make reforms where they could, "without troubling a Parliament," which "would go a very great way in the reformation of things amiss in the law." Even when legislators did want to act, he urged them to consult with judges on the first drafts of the laws.[51]

Thus, as with Coke, Hale's extensive interest in legal history grew partly out of his desire to shape the present. Hale went even further in contending that judges were the best reformers of the law. Also like Coke, Hale published in English. He advocated, while a member of Parliament during the Interregnum, for legal proceedings to be in English rather than the French or Latin in which most court proceedings were held. Although Parliament passed this reform in 1650, it was reversed after the Restoration of Charles II in 1660. Not until 1731 did Parliament again pass a law that allowed most court proceedings finally to be heard in English.[52]

Blackstone was more moderate ideologically than Coke and Hale, yet he played a critical role in introducing Enlightenment reforms at the same time as he justified older status relationships. In his compromises, he sought to

50. On this commission in general and Hale's role in particular, see, among others, Cotterell, "Interregnum Law Reform," *English Historical Review,* LXXXIII (1968), 689–704; Shapiro, "Law Reform," *American Journal of Legal History,* XIX (1975), 280–312, esp. 298.

51. Hale, "Alteration of Lawes," in Hargrave, ed., *A Collection of Tracts,* I, 266, 272–273.

52. Shapiro, "Law Reform in Seventeenth Century England," *American Journal of Legal History,* XIX (1975), 295, 307.

make the law more comprehensible and uniform. One scholar has argued that Blackstone was very conservative and that he compromised with Enlightenment reformers only to pacify critics of the English legal system. But he cannot be labeled simply conservative, because he moderated his metaphorical crowning of "custom" with reason and natural law. Blackstone held that custom that did not conform to "reason" was invalid: any "precedent" that contradicted reason was not precedent, was simply "not law." By this logic, any judge could dismiss any precedent as "bad law" and ignore it if it did not fit his ideas about justice. In short, Blackstone honored precedent but also undermined it; his invocation of natural law allowed and even encouraged innovation. And he often defined this reason explicitly in terms of the natural law theories of Grotius, Pufendorf, Locke, Jean Barbeyrac, and Montesquieu.[53]

Blackstone was not, of course, the first common lawyer to trump precedent with reason, thereby conflating reason with custom. This injunction from Blackstone was expressed as early as the late fifteenth century in Thomas Littleton's *Treatise on Tenures*: "Pur ceo que cest prescription est encounter reason ceo est voyd." On this passage Coke commented: "This containes one of the Maximes of the Common Law, viz. that all customes and prescriptions that be against reason, are voyd." Given the popularity of *Coke upon Littleton*, it was an injunction with which common lawyers would have been widely familiar. Yet following it demanded interpretation, especially given the changing meanings for what was reasonable. Much depended on how one weighed the balance between reason and precedent, on which precedents one excluded as unreasonable. As norms about reason were changing, this clause opened avenues for change, into which stepped Coke, Hale, and Blackstone.[54]

Revolutionary-era lawyers in America would also conflate custom with reason, and reason with natural law and political theory. Thus, "custom" quite literally did not always mean custom in the way we idealize the term today, as normal legal practice as it has existed for, presumably, generations. Custom sometimes created a past in order to justify a future. As J. G. A. Pocock described this tension as it emerged in the early seventeenth century, "Custom was . . . always immemorial and always up-to-date." While relying on

53. Duncan Kennedy, "The Structure of Blackstone's Commentaries," *Buffalo Law Review*, XXVIII (1979), 205–382; David Lieberman, *The Province of Legislation Determined: Legal Theory in Eighteenth-Century Britain* (Cambridge, 1989), citing Blackstone, *Commentaries*, I, 69–71, 76–77. Lieberman also cites other legal treatise writers who gave similar opinions, including Hale in his *History of the Common Law*, 45–46.

54. *Coke upon Littleton*, 140.

history for precedent provided some restraints, these men, in particular, revised the law to make it fit more closely with their religious and political beliefs about justice. Their reforms tended to limit the ability of children to give voice, to consent, and to form intent. At the same time, they tended to limit the power of lords and to increase the power of parents.[55]

55. Pocock, *The Ancient Constitution and the Feudal Law*, 15, 241; James Q. Whitman, "Why Did the Revolutionary Lawyers Confuse Custom and Reason?" *University of Chicago Law Review*, LVIII (1991), 1321–1368. Also see, generally, J. R. Pole, "Reflections on American Law and the American Revolution," *William and Mary Quarterly*, 3d Ser., L (1993), 122–159, and the responses to his article in the same volume by Peter Charles Hoffer and Bruce H. Mann. Pocock describes a shift in appeal with regard to political and legal theory, from the reliance on a simpler understanding of custom and tradition to a blending of those with reason. Even the appeal to the English constitution was transformed during the seventeenth century as it became not merely (or even purely) immemorial but also rational.

CHAPTER 6

UNDERSTANDING INTENT

CHILDREN AND THE REFORM OF

GUILT AND PUNISHMENT

"Edward Flemyng, being a child, was drownid in water
by his owne default."
Sussex Coroner's Inquests, *June 1, 1577*

"There are many Crimes of the most heinous Nature . . . which
Children are very capable of committing; . . . therefore, though
the taking away the Life of a Boy of ten Years Old may savour of
Cruelty, yet as the Example of this Boy's Punishment may be a
means of deterring Other Children from the like Offences; and as
Sparing this Boy, merely on Account of his Age, *will probably*
have a quite contrary tendency, in Justice to the Publick,
the Law ought to take it's Course."
Sir Michael Foster, A Report of Some Proceedings on the
Commission of Oyer and Terminer and Goal Delivery *(1762)*

In Exeter, England, in 1641, Peter Moore, an apprentice apothecary, was executed for poisoning his master. Since he had just begun his service, we can guess that he was fourteen. But his age was not an issue in the case, nor for Moore himself in his deathbed confession, *The Apprentices Warning-Piece.* The surviving records of the assize courts from sixteenth- and seventeenth-century England, where most serious crimes were prosecuted, likewise usually lack ages for the accused, as do the colonial American records.[1] Age, even

---

1. Peter Moore, *The Apprentices Warning-Piece, Being a Confession of Peter Moore, Formerly Servant . . .* (London, 1641), esp. 3.

The surviving assize records include all indictments made for Essex, Hertfordshire, Kent, Surrey, and Sussex during the reigns of Elizabeth I and James I. They appeared in a series of eleven volumes edited by J. S. Cockburn between 1971 and 1985. J. S. Cockburn, *Introduction: Calendar of Assize Records: Home Circuit Indictments, Elizabeth I and James I* (London, 1985), provides a guide to these volumes. He also edited a volume on Western Circuit assize orders, 1629–1648, and one on Somerset assize orders, 1640–1659. I also checked T. G. Barnes, ed., *Somerset Assize Orders, 1629–1640* (Frome, 1959).

in the casual form of calling someone "boy" or "girl," was rarely recorded. Three reasons might account for this lacuna: no children committed crimes; when children committed crimes, their cases were not even heard, because the law assumed they could not form intent and therefore assume guilt; or children committed crimes, but, since the law made little distinction between children and adults, age was irrelevant. The easiest assumptions to make have been the first two, since they fit our modern norms. Yet the last is the main answer.

This chapter contends that legal guides and a careful reading of the few cases where age is mentioned (seemingly by chance) allow us to peer behind the curtain at the court proceedings themselves, despite the opacity of the court records. Children were part of this drama of crime and punishment. They were there along with the whole criminal cast in the sixteenth through eighteenth centuries, pilfering, burning, and even killing along with the rest: and hanging with them too.

By the nineteenth century, children under fourteen were largely offstage, at least when it came time for trial and conviction and, especially, punishment. They might burn a barn, steal a silver spoon, or even kill, but they were unlikely to be tried, convicted, or punished, especially by execution. In their movement off the stage, children demarcate fundamental shifts in both how guilt was adjudged (what criminal intent meant) and in how the convicted should be punished.

In the sixteenth and early seventeenth centuries, these rules defined guilt as arising from action: whether one committed the act was the most critical issue. Punishments were brutal, meant to inspire terror and blind obedience. They focused on deterrence by example. So, in England, judges of the Abingdon assizes hanged eight-year-old John Dean for burning two barns in 1629. The seventeenth- and eighteenth-century reformers, whose principles became increasingly influential, focused much more on intent: one cannot be .guilty of a crime unless one fully understands the consequences of one's actions and intends those consequences. Reformers advocated shifting punishments away from terror, away from teaching blind obedience, and toward shaping intent and understanding, toward teaching appropriate action and penitence. They sought to limit harsh bodily punishments like whipping, branding, and hanging and to replace them with transportation, prisons, and reformatories. For children, this reform movement would culminate in the creation of separate juvenile courts by the end of the nineteenth century.

These debates were part of a larger struggle over intent that related to the struggle over consent and over equality. Legal ideas about guilt and punishment changed in response to the same debates about political authority that affected children's status in other ways. Key reformers, such as Sir Matthew

Hale, linked the ability to vote to criminal responsibility: both require reason and understanding. One cannot bear the responsibility for either without reason. Issues of political consent were bound up in the debates over criminal responsibility and punishment.

Yet one element would enter the logic of debate over punishing children that was absent from the debates over whether children should vote or exercise power: their threat to society. This issue of threat had the potential to trump the concerns about understanding and intent that tended to moderate punishment. Threat could be generally invoked (to set the age of criminal responsibility) but also selectively applied in a way that had class and race overtones, reminiscent of older status-based codes of punishment. "Threat to society" could override the claims of equality and intent and the very logic of the law. The principle behind this invocation of "threat," that any person who broke a law should be taught to obey through terror and blind obedience, was not new. By making children's criminal responsibility an issue separate from other types of civic responsibility and by setting the age lower, the effect was to selectively justify the previous norms of rule without consent, even of rule by terror: children could not make the law but could be punished for not following it.

In practice, the eighteenth and early nineteenth centuries witnessed a struggle between intent and threat, between sparing the child and seeking to make the child an example. An alternative to these two extremes, developed especially for youths between fourteen and eighteen, was modified versions of the new penitentiary that tried to reform them. Paying attention to age, which judges, juries, and witnesses generally did by the early nineteenth century, reveals concern not only about a person's responsibility for a criminal act but the possibility of reforming that person and the role of education in creating understanding and responsiblity. In a way, as Jeremy Bentham put it, all children were criminals in their understanding, in that they needed to be reformed and educated. On the other hand, they could not be criminally responsible. This conundrum did not apply simply to children. In a government based on consent, punishment itself raised terrible questions about the limits of consent—specifically about the ability to dissent and disagree with norms, particularly in one's actions. If the presumption is that all reasonable people will agree on just laws, then any who do not agree and do not follow them are by definition unreasonable and need reforming. Yet, if they are not reasonable, they cannot be punished: they can bear no responsiblity. The question of punishments and the debates over them had no simple answers for political reformers, whether political radicals in England or the most reformist of the American Revolutionaries.

The child-as-criminal still presents dilemmas for us today. If a child cannot have mens rea (criminal intent), how can the child's potential threat to society be met? To what extent should a child be responsible for a criminal act? The guidelines for accountability were defined during the same era as guidelines for political participation and political rights were, and by many of the same thinkers, legislators, and judges. Questions of accountability for crime and of membership in the political community were asked and answered in the same breath. Yet that connection has been lost, even to the very informed public of judges, lawyers, legislators, and legal historians. Attention to what is now defined as juvenile crime has focused on the last century and a half. Only by telling the history of the previous three centuries do the connections between children's liability for crime and what we would now call democratic political theory or, more broadly speaking, between crime and enlightenment, become clear. The question of children illuminates larger transformations in the meaning of culpability. The changing norms about culpability—which rested on ideas about human understanding—were rooted in the religious debates of early modern England and America.

"Eight yeares of age, or above, may commit hom[i]cide, and shall be hanged for it," stated *The Countrey Justice,* the popular guide for justices of the peace by Michael Dalton, in 1618. Puritans such as John Winthrop, who had been a justice of the peace in England before leaving for America, used it as a guide in crafting legal judgments. Dalton's guide was also recommended for judges in Virginia by a statute of 1666. But were his instructions followed? Dorcas Good was accused of witchcraft at age four in Salem in 1692 and spent the next six months in chains in the Boston jail. The two examples, of Good and of eight-year-old arsonist John Dean, demonstrate that very young children might be found guilty of crimes and punished during the seventeenth century in ways that they would not be punished today.[2]

Yet ascertaining the extent of child crime and punishment is nearly impossible. In 1629 when the Abingdon assize judges hanged eight-year-old John Dean for burning two barns, his age was recorded seemingly by chance. Arson was a crime eligible for benefit of clergy (a onetime exemption if one could read), but Dean could not claim it. Occasionally a boy could claim benefit of clergy, but he had to really know how to read. Age was not the main issue. Thirty-one different assize judges rode the home circuit in England during the late sixteenth and early seventeenth centuries and heard thousands of cases, but virtually none of the surviving records mention age. Strangely, in those few cases that do, one of two assize judges (Thomas

2. Michael Dalton, *The Countrey Justice* (1618; rpt. Amsterdam, 1975), 215.

Gawdy or Francis Gawdy) usually presided. Of the cases heard by these two judges over twenty years, even they rarely mentioned youth: they did so in only seven cases, and always as an afterthought, as a footnote or a comment after the guilty verdict. Even then they sometimes described the defendant only as a "child," "a boy," or a "small boy." In four cases, they mentioned exact ages: thirteen, ten, ten, eight. In all but one of them, the child was found guilty. In that case, John Shepe of Sevenoaks, age thirteen, had burned a barn with corn in it. He was allowed, as an adult would be, benefit of clergy, upon showing that he could read a passage from the Bible. Burnt on the thumb to signify that he had claimed this onetime exemption from the full punishment for felony, he would have no recourse if convicted of a felony again; he would be hanged.[3]

In the other cases, youth might have helped to reduce the sentence. Roger Gatton, age ten, was whipped for theft. But his punishment for theft depended largely upon the value of the goods, as it did for all others. Thomas Sharpe, age eight, guilty of burglarizing a house and stealing thirteen shillings, seems to have died in jail (or escaped?) several months after his conviction. Rachel Brackley, age ten, was remanded to jail without sentencing in July 1602. She had committed two thefts when age nine and ten (a gown, a kerchief, an apron, and five shillings). She would spend at least a year in prison and, like Sharpe, probably died there.[4] Thomas Toyse, "a boy" found

3. This information derives from a footnote inserted by Sollom Emlyn, the editor of Matthew Hale's *Historia Placitorum Coronae: The History of the Pleas of the Crown*, 2d ed. (London, 1778), I, 25. Emlyn found this in the manuscript reports of the Abingdon assizes, Feb. 23, 1629. Unfortunately, a zealous clerk in the early nineteenth century carefully destroyed old and useless records—including all those of the Abingdon assizes, so the details of the case that Emlyn consulted are now lost.

To get benefit of clergy, for which only males were eligible, one had to show that one was "preparing" for the clergy and to read a passage, at random, from the Bible. By the late sixteenth century, "preparing for the clergy" was increasingly treated as a formality, but the convicted person still had to read from the Bible. Sometimes a judge forewarned the condemned of the particular passage and let the condemned memorize it. Benefit of clergy, at least in its origins, was also a reflection of status, since mostly only youths of higher status learned to read. John Shepe's case was heard before John Southcote and Thomas Gawdy at the Rochester assizes, July 3, 1581. J. S. Cockburn, ed., *Kent Indictments, Elizabeth I* (London, 1979), 184.

4. Roger Gatton's case was heard by both Thomas Gawdy and Francis Gawdy, July 5, 1585, in Cockburn, ed., *Kent Indictments, Elizabeth I*, 242; Thomas Sharpe's case was heard by John Southcote and Thomas Gawdy, March 1578, in Cockburn, ed., *Essex Indictments, Elizabeth I* (London, 1978), 166 (also see record no. 997—he was still a prisoner in July 1578); Brackley's case was heard before Francis Gawdy and Sergeant

guilty of breaking into a house and stealing a shirt, a hat, and eighteen shillings, died in the Colchester jail two years after his conviction. Henry Hide, "a small boy," spent almost two years in jail for stealing some chickens, before he was pardoned in February 1601.[5] These are the few cases where age was mentioned. In remanding these convicted children to jail without sentencing them, the judges clearly intended to be merciful. Yet the high death rate in those jails meant that these young felons' escape from death by the noose usually offered no long-term blessing.[6]

While age was not important, all assize judges mentioned the status of the accused, directly after the name, as required by law. Thomas Toyse, for example, was identified as "of Braxted, labourer." Only in a brief comment at the end did Francis Gawdy and William Daniel, the assize judges in the case, note that he was a boy as their reason for deferring sentence. Sharpe (age eight), Shepe (age thirteen), Stanley (a child), and Hide (a small boy) were also called laborers. Gatton (age ten) was a yeoman, and Brackton was a "spinster." Gatton, the only one of higher status, was also the only one of this lot to be sentenced to a whipping, and freed, for theft. To routine court procedure, status mattered much more than age—one's status was as much a part of one as one's name. Youth was mentioned only as an afterthought—and almost only by these two judges, Francis and Thomas Gawdy, both Puritans or of Puritan sympathy.[7]

——————

John Heale in July 1602, in Cockburn, ed., *Essex Indictments, Elizabeth I*, 540. She was still listed as a jail prisoner in September 1603; see Cockburn, ed., *Essex Indictments, James I* (London, 1982), 2. She might have been freed as part of a general pardon by James I shortly after his succession, but, if so, she was not listed with the others on that pardons list.

5. Toyse's case was heard by Francis Gawdy and William Daniel in March 1601, in Cockburn, ed., *Essex Indictments, Elizabeth I*, 510. He remained a prisoner (see items 3188, 3231) through lists dating to July 1602 and died in the Colchester jail in February 1603. For inquest list, see Cockburn, *Introduction*, app. 2, 149. Hide's case was heard by Francis Gawdy and George Kingsmill in March 1599, in Cockburn, ed., *Kent Indictments, Elizabeth I*, 436. He remained a prisoner in jail (see items 2695, 2736, 2780) through assizes dated June 26, 1600, and was officially pardoned on February 27, 1601. For pardon list, see Cockburn, *Introduction*, app. 7, 203.

6. Cockburn, *Introduction*, 36–37, comments on how many prisoners died of typhoid and other jail fevers. Others simply starved. He also notes that the inquests are incomplete. Prisoners did sometimes escape.

7. J. S. Cockburn confirmed in a conversation with the author that he was consistent in recording the indictment records in full and was especially sensitive to age. So the fact that only nine cases, of tens of thousands, mention age is not due to inconsistency by the transcriber and translator. Cockburn was certain that Francis and Thomas Gawdy were

Coroners' reports, which did pay more attention to age, provide an important analytical source for understanding legal norms about culpability. Like the assize court judges, the coroners for Sussex during the reign of Elizabeth I (1558–1603), for example, always stated the status of the accused. They mentioned the age of the accused more frequently—7 percent of the time. Those the coroners gave ages to were often extremely young, five or under, who had died by drowning, a common cause of death (80 percent of those who drowned, where age was mentioned, were under five). The question was whether they had feloniously drowned themselves. Without exception, the answer was no. But they were responsible for their own deaths. Mary Water, age one year and seven months, for example, drowned in a "keeler" (used for cooling liquids) filled with water six inches deep and eighteen inches wide. The two servants who had left her alone in the kitchen with the keeler in order to "settle" a swarm of bees outside were not held accountable. Instead, the "misadventure" was by Mary herself, who caused her own death.[8]

Puritan. On this question also see *Dictionary of National Biography*, s.v. "Gawdy, Sir Thomas": he "distinguished himself from his colleagues as the 'only favourer' of the protestants."

Two other cases were not heard by one of the Gawdys: Joseph Griffen "a little boy," accused of stealing twelve pence in 1648, in Somerset assizes; William Andrewe, "aged 10 years," for stealing several yards of cloth, a pair of hose, and four pounds in 1594, at Chelmsford assizes. Griffen was found not guilty by the jury (his master had received much more money from his father to take him as an apprentice, and seemed to have brought the charge in order to keep it without obligation). Andrewe, "a husbandman," on the other hand, was found guilty and sentenced to hang. But then he was "remanded after sentence because he is a boy aged 10 years." His ultimate fate is unclear, but he was probably hanged at the next assizes. J. S. Cockburn, ed., *Somerset Assize Orders, 1640–1659* (Frome, 1971), 28–29; Cockburn, ed., *Essex Indictments, Elizabeth I*, 412–413.

Paul Griffiths, a historian who has examined many court records of early modern England looking specifically for evidence about youth, found little except in Norwich. He confessed himself frustrated, commenting, "Courtbooks like those of the Norwich Court of Mayoralty, which in some cases record the age of offenders, are unfortunately rare." Norwich was a center of Puritanism and a French Huguenot refuge in the late sixteenth century. *Youth and Authority: Formative Experiences in England, 1560–1640* (Oxford, 1996), 32.

8. R. F. Hunnisett, ed. and trans., *Sussex Coroners' Inquests, 1558–1603* (Kew, 1996), 54. Other drownings ruled "by misadventure": girl age 3 (no. 15); girl age 13 (no. 17); girl age 3 (no. 34); boy "about 5," fell into a moat (no. 57); boy "under 14," fell off a ship (no. 61); boy age 2, fell into a pond while playing by himself (no. 90); boy age 4, in tub, tub was deodand (no. 110); boy age 3 (no. 121); girl "an infant," fell off a bridge (no. 133); girl age 1 year, 11 months (no. 176); girl age 8, (no. 201); girl "aged over 4½" (no. 214); boy

Indeed, in none of those cases did adults bear any legal responsibility for the children's deaths. Susan Neve, age six months, was left on a chair near the fire by a servant who went to milk the cows. Susan "by misadventure and from lack of prudence, moving the chair, turned it over and she fell into the fire." The chair and Susan's own "lack of prudence" were held responsible for her death. The chair was forfeit as deodand. It was six-month-old Susan's misadventure, and the responsibility for her death lay only with herself and with the chair. "Edward Flemyng, being a child, was drownid in water by his owne default." The question for the coroner was, Did someone else cause the death? Inadequate supervision was never an issue: the responsibility for a death lodged only in someone who had actively hurt another.[9]

Things and animals were often partly responsible too, just like Susan's chair. A sixteen-year-old boy was driving a cart "laden with dede leaves" when " 'the further wheel of the cart' by misadventure 'did go over and crushe' the head of Joan Hide," age seven, who had been playing in the street. The cart in this case was held partly responsible for Hide's death and consequently forfeit as deodand.[10] During the sixteenth and seventeenth centuries, any *thing* that caused the death of a human being was considered "deodand" and forfeit to the king or lord or locality. Both Coke and Dalton devoted sections of their treatises to deodand. Coke defined a deodand as "any moveable thing inanimate, or beast animate, doe move to, or cause the untimely death of any

---

age 8 months (no. 215); girl "over 1½" (no. 225); girl age 2 (no. 234); girl age 5 (no. 246); girl age 14, fell on slippery steps (no. 256); girl age 1½, actually scalded by the keeler, keeler was deodand (no. 259); "a boy" (no. 260); a boy "aged over 3½" (no. 261); boy age 3 (no. 378); boy age 2 (no. 401); boy age 2 (no. 428); "a boy" (no. 433).

Others died from a fall, their deaths ruled misadventure: a boy age 10, climbing a plum tree (no. 117); a girl age 3, climbing onto a cart and falling onto stones, cart was deodand (no. 125). A five-year-old boy fell into a privy "by misadventure" when the boards broke (no. 83).

9. Hunnisett, ed. and trans., *Sussex Coroners' Inquests,* no. 177.

10. Ibid., no. 543. Cases where an animal or thing was held partly responsible for the death "by misadventure" of children include the following (in many other cases with deodands responsible, the age was not mentioned). *Sussex Coroners' Inquests:* John Allen, "about eleven," fell off a horse that went into a pond, and drowned; horse was deodand (no. 100). Thomas Bull, age 12, fell off a cart while driving it; cart was deodand (no. 131). Thomas Thomas, age 10, run over by cart he was sitting in; cart was deodand (no. 169). Simon Watle, "youth," killed by a wheel for a furnace; wheel forfeit as deodand (no. 447). Thomas Whyttur, age 11, "killed by the steers and plough" he was driving after he fell off, which were forfeit as deodand (no. 461). Elizabeth Phillipes "stumbled and fell in front of the cart of 'Roger Alderton, gent.' "; wheel was forfeit as deodand (no. 520). Also see no. 543, where horses, cart, wheels, and even the dead leaves in the cart were deodand.

reasonable creature by mischance . . . without the will, offence, or fault of himself, or of any person." Deodands could include not only animals but stones, carts, or logs.[11] Some early-seventeenth-century examples of deodands from Maryland, Plymouth, and Virginia included a tree that had fallen upon a man and killed him, a canoe that failed "to make way in a storm," and the chain with which a boy hanged himself. Puritans put to death the animals who participated in sexual acts with humans as well as the humans, who, we would now say, were the only ones who could intentionally commit the act of bestiality. Animals were occasionally tried in England as well (although not as frequently as in medieval or contemporary France). The very concept of deodand and the trial of animals suggest that intent was broadly defined.[12]

Some youths, at least, were held culpable for their own death: a fourteen-year-old boy "feloniously hanged" himself on a tree branch; a fifteen-year-old girl "feloniously" threw herself off a cliff; John Peach, age eighteen, "feloniously hanged himself in the barn of his master." Occasionally the ages of older accused were mentioned: Richard Willfford, "aged 40," feloniously hanged himself in his bedroom. It seems that only those over fourteen could be found guilty of felonious suicide. But, given that many cases mentioned no age, even that conclusion is tentative. A "girl" convicted of felonious suicide such as the following, for example, might well have been younger:

11. Dalton, *The Countrey Justice*, 218; Edw[ard] Coke, *The Third Part of the Institutes of the Laws of England . . .* (London, 1660), 57–58; William Blackstone, *Commentaries on the Laws of England* (London, 1765–1769), I, 290–292. Dalton defines deodand as follows:

> Next, what shall bee forfeited and taken for a Deodand; The olde rule is, *Omnia quae movent ad mortem, sunt Deodanda* [all things that cause a death, are deodands]: And yet besides, Deodands may bee of some things that a man shall moove or fall from, though the thing it selfe moves not; as to fall from a shippe, cart, mow of corne or hay, etc. So as Deodands are any good which doe cause, or are the occasion of the death of a man by misadventure.

According to a footnote in the 1916 edition of Blackstone, the last significant case of a deodand in England involved a steam engine in 1842. Deodands were formally abolished by statute in 1846 in England (9 and 10 Vict., c. 62). It is a measure of the obsolescence of deodand in America during the last two centuries that Lawrence M. Friedman's encyclopedic *Crime and Punishment in American History* (New York, 1993) contains no reference to deodands in the index.

12. Bradley Chapin, *Criminal Justice in Colonial America, 1606–1660* (Athens, Ga., 1983), 35; Walter Woodburn Hyde, "The Prosecution and Punishment of Animals and Lifeless Things in the Middle Ages and Modern Times," *University of Pennsylvania Law Review and American Law Register*, LXIV (1915–1916), 697–730; E. P. Evans, *The Criminal Prosecution and Capital Punishment of Animals* (New York, 1906); Keith Thomas, *Man and the Natural World: Changing Attitudes in England, 1500–1800* (New York, 1996), esp. 97.

"On 8 Nov. 1581 Joan Bray, a girl late of Cliffe, 'spynstar' [which refers only to rank, not to age], bought a portion of poison called 'ratsbane' worth ½d at Cliffe, mixed it with a draught and drank it, thereby murdering herself. At that time she had not goods or chattels beyond her clothes."[13]

Two points are clear here: (1) some "default" was on the part of the children for their own death even when they were not found guilty of suicide, and (2) coroners often mentioned the age of the deceased in order to justify a verdict of misadventure (so that their deed was not felonious suicide, which would forfeit their goods and deny them burial in hallowed ground). The coroners' juries found many of those whose ages were not listed to have "feloniously" killed themselves, whether by drowning or otherwise. Indeed, given that the belongings of those who committed suicide (felo de se) were forfeit (sometimes to the locality, sometimes to the lord, sometimes to the king), coroners' juries might have been encouraged to bring verdicts of felonious suicide in cases when a person owned goods. The fact that most children, especially five and under, had none of their own meant that incentive was absent in their cases.[14]

These coroners' rolls do show a pattern for the extremely young: if under age five, indeed, generally under age fourteen, one would probably not be held guilty of felonious suicide.[15] But intent was formulated differently during this period, which can be seen by examining the six different types of killing (and their punishments) that emerge from the legal manuals: (1) murder of superior, as of master, husband, lord: the status crime of petty treason for which the punishment was death, with either drawing and quartering for males or burning alive for females, no benefit of clergy allowed; (2) other murder: death, goods confiscated, no benefit of clergy; (3) manslaughter:

13. Hunnisett, ed. and trans., *Sussex Coroners' Inquests:* James Bacheler, 14-year-old boy (no. 52); Denise Dannyell, 15-year-old girl (no. 8); Peach (no. 66); Willfford (no. 64); Bray (no. 270).

14. A classic case of felonious drowning is the following: "Henry Michell feloniously killed himself by throwing himself into the salt water of the sea in the strand at Rye. At that time he had 'a dublet, a cloke, a payre of breches, a shert, a hatt, a gerdle and a payre of stockings' worth 20s, and 6 s in money, all of which the Rye chamberlain was ordered to seize for the town's use." Ibid., no. 548.

15. Later guides clearly specified "discretion," or "fourteen" for guilt in suicide. To be guilty of suicide, the person must be "1. Of the Age of Discretion. 2. Compos Mentis. 3. The Act must be voluntary." The punishment would be that the goods would be forfeit to the king for depriving him of a subject. *Conductor Generalis; or, The Office, Duty, and Authority of Justices of the Peace* . . . (Philadelphia, 1722), 85. Thomas Wood explicitly excused those under fourteen from liability for suicide, in *An Institute of the Laws of England* . . . , 6th ed. (London, 1738), 352.

benefit of clergy, but only for men who could read, and burning on hand; otherwise, death by hanging, goods confiscated; (4) misadventure: the person accountable for own death, by accident, goods usually not forfeit; (5) felonious suicide: the person held responsible for own death, done on purpose, goods confiscated; (6) death from natural causes: no one and no thing responsible.[16]

An important clue about the weak way in which *intent* was understood is that juries and judges were inconsistent in practice about distinguishing the boundaries between murder, manslaughter, and misadventure, especially when someone had actually caused physical harm to another with a sharp object or a gun. Even though death by misadventure was seemingly not supposed to result in forfeiture of goods (except deodands), some coroners' juries seemed to think that it might.[17] Edward Putland picked up a gun not knowing it was loaded, which killed Elizabeth Salter. This was called a "misadventure," but punished more harshly, with confiscation of goods, than some other deaths by misadventure (Putland's belongings, appraised at 30s., and the gun appraised at 6s. 8d., were all forfeited). A similar case is that of George Stephen, "laborer, aged 15," who killed Joan Baylye "by misadventure and against his will" when he picked up someone else's "goone," which he did not realize was loaded. Even though ruled misadventure, his goods would have been forfeit had he owned any. Dueling was usually considered manslaughter (so eligible for benefit of clergy), but there was some question among the coroners' juries over it. Obviously, duels were planned. Those who killed in self-defense were found guilty of murder but then bailed and urged to obtain a pardon. After Katharine Lucas attacked and killed Alice Tuppen with a wool card, the coroner ruled "felonious," but then the jury acquitted Lucas, on the grounds that "John Card" was "said to have killed" Tuppen. No "John Card" was prosecuted, and the jury seems to have found the wool card guilty. Anthropomorphizing happened in other cases, when people were acquitted of murder on the grounds that "John in the Wind" or "John Death"

16. But, for misadventure, see Hunnisett, ed. and trans., *Sussex Coroners' Inquests*, no. 433. Occasionally the jurors seem to have valued their goods anyway, meaning they weren't really distinguishing between misadventure and murder.

17. See, for example, ibid., no. 74: "John Nele accidentally killed himself. Therefore felo de se. He had not lands or tenaments, goods or chattels." So accidental death could be felo de se. On the other hand, no. 247: "On 25 May [1580], when Christopher Bristowe and Humphrey Blackfane were wishing to wash in a pond or pit in East Grinstead, they were drowned in it by misadventure and not by their intention or that of any other person." Their goods were not evaluated, and no effort seems to have been made to evaluate them.

was "said to have killed" the person in question, thus shifting responsibility from a person to a thing.[18]

The general point is this: intent had a different meaning and weight than it does in the law today. Whether the killing had been planned in advance ("malice prepensed") sometimes helped to differentiate murder from manslaughter. But that distinction, so fundamental to our law today, was much less important than the simple fact of who or what directly caused the death (intentional or not). The proximate causer of the death was critical to accountability, and "causer" was quite broadly defined. Murder and manslaughter, particularly, had a very thin line between them, with even manslaughter punished by death, unless one could plead benefit of clergy. Indeed, only during the sixteenth century, arguably in response to the Reformation, did manslaughter begin to be distinguished from murder. The distinction rested on premeditation.[19] Despite these emerging distinctions between manslaughter and murder, the legal definitions of different kinds of killing depended to a great degree on ideas about direct causation. Even accidental deaths bore some degree of responsibility. It was important whether a person had meant to commit a crime, but not important whether a person understood its consequences. Even if someone had not meant to commit the crime, that person still bore a residual accountability: although youths seemed to bear reduced responsibility for suicide, for example, they could still be at fault in their own death.[20]

18. Ibid.: Putland, no. 444; Stephen, no. 168; dueling, no. 527 ("And whether this be murder or manslaughter we referre yt to the lawe and as it shalbe adjudged so we finde"); self-defense, no. 464; John Card, nos. 417, 422, 448, 479 ("John in the Wynd"), 481 ("John at Noke"), 96 ("John ap Nokes").

19. J. M. Kaye, "The Early History of Murder and Manslaughter," *Law Quarterly Review*, LXXXIII (1967), 365–395, 569–601. Kaye argues against discerning modern murder distinctions in the Middle Ages. He shows, among other things, how men who killed others in spontaneous fights were found guilty of homicide in the fourteenth century and how phrases such as "malice prepensed" meant something very different in the late Middle Ages than modern legal commentators have assumed. J. M. Beattie, *Crime and the Courts in England, 1660–1800* (Oxford, 1986), 91–106, effectively continues where Kaye left off. Beattie finds an increasing distinction, based on intent, between murder and manslaughter during the eighteenth century.

20. Dalton's *Countrey Justice*, 205–223, reveals how confusingly the distinctions were drawn between homicide, manslaughter, misadventure, and chance-medley. Consider, even, the confusion evident in the Massachusetts laws of 1641: "If any person committt any wilfull murther, which is manslaughter, committed upon premeditated malice, hatred, or Crueltie, not in a mans necessarie and just defence, nor by meere casualtie against his will, he shall be put to death." In Edwin Powers, *Crime and Punishment in Early Massachusetts, 1620–1692* (Boston, 1966), 545.

Distinctions between different grades of murder were based to a great degree, as well, on status (a servant's killing a master was punished much more harshly than vice versa). It was assumed, for example, that a mistress or master who killed a servant while punishing him or her had not planned the death, whereas a servant killing a master or mistress was guilty of petty treason (a murder as well as a status offense).[21]

Despite the general disregard of age, a few English laws exempted children from punishment, usually at very young ages, with the exemption varying by the type of crime committed. According to William Lambarde in 1581, those over six could be punished for not wearing English-made woolen caps on Sundays and holidays, and every "man childe" over seven could be punished for not owning a longbow with two shafts (so he could serve in the militia).[22] Yet actions of the peace could be made against them regardless of their age. Those over age sixteen could be punished for not attending church. The highest age limit I discovered was a statute of Henry VIII's that encouraged leniency to servants under age eighteen and all apprentices who stole from their masters or mistresses; it was cited by many early law books. But that statute still left such servants and apprentices culpable.[23]

21. See, for example, Hunnisett, ed. and trans., *Sussex Coroners' Inquests*, no. 5, where a mistress who hit and killed her eight-year-old servant was found not guilty of murder. This is a common pattern. Dalton's *Countrey Justice*, 149, made it clear that killing a servant or child in the act of punishing her or him "in a reasonable and moderate manner" was not murder, because some people have a "naturall" or "civile" authority over others.

> Also though Assaults and Batteries bee for the most part contrarie to the peace of the realme, and the lawes of the same, yet some are allowed to have a naturall, and some a civile power (or authoritie) over others; so that they may (in reasonable and moderate manner only) correct and chastice them for their offences, without any imputation of breach of the peace, yea they may (by the law) justifie the same.

> And therefore the parent (with moderation) may chastise his child within age.

> So may the master his servant, or apprentice.

22. William Lambarde, *Eirenarcha; or, Of the Office of the Justices of Peace* (1581; rpt. Amsterdam, 1970), 373. "If any person above six yeres of age (except Maydens . . . Nobles . . .) have not worne upon the Sunday and Holiday . . . upon his head, one Cape of Wooll, knit, thicked, and dressed in *Englande*," that person would be fined. Every man under sixty "being the Queenes subject" should have a longbow, and "everie man childe in his house betweene seaven yeres and seaventeene of age a Bow and two Shaftes, and for everie such being above seventeene yeares, a Bowe and foure Shaftes" (378).

23. Ibid., 200; Wood, *Institute of the Laws*, 403; 21 Hen. VIII, c. 7; Antho[ny] Fitzherbert, *Loffice et aucthoritie de justices de peace . . .*, enl. R[ichard] Crompton (1584; rpt. London, 1972), 39; [Matthew Hale], *Pleas of the Crown; or, A Brief, But Full Account of Whatsoever Can Be Found Relating to That Subject* (London, 1678), 51; *Conductor Generalis*, 88.

The coroners' rolls reveal that what the laws said did matter: they paid attention to the age restrictions where they existed, especially with religious crimes (which included suicide) where age limits for culpability were higher. One case of recusancy appeared in the coroners' rolls because the convicted man died in prison, but it showed keen attention to the age limit for prosecution: Simon Godfreye "being over 16" was arrested in 1588 for not attending any "church or chapel" for two months. He died on March 30, 1599, eleven years later, still in the Horsham jail, for refusing "to satisfy the penalties laid down in the statute."[24]

But there was not a solid rule even for religious cases: the medieval canon law incorporated different opinions on this issue that engendered new debate during the Reformation. Under fourteen, the age of discretion in the Marian heresy trials, one was supposed to be able to change one's mind about religious affiliation. Yet at least one heretic was only eleven: John Davis escaped martyrdom by Henry VIII's death. (At the accession of a new king, general pardons were issued to all those awaiting trial or execution.) Davis spent months in chains in prison and underwent several inquisitions to force him to recant; the inquisitors tested his resolution to burn for his religious beliefs by holding his hand in a candle flame.[25]

Untangling culpability is not a simple matter even in legal guides used by contemporaries. Consider the guides for justices of the peace published in England in the late sixteenth and early seventeenth centuries, widely used by justices, often as their only form of legal training. Andrew Horne's *Mirrour of Justices*, a text on English law, was originally composed in French (as "La somme appele mirroir de justices vel speculum justiciariorum") in the fourteenth century but translated and published in English in 1646, during the Interregnum. According to Horne, the age of discretion was over seven years, and he excused those under that age from culpability for murder.[26] Christopher Saint-German's *Dialogue betweene a Doctor of Divinity and a Student in the Laws of England,* a fifteenth-century legal guide reprinted many times during the seventeenth century and cited by later manuals, offered no age but

24. Hunnisett, ed. and trans., *Sussex Coroners' Inquests*, no. 530.

25. John Foxe, *Book of Martyrs; or, An Universal History of Martyrdom* (1563; rpt. New York, 1965), VIII, 554.

26. Andrew Horne, *The Booke Called, The Mirrour of Justices* . . . (1300s), trans. W. H. (London, 1646), 195. Those excused from liability for murder include "those who kill without Judgement, and without offence, as it is of those who are without discretion and kill men, as Mad-men, Idiots, Infants within the age of seven yeares." Horne was cited as an authority by St. George Tucker, *Blackstone's Commentaries: With Notes of Reference, to the Constitution and Laws, of the Federal Government of the United States; and of the Commonwealth of Virginia,* 5 vols. (Philadelphia, 1803), IV, 23.

emphasized that, if the perpetrator was "within yeeres of discretion to know good from evill," she or he should be excused from corporal punishment. In the same paragraph, Saint-German used the phrase "discretion to know the law," implying that knowing good from evil was similar to the ability to simply "know the law." William Stanford's *Les plees del coron* (1567) held that the age should be twelve but that under that age a child might still be guilty if she or he understood the difference between good and evil. William Lambarde's 1581 *Eirenarcha*, although it made no mention of age, elaborated slightly on the question of capacity. He argued: "[If] a childe tht apparantly hath no knowledge of good nor evil, do kil a man, this is no felonious acte, nor any thing forfeited by it. For they cannot be said to have any understanding wil. But if upon examination it fal out, tht they knew what they did, and tht it was ill, then seemeth it to be otherwise." His emphasis was thus on whether the perpetrator had "knowledge of good [or] evil." But his comments about "understanding wil" are different from the others'.[27]

By the early seventeenth century, Dalton's guide elaborated on these issues. The general rule, according to *The Countrey Justice* (1618), was, "If one that is *Non compos mentis,* or an Ideot, kill a man, this is no felonie; for they have no knowledge of good and evill, nor can have a felonious intent, nor a will or mind to do harme: And no felony or murder can be committed without a felonious intent and purpose." Despite these epistemological elaborations, Dalton repeated the earlier low age limit: a person could be guilty of murder if over seven. "Eight yeares of age, or above, may commit hom[i]cide, and shall be hanged for it, *viz.* If it may appeare (by hyding of the person slaine, by excusing it, or by any other act) that he had knowledge of good and evill, and of the perill and danger of that offence." He thus excluded, along with children under age eight, lunatics, natural fools, and those born deaf-mute. He emphasized that "an infant of such tender yeares, as that he hath no discretion or intelligence, if he kill a man, this is no felonie in him."[28]

"Age of discretion" evidently had more than one meaning. To Dalton and Horne, it meant passing seven years; to Stanford in *Le plees del coron*, it meant

27. [Christopher Saint-German], *The Dialogue in English; between a Doctor of Divinity, and a Student in the Laws of England* (London, 1638), chap. 46, 147b; [William Stanford], *Les plees del coron . . .* (London, 1567), 16. "Mes si un del age de. 12. ans, ou outer, tua auter ceo est felony, mesme ley est sil ne soite que de. 9. ans al temps del tuer, si issint soit que per ascun signes poit estre intendu que il ad conusance de bien et male, come per son excuse, ou per ascun act que il fesoit apres le tuer. s. in occultant le mort in ascun secret" (citing 3 Hen. VII, fo. 2). Lambarde also excused a "mad man or a naturalle foole, or a lunaticke in the time of his lunacie," citing two laws, 21 Hen. VII, c. 31, and 3 Hen. VII, c. 1 (*Eirenarcha*, 218).

28. Dalton, *The Countrey Justice*, 215, citing 3 Hen. VII, c. 1, c. 1b (statutory).

attaining age twelve. Saint-German and Lambarde specified no age. Age eight seems to have been the norm specified in Tudor homicide law as well as in pre-Reformation Catholic canon law. The canon law, in particular, was murky. While canon law had set six or seven as the minimum age for accountability in the late Middle Ages, it was strongly influenced during the fifteenth and sixteenth centuries by Justinian's *Institutes* and *Digest* of Roman laws, which gave twelve for girls and fourteen for boys as the ages of entering adulthood, which influenced canon law on marriage. But canon law attached great importance to age seven in marriage law as well (the minimum age to consent to marriage). It is possible that these ages from canon law of seven (or having finished seven years, which is eight), twelve, and fourteen influenced the discussion here. Coke linked the age of discretion to the age of fourteen with respect to homicide. In that, he was unusual, apparently consciously advocating a change in policy.[29]

Even in the late seventeenth century, however, Coke's injunction was not the norm followed, not even for the less serious crime of theft, as pamphlets that summarized trials at the Old Bailey and other assize courts surrounding London in the late seventeenth century reveal. Most of these pamphlets also ignored age completely, but a few referred to it in passing. At the Old Bailey in August 1679, for example:

> Four young gentlemen scholars of Westminster school, charged with killing a Bailey that came to make an arrest near that school . . . should likewise have been tried this sessions; but the Coroner declaring, that the

29. For ages in Tudor homicide trials, see Peter C. Hoffer and N. E. H. Hull, *Murdering Mothers: Infanticide in England and New England, 1558–1803* (New York, 1981), xiii. They cite, specifically, 3 Hen. VII, c. 1, which early legal treatises do sometimes as well—but this law is very vague and certainly does not give a specific age to liability. They do not cite specific court records. Steven Ozment, *When Fathers Ruled: Family Life in Reformation Europe* (Cambridge, Mass., 1983), gives six or seven as the appropriate age (144). Edward Britton, *The Community of the Vill: A Study in the History of the Family and Village Life in Fourteenth-Century England* (Toronto, 1977), examining the late-medieval English village of Broughton, in Huntingdonshire, concludes that the youngest offenders were "presumably teenagers" and over twelve but gives no supporting data (39). Robert B. Shoemaker, *Prosecution and Punishment: Petty Crime and the Law in London and Rural Middlesex, c. 1660–1725* (Cambridge, 1992), does not address ages of the convicted.

Coke: *Third Part of the Institutes* (1660), 47; *The First Part of the Institutes of the Laws of England* . . . , 4th ed. (London, 1639), 247b. In this chapter in the *First Part* on whether a person could make a feoffment of land, he stated that the age of discretion for criminal matters was fourteen.

King's evidence was not ready . . . they were put off to the next sessions; and in the mean time, after some mature consideration of their youth and quality, to prevent the inconveniences that might attend their continuing so long amongst ill company in custody, were admitted to extraordinary Bail.

The pamphlets mentioned no further prosecution. All four "young gentlemen" were presumably under thirteen and conceivably as young as seven (the ages when one would attend Westminster). But their "extraordinary" treatment had to be due primarily to their status. At the same sessions Margaret Taylor, "a girl," received a death sentence for robbing her mistress (a verdict despite the statute mentioned above that encouraged leniency in such cases). And in January of the same year, a report on the executions at Tyburn noted that one of those executed was "young in years."

> The next in this dread sceen of Fate was John Maccarty, a notorious offender, who tho but young in years, yet old in sin, he was indicted for stealing a piece of twelve-penny-broad ribbon, valued at 10s. . . . and being brought in guilty of the same, the Executioner going to search his hand, found that he had formerly been burned, so that he being an incorrigible offender, the court passed sentence of death upon him.

"Young in years, yet old in sin" was not an uncommon expression. That he had stolen a ribbon after previous conviction confirmed to the court that he was "incorrigible."[30]

A case similar to that of the "four young gentlemen scholars of Westminster school" illustrates beautifully the way that status trumped age. Just as with the "young gentlemen scholars," this case involved the murder of a "Bailey," or a "beadle." In late February 1670/1 Christopher Monck, duke of Albemarle, was involved, with other young lords, including the duke of Monmouth (Charles II's illegitimate son) and the duke of Somerset, in a wild party at a "scandalous" house in Whetstone Park, then a seedy part of London. At a "very unseasonable" hour of the night, they making "shrill noises," the watch came to quiet them. "In came the watch, disturbed with sleep and ale. . . . Then fell the Beadle by a ducal hand." Christopher Monck, then seventeen, seemingly with the aid of Monmouth (twenty-one), and Somerset (thirty-six), killed a beadle, one of the watch, apparently with a sword or knife, since Monck was "all daubed with lace and blood." Even these powerful

30. *The Proceedings at the Sessions at the Old-Baily, August the 27th and 28th, 1679* (n.p., n.d.), 3–4; *A True Narrative of the Confession and Execution of the Three Prisoners at Tyburn* [*January 1679*] (n.p., n.d.).

young men realized the danger they were in, and they hurried at once to the king to beg a pardon. Despite the heinous nature of the crime—essentially equal to killing a policeman who came to quiet a party—Charles II pardoned all involved within the month, Monck first, he being most at fault (his pardon was the fullest). The populace of London was so angry at the actions of these young lords that Charles II canceled a ball he had planned for the next weekend. Not simply the pardons but also letters, and even a poem, recorded the story as a kind of oral history. It was clearly a widespread scandal. The oral history reproved the king's pardon.

> Near t'other park there stands an aged tree
> As fit as if 'twere made o'th'nonce for three
> Where that no ceremony may be lost
> Each Duke for state may have a several post.

Deference to the status of the three dukes could be maintained by giving each his own branch to hang from. For lesser men or youths, killing a beadle would have meant precisely that. For murder there was no benefit of clergy, no onetime exemption, and only very rarely a pardon from the king. A pardon would usually be granted, if at all, only after a trial, conviction, and a recommendation by the judge to the king that the person in question be pardoned. They should have been judged by their peers in the House of Lords (where they would, one assumes, have been less likely to be convicted than if tried by a regular jury), but the king did not even let the trial take place.[31]

Comparing the punishment of John Maccarty for stealing a ribbon (death) to that of Christopher Monck for killing a beadle (nothing) shows the powerful role of status. The "young in years" Maccarty was almost certainly younger than seventeen-year-old Monck. Unlike the prominent Monck, however, whose birth date is easy to trace, Maccarty's is almost impossible. Examining other uses of the words "young in years" in these records gives clues to his age. If a report specified the accused as "young," he or she was probably very young, under twelve, at least, and perhaps eight or ten.

Indeed, it seems clear that a child of eight or above should be held liable for

31. Estelle Frances Ward, *Christopher Monck, Duke of Albemarle* (London, 1915), 47–50. By the eighteenth century, at least, the norm was for a judge to recommend a pardon, and the king perhaps to give it, at some point well after the trial. On pardons, see, particularly, Douglas Hay, "Property, Authority, and the Criminal Law," in Hay et al., *Albion's Fatal Tree: Crime and Society in Eighteenth-Century England* (New York, 1975), 17–63. On trials of peers in the House of Lords, see Andrew Swatland, *The House of Lords in the Reign of Charles II* (Cambridge, 1996).

theft, according to most authorities. In justice of the peace guides, the discussion of the age of culpability for theft and other felonies was similar to that for murder. The one exception was Dalton, who introduced fourteen as a minimum age for liability for theft. "It is not Burglary in an Infant of fourteene yeares of age; nor in poore persons that upon hunger shall enter a house for victuall under the value of twelve pence; Nor in natural fooles, or other persons that bee *non compos mentis*." In his guidelines to juries about whether they should convict a person of a crime, Dalton noted that the jury should take into consideration many things, including whether the accused was an "infant."[32] Hale's *Pleas of the Crown* (1678) partially followed Dalton, but equivocated. "An Infant under fourteen years may commit Larceny, but prudence to respite Judgment; yet under fourteen burnt in the hand." After Dalton, fourteen seemed to become a possible exemption and a specific issue. But his strictures do not appear to have been widely accepted in the late seventeenth century.[33]

The late-seventeenth-century London reports indicate that, despite Dalton's advice, many "boys" and "girls" and "young girls" and "young youths" were punished for theft with transportation or death. In 1686, Nathaniel Johnson, "a boy about ten years of age," was indicted for stealing thirty pounds and convicted. As punishment, he was transported to the colonies. Thomas Jones, "a boy," was found guilty of theft and sentenced to death.

> Thomas Jones, a boy, Jane Bowman, and Thomas Davis were tried for breaking the house of . . . taking away two silver spoons value 12 s., a piece of angel gold, and other goods, some of which were found about Jones [and he confest] . . . yet the latter two were acquitted, but Jones was found guilty.

Mary Williams and Elizabeth Burkin were convicted, on slim evidence, of picking pockets. Nothing was found on either prisoner (supposedly because they had conveyed the booty to another, who had "run away"), and "they both denied the fact, but they were known to be old offenders, tho very young." Both received a sentence of death. In the same sessions, Walter Stephens, "a

32. Dalton, *The Countrey Justice*, 226, 267. [Stanford], *Les plees del coron*, specified guilt in larceny in the same way he defined a child's guilt in a murder trial: that is, if the child were under twelve, she or he might be guilty if able to tell the difference between good and evil (27).

33. [Hale], *Pleas of the Crown*, 53. Hale argued that one had to have reached discretion to be guilty of treason (10). He cites 3 Hen. VII, c. 7. But of course the reliability of that reference is compromised if "discretion" does not have a stable age definition.

young youth," received a sentence of death for stealing a sword worth forty shillings.[34]

Other children were burned on the hand. Mary Middleton, "a child, aged about seven or eight years," was found guilty of stealing two silver spoons and other things, "to which she pleaded guilty," so was "burnt in the hand." William Carter, "a little boy, about ten years of age," was convicted of stealing two gold rings and some money (total eighty-six shillings), for which his hand was branded. Two "young girls," Rebeka Cook and Sarah Tomson, were found guilty of stealing fifty yards of silk. The jury moderated their punishment by falsely valuing the silk at only nine shillings (when it was really worth about forty shillings) as juries frequently did in any theft case, regardless of age, in the eighteenth century. As a consequence, both were punished only by being "burnt in the hand." Being burned on the hand, however, literally branded one for life. If any of these children were convicted of another crime, their hands, like those of John Maccarty, above, would be searched, the brand would be found, and they would be seen as "old offenders, tho very young."[35]

Other boys and girls were whipped. The difference in punishment was based largely on the value of the goods. Lawrence Nonny, "a black boy," stole a staff with a silver head valued at more than four pounds. The jury undervalued it at ten shillings. He was sentenced to be whipped "from Newgate to the Royal Exchange." Thomas Turner, "an idle young boy," confessed that he broke into a house by removing a pane of glass, put in his hand and took a cane valued at two shillings, for which he was whipped. Jane Peel, "a girle," accused of stealing nine shillings, convicted by the jury of stealing ten pence, was whipped. Peter Gough, indicted for stealing nine yards of bone lace valued at fifteen shillings, was convicted by the jury "to the value of 10 d." The judges sentenced him "to be whipt from Newgate to Holborn bar."[36]

Just like adults, some children were acquitted or pardoned. Ruth de-Pree, "a little girl, aged 8 or 9 years," was accused of stealing a silver tester and a little money. The Old Bailey reporter called the evidence "weak" (no one had seen her, the goods were not found, and she had not confessed), and thus she

34. The Proceedings on the King's Commission of the Peace . . . in the Old-Bayly [May 20–22, 1686] (London, 1686), 1, 4; The Proceedings . . . [Feb. 18–20, 1690/1] (London, 1690), 2, 4; The Proceedings . . . [Apr. 26–29, 1693] (London, 1693), 3, 6.

35. Proceedings [Apr. 26–29, 1693], 3, 6; The Proceedings . . . [May 1–2, 1690] (London, 1690), 4; The Proceedings . . . [July 17, 18, 1690] (London, 1690), 3. For regular undervaluation by juries, see Peter Linebaugh, The London Hanged: Crime and Civil Society in the Eighteenth Century (Cambridge, 1992), esp. 81.

36. Proceedings [May 1–2, 1690], 1, 4; The Proceedings . . . [Sept. 3–5, 1690] (n.p., 1690), 1, 4; Proceedings . . . [Dec. 11–14, 1689] (London, 1689), 3.

was acquitted. Susannah Tyrrell, "a girl about ten years old," confessed to stealing two gold rings and fourteen shillings. Although initially sentenced to be transported for the theft, she was pardoned in the next sessions, along with twenty-nine other people (as part of a general pardon of all convicts by William and Mary near the time of their accession to the throne).[37]

Youth did not necessarily even moderate the punishment. Consider this case heard before the Old Bailey in 1690: "Richard Eaton and James Ardon were both indicted for robbing Henry Meseles of Stepney. . . . All of which the boy, Eaton, confest before Justice Withers. . . . Upon the whole, Arden was found to entice the Boy to rob his master; yet in the conclusion they were both found guilty." Both Arden and the "boy" were then punished identically, sentenced to be transported to the colonies. Nicholas Carter and Giles Webb, "two pick-pocket boys," "were tryed for taking the beaver hat off the head of one Mr. William Cummins, value 3 £ 2 s." Carter confessed and was sentenced to death. Webb was acquitted because of insufficient evidence. In Carter's dying speech, he pleaded that "if he might be spared he resolved to amend his evil life." The ordinary described him as "about fourteen years of age."[38]

Age was alluded to in a seemingly random way. Some of the Old Bailey reporters seemed to care more about it and would report it occasionally. Others might mention age obliquely when describing the evidence:

Thomas Finch . . . was indicted for stealing a quart pot. . . . The evidence set forth that the prisoner and another boy were seen in an alley that goes up to the house and the prisoner had the potts upon him.

Many other reports from the Old Bailey during the late seventeenth and early eighteenth centuries gave no clue to the age of any of the accused whose cases they listed. Others might say something vague, such as an ordinary's describing the execution of John Benlose for burglary "and attempting to kill his master," as "cut off in the flower of his youth." In 1690 a reporter described some of the accused as "boy" or "girl," but not Constance Wainwright. Yet her dying speech revealed her age as sixteen. She was condemned to death for "stealing a teapot and other things."[39]

37. *Proceedings [Sept. 3–5, 1690]*, 2, 4; *The Proceedings . . . [Oct. 15–18, 1690]* (London, 1690), 4.

38. *Proceedings [Sept. 3–5, 1690]*, 2, 4; *The Proceedings . . . [Jan. 15–19, 1690/1]* (London, 1690[/1]), 3, 4; *A True Account of the Behaviour, Confession, and Last Dying Speeches of the Eight Criminals That Were Executed at Tyburn [Jan. 26, 1690/1]* (London, 1690), 2.

39. *The Proceedings . . . [Dec. 10–13, 1712]* (London, 1712), 1 (Finch was sentenced to be whipped [6]); *A True Account of the Behaviour, Confession, and Last Dying Speeches [Jan.*

Unsurprisingly, the colonial American records reveal a similar picture with regard to the ages of the accused. Colonial courts and judges used the same English legal guides by Dalton and others. But the Puritans in Massachusetts, in particular, crafted their own, elaborate criminal code. The Massachusetts Body of Liberties provided some guidelines about children's liability for crime, which exempted children more from punishment, along with others who might not know the rules. "Children, Idiots, Distracted persons, and all that are strangers or new commers to our plantation, shall have such allowances and dispensations in any Cause whether Criminall or other as religion and reason require." This Massachusetts policy showed some correspondence to English guides for justices of the peace such as Dalton's. Yet few of these earliest laws contained explicit legal exemptions based on age.[40]

One peculiarity of Puritan laws was that young children could be sentenced to be punished by their parents. For example, according to the Massachusetts laws of 1660, those over fourteen who lied could be fined, but those under age fourteen were to be given "correction" by their parents under the supervision of a magistrate. The same general guidelines applied to children's proper observance of the Sabbath. Yet, as a 1668 law made clear, Massachusetts policy would be that "in all Criminal cases, every person younger as well as elder, shall be liable to answer in their own persons, for such misdemeanours as they shall be accused of, and may also inform and present any misdemeanour to any Magistrate," even though in civil cases those under twenty-one were to be represented by a guardian, parent, or master. So, while Massachusetts distinguished limits for culpability in some ways, it did not in others. One might even argue that the 1668 law made children explicitly culpable.[41]

Indeed, Massachusetts, like England during the same period, largely disregarded age. Dorcas Good, seen earlier, was only four years old when accused of witchcraft in Salem in 1692. She was arrested and sent to the Boston jail "upon suspition of acts of Witchcraft by her committed." The actual court

---

26, 1690/1], 1; *Proceedings [Oct. 15–18, 1690]; A True Account of the Behaviour, Confession, and Last Dying Speeches of the Criminals Executed at Tyburn on Friday, the 24th of October, 1690* (London, 1690), 2; *Proceedings [Dec. 10–17, 1690]* (London, 1690), 3–6.

40. Quoted in Powers, *Crime and Punishment,* 440, from the Body of Liberties (1641), article 52. Also see Ross W. Beales, Jr., "In Search of the Historical Child: Miniature Adulthood and Youth in Colonial New England," *American Quarterly,* XXVII (1975), 379–398; John Demos, *A Little Commonwealth: Family Life in Plymouth Colony* (New York, 1970).

41. Joseph M. Hawes, *Children in Urban Society: Juvenile Delinquency in Nineteenth-Century America* (New York, 1971), 15; *The General Laws and Liberties of the Massachusetts Colony: Revised and Re-printed* (Cambridge, Mass., 1672), 2.

records do not give her age but refer to her only as "the daugter of W'm Good" on her arrest warrant and as "Sarah goods daughter" in the testimony against her. Other arrest warrants referred to people by their family status, as "Rebeca Nurce the wife of franc's nurce." "Daughter" could refer to a girl or young woman of any age before, one supposes, marriage. Dorcas spent six months in chains in the Boston jail before she was allowed bail. Still, proceedings against her did not progress as quickly or as far as those against Rebecca Nurse, who was arrested at the same time, convicted of witchcraft, and executed. Dorcas was probably accused, at least in part, because her mother already stood accused of witchcraft. There was some suspicion that her mother might have tainted her daughter (following witchcraft beliefs of that time: if demons could suckle off a witch's teats, a child might similarly suckle evil through her mother's milk). Mary Lacey, Jr., was fifteen when she was arrested for witchcraft a few months later (her age appeared only in her recognizance). Like Dorcas, she was referred to in her arrest warrant as "daughter of Lawrence Lacy." She was not convicted, because the witchcraft proceedings as a whole collapsed.[42]

Looking only at these two cases and at the few laws that exempted the very young, one could argue that, in Massachusetts, youth were prosecuted more lightly than adults in the seventeenth century. Others tried in the same courtrooms as Dorcas Good during the Salem witch trials of 1692 suffered death, but Dorcas escaped with only chains and imprisonment. Edwin Powers's careful study of the records of seventeenth-century Massachusetts acknowledged, "Rarely does the age of the offender appear in the records." But he did find a few examples where children, instead of being sent to the public whipping post, were given to their parents to be punished in conformity with the laws. The youngest confirmed conviction and execution for any felony (in this case "buggery" with a selection of barnyard animals ranging from a mare to a turkey) was of Thomas Granger, "16 or 17" years old, in 1642. We know his age only from William Bradford's corresponding account of his case. Powers concludes with a sentence that hides a powerful assumption: "There is no evidence that anyone under the age of fifteen was executed in the Bay Colony." Yet there is *little* evidence that anyone *over* age fifteen was executed.

42. Paul Boyer and Stephen Nissenbaum, eds., *The Salem Witchcraft Papers: Verbatim Transcripts of the Legal Documents of the Salem Witchcraft Outbreak of 1692* (New York, 1977), I, 255, II, 351–353, 519, 533, 583, 662; Boyer and Nissenbaum, *Salem Possessed: The Social Origins of Witchcraft* (Cambridge, Mass., 1974), 5. Also see Carol F. Karlsen, *The Devil in the Shape of a Woman: Witchcraft in Colonial New England* (New York, 1987), 64. Of the 156 witchcraft prosecutions where Karlsen could estimate the age of the women accused (or 60 percent of witchcraft cases involving women in New England before 1725), she identifies 3 as under ten (one of whom was Dorcas Good).

We have no proof, to flip Powers's assumption on its head, that someone under age fifteen was *not* executed.[43]

The minimal concern with ages in these criminal records is more than a curtain: it reveals that age was not central in assessing culpability. Given that the criminal laws and legal guides made no exception for children in most cases and that ages were generally ignored, we should assume that children younger than fifteen probably were prosecuted and convicted in some cases. Consider, for example, the cases of Nicholas Favor and Robert Driver, convicted of murdering their master in Massachusetts in 1674. Both were described as apprentices. Their ages were ignored. As later chapters will show, apprentices were often younger than fourteen. Both were hanged.[44]

Virginia made much less effort than Massachusetts to craft its own criminal code, following English criminal laws more closely. Virginia law defined few crimes for itself, with the significant exceptions of its slave code (which had no age exemptions) and a smattering of laws about not tampering with tobacco casks, for example. Three cases from Virginia in the 1620s and 1630s illustrate its adherence to English practice. In 1628 William Reade, "labourer," was indicted for "felloniously" giving John Burrows a mortal wound. We know his age, thirteen or fourteen, because he gave it during his testimony. According to Reade, Burrows took Reade's knife from him, and then, when Reade accused him of taking the knife, Burrows dropped it and "strooke [Reade] uppon the brest with his fist." Reade then grabbed the knife just before Burrows attacked him again, this time landing on the knife: "He ran his belly [upon] the knife." The other witness, another servant, gave much the same account, except he thought Reade too ingenuous about Burrows's running on the knife: Reade "stabbed *Burrowes* into the belly." Regardless of Burrows's intentions in the middle of the fight, this was clearly a brawl that had turned ugly and thus fell into the manslaughter category: "The said *Reade* was guilty of Manslaughter whoe being asked what hee had to say for himselfe that he ought not to dy demanded his Clergy whereuppon he was delyvered to the ordinary, etc." Reade, whose age was not part of his indictment (but whose status was), was convicted of manslaughter in a routine way and would have been executed had he not been granted benefit of clergy.[45]

43. Powers, *Crime and Punishment*, 178, 303, 443. This case is cited in many other places; see also, for example, Friedman, *Crime and Punishment*, 34–35. For Bradford's original comments, see *Of Plymouth Plantation*, 1642.

44. *Records of the Court of Assistants of the Colony of Massachusetts Bay, 1630–1692* (Boston, 1901–1928), I, 30–32.

45. H. R. McIlwaine, ed., *Minutes of the Council and General Court of Colonial Virginia*, 2d ed. (Richmond, Va., 1979), 183–184. The testimony was included rather arbitrarily in

Other Virginia cases, one a suicide, the other a petit treason, reinforce Virginia's lack of concern with age and its close adherence to the English criminal code as it related to intent. John Verone, "a boy," was found by a jury to have hanged himself in March 1628: he "was giltie of his owne death. And that the Cheayne where with he hanged himselfe doth fall to the kinge for A diadon [deodand]." The testimony concerned whether his master might have hanged him. Did Verone have evidence of blows or stripes on his body? Could he have attached the rope? "He might easely have saved him self by the stanchione" in his master's barn where he hanged, stated one witness, meaning, it seems, that, if another had done this, Verone could have saved himself. His age was never asked; it was not critical to the verdict. Yet the witnesses who described him referred to him repeatedly as "the boy." The deodand and the lack of consideration of age both typify English practice (indeed, coroners in England paid more attention to age in cases of suicide). In a 1630 case (about which we have only notes taken before the records burned in the Civil War) a "servant" received the full and appropriate punishment for petit treason after killing his master. "William Mathews Servant to Henry Booth Indicted arraigned and found guilty of petit treason by 14 Jurors. Judgment to be drawn and hanged." A servant might have been older but was likely under twenty-four and might have been as young as ten or twelve. This servant had his bowels drawn out before being hanged because he had not simply committed murder but had committed the status crime as well, which made it worse.[46]

Pennsylvania more closely resembled Massachusetts in that it crafted its own criminal code, distinct from England's (with many fewer crimes punishable by death), passed more laws meant to encourage morality, and sometimes created age distinctions within those laws. Pennsylvania laws from the early eighteenth century stated, for example, that those under age sixteen were to be whipped for swearing, whereas those sixteen and over were to sit in the stocks for three hours. But its actual legal records, like those of Virginia, Massachusetts, and England, were almost silent on the question of age during the colonial period (and, indeed, through the early national period). Few court cases specifically mentioned the age of the accused.[47] According to the main legal guide published and used in Pennsylvania, *Conductor Gener-*

---

this early period, the record later becoming more formal. Most of the general court records, were, of course, burned. See also Chapin, *Criminal Justice in Colonial America,* 43 n. 80, who does not directly address the issue of age.

46. McIlwaine, ed., *Minutes of the Council and General Court of Colonial Virginia,* 53–54. On Mathews: 479 (words abbreviated in the notes are spelled out, and punctuation is added).

47. *Conductor Generalis,* 208. (My research focused on the quarter session records of Chester County during the 1750s, 1780s, and 1810s.)

alis (1722), those under fourteen could not be punished for rioting. Yet, as in England, they could be bound to keep the peace if they assaulted someone. It also remarked simply and unequivocally, as if to clarify a debate, that persons under age fourteen could be found guilty of stealing, without specifying any further guidelines. Only those fourteen and older, however, could be fined for forcible entry. It was, in short, entirely in line with the early-seventeenth-century guides discussed above.[48]

By the early eighteenth century a new consensus was emerging in England. It would profoundly influence the colonists, and American reformers would take it even further after the Revolution. Following Coke and (to a lesser degree) Dalton, common law reformers began to build an argument that fourteen was the age of discretion and that under that age a child could not be guilty of a felony.

In his *Pleas of the Crown*, Hale followed Coke to define the "age of discretion" for homicide as unequivocally fourteen. However, unable to ignore precedent, he acknowledged that in some cases those older than seven might be convicted, and cited Dalton. Hale thus created, for the first time, a range of ages of legal culpability. Yet those who were under fourteen and found guilty, he argued, should be pardoned. "An infant within years of discretion kills another, no felony; as if he be nine or ten years old. But if by circumstance it appeareth he could distinguish between Good and Evil, it is felony: as if he hide the body, make excuses, etc. But in such cases Execution in prudence respited to get a pardon."[49]

He discussed this issue extensively in his *History of Pleas of the Crown*. There he cited few English precedents, and those he did cite included Anglo-Saxon laws. His goal was to reconcile a variety of legal authorities to establish a new rule about when a young person should be liable for a crime. After discussing Roman law, Continental civil law, and some English precedents as far back as a law passed by King Ine (d. 726), he concluded, "Fourteen years of age therefore is the common standard, at which age both males and females are by the law obnoxious to capital punishments for offenses committed by them." Although he had mentioned a broad variety of ages (and had

---

48. *Conductor Generalis*, 96–97, 100, 147, 198. "Peace may be granted . . . against an Infant, tho' under 14 years of age." While the text makes clear that married women cannot post bond on their own behalf and so must be committed to jail if no one posts bond for them, it is unclear whether those under fourteen can actually post bond. Instead, they might have to stay in jail if someone swears a violation of the peace against them and none will post bond on their behalf.

49. [Hale], *Pleas of the Crown*, 35.

carefully chosen his examples), he generalized from the many examples and provided an epistemological basis for his conclusions. He sought excuses for the evidence that the common law on this issue had been different in the past: the law had "received a greater perfection, not by a change of the Common Law, as some have thought, for that could not be but by act of parliament: but men grew to greater learning, judgment and experience, and rectified the mistakes of former ages and judgments." Hale's legal sleight of hand here was remarkable. Clearly, he had been criticized for trying to change standards for accountability without involving Parliament, a just charge. (Such was the plan he advocated elsewhere in his essay "Considerations touching the Amendment or Alteration of Lawes.") His response was that his new standards "rectified the mistakes" of the common law rather than changed it.[50]

Although Hale offered some of the same guidelines as had earlier treatise writers, that the child "could discern between good and evil at the time of the offense committed," he led up to a higher standard of guilt. "It is necessary that very strong and pregnant evidence ought to be to convict one of that age, and to make it appear he understood what he did." Hale thus did not end where others did: he stretched both the age and the basis of determination, from knowledge to understanding. Hale was not completely without precedent: Lambarde had suggested that children must have an "understanding wil," and Coke had suggested that they should have attained fourteen (at least for homicide). Yet Hale justified these higher and stricter guidelines much more thoroughly and consistently than any English writer had done before.[51]

Not only did he define a later age of discretion than all earlier legal authorities except Coke (and extend it beyond homicide) as well as urge the pardon of all those under age fourteen who might be convicted anyway; he even considered excusing those under age twenty-one from liability for crime. But he rejected this extension on the grounds that youths between fourteen and twenty-one posed too much of a threat to society, an issue he did not raise for those under fourteen. With any such move, "the kingdom would come to confusion."

> Experience makes us know, that every day murders, bloodsheds, burglaries, larcenies, burning of houses, rapes, clipping and counterfeiting of money, are committed by youths above fourteen and under twenty-one;

50. Hale, *Historia Placitorum Coronae: The History of the Pleas of the Crown* (London, 1736), I, 16–29, esp. 24–25; Hale, "Considerations touching the Amendment or Alteration of Lawes," in Francis Hargrave, ed., *A Collection of Tracts relative to the Laws of England, from Manuscripts* (Dublin, 1787), esp. 272–273.
51. Ibid., 26, 27.

and if they should have impunity by the privilege of . . . their minority, no man's life or estate could be safe.[52]

It is remarkable that Hale took this idea as seriously as he did, given the precedents with which he was working. It is a measure both of his attempt to promote consistency about "full age" and of his attitudes toward the abilities of children under age twenty-one. Hale was saying, in effect, that, even though teenagers between the ages of fourteen and twenty-one could not really understand the consequences of their actions, they had to be punished like adults because they could commit so many crimes and were such a threat to society.

Many later manuals cited Hale, quoting him almost exactly, although they usually added more detail and sometimes a different emphasis. They included William Hawkins's *Summary of the Crown-Law* (1728), Thomas Wood's *Institute of the Laws of England* (1738), William Blackstone's *Commentaries* (1765–1769), St. George Tucker's Virginia version of Blackstone (1803), and Matthew Bacon's *New Abridgment of the Laws* (first American edition, 1813).[53] By 1728, Hawkins had used the basic distinction between guilt and innocence outlined by Hale as the introduction to his treatise on crown law. He added detail to Hale's earlier description but retained the substance of his comments.

> To make a man liable to a criminal prosecution, two things are required,
>   1. That he have the use of his reason.
>   2. That he be sui juris.
> . . . On this account the Law indulges Infants under the Age of Discretion, Ideots and Lunaticks. . . . And if it appear that an infant under the age of Discretion could distinguish between good and evil, as if one of nine or ten years of age kill another, and hide the body, or himself, etc. he may be convicted and condemned, etc. But the judges in prudence will respite the execution.

The whole discussion repeated Hale almost exactly.[54]

52. Ibid., 25.

53. William Hawkins, *A Summary of the Crown-Law* . . . (London, 1728), I, 1–2; Wood, *Institute of the Laws*, 352. "One under the age of Discretion, or One Non Compos Mentis, cannot be Guilty of the Murder of Another. But if it appears by Circumstances That the Infant did Hide the Body, etc. it is Felony." Blackstone, *Commentaries*, IV, 23–24; Tucker, *Blackstone's Commentaries*, V, 19–24 (chap. 2); Bacon, *A New Abridgment of the Law*, 1st American ed., from the 6th London ed. (Philadelphia, 1813), 590.

54. Hawkins, *A Summary of the Crown-Law*, I, 1–2. Hawkins also added one comment, however: "As to an offender's being sui juris, neither a Son, nor a Servant, nor

In 1738, Thomas Wood baldly asserted that children under fourteen could not be guilty of crimes:

In Criminal Cases, the act of an Infant shall not be imputed to him; no not in Case of High Treason, 'till he is of the age of Fourteen; which (as hath been said) is accounted the Age of Discretion. In some Cases of Extraordinary Malice, an Infant under 14, comes within the Censure of the Law.

He then justified his strong stand with theories about the development of a child's understanding, acknowledging at the same time that this represented a shift in the common law: ". . . the Law was anciently otherwise."

Those that are to be esteemed Guilty of any Offenses must Have the Use of their Reason, and be at their own Disposal or Liberty. For 1. Those that want Reason, to distinguish between Good and evil (as Infants under the Age of Discretion . . .) ought not to be prosecuted for any Crime . . . tho' the Law was anciently otherwise. . . . . But as to Infants, their Understanding and Discretion ought to be Examin'd. For if they appear to have Knowledge equal to those that are of Years of Discretion, they may be Prosecuted. But it is proper to respite execution in order to obtain a Pardon.

He thus followed Hale in recommending that, even if a child under fourteen had the "Understanding and Discretion" of someone older than "Years of Discretion," that child should not be executed, but should be given a pardon. While earlier commentators had emphasized the ability to have knowledge of good and evil, Wood emphasized the development of the understanding.[55]

William Blackstone's arguments about responsibility drew on Hale and Hawkins but incorporated more elaborate arguments about the development of the human understanding. Of the "Conditions exempting responsibility for crime" the first and most important is "where there is a defect of understanding."

For where there is no discernment, there is no choice; and where there is no choice, there can be no act of will, which is nothing else but a determination of one's choice, to do or to abstain from a particular action: he therefore, that has no understanding, can have no will to guide his conduct.

------

any other Person, except a Feme Covert, is excused on that Account, as acting by the Command or Coercion of another."

55. Wood, *Institute of the Laws*, 13, 339–340. "An infant under twelve years of age cannot be outlawed" (578).

His words, sharply reminiscent of the seventeenth-century religious debates over baptism and conscience, would be increasingly used in later-eighteenth-century cases.[56]

By the late eighteenth century, judges paid much more attention to age in deciding punishments and even whether children should be tried. Clerks of the court were more likely to record the ages of the accused, juries to find children (especially under fourteen) not guilty, and judges to seek a pardon. A mid-eighteenth-century English case cited by most manuals afterward, from Blackstone's *Commentaries* and Hening's *Virginia Justice* to early-nineteenth-century cases discussed below, served as a model of Hale's and Wood's advice: even if the boy knew that the murder he committed was evil, he should be pardoned because of his age. Under age fourteen, irrespective of whether he knew the difference between good and evil, he could not fully understand the consequences of his actions.

In 1748, at Bury, in England, a ten-year-old boy named William York killed a five-year-old girl. Both were "parish children" (poor apprentices) and were the only children living with a parishioner and his wife. When the couple had gone for the day and the two children were left home alone, the girl disappeared. Initially, William claimed he had no knowledge of what had happened to her. After the body was found, he was questioned but continued to deny any knowledge, even to a coroner's jury. "At length, being closely interrogated, he fell to crying, and said he would tell the whole Truth." According to his confession:

> He took her out of the Bed, and carried her to the Dung Heap; and with a large Knife, which he found about the House, cut her in the manner the Body appeared to be mangled, and buried her in the Dung Heap; placing the Dung and Straw that was bloody under the Body, and covering it up with what was clean; and having so done, he got Water and washed himself as clean as he could.

The judges did not initially want to accept his confession. By hiding the body, however, he indicated that he understood that he had committed a great wrong. The judges decided that a jury should make the judgment, and the jury convicted him.[57]

The judges initially agreed. They reflected that he had undoubtedly shown "Tokens of what my Lord Chief Justice Hale, somewhere calleth Mischievous Discretion, that he is certainly a proper Subject for Capital Punishment,

56. Blackstone, *Commentaries*, IV, 21.

57. Michael Foster, *A Report of Some Proceedings on the Commission of Oyer and Terminer and Goal Delivery* . . . (Oxford, 1762), 70–73.

and ought to suffer." They hesitated to take away his life but reasoned that they should.

> There are many Crimes of the most heinous Nature, such as in the present Case the Murder of Young Children, Poisoning Parents or Masters, Burning Houses, etc. which Children are very capable of committing; and which they may in some Circumstances be under strong Temptations to commit; And therefore, though the taking away the Life of a Boy of ten Years Old may savour of Cruelty, yet as the Example of this Boy's Punishment may be a means of deterring Other Children from the like Offences; and as the Sparing this Boy, *merely on Account of his Age,* will probably have a quite contrary tendency, in Justice to the Publick, the Law ought to take it's Course.

The ability to commit "Crimes of the most heinous Nature," in addition to evidence of "Mischievous Discretion," for these judges meant that children should be punished, even though their understanding was incomplete. The general threat of such children motivated the judges to seek his execution.[58]

However, the law did not take its course. Although all of the judges agreed with the reasoning offered above, two judges urged a delay in his execution (in case evidence emerged that he was acting under the direction of another). They deferred his execution several times, until the secretary of state stepped in to extend his respite indefinitely. Finally, at age nineteen, he was pardoned by George II on condition that he join the navy. Thus, although the jury found him guilty of committing a "heinous" crime and the judges confirmed that he had "Discretion," the judges, secretary of state, and finally the king hesitated to execute him as they would an adult.[59]

Through the middle of the eighteenth century, many youths younger than fourteen continued to come before the English courts, but they seem increasingly likely to have obtained reprieves from execution. In 1741, for example, Charles Shooter, a "quill boy," was sentenced to death for stealing a purse from his master. His age, twelve, came out by chance; it was not an explicit issue in the case. But, perhaps following Hale's and Wood's guidelines, the jury who found him guilty "desired he might be recommended by the court for his majesty's mercy." It was certainly in response to the harsh criminal laws of eighteenth-century England, and perhaps partly in response to a desire to find alternatives to the noose for younger felons, that Parliament passed the Transportation Act in 1718. It offered transportation as a substitute to hanging for many of the convicted. The convict would be transported to the

58. Ibid.
59. Ibid.

American colonies, where he or she would have to perform forced labor as a servant for seven or more years. About fifty thousand such persons were sent from England to its North American colonies between 1718 and 1776, many to Virginia, yet we rarely know their ages. One scholar who has examined transportation lists notes, "Information on the ages of transports is scarce." A few pieces of evidence from Maryland suggest that few children under fourteen were transported. Undoubtedly, the fact that the punishment for a first offense was usually branding pushed the ages of transports slightly higher. Perhaps different rules about service in different colonies, however, influenced where convicts were sent (Virginia's laws, for example, had longer service for youths under nineteen, which might have encouraged the transporters, who operated privately after picking up their human cargoes, to sell the younger convicts there). The data are so scarce it is difficult to see beyond them, but there might already have been some changes in the conviction patterns of those under fourteen by the middle of the century.[60]

Regardless, the crimes of children remained a significant problem in London, with many under fourteen still appearing before the courts, and many under twenty-one hanging. A welfare system that did not fulfill the needs of the poor, a socially stratified society, with much wealth on display, inadequate employment of youth: all of these factors helped to fuel the involvement of many youths in theft in particular, which was usually a hanging offense (depending on the value stolen). According to the solicitor general in 1785, nine-tenths of those hanged in London were under age twenty-one. Even assuming he exaggerated, it is a startling statement. In 1758, Sir John Fielding, after seeing many boys under fourteen years old come before his courts for stealing, sought to remove their motivation for theft by providing jobs as cabin boys on ships for boys between twelve and fifteen who lived in the streets, so that they would not have to steal to live. A report to Parliament in 1778 proposed allowing boys under fourteen to serve in the navy or army for three years instead of being executed or transported.[61]

60. *The Proceedings at the Sessions of the Peace, and Oyer and Terminer, for the City of London, etc. [Jan. 16–20, 1741]* (London, 1741). The data in a 1755 Maryland census suggest that those under sixteen formed 4.4 percent of the transports. Lists of two transport ships that arrived in Maryland in 1721 and 1724 reveal that, of 153 felons for whom age can be determined, only 1 was between ten and fourteen; 24 percent were between fifteen and nineteen. Peter Wilson Coldham, *Emigrants in Chains: A Social History of Forced Emigration to the Americas* . . . (Baltimore, 1992); A. Roger Ekirch, "Bound for America: A Profile of British Convicts Transported to the Colonies, 1718–1775," *William and Mary Quarterly*, 3d Ser., XLII (1985), 195.

61. Leon Radzinowicz, *A History of English Criminal Law and Its Administration from*

At the end of the eighteenth century, some judges began to pay more attention to age in determining guilt and punishment. One court clerk began routinely to record the ages of offenders in London between 1782 and 1787. In analyzing these data, Peter King concludes, "Youth in itself was considered to be a strong mitigating circumstance." Fewer than 2 percent of the accused were under age fourteen. Only 19 percent of those accused were under age nineteen. About 47 percent were under age twenty-five. While more than half of those convicted of burglary and housebreaking who were fourteen to eighteen were sentenced to death, only a quarter of those sentenced to death who were fifteen to sixteen were actually hanged. Still, juries seemed to use youth as a mitigating factor, according to one contemporary critic.

> But perhaps he happens to be young—it appears to be his first offence—he has, before the fact that was proved against him, had a good character—he was drawn in by others—was in liquor—or some other circumstance of the like kind strikes the minds of the jury.

The suspicion that he might have been "drawn in by others" was precisely the concern that two judges had expressed after ten-year-old William York's conviction: this and the other concerns were ways of exonerating a child from responsibility.[62]

This wonderfully rich span of records from 1782 to 1787 when ages suddenly began to be mentioned was interpreted by Peter King to be representative of juvenile crime and punishment in seventeenth- and eighteenth-century Britain. Yet the very act of routinely recording age indicates that age was important to the outcome of these cases as it had not been before. These cases, therefore, were hardly typical of the preceding two centuries.

What happened was that the American Revolution put a halt to England's alternative to death by hanging. In doing so, it provided a powerful spur

---

1750 (London, 1948–1986), I, 14; Ivy Pinchbeck and Margaret Hewitt, *Children in English Society*, I, *From Tudor Times to the Eighteenth Century* (London, 1969), 110, 124. Peter Linebaugh's close examination of those hanged in London during the eighteenth century focused on social class but offers some clues about age. Of those hanged at Tyburn between 1703 and 1772, where he could determine something of their status, 27 percent were apprentices, and only 21 percent were qualified artisans (probably over twenty-one). Some of those listed as laborers (9 percent) and servants (7 percent) were probably very young. The rest were sailors, soldiers, and unknown. *The London Hanged: Crime and Civil Society in the Eighteenth Century* (Cambridge, 1992), 97.

62. [Martin Madan], *Thoughts on Executive Justice . . .* (London, 1785), 137–138; Peter King, "Decision-Makers and Decision-Making in the English Criminal Law, 1750–1800," *Historical Journal*, XXVII (1984), 25–58, esp. 36–41.

to bring a half-reformed system to account, to create alternative forms of punishment and sentencing, particularly for children who might bear only partial responsibility, and thus deserve milder punishment, according to the new ideas about culpability. England's bloody code, which gave the death penalty for more than two hundred crimes, some as petty as chopping down a tree in a lord's forest, had been moderated throughout the eighteenth century by commuting many of these sentences to transportation. Between 1760 and 1764, only 13 percent of those convicted of felonies were actually executed; 74 percent, however, had their sentences commuted from death to transportation. Of the remainder, 12 percent were whipped (for lesser crimes), branded, or fined, and only 1 percent were imprisoned.

The clerk began keeping track of some ages in 1776, the year that transportation of convicts to the North American colonies was dramatically interrupted by the rebellion that created the United States. By 1782, when the clerk began to record all ages, the crisis had become acute. While judges continued to sentence convicts to "transportation," they had nowhere to go between 1776 and 1786 (when convicts began to be sent to Australia) and instead filled and overfilled floating prison barges on the Thames and the local jails. The rate of executions for those found guilty at the Old Bailey skyrocketed, from 13 percent in 1760–1764 to 26 percent in 1780–1784. The other convicts between 1780 and 1784 went to the prison ships to await transportation (24 percent), to jail (35 percent), or were whipped, branded, or fined (16 percent).[63] This clerk began keeping track of age, it seems clear, because it was a more important factor in punishment once transportation became impossible and "imprisonment" an uncertain and overcrowded alternative to death. If the accused were a child under fourteen, given the new rules about accountability, then such a child would be less likely to be convicted, without this key alternative to death as a punishment. Juries might also be less likely to convict youths between fourteen and twenty-one, but, if they were convicted, then hanging became more likely. If imprisoned, a youth might simply learn evil ways from the older felons already imprisoned. Age, thus, could also help determine the treatment of prisoners.

63. While King notes that his statistics derive from the chance notations of the clerk of the home circuit, whose "enthusiasm for this practice [keeping track of ages] rose and fell with the crisis over transportation," he does not connect the "crisis over transportation" logically with the clerk's attention to age ("Decision-Makers and Decision-Making," *Historical Journal*, XXVII [1984], 34). Michael Ignatieff, *A Just Measure of Pain: The Penitentiary in the Industrial Revolution* (New York, 1978), 80–91, 81 (for all statistics).

Although in 1787, the year after the first prison ship went to Australia, the home circuit clerk stopped noting age, the English courts would pay increasing attention to the age of young offenders over the next fifty years, an interest that corresponded to the reform of punishment and the birth of the penitentiary. In 1791 the Old Bailey began to note age routinely, and made it a permanent policy. By 1800, several counties were keeping track of the ages of offenders. And in 1834, at roughly the same time as political reform reshaped British government—and a full-blown penitentiary system was finally established—a new law mandated tracking all of those indicted and convicted of crimes who were under age sixteen. Thus the development of the prison was connected temporally with questions of age, accountability, and appropriate punishment for children.[64]

But transportation, penitentiaries, and making age a critical issue in assessing both culpability and punishment were interwoven not simply in timing but also in principle. All drew on the idea that a person who commits a crime is not necessarily permanently evil, and especially not born evil. Those convicted of crimes have the potential to reform, especially the young. That principle of reform privileged nurture over nature, environment over hereditary character. The crisis in transportation spurred many people to reconsider England's bloody criminal code, which had been softened only by transportation. Some of the most important reformers, whose plans gave birth to the penitentiaries as an alternative form of punishment, especially John Howard, Blackstone, and Jeremy Bentham, were deeply disturbed by the overuse of the death penalty and the inadequacy of alternatives after 1776. Blackstone and Howard worked together on England's 1779 Penitentiary Act. Transportation itself, increasingly relied on by English authorities during the eighteenth century, was, of course, a type of imprisonment. But it was also expedient and cheap. There was little effort made to reform the person in a conscious way, although forcing a thief to labor might conceivably teach "good" habits. Still, transportation was a simple model of reforming criminals, providing them with a second chance, even if forced to endure temporary slavery.[65]

John Howard, whose efforts to reform English jails were so critical to the birth of the penitentiary, equated the conversion experience with the reformation of criminals; since all people have the potential to sin, so also could

64. Peter King, "The Rise of Juvenile Delinquency in England, 1780–1840: Changing Patterns of Perception and Prosecution," *Past and Present*, no. 160 (August 1998), 119. King was trying to find runs of data with which to track juvenile delinquency rates.

65. Ignatieff, *A Just Measure of Pain*, 93.

anyone be saved. He believed that criminals, like children, could not exercise judgment and should be guided toward good behavior. According to his friend and biographer John Aikin, Howard thought "calm and gentle" coercion necessary to reform and shape both children and criminals:

> Regarding children as creatures possessed of strong passions and desires, without reason and experience to control them, he thought that nature seemed, as it were, to mark them out as the subjects of absolute authority; and that the first and fundamental principle to be inculcated upon them, was implicit and unlimited obedience. This cannot be effected by any process of reasoning, before reasoning has its commencement; and therefore must be the result of coercion. . . . The coercion he practiced was calm and gentle, but at the same time steady and resolute.

His attitude toward children, as without "reason and experience," without "any process of reasoning," and having "strong passions and desires," shaped his approach to the reform of criminals that underlay his proposals for penitentiaries and for special treatment of childhood criminals. Benjamin Rush, who was critical to the birth of the penitentiary in Pennsylvania (which became an international model for punishment in a republic), expressed similar ideas. Indeed, Howard's writings on punishment influenced Rush and were widely discussed in Pennsylvania.[66]

The culpability of children helps us understand the ideals underlying the "republican" form of government and the connections between that form of government and punishment itself. Both the ability to consent and not to do wrong rested on the understanding. The understanding could be cultivated and formed. It was thus that the underlying ideology of the Revolution led to a different type of punishment. Blackstone was directly influenced by How-

66. Ibid., 47–56, 48; John Howard, *The State of the Prisons in England and Wales*, 2d ed. (Warrington, 1780), esp. 10, 34–35, 47; John Aikin, *Life, Travels, and Philanthropic Labours of the Late John Howard* (1792; Boston, 1794), esp. 29–30; Hawes, *Children in Urban Society*, 20–23. In fact, there had been earlier efforts to remove the children of the prisoners of Newgate; see W. J. Sheehan, "Finding Solace in Eighteenth-Century Newgate," in J. S. Cockburn, ed., *Crime in England, 1550–1800* (London, 1977), 237.

On Rush, see Benjamin Rush, *An Enquiry into the Effects of Public Punishments upon Criminals, and upon Society* (1787) and "Thoughts upon the Amusements and Punishments Which Are Proper for Schools" (1790), both in Benjamin Rush, *Essays: Literary, Moral, and Philosophical*, ed. Michael Meranze (Schenectady, N.Y., 1988), esp. 37, 84–93. On Howard's many connections to the Quaker reformers in Pennsylvania who led the movements to reform punishment and establish penitentiaries there, see Michael Meranze, *Laboratories of Virtue: Punishment, Revolution, and Authority in Philadelphia, 1760–1835* (Chapel Hill, N.C., 1996), 140–143.

ard's ideas, in their roles as joint authors of the Penitentiary Act of 1779, but he was clearly open to that influence even before. Blackstone began his 1769 volume *Of Public Wrongs* (volume IV of his *Commentaries*) with a précis of Locke's "Second Treatise" that explained the connection between the ability to consent to government and to be responsible for crime. The capacity to punish crimes "against the law of nature, as murder and the like, is in a state of mere nature vested in every individual." When people live in a "state of society," however, they transfer that power to "the magistrate alone; who bears the sword of justice by the consent of the whole community." Especially for crimes that are not *"mala in se"* (bad in themselves, like murder) but only *"mala prohibita"* (prohibited by the laws, like property crimes), the only basis of punishing violators rests on this principle, "that the law by which they suffer was made by their own consent." For Blackstone, the ability to consent to laws and legislators correlates directly to the capacity to commit a crime (indeed, to the very definition of what is criminal), and only a person's initial consent to the laws creates in the legislator or judge the ability to punish the transgressor. Blackstone went so far in his discussion of criminal capacity as to call it "contracting guilt" and thus to directly correlate the capacity to contract with the capacity to be guilty.[67]

Blackstone's attack on the death penalty, which he built on this logic of consent and capacity, is staggering, given its context: he was supposedly chronicling the common law and England's existing laws. The red robes of the hanging judges would be stained with blood that indicted them and the legislators behind them if they executed any without a clear mandate from God. Those who "shed the blood of our fellow creature" must have the "fullest conviction of our own authority." "For life is the immediate gift of God to man" and cannot be taken but "by clear and indisputable demonstration" that God would command it. Not the lawbreaker, but the legislator is the criminal with blood on his hands if he levies the death penalty without this warrant from God. "The guilt of blood, if any, must lie at their doors, who misinterpret the extent of their warrant; and not at the doors of the subject, who is bound to receive the interpretations, that are given by the sovereign power." Not until 1778, however, when already in conference with Howard over what would become the Penitentiary Act, did Blackstone begin to lay out clear alternatives to the bloody code, amending his *Commentaries* to include them.[68]

While some like Howard, or arguably many of the Quaker reformers in Pennsylvania, were acting from partly or even largely religious motives, they

67. Blackstone, *Commentaries*, IV, 7–8, 23.
68. Ibid., 10–11; ibid. (Dublin, 1788), IV, 437.

were also influenced by more overtly political ideals. Thomas Paine, Thomas Jefferson, and Benjamin Rush agreed that the system of punishment was very closely related to the form of government of a nation. As Benjamin Rush put it so clearly: "Capital punishments are the natural offspring of monarchical governments," of those who, thinking they bore God's authority, ruled as tyrants, by fear. Jefferson distinguished between harsh capital punishments as the instruments of despotic monarchy, where government ruled by fear, and a uniform and routine set of laws with moderate punishments that fitted the crime, which suited a republic. Both Jefferson and Rush were inspired by Montesquieu and also Cesare Beccaria's famous 1764 treatise *Crimes and Punishments* (which Montesquieu had also inspired). "Severity in penalties suits despotic government, whose principle is terror," wrote Montesquieu. "It would be easy to prove that in all or nearly all the states of Europe penalties have decreased or increased in proportion as one has approached or departed from liberty." Paine addressed questions of age explicitly: "When, in countries that are called civilized, we see age going to the workhouse and youth to the gallows, something must be wrong in the system of government." "Civil government does not consist in executions, but in making that provision for the instruction of youth, and the support of age, as to exclude, as much as possible, profligacy from the one, and despair from the other."[69]

Even in England, radical Whigs who supported the American Revolution, like Richard Price and Jeremy Bentham, used England's harsh punishments as evidence of the need to push for broader political reform, of commons, lords, and the monarchy. In response, Parliament stopped public whippings as well as the public processions of the condemned to their hangings at Tyburn. Branding was abolished in the same law that was to create the first "penitentiaries" in London in 1779, the act coauthored by Howard and Blackstone. Jeremy Bentham, who in 1776 wrote "A Comment on the Commentaries" and *A Fragment on Government*, which accused Blackstone of not reforming enough, particularly with respect to the right to consent to government, did approve of his plan for penitentiaries and wrote a treatise on peni-

69. Benjamin Rush, *Considerations on the Injustice and Impolicy of Punishing Murder by Death* (Philadelphia, 1792), 18; Thomas Paine, *Common Sense*, 99, 108, and *The Rights of Man*, 314, in Michael Foot and Isaac Kramnick, eds., *Thomas Paine Reader* (London, 1987); Montesquieu, *The Spirit of the Laws*, ed. and trans. Anne M. Cohler, Basia Carolyn Miller, and Harold Samuel Stone (Cambridge, 1989), 82–83, 191; Thomas Jefferson, *Notes on the State of Virginia*, ed. William Peden (Chapel Hill, N.C., 1954), query 14. Also see his revisal of the laws, bill no. 64, "A Bill for Proportioning Crimes and Punishments in Cases Heretofore Capital," in Julian P. Boyd et al., eds., *The Papers of Thomas Jefferson* (Princeton, N.J., 1950–), II, 492–499; Kathryn Preyer, "Crime, the Criminal Law, and Reform in Post-Revolutionary Virginia," *Law and History Review*, I (1983), 53–85.

tentiaries himself. Neither Bentham nor Blackstone was directly inspired by his religious beliefs. Instead, their thinking about authority, consent, crime, and punishment was filtered through the writings of the Enlightenment.[70]

The possibility of reforming criminals grew out of the Enlightenment promise of education. Yet while Bentham called criminals "froward children, persons of unsound mind," who could not control their passions but could be taught to, there was hardly one answer about how reform could be accomplished, just as there was no one principle about how a child should be taught to reason.[71] Education and "reform" could likewise, of course, teach blind obedience. So, while the impetus for reforming criminals rather than executing them originated in egalitarian principles of consent and possibility, it could be twisted into something far different. "Reforming the mind" of someone who broke a law had many different means and ends: far from a single answer, it opened a multiplicity of strategies and options. Some of these, such as long-term solitary confinement, were undoubtedly cruel: worse, perhaps, even than death by hanging. But many—if the transgressor were to choose—were better, offering, at least, hope.

The American Revolution thus spurred reform in more ways than one. In England, the halting of transportation was critical, but so too were the ideas underlying that revolution, with which many of the reformers were sympathetic. Revolutionary ideas encouraged the reexamination of consent, intent, and appropriate punishment. Americans, likewise, were affected not only by British reformers, especially common law reformers like Hale and Blackstone, but by these ideas themselves. The decades after the Revolution would lead the new American states to reconsider their entire criminal codes.

Although the colonies made a few reforms before the Revolution, they still paid almost no attention to age. County court records for Massachusetts,

70. On English radicals and the other reforms, see Ignatieff, *Just Measure of Pain*, 63–65, 90.

Jeremy Bentham condemned Blackstone's *Commentaries* sharply on the grounds that Blackstone merely compiled the law as an "Expositor" but did not criticize it even when it needed criticizing, as a "Censor": he thought, in short, that Blackstone relied wholly on custom, not reason. Yet Bentham did not realize that Blackstone was reforming the law as he was compiling it (thus tempering custom with reason), undoubtedly because Bentham had learned the law from Blackstone's lectures at Oxford in the early 1760s. Blackstone's reforms, thus, were invisible to Bentham. Bentham approved completely, however, of Blackstone's prison reform. Bentham, *"A Comment on the Commentaries" and "A Fragment on Government"* (1776), ed. J. H. Burns and H. L. Hart (London, 1977), 398, 406, 542–544 (Bentham's comments on Blackstone's prison reform).

71. Ignatieff, *A Just Measure of Pain*, 66, 74.

Pennsylvania, and Virginia in the 1750s always indicate the status of the accused, but only rarely age. In the revisions that followed the Revolution, many laws excluded children from culpability for individual crimes. The early-eighteenth-century Pennsylvania law, for example, that based different punishments for swearing on whether one was older or younger than sixteen, with the younger whipped and the older set in stocks, was dramatically revised by 1794. Swearing was still punished for those over sixteen, but only by a fine. Those under sixteen were to receive no punishment at all. Age became more crucial in deciding cases. Testimony makes it clear that even witnesses were considering age more closely.[72]

Early-nineteenth-century American state superior court cases illuminate a profound transformation in attitudes toward culpability. Age was becoming critical to deciding not only punishment but guilt itself. In Tennessee in 1806 a twelve- or thirteen-year-old girl was found innocent in a case where an older woman almost certainly would have been found guilty. Probably only the extreme butchery of the crime brought Mary Doherty to the court in the first place. She was accused of murdering her father, whose body had been cut up and hidden under the floorboards of their house. Blood covered an ax, his bed, and his head. The family of four children and their drunkard father had lived outside town. Two additional children had run away. Mary was the eldest remaining. When the body was found, none of the children appeared surprised or upset. On the witness stand Mary refused to speak. Her ten-year-old brother was barred from testifying because he "had not any sense of the obligation of an oath." Mary had confessed to a member of the coroner's inquest, but the judges refused to hear her confession secondhand, arguing that "no confession obtained from the prisoner by hope or fear should be given in evidence." (The member of the inquest, John Miller, had promised her that no harm would befall her if she told him what had happened.) In excluding her confession, the judges cited Hale's *History of Pleas of the Crown,* where Hale had written: "If an infant under the age of twenty-one shall confess an indictment, the court in justice ought not to record the confession, but put him to plead *not guilty,* or at least ought also to have inquired by an inquest of office of the truth and circumstances of the fact." They thus used Hale to bar a confession that she had given outside of court. However, they expected her to testify within the courtroom.[73]

Hale's authority was invoked not only in deciding when the confession of a

72. *Conductor Generalis,* 208; Collinson Read, *Precedents in the Office of a Justice of the Peace*...(Philadelphia, 1794), 16.

73. Hale, *Historia Placitorum Coronae: History of the Pleas of the Crown* (1736), I, 24.

child might be accepted but in determining the range of ages for culpability. The judges stated "the law on this point" to the jury before they retired to confer.

> If a person of fourteen years of age does an act, such as stated in this indictment, the presumption of law is that the person is *doli capax*. If under fourteen and not less than seven, the presumption of law is that the person cannot discern between right and wrong. But this presumption is removed, if from the circumstances it appears that the person discovered a consciousness of wrong.

Even though she had cut up the body and hidden it (like William York), indicating she was conscious of the wrong, the jury found Mary Doherty not guilty, apparently based on the "presumption of the law" that a person under age fourteen "cannot discern between right and wrong." Mary's silence on the witness stand, coupled with her refusal to speak while in jail, probably helped to convince the jury that she was not mentally aware. Two factors worked on Mary's behalf that would not have had she been older: her confession was not admitted as evidence, and the prosecution had to prove not only that she committed the act but that she knew the difference between "right and wrong."[74]

Although children under fourteen continued to be tried, they were presumed innocent. The presumption of innocence based on inability to reason is most clearly stated in the 1827 Massachusetts case of Thaddeus P. French, who had stolen a watch. During the trial, the storekeeper from whom Thaddeus had stolen the watch admitted that he had also sold him a "Tom and Jerry," a drink that contained plenty of rum. The storekeeper acknowledged that "he sold this composition to all who wanted it, children as well as men, and that it was usually sold in shops similar to his own." The judge directed the jury to blame the shopkeeper for the theft of his own shop:

> It is an immoral act in the prosecutor to sell to these children such a vile composition, and it might well have happened that the combined influence of the liquor and cigar, on a child of so tender years, would produce a temporary insanity. This case essentially differs from that where a crime is committed by a person, who by a free indulgence of strong liquors, has at the time voluntarily deprived himself of his reason.

In other words, although the boy bought the rum punch of his own accord, he did not "voluntarily deprive himself of his reason." Instead, the shopkeeper

74. *State v Mary Doherty*, 2 Tenn. (2 Overt.) 80 (1806).

committed an "immoral act" by selling the boy the rum drink. The case hinged on the judge's estimation and the jury's agreement that a thirteen-year-old boy could not "voluntarily deprive himself of his reason."[75]

In the two last cases in the United States where children under fourteen were executed, the children, unsurprisingly, were distinguished as nonwhite. The state of Connecticut executed Hannah Ocuish, a part-Indian girl, in 1786, when she was twelve. New Jersey hanged James Guild, a "coloured" boy, in 1828 at the same age. With Ocuish, the very fact that her exact age, "twelve years and nine months," was put in the title of the pamphlet that contained her death confession reveals how much more interested the public had become in these issues.[76] Guild's case was written up in an extensive report. James Guild, a "servant" of Joshua Bunn, confessed to killing an elderly neighbor, Catherine Beakes. Guild said that he went to her house to borrow a gun, but she refused to let him have it. She "accused him of things not true. She accused him of killing fowls or chickens, and letting out pidgeons." As he was leaving her house, he saw a yoke by the door. Picking it up, he went over and struck her three times as she was bending down to blow the fire. After she fell at the second blow, "he then went toward the door, and then he thought if she got well, she would tell his mistress, and his mistress would thrash him. He then went back to kill her." The main issues in his trial were whether his confession could be admitted (since otherwise there was little evidence) and whether he had sufficient understanding to be held responsible for the murder. After substantial debate, Justice George K. Drake decided to admit his confession, even though it had been coerced by both threats and promises and he was so young: it was recited in court as he had told it to others. He did not testify himself.[77]

James's life then depended on whether he had enough "understanding" to be culpable. The testimony on this subject was thus extensive. One witness testified, "He has as much sagacity as any boy I know of his age; was always accounted a smart, cunning mischievous kind of boy." Another accepted his confession after determining that he knew something about the "nature of an oath" and had "a great deal of understanding."

75. *Commonwealth v Thaddeus P. French* (1827), Peter Woodman, ed., *Reports of Criminal Cases Tried in the Municipal Court of the City of Boston, before Peter Oxenbridge Thacher* (Boston, 1845), 163–165.

76. Henry Channing, *God Admonishing His People of Their Duty as Parents and Masters: A Sermon . . . Occasioned by the Execution of Hannah Ocuish, a Mulatto Girl, Aged Twelve Years and Nine Months . . .* (New London, Conn., 1786). See also Louis P. Masur, *Rites of Execution: Capital Punishment and the Transformation of American Culture* (New York, 1989), 36.

77. *The State against James Guild*, 10 N.J.L. (5 Halst.) 163–190, esp. 164, 167–169.

Before taking his examination, I asked him if he knew any thing about the nature of an oath. He said he did not. I told him he must tell nothing but the truth; if he did, when he come to die, he would go to punishment. He said he knew that well enough. He has a great deal of understanding; as much as any black boy I am acquainted with.

This witness seemed to make reason somehow racially specific. Others offered similar comments: "He is reputed a cunning smart boy"; and "He is accounted smarter than common for black boys of his age; full of mischief; think him a cunning boy; ingenious to get out of a scrape." Another said: "I thought him full as acute as boys in common. His memory seemed to be correct."[78]

Other witnesses, however, disputed these analyses of his understanding. One who had heard his confession said, "He appeared to have considerable wit, but wanted discretion and good sense." Another one said, "He did not appear to realize his case as a discreet or rational person would." A third stated more fully: "I have seen many boys of his age having a greater share of understanding than he. I do not think he had hardly an ordinary share of it. . . . He had intelligence enough to know when he did wrong, but was wanting in discretion, and could not fully appreciate the consequences of crime." When cross-examined, the same witness acknowledged: "He has capacity enough to distinguish between right and wrong; but I do not think he considers or reflects as much as some. . . . I think his bad actions proceed more from passion than from malice." His master generally corroborated. "I have endeavored to give him good instruction, and in some respects he knows the difference between good and evil. . . . He is passionate, mischievous, insolent, but does not bear malice."[79]

In his instructions to the jury, Justice Drake urged them to consider a low level of understanding as sufficient for criminal responsibility. He began by admitting that fourteen was the general age below which a person was presumed innocent. "With respect to the ability of persons of his age, to commit crimes of this nature, the law is, that under the age of seven, they are deemed incapable of it. Between seven and fourteen, if there be no proof of capacity . . . the presumption is in their favour." Drake then backtracked to effectively challenge this counsel. This presumption of innocence was "a presumption however growing weaker and more easily overcome, the nearer they approach to fourteen."

And at the age of this defendant, sufficient capacity is generally possessed in our state of society, by children of ordinary understanding, and having

78. Ibid., 167, 169.
79. Ibid., 169–170.

the usual advantages of moral and religious instruction. You will call to mind the evidence on this subject; and if you are satisfied that he was able, in a good degree, to distinguish between right and wrong; to know the nature of the crime with which he is charged; and that it was *deserving of severe* punishment, his infancy will furnish no obstacle, on the score of incapacity, to his conviction.

Drake thus set up a situation where the jury could find James guilty, undermining the advice of Hale, although he had begun with it. All the jurors had to do once they decided he had committed the act was to decide whether he had ordinary understanding for a twelve-year-old and whether he could "in a good degree . . . distinguish between right and wrong." It is impossible to say whether this judge generally disapproved of the emerging guidelines about the guilt of children or was simply prejudiced against the accused boy. It certainly seems ironic that, while so many other people in the early nineteenth century were trying to prove that blacks were mentally inferior (in order to justify slavery and racism), many of the witnesses in this case vied to grant Guild an understanding equal to or greater than other boys his age, since only possession of that understanding would make him responsible: he had to be "cunning" to be hanged.[80]

One is left finally with the puzzling logic that allowed these two young nonwhite children to be convicted when white children of the same age were not. It seems in the latter case, at least, that the judge relaxed the emphasis on "understanding" and emphasized "malice" instead. Indeed, the final sentence of the judge's instructions equated malice with a sudden passion. "If a man kill another suddenly, without any, or without considerable provocation, the law implies malice, and the homicide is murder." The judge's instructions, whether motivated by sincere disagreement or simple racism, elaborate the loophole left by Hale to enable the punishment of children over age fourteen and under twenty-one, a loophole that emphasized the needs of society—and the potential danger to society of the accused—rather than the "intent" of the defendant. When Guild's case was appealed to the Supreme Court of New Jersey on the grounds that he was too young to be executed, the judges quoted Blackstone's discussion of the 1748 English case of William York, who had killed his five-year-old fellow apprentice (summarized above), in which some judges had emphasized the needs of society over the understanding of the child in order to uphold the verdict.

In very modern times, a boy of ten years old was convicted on his own confession, of murdering his bed fellow, there appearing in his whole

80. Ibid., 174.

behaviour plain tokens of a mischievous discretion, and as sparing this boy merely on account of his tender years, might be of dangerous consequence to the public by propagating a notion that children might commit such atrocious crimes, with impunity, it was unanimously agreed by all the judges that he was the proper subject of capital punishment.

Blackstone (and the New Jersey judges who quoted him) misstated the case in arguing that the judges "unanimously" agreed that the boy should be hanged (rather, they unanimously agreed he was guilty), in order to strengthen an argument based on the perceived consequences "on the public" rather than the understanding of the child. Their invocation of the needs of society illustrates how different rules could be applied and bent, depending on the identity of the criminal and the attitude of the judge.[81]

These arguments about understanding and youth, however, although less consistently applied than for white children, did sometimes offer greater leniency even for black children. Youth began to be mentioned as a reason for absolving black slaves from the full punishment for crimes that they were accused of. While youth had not generally been an issue for slaves in the seventeenth and early eighteenth centuries, it began to be by the end of the eighteenth century. In Virginia in 1785, Will, the slave of Edward Dodson, although found guilty of "plotting, advising and consulting" a slave insurrection, for which the usual punishment was death, instead received only thirty lashes, "taking into consideration the extream youth of . . . Will." In 1796, when William, the "thirteen or fourteen year old slave" of Frederick County planter Rawleigh Colston, was condemned by the slave court judges to die for arson (burning Colston's house), ninety-two Frederick County residents petitioned the governor to pardon him, much to Colston's anger. In 1818, in a trial for the murder of his master, Robert Berkeley, a young black boy, Landon, might have received a lesser punishment in response to the plea of a witness. "He was young, and [the witness] hoped that if he had any hand in killing his master, he was drawn into it by some of the older ones and perhaps the court on account of his youth would have mercy on him."[82]

By the mid-nineteenth century, Hale's and Blackstone's dictum that those under age fourteen generally should not be held responsible for their crimes

81. Ibid., 189, referring to Blackstone's *Commentaries*, IV, 24. See my discussion of the case above; not all of the judges agreed, and the boy was not killed but instead eventually pardoned.

82. Philip J. Schwarz, *Twice Condemned: Slaves and the Criminal Laws of Virginia, 1705–1865* (Baton Rouge, La., 1988), 189–190, 323; Frederick County Order and Minute Books, 1750–1820, 1817–1820 (May 25, 1818), 77, Library of Virginia, Richmond.

had become the standard guideline, repeated in the superior courts of most states.[83]

What I have traced here is a fundamental shift in the way that culpability was assigned. In the sixteenth century, guilt depended only partly on intention but more on direct causation and on status. The question was less whether one meant to do something than whether one actually had done it. Culpability increasingly became linked to ideas about human understanding and to the age of fourteen instead of seven or eight. The definition of culpability was profoundly influenced by religious arguments about human understanding that flourished in the wake of the Reformation. The emphasis by such Puritans as William Lambarde, Sir Mathew Hale, and and Sir Edward Coke was on, to use Lambarde's simple expression, the "understanding wil." The religious debates about the role of understanding in religious choice, particularly about church membership and church authority, framed larger questions about the ability to choose itself and directed focus toward the development of the human understanding. Ideas about human understanding and its role in framing human consent, whether to laws or to breaking the laws, were intertwined in the works of John Locke and others. Locke wrote, for example: "The *Freedom* then of Man and Liberty of acting according to his own Will, *is grounded* on his having *Reason,* which is able to instruct him in that law he is to govern himself by. . . . This is that which puts the *Authority* into the *Parents* hands to govern the *Minority* of their Children." He argued first that government should not be based on inherited right, on status, but should instead be based on consent (in his *Two Treatises*), and only then did he write lengthy treatises on how consent can be formed, through education and the development of the human understanding. While the religious and political debates themselves framed Coke's and Hale's concerns about children's intent, later legal scholars such as Blackstone were influenced more directly by Locke.[84]

These transformations in culpability shared their origin with republican political ideology. The reformers who reshaped the meaning of culpability in the sixteenth and seventeenth centuries, like those who argued for govern-

83. See, in general, *The American Digest: A Complete Digest of All Reported American Cases from the Earliest Times to 1896,* Century edition (St. Paul, Minn., 1897–1904), XXVII, 1187–1198, particularly 1188–1190.

84. Walter Scott, ed., *The Somers Collection of Tracts: A Collection of Scarce and Valuable Tracts, on the Most Interesting and Entertaining Subjects: But Chiefly as They Relate to the History and Constitution of These Kingdoms . . . ,* 2d ed. (London, 1811), VI, 218; John Locke, *Two Treatises of Government,* ed. Peter Laslett (Cambridge, 1988), 309 ("Second Treatise," chap. 6, sect. 63). On Locke and legal scholars, see discussion at end of Chapter 5, above.

ment based on consent, were religious Nonconformists. During the seventeenth century many judges who introduced changes were also devoted to political efforts at reform, generally trying to replace authority based on inherited right. Hale, for example, claimed to be simply "recording" the common law, yet was a reformer who had headed the Rump Parliament's Commission of 1652 to revise the English code of laws. He urged many changes that privileged age over status, including raising the age requirement (and dropping the property requirement) for jurors.

Until children have understanding, they do not comprehend the laws they should be governed by. They cannot then be responsible for their own actions. Instead, it is the parents who should be responsible for them. Saying this seems normal to us. But going back, however briefly, to the Sussex coroners' rolls for the sixteenth century should make us think: those very young children who died in tubs of water, although not held liable for suicide, were responsible for their own deaths (and so were the tubs). No adult, in any of those cases, was held responsible. Now those who are "responsible" for children are at least in part culpable for such "accidents." Just so, in reallocating culpability away from children, we give part of the responsibility for their behavior to their parents. So too did Puritans in New England (consider their laws and even calling Dorcas Good "daughter" of William Good, rather than "spinster" as she would have been in England).

This era witnessed not simply a shift in punishment of children or an increase in pardons granted. It was a shift in their very ability to be considered guilty of an act. Even the young children granted leniency by the Gawdys in sixteenth-century assizes had been found guilty by juries. According to the new orthodoxy, they could not be not guilty in the same way an adult could be. The reasoning behind this exclusion was related to the development of the notion of intent. Without intent, without not only meaning to commit a crime but understanding the full consequences of one's actions, judges increasingly believed, a person could not be guilty of a crime. In the sixteenth century the most important distinctions in punishing crimes such as murder lay in whether an act had been committed by accident or was a crime of status. Status mattered much more than age in assessing guilt. By the early nineteenth century, legal treatises and legal decisions focused increasingly on intent: not simply on whether one meant an event to happen but on whether one understood the full consequences of one's actions. According to Blackstone: "Where there is no discernment, there is no choice; and where there is no choice, there can be no act of will, which is nothing else but a determination of one's choice to do or to abstain from a particular action: he, therefore, that has no understanding, can give no will to guide his conduct." Thus responsibility for crime became elaborated beyond the sixteenth-century ability to distinguish "good" from "evil."[85]

Behind this removal of culpability lay a broad shift in "social judgment." Children could not be guilty of criminal behavior, but could be guilty only of criminal potential, inasmuch as they were shaped by their surroundings and could not exercise their own understanding. Although some children, even under age fourteen, continued to be convicted of petty crimes, they began to be placed in special "reformatories" for children that would shape their minds. Thus judges redefined the boundaries of criminal responsibility to exclude children.[86]

Not only the definition of crime and the character of punishment but even the allocation of guilt mutated during this same era. The issue of a child's liability for a crime best shows the reasons and extent of this new allocation of guilt but also in some sense its limits. Logically, if a person did not have enough reason to vote until age twenty-one (or, indeed, to manage an estate), could that same person exercise enough reason to intentionally commit a crime and become liable for the full consequences of that action? After considering this question, Chief Justice Matthew Hale (1672) argued that fourteen should be the minimum age for liability for a crime, explaining that it would be too dangerous for society to follow the logical boundaries of minority (twenty-one) that he was advocating for other forms of responsibility. Hale was essentially arguing that children between fourteen and twenty-one were innocent, but dangerous, so they could be punished regardless. This same argument could be applied to other peoples that could not exercise political authority, such as women, poor men, and those enslaved whose situations presented the same logical dilemmas.

If they have no voice in the laws, how can they be bound by them? For children, the dilemma would be directly addressed in 1899 with the creation of the first juvenile court in Illinois.

Legislators in England and America transformed the character of punishment during the late eighteenth and early nineteenth centuries in response to changing norms about the purpose and nature of political authority. Revolutionaries in America initiated a sudden transformation away from such bodily punishments as branding, whipping, cutting off ears, castrating, and hanging toward imprisonment in its varied forms as the punishment for all crimes. A similar metamorphosis transformed the categories of crimes pros-

85. Blackstone, *Commentaries*, IV, 21.

86. In 1823, according to a report on "juvenile delinquents" in New York, between one hundred and two hundred youths between the ages of seven and fourteen appeared before the New York courts. Hawes, *Children in Urban Society*, 27–28.

ecuted. A range of offenses previously defined as crimes became redefined as not criminal or as not to be punished as harshly—including bestiality, non-attendance at church, and sedition. Other crimes, such as murder, continued to be punished harshly, but often by imprisonment instead of hanging. These redefinitions of crimes and punishments follow a particular pattern because they were part of a shift in political authority, both of the church and of the state itself.

Changing children's culpability for crime was part of the same transformations. Beginning about the time of the Revolution, in the same places where prisons were becoming the standard form of punishment, children began to be distinguished from adults in both kind and place of punishment. Pennsylvania had the earliest and most extensive reforms and moved the most vigilantly to treat juvenile offenders differently from adults. By the 1830s, all but two states had set up penitentiaries. The rethinking of the legal codes encouraged the replacement of the death penalty and other forms of bodily punishment with "penitentiaries" that sought to shape the mind. This transition reflected a shift in thinking about human nature: a child—nay, even an adult—is not irredeemably evil, even if that person has committed a grave crime. The emphasis on mental shaping applied particularly to children, the most malleable and with the most undeveloped understanding; they could only partly comprehend what they did, incompletely "intend" their actions, and were much more susceptible to temporary evil influences as well as to beneficial ones. The reasoning behind the penitentiary movement was that almost all criminals could be reformed and turned into better human beings. Children became the model and the main beneficiaries of these reforms.

CHAPTER 7

THE EMERGENCE OF PARENTAL CUSTODY

CHILDREN AND CONSENT TO CONTRACTS
FOR LAND, GOODS, AND LABOR

*"And an infant of the age of four years may make a will, and it
shall be good for all his goods and chattels."*
John Perkins, Treatise of the Laws of England on
the Various Branches of Conveyancing *(circa 1540)*

"Our children be not in potestate parentum, *as the children
of the Romans were: but as soone as they be* puberes,
*which we call the age of discretion, before that time nature
doth tell they be but as it were* partes parentum. *That which
is theirs they may give or sell, and purchase to themselves other
lands and other moveables the father having nothing to doe
therewith. And therefore* emancipatio *is clean superfluous,
we knowe not what it is."*
Sir Thomas Smith, De Republica Anglorum *(1583)*

In February 1752, the churchwardens of Frederick Parish, in Virginia, bound
four white children whose father had died into apprenticeships: Jonathan
Rose (age thirteen), Hannah Rose (nine), Abigail Rose (five), and Isaac Rose
(one). Likewise, they bound John Smith (three) and his sister Eleanor (six) in
August 1752 (both also white) to learn the "skills" of "husbandry" and spin-
ning and sewing, respectively. Only the mother of the Rose children lived;
both parents of John and Eleanor Smith were alive but poor. The records of
colonial Virginia are full of such apprenticeships for white children, which
almost always split families apart and were done without concern for the
consent of either the parents or the child. These cases show little concern for
parental "custody" as we would think of it. Note also that the children were
not "adopted" or in "foster care" or orphanages, but bound to labor for others
until they reached age eighteen (for girls) and twenty-one (for boys). "Family"
and parental custody had very different meanings in the common law prior to
the late eighteenth century. It was not simply that poverty could abrogate
parents' or even the child's rights, but that family had a legal meaning that
was interwoven with rank in society. This was a society where the rights of

masters trumped those of parents, and it grew out of much older feudal norms preserved in the law books that the Virginians brought with them. Indeed, the binding of these white children, even though it was for a limited time, parallels the sale of black children who were enslaved, a practice occurring at the same time in the same county. While there were some differences in future opportunities for these black enslaved children from those for white ones, both practices shared common origins and principles.[1]

Custody as a principle of law as we know it today did not exist four centuries ago in England or America. Parents had some authority over their children, and it became, increasingly, the subject of important public debates. The legal principles that parents or others are "responsible" for their children if they are hurt (explored above in discussing criminal intent) or that parents should legally make decisions for them were simply not there. Parents often influenced their children's decisions, of course: that is partly what this chapter is about. But most law books said nothing about custody. The only place that the term appeared in the law was with respect to guardians, but guardians existed only for heirs. Likewise, their powers, which varied depending on the nature of the guardianship, were very different from guardians' powers today. Masters' or lords' rights, on the other hand, though not called custodial, were firmly established. Parental custody, in short, was not much of a legal issue—except in the case of heirs. Even then it was different.

It was different in part because birth status was in many ways more important to the law than consent in the sixteenth century. To the extent that consent was important, children's consent was in many cases valid. The rights of "lords" predominated except when a child was an heir. Yet these legal principles have been difficult for scholars to imagine because our modern legal norms are so powerful. Writing in nineteenth-century England, Sir Henry Maine noted that the shift that characterized the transition away from feudalism toward a "modern" social order was one from status to contract: formerly one's position and legal rights were associated with one's status, but they began to be based on the rules of contract instead. Despite this immense shift in norms, he saw children's legal abilities as outside this shift. Children cannot make contracts (and always could not), he contended, because they

1. Frederick County Order Books, IV, 117, 264, at Library of Virginia, Richmond (hereafter FCV OB; and Minute Books, MB). John K. Nelson, *"A Blessed Company"*: *Parishes, Parsons, and Parishioners in Anglican Virginia, 1690–1776* (Chapel Hill, N.C., 2002), chap. 8, counted 7,470 such bindings in his survey through some of the surviving records of thirty-one Virginia counties. Virtually all of them were white children. On the absence of adoption in early America, see Yasuhide Kawashima, "Adoption in Early America," *Journal of Family Law*, XX (1981–1982), 677–696.

cannot exercise judgment. "The great majority of Jurists," he asserted, "are constant to the principle that [children and the insane] are subject to extrinsic control on the single ground that they do not possess the faculty of forming a judgment on their own interests; in other words, that they are wanting in the first essential of an engagement by Contract." Although Maine noted that consent had become more important than status, he did not address what the earlier period had meant for children: he assumed (as have most scholars), in fact, that fathers had had extensive and unlimited power. But neither the principle that children should be "subject to extrinsic control" because they cannot form judgments of their own interests nor the principle that fathers had extensive and unlimited powers over their children existed within the early law. Nor did "contract law" yet exist as a unified body of thought. To tell the story of children's ability to make and unmake contracts (and of granting parents the ability to act on their behalf) is to tell the story of contract law itself. It is about how meaningful, legitimate, and reliable consent became central principles of the common law.[2]

In the late sixteenth century, most children had no "custodian," whether guardian, master, or parent. Parents normally had no custodial power. Masters obtained their authority by contract. Only guardians had what they called custodial power, and that usually ended at age fourteen. Children were "responsible" for themselves in the sense that they could form many valid contracts—influence from their "friends" (parents or others) was common, but parents did not legally make the decision. In some cases children were allowed to annul their contracts, but not in others. By the early nineteenth century, in England and the various states examined here, virtually all children had custodians to make decisons for them during a custody that usually ended at a standard age of twenty-one. This period demarcates many significant changes, the most important being the emergence of parental custody as we know it, in the wake of challenges to birth status and a decline in children's ability to form all types of contracts, even for labor. Its roots were in changing ideas about what constitutes meaningful consent, which were coupled with an emphasis on parental authority as most "natural."

Custody in the Late Sixteenth and Early Seventeenth Centuries

The term "guardian" evokes images of a standard idea of minority, with consonant privileges and restrictions. However, guardianship was actually suprisingly different in the sixteenth and early seventeenth centuries. The

2. Henry Sumner Maine, *Ancient Law: Its Connection with the Early History of Society and Its Relation to Modern Ideas* (1861), new ed. (London, 1930), 180–181.

most important single fact is this: only heirs had guardians; indeed, mostly only heirs of land had guardians. In a society where inheritance of land was governed usually by primogeniture, then, only a small minority of orphans had guardians.

A father or mother could be guardian to the heir (assuming the heir inherited land from a more distant relative). But normally the idea of custody did not even apply to the rights of parents but concerned only the rights of this small group of guardians. Such a thing as a "guardian for nurture" did exist but was relatively unimportant. That the law books say almost nothing about it is perhaps the most important point. Today such guardians, including parents, are responsible for the nurture and care of a child and make decisions on their behalf. Then, most children had no such person, and such a person was not perceived as legally necessary. Young children were viewed as needing care and nurture, but not as belonging to a parent, who made decisions for them. And the sense of adult responsibility was much less.

Those who were heirs of land did get guardians. But the role varied dramatically, depending on the way the land was held. And here the reader must absorb some strange terms, because they formed the very core of the land law during this period: knight's service, copyhold, and socage. Land could be held in a variety of ways. If one held an estate in "knight's service" (virtually all of the land that Henry VIII acquired from the monasteries was sold with this restraint on it), then the understanding was that one owned the land in exchange for serving as a knight for the king (or any lesser lord if one held the land directly of him) when he so commanded. If one was unable to serve (as with a male under twenty-one), then the king reclaimed that land until one was able. For boys who married, who sought knighthood, or who literally bought their own wardships from the king or queen, wardship ended earlier. For girls it ended earlier still: it never started if they were fourteen when they inherited the land; if under fourteen, it ended when they married or at sixteen. The presumption was that they would marry a knight to serve the king.[3]

But the twist here is that guardianship in knight's service actually comprised three components: guardianship of the land; guardianship of the body of the ward; and, as an extension of the guardianship of the body, some

3. Sue Sheridan Walker, "Proof of Age of Feudal Heirs in Medieval England," *Mediaeval Studies*, XXXV (1973), 306–323; Edward Britton, *The Community of the Vill: A Study in the History of the Family and Village Life in Fourteenth-Century England* (Toronto, 1977), 46–47; Joel Hurstfield, *The Queen's Wards: Wardship and Marriage under Elizabeth I* (London, 1958), 137, 166. For an example of full age, see Marian K. Dale, ed., "Court Roll of Chalgrave Manor, 1278–1313," *Bedfordshire Historical Record Society*, XXVIII (1950), 46. For estimate of Charles I's income from the court of wards, see Christopher Hill, *Intellectual Origins of the English Revolution Revisited* (Oxford, 1997), 321.

influence over the ward's marriage. A guardian in knight's service could (and often did) sell the rights separately. Under knight's service the king or queen (or sometimes a lesser lord) was entitled to all of the profits from the estate (out of which he or she remitted a small amount to maintain the child in question). The lords of manors exercised similar control over the bodies and lands of heirs of those who held copyhold land from them (who were their tenants). In other words, the land returned, temporarily, to the lord. This practice can be seen as a kind of tax. Indeed, by one estimate, this type of guardianship—and the sales of the profits of wards' lands and bodies—had brought Charles I more revenue than the rents from all of his crown lands (which he owned directly).[4]

The most common type of guardianship, however, was of wards who held land in "socage" (that is, freehold). In this case, the heir would automatically be given a guardian of his or her body and land until reaching the age of fourteen. This guardian would not be a lord or king; instead, the guardian had to be the closest relative of the child to whom the property could not descend. Elaborate descriptions explained who this person had to be. When the property was inherited via the father, for example, the guardian would be the mother if she lived, her eldest brother if she did not, and so on. A father could be guardian in socage if, for example, his son inherited land from a maternal grandfather. Guardians in socage, unlike guardians in knight's service, did not keep the profits of the estate. Instead, they had to make a careful accounting to the ward when the ward reached fourteen. Neither did such guardians get to arrange or encourage a ward's marriage. The guardian's rights, in other words, were relatively limited. After the heir reached fourteen, he could "oust the Guardian . . . and occupy the Land himself if he will" and could choose a guardian (and rechoose), if he wished.[5]

4. Hill, *Intellectual Origins of the English Revolution Revisited*, 321.
5. Edward Coke, *The First Part of the Institutes of the Laws of England . . .* , 11th ed. (London, 1719), 79a, 88a–90b (hereafter referred to as *Coke upon Littleton*); Coke, *The Complete Copyholder . . .* (1641), 35 (hereafter referred to as *Complete Copyholder*), in *Coke upon Littleton*. "The next Friend unto the Heir, to whom the Inheritance cannot descend, shall have the Ward of the Heir's Body, and of his Land until the Age of fourteen." (Coke is here commenting upon Littleton's treatise of almost two hundred years earlier.) The 11th edition of 1719 is virtually identical to the 2d edition of 1629 in text (unlike editions of Blackstone, which were continually updated).

When a parent had wardship of the heir, Coke called this "guardianship by natural law": "*Legitimus jure naturae*, as where the Father or the Mother hath the Wardship of their Heir apparent." *Complete Copyholder*, 35.

For examples of fourteen (or reaching fifteen) as the key age, see Walker, "Proof of Age of Feudal Heirs," *Mediaeval Studies*, XXXV (1973), 313, 317.

Although there were ten different types of guardianship in England by the sixteenth century, most of them corresponded to one or the other of these two main types. In almost all cases, guardians existed only for those "orphans" (usually fatherless children) who inherited landed property.[6]

The one unusual type was set up for heirs of merchants in London. London was allowed a special exemption (and had to pay for it) to disbar any lord from claiming wardship over a child, even if the lord might otherwise have rights by the way the heir owned land. Instead, the court of orphans took the goods and lands of such an heir and set up an elaborate system of paying interest on the money, one from which city officials seemed to make a tidy profit. It was unusual in several respects, most importantly in that it assigned guardians for heirs of goods. Also, because the custom of London divided (of necessity) a father's estate in goods among his children and his wife (one-third to be divided among his children, one-third to his wife, one-third to be disposed of by testament), more of his children would be his heirs than was the norm elsewhere, where primogeniture tended to govern the distribution of land. Still, only the most elite orphans got guardians. The average estate in the London Court of Orphans in the year 1662–1663, for example, totaled more than £1,665. The children in question had guardians of their body (usually their mother, if she were alive) as well as for their estate and were wards until they reached twenty-one.[7]

In none of these cases could the father (or mother if she owned land) determine the custody of the child. According to Coke in 1628 (who was clearly trying to modify the system to give fathers more power), a father could designate custody of the land past his heir's age of fourteen. Likewise, if they wanted (presumably in order to make a more secure rental or sale), heirs in socage could choose someone to be guardian for their land after they reached the age of fourteen. But such heirs did not need a guardian for their land. And no one could have custody of the body of an heir in socage after the heir had reached age fourteen.[8]

6. On other types of wardship, and the rights granted by them, see, generally, Stephen Edward Jess, "Orphanage in Tudor-Stuart England: The Law and the Practice, 1509–1660" (Ph.D. diss., University of Nebraska, 1974), esp. 98–101. On guardianship in socage, see 34–35. Also see Frederick Pollock and Frederic William Maitland, *History of English Law before the Time of Edward I*, 2d ed. (1898; Cambridge, 1968), II, 443–444.

7. Charles Carlton, *The Court of Orphans* (Bristol, 1974), 46–47; Barbara Hanawalt, *Growing up in Medieval London: The Experience of Childhood in History* (New York, 1993), 51, 202–203.

8. See Coke, *Complete Copyholder*, 34. If a father appoints a guardian, "and withal committeth the Care of his Child's Body and Disposition of his Substance unto some friend . . . until he accomplish the full age of fourteen years; and then immediately he

Although parents were allowed a few privileges over their children, these privileges were not central to the law and were of short duration. Parents could punish their children "in reasonable and moderate manner only" according to Michael Dalton's 1618 *Countrey Justice*. Although Dalton allowed that "Assaults and Batteries be for the most part contrary to the peace of the realm," parents and masters were allowed this privilege on the grounds that they had "a natural authoritie" over their children "within age." But it seemed to end at fourteen. "Guardianship by nurture" (the only type of guardianship that at all approximates our own), the guardianship of parents that assumes they will nurture their child, ended at fourteen, according to Coke. (And Coke, as will be shown below, was trying to strengthen ideas about parental custody.) Sir Thomas Littleton himself, upon whom Coke was commenting, said nothing about "guardian per cause de nurture" when he wrote in the fifteenth century: it was present only in Coke's commentary. Most law books of this period, although they dealt extensively with land law, conveyancing law, criminal law, and the powers of guardians over wards, said virtually nothing about the powers of parents.[9]

So what happened to the majority of orphans? Who had "custody" of them? Someone must, one assumes, have cared for them as a guardian would today. Not quite. Status runs through the answer to this question as it runs through the law during this entire period. The law did not care about children's welfare, but about their land and money. Children in elite and middling families whose father had died usually lived with their mother. No great effort was made to provide legal guardians, although a father could, particularly if he left his child a landed legacy. If he did, the wardship of the body ended by fourteen. But formally assigning a guardian did not seem to be necessary. The executor of the estate, often the mother, would typically handle the payments due out of it, to be paid at the appropriate times. If the mother was also dead, then the children might live with a relative or godparent who would care for them. For middling or poorer children, the death of a father could bring significant economic distress, not only because the father's trade

---

shall be out of Ward for his Body, but his goods may be kept longer; for as for them they shall remain in the Trustees Hands so many Years as the Testator appointed by his last Will and Testmament: For tho' it be not in the Father's Power to restrain the Liberty of his Child's Body longer than to the age of fourteen, yet the disposing of his Goods he may commit to any for as long Time as himself shall think expedient." This does not apply to land held in knight's service or copyhold, when the father cannot appoint any guardian, for land or body, since the lord's rights are superior to his.

9. Michael Dalton, *The Countrey Justice* (1618; rpt. Amsterdam, 1975), 149; Coke, *Coke upon Littleton*, 89a. Also see Coke, *Complete Copyholder*, 34; and *Ratcliffe's Case*, in George Wilson, ed., *The Reports of Sir Edward Coke* ... (London, 1777), 5 Co. 37, II, 37–42.

or labor had provided the money to support the family but because the inheritance practices often left all the children but the heir with no claim to the land. Their mother might be able to support the other children out of her dower right or jointure, were she still alive. The father's goods, after his widow's one-third, were also usually apportioned between the children, with a double share to the eldest son, but the goods represented only a portion of the family's former estate. The smaller the family estate, the more likely such children would fall on the poor relief system: they might go begging; they might be forced to work. Thus the majority of orphans did not get guardians; if they got anything legally constituted, they got masters. And those masters, like the lords in knight's service, had real power over them.

Children's Consent to Contracts in the Late Sixteenth and Early Seventeenth Centuries

The late eighteenth and early nineteenth centuries have been called the period of the "rise of contract." Only then did ideas about contracts become central to the law and receive their own legal treatises. But changes in contract law were happening during the earlier two centuries as well and are intertwined with the struggles over justice and power that followed the Reformation. These legal transformations originated with lawyers and judges directly involved in the religious and political debates over consent that convulsed England in the seventeenth century. In many cases, these men sought to bring changes via judicial fiat—which disguised the change—even in the face of unsuccessful legislative reform. In other cases, they sought and achieved open legislative reform.[10]

But whether open or not, these common lawyers changed the grounds for making legal contracts to exclude force, influence, *and children* as part of a general effort to create a unified law about valid consent. They sought one rule that applied to all types of promises, vows, and agreements, including the ability to vote; they sought to unify a mishmash of varying norms for consent into one consistent principle that determined when consent was valid and binding across all kinds of contracts, whether for goods, land, labor, marriage, or power. Only when the transitions in all these categories are placed side by side does their full scope become clear. For men such as Edward Coke in the early seventeenth century or Gouverneur Morris at the United States Constitutional Convention, the logic of the law should be consistent about the ability to consent.

While some common law reforms about children's consent preceded other

10. P. S. Atiyah, *The Rise and Fall of Freedom of Contract* (Oxford, 1979).

statutory reforms (such as those about suffrage), they seem to have done so in part because the judges could manipulate certain parts of the common law more easily in response to their principles of justice. Common law reformers used the law to influence the larger ideological debate over political power: who should have power, and why? Coke, as we shall see, overreached himself—to adjudicate about the sources of political power—and failed. He did shape, however, reforms in areas perceived to be more purely "common law." Coke and others did not see these changes in contractual ability simply as useful tools for reforming political power: they consciously sought to systematize, to unify, to justify a whole new system of thought that made consent central. At the same time, that system excluded some from the right to consent based on a logic of inability: those persons became subject to custody.

In the early sixteenth century very different guidelines circumscribed the ability to contract. Although the age of twenty-one in some cases defined "minority," it did so only loosely as an outside delimiter, and only within the common law. Because the jurisdiction of the common law was much narrower, many contracts, including wills and marriages, were governed by ecclesiastical courts, for which the age of full majority was fourteen for boys and twelve for girls. The key issue here is *not* that the ages of twenty-one or fourteen or twelve existed as reference points, but that the meaning of those boundaries shifted. Depending on the nature of the legal contract, the consent of those under age twenty-one was often revocable at their own desire before they turned of age; in many other cases children under that age entered binding contracts. The one area where the contractual ability of children seemed to change least was in their ability to sell, rent, or make a testament of land. But even there the illusion of similarity masks real differences over what would make a valid contract.

Contracts were not as central to law in the Middle Ages; the word, in fact, hardly existed. What we would call contracts of course existed; they were called deeds (*faits* in the law French) or indentures or feoffments (wills) or vows (for marriage, to become a monk or nun, and so forth).[11] But no unified law governed these various agreements. The modern conception of a contract as a legally binding agreement only when a person was qualified to enter such an engagement, wherein the promise itself made the covenant binding,

11. Sir Thomas Littleton died in 1481. His treatise was first published in 1481 or 1482 (A. W. B. Simpson, ed., *Biographical Dictionary of the Common Law* [London, 1984], 316). His treatise did not use the word *contract*. Coke uses it in his commentaries on Littleton to refer, for example, to a deed to rent land from one person to another, but only rarely, and it was clearly not the best legal term (47b, 162b).

existed in the Middle Ages in very different and less generalizable forms. Certain legal rules did govern exchange relationships. However, these rules paid less attention to age or maturity. Very young children consented to valid contracts of different types; they placed their marks at the bottom of indentures for apprenticeship and on wills and on deeds for goods and land, and they repeated after the minister in marriage ceremonies. In a few cases their consent was void, but usually their consent was either voidable (at their own discretion) or binding, depending on the age of the child and the type of contract.

Fulfilling the formalities made a deed good. All deeds and indentures for land, the most important category, needed to be formally rendered on paper; the law recognized no other surface, because other surfaces that people might write on, such as wood, were more likely to deteriorate. To be valid, such contracts had also to be accompanied by the seals of those who agreed to the covenant and had to be written with specific words. At least two copies had to be made, one for each party who agreed.[12]

Coercion to obtain the consent of the seller or the buyer did not make a deed void so long as these formalities were met. When he wrote his legal treatise on "conveyancing" sometime before his death in 1545, John Perkins generalized about deeds and wills to transfer land. If properly performed, in the sense that they are written and sealed, such agreements are voidable, but still valid, even when made under duress. "All Feoffments, Leases, gifts or grants, made by duresse are voidable; and not void"; they can be voided by "the parties themselves, by their heires, and by those who have their estates." In other words: if someone forces me to sign a deed to sell or rent him land, it is valid unless and until I or my heirs or my guardian protests it formally. This may sound like a trivial distinction, but consider its implications: only a limited number of people could actually void such agreements. And agreements had to be actively avoided. Force, in short, was given, not full legitimacy, but a measure of it.[13]

The strongest constraints on the contractual power of children were with respect to their selling land. Even here, however, they had considerable dis-

12. All examples of indentures and deeds given by Littleton (pre-1481) concern land. See *Coke upon Littleton*, 143b, 229a–230b. These requirements are in Littleton. Coke defines *fait* as "a deed, and signifieth in the Common Law, an Instrument consisting on three things, viz. Writing, Sealing and Delivery, comprehending a Bargain or Contract between Party and Party, Man or Woman" (172a–172b).

13. John Perkins, *A Profitable Book . . . Treating of the Lawes of England* (London, 1642), par. 16. (Different editions of Perkins I checked contain text with the same meaning but have different titles and appear in three languages, Latin, law French, and English.) Perkins's book was also called by such names as *On Conveyancing.*

cretion, and the rules varied by locality. According to the mainstream common and canon law of the sixteenth century, children could not make wills to give away land until age twenty-one, but they could rent or sell it by deed (so long as they did not violate other encumbrances on the estate). Although they could avoid those deeds at any time before age twenty-one, their heirs could not. In many localities this guideline varied such that at age fifteen a child's devise of land was binding and unavoidable.[14]

Buying land was easier than selling it and was admissible even for Coke. "An infant or minor (whom we call any that is under the Age of 21 years) hath without Consent of any other, capacity to purchase, for it is intended for his Benefit, and at his full Age, he may either agree to it, and perfect it, or without any Cause to be alledged, waive or disagree to the purchase." Littleton as well as Coke discussed this issue under the category of joint heirs to land, where the land was divided among all the children while some were younger than twenty-one. The voidability clause provided an avenue for the child to disagree later if the partition were unfair.[15]

Most other contracts did not have to be as formal as those for land. Apprenticeships and other labor contracts usually required formal deeds. But most personal items (goods and chattels) required no formal indenture to exchange them. Although some exchanges of goods used formal deeds when they were for the future, many transactions for goods were completed at one time, as on a market day, and did not require a deed. Other types of contracts, such as marriage, accepted oral promises rather than written ones. Although narrow rules circumscribed their validity as well, they were different rules. Wills fell in between the two categories; they could be oral or written.[16]

The law distinguished between children's abilities to buy and to sell goods and chattels. All of their immediate exchange for goods or chattels was binding; it was done. But if a child wanted to be obliged to pay in the future (important, since a child might not have immediate control of lands or money

14. Ibid., par. 504: "But if there be a Custome, that all lands and tenements within such a precinct etc. are devisable by all manner of persons, which are of the age of 15 years, or above such age. A devise made of lands or tenements by one of such age is good."

Perkins was cited by William Blackstone as unusual in allowing a four-year-old to make a will by the late-eighteenth century. See Blackstone, *Commentaries on the Laws of England* (1765–1769; rpt. Chicago, 1979), II, 497 (chap. 32) (the reference remained in editions published through 1778, that is, until Blackstone's death in 1780).

15. *Coke upon Littleton*, 2b, 171b.

16. A. W. B. Simpson, *A History of the Common Law of Contract: The Rise of the Action of Assumpsit* (Oxford, 1975), 23–25, 35–36, 199–207; Henry Swinburne, *A Briefe Treatise of Testaments and Last Wils . . .* (1635; rpt. Amsterdam, 1979), part 1, 5, 43.

but would inherit later), then the agreement could in some cases be voided. In many other cases, it could not. The ability to purchase by bond (or formal agreement to pay in the future) was binding so long as one "needed" the item one bought: "If an infant at the years of discretion make a bond for his necessary meat and drink, or for his necessary apparel, or his schooling, he shall not avoid the same." Usually only the child could avoid the promise, and only within a narrow window. When exchange was immediate or for necessities, it was presumed binding on the grounds that children often had to provide their own necessities, especially if older than fourteen.[17]

Sales by infants gave them greater possibilities to avoid the exchange, but they were still good, so long as the "infant" gave "delivery of his own hand," that is, freely. Force to extract a sale from a child would void it completely. A child under the age of twenty-one had to give a horse freely when asked in order to confirm its sale by deed, for example. Such exchanges "are voidable by himself, and his heirs, and by those which shall have his estate." In other words the child, his heirs, or the guardian of his land (or the executor of the estate, if the land was still in the executor's hands) could void the sale of goods. Most conveyances by children were voidable, although their validity varied widely by the nature of the contract—for what, for when (present or future), via what medium (oral or written), and the age and sex of the child.

Testaments by children to give away their goods, money, and chattels, however, were binding once the child died. Children of four or older could make wills for their goods and their chattels, according to Perkins, one of the most widely read treatise writers on conveyancing; Henry Swinburne, another, later, judge, stated that the minimum age to write such a will should be fourteen for boys and twelve for girls. The City of London had its own rules. There, children under twenty-one could not make valid wills, whether for land or for goods and chattels. But, outside London, it appears that very young children, even under puberty, might make binding wills.[18]

17. Perkins, *Treating of the Lawes of England,* pars. 13, 14; 16 (on force); 503, 504 (on testaments); 13, 14, 19 (on voidability).

18. Carlton, *Court of Orphans,* 62. "And an infant of the age of foure yeares may make a will, and it shall be good for all his goods and chattells" (Perkins, *Treating of the Lawes of England,* par. 503). The same age of *four* appears in the editions of 1565 (in law French), 1642, and 1757; 1565: "enfant del age de iiii ans poit faire testament e serra bon" (fol. 97). Also see Swinburne, *Treatise of Testaments and Last Wils,* part 2, 61–62. Note that this concerns only testaments for goods, not lands: "A boye cannot make his Testament before hee have accomplished the age of 14. yeares, nor a wench before she have accomplished the age of 12. yeares. In so much that if before these foresaid yeares they were of that ripenesse of wit, that they were *doli capaces,* capable of deceit, or able to discerne betwixt good and evill, and betwixt truth and falshood; yet could they not make

According to Sir Thomas Smith, who summarized English law in 1583 and compared it to Roman law, English children could and did exchange goods and lands even when their fathers were alive. He argued that, unlike Roman law, English law recognized no age of emancipation.

> Our children be not *in potestate parentum,* as the children of the Romans were: but as soone as they be *puberes,* which we call the age of discretion, before that time nature doth tell they be but as it were *partes parentum.* That which is theirs they may give or sell, and purchase to themselves other lands and other moveables the father having nothing to doe therewith. And therefore *emancipatio* is clean superfluous, we knowe not what it is.[19]

Although children before puberty did not seem to have the same liberties to "give and sell, and purchase" as those past puberty, the very fact that puberty rather than intellectual capabilities provided the only partial guideline is important. Smith's statement, that *"emancipatio* is clean superfluous, we knowe not what it is," provides a distinct contrast to later policy, which did set an age of emancipation, at an age well beyond puberty. Infants could possess land as well as exchange it; they did not need to be represented in court by anyone, but appeared in their own right. Far from having to sue by representation of their guardian, they could actually sue their own guardian. They were responsible for their actions. "Any speculative objection that there may be against the attribution to infants of an *animus possidendi* [a will to possess], runs counter to English habits."[20]

Their ability to bind themselves by their own consent is clearest with respect to their ability to bind themselves, their own bodies, in labor contracts. The primary sovereignty over their own selves was within their own discretion. Yet others were expected to have influence over them: force and

---

any Testament, nor dispose of their goods." "Howbeit a boye after the age of 14. yeares, and a wench after the age of 12. yeares, may make a Testament and dispose of their goods and cattels, and that *not onely without the authoritie or consent of their Curator or guardian, but also without the authoritie and consent of the father,* if hee or shee have any goods of his or her owne" (my emphasis).

19. Thomas Smith, *De Republica Anglorum: A Discourse on the Commonwealth of England* (1583), ed. L. Alston (1906; rpt. New York, 1979), book 3, chap. 7, 128–129.

20. Pollock and Maitland, *History of English Law,* II, 440. They did find one situation where "minors" had particular privileges: "During infancy the possessory status quo is to be maintained." In other words, the young heir's or heiress's lands could not be taken to pay debts, and a lease could not be broken by others until he or she had emerged from guardianship.

persuasion did not make their contracts void. In sixteenth-century England, children were allowed to contract directly with a master in order to bind themselves into an apprenticeship. All contracts signed by apprentices, even under the age of seven, were declared valid and enforceable by law in 1563 "as amply and largely to every intent as if the same Apprentice were of full Age at the time of the making of such Indentures."[21]

Even then some judges questioned whether those under twenty-one could be bound by their mark and seal on an apprenticeship contract, but any question was resolved firmly in favor of their ability to consent and become permanently bound. The above law was passed "because ther hath bene and ys some Question and Scruple moved, wether any person being within [the age] of one and twentye yeres . . . shoulde bee bounden accepted and taken as an Apprentyce." It should replace "any lawe, usage or Custome to the contrary" and applied to all apprenticeship and labor contracts (except those of London and Norwich) and was repeated in legal guides over the next two centuries.[22]

Coercing the child's own consent to a labor contract was acceptable, so long as a justice approved. "Yf the said person refuse to bee bounde as an Apprentice, to commit him unto Warde [prison], *there to remayne untill he be contented and will bee bounden to serve as an Apprentise* should serve" at least seven years or up to age twenty-four. Thus children under age twenty-one could be committed to prison until they agreed to be bound as apprentices. This law is remarkable for the very ease in which it wrapped these assumptions: no question was raised about parental consent; the force used was made legal (although otherwise it might be questionable).[23]

While age shaped the length of service and whether one got paid, it was rank, and rank alone, that determined whether one could be forced to sign a labor contract. Others (men between twelve and sixty and unmarried women between twelve and forty) could also be forced by threat of prison to sign labor agreements, but only for a year or less. Here was an almost universal category, with married women alone exempted, but one other major exemption existed: no person could be forced to labor who had "an Auncestour whose Heire Apparant he [or she] ys" or who had more than ten pounds worth of property. If one did inherit, one's labor contract was void, whether that con-

---

21. 5 Eliz. I, c. 4, sect. 35. I have modernized the spelling slightly.

22. For example, see Thomas Wood, *An Institute of the Laws of England* . . . , 6th ed. (London, 1738), 13. "An apprentice shall be bound by his indenture notwithstanding his Nonage."

23. 5 Eliz. I, cc. 4, 17, 28, 29.

tract was for a year or an apprenticeship. As these extensive status exemptions make clear, one's status as poor legitimated coercion to obtain consent. Heirs, on the other hand, were exempt from forced service.[24]

The length of service might seem to define a kind of childhood. Children under twenty-one could be bound apprentices to husbandry "as the parties can agree" until age twenty-four or to skilled trades for seven years.[25] Does this mean that the law sought to control youth under twenty-four, particularly poor youth? Obviously, yes. But why? The answer is not simply that it assumed them not to be adults. On some deep level their status in age interacted with their status in rank. Perhaps young people of the lower orders needed longer coercion to adjust themselves to their rank. In other words: it was a process of forcing them to accept their place in society, of restraining them from theft and vagrancy, at the same time as it provided some nurture and skills. The phrase "as the parties can agree" reveals much and little: how much agreement was sought? How much choice would the young person really have? The law itself both proffered choice and—in allowing imprisonment for as long as necessary to get the child to agree—took it away. Its implementation could have varied dramatically by region and by the justice of the peace or churchwarden who oversaw each contract. We cannot recover the negotiations that lay behind these formal contracts.

This law sought the child's consent, as mediated by justices of the peace, and parents were left out of the equation altogether. Parents might well have influenced their children's choices, either through affection or money (better trades, especially, required a fee to the master). But their influence was indirect and reflected the money, connections, and persuasion at their disposal. Indeed, the many variations on this law, commonly known as the Poor Law, or Statute of Artificers, which was repeated in various forms by statutes and legal manuals in England and its colonies over three centuries, rarely mentioned parental consent for a child's apprenticeship, as we shall see. Parents had no formal claim even to keep their children with them, let alone control their labor, except, of course, in the case of heirs.

Putting this all together reveals a startling picture. The idea of parental custody was not important to the law (nor, at best, even carefully consid-

24. Ibid., cc. 2–5, esp. 4.

25. "No person shall by force or color of this [statute] bee bounden to enter into any Apprenticeshippe other then suche as bee under the age of one and twentye yeres" (5 Eliz. I, c. 4). Adults could also be forced to work, but only for periods of up to one year. Paul Slack, *Poverty and Policy in Stuart England* (London, 1988); A. L. Beier, *Masterless Men: The Vagrancy Problem in England, 1560–1640* (London, 1985), chaps. 2–4; Paul Griffiths, *Youth and Authority: Formative Experiences in England, 1560–1640* (Oxford, 1996), esp. chap. 7.

ered, certainly not recognizable). The closest one comes is a quote such as Sir Thomas Smith's that assumes that children before puberty (presumably twelve for girls and fourteen for boys) were "partes" of their parents. Most of those with dead fathers or mothers did not have guardians. Of those who did, the purpose of guardianship differed substantially. Guardians in knight's service were frequently called simply the heir's "lord" (not the guardian). This relationship, in particular, bespeaks a feudal obligation. And so it was called when it was abolished in the seventeenth century. Most guardianships over the bodies of heirs ended by fourteen. Many guardianships of land would have ended soon afterward, depending on a variety of factors. Some guardianships, especially in knight's service, could last until twenty-one. In the latter case in particular, the ward was not held to "own" the land at that time (the ownership was suspended until the boy could become a knight in the king's service). So we cannot think about this type of guardianship as being justified on the grounds that the heir was not properly able to manage the land, nor was such an explanation offered.

In sum, children had the greatest possibilities of voiding their contracts when they were wealthier and the contracts were over land. In no case was the contract of a child actually void except if a good (such as a horse) were taken by force, or for a will over land. In a society that placed many other constraints on the ability to alienate land from the family (the presumption was that one would allow one's heir to have the land), the fact that land transactions, particularly involving the transfer of family land, were the most sharply constrained is hardly surprising. The laws and customs aimed to keep land within the family; it was critical to the family status. Those who owned copyhold land could neither sell it nor will it. Those who owned entailed land could only rent it (though legal maneuvers to get around this were already being tried in the late sixteenth and early seventeenth centuries). Those most elite members of society who were wards in knight's service took longer to obtain control over their land. But does this mean that they thought of children under twenty-one as minors? In some ways, clearly. Yet that boundary meant something different when their deeds, even over land, were only voidable. They could and did contract in many cases, even with this most sovereign good in this society, land.

Children were more strongly bound by contracts if they were buying instead of selling or if granting their own labor. Who benefited from these rules? Not most parents, certainly. The obvious answer is that these rules were skewed in favor of those with privilege. These were rules that allowed masters to obtain servants who might be coerced into labor. But they cushioned elite families from losing their land especially. They were rules that allowed wealthy young men who would inherit in the future to pledge part of their future inheritance (which they knew they would inherit in many cases, especially if the land were entailed) for goods. They gave them power and access earlier. But they also protected their future estates.

So was this "free consent"? Hardly. One needed money or land or the expectation thereof in order to buy and sell. The more wealth and influence, the greater the credit that might be extended. The contracts of wealthy heirs, even still, were often avoidable by themselves and sometimes by others; the contracts of poor children, however, over the main commodity they had—their own labor—were not avoidable, and force and influence were acceptable, explicitly so, in their forming of that contract. Real choice was skewed sharply by rank.

Throughout this period, poor parents did not even have the right or obligation to nurture their children, though actual practice clearly depended on the administration of poor laws in particular regions. The poor laws offered a mixed set of payments to some of the poor, and forced labor for others. Each locality was to be responsible for its own poor (determined largely by whether they were born there or had established residency). By the early seventeenth century, children under age seven had the same residency as their parents: over that age, however, they should be sent to the locality of their birth. The poor law in operation thus presumed that poor parents and their children should stay in the same parish only until the child was seven. And it did not give such parents control over their children's labor. What changed was the effort to obtain the child's own consent: it vanished. During the same period, while children began to be settled in the same parish as their parents until they reached age fourteen, this increasing sense of custody for poor parents was undercut by allowing children to be bound at ever younger ages.[26]

Shifting Ideas about Contracts and Custody: The Role of Coke

Sir Edward Coke made at least three alterations in these earlier patterns, which are actually fairly obvious given that he was commenting, in the first volume of his *Institutes of the Laws of England*, on a law book written almost

---

26. William Lambarde, *Eirenarcha; or, Of the Office of the Justices of Peace* (1581; rpt. Amsterdam, 1970), 370; Wood, *Institute of the Laws*, 52. A directive from Chief Justice John Popham issued at the beginning of the seventeenth century stated that all vagrants over seven were to be whipped and sent to their own proper place of settlement (determined by a complicated equation of place of birth and last residence), whereas those under that age could be sent with their parents, to their parents' place of settlement. "Place of settlement" determined the parish responsible for their welfare. Ivy Pinchbeck and Margaret Hewitt, *Children in English Society*, I, *From Tudor Times to the Eighteenth Century* (London, 1969), 100–101.

two centuries earlier. His treatise contains, throughout, Littleton's original *Tenures* in law French, Coke's translation of Littleton, and then Coke's commentary thereon. His alterations might seem minor, yet he made consistent changes that tended toward (1) universalizing a law of contracts, (2) making minority more of a consistent boundary, and (3) giving fathers especially, and parents generally, more custodial power.

With regard to guardians, for example, Coke tried to make the age of twenty-one much more of a fixed boundary for ending males' wardship in knight's service. Coke's translation of Littleton reads: "And also if such Heir be not married at the Time of the Death of his Ancestor, then the Lord shall have the Wardship and Marriage of him." The clear implication of Littleton was that marriage ended wardship of the body. Practice in the late sixteenth century in the Elizabethan court of wards was to end both the wardship of the land and the body at the ward's marriage, whether male or female. While Coke admitted that marriage ended wardship for females for both their land and their body and of the body for males, he claimed that the male heir's land should be retained by the guardian until he reached age twenty-one: "The Guardian shall have the Custody of the Land until the Heir come to his full Age of one and twenty Years." He urged a similar change for another exemption that had allowed males to end wardships early when the land was entailed (so it could not be sold) or when the heir had to provide dowers and provision for siblings. According to Coke, current practice was that the lord would have wardship of one-third of the lands and of the body of the ward until twenty-one: "But now in all these cases the Heir shall be in Ward for his Body, and a third Part of the land." Before then, when the male or female heirs were married at the death of the ancestor, the land was entailed, or they had to provide for younger siblings, they did not usually enter wardship for their land or body. Partly under Coke's influence, wardships for both land and body began to continue longer. Given that child marriages were possible during this period and some parents encouraged their children who would inherit land in knight's service to marry (or entailed their land) so as to avoid wardship altogether, Coke's statements encouraged a significant change, toward not ending this type of guardianship for boys until age twenty-one.[27]

Coke urged a similar reform, subtly, for guardianship in socage. Littleton had stated unequivocally: "And when the Heir cometh to the Age of 14 Years compleat, he may enter and oust the Guardian in Socage, and occupy the Land himself if he will." While Coke acknowledged this passage, he emphasized (as Littleton did not) that, after the age of fourteen, heirs in socage could

27. Hurstfield, *The Queen's Wards*, 137, 166 (for earlier policy); *Coke upon Littleton*, 74b, 78a–79a.

choose a guardian until they reached age twenty-one. He also argued that the owner of socage land could designate a guardian by will for his child, for his body up to fourteen only but longer for his land. Neither of these changes was entirely of Coke's doing. He could not completely reform the common law in one breath; he had to pay attention to precedent. But he could interpret precedent in such a way as to open paths and magnify inconsistencies. In doing so he provided direction for others to follow.[28]

With regard to contracts for goods, the changes that Coke made were very smooth. Littleton's treatise was only about land law. Coke's translation of Littleton's comments about an infant's ability to sell land was very close to the original: "For if before such Age [of twenty-one] any Deed [fait] or Feoffment, Grant, Release, Confirmation, Obligations, or other Writing be made by any of them etc. . . . all serve for nothing ["tout serve pur nient"], and may be avoided ["et poit este avoyde"]." But, whereas Littleton specifically limited the application to land, Coke broadened the application of this sentence considerably—to all goods and chattels—in his commentaries. "The Law hath provided for the Safety of a Man's or Woman's Estate, that before their Age of twenty-one Years they cannot bind themselves by any Deed, or alien any Land, *Goods or Chattels.*" Coke likewise shifted the implication of this sentence, from voidable "may be avoided" to read "cannot bind." He acknowledged in his commentaries on this section that Littleton had meant only that the deed would be voidable. And he acknowledged that children could be bound by their contracts for necessities. But he made it seem as though these were exceptions to a general rule about their inability to bind themselves. He thus changed the presumption of the law.[29]

"They cannot alien any Land, Goods, or Chattels" was a very strong statement, differing considerably from the earlier lawyers. Whereas Littleton was considering only land, Coke interpreted it as applying to everything. Yet as Henry Swinburne and John Perkins made clear (as discussed above), very different rules had applied to other types of contracts.[30] Littleton gave exam-

28. *Coke upon Littleton,* 78b, 88a, 89a; Coke, *Complete Copyholder,* 34–35.

29. *Coke upon Littleton,* 171b, 172a–b, emphasis added. Coke writes that some exceptions to this rule exist: "An Infant may bind himself to pay for his necessary Meat, Drink, Apparel, necessary Physick, and such other Necesssaries, and likewise for his good Teaching or Instruction, whereby he may profit himself afterwards: But if he bind himself in an Obligation or other Writing, with a Penalty for the Payment of any of these, that Obligation shall not bind him . . . and generally whatsoever an Infant is bound to do by Law, the same shall bind him."

30. Ibid., 172a–b. But note at the end of this that Littleton writes that those under twenty-one should not be jurors for an "enquest" (Littleton seems to have meant by this a civil jury considering land issues).

ples elsewhere in his treatise of infants' deeds to rent land (part of a complex example relating to various levels of renting—if an infant rents to one person, who rents it to another, can recovery be had by the infant?). "If I being within Age, let land to another for Term of 20 years, and after he grant the land to another for Term of ten years, so he granteth but Parcel of his term: In this case when I am of full Age . . . if I confirm his Estate, then this confirmation is good." Coke's comment on this was simply, "That the Lease of an Infant in this Case is not void but voidable." He had to acknowledge it because it was part of Littleton's treatise, even though it did not fit the shape of the presumptions he was urging elsewhere.[31]

One last example should provide proof of Coke's general mission to provide an older and consistent age of majority: his claim in volume IV of his *Institutes* that those under twenty-one could not be elected as a "Knight, Citizen, or Burgesse of Parliament." "One under the age of 21 years is not eligible [for election to the House of Commons], neither can any Lord of Parliament sit there [in the House of Lords] untill he be of the full age of 21 years." Volume IV was published after Coke's death, during the Interregnum. Unless someone altered his manuscript (possible but unlikely), Coke was consciously trying to change the law. Consider only this: in the Parliament of 1621, Coke supported a bill to reform the voting laws. This bill sought to set the qualifications for those elected to the House of Commons: one should have at least six months' residency in the place electing him; one should not treat or influence the voters ("verball sollicitacion to be restrayned aswell as sollicitacion by Letters"); and one should be at least twenty-one years old ("None to be chosen Under age as Unfitt to be trusted to make Lawes for other mens estates that are not trusted with their owne"). He was present at the debate on this bill and tried to get it passed, urging that it not be bogged down with extra requirements when someone proposed adding a property qualification. But the bill did not even make it out of the Commons. Coke knew it did not pass; such a law did not pass until after the Glorious Revolution. Many teenage members of Parliament were elected before and afterward—and were present at that Parliament. So why, then, did he try to make the law seem different from what it actually was? His was a startling attempt at judicial fiat, which, given the popularity of his *Institutes* over the next two centuries, probably had real influence.[32]

31. Ibid., 308b.

32. Edw[ard] Coke, *The Fourth Part of the Institutes of the Laws of England: Concerning the Jurisdiction of Courts* (London, 1644), 46–47; Wallace Notestein, Frances Helen Relf, and Hartley Simpson, eds., *Commons Debates, 1621* (New Haven, Conn., 1935), IV, 446 (Nov. 28, 1621). Puritans made another attempt to exclude those under twenty-one from

Coke died in 1634. As judge and member of Parliament, he was part of a broader mission of Puritan reform that would help to transform custody and minority. The very idea of guardianship would change in 1645. In the midst of the Civil War, the House of Commons abolished guardianship in knight's service and all the courts and procedures associated with it. In 1660, Charles II was required to ratify this abolition as a condition for assuming his throne. Only then did the terms of all guardianship change substantially. By the law of 1660, fathers, and fathers alone, were granted the right to designate who would be guardians of all their children, of both their lands and bodies, up to the age of twenty-one.[33]

This law marked a pivotal transition in legal norms about guardianship and custody. It universalized guardianship, making all children potential wards, and gave fathers significant power over their children. In the process, it extended the length of wardship in all cases to as late as twenty-one. At the same time, it denied that power to social superiors. Thereafter, a father's rights to determine the "custody" of his children would be legally paramount. It replaced a lord's power with a father's, created a kind of equality among adult men and gave them superiority over their children (and, by implication, over women, by not giving them that power over their children). Establishing the father's right to designate a guardian for all of his children until age twenty-one extended the institution of guardianship to cover most fatherless children, lengthened the span during which most guardianships lasted, gave fathers more power, and set a more uniform principle of custody.

This statute, thereafter referred to as the "abolition of feudal tenures," could just as easily be called "establishment of paternal custody" or, to use Blackstone's words of a century later, creation of the "empire of the father." The reason this statute was a critical negotiating point for restoring monarchy was that it cut through the monarchs' and lords' powers and elevated

---

election to the House of Commons in 1626. See William B. Bidwell and Maija Jansson, eds., *Proceedings in Parliament, 1626* (New Haven, Conn., 1991–1992), II, 25 (Feb. 13, 1626).

33. 12 Car. II, c. 24, esp. par. 8. "Where any person hath or shall have any Child or Children under the age of twenty one yeares and not married at the time of his death that it shall and may be lawfull to and for the Father of such child or children . . . [by deed or will] to dispose of the custody and tuition of such children or children for and dureing such time as he or they shall respectively remaine under the age of twenty one yeares or any lesser time." Hill, *Intellectual Origins,* calls this law "one of the unspoken conditions of the restoration" (321).

the authority of the father. Income from lordships had supplied Charles I's main source of income prior to the Civil War. In getting rid of that income, it also undercut some key feudal principles of obligation, substituting a lord's might for a father's and setting a limit to that authority of twenty-one. Yet in creating that boundary, it made that age a much more important distinction. Indeed, age became more important than rank.

Yet the issues raised by this pivotal law were far from resolved. During the late seventeenth century, for example, it was debated whether heirs who held land in socage needed a guardian after they reached age fourteen, the earlier limit. *The Infants Lawyer* (1697) still said that all guardians in socage had authority only until the heir reached age fourteen. However, it then noted that, after the 1660 law, fathers had the power to grant the custody of their children to any person until the child reached age twenty-one.[34]

Because land in the colonies was held in socage before 1660 and the new law, the duties of most guardians, assigned according to socage rules, officially ended when the ward reached the age of fourteen.[35] But not in Massachusetts. In 1641, as war began to convulse England, the Massachusetts colony for the first time circulated its own body of laws. The first section of the Massachusetts Body of Liberties established a man's right to keep his family with him: "No man shall be deprived of his wife or children." This clause was listed with his rights to his goods and estate, his life, and his honor. Only a man's violation of a law duly passed by a popularly elected General Court and well publicized could take these privileges away from him. Although it does not say "have power over them," it does imply that in part (it is unclear whether the children or wife may leave of their own accord). The law contradicts the Statute of Artificers, at least insofar as it had allowed children to bind themselves to others without their father's consent. Still, it permitted children to be removed from their parents if the parents were not educating them properly. The Body of Liberties prohibited wardships and other feudal impositions. Instead, it gave the following guidelines for orphans: "No Orphan dureing their minoritie which was not committed to tuition or service by their parents in their life time, shall afterwards be absolutely disposed of by any kindred, freind, Executor, Towneship, or Church, nor by themselves without the consent of some Court." While this did not privilege fathers over mothers, it did imply that such orphans should be committed to someone's custody during their minority, which Nathaniel Ward, the author of the Mas-

34. *The Infants Lawyer; or, The Law (Both Ancient and Modern) Relating to Infants, Setting Forth Their Priviledges, Their Several Ages for Divers Purposes* . . . (London, 1697), 46–47.

35. Hurstfield, *The Queen's Wards,* 23.

sachusetts Body of Liberties, defined elsewhere as twenty-one. They were not permitted to choose their own guardian until age fourteen: others chose for them. It also universalized the application of rules for all orphans, not only heirs. (The category of heirs would have been broadened regardless, because estates were to be divided among the children and wife, rather than going to the elder son, with the wife having only a temporary dower right.) It thereby established a firm minority during which consent was inappropriate. The Body of Liberties also stated clearly that the age of twenty-one would be the "age of discretion for passing away lands or such kinde of herediments, or for giveing, of votes, verdicts or Sentence in any Civill Courts or causes." It did permit children under twenty-one to alienate land if, and only if, that conveyance were ratified directly by the General Court.[36]

Although Massachusetts law allowed fathers to assign custody of their children (both their body and lands) up to twenty-one, not all fathers in Massachusetts actually did so. Nor, indeed, did all Virginia fathers after 1660. (In the absence of their own law, Virginians followed the 1660 English law, as put forth in legal guides that they used such as the *Infants Lawyer*.) As examples from both Massachusetts and Virginia illustrate, fathers during the seventeenth and early eighteenth centuries who designated when their children should control their land gave a variety of ages for inheritance (when they said anything), often younger than twenty-one and as young as fifteen. These included ages of fifteen, sixteen, and seventeen. Suits from the Virginia General Court during the early eighteenth century (over issues unrelated to guardianships) show sixteen- and seventeen-year-olds managing estates without guardians.[37]

36. Edwin Powers, *Crime and Punishment in Early Massachusetts, 1620–1692: A Documentary History* (Boston, 1966), 533, 534, 539, 542–543 (sections 1, 10, 11, 14, 53, 81–84).

37. John Demos, *A Little Commonwealth: Family Life in Plymouth Colony* (New York, 1970), 149. Demos noted that, while many Puritan wills specified that sons should have the land at twenty-one, all other wills designated younger ages. The 1647 will of Alexander Winchester designated that his children should have the land when they arrived at fifteen years. Also see Darrett B. Rutman and Anita H. Rutman, " 'Now-Wives and Sons-in-Law': Parental Death in a Seventeenth-Century Virginia County," in Thad W. Tate and David L. Ammerman, eds., *The Chesapeake in the Seventeenth Century: Essays on Anglo-American Society* (Chapel Hill, N.C., 1979), 153–182: "John Sumner, for example, in 1703, specified that his son of sixteen was of age to dispose of his estate with the advice of designated executors, while Thomas Norman, in 1727, declared it to be his will that his seventeen-year-old son Robert 'Act and do for himself' " (170).

On suits from Virginia General Court: *Case Int. Hallows and Manly* (1722), B26–B27, where a will made in 1687 by a widow named Restitute Whiston Manly specified that her three children should inherit when they turned sixteen: they in fact did so. In another case, Daniel McCarty left his estate to his three sons and appointed executors in trust for

Critical to understanding custody is the practice of naming heirs as executors. If the legal guides are any gauge, it was normal for heirs and heiresses to be executors, regardless of their age. The acts of executors, even over land, were binding if they had reached age seventeen. Executors could, however, be much younger. Swinburne's 1635 *Testaments and Last Wils* held that it was even lawful to make "the childe in the mothers wombe, and unborne at the death of the Testator" an "Executor." So, too, "if the Infant be so yong that he hath no discretion," he still could be executor. But, in these cases, an "Administrator" would then manage the estate "for the childes behoofe, until he be able to execute the same himselfe," until the child was seventeen years old (or even younger). Some protections were prescribed. A younger child acting as executor was not permitted to forgive debts without payment. Making a very young child an executor seemed to put the estate into a holding pattern that did not give the administrator much real power. The administrator "cannot sell or alienate any of the goods of the deceased, unlesse it be upon necessitie, as for the payment of the deceaseds debts, or that the goods would otherwise perish: nor let a lease for a longer term than whilest the Executor shall be in minority."[38]

At his death in 1690, for example, John Carter (Jr.) left his only child, a daughter named Elizabeth, as his main heir and "executrix." She was under fourteen, for the will stated that when she "arrives to 14 yrs. age" she was supposed to be able to choose whether she wanted to live in Virginia or England; if she stayed in Virginia, she could choose whether she wanted to live with her grandmother, mother, or a Mr. Morris. She was to be given, at that point, some of the money from her inheritance for her own use. Carter did not mention any "guardian" or "administrator." He appointed four people, Elizabeth's grandmother and mother, his brother Robert, and Mr. Morris, as "overseers" of his will. Her mother would be her guardian under the rules about socage land until Elizabeth reached fourteen. Although Elizabeth did not receive all of her estate at fourteen, she would by seventeen, as executrix. In her case, most of her estate was in money (which her father could designate control over longer), not land: her grandfather John Carter had entailed his land in tail male, so she could not inherit it (her uncle Robert, later known

---

the estate until the eldest son turned seventeen, when by the common law he could become full executor of the estate (*McCarty ag't McCarty Extors* [1733], B34–35). R. T. Barton, ed., *Virginia Colonial Decisions: The Reports by Sir John Randolph and by Sir Edward Barradall of Decisions of the General Court of Virginia, 1728–1741* (Boston, Mass., 1909).

38. Swinburne, *Testaments and Last Wils*, part 5, p. 6. Swinburne cites *Coke upon Littleton* and Coke's argument in Russel's case as important authorities in this section. So these rules about executorships already bear Coke's stamp.

as King Carter, did). (Within four years Elizabeth married and then died. Her husband, Julian LLoyd, appeared in court to request that he assume her resposibilities as executor in March 1693/4.) Many testators in Virginia were leaving their heirs as executors of their estates during this period instead of appointing guardians, even when their heirs were under twenty-one. This practice needs to be central to our understanding of custody in the seventeenth and eighteenth centuries.[39]

By the mid-eighteenth century, both Pennsylvania and Virginia seemed to follow common law guidelines that formed the new, post-Cokean variant on socage guardianship: a guardian is appointed (following the rules about next of kin who cannot inherit), and at fourteen the children can choose their own guardian until the age of twenty-one. Only heirs had guardians, but in Pennsylvania this was a broader category than in Virginia, because the rules of inheritance differed. In cases of intestacy the difference is most clear: Pennsylvania gave one-third of real and personal property to the wife (as dower) and divided the remainder among the children, with a double share for the eldest son. In Virginia, the eldest son would receive all of the land and slaves (with the wife's having a use right to one-third) and only goods would be divided among the wife (one-third) and the children, in which case, despite receiving all of his father's land, the eldest son also got an equal share. But personal goods (especially once debts were subtracted) did not usually amount to enough to educate and feed a child for long. Younger siblings in Virginia, therefore, might be bound out, a pattern that was rarer in Pennsylvania except when the bindings were "real," that is, of boys at fourteen to learn a skilled trade. In this sense Virginia was more similar to England.

It had become more common, by the mid-eighteenth century, for orphans to have guardians until age twenty-one and for fathers to assign guardians. Even then it was unclear whether fathers could assign guardians for the entire period—to do so was relatively uncommon in Virginia and Pennsylvania. In one Pennsylvania orphan's court case from the 1750s, for example, the guardian appointed by the court tried to bind Samuel Sharp into an apprenticeship, whereupon someone produced the will of Samuel's father, who had chosen a different guardian for him. When Samuel reached age

39. On Carter: "Will of John Carter [Jr.] of Corotoman, 1690," *Virginia Magazine of History and Biography*, XVII (1909), 217–218. On the entailing of this property, see Holly Brewer, "Entailing Aristocracy in Colonial Virginia: 'Ancient Feudal Restraints' and Revolutionary Reform," *William and Mary Quarterly*, 3d Ser., LIV (1997), 322–323 n. 49. For Elizabeth's husband's appearance, see "Abstracts from Records of Richmond County, Virginia," *William and Mary College Quarterly Historical Magazine*, 1st Ser., XVII (1908–1909), 73–74.

fourteen soon afterward, he proceeded to choose his own guardian (neither his father's choice nor the court's), who did not seek to bind Samuel into an apprenticeship (via the court's authority). The lesson here is that, after fourteen, Samuel's choice of guardian trumped his father's but that before fourteen Samuel's choice did not matter, whether to guardian or master. If his father had not named a guardian, Samuel would have been locked into a labor contract not of his choice until age twenty-one. The middle- and late-eighteenth-century court records of Virginia and Pennsylvania are full of orphan heirs choosing their guardians at age fourteen.[40]

Virginia's laws from the very beginning followed those of England more closely on questions of custody. Acknowledging that "for the most part the parents, either through fond indulgence or perverse obstinacy, are most averse and unwilling to parte with theire children," Virginia's first version of the poor law in 1646 confirmed the "great wisdom [of the English statutes] . . . for the better educateing of youth in honest and profitable trades and manufactures, as also to avoyd sloath and idelnesse wherewith such young children are easily corrupted." It thereby specifically dismissed parental custody (the contrast to Massachusetts laws of the same era is especially striking). When Virginia in 1730 finally passed its own version of England's guardianship law of 1660, giving fathers the power to determine the custody of the children up to the age of twenty-one, it made clear that this should not interfere with apprenticeship: "*Provided*, That this act shall not extend to discharge any apprentice from his apprenticeship."[41]

Justices of the peace could bind at their own "discretion" all children whose parents' "poverty extends not to give them breeding"—a flexible and broad category. In the eighteenth century, Virginia seemed to bind more children and at younger ages than Massachusetts and Pennsylvania. One study of county records from eighteenth-century Virginia has counted 7,470 children (mostly white) bound out. My own examination of the records of Frederick

40. In Virginia, the orphan's court records are mixed in with those of the quarterly courts; see FCV OB, MB. For Pennsylvania, see Dorothy B. Lapp and Frances B. Dunlap, comps., *Records of Orphan's Court for Chester County, Pennsylvania, 1747–1761* (Danboro, Pa., 1975), 14 (Mar. 15, 1747/8), 39 (Dec. 20, 1748), 52 (Sept. 19, 1749). Lois Green Carr has a rich analysis of the orphan's court in late-seventeenth-century Maryland, which followed a similar practice: guardians could be appointed until age fourteen; after that age the youth could choose. "The Development of the Maryland Orphans' Court, 1654–1715," in Aubrey C. Land, Lois Green Carr, and Edward C. Papenfuse, eds., *Law, Society, and Politics in Early Maryland* (Baltimore, 1977), 41–62.

41. William Waller Hening, ed., *The Statutes at Large: Being a Collection of All the Laws of Virginia . . .* (rpt. Charlottesville, Va., 1969), I, 336, IV, 285–286.

County in the 1750s estimates that fully 7.3 percent (161) of the children (virtually all white) in that decade alone were bound by the churchwardens.[42]

Those same records reveal a great deal about what happened to those whose fathers had died. In the decade 1751–1760, more orphans (those whose fathers had died but whose mothers usually lived) were given masters than guardians. While only fifty-seven had guardians (assigned or chosen), seventy-four were bound by the churchwardens. Whether because fathers were splitting inheritances more evenly or because different poor law policies tended to support mothers with young children, fewer orphans, proportionately, were bound out in Massachusetts and Pennsylvania. Indeed, the Frederick County churchwardens bound children—orphans, children of simply poor parents, and illegitimate children—in the 1750s at an average age of 7.9: this was the welfare policy for children, which did not value keeping such families together.[43]

Can Virginia's policies about fatherless and poor children be understood as the traditional policy about poor parents' custody of their children? To some great degree, yes, although it is likely that fewer young children, proportionately, were bound in England. The average age of binding undoubtedly varied by parish and over time. The frequent disputes about proper settlements for children and their parents in England show that the traditional pattern sometimes did provide for families with very young children, perhaps under seven. Yet the Elizabethan poor laws had no lower age limit for binding children, suggesting that in England itself some children were bound at extremely young ages.[44]

Indeed, the attempt to keep young children with their parents may well

42. Hening, ed., *Statutes at Large,* I, 336 (October 1646); Nelson , *"A Blessed Company,"* chap. 8.

43. FCB OB, 1751–1760 (IV–IX). While 74 "orphans" were bound and 46 were "bastards," only 41 were simply "poor," indicating that their father lived. So only one-fourth of those bound (41 of 161) had a father.

44. 39 Eliz. I, cc. 3–4 (1597/8); 43 Eliz. I, cc. 1, 2 (1601). Although most early modern English poor-apprenticeship records "do not include the ages" of those bound, some tentative estimates have been made. Ann Kussmaul, *Servants in Husbandry in Early Modern England* (Cambridge, 1981), 14. See Paul Slack, *The English Poor Law, 1531–1782* (Cambridge, 1995), 19, 31–32; and, especially, Ilana Krausman Ben-Amos, *Adolescence and Youth in Early Modern England* (New Haven, Conn., 1994), 260 n. 125, where she estimates from a sample of ninety-five Southampton records for the seventeenth century that only 20 percent were younger than ten. K. D. M. Snell has some interesting observations about apprenticeship in *Annals of the Labouring Poor: Social Change and Agrarian England, 1660–1900* (Cambridge, 1985) 287–289, and table for 1609–1708. Also see O. J. Dunlop and Richard Denman, *English Apprenticeship and Child Labor: A History* (New York, 1912).

explain the frequency of families' being "warned out" of Massachusetts and (to a lesser degree) Pennsylvania communities in the 1750s, a practice not used much in Virginia. If Massachusetts tended to support families with young children with monetary payments in order to allow them to stay together, having a new poor family in the community would be an expensive proposition. If, on the other hand, Virginia did not—and instead bound out the children of the family and left the parents free to work unencumbered by the care of their children—then the poor family cost it nothing (and in fact just meant extra laborers). The average age at binding was critical to the cost each community would pay in poor relief.[45]

This contrast also puts Massachusetts's notorious auctions of the poor in a new light. What the auctions did was see who would accept the lowest amount for caring for a family or individual within their own home or for renting a house for them. While an auction does seem embarrassing, in practice it allowed the family to remain together; the lowest bidder for individual children was often a relative. No such practices existed in Virginia, and transfer payments of that sort were very rare. Instead, Virginia bound children individually into apprenticeships (thus separating them from the par-

45. The literature on "warning out" in New England, particularly, is extensive. The Plymouth General Sessions records (David Thomas Konig, *Plymouth Court Records, 1686–1859* [Wilmington, Del., 1979]) are full of instances of the warning out of families, as too is the "Goshen Township Book" of Chester County, Pennsylvania (Pennsylvania Historical Society), for example. The "Quarter Sessions Dockets and Indictments" for Chester County also contains numerous disputes over the "proper residency" of pauper families (and of individuals within them). In virtually all cases, the townships did not want the families and sought to make them go back to their "legal place of settlement." On Massachusetts, see, especially, Ruth Wallis Herndon, *Unwelcome Americans: Living on the Margin in Early New England* (Philadelphia, 2001), which focuses on warning out. On Pennsylvania see Duane Eugene Ball, "Dynamics of Population and Wealth in Eighteenth-Century Chester County, Pennsylvania," *Journal of Interdisciplinary History*, IV (1975–1976), 621–644; Lucy Simler, "The Township: The Community of the Rural Pennsylvanian," *Pennsylvania Magazine of History and Biography*, CVI (1982), 60.

Similar directives to those of Chief Justice Popham from the early seventeenth century appeared in many later legal treatises, beginning to specify age fourteen instead of seven. According to *Conductor Generalis; or, The Office, Duty, and Authority of Justices of the Peace* (Philadelphia, 1722), 219, those over fourteen should be sent to their place of legal settlement, and those under fourteen to their parents. This clearly derived from an older policy that punished those over fourteen for "begging or wandering." Lambarde, *Eirenarcha*, 192, 244. Also see Pinchbeck and Hewitt, *Children in English Society*, I, 97.

On the later period, see John R. Sutton, *Stubborn Children: Controlling Delinquency in the United States, 1640–1981* (Berkeley, Calif., 1988), 69–71; Allen Steinberg, *The Transformation of Criminal Justice: Philadelphia, 1800–1880* (Chapel Hill, N.C., 1989), 179–180.

ents as well as siblings); the children's future labor would pay for their present keep. Although Massachusetts occasionally bound children separately to labor (as did Pennsylvania), reading through these three sets of records reveals clear differences.[46]

Already, by the 1750s, Massachusetts and, to a lesser degree, Pennsylvania had altered practices so as to give more weight to keeping children, especially those below puberty, with their parents: in Massachusetts by giving fathers more power in wills (to designate guardians rather than follow the socage laws), in both Massachusetts and Pennsylvania by splitting up inheritances such that more children were heirs and had some money to live on in case of their parents' death, and by administering the poor law differently so as to keep young children with their mothers.

How much real control did these various custodians have or even want? In gauging control, the question of acceptable punishment is critical. This was partly due to the crowning of custody at that point, and partly due to religious ideology (and beliefs about children's sinfulness). Parents and masters both had more power over the bodies of children than did guardians (with the possible exception of the guardians in knight's service and the variant of copyhold guardians, both of whom were considered "lords"). Both parents and masters, according to guidelines for justices of the peace, had the right to "chastise" their children and servants without being charged with assault;

46. See, for example, Charles H. Bricknell's typescript, "Records of the Town of Plympton," book 2 (vol. I, 1731/2–1781; II, 1781–1802), Widener Library, Harvard University, Cambridge, Mass. Many families were supported intact via levies voted by the town. See, for example, Oct. 24, 1781: "Voted and raised 25 pounds in hard money to supply Noah Eaten's wife and family and for clothing for the poor of said town." A more exhaustive search through the various Massachusetts records that were kept and survive indifferently would surely have yielded more information, but the impression is rather strong: the rate of children bound was lower in Massachusetts, and they tended to be older (that is, teenagers). Herndon, *Unwelcome Americans*, chap. 1, gives several examples of children bound very young (at age three or four).

Nelson, in *"A Blessed Company,"* counted apprenticeships and examined the vestry records for other counties in Virginia and reinforces the findings. Only rarely did the vestry support families. It supported only those incapable of work (for example, under about age two to four), and virtually no individual children longer than four years. The norm seemed to be two to three years, and most of these were illegitimate children whose mother or father had paid a fine, which paid for their first two to three years of support and did not go to the natural parents (at least in the 1760s). See the "Vestry Book for Frederick Parish," MS, Library of Virginia; Wilmer L. Hall, ed., *The Vestry Book of the Upper Parish, Nansemond County, Virginia, 1743–1793* (Richmond, Va., 1949), 48–49, 56–57, 86–91, for example.

guardians did not have that right. The rights of parents to discipline their children (and the duty of children to obey their parents) were made explicit by laws in Massachusetts and New York (which would later become part of Pennsylvania's laws): teenage children who "smited" their parents could be put to death. Penn's charter (and later laws) modified this rule such that children who "assault or menace" their parents could be committed to a house of correction (original charter) or put in prison for six months at hard labor (law of 1700). Dalton's *Countrey Justice*, popular in all colonies, instructed that parents might chastise their children and that masters might punish their servants "in a reasonable and moderate manner only."[47]

Similar injuctions appeared in Pennsylvania's guide of 1722, *Conductor Generalis*. It is no assault "where men have a natural power over others . . . as parents have over their children 'till they come of age, for till then they may chastise them for offences without a breach of the peace." George Webb's Virginia manual of 1736, *Office and Authority of a Justice of Peace*, repeated these clauses. Neither, however, contained the clause limiting parental punishments to what was "reasonable and moderate." If a child died as a result of being "chastised" by a master or parent, these guides did not deem the action homicide, but only "chance-medley" or accident. Later guides, such as Blackstone's *Commentaries on the Laws of England* of 1765 and Hening's *Virginia Justice* of 1825, reinserted the clause about reasonable and moderate punishment. Parental punishment seemed to be actually increasing over time, a movement linked to evangelical Christianity. Historians who have examined diaries over this entire period reveal that discipline was harshest in evangelical families in the early nineteenth century.[48]

47. Dalton, *The Countrey Justice*, 149. On the "stubborn child law" in Massachusetts, see Sutton, *Stubborn Children*, 16. The duke of York (the future James II) signed the first law that gave public authorities in the future Pennsylvania the power to punish children over sixteen who had been disobedient to their parents. Staughton George, Benjamin McNead, and Thomas McCamant, comps., *Charter to William Penn, and the Laws of the Province of Pennsylvania* . . . (Harrisburg, Pa., 1879), 19–20, 113; James T. Mitchell and Henry Flanders, comps., *The Statutes at Large of Pennsylvania from 1682 to 1801* (Harrisburg, Pa., 1896–1911), II, 13. There is no evidence that any child was actually executed as a result of the stubborn-child laws. On the circulation of legal texts in early America, see Appendix.

48. *Conductor Generalis*, 18, 131, 161–162; George Webb, *The Office and Authority of a Justice of Peace* . . . (Williamsburg, Va., 1736), 27; Blackstone, *Commentaries*, I, 440. See, especially, Linda A. Pollock, *Forgotten Children: Parent-Child Relations from 1500 to 1900* (Cambridge, 1983), 269. Although Philip J. Greven, Jr., ignores the time dimension in his analysis, his main examples of harsh evangelical discipline are from the early nineteenth century (for example, Francis Wayland, p. 39) (*The Protestant Temperament: Pat-*

The clause about "reasonable and moderate" is actually important, because the issue of parental power to punish harshly and to kill their children was part of the debate about absolute power for monarchs. If a monarch's power paralleled a father's, the reason this was contested sharply in the various political treatises of the seventeenth century is obvious. Can a king execute his subjects who break a law? It could be used to separate the two powers (kings can kill, fathers not)—or to highlight the authority of both (kings and fathers can kill).

One significant difference separated the privileges of parents and guardians from those of masters: children could legally leave a parent; they could choose a new guardian, at least if over fourteen (in the places where socage law was followed); they could not leave a master. Having a guardian and having a master or a parent were not, of course, exclusive categories. During the earlier period, a child could not have both a guardian and a master. (The Elizabethan Statute of Artificers released a child from an apprenticeship contract if the child became an heir or heiress.) The powers of parents, guardians, and masters were different on other levels as well. Heirs over fourteen could not only choose their guardian, but they could rechoose as often as they liked and even sue their guardian for damages (via, by the late eighteenth century, a "next friend"). Poorer orphans, by contrast, were assigned to a master. And that assignation was almost irrevocable (barring the death of the master or gross cruelty). Masters not only had privileges to chastise a child, but their provision of necessities was much less closely overseen by the courts. Guardians had to post a bond for their management of the estate and their treatment of their ward and were supervised by special orphan's courts; their provision for their wards was supposed to be proportional to the profits from the wards' estate and suitable to "their station in life." But the majority of children, even many orphans, still formally had neither master nor guardian.

Overall, the clearest transition in the law of custody during the eighteenth century was that parental custody (as opposed to custody of masters or guardians) became more idealized and strengthened, over a minority that stretched to twenty-one. Blackstone's *Commentaries on the Laws of England* was the first to lay out a theory of parental custody in a comprehensive form as something

---

terns of Child-Rearing, Religious Experience, and the Self in Early America [New York, 1977]). On this issue also see Greven, "The Self Shaped and Mis-shaped: The Protestant Temperament Reconsidered," in Ronald Hoffman, Mechal Sobel, and Fredrika J. Teute, eds., *Through a Glass Darkly: Reflections on Personal Identity in Early America* (Chapel Hill, N.C., 1997), 348–369.

within the common law. Yet his citations, aside from Coke, a few later court decisions, and seventeenth- and eighteenth-century statutes, were to Roman civil law and to such natural law philosophers as Samuel von Pufendorf and Hugo Grotius. He even cited Montesquieu. He maintained that parents owe their legitimate children three things: "their maintenance, their protection, and their education."

> The duty of parents to provide for the *maintenance* of their children is a principle of natural law; an obligation, says Puffendorf, laid on them not only by nature herself, but by their own proper act, in bringing them into the world. . . . By begetting them therefore they have entered into a voluntary obligation, to endeavour, as far as in them lies, that the life which they have bestowed shall be supported and preserved. And thus the children will have a perfect *right* of receiving maintenance from their parents. And the president Montesquieu has a very just observation upon this head: that the establishment of marriage in all civilized states is built on this natural obligation of the father to provide for his children; for that ascertains and makes known the person who is bound to fulfil this obligation.[49]

Blackstone thus appealed to natural law principles that make a father's obligation to take care of his legitimate children the fulfillment of a contractual agreement on his part (both his marriage and his "begetting" them indicate his assent to the contract).

But Blackstone supported the poor laws, which removed poor children from their parents, on the grounds that those children thereby got a better education, suitable to their "several stations" (that is, to their status). He claimed the poor laws removed only children past "the age of nurture." While he argued that parents should have to educate their children, he admitted that this duty was not generally part of the laws of England at that time: "Their [the laws'] defects in this particular cannot be denied." Blackstone sought to shape the law into what it should be—in terms of his principles of justice—by appealing to natural law and political philosophy, particularly to ideas about consent.[50]

Although he acknowledged that Coke had allowed "guardianship by nurture" to last only until fourteen, he interpreted the 1660 law (12 Car. II, c. 24) as granting fathers power over their children until twenty-one.

> The legal power of a father (for a mother, as such, is entitled to no power, but only to reverence and respect) the power of a father, I say, over the

49. Blackstone, *Commentaries*, I, 435.
50. Ibid., 439.

persons of his children ceases at the age of twenty one: for they are then enfranchised by arriving at years of discretion, or that point which the law has established . . . when the empire of the father, or other guardian, gives place to the empire of reason. Yet, till that age arrives, this empire of the father continues even after his death; for he may by his will appoint a guardian to his children.

What is so marvelous about this passage is the way that he both appealed to natural law ideas and to past authority without acknowledging the historical groundings of that past authority: the law of 1660 is made to affirm "The empire of the father [which] continues even after his death"—as if the father's ability to appoint a guardian for his children until they reach twenty-one was buried in time immemorial. In trying to give sense to the law, he reified fathers' power and made it timeless. He did not even bother to explain, by natural law principles or otherwise, why a mother has no "legal power," though the sense of his earlier argument would seem to grant it to her. His language makes the point unmistakably: A child goes from "the empire of the father" to "the empire of reason."[51]

By the time he compiled his influential *Commentaries on American Law* (1826–1830), James Kent had naturalized parental custody, particularly paternal custody, even further. He associated it with twenty-one unequivocally—like Blackstone, making it seem a permanent part of the common law. In one place Kent even neglected to mention that the statute he referred to was passed in 1660 (after the colonies were settled, which usually meant that it would not apply to them, at least according to post-Revolutionary approaches to this question). He too interpreted this statute to mean that fathers had guardianship and control over their children until twenty-one. He also increased their powers. The language and the natural law theory supporting his arguments make his writing almost poetic.

The duties that reciprocally result from this connexion [of parent and child], are prescribed, as well by those feelings of parental love and filial reverence which Providence has implanted in the human breast, as by the positive precepts of religion, and of our municipal law.

A father's house is always open to his children. The best feelings of our nature establish and consecrate this asylum. Under the thousand pains and perils of human life, the home of the parents is to the children a sure refuge from evil, and a consolation in distress. In the intenseness, the lively

51. Ibid., 441, 450.

touches, and unsubdued nature of parental affection, we discern the wisdom and goodness of the great Author of our being, and Father of mercies.

He called parents "the natural guardians" of children.[52]

Kent claimed that fathers are "entitled to the custody of the persons, and to the value of the services and labour of his children, during their minority" as though this right had always been true (though he admits that even Blackstone had said that fathers were due the labor of their children only while they lived with him). Blackstone's comment was in passing, relating directly to the father's then support. It was not a clear concept in the common law before Blackstone, although children who lived with their parents were expected to labor with the family. In broadening the application this way and in attaching it firmly to minority and twenty-one, Kent thereby expanded "the empire of the father" considerably. Yet in doing so he built not only on Blackstone but on post-Revolutionary American precedents set in Massachusetts and New Hampshire.[53]

Even in the new Republic, however, the empire of the father had limits; the empire of the mother, if such an expression can be used, even more. Poverty, in short, continued to allow the removal of children from their parents, even in the 1810s; poor fathers and mothers often lost their children to apprenticeships at very young ages. The records of Chester County, Pennsylvania, and of Frederick County, Virginia, are full of such bindings, often when both parents lived. Still, the majority of those bound were the fatherless. While the average age increased to over eleven years in Frederick County, apparently as a result of efforts to keep such families together (via such policies as soldiers' pensions and enforcing paternal maintenance of illegitimate children), the practice was still common. But the ratio of those assigned guardians as opposed to those bound shifted dramatically in Virginia: many more orphans were allowed to stay with their mothers in the 1810s.[54]

But the real limits were for black parents, particularly black parents who were enslaved. There, sixteenth-century rules about children's status and masters' rights remained anywhere that slavery continued, with *masters*, not parents, having custody. In South Carolina in 1809, the court ruled that

52. James Kent, *Commentaries on American Law* (New York, 1826–1830), II, 159–163; Blackstone, *Commentaries*, I, 441.

53. Kent, *Commentaries*, II, 163. Kent cites *Day v Everett* in 7 *Massachusetts Reports* 145, and *Gale v Parrott* in 1 *New Hampshire Rep.* 28.

54. For evidence on changing attitudes about pensions and child support, see Holly Brewer, "Constructing Consent: How Children's Status in Political Theory Shaped Public Policy in Virginia, Pennsylvania, and Massachusetts before and after the Revolution" (Ph.D. diss., University of California, Los Angeles, 1994), chap. 6.

children of enslaved mothers were also slaves of the person who owned their mother at the time of their birth. The enslaved had as much right to their children as did cattle: "The young of slaves . . . stand on the same footing as other animals." They thus effectively closed the door to fraternal equality among white and black fathers—by comparing the rights of enslaved fathers to those of animals. Free black children in Virginia, meanwhile, were much more likely than free white children to be bound out by the overseers of the poor, sometimes in the face of a protracted struggle with those children's mother or father, a struggle clear in the court records. This binding out was undoubtedly due, in part, to their poverty, which in Virginia clearly negated parental custody (and to the fact that more black children might have lacked legal fathers, either because such fathers were enslaved or white and could not have legally married a black mother, even had they wanted to). In Pennsylvania, the plan for gradually abolishing slavery by definition split black parents from their children. If they had any children before they reached the age of twenty-eight and their freedom, those children would in turn have to stay with the master until their own age of twenty-eight. At the very least, we can say that the black family was not protected in the same way as the white, although policies varied by state.[55]

Children's Contracts Made Void: Fathers (or Others) Contract on Their Behalf

Early- and middle-eighteenth-century lawyers consolidated Coke's synthesis but moved gradually toward a position that children could not make contracts

55. *M'Vaughyter's Administrators v John Elder,* in Joseph Brevard, *Reports of Judicial Decisions in the State of South Carolina . . . 1793 to 1816* (Charleston, S.C., 1857), II, 12 (2 Brevard 313). Also see Margaret A. Burnham, "An Impossible Marriage: Slave Law and Family Law," *Law and Inequality Journal,* V (1987), 187. In Frederick County in the 1810s, 37 black children were bound, compared to 187 white children, but the white population was much higher. By my calculations, based on the censuses for 1810 and 1820, 28.4 percent of all free black boys were bound in that decade, compared to 6.4 percent of black females, and only 6.1 percent and 1.5 percent of white males and females, respectively. See Brewer, "Constructing Consent," chap. 6, esp. 385–386, 394. Ira Berlin, *Many Thousands Gone: The First Two Centuries of Slavery in North America* (Cambridge, Mass., 1998), 232–233, has examples of masters of these children controlling the parents as well, owing to the parents' desire to be near their children; thus parents consented to long-term labor contracts.

On Pennsylvania's gradual abolition of slavery and the semislave status of those born to slave parents after 1780, see Gary B. Nash and Jean R. Soderlund, *Freedom by Degrees: Emancipation in Pennsylvania and Its Aftermath* (New York, 1991).

at all, particularly over land. During the early eighteenth century, legal treatises such as Thomas Wood's *Institute of the Laws of England,* popular in the
colonies, followed Coke in distinguishing between the ability to buy and the
ability to sell land, but they hardened the earlier distinctions. On the one
hand, Wood claimed that "at Twenty-one [a man] may alien his Lands, Goods
and Chattels, but not before," and designated the same for women. On the
same page, however, Wood cited the passage from Coke that allowed an
infant to purchase "without consent of any other, for it is intended for his
benefit."[56]

In practice, a Virginia court case of 1731 offered conflicting precedents
about whether the deed of someone under the age of twenty-one should be
binding, but finally ruled that it should. One justice cited a recent English
court decision to the effect that "the Deeds of Infants have only the form but
not the Operation of Deeds." The Virginia General Court ultimately decided,
however, that an eighteen-year-old's deed of slaves to his half brother was not
voidable, since Virginia law allowed an eighteen-year-old to make a will over
land. Slaves (like land) were legally real estate, and he had made a will on the
same day that he made the deed. Several Massachusetts local court decisions
from the mid-eighteenth century also held, like some English decisions, that
those under age twenty-one could simply not form valid contracts over land.
Thus Virginia held on longer to the older norms.[57]

In the longer term, this movement toward the absolute invalidity of an
infant's deed for land extended into the idea that infants should not be held
liable for failing to uphold their side of a contract over goods, even when other
persons had performed their part. This stance made contracts with minors a
considerable risk. Those under age twenty-one had been allowed at their own
discretion to evade contracts they perceived to be detrimental to them, but
they were liable to return the goods they had purchased (or the money they
had received) and liable for damages. Gradually, legal authorities began to
argue that persons under twenty-one should be unable to make any contracts
for land or purchases, and that anyone who formed such a contract with a
minor deserved to be burdened with the liability if the minor did not fulfill
the bargain.

56. Wood, *Institute of the Laws of England,* 12.

57. *Waughop v Tate and Ux'r,* in R. T. Barton, ed., *Virginia Colonial Decisions,* R76–
R77. For Massachusetts, see William E. Nelson, *Americanization of the Common Law:
The Impact of Legal Change on Massachusetts Society, 1760–1830,* (Cambridge, Mass.,
1981), 199 n. 47, 245 n. 249. The law in Massachusetts seemed to go back and forth, in
that some early-nineteenth-century Massachusetts local court decisions held that such
contracts were only voidable.

Most agreed, throughout this entire period (1550–1830), that children had to be responsible for contracts for their "necessities," but children began to be excluded from even this contract by some judges and legal treatise writers, particularly American authorities, by the early nineteenth century. As the vagueness of the term implies, "necessities" could mean both everything and nothing, depending on the judge and the jury. But, over time, the term began to include less. Coke included as necessities "Meat, Drinke, Apparel, necessary Physicke, and such other Necessaries, and likewise . . . good Teaching or Instruction." Seventy years later, the *Infants Lawyer* shortened the list, but kept it substantially the same: "diet, apparel, Learning, and necessary Physick." A popular early-nineteenth-century English legal guide illustrated the ways in which the term "necessaries" could be stretched. In a widely reported 1793 English decision, for example, Chief Justice Lloyd Kenyon ruled, "A captain in the army, being under age, is liable to pay for a livery ordered for his servant, as necessaries, but not for cockades ordered for the soldiers of his company." Kenyon's was a broad definition of necessities, reflecting the responsible positions that elite young men often still held in late-eighteenth-century England.[58]

But, increasingly, nineteenth-century American decisions began to view necessaries in very narrow terms. The most important change about these contracts for necessities was expressed by James Kent in his 1827 *Commentaries*. When discussing necessities, Kent redefined the entire basis of the question. It was not whether the infant should be liable for necessities, but whether the father was liable for the contracts that the infant formed for necessities. Kent held that, except in extreme cases, the father was not. Only if a child was not living with its father or guardian could the father or guardian be held liable for necessities. "If the infant lives with his father or guardian, and their care and protection are duly exercised, he cannot bind him[s]elf even for necessaries." Otherwise, the law assumed that the father provided them. Kent's standing on this reveals the development of both custody law and contract law. The assumption of the law had shifted to deny the identity of a child altogether, up to age twenty-one: society should see the child only as part of a family, with a father at its head. A child could not contract by himself or herself: the father had to contract on the child's behalf.[59]

For children's contracts beyond necessities, the biggest question during

58. *Infants Lawyer*, 119; *Coke upon Littleton*, 172a; Samuel Comyn, *A Treatise of the Law relative to Contracts and Agreements Not under Seal: With Cases and Decisions Thereon in the Action of Assumpsit* (London, 1807), I, 155.

59. Kent, *Commentaries*, II, 196, especially, and also generally his whole section "Of Infants," II, 191–200.

the seventeenth and eighteenth centuries was about liability where an infant took possession of goods and then could not return them and refused to pay for them. If a child ate the food, rented the house, or damaged the horse, should the child be responsible for paying the costs as promised? Should the minor be able to keep goods not paid for? *The Infants Lawyer* (1697) debated this question at length, acknowledging that judges had offered arguments on both sides. On the one hand, some lawyers thought that an infant should be responsible for the return of goods if he or she decided to void the contract. If the child could not return the goods, then he or she was responsible for the damage caused. "It was the opinion of some, that an Infant is chargable for a Tort; and therefore Trover and Conversion being a Tort, an Infant is chargable with it, and that therefore Trover lies against him, and he cannot plead *diens age* [within age]." Other lawyers distinguished between violent actions ("vi et armis") and "such torts which concern Contract, Lending, Finding and Conversion, the Original cause whereof is not *Vi et armis,* or such as found in Deceipt." If the damage arose only from a violation of contract, then "no action lies" against the minor. The author of *The Infants Lawyer* finished this analysis with two cases that showed that infants were unquestionably responsible for the payment of rent, even though leases arose from a contractual arrangement. He concluded that infants should generally be held responsible for damages, even if they arose simply over a contract. The *Infants Lawyer* was in this sense typical. It was generally agreed during the early eighteenth century that infants should be liable in cases where they intentionally caused damage or acted deceitfully, such that they, for example, sought to sell goods not their own or pretended that they were of age.[60]

By the early nineteenth century, children had largely lost this liability. The denial of any liability, even in cases of fraud and damage, undermined children's ability to make contracts, since enforcement, even when the other party had fulfilled its part of the bargain, became impossible. Samuel Comyn's popular *Treatise of the Law relative to Contracts and Agreements* (1807) began by stating, "All contracts with infants, except for necessaries, are either void or voidable: the reason of which is, the indulgence the law has thought fit to give infants, who are supposed to want judgment and discretion in their contracts

---

60. *Infants Lawyer,* 68–70. In the early eighteenth century, children were clearly supposed to be held liable for damage they committed, including damage that resulted from a violation of a contract. William Hawkins, *A Summary of the Crown-Law . . .* (London, 1728), wrote, "Want of reason shall not screen a defendant in any civil action, from satisfying the actual damage" (I, 2). Wood agreed: "Yet if an Infant or Non Compos commit a Trespass against the Person or Possession of another, he must answer for the damage in a Civil Action" (*Institute of the Laws,* 340). Also see the *Infants Lawyer,* 67–68.

and transactions with others, and the care it takes of them in preventing them from being imposed upon or overreached by persons of more years and experience." Comyn added the "void" to where only "voidable" had been for Littleton and Perkins in the sixteenth century—an important distinction—and offered an elaborate justification for why children should not be able to make such contracts. "Lord Kenyon [chief justice] said, 'Nothing is clearer in the law than that an infant cannot contract a debt except for necessaries.' " He gave examples of judges who ruled that "the law will not allow an infant to trade," and "that if one deliver goods to an infant on a contract knowing him to be an infant, the infant shall not be charged for them in trover and conversion; for by that means all infants in England would be ruined." He thought that those under age twenty-one would make such disadvantageous contracts, because of their youth, that, if held liable for their performance as were adults, such infants' fortunes "would be ruined." Comyn also emphasized an earlier decision by Lord Chief Justice John Kelyng (1666), who had argued that a judgment against a minor for three hundred pounds damages (resulting from a broken mortgage contract) undercut the major basic principles of contract law. In appeal Comyn urged that the judgment against a minor should be stayed (suspended): "The judgment will stay [not go into effect] for ever, else the whole foundation of the common law will be shaken." For Kelyng in 1666, the issue had to do with the particular issue of an infant's deciding to void a land sale (even though he had lied about his age). For Comyn, the idea that a child could not make a valid contract had become a universal principle, regardless of the type of contract—he did not even mention that it was a mortgage. Comyn argued that "the whole foundation of the common law" rested on the principle of competency.[61]

While judges in England were beginning to adhere to a strict denial of liability for children who made contracts, judges in the United States continued to offer a range of opinions about whether infants were liable for costs when they broke a contract. When were their contracts binding? After he had surveyed the situation in 1827, Kent admitted that he saw "much contradiction and confusion." Kent himself could not help repeating that confusion and offering contradictory advice. After giving the above judgment about

61. Comyn, *Contracts and Agreements*, I, 149, 151, 157; *Manby v Scott*, 1 Sid. 129. The Kelyng case is *Johnson v Pye*, 1 Keb. 905. Children may still make contracts to purchase goods or services or to buy or sell land in many states. Their contract, however, is voidable at their own wish any time before they reach the age of majority (usually twenty-one). A modern legal scholar therefore advises that, practically speaking, children do not have this right, and property left to them should be managed by a trust or a guardian and not by the child. Robert Mnookin, *Child, Family, and State: Problems and Materials on Children and the Law* (Boston, 1978), 217, 681.

children's contracts for necessities, Kent also cited Joseph Story, whose opinion he clearly regarded highly, as giving the argument some precision: any contract that went against the interest of the child should be void; if for the child's benefit, it should be good; and, if unclear, it should be voidable at the child's own discretion (and none other's). The decentered nature of American decisions probably accounted, at least in part, for the contradictory judgments.[62]

American state superior court decisions reflect the extensive uses to which contracts were put by the early nineteenth century. These decisions varied by state and by type of contract as well as by the behavior of the child. For example, some judges held that a negotiable note executed by an infant was void from the beginning, whereas other judges held that it was only voidable.[63] With regard to the key questions of liability, the general opinion of American judges began to adhere to the English consensus that the minor should not have to be responsible for returning money received for an item even after rescinding the contract (and receiving the item back). Infants could also not even be liable for contracts they had purposely violated. In a New Jersey case of 1818, for example, two infants "wilfully" broke a riding chair they had borrowed by using it on a rough road and a long journey very different from the road and journey they had promised to take. Despite this intentional violation of the contract, Justice Samuel Southard concluded, "That infants are not liable upon contracts, is too well established to admit of argument." The intentional part could also be difficult to prove, for, if an infant could be said to have altered an agreement based merely on insufficient knowledge of the situation, then a suit for recovery of damages could not be won.[64]

62. Kent, *Commentaries*, II, 191, 193.

63. *The American Digest: A Complete Digest of All Reported American Cases from the Earliest Times to 1896*, Century Edition (St. Paul, Minn., 1897–1904), XX, 1136. "Void" decisions were made in Kentucky in 1809, *Beeler v Young*, 4 Ky. (1 Bibb) 519; New Hampshire in 1831, *Wentworth v Wentworth*, 5 N.H. 410; New Jersey in 1818, *Fenton v White*, 4 N.J.L. (1 Southard) 100; and Tennesee in 1834, *McMinn v Richmonds*, 14 Tenn. (6 Yer.) 9. Decisions that said an infant's note was not void were made in Kentucky in 1842, *Best v Givens and Wood*, 42 Ky. (2 B. Mon.) 72; Massachusetts in 1840, *Reed v Batchelder*, 42 Mass. (1 Met.) 559; and New York in 1837, *Everson v Carpenter*, 17 Wend. (N.Y.) 419. The second batch actually overlapped in the same states as the first batch, but appeared slightly later: the absolute "void" nature of infants' contracts appears to have had fewer adherents by the mid-nineteenth century. Most decisions were that the minors could avoid these contracts without liability.

64. *Abraham and Jacob Schenk v Stephen Strong*, 4 N.J.L. (1 Southard) 97–98 (February 1818).

Even this limited liability, however, began to be questioned during the late eighteenth and early nineteenth centuries. The process of change can be seen in one exemplary case from Connecticut, where a lower court held to the older norm and the supreme court to the newer. *Brown v Dunham* (1791) turned on whether a minor under age twenty-one could be liable for a contract if he pretended to be of age. A lower court ruled that his contract of sale should be upheld on the grounds that the "defendant had the appearance of a man of full age and was allowed by his father to trade." The Connecticut Supreme Court judges overturned that decision, calling that decision a "manifest error," since the "defendant being a minor under the care of his parent, was incapable of making a contract, except for necessaries, therefore could not be guilty of a fraud in contracting."[65]

One notable exception, albeit limited, was made by the United States Supreme Court in 1810, which overturned a circuit court decision. In *Vasse v Smith*, the Court decided that nineteen-year-old Joseph Smith was liable for the goods of another that he had engaged to sell by contract. He had agreed to sell them in Alexandria, Virginia, but instead shipped them to the West Indies. Unfortunately, the ship sank before the goods arrived. Afterward, Smith pleaded that he was not responsible for the loss, because he was an infant when he entered the contract. Chief Justice John Marshall ruled that he was liable, since he had intentionally violated the original contract.[66]

Within the debates several general points of consistency emerge. First, most contracts with infants went from voidable to void. Second, by the nineteenth century, whoever entered into a contract with an infant could lose substantial amounts of money—amounts not at risk earlier because the infant then would have been liable for damages. Third, those cases where contracts with infants had been binding, especially for necessities, became, for the majority of judges, either void or voidable. The assumption of the

65. *Brown v Dunham*, in Jesse Root, *Reports of Cases Adjudged in the Superior Court and Supreme Court of Errors [1789–1793]* (Hartford, Conn., 1798), I, 272–273. Also see a similar case, where the supreme court overturned a lower court's judgment, in the same volume, *Geer v Hovy*, I, 179. This issue continued to be debated during the nineteenth century. See *American Digest*, XXVII, 1186: "An infant is answerable for falsely representing himself to be of full age, and thereby inducing a person to sell him goods on credit" (citation to *Fitts v Hall*, 9 N.H. 441 [1838]).

66. *Vasse v Smith*, 10 U.S. (6 Cranch) 226. Chief Justice Marshall ruled that Smith should be liable in this case because he had committed "not an act of omission but of commission." In other words, Smith did not just fail to sell the goods but actively chose to take a different course in sending the flour to the West Indies. If the former, he would not have been liable. This opinion differed from the English decisions.

law was that someone else, usually the father, was always supposed to act on their behalf; the consent of the infants themselves became almost irrelevant. When necessities were permitted, what they included varied by judge and by state but became increasingly narrow. They could include a primary education but not a college education; clothes, if not extravagant and if the parents (or others) did not already buy them sufficient clothes.

Thus, what had earlier been a limited application of voidability, meant to apply mostly as a safety clause that assumed that children made contracts, was applied much more broadly by the early nineteenth century, such that it became almost impossible for children to form any contracts. At a time when contracts were more important for the basic transactions of society, contracts directly with infants themselves became much riskier for those who made them. Court decisions usually favored infants in questions of liability, with the argument that they should be able to receive back exactly what they had sold but did not have to return (especially in the same form) the goods or money they had received. This high risk made infants effectively unable to form contracts.

Labor Contracts

The evidence from the shipping records and a few contracts in the colonies confirms that many children were consenting to their own labor contracts in the seventeenth century. In 1634 a "servant" in Plymouth Colony agreed to serve a master for twelve years, until he turned twenty-three, so he was eleven when he bound himself. In Middlesex, England, in 1683–1684, children as young as eleven were putting their mark to such contracts. In a few cases where children were very young, a parent signed the contract instead of or in addition to the child. In Massachusetts in the 1660s, a father bound his daughter for more than fourteen years of labor (she was probably three). In 1701 in Virginia, six-year-old Elizabeth Bartlett's contract was signed only by her mother and her new master. Is this failure to consider her consent part of a transition to parental consent? Or due to her very young age? Regardless, it seems that, during the late seventeenth century, the contracts of even those under fourteen were still valid but becoming less necessary and that parental consent was allowed in some cases instead.[67]

67. Lawrence William Towner, "A Good Master Well Served: a Social History of Servitude in Massachusetts 1620–1750" (Ph.D. diss., Northwestern University, 1955), 69. Unfortunately for my study, Towner's extensive survey of servants and apprenticeship was not concerned generally with questions of consent. On Middlesex, see

By the early seventeenth century, poor children no longer had to be coerced into consenting to labor contracts; instead, the laws simply allowed justices of the peace or churchwardens to bind them. But children could still bind themselves. This change can be glimpsed in the first shipments of children to Virginia, shipments that mark the beginning of indentured servitude itself.

Between 1617 and 1622, the City of London sent three boats of children to the colony of Virginia, accompanied by agreements with the Virginia Company about their term of service. These children were all poor "vagrants," mostly boys, ranging in age from eight to sixteen. One was Nicholas Granger, who arrived at the age of nine in 1619 and was one of the few to survive his apprenticeship. When asking for a second batch, the Virginia General Court requested that all children be over age twelve. Some scheduled to be sent in the second batch were "obstinate" about not wanting to go to Virginia. The City of London, it turned out, needed the children's consent to convey them to Virginia. In order to force the children (who refused to agree), they had to obtain the special permission of the Privy Council, which granted the request for two reasons: the transportation would be to the youths' benefit (on the grounds that they would obtain land when their service finished), and these children were rogues and vagabonds.[68] James I described them as "divers idle young people." Because these children had "noe employmente" and were seen to have no legitimate means of supporting themselves, they were forced to enter these labor contracts—in this case, across the ocean. In effect, in the eyes of both English and colonial authorities, their poverty invalidated the need for their consent (even coerced); their consent was obviated both legally and sometimes illegally but with the complicity of English authorities.[69]

David W. Galenson, *White Servitude in Colonial America: An Economic Analysis* (Cambridge, 1981), 76.

The Massachusetts contract is cited by Towner, "A Good Master Well Served," app. A, 377. Virginia: York County Records Project, Colonial Williamsburg Foundation, Williamsburg, Va. (hereafter cited as YCRP), citing York County, Deeds, Orders, and Wills (11) 528 (DOW).

68. Robert C. Johnson, "The Transportation of Vagrant Children from London to Virginia, 1618–1622," in Howard S. Reinmuth, Jr., ed., *Early Stuart Studies: Essays in Honor of David Harris Willson* (Minneapolis, Minn., 1970), 137–151, esp. 144, 148; Grace Abbott, ed., *The Child and the State . . . : Select Documents* (Chicago, 1938), I, 196, citing *The Records of the Virginia Company of London;* Abbot Emerson Smith, *Colonists in Bondage: White Servitude and Convict Labor in America, 1607–1776* (Chapel Hill, N.C., 1947), 147–151. The Virginia court's request is reprinted in Abbott, *The Child and the State,* I, 195–198. See also Pinchbeck and Hewitt, *Children in English Society,* I, 106.

69. Pinchbeck and Hewitt, *Children in English Society,* I, 106. For other, similar

Clearly, however, not enough "servants" could be obtained legally with the aid of local authorities, whether City of London officials or parish officers in charge of the poor laws. But English authorities did for most of the century turn a blind eye to a thriving trade in what came to be called, by midcentury, "kidnapping." Thousands of people, both children and adults, were kidnapped, or assaulted and put on board ships without their consent, to be sent to the colonies and sold as servants during the seventeenth century. English court records are full of complaints: such theft of persons was technically illegal but was only lightly punished with a small fine, obtainable only when an individual brought suit and, usually, captured the kidnapper as well. A variety of statutes sought to prevent kidnapping by securing the consent of all immigrants, especially young ones. Barbados required in 1661 no one should transport any "servants, under the age of fourteen years unless they can produce a good Certificate, or an Indenture, or Writing from the principal person of the Parish, wherein the child last lived, that it was done with their consent, or at the request of the parents of such child." For violating this, they were to be imprisoned and forced to return the child at their cost. Massachusetts and Pennsylvania heard a few petitions from such kidnapped children and sometimes released them.[70]

Seventeenth-century Virginians, however, condoned the practice, passing laws about how long such "servants" who arrived without contracts should serve—laws that, with every iteration, increased the length of service. The first law, passed in 1643, stated that "such servants as shall be imported haveing no indentures or covenants either men or women if they be above twenty year old to serve fowre year, if they shall be above twelve and under twenty to serve five years, And if under twelve to serve seaven years." By 1666, those over age nineteen had to serve for five years (one more year), and those under that age had to serve until they reached age twenty-four. For those "under twelve," who had to serve seven years by the 1643 act, the 1666 act meant an additional six or more years of service. A twelve-year-old, meanwhile, who had to serve only until seventeen in 1643, by 1666 had to serve until twenty-four. Virginia judges assessed their ages. So, in 1679, "James Browne a servant coming in without indentures consigned by Mr. William Smith of London to Captain Francis Page . . . is adjudged eleven years of age and is ord. to serve according to act," which meant thirteen years. By forcing such persons to labor for long terms without contracts, Virginians were condoning kidnap-

---

examples, see James Horn, *Adapting to a New World: English Society in the Seventeenth-Century Chesapeake* (Chapel Hill, N.C., 1994), 62–65, 253–255.

70. Richard B. Morris, *Government and Labor in Early America* (New York, 1946), 340–345; Richard Hall, ed., *Acts, Passed in the Island of Barbados . . .* (London, 1764), 35.

ping of English subjects, adults as well as children, and completely ignoring whether those persons had consented to that labor. (The similarities to the capture and sale of Africans in Virginia are striking.)[71]

To prevent such practices, English courts set up some policies to ensure that those taking ship for the New World had chosen to go, but they were weakly enforced. The first prosecution of kidnapping began during the Civil War, amid heightened tensions between Parliament and the king. In 1643 Elizabeth Hamlyn was committed to Newgate Prison, where she was whipped, "for taking diverse little children in the street and selling them to be carried to Virginia." In 1645, Parliament enacted an ordinance that those who "in a most barbarous and wicked Manner steal away many little children" should be pursued and publicly punished. Even so, when four-year-old Richard Har-ñold, heir to eight hundred pounds a year, was stolen and sent to Virginia in 1657, the courts were more concerned than over most poor children. With the Restoration, the penalties were relaxed considerably, despite the institution of a formal registry of all outgoing passengers and sending "Searchers," or English officials, to visit servant ships before they left to determine whether emigrants were on them against their will. If the children "had been properly signed on," that is, if they had consented to go, then "the parents could not distress [the] ship owners," but must let them go to the colonies.[72]

Enforcement of the antikidnapping laws gained some teeth in the 1680s, but kidnapping was still fairly widespread and only lightly punished through the first half of the eighteenth century. In 1682, Charles II ordered that persons over twenty-one should bind themselves as servants in the presence of a justice of the peace and that those under twenty-one could bind them-selves only with the additional consent of parents or masters. If under four-teen, such parents or masters had to be present at the making of the new contract. Although renewed under James II, this order was only sporadically enforced. In 1717, in response especially to pressure from merchants, who feared being sued by irate masters deprived of apprentices or by wives de-serted by husbands, Parliament issued its first proclamation on the subject, albeit with lower ages than Charles II's original order. Those over fifteen had to give assent in person to a magistrate, which would be irrevocable; those under that age apparently had to have their parents present as well. Frequent evasion of these acts was still occurring in the eighteenth century, however.

71. Hening, ed., *Statutes at Large*, I, 257 (1643), 441–442 (1658), II, 113–114 (1662), 240 (1666); YCRP citing DOW (6) 112 (Aug. 24, 1679). Many other such cases appear.

72. Peter Wilson Coldham, "The 'Spiriting' of London Children to Virginia, 1648–1685," VMHB, LXXXIII (1975), 280–287, esp. 281, 286; Morris, *Government and Labor*, 342, 344; Smith, *Colonists in Bondage*, 73.

That children were still coming into Virginia without indentures in 1705 is evidenced by an act of that year concerning tithables.[73]

A pamphlet published in London in 1715 announced that two kidnappers had been discovered, caught, and were awaiting trial—caught only through the endeavors of bereaved parents. The two kidnapping ship captains, Azariah Daniel and Edward Harrison, preferred boys between the ages of ten and twelve. Two boys of "about the age of twelve," kidnapped by Daniel, had been found "bound in a garret." Meanwhile, the others he had kidnapped had already been placed aboard ships. The father who had tracked down the other captain, Harrison, had found him too late: Harrison had put his son on a frigate that had already departed for Barbados. Harrison admitted to putting "above 150 more aboard several other ships in the said river bound to his Majestys Plantations." In other locales, such as Aberdeen, Scotland, in the 1740s, the judges colluded with those who captured boys under fourteen, in particular giving them false contracts that stated that parent and child consented.[74]

By the eighteenth century, the colonies had begun to follow very different policies toward young servants and apprentices in response to increasing emphasis on contracts themselves and growing doubts about the ability of children to make contracts. Apprenticeship contracts from Virginia and Pennsylvania during the eighteenth and early nineteenth centuries demonstrate that Pennsylvanians put a higher value on the consent of the child (of whatever age) as well as of the child's parent. Not only were Virginia's children much more likely to be bound by overseers of the poor on the basis of poverty (in which case their consent was considered irrelevant), but children were much less likely to sign other labor contracts in Virginia. In only two contracts in the 1750s did a boy explicitly sign his own indenture; in later contracts, children of both sexes were bound only by their parents, and their consent was not an issue.[75]

73. Morris, *Government and Labor*, 340. Although the contracts were identical in other respects for persons of all ages, the contracts of servants under twenty-one were more likely to include training in a trade or education. Galenson, *White Servitude*, 200–203.

74. Hening, ed., *Statutes at Large*, III, 259; *The Grand Kidnapper at Last Taken . . .* (London, [1715]), British Library; Peter Wilson Coldham, *Emigrants in Chains: A Social History of Forced Migration to the Americas . . .* (Baltimore, 1992), chap. 7.

75. Indenture of Thomas Pollard, dated June 14, 1751, age seventeen; no parents, guardians, or others signed. Indenture of John Tucker, dated July 20, 1753, age unspecified; both he and his mother signed (Lancaster County, Va., Apprenticeship Records, Library of Virginia). Apprenticeship contracts were not formally kept, so it is difficult to provide a comprehensive sample.

In Pennsylvania, on the other hand, children usually signed their contracts, regardless of their age. In all of the cases where children were under fourteen, a parent or other family member signed the contract as well. In one case, two-year-old Phebe Stuart's mark appeared next to her name at the bottom of the contract. In two others, a four-year-old and a five-year-old signed their own contracts. Nine-, ten-, and twelve-year-olds also signed their own apprenticeship contracts. Even the wording of the contracts in Virginia and Pennsylvania was different. In nearly all the Pennsylvania contracts, the words "doth voluntarily, of his [or her] own free will and accord, put himself apprentice to . . ." appeared, even in the apprenticeship contract of four-year-old David Wilson, for example: "This indenture witnesseth that David Wilson . . . by and with the approbation of his father James Wilson . . . hath put himself and by these presents doth thereby put, place, and bind out himself." In Virginia, however, the wording appeared differently. Instead of the consent of the child, the contract laid stress on the consent of a parent, either the father or the mother, to binding the child. "Nicholas Hardin . . . hath of his own free will put and by these presents doth bind his son Henry Hardin apprentice." Still, these seem to have been a minority of contracts: most were made by the churchwardens or overseers of the poor.[76]

Thus, two different types of contracts had emerged: the older contract, which involved the consent of the parties involved, and that between the vestrymen of the parish and the master, which could bind the poor against their will. The one involved the direct consent of the child to labor, and the other avoided the child's consent—just as it avoided the consent of adults—on the basis of poverty. The nature and use of both types of contracts would change over time. With respect to both, there was an increasing consensus, as with contracts for goods, lands, and marriage, that young children should not have to be bound by their own contracts but that others could bind them during their minority. The minimum age to form a binding labor contract inched upward during the seventeenth and nineteenth centuries, with different colonies/states following different rules. Most labor contracts involv-

76. Contract of Phebe Stuart, dated Oct. 15, 1811, Apprenticeship Records (AR), Chester County Historical Society, Chester, Pa. (CCHS); David Wilson (age four), dated June 27, 1818, AR, CCHS; James Keegan (age five), dated Dec. 19, 1748, record 32020, CCHS; Hannah Field (age twelve), dated June 27, 1811, record 32812, CCHS; Lydia Morton (age nine), dated June 24, 1822, AR, CCHS; Johnson Walters (age ten), July 10, 1814, AR, CCHS; Benjamin Webb (age ten), Aug. 3, 1775, AR, CCHS; Indenture of Henry Hardin (aged eleven), dated Jan. 20, 1787, FCV, AR.

For an earlier contract, see that of Robert Wilson (1732), "With the advice and consent of his mother and father in law Joseph Stringer and Mary String . . . of his own free and voluntary will and accord put and bind himself . . ." (AR, CCHS).

ing children were apprenticeships where the child learned a skill and was taught to read, write, and cipher. Therefore, if the contract was voidable at the child's wish, as became the rule by the late eighteenth century, then masters or mistresses would be less willing to invest in the child in the early years as their part of the contract. This voidability without liability thus effectively limited the opportunities for children to make their own contracts. The growing legal consensus that these contracts could be void at the request of the child encouraged the use of parents as coguarantors or even as sole guarantors as well as the apprenticeship of children by the vestry or county courts. Children's own consent became irrelevant. The question became who should consent for them: Parents? Guardians? State authorities?[77]

By the early nineteenth century, as part of a broad strengthening of notions of custody, parents began to be given a property right in their children and in some states could even sell their children's labor. Several cases illustrate the developing tensions over children's consent in Pennsylvania. In 1748, two guardians petitioned the Pennsylvania court, praying the court to allow them to bind two orphan boys. "Rich Richard and David Richard, two of the children of the deceased being minor yet being obstinately inclined, refuse to be bound to trades pursuant to the direction of their late father's will or to follow any other employment whatsoever, which in the method they are in must inevitably end in their ruin." The guardians promised to bind them only to such masters as the boys "may judge proper or convenient to them," but could not legally do so without a court order authorizing them to bind the orphans. There is no record of their age, yet they were both called "minors." In 1753, another case reinforced the principle that a boy's consent was normal and accepted for a labor contract. Seventeen-year-old Thomas Ralph petitioned the court that he should be released from the indenture he had signed two years previously with one Arthur Kennedy in Ireland, who used "many persuasions and fair promises, to entice your petitioner to leave his parents, and go to Pennsylvania." He was only fifteen years old at that time, and his parents "knew nothing of the agreement." He also noted that the master to whom Kennedy had sold him had forced him to sign a new indenture with more time on it. The court ignored the issue of parental consent but responded to the claim about a coerced second contract and made him serve his master only until the time first set. Clearly, the court thought that a fifteen-

77. On changes in labor law generally during this period, see Robert J. Steinfeld, *The Invention of Free Labor: The Employment Relation in English and American Law and Culture, 1350–1870* (Chapel Hill, N.C., 1991); Christopher L. Tomlins, *Law, Labor, and Ideology in the Early American Republic* (Cambridge, 1993); Karen Orren, *Belated Feudalism: Labor, the Law, and Liberal Development in the United States* (Cambridge, 1991).

year-old did not need the consent of his parents in order to enter a binding agreement. In 1811 Elizabeth Rope petitioned the court to dissolve her apprenticeship on the grounds that she was bound to learn housewifery by a man who claimed to be but was not her guardian, at age fifteen, without her consent. Her new master and mistress beat her severely. Although the outcome of the case is not known (it might have been resolved out of court), the question of valid consent (including her own) was central to the petition. In these cases Pennsylvania norms tended to privilege the consent of the child.[78]

In Virginia in 1789, however, a boy was released from his contract—despite the fact that his master had paid for his passage from Ireland—on the grounds that his parents had not consented. Eighteen-year-old Humphrey Murphy petitioned the court to be set free from his apprenticeship because he had signed his own indenture when about age thirteen in 1784 in Ireland, without his father's consent. The court, after examining his indenture with his own mark at the bottom, as well as that of Timothy Parker, to whom he had originally indented himself, released him from his service on the grounds that he had made the contract "when a minor and uncapable of entering into any transaction obligatory." Murphy's master, who had bought his indenture, apparently astounded at the verdict, appealed to the Frederick District Court, where the lower court's judgment was upheld. Thus the labor contracts of those under fourteen, at least, were held to be invalid in Virginia in 1789. Indeed, the court's blanket use of the term "minor" indicates that, had he been any age under twenty-one when he signed the contract, he could also have voided it at his wish.[79]

By the early nineteenth century in most states the decision rendered by the Virginia court had come to be typical. A Massachusetts statute of 1794 held that parental consent was necessary to the labor contracts of all those under age twenty-one (as well as the consent of the child if over fourteen). If the father was not living or if the child was illegitimate, the mother could bind the child. If children had no parent, then their "legal guardian" could bind them. If they also had no guardian, then they could request to be bound by the town selectmen if over age fourteen. In other words, some adult always had to consent for them; if they were under fourteen, then that adult would provide the sole authorization. In some states, in fact, it became normal for a father to have the right to the labor of his children, including any wage or profits a child might earn. Two contracts from Connecticut in 1815 show fathers bind-

78. Chester County, Pennsylvania, Quarter Session Indictments, May 1753, petition of Thomas Ralph; November 1811, complaint and petition of Elizabeth Rope.

79. *Murphy v Magill*, FCV Ended Cases, June 1789. Also see FCV MB, 1786–1790, June 1789, 281–282.

ing out several of their children to the Slater Cotton Mill and having the right to their wages, although one father agreed to give his two oldest sons one-half their wages. The contracts do not specify ages, but the newly accepted rule was that fathers had the right to their children's labor until the child reached twenty-one, following Blackstone (discussed above). That this right was becoming clearer in the common law is shown by Kent's dictum about the property rights of fathers in their children.[80]

The best illustration of Pennsylvania's exceptional stand—even better than the very young children's signatures on labor contracts—is the 1793 Pennsylvania Supreme Court decision of *Respublica v Catharine Keppele*. In this case Peter Dehaven bound his ward Benjamin Hannis, age ten, to Catharine Keppele for five years, for which Keppele paid Dehaven. The judges released Benjamin and maintained that guardians could not bind their wards as servants—and that even parents could not bind their children as servants. Although they granted that "a parent may have a right to the personal service of his child," they held that "no parent can make his child the servant to another," since such a contract "cannot be for [the child's] benefit." They implied that the child must always consent as well and specified that the "personal service" of a child could not translate into selling the child's service. The justices in Pennsylvania thus set a completely different precedent at this juncture, separating their policy decisively from that of Massachusetts and Virginia, who were wrestling with the same questions.[81]

Over three centuries a broad change occurred in the ability of children to consent to their own labor contracts. Whereas in the Elizabethan period the labor contracts of children under seven were held to be valid, and unavoidable even at the child's own request, by the late eighteenth century the courts were beginning to rule (and the laws to state explicitly) that a father, mother, guardian, or the overseers of the poor should make that contract for them. Contracts signed only by minors became seen as not binding on them. This change did not happen overnight, but began in the seventeenth century with the change in the poor law itself.

80. *The Revised Statutes of the Commonwealth of Massachusetts, Passed November 4, 1835* . . . (Boston, 1836), 494; Slater Company Records, University of Connecticut Library, record nos. p2243 (March 1815), p2245 (May 1815) (thanks to David Zonderman for this reference). On the Virginia decision, see generally the *American Digest*, XXVII, 1120–1122. There seems to be little dispute on this issue in the nineteenth century. None of the state cases that upheld minors' rights to dissolve their labor contracts in the nineteenth century appeared in Pennsylvania.

81. *Respublica v Catharine Keppele*, Pa. (1 Yeates 233–237) (1793); Kent, *Commentaries*, II, 163.

The process of change on the individual level can be seen in the notes made in the margins of the practice book of a man who would later become a Massachusetts Supreme Court justice. Young Theophilus Parsons, when first learning the law in 1775, copied out a form (or precedent) against an apprentice for an action of covenant broken, for which the injured master could obtain damages. After copying out the routine form, which served as the basic pattern for masters' seeking damages, however, he wrote in the margin: "Quere whether this action his [against] the [person] who was a minor when he sealed the deed?" In other words, Parsons questioned whether the master had the right to damages from his former apprentice. If not, of course, any apprentice could annul a contract he had signed at his own discretion. These are the questions that haunted all of contract law as it began to cohere into a unified body of thought in the eighteenth century. Under what circumstances could a minor's contract be valid and enforceable? If a father consents for his children in the political arena, because his children cannot sufficiently exercise their understanding (as the republican political theorists had argued), should he not consent on their behalf to other contracts as well?[82]

In England the law of contract, as we now know it, was influenced profoundly by seventeenth- and eighteenth-century natural law and political theory, and gained the central place in the common law it now occupies only in the late eighteenth and early nineteenth centuries. The first treatise that elaborated the centrality of a law of contract in its own right was John Joseph Powell's *Essay upon the Law of Contracts and Agreements* (1790).[83]

Both the "rise of contract" in the law and the rise of democratic-republican political ideas and institutions relied on consent, whether to political or legal contracts. Both also relied on the development of a concept of meaningful, uncoerced, and uninfluenced consent. Children, especially young children, can be both coerced and influenced. Legal contracts thus began increasingly to require the "full development" or "maturity" of the understanding; they also changed substantially in their attitude toward coercion and in their requirements for formality.

These ideas about contracts were expressed variously by New England

82. Theophilus Parsons, "Precedents book of the Massachusetts Law, 1775," MS, Harvard University Law Library, Cambridge, Mass. Also see Nelson, *Americanization of the Common Law,* 199 n. 47, for examples in late-eighteenth-century Massachusetts where the contracts of apprentices were held to be invalid on the grounds that the parent or guardian had failed to sign the indenture. Fathers were also granted the right to their children's wages in several decisions.

83. Atiyah, *Freedom of Contract,* 102–103.

Puritans, by the English Puritans under Cromwell, by the supporters of the Glorious Revolution such as Locke and Algernon Sidney, and they were embodied in much of what we have come to call the Enlightenment. They thus show the connections between these earlier religious and political ideas and democratic-republican thought. They would transform not only the basis of political power but the basis of personal power explicitly, by writing new statutes and, implicitly, by rewriting the common law.

Both similarities and differences exist between ideas about custody and consent embodied in Locke's *Two Treatises of Government* and the common law as codified by Blackstone and treatise writers who followed him. In "The Second Treatise" Locke distinguished adults who could reason and form political contracts from the children who could not. "Their Parents have a sort of Rule and Jurisdiction over them . . . [though] but a temporary one." Parents must "govern the Actions of their yet ignorant Nonage, till Reason shall take its place." Although Blackstone (and other common lawyers after him such as Kent) implied that fathers, in particular, had a property right in their children, Locke did not. In a weird way, then, the common law, in retaining allegiance to the property rights of lords and masters in their villeins and servants, was transferring those rights to parents (and the obligations to children). This comparison drew on the logic of Locke and other natural law theorists to some degree but carried the implications of those arguments significantly further. Locke had been careful to distinguish the limits of parents' power over their children "to the Childrens good," limits that carefully exclude a property right of fathers or mothers in their children.[84]

That important technicality aside, it is clear that contract law as it formed in the eighteenth and nineteenth centuries drank deep from the philosophical debates about justice and political power. Consider Blackstone's comments about custody: The power of the father "ceases at the age of twenty one . . . when the empire of the father, or other guardian, gives place to the empire of reason." Only when they have reached the empire of reason can they consent to any contract: they are then enfranchised.[85]

Blackstone gave more power to the father (as opposed to the mother) than did Locke, but both used the same justification: the father's provision of nurture and support justified his power. Yet that logic was subject to an internal critique that would surface in custody disputes of the late eighteenth and early nineteenth centuries: perhaps the mother, not the father, provided the most nurture. Custody disputes between parents would become more

84. John Locke, *Two Treatises of Government*, ed. Peter Laslett (Cambridge, 1988), 304, 306, 309 ("Second Treatise," chap. 6, pars. 55, 58, 63).

85. Blackstone, *Commentaries*, I, 441.

important as divorce was legalized in the wake of the Revolution, but they also need to be seen in the context of (1) the waning power of the "lord," as embedded, in part, in the removal of the old guardianship rules and (2) the increasing importance of custody itself as "children" became defined as needing someone else to make decisions for them.

Even as paternal power strengthened, challenges to it also arose. The questions increasingly became, Who would act in the children's best interest? Who could act for them? William Murray, Lord Mansfield (chief justice of England, 1756–1788), challenged the emerging emphasis on paternal custody in two key rulings in 1763 and 1764, one of which gave a daughter (who had been apprenticed into prostitution) freedom from her father's custody and set her "at liberty to go where she will" (she was eighteen). In the second, more important case, Mansfield held that, while "the natural right [to custody] is with the father," if the father is a bankrupt, for example, or mistreats the child, then he voids his right to custody. "The court," he held, "will do what shall appear best for the child." A parent's love for the child began to enter into the legal debate as part of this question of best interests. In 1827 Kent, for example, invoked the "unsubdued nature of parental affection" in justifying the custody and responsiblities of parents.[86]

Joseph Story, an associate justice on the United States Supreme Court (1812–1845), voiced a critique of the emerging common law doctrine of paternal custody that would have broad impact, in his important treatise *Commentaries on Equity Jurisprudence* in 1836. He drew on equity court (or Chancery) decisions in England, which provided alternatives to common law verdicts. It was in the equity courts (which influenced decisions in the United States, partly via Story's treatise) that limits on paternal custody developed furthest through the doctrine of "parens patriae" (that the state is the ultimate parent). He searched in vain for any precedents in those courts prior to 1690 concerning parental custody (for reasons that the reader of this chapter will understand). Based on these later decisions, he contended that a father is entrusted with the custody of his children solely on the grounds that "he will best execute the trust reposed in him" for their care. A father's "corruption," "gross ill-treatment or cruelty," or even his "irreligion" might "deprive him of the custody of his children." By the mid-nineteenth century, with the argument that the mother provided better nurture than the father, some judges began to hold that she should be given custody in case of separation or divorce. Other judges emphasized the "natural right" of the father to his

86. The key Mansfield cases are *Rex v Deleval*, 97 Eng. Rep. 913 (3 Burr 1434) (1763) (*The English Reports* [Edinburgh, London, 1900–1932]) and *Blissets Case*, 98 Eng. Rep. 899 (Lofft 748) (1774); Kent, *Commentaries*, II, 159–164.

child. These varying viewpoints circumscribed the nineteenth-century debate about the rights and powers of fathers.[87]

Comyn's popular 1807 treatise on contract law ascribed the reason for the changes to "the care [the law] takes of [children] in preventing them from being imposed upon or overreached by persons of more years and experience." Yet these changes did not simply "protect" children—they protected the very principle of legitimate consent. The phrase "imposed upon" implies illegitimate influence. Hobbes had allowed influence and force to be natural in forming all contracts. Children gave "implied" consent to their father's authority. Locke's distinction between children and adults allowed adults to consent explicitly. While Blackstone allowed for implied consent, he was also very concerned with separating children from adults in their ability to contract. In that sense, Blackstone based his synthesis of the common law not only on contracts and consent but allied himself more closely with Locke than Hobbes. Indeed, only when force and illegitimate influence are excluded does "consent" to government become something we recognize as democratic.[88]

The early-nineteenth-century treatises on the law of contract acknowledged that, practically speaking, these restrictions on liability, these "protections," actually disabled minors from making contracts.

> Miserable must the condition of minors be; excluded from the society and commerce of the world; deprived of necessaries, education, employment, and many advantages, if they could do no binding acts. Great inconvenience must arise to others, if they were bound by no act. The law therefore, at the same time that it protects their imbecility and indiscretion from injury through their own imprudence, enables them to do binding acts for their own benefit, and without prejudice to themselves, for the benefit of others.[89]

87. Joseph Story, *Commentaries on Equity Jurisprudence, as Administered in England and America* (Boston, 1836), II, 572–585, esp. 575–576, 579–580; Michael Grossberg, *A Judgment for Solomon: The D'Hauteville Case and Legal Experience in Antebellum America* (New York, 1996), 52–55, 150, 159–167. Note that in *Blissets Case* of 1774 (cited above), Mansfield's innovative decision was influenced by what he called the "late remarkable cause of *Giffard and Giffard* before the Lord Chancellor," which was, of course, an equity case.

88. Comyn, *Contracts and Agreements*, 154. Children may still make contracts to purchase goods or services or to buy or sell land in many states. Their contract, however, is voidable at their own wish any time before they reach the age of majority (usually twenty-one). A modern legal scholar therefore advises that, practically speaking, children do not have this right, and property left to them should be managed by a trust or a guardian and not by the child. Mnookin, *Child, Family, and State*, 217, 681.

89. Comyn, *Contracts and Agreements*, I, 154.

They understood, in other words, that only the binding nature of contracts for necessities allowed minors, practically, to make those contracts. Thus by excluding those under twenty-one from making contracts even for necessities, as many judges began to do, the judges knew they were banishing them from "the society and commerce of the world" and from a legal identity of their own.

What makes a valid contract or what constitutes consent was being debated both inside and outside the law over these two centuries. While Edward Coke helped make these connections about an age of consent to contracts in the early seventeenth century, William Blackstone played a more important role in the late eighteenth century. His contribution was not so much in what he said about children and contracts, but in the ways that he made explicit the connections between political contracts and legal ones. Blackstone adapted the common law to highlight the centrality of contract. He openly incorporated republican political theory, especially the emphasis on consent and contract, into his synthesis of the "common law." Yet he left openings that could permit coercive or illegitimate authority. For Blackstone, even if a person did not specifically agree, that person "hath virtually agreed" to the "general contract" of society or, as he states later, to the "implied original contract to submit to the rules of the community, whereof we are members." As the American Revolutionaries would confirm, "virtual" consent and "implied" contracts are a tricky business. It was exactly on these grounds that many pamphleteers in the decades leading up to the Revolution debated the colonists' obligation to pay the various taxes imposed by Parliament: Did the colonists consent "virtually" to Parliament via others' votes on their behalf? Or did all who paid taxes need to vote explicitly? Blacksone's position on children—that they are, in essence, unable to consent—helped to shape the debate.[90]

The implicit answer of Blackstone for who represented those, like children, who did not vote (the vast majority of the population in England when Blackstone wrote in the 1760s) was fathers or masters, because they possessed a kind of "property" or custody in them. Coke, Blackstone, and, of course, Kent would help shape ideas about custody, the importance of which went hand in hand with the decline in children's ability to contract. Children

90. Blackstone, *Commentaries*, III, 158, 159; Blackstone refers to Locke, and his influence is evident, throughout his treatise. See, for example, I, 7, or I, 122. "Blackstone [was] an important propagator of social contractarianism in the Locke tradition. If anybody was needed to convert Locke's ideas into an influential tool for lawyers—and perhaps none was needed, for every educated lawyer must have read Locke—this part was played by Blackstone." Atiyah, *Freedom of Contract*, 59, 215–216.

began to be seen, especially in America after the Revolution, increasingly as the "property" of parents (or others in the absence of parents). "The child hath no property in his father or guardian; as they have in him, for the sake of giving him education and nurture." By this principle, according to Blackstone, a father could sue another for damages for the lost labor of his child if that child were injured, but a child could not sue if his father were injured, because he had no right to his father's labor. Likewise, Blackstone used the word "property" in justifying a man's recovering his wife, child, or servant from anyone who "wrongfully detain[ed]" them. Like his "property in goods or chattels personal," he could recapture them as long as doing so did not involve a serious breach of the peace. Kent went further in certain respects by challenging even the right of children to form binding contracts for necessities on the grounds that their fathers would provide for them.[91]

Although Blackstone paid more attention to contracts than those who preceded him, he separated his discussion of contracts into separate categories with different rules, unlike later legal treatises.[92] By the early nineteenth century, however, the same rules began to apply to all contracts. Assumpsit actions, for example, were contract suits based only on the oral promises between two partners but unaccompanied by any corroborating actions. In this sense, as we shall fully understand only after the next chapter, contracts for property were influenced by ideas about vows, particularly vows of marriage. The biggest change, however, occurred with respect to the adjudication of contracts: judges began to focus increasingly on the intent of the parties contracting. Did they understand what they did? We can see that shift fully only by focusing on the capacity of children.[93]

Without question, these changes in the ability to make legal contracts had other consequences. They probably aided the growth of capitalism, for example. Yet a simple argument that these changes were driven by the needs of capitalism for reliable contracts does not explain the nature of the changes, the fierceness of the debates, and the sometimes anticapitalist positions taken in deference to the logic of competency. The arguments used to revise the legal rules grew out of and in turn grew into the ideological debates over who could consent. But these changes were also tied into religious ideas and debates, especially under the unifying influence of the common law. As

91. Blackstone, *Commentaries*, III, 4 (citing Coke, *Insititutes*, III, 134), 143.

92. Atiyah, *Freedom of Contract*, 102–103, referring to Blackstone, *Commentaries*, II, chap. 30, III, chap. 9. Also see Atiyah, 215–216.

93. Atiyah, *Freedom of Contract*, 139; Nelson, *Americanization of the Common Law*, esp. 136–144; Morton Horwitz, *The Transformation of American Law, 1780–1860* (New York, 1977), esp. 160–210.

contracts formerly under the control of the ecclesiastical courts, such as marriage vows and wills, became part of the common law, some of their rules began to apply to other types of contracts, such as those making any type of verbal commitment (regardless of whether it was written on paper and regardless of whether it bore the proper seals) binding.

But the meaning of religious vows was also changing, partly in response to the Reformation and partly in response to the same arguments that were reshaping the idea of consent within the common law. Consider *Cases of Conscience*, by William Perkins, the Puritan scholar so influential on New England ministers and many others. In 1606 he meditated on promises: when are they binding?

> [A vow] must be *voluntarie*, and *free*. And that it may be so, three things are necessarily required. First, that it be made in Judgement, that is, with reason and deliberation. Next, that it be done with consent of will. And thirdly, with libertie of Conscience.
>
> Hence it appeares, that the Vowes of children, mad-men, and fooles, or such as are taken upon rashnes, or constraint . . . are all utterly unlawfull.[94]

For Perkins, only reason created the conscience that could be bound. Promises should be good only when made voluntarily and freely by those who fully understand the nature of their commitment and who are not under the "government of a superiour." Perkins represented one edge of a debate about the meaning of consent. His position differed dramatically from the ecclesiastical and the common law at that point (in allowing a father to void a vow made without his consent, or in their emphasis on free will, or calling the vow of a child "utterly unlawfull"). What is most important about his meditations on vows is how much they represented what the law of contract would become. They are also important for what he left unsaid: Who is a child and when does childhood end? What constitutes reason? Much remained, in 1608, still to be debated.

Although the shift in children's ability to form contracts did not happen suddenly with the American Revolution, the intellectual roots behind these shifts are the same as those behind the Revolution. The epistemological debates of the seventeenth and eighteenth centuries were not merely abstract theorizing about religious faith, human potential, and the laws of nature. They were central to Lockean and republican political ideology. Although earlier Christian authors such as Aquinas had introduced the concept of an "age of reason" and classical authors such as Aristotle had similar concepts,

94. W[illiam] Perkins, *The Whole Treatise of the Cases of Conscience* . . . (Cambridge, 1606), 406–407, book II, chap. 14.

seventeenth-century Continental natural law theorists and English Dissenters and revolutionaries of the seventeenth century, upon whom Blackstone and other legal reformers drew, developed this concept, granting it much greater definition and weight. The separate status of childhood is in many respects a consequence of this emphasis on an age of reason, a distinction that became critical to the political legitimacy of government based upon consent.

Martha Minow summarizes the chasm that characterizes the division in modern law between "persons who are mentally competent and persons who are not."

> The competent have responsibilities and rights; the incompetent have disabilities and, perhaps, protections. The competent can advance claims based on principles of autonomy; the incompetent are subject to restraints that enforce relationships of dependence. These "two tracks" of legal treatment reflect the traditional Western idea that responsibility follows only from voluntary, knowing, and intelligent choice. Mental competence signifies the ability to appreciate the consequences of one's actions, to protect oneself from manipulation and coercion, and to understand and engage in transactions of property and commerce.[95]

While Minow, speaking from the perspective of today, can write of the "traditional Western idea that responsibility follows only from voluntary, knowing, and intelligent choice," we have seen that such sharp distinctions were not traditional in the eighteenth century. These distinctions developed only gradually as a consequence of the law's focus on "voluntary, knowing, and intelligent choice" and were deeply intertwined with the body of ideas that would come to be called democratic.

95. Martha Minow, *Making All the Difference: Inclusion, Exclusion, and American Law* (Ithaca, N.Y., 1990), 126.

CHAPTER 8

"PARTLY BY PERSUASIONS AND PARTLY BY THREATS"

PARENTS, CHILDREN, AND CONSENT TO MARRIAGE

*"Mrs. Mary Hathaway a minor humbly Sheweth . . . how she at
or about the age of nine years and under the age of Consent partly
by Persuasions and partly by threats of her mother did de facto
Marry Mr. William Williams of this County but now being
arrived at some more mature discretion [age 11] . . . humbly Prays
a final determination of the same."*
Stafford County, Virginia, Order Books, December 16, 1691

*"Every Child who has a capacity that qualifies him or her to
make the marriage contract is (naturally) in this respect* sui
juris. . . . *The right cannot lie in the Parent. For although the
being of the child comes from the parent, the rights of the child as
a distinct individual do not."*
[Dr. Henry Stebbing], An Enquiry into the Force and
Operation of the Annulling Clauses in a Late Act for the
Prevention of Clandestine Marriages *(London, 1754)*

In Virginia, in 1689, Mary Hathaway, only child and heir of Thomas Hathaway, deceased, married William Williams. She was nine years old. Two years
later, accompanied by two lawyers well versed in the law, she appealed to the
Stafford County Court to release her from the marriage on the grounds that
"never any further rites of Marriage have passed betwixt us but the bare
verbal Ceremonies" and that she could "by no means . . . entertain a thought
of ever receiving him for a spouse or husband." If they had consummated the
marriage, it would have been unbreakable by the canon laws of England. So,
too, would it be if she did not renounce it soon after turning twelve, then the
age of consent to marriage: the court would see her as married according to
the vows she had made at age nine. Even still, the court divided three to two
over her petition for divorce, the minority registering their strong dissent.
"Mr. John Withers and Mr. Matthew Thompson did Publickly and openly in
Court dissent from the said Judgment and for that they are of opinion that the
said Mary Hathaway is the wife of the said William Williams not only [now]
but alsoe when she shall arrive at the age of Twelve . . . it appearing to

them that she was married by the said Mr. John Waugh clerk [minister] as af[ore]s[ai]d and that by the consent of her guardian." Their objection was so strong that they "did therefore order the clerke [of the court] to enter their dissent upon the records accordingly."[1]

In agreeing that she could be released, the Stafford County Court postponed its verdict upon the appeal of Williams's lawyer that she "wanted Ten days of being Twelve years old, and that before she was of that age fully her assent or dissent could not determine the matter nor could this Court judge it." Mary Hathaway, however, was afraid that this ten days might be too long. She reported that Williams "did threaten or at least she was afraid of being by him violently seized both in Person and Estate and did therefore most humbly Supplicate their honors to take such order and give such directions to hinder the force she feared a sin." If he had forced her to consummate the marriage, the judges would probably have prevented her from voiding it, or so the canon law implied, a law Williams clearly understood. The court then promised that during the short delay they would make sure that "noe force [could be] committed nor opportunity of force given." They convened the court on her birthday, December 28, "the very day by the mercy of God that I am twelve years old," to hear her formal "Protestation" and to release her from the covenant she had made at nine.

In a world where most divorces were extremely difficult (if not impossible), she had followed precisely the procedures necessary to dissolve her marriage: she had not shared her husband's bed and had appealed for the separation immediately upon reaching her age of discretion. She made clear, in her appeal, that her "Solemn declaration and Protest proceed[ed] Purely from my own Judgment and desire and not by any Enducement either by Persuasions force or fraude from any Person or Persons whatsoever." Annulling such an unconsummated marriage was easier when it had been made by a child. Yet medieval canon law had typically allowed annulments in cases of nonconsummation regardless of age, and English codes continued this practice after the Reformation.[2]

Was "Mrs. Mary Hathaway's" case unusual for seventeenth-century Virginia? The divorce probably was. The court divided over the question. She had

1. "Notes from the Records of Stafford County, Virginia, Order Books," *Virginia Magazine of History and Biography*, XLV (1937), 370–375, 379–381 (Dec. 16, 28, 1691), for account of Mary Hathaway case here and below. John Withers, interestingly, was Mary's maternal grandfather and had probably helped to encourage the match.

2. James A. Brundage, *Law, Sex, and Christian Society in Medieval Europe* (Chicago, 1987), 288 (and see note 11, below); Martin Ingram, *Church Courts, Sex, and Marriage in England, 1570–1640* (Cambridge, 1987), 172–174; Lawrence Stone, *Broken Lives: Separation and Divorce in England, 1660–1857* (Oxford, 1993), 21–22.

to write a petition to the Governor's Council and then to hire two lawyers. The governor and his Council decided that the county court had jurisdiction in this case on the grounds that it could try ecclesiastical causes generally; her petition and the response suggest how unusual it must have been. But with the help of her lawyers, who "brought divers book cases of good authoritie" from the "Common law, Statute law, and . . . Canon Law" and even translated, in court, several canon law cases from the Latin, she succeeded in the anulment. Without considerable resources, including good advice, protection from her husband's potential forcing of his right, and fees for her lawyers and to the governor (to record this divorce in the records of the general court), it would not have happened. Mary Hathaway would have remained married to William Williams. And we would know nothing of her story.[3]

It was not, however, unusual for girls to marry so young. Note that no one questioned the validity of her consent at age nine. Mr. John Waugh solemnized and recorded her marriage as apparent routine. No hullabaloo accompanied her marriage; everyone accepted her marriage as valid. The debate surrounded only the divorce.

Although he argued for Mary Hathaway's ability to divorce, Mr. William Fitzhugh, her lawyer, had himself married a young bride. In 1674, or fifteen years earlier, he had married eleven-year-old Sarah Tucker. By 1684, when Sarah was only twenty-one, she had already borne him five children. Within a year after this trial, in 1692, one of those children, William Fitzhugh, Jr., then twelve (the same age as Mary Hathaway), married an eight- or nine-year-old heiress named Ann Lee, a girl about as young as Mary herself had been. Both Fitzhughs' marriages, unlike Mary Hathaway's, would last. How could a twelve-year-old marry an eight-year-old? Their stories reveal a great deal about the meaning of consent in seventeenth-century Virginia and early modern England and America generally.[4]

This chapter will trace the transition in acceptable norms and ideals, particularly as it intersects with the legal codes, in both England and in three of its colonies, from the allowance and expectation of semiarranged marriages for children (especially among the elite) to the idealization of a different kind of choice to marriage. It thus is about what consent to marriage means, and

3. "Stafford County Order Books," *VMHB*, XLV (1937), 370–375, 379–381.
4. Richard Beale Davis, ed., *William Fitzhugh and His Chesapeake World, 1676–1701: The Fitzhugh Letters and Other Documents* (Chapel Hill, N.C., 1963), 10–11, 45. While he acknowledged Sarah Tucker's young age (in the face of strong evidence in the court records), Davis discounted the family record of the son's marriage to Ann Lee in 1692, as many historians have done when confronted with such evidence, on the ground that it does not fit modern assumptions.

about what law and society think marriage should be. It is also the final chapter in the broader debate about children's ability to form contracts.

Marriage under the Age of Consent

Marriage is a critical contract in Western tradition. It was one of the most important contracts within medieval canon law and Roman civil law, two important sources for the English common law. Marriage was a sacrament, and the contract itself had many dimensions of cultural meaning within the medieval church. It also had critical material consequences as well as religious, doing much to shape people's lives and prospects. In both England and its colonies, the contract of marriage would undergo a real transformation from the sixteenth through the late eighteenth centuries that paralleled shifting norms for contracts: where the marriage contracts of girls under twelve and boys under fourteen had once been voidable at their discretion, their contracts became void, and they became unable to contract matrimony at all. By the late eighteenth century, Mary Hathaway, for example, would have been unable to marry at nine; if she had somehow managed to (with aid), then simply admitting her age would likely have voided the marriage. She would have had no need to formally annul the marriage. The other transition was just as important: those considered old enough to consent (girls at least twelve and boys at least fourteen) began to need the consent of a parent or guardian to validate the contract if marrying before age twenty-one. Some states (and England itself) even experimented with giving parents the ability to void their child's marriage if made without their consent (if the child was under age twenty-one). Marriage contracts also increasingly had to be formal, with accompanying public rituals, in order to be valid.

A contract for marriage, of course, was very different from a temporary contract for goods. Most contracts for goods or even for land were not as important to people's lives as commencing a marriage, nor was a contract for goods or land as intimate in its consequences. Although marriage contracts often included exchanges of goods and land, marriage involved people, culture, and beliefs more fundamentally. These differences help to frame what ultimately became a different debate, but one involving many of the same issues of mental ability, informed personal consent, and judgment.

The shift in ideas about personal competency to consent helps to answer important questions about parental control over marriage during this period and whether that control was waxing or waning. Parents gained different methods of control as child marriages came to be seen as illegitimate, methods in some ways more powerful (legally at least) but that spawned their own reaction. The laws over three centuries reveal, not a steady decline in parental power, but a general growth in such power, beginning with the Reformation. Parental influence went from being implicit to being explicit as parents gained increased control, especially in America, over inheritance as a method of influence. This control led to a strong public reaction (embodied, for example, in romances) toward holding that parents' judgment should not overpower their child's choice of mate. Marriage contracts, especially, required something more than a parent's—or a child's—reason. The role of physical attraction went from "fansy" and "love" to a romantic blending of reason and passion with individual choice. No one denied the necessity of a person's own consent to marriage throughout this period. The questions were, How much influence should be given to parents over the choice? What was a marriage supposed to be? and, What qualities did one need in order to consent? The answers to these questions would change over time and would become increasingly controversial; resolving them occupied the pens of political theorists, lawyers, ministers, and many of the first novelists (as that form of writing originated) in the eighteenth century.

Many marriages were encouraged or even arranged by parents in the sixteenth and seventeenth centuries. Although young women such as Mary Hathaway had to consent to the marriage to make it valid and their consent was critical, children's consent was clearly influenced in a variety of ways; one might even argue that some parents actually had more influence over marriage choices with such youthful marriages. Influence was expected over a child's choice, sometimes explicitly. Guardians of wards in knight's service, for example, were allowed to arrange the marriages of their wards through 1660, when such guardianship was abolished. But in many cases wards were allowed simply to pay a fine to make their own choice, almost routinely. In other cases they married following their guardian's suggestion. So coerced choice of one kind or another was not invalid per se (although it depended, to some degree, on the "persuasions" and "threats" invoked). Questions about valid consent to marriage intertwine themselves through Mary Hathaway's case. Does force, fraud, or persuasion invalidate consent? (There is a hint that it might.) But she claimed that her mother initially obtained her consent only "partly by Persuasions and partly by threats," and the judges still saw the marriage as valid (though voidable). On the other hand, does forced sex count as consummation? The implication of this case and of canon law generally is that it would (if both had already said the vows, they had consented). Yet Mary, obviously following the advice of her lawyers, argued that her vows had been coerced but that her current opposition to the marriage was of her own free will. Although persuasion did not invalidate her consent, it did open the possibility of annulment; it helped to make the marriage voidable, not void (an important distinction).

Mary Hathaway's young marriage was not unique to Virginia; the marriage of one of Charles II's illegitimate sons (whom he created duke of Southampton) in 1671 to Mary Wood, when he was nine and she seven, for example, was similar. Some sense of Mary's wealth (she was an only child) can be seen in her father's agreeing with the king in a premarriage contract to pay the duke twenty thousand pounds if Mary refused to follow through on the planned marriage. Such *premarriage* contracts were not uncommon in the sixteenth and seventeenth centuries. Among the elite in England, in fact, semiarranged marriages were the norm: children would be given some choice, but marriages were actually brokered and negotiated by parents and usually involved complicated settlements. The emphasis in marriage choices was on status, on economic resources, and to a certain extent on "fansy."[5]

William Shakespeare's *Romeo and Juliet* (circa 1597) (while set in Verona) reveals much about the cultural underpinnings surrounding such marriages in England at the same time as it reveals some of the tensions surrounding them. Juliet is just thirteen at the beginning of the play; her mother calls her almost an old maid: "By my count I was your mother much upon these years that you are now a maid" (which makes Lady Capulet herself only twenty-six). When asked by Paris whether he would approve his courting her, her father answers: "Woo her, gentle Paris, get her heart, / My will to her consent is but a part; / And she agree, within her scope of choice / Lies my consent and faire according voice." Her father had been somewhat concerned over her age: "She hath not seen the change of fourteen years; / Let two more summers wither in their pride / Ere we may think her ripe to be a bride." Paris responds: "Younger than she are happy mothers made," to which Capulet responds: "And too soon marr'd are those so early made." But he admits his objection originates in his loss of other children. He then relents, encouraging Paris to court her. Her mother then urges Juliet to consider Paris for a husband. "What say you. Can you love the gentleman?" Juliet instead falls in love with Romeo: in one evening they meet, they dance, they touch, they kiss,

5. John Habakkuk, *Marriage, Debt, and the Estates System: English Landownership, 1650–1950* (Oxford: 1994), 145–240, esp. 189. Also see Barbara J. Harris, "Marriage, Property, and Patriarchy: Aristocratic Marriage Contracts in Yorkist and Early Tudor England," paper at the annual meeting of the American Historical Association, December 1992. On jointures, see Susan Staves, *Married Women's Separate Property in England, 1660–1833* (Cambridge, Mass., 1990); and Marylynn Salmon, *Women and the Law of Property in Early America* (Chapel Hill, N.C., 1986), esp. 88–89. On romantic love, see Lawrence Stone, *The Family, Sex, and Marriage in England, 1500–1800* (London, 1977); John R. Gillis, *For Better, for Worse: British Marriages, 1600 to the Present* (Oxford, 1985).

and then later (the balcony scene) promise marriage. They sanctify those vows the next day, still secretly, before a priest who with "holy church incorporate[s] two in one," and consummate the marriage soon after. Juliet's youth, the impulsiveness of their love (based mostly on physical attraction), her parents limited control over her actual marriage choice, the role of the priest in the marriage: all conformed with the actual legal rules of this period.[6]

How common such marriages were (of children younger than, say, fourteen) is difficult to answer. The statistics that demographic historians have compiled for the seventeenth century, which point to average marriage ages in the late teens to early twenties, seem to indicate that these marriages were uncommon. However, there is considerable evidence that demographic historians assumed such marriages were impossible and therefore excluded them from their statistics.[7]

6. William Shakespeare, *Romeo and Juliet*, 1.2, 3; 2.2, 6.

7. The data that pointed to these marriages were filtered out because of the power of modern norms about child sexuality and a misreading of contemporary laws. Also, most demographic historians were more interested in fertility than marriage itself, and fertility begins later than such marriages. For evidence showing why such data were excluded, see, for example, Peter Laslett, who misread the law on this question (and who was very influential on the Cambridge Group who studied English population history), "Misbeliefs about Our Ancestors," chap. 4 of *The World We Have Lost: Further Explored* (New York, 1984), esp. 81. For Virginia, Darrett B. Rutman and Anita H. Rutman conducted one of the most thorough studies. While they did not explain their assumptions on this question, the marriage tables in their *Place in Time: Explicatus* (New York, 1984) only begin with age fifteen (3, 65). In tracking their methodology, it appears that they did not link a birth date with a marriage date, even if a person bore the same last name, unless at least fifteen years separated the two. For a much fuller explanation of this issue, see my "Marriages 'Under the Age of Consent': The Perils of Demography and the Power of Ideology," *Past and Present* (forthcoming). For data on age at first marriage for England and America, see especially E. A. Wrigley and R. S. Schofield, *The Population History of England, 1541–1871: A Reconstruction* (Cambridge, Mass., 1981), 424; David Hackett Fischer, *Albion's Seed: Four British Folkways in America* (New York, 1989), 85, which provides a nice summary of the literature. Some studies that are more sympathetic to the issue of young marriages, such as that by Lorena S. Walsh in her study of marriages of Maryland orphans, find much lower average ages: see " 'Till Death Us Do Part': Marriage and Family in Seventeenth-Century Maryland," in Thad W. Tate and David L. Ammerman, eds., *The Chesapeake in the Seventeenth Century: Essays on Anglo-American Society* (Chapel Hill, N.C., 1979), 131.

Note also Wrigley and Schofield, *The Population History of England*, 20, 21 n. 12, 28, 69, 257 (esp. n. 99), 259–262, 424. Although they admit (259) that "in the absence of dependable and representative evidence about remarriage before the nineteenth century any solution to this problem must at present be arbitrary," they still entitle their results from averaging ages at all marriages, including second marriages and so forth,

Indeed, as soon as one moves away from the official averages, young marriages appear frequently, especially before about 1700, and more among the elite than other groups. Averages say little about the range of ages at marriage, which differed markedly by status, place, and time. While a young woman who came to Virginia as an indentured servant, for example, could be effectively prevented from marrying until age twenty-four by her master, an heiress such as Hathaway could marry at nine.[8]

In the long eighteenth century, from about 1660 onward, doubts increased about whether young children could (and should) marry, and such marriages became less common. By the mid-eighteenth century, marriages between children under twelve for girls and fourteen for boys came usually to be seen as illegal under the common law, which was responding to changing norms about the capacity to contract. At the same time, they became less necessary because of other legal changes, such as the abolition of the court of wards (parents had encouraged such marriages to avoid wardship). Preventing such marriages might have increased children's "real" choices, but canon laws permitting these prepubertal marriage were replaced with increasingly stringent laws mandating parental consent during a minority that extended to twenty-one.

Issues of lineage were central to why young marriages occurred at all, as the laws and practices surrounding guardianship in the sixteenth and early seventeenth centuries reveal. Guardians in knight's service (guardians of wards whose land was actually held primarily by the king) were allowed to arrange marriages for their wards if unmarried and under age fourteen (for girls) or twenty-one (for boys). Two guidelines circumscribed this right: they had to offer a potential spouse "without disparagement," which primarily meant a person from the same place (or higher) in the social hierarchy; and they must

---

as "Age at first marriage" (424). Also see R. B. Outhwaite, *Clandestine Marriage in England, 1500–1850* (London, 1995), which gives an excellent overview of the biases of the sources that Wrigley and Schofield relied upon (xviii, xxi, 1–49).

8. Habakkuk, *Marriage, Debt, and the Estates System*, 145–240. Medieval scholars also document many such marriages, as contained in, for example, *Calendar of Inquisitions post Mortem . . .* , 2d Ser., III, *Henry VII* (London, 1955), 99 (such as the case of Thomas Trygot), which were done mostly for those who left property. Sue Sheridan Walker, "Free Consent and Marriage of Feudal Wards in Medieval England," *Journal of Medieval History*, VIII (1982), 125. Walker's own study of MS records as well as the studies of J. B. Post, "Another Demographic Use of Inquisitions post Mortem," *Journal of the Society of Archivists*, V (1974), 110–114; and Josiah Cox Russell, *British Medieval Population* (Albuquerque, N.Mex., 1948), 156–158, 171, concur that teenage marriages were normal among those who inherited property.

gain the consent of both. If the ward refused consent, then the ward owed the guardian a fine based on the value of the marriage—but only if the potential mate were of the same or higher status. Proposing a spouse of lower status (or too old to bear children, blind, or lame) would constitute "disparagement" of the ward, and the guardian's right to arrange a match would be abrogated without fining the ward. The logic behind giving the guardian such powers was explained by Sir Thomas Smith, in *De Republica Anglorum* in 1583: "It was thought that most like, that noble men, good knights, and great captaines would bring up their wards in their owne feates and vertues, and then marry them into like race and stocke where they may finde and make friendes." (The terms "race" and "stocke" as referring to bloodlines and hierarchical distinctions within England are fascinating in light of their later usage.)[9]

Young marriages, in short, have everything to do with lineage, maintaining inherited status, and the ideologies underlying social stability, order, and monarchy. The main opportunity to dramatically change one's status—or, indeed, to preserve it—came at marriage, for both boys and girls. A wealthy youth might be persuaded to marry someone who sought only a fortune, who would offer "disparagement" to him. Young marriages were ways of limiting the choice of young people as well as protecting their futures (economically, at least) and the family lineage. Controlling marriages was important to stabilizing a patriarchal system of allocating power by making sure that lineage was not corrupted and that social relations remained consistent and boundaries between ranks respected. In condemning the practice in 1593, Philip Stubbes wrote, "In [Anglia] there is one great libertye permitted therein; for

9. Thomas Smith, *De Republica Anglorum: A Discourse on the Commonwealth of England* (1583), ed. L. Alston (1906; rpt. New York, 1979), 122; Joel Hurstfield, *The Queen's Wards: Wardship and Marriage under Elizabeth I* (London, 1958), esp. 187–189.

One medieval scholar argues that the payment of the marriage fine by wards was so common that obviously many, if not most, wards chose their own partners and that this should be seen solely as a tax (Walker, "Free Consent and Marriage of Feudal Wards," *Jour. Med. Hist.*, VIII [1982], 123–134). Hurstfield gives an example of a marriage contract, although privately made, between a ward and chosen mate that was upheld against the objections of the guardian. The ward, however, was fined (133). He also gives many examples of wards' "buying their own marriages" from their guardians.

Many orphans also never entered wardship or ended it early by being knighted, getting married, or literally buying their own wardship. Most other types of guardianship (and there were at least ten before 1660) did not give the guardian any control over marriage. Guardianship in "socage," the most common type of guardianship, which became the basis of eighteenth-century models of guardianship, ended at fourteen and gave no rights to offer a marriage partner before that age. Basically, then, guardians had little control over marriage, and even the one type that had some power had only a monetary lien, not a right to actually determine the mate of their ward.

little infants in swadling clowts, are often maried by their amibicious Parents and frends, when they know neither good nor evill; and this is the origene of much wickednesse."[10]

Officially, the medieval Roman Catholic Church honored any vows made between a female and male, so long as they were not related (or already married), regardless of where they were made or in whose presence. According to Gratian, the most influential of the canon lawyers, their consent was "meaningful" if the individuals were older than seven, although this point was disputed and some commentators allowed earlier marriages. Such a marriage would be permanent so long as neither party sought annulment soon after reaching puberty (presumed to be twelve for girls and fourteen for boys) and they did not consummate it. If both were older and both admitted to the vow, then the marriage would be final. What confirmed a marriage was that each had consented. Although Gratian's suggested age of seven for "meaningful consent" was not adhered to strictly, this Catholic marriage policy of the Middle Ages was followed in England, both before and after the Reformation. Not only was personal consent, at whatever age, necessary, but Catholic Church policy explicitly stated that parents could not impose marriages on their children without their consent and that informal marriage ceremonies were valid. Still, "convince" clearly had a different meaning. Force and influence were permissible elements of persuasion.[11]

10. Philip Stubbes, *Anatomie of Abuses in Ailgna* (1583), ed. Frederick J. Furnivall (1877–1879; rpt. New Shakespeare Society), 97.

11. Brundage, *Law, Sex, and Christian Society*, 183, 194, 238, 275, 364, 437–439, 448–450. Brundage summarizes the writings of Gratian, the most important medieval Catholic author on marriage law. Although Gratian emphasized the importance of consummation in ultimately confirming a marriage, "consent was an essential element of his definition of marriage, and he discussed consent issues at length." Gratian held that "both parties must have attained the age of seven before their consent could be considered binding" (238). Failure to consummate the marriage could provide grounds for annulment (for adults as well as children).

In noting that one "concern that impelled both lawmakers and law writers to uphold the validity of clandestine [private] marriages arose from their commitment to freedom of contract and their wish to enable persons to marry despite opposition from their families," Brundage follows many other scholars (*Law, Sex, and Christian Society*, 364). See also George Elliot Howard, *A History of Matrimonial Institutions: Chiefly in England and the United States* . . . (Chicago, 1904), I, 339; Alan Macfarlane, *Marriage and Love in England, 1300–1840* (Oxford, 1986), 125–126; M. Sheehan, "Choice of Marriage Partner in the Middle Ages," *Studies in Medieval and Renaissance History*, I (1978), 3–33; R. H. Helmholz, *Marriage Litigation in Medieval England* (Cambridge, 1974); Walker, "Free Consent and Marriage of Feudal Wards in Medieval England," *Jour. Med. Hist.*, VIII (1982), 123–134.

The main English seventeenth-century treatise on marriage distinguished between the marriages of those under seven and those between seven and puberty. If under seven when they said their vows, the marriage was void unless they ratified it afterward (by kisses, embraces, lying together, exchanging gifts or tokens, or calling each other husband or wife). If over that age, they were "of ripe age" to marry, but their marriage was still voidable if they did none of these things and sought a formal annulment.[12]

In the mid-sixteenth century, the ecclesiastical courts (which regulated marriage) were most concerned about the consent of the two parties directly involved, and whether they exchanged vows in front of a priest or other witnesses was not determinative of the marriage. The new Anglican Church, like the Catholic Church before it, honored "trothplights" and "clandestine marriages." So long as both parties consented, the marriage was valid. No formal ceremony was necessary, nor were banns or a priest. In the following trothplight enforced by the sixteenth-century courts, for example, the words were spoken one evening in front of three friends, with no minister present.

> The said George Johnson did take the said Anne by the hand; [and] when they held hand in hand, George Kay said, "art thou, George, contentid to take Anne to thie wief, and so to use her?" and George Johnson answerid, "Yea, by my faith and trowth" and likewise the said George Kay said, "Anne, art thou contentid to take George Johnson to thi husband, and so to use hym?" and she answerid, "yea, by my faith and trowth."[13]

The couple thereafter "used each other" as husband and wife and exchanged tokens of their affection (no ages were given). It is a model of what was then necessary to a valid contract.[14]

12. Henry Swinburne, *A Treatise of Spousals, or Matrimonial Contracts* . . . (London, 1686). Judge of the prerogative court at York, Swinburne died in 1624 (or long before publication). "In the *Civil* and *Ecclesiastical Laws*, by Infants (most commonly) are understood those Children which have not as yet accomplished the Age of *Seven* years; and so is the word accepted in this place." "Spousals contracted during infancy are utterly *void*" and "so they cannot [contract] Matrimony" except if they ratify it in some way "after they have accomplished their several Ages of Seven years" (19–21). See also esp. 27, 40.

13. Frederick J. Furnivall, ed., *Child-Marriages, Divorces, and Ratifications, etc. in the Diocese of Chester, A.D. 1561–6* . . . (London, 1897), 58.

14. In his magisterial three-volume study, still thorough in its coverage for England and America, Howard writes: "There was no absolute requirement of parental consent or of a certain age. All persons on reaching the years of puberty were declared capable of [binding] wedlock solely on their own authority. No religious ceremony, no record, or witness was essential. The private, even secret, agreement of the betrothed, however expressed, was declared sufficient for a valid contract." *Matrimonial Institutions*, I, 339.

Many children between ages two and fourteen (usually over seven) married formally during this period, sometimes via a contract arranged between the parents or at the urging of "frendes" (which could include parents) who told them that their potential spouse was likely to inherit (or had inherited) and would make a good match. "They were maried biecause she shold have had bie hym a pretty bargane, yf they cold have lovid, on[e] the other," testified the father of one girl. Other marriages involved children with some wealth or prospects: one boy had served an apprenticeship; another attended school and was "in service to" an earl (his squire?); a third's father owned "Hatton Hall." At six, Elizabeth, daughter of Thomas, Lord Clifford, of Skipton Castle, married Sir Robert Plumpton of Plumpton Castle, of about the same age.[15]

However, like Mary Hathaway (and seemingly with more ease) these children could, at puberty, refuse the marriage, and the marriage would be formally annulled—so long as the parties had not consummated the marriage or reinforced their vows after puberty. The ecclesiastical records for Chester Diocese contain twenty-seven such petitions for annulment between 1561 and 1564. Although probably neither as expensive nor as uncertain as Mary Hathaway's case, the suits did cost money. When the judges asked Jane Leyland why she had not requested an annulment earlier, she answered that "she was poor, and had no money; and nowe she hath gotten somewhat in Service, and nowe spendes hit in triall of the Lawe." Yet the knowledge of the ability to annul these marriages was widespread and an expected escape hatch. During the marriage of a twelve-year-old boy and a nine-year-old girl, a witness "h[e]ard the mother of Peter Hope, callid Christian Hope, say to Peter Hope, that yf he and Alice Ellis, alias Mathue, cold not agree when they comme to Lawfull age, that the said Peter shuld be at Libertye, and the Matrimony shuld be void."[16]

The main questions of the court focused on consent, as discerned through both behavior and words. Did they exchange love tokens (like rings) or kisses? Did they consummate the marriage? Did they reaffirm after puberty in any way the vows they had made when younger? In response, one witness answered:

The said William and Anne did never, either afore they came to yeres of consent, or after, cohabitt and dwell together,—as this deponent, beinge houshold Servaunt to Sir John Sothworth, well knowes,—nor ever used either other, as man and wief, in wordes or otherwise. And further this

15. Furnivall, ed., *Child Marriages:* case of *Joan Leyland v Rafe Whittall*, 12; apprentice (George Hulse, married at seven), 4; William Stanley ("in Service with therle [the earl] of Derby"), 48; Roland Dutton (Hatton Hall), 43; Elizabeth, xxxii.

16. Ibid., 12, 21.

deponent saies, that about a yere and a half ago, John Westby, father to the said William, in the presence of Sir John Sothworth, knight, and the Ladie Mary Sothworth his wief, parentes to the said Anne, and of diverse others, did demaund of the saied Anne, whether she cold be content to take the said William as her husband; and the said Anne answerid that "she wold not take hym as her husband; nor she cold not fansy hym, or consent to the said Mariage."

In order to divorce, they had to establish that they had not "used either other as man and wief, in wordes or otherwise." In practice, this criterion must have meant less choice for girls, if the husband were older, because of the possibility of rape. But this was not the case here. William Westby and Anne Sothworth had been nine and ten, respectively, when they said their vows in the church of Samsbury.[17]

That the child consented only to please a parent was offered sometimes as evidence to support separation. In *Ellen Dampart v. John Andrews*, in order to prove that neither child had wanted to marry out of natural inclination, two witnesses testified that the fathers of Ellen (age seven) and John (age ten) encouraged them to marry because Ellen was to inherit one half of a house, and John the other. If Ellen and John married only at the urging of their parents to make the house whole, said one witness, then "the parties [themselves] never consentid thereto." To persuade John to marry, the witness continued, his father had promised him that he could divorce later.[18]

Thus in England in the 1560s, judges honored marriages based on mutual consent of young children, some even younger than the seven that Gratian offered as the minimum age for meaningful consent. Indeed, the marriage vows of two-year-old Jane Brerton and three-year-old John Somerford, which others helped them speak, were valid: they had to seek a "causa divorcii" in order to annul their marriage. Though obviously these very young children could be controlled by adults, parental consent was not necessary to any of these marriages. The authority to make the marriage commitment was vested in the children, as was annulment.[19]

Parental Authority and the Reformation

Strengthening parents' legal power was only one of the many ways in which the leaders of the Reformation sought to reshape the grounds and conditions

17. Ibid., 37. This record contains only depositions, not verdicts.
18. Ibid., 13.
19. Ibid., 25–28 (divorce was not necessary for spousals [that is, engagements]).

for valid marriage. They also sought to raise minimum marriage ages, usually to several years beyond puberty, to make valid only those marriages that were formally performed, and to dethrone marriage's status as a sacrament by turning it into a civil and thus breakable contract. Many of the leaders of the Reformation objected to the lax regulation of marriage within the Catholic Church. Medieval Catholic theology had held that the consent of the partners to the marriage made the marriage valid: private vows were legitimate, and parental consent was irrelevant to the validity of the contract. Martin Luther, on the other hand, argued not only that parental consent was critical to a marriage but that failure to obtain it should make the marriage void. He justified his position with biblical examples of parental authority as well as a contention that parents provided "good advice and sound judgment." Both John Calvin and Ulrich Zwingli wrote legislation that rescinded marriages contracted without parental authorization, under which laws many parents petitioned to void the marriages of their children. The reformers also sought to raise the minimum marriage ages: in Zurich, for example, the minimum ages were sixteen and fourteen, and parental consent was necessary until nineteen.[20]

Ultimately, their justification for parental consent originated, at least in part, in the notion that children should not make their own decisions about such an important event, especially when very young. Although they worried that arranged marriages, among young children in particular, would lead to sin because the partners to the marriage might have no true affection for each other, they were unwilling, at the same time, to rely on young people's own fancies. They appealed to both parental power as justified by the fifth commandment and other biblical sources and to ideas about judgment.

Youthful marriages allowed parents some control over marriage, but with limits. Parents also could control their children through inheritance. When parents had little to offer their children (to bribe them with, to put it most crudely), they had less leverage. An example from the life of Sir Edward Coke gives some sense of the practice at the same as it shows some of the increas-

20. Steven Ozment, *When Fathers Ruled: Family Life in Reformation Europe* (Cambridge, Mass., 1983), 36–44. Brundage, *Law, Sex, and Christian Society,* 552–553. The laws written by John Calvin can be found in his *Ecclesiastical Ordinances of 1541;* by Zwingli, in Ulrich Zwingli, *Zurich Marriage Ordinance* (1525), in Samuel Macauley Jackson, ed., *Selected Works* (1901; Philadelphia, 1972), 120. Also see David Hunt, *Parents and Children in History: The Psychology of Family Life in Early Modern France* (New York, 1972); Natalie Zemon Davis, "Ghosts, Kin, and Progeny: Some Features of Family Life in Early Modern France," *Daedalus,* no. 106 (Spring 1987), 105–108; Ruth H. Bloch, "Untangling the Roots of Modern Sex Roles: A Survey of Four Centuries of Change," *Signs,* IV (1978), 237–252.

ing tensions surrounding it. In 1598 at age forty-six he married (without license) for the second time to a widow, Lady Elizabeth (Cecil) Hatton, then twenty (who kept the name of her first husband, who was of higher status than Coke). Their daughter Frances, partly because of her mother's wealth, was a considerable heiress. In order to further favor with James I, Coke promised Frances, then fourteen, to Sir John Villiers, the brother of James I's favorite, the duke of Buckingham. (Villiers was then about thirty.) Lady Hatton, whether siding with her daughter or convincing her, then ran away with her to the house of some of her Cecil relatives. At some point, Frances wrote a letter (perhaps at her mother's urging) promising herself in marriage to someone else. Coke then got a writ from a member of the Privy Council to search the Cecil relative's house and retrieve his daughter. In response Lady Hatton proceeded posthaste to London, where she received aid from Sir Francis Bacon, who was lord keeper, disliked Coke, and had great influence. The Privy Council met to hear the case and appeared to be leaning in favor of Frances and Lady Hatton. At this point, the same member who had given the writ to Coke pulled a personal letter from James I out of his pocket, indicating that the king wanted this marriage to go forward and that he thought Frances should obey her father.[21]

Frances was left with her father, who convinced her that she should go through with the marriage. One rumor at the time contended that he had tied her up and whipped her. Her own letter to her mother, however, stated simply otherwise. "Dear Mother believe there has no violent means been used to me by word or deed." Instead, her father convinced her that her wishes should not count: "I being a mere child and not understanding the world nor what is good for myself." Villiers, her intended husband, was, after all, a "gentleman well born." Possible violence notwithstanding, she consented. Frances was then duly married, in the presence of James I and a huge royal assembly, at age fourteen, as her father had wanted.

During the next few years, however, the marriage foundered. Buckingham had Frances put on trial for adultery (for bearing a child not her husband's, that is, not his brother's). On her way to trial, she was said to have "marvelled what these poor old cuckolds had to say to her." Though convicted, she was not punished. Coke's desperate struggles to control his daughter's choice were successful, to some degree, but not without the king's explicit intervention. His attitude toward his "right" to control his daughter is especially

21. For the Coke episodes: Catherine Drinker Bowen, *The Lion and the Throne: The Life and Times of Sir Edward Coke (1552–1634)* (Boston, 1956), chap. 29, 529–531. Also see Staves, *Married Women's Separate Property in England*, 26; Antonia Fraser, *The Weaker Vessel* (New York, 1984), 12–19.

revealing, given his Puritan bearings and his attempts to strengthen legal "custody" itself discussed in the last chapter. In the end, Frances chose her own path.

The extent of parents' control depended not only on the status of the parents and their wealth but also on the age of the children: fourteen-year-old Frances Coke, for example, put up a struggle that a four-year-old Frances would not have.[22]

The fact that many parents provided the money and land that a couple needed to set up house gave parents influence over the marriages of their children. For daughters, dowries were usually negotiable throughout this whole era. A father's power to negotiate her dowry could shape her prospects and her final choice considerably. This was also important for younger sons, whose inheritance was less assured (because the land was often entailed on the oldest son). But, as historians have shown for England, because daughters' dowries went further in obtaining a good match, fathers were more willing to invest their money there than in younger sons, for whom they usually only purchased career opportunities in the church, the law, or the military. In Virginia, where entails were also common, fathers had less control over their estates, and thus had less ability to shape their children's choices, particularly for the eldest son. The ability to disinherit increased after the Revolution when entail was abolished in Virginia, thereby increasing fathers' ability to influence their sons' choices. But this change did not affect only sons: the general freeing up of the estate meant that fathers had greater flexibility over which children to endow, and with how much. In New England and Pennsylvania, where entails were rare, most land and property were controlled by fathers (who also lived longer); thus they had stronger control in that way throughout.[23]

Historians have tended to overemphasize parental control over marriage

22. Stone, *Family, Sex, and Marriage*, 180, 183. Also see Edward Shorter, *The Making of the Modern Family* (New York, 1975), 148–149. Stone gives some examples, lasting through the seventeenth century, of parents who, through threats and promises, successfully persuaded their children to make particular matches. The most effective control, he argues, was exercised by the parents of the wealthy, who could threaten to disinherit their children.

However, in England (especially before the inheritance taxes of the early twentieth century) a large proportion of land was entailed, meaning that the father could neither grant the land nor refuse to grant it. In these cases the father possessed no power based on inheritance. For younger sons and most daughters, a wealthy father held greater monetary leverage: to set them up in a career or to give them a dowry. For children of middling and lesser circumstances, parental support was important as well.

23. Habakkuk, *Marriage, Debt, and the Estates System*, esp. 156–157.

by quoting from religious manuals as though they were gospel, without realizing the political context of the debates over parental authority. In *The Whole Duty of Man* (1658), Richard Allestree, for example, gave parents a property right in their children and described their marrying without parental consent as "a kind of theft." "Children are so much the goods, the possessions of their Parent, that they cannot, without a kind of theft, give away themselves without the allowance of those that have the right in them." Yet he did this in order to justify the power of the king as highest father. Indeed, such arguments probably helped to make him a favorite minister of Charles II.

> The Civil Parent is he whom God hath establisht the Supreme Magistrate, who by a just right possesses the Throne in a Nation. This is the Common Father of all those that are under his authority. The duty we owe to this Parent, is first Honour and Reverence, looking on him, as upon one, on whom God hath stamped much of his own power and authority, and therefore paying him all honour and esteem, never daring upon any pretence whatsoever, *to speak evil of the Ruler of our People.*

Because the king bore God's "own power and authority," he should always be obeyed. In the extreme case where his commands were obviously against the word of God, then we need not actively obey, but "even this is a season for the Passive Obedience, we must patiently suffer. . . . They that resist shall receive in themselves damnation."[24]

24. [Richard Allestree], *The Whole Duty of Man* . . . (London, 1703), 107–108, 112. For more on this tract, see Gordon J. Schochet, "Patriarchalism, Politics, and Mass Attitudes in Stuart England," *Historical Journal,* XII (1969), 430–431.

American historians have drawn on the conclusions by British historians to argue that fathers exercised considerable control over marriage before the mid-eighteenth century. Daniel Blake Smith, in his study of eighteenth-century southern family relations, for example, summarizes: "The ability to choose a marriage partner is a fundamental aspect of personal autonomy. But few sons and daughters in early America exercised this independence of choice" (*Inside the Great House: Planter Family Life in Eighteenth-Century Chesapeake Society* [Ithaca, N.Y., 1980], 140). In a similar vein Carl N. Degler's grand study of women and the family in America since colonial times asserted: "In the half-century after the Revolution the bases of marriage began to change in a decidedly modern direction. Increasingly, free choice by the partners became the basis of family formation" (*At Odds: Women and the Family in America from the Revolution to the Present* [New York, 1980], 9). In support of their "before" picture of strong parental power, these authors rely on Stone, a quote from *The Whole Duty of Man* cited by Stone, Greven's work on early New England inheritance practices, and two demographic studies of New England towns.

They have argued that, over time, especially under the liberalizing and radical pressures set free by the American Revolution, parental power over marriage relaxed. These

Allestree, who fought with Charles I against Cromwell and who delivered numerous sermons to Charles II himself in the decade following the Restoration, was offering a highly politicized version of the duties of people, including children, one aimed especially at the "meaner" sort. He also wrote numerous conduct books for gentlemen and ladies, such as *The Government of the Tongue,* that helped to define and reify status. His views were neither uncontested nor traditional: his book was one of the few to so strongly imply that children were the "property" of their parents. *The Whole Duty of Man* went through many editions in England, particularly in the late seventeenth century. The only colony to reprint it was Virginia, in 1746, indicating that Virginians found patriarchal ideology as advocated by this popular Anglican minister more palatable. Six editions of George Whitefield's radical sermons were printed in the same year—and no Allestree—in Boston and Philadelphia. Allestree, in short, was supporting an extreme version of parental authority in order to justify patriarchal/absolutist political ideology, and Virginia's reprinting is revealing about how its religious and political ideas differed from those in Massachusetts and Pennsylvania. Although both "patriarchalism" and "Puritanism" had common origins in the Reformation, with its emphasis on the fifth commandment, no other moralist went so far as to see children as so clearly their parents' property with respect to marriage.

Despite Virginians' reading these sermons that emphasized more fatherly power, the main way that parents influenced their children was through inheritance, which many fathers did throughout the colonies. Some fathers in Massachusetts, for example, retained control over their property until they died, and many others dispersed property and money to their sons and daughters at the time of their marriage, some of those only "confirming" the settlement of property to the son or daughter in their will. Among the southern elite, fathers threatened to disinherit daughters or sons who married against their wishes. An egregious example is William Byrd II in 1723: he sought his daughter's allegiance to his wishes and threatened to disinherit her if she disobeyed. Letters exchanged between two fathers in Virginia discuss how much they would settle upon their courting children, should they decide to marry. The young man's father hoped that his son was agreeable to

---

assumptions have become so commonplace that their conclusions are cited in recent books for which the issue of parental control over marriage is only a minor point. See, for example, Gordon S. Wood, *The Radicalism of the American Revolution* (New York, 1992), 48–49. Wood is more tentative in making these broad claims than Degler and Smith. But they are too simplistic, particularly in terms of their "before" picture. They do not fully realize the ways in which the debate over consent to marriage is connected to the struggle over the basis of political authority.

"yourself, lady, and daughter," and the young woman's father gave his agreement and support to the match if the young man "succeeded" in his courtship. Many similar examples exist for England.[25]

Aside from monetary leverage, which many parents employed, the legal story is very different. Parents had no effective legal power over marriage in England, except briefly during the Interregnum, until 1753. This power almost always ceased with the father's death. In one case, a father sought to reach out his hand from the grave. He had altered his daughter's bequest, dependent on whether she followed the advice of the executors of his estate in choosing a mate. This restriction seems to have been rare, however, and clauses in wills that gave specific instructions about marriage (to either bar it or direct a specific choice) were usually invalid. Most children did not have guardians, and the one type of guardianship that had allowed guardians some power over marriage, guardianship in knight's service, gave them only a limited financial leverage.[26]

The one situation where parents emphatically had more control over marriage was when their daughter was an heiress and under age sixteen. By a law of 1558 (the abduction statute, 4 and 5 P. and M., c. 8), parents were granted power over the marriages of daughters who would inherit property: men who "abducted" heiresses under sixteen and married them without their parents' or guardian's consent would be punished by five years' imprisonment and withholding the girl's fortune during his lifetime. Whereas men who abducted such a girl or woman and coerced her into marriage against *her own* will were punished more harshly—with death, without benefit of clergy—this law explicitly connected, for the first time, parental consent to the marriage of

25. John Demos, *A Little Commonwealth: Family Life in Plymouth Colony* (New York, 1970), 164–169; Philip J. Greven, Jr., *Four Generations: Population, Land, and Family in Colonial Andover, Massachusetts* (Ithaca, N.Y., 1970), 168; Daniel Blake Smith, *Inside the Great House*, 141, 145–150; Edmund S. Morgan, *Virginians at Home: Family Life in the Eighteenth Century* (Williamsburg, Va., 1952), 32–33; Lawrence Stone, *Road to Divorce: England, 1530–1987* (Oxford, 1987), 55–58.

26. For the case, see Stone, *Family, Sex, and Marriage*, 182. Macfarlane has argued that England was unique in granting personal autonomy to sons and daughters with regard to marriage choice between 1300 and 1840. "Thus from the twelfth to eighteenth centuries marriage for men from fourteen, for girls from twelve, was valid against all pressures from the outside world." Macfarlane goes so far as to deny the significance of even the British Marriage Act of 1753, arguing that, according to Blackstone, it did not render the marriages of those under twenty-one void. However, his quotation from Blackstone originates in an edition of 1829, after the Marriage Act was repealed, and his *Commentaries* had been updated by others to reflect that repeal. Macfarlane, *Marriage and Love in England*, 119–147, esp. 127; Blackstone, *Commentaries on the Laws of England* (1765–1769; rpt. Chicago, 1979), I, 440–441.

girls. Abduction in order to coerce marriage was a crime closely related to rape in early modern and medieval English law. A 1488 law (3 Hen. VII, c. 3), for example, gave the same punishment for abduction, even if it ended in marriage, as for rape. The presumption was that the abduction could enable rape and threats to coerce her consent. Likewise, the 1558 law compared the lack of parental consent with the lack of personal consent that defined the crime of rape.[27]

The 1558 law thus established parental authority over marriage in a limited case. It presumed that a girl younger than sixteen who would inherit money and property might be inveigled, for the wrong reasons, into marriage by a man who wanted only her property and had little interest in her person. Marriage of young heiresses without parental consent was a kind of property theft (not of the girl, but of her fortune): by the laws of England, husbands often gained control over their wife's property. Thus in amending the inheritance laws of that time that often restrained the father's control (as when land was entailed in *tail general* and a man had only daughters), it strengthened parental power. Because such marriages were tempting to those who sought an easy fortune, the law sought to withdraw that temptation by preventing the transfer of wealth. Still, the law gave parents this extra control only until their daughters were sixteen.[28]

27. 3 Hen. VII, c. 3: "Where Wymmen aswell [Maydens] as Wydowes and Wyfes havyng substaunce somme in goods moveable, and some in landes and tenants, and sume beyng heires apparaunt unto their auncesters, for the lucre of suche substaunce been oft tymes taken by mysdoers countarie to their Will, and after maried to such mysdoers or to other by their assent, or defoulled, to the greate displesire of God and contarie to the Kyngs lawes and disparagement of the seid Women and utter hevynesse and discomforte of their frendes and to the evyll example of all other." Sir Edward Coke's discussion of the abduction statute also includes the "deflowering" of heiresses in the same category as forced marriage. *The Third Part of the Institutes of the Laws of England* . . . (London, 1644), 62.

28. 4 and 5 P. and M., c. 8. This emphasis on the girls' inheritance was reiterated in later legal treatises. Coke claimed that this statute applied only to heiresses, as did Sir Matthew Hale (Coke, *Third Part of the Institutes*, 62; [Matthew Hale], *Pleas of the Crown; or, A Brief, but Full Account of Whatsoever Can Be Found Relating to That Subject* [London, 1678], 101). According to William Blackstone, the punishment varied sharply depending on whether the abducted were an heiress: if so, then the abductor would be punished with death if found guilty (without benefit of clergy), and her inheritance would go to her next of kin; if not, then the abductor would be punished with a prison term of two to five years. But the text of the law is somewhat obscure on the last point, as shown by Coke's and Hale's interpretation that this law applied only to heiresses (Blackstone, *Commentaries*, IV, 208–210). George Webb, *Office and Authority of a Justice of Peace* . . . (Williamsburg, Va., 1736), 219, construed this statute as did Blackstone. The 1598 statute

In granting parents control over young heiresses' marriages, this law broke new ground. Why then? Queen Mary, who was in power in 1558, was Catholic. This law actually coincided with the Catholic Church's deliberations at the Council of Trent over marital issues, which resulted in requirements that all marriages had to be formal to be valid. The Council of Trent was the core of the Counter Reformation response to Protestant challenges, some of which addressed marriage norms. Second, this law makes more sense in the context of increasingly entailed estates, since the heiress's father in these cases could not disinherit her. At its base, the law raised the issue of when a girl's consent to marriage could be valid. Girls under the age of sixteen on some level were presumed incapable of exercising sufficient judgment about an appropriate marriage partner, especially when a man had a strong incentive to disguise his true intentions.[29]

The second move toward strengthening parental power over the marriages of sons and daughters grew out of the English ecclesiastical councils, but it was halfhearted. In an attempt to bring the Church of England more in line with both the Catholic Church (since the Council of Trent) and with Puritan concern about parental consent to marriage, in 1604 the Church of England encouraged its ministers, under threat of suspension for three years, to gain parental consent to each marriage that involved a son or daughter under age twenty-one before posting the banns. However, it had a glaring defect in that the older clandestine marriages were still valid. Thus, although formally the Anglican Church, by the early seventeenth century, encouraged the consent of parents to the posting of banns, since private promises were still binding in the eyes of the ecclesiastical courts that upheld or dismissed marriages, such a guideline provided little more than an exterior patch. Even in the early eighteenth century in England, many ministers married those under twenty-one without their parents' consent. These ministers argued that they upheld the true guidelines of the church: only the personal consent of those marrying was necessary.[30]

(39 Eliz. I, c. 9) specified only heiresses and women who were property owners (widows and such) but also stressed the woman's rather than her parents' consent: "Marrying or defiling [any woman] against her will is felony without clergy."

29. On the deliberations (which lasted more than fifteen years) at the Council of Trent about parental consent to marriage and clandestine marriages, see Brundage, *Law, Sex, and Christian Society*, 563–565.

30. *Constitutions and Canons Ecclesiastical, Treated upon by the Bishop of London* . . . (London, 1678), 28–29.

No minister, upon pain of Suspension per triennium ipso facto, shall celebrate Matrimony between any persons . . . when Banns are thrice asked . . . before the

Realizing this broader religious context sheds light on the efforts to enforce parental consent to marriage in British North America. There, aside from a feeble attempt by Virginians to follow the Canons of 1604, Puritans set the pattern: the first laws that enforced parental power were made by the Puritans in New England, and similar laws were passed in England during the Interregnum. While Virginia legislators were the first to bow toward parental consent, private (or clandestine) marriages were still freely practiced, so that the law about parental consent to public marriages could be evaded, just as in England. In Massachusetts and Plymouth, however, as in Pennsylvania later, private (or clandestine) marriages were punished, effectively making the rules about parental consent stronger. Also, over the long term, largely through common law reforms, the minimum ages for marriage were raised, first by making the canonical ages to confirm marriages (of twelve for girls and fourteen for boys) the minimum ages, and then by raising those ages still farther.

Virginia encouraged parental consent to the marriages of minors along lines that essentially echoed the ecclesiastical guidelines of the English canons of 1604. A 1632 law provided that formal marriage celebrations should include parental consent (via either the banns or the license) for children under twenty-one. However, it did not void or otherwise invalidate clandestine marriages, which remained valid in the eyes of the Anglican Church. Neither did it provide any punishments for private marriages or punish ministers or children who violated the law. In 1646 Virginia gave some teeth to the 1632 law when it began to fine ministers who violated it. Virginia also added, in 1643, 1658, and 1662, requirements for the consent of masters and mistresses to the marriages of servants, the violation of which punished the servants themselves. According to the 1643 law, a marriage without the consent of the master or mistress would lengthen the servant's term of indenture: for men by "one complete year," and for women by doubling their entire term of service. Thus Virginians provided a means to punish the participants in informal marriages in this situation, at least. Since most indentured servants were under twenty-four—indeed, many were as young as ten or twelve

---

Parents or Governours of the Parties to be married, being under the age of twenty and one years, shall either personally, or by sufficient Testimony, signifie to him their Consents given to the said Marriage.

Marriage licenses, however, could also avoid the requirement for parental consent. My thanks to Ruth Bloch for bringing my attention to this ecclesiastical policy.

On marriage licenses: Gillis, *For Better, for Worse*, 94; Swinburne, *Treatise of Spousals*, esp. "Of Publick and Private Spousals," 193–202.

when the indenture began—these laws prohibited the marriages of many young people. In 1662 they also briefly sought to invalidate clandestine marriages, but this law seems to have expired and was not repeated.[31]

A law of 1696 provided a much heavier fine, five hundred pounds, for ministers who married "any person or persons" without parental consent, and it added the same fine for clerks who issued licenses without parental consent. The 1696 law removed any mention of age. A law of 1705 went even further: Virginia ministers who married people outside of Virginia would still be punished if they violated Virginia's provisions, and clerks who issued licenses without parental consent could be punished for forgery in addition to the five-hundred-pound fine. It reinserted, however, an emancipation age of twenty-one. The 1662 attempt to invalidate private marriages was not repeated in later laws or the Virginia legal guide, and such mariages continued to be valid in Virginia as in the Church of England. Still, it is clear that formal marriages were much more legally sound and that informal marriages could pose threats to inheritance and legitimacy.[32]

Virginia also passed two different versions of the English abduction statute, in 1696 and then in 1789. The English law was also included in eighteenth-century legal guides for justices of the peace for Virginia and Pennsylvania and in the most-used manuals on the common law. It is unclear how consistently the law about abduction was enforced in any of these colonies. There

31. 1632: William Waller Hening, ed., *The Statutes at Large: Being a Collection of All the Laws of Virginia* . . . (rpt. Charlottesville, Va., 1969), I, 156–157: "No mynister shall celebrate matrimony betweene any persons without a facultie or lycense graunted by the Governor, except the baynes of matrimony have beene first published three severall Sundays or holydays in the time of devyne service in the parish churches where the sayd persons dwell accordinge to the booke of common prayer, neither shall any mynister under any pretense whatsoever joyne any persons soe licensed in marriage at any unseasonable tymes but only betweene the howers of eight and twelve in the forenoone, nor when banes are thrice asked, and no lycense in that respect necessarie, before the parents or guardians of the parties to be married beinge under the age of twenty and one years, shall either personally or by sufficient testimony signifie unto him theire consents given to the said marriage."

1643: I, 252–253; 1646: I, 332; 1658: I, 438–439; 1662: II, 50–57, 114.

32. 1696: ibid., III, 150; 1705: III, 441–446; 1748: VI, 80–85. Webb, *Office and Authority of a Justice of Peace*, 219-221. On this question see also James Horn, *Adapting to a New World: English Society in the Seventeenth-Century Chesapeake* (Chapel Hill, N.C., 1994), 201–213; Kathleen M. Brown, *Good Wives, Nasty Wenches, and Anxious Patriarchs: Gender, Race, and Power in Colonial Virginia* (Chapel Hill, N.C., 1996), esp. 93–94. Brown interprets a 1624 order as a broad condemnation of private vows, but it might well have referred only to improper vows when the correct words were not spoken (a common theme in ecclesiastical cases of this period).

probably was less call for it in Pennsylvania or Massachusetts, where entail was less common. Yet this is an important omission, since both colonies (unlike Virginia) passed comprehensive criminal codes. When judges did invoke this law in Virginia in 1784, the jury found the abductor not guilty.[33]

Virginia's marriage laws were more focused on controlling property, particularly servants and slaves. Most of the laws affecting marriages can be better described as trying to consolidate patriarchal control, or the power of masters, than as trying to consolidate parental or even paternal control. Virginia was controlling poorer white young people's labor by preventing their marriages (at the same time as masters had unparalleled control over their servants' bodies, because of the long-term contracts in Virginia and no real laws protecting them). By not recognizing the marriages of slaves as valid, masters likewise gained greater flexibility and control over those enslaved. But parents could only suggest children's marriages, subject to the same restraints as the old Catholic marriage law, at least until Virginia passed its 1696 law. Throughout, Virginians seemed less concerned with who had the capacity to contract (in reason, judgment, reaching puberty, "fansy," or other qualities) than with implementing and absorbing patriarchal power in its various dimensions (which fitted with Allestree's sermons). Virginia's laws appealed, for their legitimacy, to the rightfulness of parental and hierarchical power generally. By reinstating the age of twenty-one into laws giving parents control over marriage, Virginia was cautiously equating the legitimacy of this law with an ability to consent. But this nine-year space when parental control had no age boundaries is very revealing.

Because masters could effectively prevent their servants' marriages until age twenty-four with harsh penalties for those who married earlier, indentured servants usually did not marry until about that age, meaning that their ages at marriage can be seen as legislatively determined. In other words, there was a fundamental difference between when, in human life, one might be attracted to a member of the opposite sex and when they actually marry, both for the wealthier and for the poorer members of Virginia society: one group was marrying sometimes even before puberty, the other marrying

33. See Hening, ed., *Statutes at Large*, III, 150 (1696), XIII, 7–8 (1789). The 1696 statute reiterated only part of the 1558 abduction statute from England. Any girl between the ages of twelve and sixteen who contracted matrimony automatically forfeited her inheritance until the husband died. Unlike with the English statute, however, the husband was not punished.

The English law was cited, for example, in Wood, *Institutes* (1738), 425. The 1789 Virginia law could in fact have been a response to the 1784 case (involving twelve-year-old Susannah Brown, discussed in Chapter 5), since, after it was dismissed, the girl's father wrote a petition to the Virginia legislature.

substantially later. And through that difference runs status. Indeed, one must only acknowledge the similarities between England and Virginia in this pattern of both poor and elite marriage in the sixteenth and seventeenth centuries to understand that the shortage of women in seventeenth-century Virgina cannot be the sole explanation for such marriages of girls, especially since elite boys could (and did) marry so young as well.[34]

The Puritans, on the other hand, sought to revise the performance of the marriage ceremony in a variety of ways. In New England, as they would in England later, they abolished ecclesiastical courts and gave the common law courts, and justices of the peace, control over marriage, thus making it a civil ceremony. Massachusetts also gave parents control even over courtship, with enforceable legal remedies, in 1647.

> And whereas God hath committed the care and power into the hands of parents for the disposing their children in marriage, so that it is against rule to seek to draw away the affections of young maidens, under pretence of purpose of marriage, before their parents have given way and allowance in that respect; and whereas it is a common practice in divers places for young men irregularly and disorderly to watch all advantages for their evil purposes, to insinuate into the affections of young maidens, by coming to them in places and seasons unknown to their parents for such ends. . . .
>
> It is further ordered, that whatsoever person from henceforth shall endeavor, directly or indirectly, to draw away the affection of any maid in this jurisdiction, under pretence of marriage, before he hath obtained liberty and allowance from her parents or governors or, in absence of such, of the nearest magistrate, he shall forfeit for the first offence five pounds.

That parents had the right "for the disposing their children in marriage" is strong language, implying that parents have a sort of property right, in their daughters in particular (though this is not as strong as Allestree's language). Notice also that this right was extended to their "governors" (guardians) in the absence of parents. Massachusetts never repealed this law, and fathers invoked its provisions on several occasions during the seventeenth century.[35]

34. See, for example, Lois Green Carr and Lorena S. Walsh, "The Planter's Wife: The Experience of White Women in Seventeenth-Century Maryland," *William and Mary Quarterly*, 3d Ser., XXXIV (1977), 542–571.

35. *The Charters and General Laws of the Colony and Province of Massachusetts Bay* (Boston, 1814), 151. For such laws in other New England colonies as well as prosecution under such laws, see Ruth H. Bloch, "Women and the Law of Courtship in Eighteenth-

Comparing the laws passed in early Massachusetts with those in Virginia reveals that Virginians were more concerned about status than parental powers per se, and vice versa for Massachusetts. In Massachusetts, the Puritan ideology led to a more universal application of parental power. Massachusetts was not concerned only with heiresses and initially gave no age limit to parental control. Massachusetts laws also strove to prevent clandestine marriages. Laws of 1692 and 1695 gave justices of the peace the power to solemnize all marriages and required parental consent, without which the justice could be fined fifty pounds. By regulating courtship itself, Massachusetts sought more control over private marriage vows, although they never explicitly rejected them.[36]

The Puritans in the Rump Parliament under Cromwell went much further than Massachusetts to punish those who married without parental consent (at least under age twenty-one). During the Interregnum, parental consent was made mandatory before a marriage could be performed, and then it was to be performed only in front of a justice of the peace. All other marriages, including informal marriages, were outlawed. Parents were given the power to initiate harsh punishments against those who "stole" sons or daughters under age twenty-one in order to marry them. Thus, in effect, the Rump Parliament not only formalized the marriage process, so that valid marriages had to be performed before a justice of the peace with such verified parental consent, but also mandated that any person who sought to marry a partner under age twenty-one without that consent could be prosecuted by the parents, guardian, or overseer.

> If any person by violence or fraud shall steal and take away, or cause to be stolen or taken away, any person whatsoever, under the age of One and twenty years, with intent to marry the said person in this Commonwealth, or in any other place; such person or persons so stealing or taking away, or causing to be stolen or taken away, shall forfeit his and their whole Estate real and personal, one half thereof to the Commonwealth, and the other half to the use of the party so taken away, to be recovered by any suit on behalf of the Commonwealth, or by any Action in a court of Record, brought by their Parent, Guardian or Overseer, and shall farther suffer strict and close Imprisonment, and be kept to hard labour in some House

Century America," in Bloch, *Gender and Morality in Anglo-American Culture, 1650–1800* (Berkeley, Calif., 2003), 78–101. The penalties increased with each additional violation.

36. *Acts and Resolves of the Province of Massachusetts Bay* (Boston, 1869), I (1692–1714), 61 (1692), 210 (1695); Bloch, "Women and the Law of Courtship," in Bloch, *Gender and Morality in Anglo-American Culture*, 79–80, 84.

of Correction or other publique Work-house during life; ... any pretended Marriage that at any time hereafter shall be obtained by any such violence or fraud, is hereby declared null and void.[37]

The punishment for the offender would be to forfeit all his or her property and money and be imprisoned at hard labor for life. Furthermore, such "pretended marriages," made without parental consent, were "null and void." The Long Parliament also made all clandestine marriages and all marriages made by boys under sixteen and girls under fourteen completely void. With these reforms, they followed Protestant reformers on the Continent and the advice of John Calvin.

This law by itself reveals the tensions within Puritan thought between egalitarianism and hierarchy: it asserted parental power; it also raised the minimum age of consent. But in circumscribing children's consent and giving a great degree of power to parents, it drew on older norms that had belonged to lords. This strong language of "stealing" proclaims a kind of property right of parents in their children.

This law was repealed, as was all Interregnum legislation, with the restoration of Charles II in 1660, and clandestine marriages were common in England during the seventeenth century; indeed, through the mid-eighteenth century. Marriage licenses were also frequently issued without parental consent. Despite at least twenty-one bills, especially in the decade after the Glorious Revolution, when eight different bills arose from either the House of Lords or the Commons, Parliament could not agree on reform until 1753. This was largely because the Lords and Commons had different concerns: the Lords was more concerned about father's or guardian's consent in order to prevent socially unequal marriages; the Commons was more concerned about raising the minimum age to marry.[38]

Pennsylvania's policies were clearly influenced by these unsuccessful English attempts. Pennsylvania prescribed fairly strict parental consent laws from its very inception, although the first pre-Penn laws specified parental consent only to the marriages of daughters. In fact, the laws of the duke of York from 1676, possibly reacting to the Dutch Calvinist background of the colonists, specified eighteen for women and twenty-one for men as the minimum ages for marriage: "All persons to bee accompted of fitt age to Marry, when the

---

37. C. H. Firth and R. S. Rait, eds., *Acts and Ordinances of the Interregnum, 1642–1660* (London, 1911), II, 715–718. "Any Contract or Marriage had or made before the respective ages aforesaid, shall be void and of none effect."

38. See, especially, R. B. Outhwaite, *Clandestine Marriage in England, 1500–1850* (London, 1995), chap. 3, and 88; also Gillis, *For Better, for Worse,* chap. 3; Macfarlane, *Marriage and Love in England,* chap. 7.

Man shall attaine to the age of twenty one and the Women of Eighteene years." Some people taking this to mean that women over eighteen did not need parents' consent, a few months later the law was revised: "Itt is to bee understood, of such persons onely as are under guardianship, and itt is not in any wayes to take of the naturall bounds of Duty and obligation which Children owe to their parents."[39] Parental consent to the marriages of sons as well as daughters was made mandatory and given sharp teeth by laws of 1700 and 1701, which fined both the ministers (twenty pounds plus damages to "parties grieved") who performed marriages without parental consent and the participants (ten pounds). "All marriages not forbidden by the law of God shall be encouraged, but the parents or guardians shall, if conveniently [they] can, be first consulted with, and the parties' clearness of all engagements signified."[40]

However, the law neglected to mention justices of the peace, who could also perform marriages, and thus left a glaring loophole and allowed the provision to be systematically flouted. A law of 1730 remedied that:

> Whereas the good intention of an act of assembly of this province, entitled "An act for preventing clandestine marriages," hath been very much eluded, by reason that no proper penalty is by the said law imposed upon [the] justice of peace . . . : Be it enacted . . . That no justice of the peace shall subscribe his name to the publication of any marriage . . . unless such justice shall likewise have first produced to him a certificate of the consent of the parent or parents, guardian or guardians, master or mistress of the persons whose names or banns are to be so published, if either of the parties be under the age of twenty-one years or under the tuition of their parents or be indent[ur]ed servants, if such parent, guardian, master or mistress live within this province.[41]

Not only parents, then, but also guardians and masters were given authority to dissent from—and thus to prevent—marriages of those under twenty-one. Through these laws, the concept of a minority, during which young persons could not make their own decisions, was taking more definitive shape. This inclusion of guardians and masters, of course, follows earlier such legislation during the Interregnum and in Virginia and Massachusetts. This 1730 law

---

39. Staughton George, Benjamin M. Nead, and Thomas McCamant, comps., *Charter to William Penn, and the Laws of the Province of Pennsylvania, Passed between the Years 1682 and 1700, Preceded by the Duke of York's Laws in Force from the Year 1676 to the Year 1782 . . .* (Harrisburg, Pa., 1879), 37, 65.

40. James T. Mitchell and Henry Flanders, comps., *The Statutes at Large of Pennsylvania, from 1682 to 1801* (Harrisburg, 1896–1911), II, 21, 22, 161–162. It is clear that, though these marriages were punished, they were still valid.

41. Ibid., IV, 152–153.

was the first that provided a minority age limit to parental power in Pennsylvania. Even this age limit, however, could be more broadly construed, since "under the tuition of their parents" could last longer. Parental power was thus circumscribed by maturity.

The Reform of 1753

England finally passed marriage reform—a dramatic one—in 1753 via a coalition between the elite (especially in the House of Lords) and the lawyers. An Act for the Better Preventing of Clandestine Marriages (26 Geo. II, c. 33) not only enabled parents actually to void the marriage of their children if they were under age twenty-one when they promised marriage, but it invalidated all clandestine marriages. From then on, only formal marriages would be legal. The provision of voidability actually echoed the initial calls of the Reformation and reinstated a measure of the reforms of the Interregnum. This act responded less to concerns about parental power per se and more to concerns about the ability of teenagers to make judgments about appropriate marriage partners. These debates illuminate the centrality of the discussion of children's rationality to these reforms. The debates and this law echoed across the Atlantic through the legal treatises that Americans followed during the late eighteenth and early nineteenth centuries.

Of the bills to reform marriages between 1660 and 1753, most had originated in the House of Lords and were concerned principally with young heirs or heiresses who married beneath their rank. The bills that began in the House of Commons usually sought to raise the minimum age of marriage and to control clandestine marriage (they were less eager to impose firm patriarchal control). The Reform of 1753 was a Lords' bill, and it was debated over many days, with frequent late-night sessions. One member remarked that "it has been harder fought than ever matter was in my Father's memory." That it carried the day in the Commons, despite the vocal opposition of cogent critics such as Charles James Fox (who had himself married Caroline, the daughter of the duke of Richmond, without the duke's consent, causing an uproar), was thus in many ways a victory for the elite. Yet it succeeded because its compromises, especially the general ban on clandestine marriages, had broader appeal.[42]

42. Outhwaite, *Clandestine Marriage*, esp. 1–17, 86. I also examined drafts of bills proposed in 1719 and 1736 (*Reasons for Passing the Bill to Prevent Clandestine Marriages* [London, 1719]; *A Bill for the More Effectual Preventing Clandestine Marriages* [London, 1736]). Earlier debates include Henry Gally, *Some Considerations on Clandestine Marriages* . . . (London, 1750); *A Vindication of Mr. Fisher's Private Missive* . . . (Glasgow, 1751). For the

The debates over the bill, both inside and outside Parliament, centered on whether giving such control to parents would lead to vast consolidations of wealth among the aristocracy, on what marriage meant, and at what age a person was capable to consent to it. They also dwelt at length on whether parents could consent for children in such a weighty and permanent matter. Many were also concerned about the consequences of banning private marriages—the poor might find it too costly to marry, and unwary girls could be seduced by false promises that before would have been binding.[43]

Many pamphlets appeared in the wake of this controversial bill. *A Letter to the Public for the Better Preventing Clandestine Marriages* summarized "the substance of what hath been offered in the late debates" in Parliament at the same time as it justified the act's stand on clandestine marriages.

> Men and Women grown to Maturity, must be left to judge in this Matter for themselves; because nobody can, in common Sense, be appointed by

---

1753 debates in Parliament, see Outhwaite, *Clandestine Marriage*, chap. 4, esp. 86, 88, 93; *Commons Journals*, XXVI, 827, 830, 832–834; and *Parliamentary History of England*, XV (London, 1813), 1–87, wherein some of the speeches are reprinted. The Marriage Act and the controversy surrounding it were also discussed in some newspapers; see *Boston Post-Boy*, Jan. 14, 1754; *Boston Weekly News-Letter*, July 11, 1754; and *Boston Evening-Post*, Jan. 28, Mar. 11, 1754.

43. Outhwaite, *Clandestine Marriages*, 86–93. None of the following tracts appears to have been republished but might well have circulated in America. Alexander Kith, *Observations on the Late Act for Preventing Clandestine Marriages* (London, 1753); *A Letter from a By-Stander Containing Remarks . . . for the Better Preventing of Clandestine Marriages* (London, 1753); *A Letter to the Public . . . for the Better Preventing of Clandestine Marriages* (London, 1753); [Henry Stebbing], *An Enquiry into the Force and Operation of the Annulling Clauses in a Late Act for the Prevention of Clandestine Marriages . . .* (London, 1754); *Some Considerations on the Act to Prevent Clandestine Marriages . . .* (London, 1754); Henry Stebbing, *A Dissertation on the Power of States to Deny Civil Protection to the Marriages of Minors Made without the Consent of Their Parents or Guardians* (London, 1755); Henry Stebbing, *A Review of the Principles of the Enquiry concerning the Operations of the Annulling Clauses . . .* (London, 1755); Tanfield Leman, *Matrimony Analysed . . .* (London, 1755); Joseph Sayer, *A Vindication of the Power of Society to Annull the Marriages of Minors . . .* (London, 1755); [James Ibbetson], *Some Observations on Two Pamphlets Lately Pubished . . .* (London, 1755); [William Dodwell], *A Letter to the Author of Some Considerations . . .* (London, 1755); James Tunstall, *A Vindication of the Power of States to Prohibit Clandestine Marriages . . .* (London, 1755); John Fry, *The Case of Marriages between Near Kindred Particularly Considered . . .* (London, 1756).

Later tracts include Charles Lind and James Lind, *Essays on Several Subjects: Viz. I: On the Late Act to Prevent Clandestine Marriages . . .* (London, 1769); Francis Douglas, *Reflections on Celibacy and Marriage* (London, 1771); [Francis Douglas], *Considerations on the Causes of the Present Stagnation of Matrimony . . .* (London, 1772).

Law to think for the rest of the Nation. But Infants or Minors, may and ought to be restrained, as wanting the degree of Judgment necessary to discern the Consequences of their Actions.

By way of evidence, the author offered several examples of youths who might, under the sway of passion or false ideas of "love," succumb to matches below their appropriate station in life—"a young Girl of fifteen, for instance, one of the Daughters of a gentleman, happening to fall in Love with her Fathers's Butler," or "a boy of sixteen, heir apparent to an Estate, whose Fancy is captivated with his Mother's Maid"—one of the chief concerns of the promoters of this legislation.[44]

The author sought to avoid such unequal matches by giving parents more control over their children, using arguments that the understanding and reason of those under twenty-one are not fully developed, whether for marriage or any other contract.

> We find, that the understanding grows, by Time and Years, from the first dawn of Reason thro' several gradations to maturity. Would it then be just, in a government, to leave a human creature to its own guidance and direction, before this Faculty hath acquired any considerable degree of strength? Would it be reasonable, in a legislature, to let a Girl, at ten years old, have the management of her fortune, with liberty to lend it to whom she pleased; and to determine for herself upon the Nature of the Borrower's Security? At what Time then shall she be trusted with this Power? When she attains sufficient judgment to resolve with Prudence how she shall dispose of her fortune.[45]

In comparing the ability to contract marriage to the ability to make other types of contractual arrangements (such as those involving goods and money), he was insinuating that marriage was largely a financial contract. He was also seeking a unified law of contract.

Since decisions about marriage are even more important than decisions about money, any youth under twenty-one needs help:

> But if Minors ought not, for their own Sakes, to be invested with the Disposal of themselves in Marriage, there can be no Doubt in whom the Authority shall be placed to controul them. . . . Parents or Guardians: who, by the Relation they stand in, cannot but be of Years to judge, and are at the same time the most likely of all others to have the Welfare of the Infants at Heart.

44. *A Letter to the Public for the Better Preventing of Clandestine Marriages*, 33–35.
45. Ibid.

Those who should aid them are parents and guardians, who have "a Disposition to promote their welfare, with judgment and Experience to discern the method of doing it, promising much greater probability of attaining this end, than what in Reason can be expected from their own casual, undirected, inconsiderate inclinations."[46]

Henry Stebbing, an orthodox minister of the Church of England, launched the most vocal opposition to the Marriage Act in a series of three pamphlets. Like the anonymous author above, Stebbing agreed that a unified capacity to contract should exist, regardless of type of contract. He denied, however, that parents should have any role in their children's contracts, championing a position similar to the pre-Reformation Catholic stance. His opposition to the Marriage Act initiated a fierce debate (outside Parliament) about the meaning of consent to marriage. His initial discussion of contract sounds as though it came directly out of an eighteenth-century legal treatise.

> In every Contract there is supposed a capacity of contracting: and therefore all Contracts made where there is no capacity are *ipso facto* null and void. It must be considered then what the capacity is which qualifies persons to make the marriage contract; and this I take to be the very same (neither more nor less) with that which qualifies them to make any other contract; viz. 1. That they be *sui juris,* or that the thing about which they contract be in their own power; and 2. that there be a sufficiency of Reason or Understanding to enable them to discern what it is about which they contract, and what is the proper End, Use and Effect of such a contract.

His discussion of the general ability to form legal contracts led to a specific analysis of consent to marriage:

> This capacity [to contract] follows close at the heels of the capacity of Procreation, and the natural appetite to marriage. Every man confesses this who marries his daughter at fifteen, sixteen, or seventeen years of age (which there is scarce a Parent in the Kingdom who would not do so for the sake of an advantageous match) and the reason is plain. For the contract arises, not from the parents consent, but from the Consent and will of the child; which consent, if the child were not in a capacity of contracting, would be absolutely of no force.[47]

46. Ibid., 36, 42 (mislabeled 34).

47. [Stebbing], *An Enquiry into the Force and Operation of the Annulling Clauses,* 6. He also had written against, among others, George Whitefield and Benjamin Hoadly, champions of toleration.

Only the persons directly entering the contract can give valid consent: parents cannot contract on their behalf. To Stebbing, the in-between compromise of their parents' providing the judgment for them misses the main element of the nature of any contract: the consent between the two parties involved. Stebbing especially objected to the power of parents to annul marriages: children should be able to choose their own marriage partners when they are old enough to have "the natural appetite to marriage," to wit, "at the heels of the capacity of Procreation" (puberty).

Joseph Sayer responded to Stebbing: parents should have power over their children until "children are capable of knowing and avoiding danger." "I do not mean to compare Matrimony to being burned or drowned; but it may be said, that it had been better for either of these to have happened to him in his infancy than to enter imprudently into it." Parents are responsible, he thus implied, if their children are burned or drowned while young—or make a wrong alliance. He then generalized: "Parents have in a state of nature a dominion over all the actions of their children till they attain the use of reason: and that so far as to make what is done without their consent void." Until children reached roughly twenty-one, their parents should be able to void any agreements made without their consent. Though he does not mention Locke or Pufendorf, Sayer was drawing on their political and philosophical theories about the capacity to contract within the state of nature.[48]

Another response to Stebbing's pamphlet, by James Ibbetson, cited Pufendorf, Locke, and Hooker by name, invoking some of the same arguments used to justify the American Revolution. He thus applied democratic-republican political theory (which gave fathers the power to consent for their children to political contracts, based on an argument that they could not sufficiently exercise reason) to this more private contract. They could act only in concert with the child.

> But an appeal is made [by Dr. Stebbing] . . . to the Friends of Liberty, whether the annulling clauses as to Minors will stand with the Principles of Liberty. The natural Liberty of man to be free from any superior Power upon Earth, and to have only the Law of Nature for his rule, and the liberty of man in society to be under no other power but that established by consent, nor under the restraint of any law but what the legislative shall enact according to the trust reposed in it: again; *the liberty of a Man at years of discretion, and the subjection of a child in his nonage, are so consistent and so distinguishable,* that I do not see how liberty, natural or civil, is at all con-

48. Sayer, *The Power of Society to Annull the Marriages of Minors,* 11, 24.

cerned in the Question. . . . But *there must be a fixed time in Society, when Men are to begin to act like free Men; and till that time, no acts of Manhood are required or allowed of; no oaths of fidelity or allegiance to the government are exacted, no voluntary contracts are esteemed valid.*[49]

"The liberty of a Man . . . so distinguishable" is a near-direct quotation from John Locke's *Two Treatises of Government*, which, with Ibbetsons's citing of other authorities, shows the influence of republican political theory and its handmaiden natural law on these marriage debates.

Ibbetson was also conscious of the problems with applying Locke and other natural law theorists in this case: the marriage contract was perpetual, while other contracts were not. Locke had said that parents could not make perpetual contracts for their children, only temporary ones, which ceased with the maturity of the child. Ibbetson might have thought that the additional consent of the child eliminated this logical difficulty: but it is a difficulty at the core of this theory. Thus the debate over the Marriage Act confronted the central issues related to the transition from authority based on inherited right to authority based on the consent of the reasonable.

Stebbing's third pamphlet critiqued, sentence by sentence, each of the pamphlets written in response to him. Citing the passage that Ibbetson had taken from Locke, Stebbing commented on it at some length. His main point was, not to disagree with the comment itself, but to disagree with what characterized reason and understanding. Stebbing argued that puberty was the appropriate age at which a person had sufficient understanding to choose a marriage partner, and thus recalled older Catholic ecclesiastical policy. Yet he gave a different authority to that older policy, to try to make it more compatible with natural rights theories, by claiming that children reached puberty at the same time as they attained the "full use of their understanding."

> [The author states] that "the Liberty of a Man at Years of Discretion, and the Subjection of a Child in his Nonage, are so consistent and so distinguishable," that he does not see how Liberty natural or civil, is at all concerned in the question. It is familiar with these writers to treat all, whom laws declare to be minors, as mere babes, who scarce know their right hand from their left: as if the ordinances of states could create common sense, and GOD himself could not give it. But the Author should have remembered, (and the Reader, I hope, will not forget) that the Persons, whom we have been considering under the appellations minors, are those who have ar-

49. [Ibbetson], *Some Observations on Two Pamphlets*, 23–24 (my italics); cf. Locke's "Second Treatise of Government," pars. 61–62.

rived to the FULL USE of their UNDERSTANDING, though not furnished (perhaps) with that cunning and worldly policy, which some seem to think necessary to qualify them to chuse husbands or wives.[50]

Stebbing thus implied that parents had only more "cunning and worldly policy," not more understanding, than their children. Even though he disagreed about when understanding could be obtained, all of these authors agreed that someone's fully developed understanding was necessary to a contract: all of those who supported the Marriage Act put this age significantly beyond puberty, at twenty-one. Although the law stayed in force, debate continued for the next seventy years over whether parents should have the power to void the marriages of underage children. Parliament finally repealed the provision allowing parents such powers in 1823 (while attaching other penalties to such marriages).[51]

Blackstone reviewed these arguments in his *Commentaries*. "Much may be, and much has been, said both for and against this innovation [the Marriage Act] upon our antient laws and constitutions," he began. He sought— along with the authors of the pamphlets—to generalize about a law of contract that should apply to marriage as well as to other contracts: What are the boundaries of children's capacities and of the responsibilities of parents? When do some incapacities end and others begin? What should be done when a permanent contract extends across the boundary of children's "incapacities" into their later adult capacities? He concentrated on the ability to contract in a way that incorporated the new epistemology: an entire section in his discussion of legal marriages concerned the "capacity of parties" to contract. Four conditions could bar parties from marrying who were willing to consent: an existing prior marriage, mental incapacity, want of age, and lack of consent of parents. All but the first related to the question of children's contracts. Before a particular age and level of judgment are obtained, "no voluntary contracts are esteemed valid": no contract can be valid without "reason; without a competent share of which, as no other, so neither can the matrimonial contract, be valid."[52]

Blackstone did not fully rationalize the marriage law in that he encountered the same difficulty about the dual age of consent over which Ibbetson stumbled. Blackstone defined "want of age" as boys under fourteen and girls under twelve. If contracted before those ages, their marriage could be voided at their discretion after they reached them (Blackstone held that a divorce was unnec-

50. Stebbing, *A Review of the Principles*, 50.
51. 4 Geo. IV, cc. 16, 23, 76 (1823).
52. Blackstone, *Commentaries*, I, 426.

essary). He emphasized, not puberty as the logic for those ages (which had served to justify those ages under the Catholic Church with respect to marriage agreements), but "imbecility of judgment"—so far, he was in agreement with those who supported and those who opposed the Marriage Act. But he still had to confront the sticky question of whether parents should be able to consent once that "imbecility of judgment" had been cured, presumably, by reaching those ages. And he was in the awkward position of summarizing a recent and controversial law, which he could not, for obvious reasons, openly attack. Instead, he assumed a contradictory stance that partly justified it, by blurring the extent of the changes it had introduced. He also effectively co-opted what had been ecclesiastical jurisdiction for the "common law."

In smoothing over the abrupt change, he made it seem that consent had always been the primary issue in officiating marriage, which to a certain degree it had: "Consent, not cohabitation, makes the marriage." But this emphasis on formal, informed consent rather than actions did blur the ways in which both had been seen as essential to the marriage, especially since consent had often been informal. More critically, Blackstone acknowledged that lack of parental consent had not traditionally been a bar to marriage. "By the common law, if the parties themselves were of the age of consent, there wanted no other concurrence to make the marriage valid: and this was agreeable to the canon law." He tried to make parental consent seem "natural" by giving examples of other nations that had parental consent laws and by interpreting previous English legislation to emphasize the continuity of the new legislation. He argued that earlier statutes had also imposed limitations by requiring banns or licenses: the banns would inform the parents by rumor, the licenses required their consent. Yet he nowhere legitimized parental power by logic: his failure to do so, indeed, is underlined by his concluding comments on this question: "Restraints upon marriage, especially among the lower class, are evidently detrimental to the public, by hindering the encrease of people; and to religion and morality, by encouraging licentiousness and debauchery among the single of both sexes; and thereby destroying one end of society and government, which is, *concubitu prohibere vago*." Blackstone's contradictory stance on this law is important, since his volumes on the English common law became the means by which most lawyers of the late eighteenth and early nineteenth centuries understood legal history and the logic of the law. Strictly by logic, Blackstone did not support the law and indeed offered a mild critique; in terms of history, he upheld it partially by emphasizing its meager precedents.[53]

53. Ibid., 422, 425–426. The statutes that Blackstone refers to as precedents were in fact not precedents, except obliquely; they require only banns and licenses for

Given Blackstone's contradictory stance on parental consent, it is difficult to measure his influence. However, post-Revolutionary legislators set firmer and often lower ages for required parental consent; in that they moved toward both Locke's and Blackstone's positions on this question. The Massachusetts laws of 1692 and 1695 were reiterated after the Revolution, except that the power of parents over boys ended at age twenty-one, and over girls at age eighteen. The 1786 law mandated that "where a male, under twenty-one years, or a female under Eighteen years of age, is to be married, the consent of the parent, guardian or other person, whose immediate care and government such party is under, if within the Commonwealth, shall be first had to such marriage." Massachusetts coupled this slightly lowered age for parental consent with a clause that voided completely marriages between a boy under fourteen and a girl under twelve. Pennsylvania's 1730 marriage law was still unchanged in 1849. The basic provisions of Virginia's marriage law continued to be reiterated, with slight alterations, by laws of 1748, 1780, and 1792.[54]

----

public marriages (and punish clergy for officiating over private marriages). While licenses required parental consent and these laws made private marriages more difficult (at least if clergy were to officiate), they did not prevent clandestine marriages or require parental consent. See 6 and 7 Will. III, c. 6 (duties on marriages, 1694); 7 and 8 Will. III, c. 35 (marriage without banns, 1695); 10 Anne, c. 19 (customs and excise, 1711).

54. *The Perpetual Laws of the Commonwealth of Massachusetts, from the Establishment of Its Constitution in the Year 1780, to the End of the Year 1800* . . . (Boston, 1801), I, 217–218, 321–322. The justice or minister was to be fined fifty pounds for such violation, with two-thirds of the fine for the county and one-third for the informer for such marriages without parental consent. In 1785, Massachusetts also had made void the marriages of those under the "age of consent," by which they almost certainly meant girls under twelve and boys under fourteen. An earlier law had more vaguely prohibited the prosecution of those who married initially within the age of consent, "that is to say, the man fourteen years of age, the woman twelve," as adulterers or polygamists because the marriages were invalid. *The Acts and Resolves, Public and Private, of the Province of the Massachusetts Bay* . . . (Boston, 1869–1922), I, 172.

On Pennsylvania: James Dunlop, *The General Laws of Pennsylvania, from the Year 1700 to April 1849* . . . (Philadelphia, 1849), 82–83.

On Virginia: Hening, ed., *Statutes at Large*, VI, 81–84 (1748), X, 361–363 (1780); Samuel Shepherd, ed., *The Statutes at Large of Virginia, from October Session 1792 to December Session 1806, Inclusive* . . . (1835; rpt. New York, 1970), I, 134–135.

Blackstone's *Commentaries* generally had a profound influence on American law, especially after 1772 upon the publication of the first American edition.

The Dilemma of Marriage for Contract Theory

Marriage posed an exquisite challenge for contract theory as laid out by John Locke and others, particularly as that theory began to shape practice. Contract theory itself said nothing about the age of consent to marriage. By implication, a child could not consent to marriage until the same age as in other contracts, that is, twenty-one. Any contract formed before that age was voidable at the age of majority, whether made by the child or the parents. Yet, given the realities of pregnancy and childbirth and a reluctance to grant divorce in such cases, this logic led to many practical problems. Contract theory gave parents some control over their children during their minority but limited that control in that parents could not make a contract that would last beyond childhood—they had only "temporary rule and jurisdiction," to use Locke's phrase. To allow parents alone to consent to any permanent contract, for example, violated the logic. Alternatively, setting the age of puberty for the ability to consent implied both that such a low age could be set respecting other capacities and gave more autonomy to teenagers than most parents wanted to give. (Perhaps a youth's judgments were not yet formed enough at fifteen to detect, for example, the difference between a fortune hunter and a lover.)

The compromise was to require parental consent for underage marriages, but such a solution still did not fit logically with contract theory, since marriage was permananent and unavoidable. Indeed, parental control over marriage, while sanctioned by many Puritans, fitted more into the arguments of patriarchal ideology than into consent-based theories. By providing age limits to that influence, the laws fitted somewhat with contract theory. Yet here were the piercing questions: How much authority should parents have over children, and for how long? Locke's "temporary rule and jurisdiction" might cover a lot or not very much. Do parents have a kind of property in their children? The emphasis on parental power that grew out of the Reformation—at the same time as the Reformation emphasized individual choice— had this same tension embedded in it. The strangest thing about these questions is that, on some fundamental level, there was a possibility of agreement between those who supported a status-based patriarchal ideology and those who supported a contractual basis for society. The Marriage Act of 1753, with its provisions actually allowing parents to void marriages by minor children, can be seen almost as an unholy alliance between the two. But it was primarily supported by those who wanted to uphold status within society, by those who worried, that "a young Girl of fifteen, for instance, one of the Daughters of a gentleman, happening to fall in Love with her Father's Butler" would marry him rather than "her equal"; or that "a boy of sixteen, heir apparent to an Estate, whose Fancy is captivated with his Mother's Maid," would marry her in order to "gratify an impetuous passion." Their central concern was about status. The Lords increasingly became the house to support that law. In 1765 and 1781 Whigs led successful votes in the Commons to repeal the 1753 act on the grounds that the law unjustly prevented love matches and promoted the wishes of parents concerned only with status, bills then blocked by the House of Lords.[55]

Thomas Jefferson's proposal to adopt the provisions of the English Marriage Act, then, indicates that Jefferson was willing to extend the arguments in contract theory to justify status in some cases. He proposed that parents be able to void marriages made by children under twenty-one, in the revision of the laws of Virginia he oversaw after the Revolution. His suggestions were not adopted by the Virginia legislature, and neither Pennsylvania nor Massachusetts considered granting parents the ability to void the marriages of underage children. Judges' decisions on this question varied, but significant decisions continued to generally uphold the right of a girl over twelve to marry, except where the minimum marriage age was raised by statute. Other decisions fined the clergymen or justices but upheld the marriages themselves.[56]

In the longer term, however, some decisions allowed parents to void marriages of children in cases where the parents could show that the child had unstable judgment. In a New York case of 1846, for example, a sixteen-year-old girl whose family "moved in the higher walks of life" married an Irishman hired by her father to make repairs on his house "who could not read or write." Her parents removed her from her new husband and committed her to the Bloomingdale Asylum for the Insane. Not relying on a straightforward argument that parents should consent to the marriages of minors, but instead making an argument about her mental capacities, the parents succeeded in annulling the marriage. As evidence of her mental incapacity, they said that she was disobedient to her parents, "her judgment weak, passions

---

55. *A Letter to the Public for the Better Preventing of Clandestine Marriages,* 33–35; Outhwaite, *Clandestine Marriage,* 96. Also see my essay "Beyond Education: Thomas Jefferson's 'Republican' Revision of the Laws Regarding Children," in James Gilreath, ed., *Thomas Jefferson and the Education of a Citizen: The Earth Belongs to the Living* (Washington, D.C., 1999), 48–62.

56. Julian P. Boyd et al., eds., *The Papers of Thomas Jefferson* (Princeton, N.J., 1950–), II, 557; Michael Grossberg, *Governing the Hearth: Law and the Family in Nineteenth-Century America* (Chapel Hill, N.C., 1985), 78, 107, 330–331 n. 40 (an excellent discussion).

violent," and "took pleasure in the sufferings of animals." By 1925, parents routinely annulled the marriages their children made while under varying ages in different states with the same arguments about mental incapacity.[57]

Parental control was also strengthened by the decreasing tolerance for informal marriages. Debate raged over the validity of informal marriages during the early decades of the nineteenth century, but in a more narrow form than it had taken in the previous two centuries: no one now argued that informal vows, by themselves, should make a marriage binding. The main voice to support informal marriages was a prominent one, James Kent, but he narrowed the definition of validity and thus reshaped the terms of the debate. Kent defended informal marriages *only* when they were accompanied by consummation. By using the term "common law marriages" he marshaled history to support him, but his definition had a stronger emphasis on *cohabitation*, and not simply on the exchange of vows. Kent's 1809 decision, popularized in his *Commentaries*, reshaped norms: some states became "common law marriage" states; others did not. (According to Chief Justice John Bannister Gibson of Pennsylvania in 1833, for example, not recognizing marriages that did not abide by the strict public ceremonies prescribed by law "would bastardize a vast majority of the children" in Pennsylvania.) A young couple could appeal to a "common law marriage" to validate informal vows in some states, so long as they had also consummated the vows. In many cases, however, courts refused to hold young men under age twenty-one liable for promises to marry in the future. So older norms legitimizing the informal vows of teenagers were largely abandoned.[58]

The practice of disallowing informal vows had begun in New England in the sixteenth century. By the early nineteenth century, Massachusetts had

57. *Reports of Select Cases Decided in the Courts of New York* (New York, 1883), I, 344–351; Mary E. Richmond and Fred S. Hall, *Child Marriages* (New York, 1925), 115. "A relatively large number of girls who are above the minimum age for marriage [without parental consent] are having their trial marriages annulled every year in the inferior courts on the ground that parental consent was lacking." They also give examples of young boys' marriages annulled by their parents (62–63, 95).

58. James Kent, *Commentaries on American Law* (New York, 1826–1830), II, 75–76; Grossberg, *Governing the Hearth*, 68–74. Bannister gave the opinion in *Rodebaugh v Sanks*, 2 Watts 9 (Pa. 1833). Of course, only since Blackstone could such informal marriages be called part of the "common law"; previous to the 1753 English Marriage Act these cases had been under ecclesiastical jurisdiction in England. See also Grossberg, *Governing the Hearth*, 40. Validating informal vows is not a simple issue, since "promises" of marriage (de futuro) were distinguished from actual marriages (de praesenti), even in the Middle Ages, by which form of the verb "will" was used in making the promise.

taken the strongest stand against them, repudiating even Kent. From the start it did not completely honor, or enforce, private contracts. While early Massachusetts laws and judges did fine persons who broke promises to marry in the future in some cases, they punished "disorderly" marriages, that is, those improperly performed. By the early 1800s their distaste for informal vows had led to strict rules. Vows not performed before an officiating justice of the peace were not legal. Indeed, in two suits where a justice of the peace witnessed the vows but did not officiate, the marriages were ruled invalid by the Massachusetts Supreme Court. In one case the couple exchanged vows in a tavern when a justice happened to be present; in the other the justice refused to solemnize the marriage, but the couple repeated the vows in his hearing. Kent's primary opponent on the subject of common law marriages during the early nineteenth century was Theophilus Parsons, chief justice in the Massachusetts court. Massachusetts, in fact, still did not accept "common law marriages" at the beginning of the twentieth century.[59]

While Massachusetts held private vows to be void by the early nineteenth century, and Pennsylvania, by the laws of 1700 and 1730, sought to eliminate private contracts, Virginia continued to honor private vows both in principle and, apparently, in practice. And in Maryland in 1786 the Reverend Henry Addison, an Anglican minister, contended, "If the rule was Established here that no marriage should be deemed valid that had not been registered in the Parish Books it would I am persuaded bastardize nine tenths of the People in the Country." This was not the Virginia legislature's preferred norm, which had moved strongly toward public marriage. Thus, in 1756, an uncle and guardian to a niece "under age" advertised in the *Virginia Gazette* that no minister should marry her to her intended husband, Mr. Snead, nor should any clerk issue a license. Even the fact that he thought it necessary to advertise, however, reinforces the notion that the marriage laws were laxly enforced. In a later court case heard in Frederick County, Virginia, in 1784, the county court upheld twelve-year-old Susannah Brown's marriage to her former tutor, even though it had been made informally, without an appropriate minister and without her father's consent. Her father wrote: "The pretended marriage was celebrated by a Peter Miskler, a Person who is neither a minister of the church of England, nor licensed to marry as a minister of any other Religious society[,] by a written form received from a Lutheran Schoolmas-

---

59. Bloch, "Women and the Law of Courtship," in Bloch, *Gender and Morality in Anglo-American Culture*, 84–85; Grossberg, *Governing the Hearth*, 71–73, where these later cases are discussed. Also see Chilton L. Powell, "Marriage in Early New England," *New England Quarterly*, I (1928), 323–324. Powell did not think that informal marriages were valid in early Massachusetts.

ter[,] without the use of the Ring, without license or publication of banns." He also claimed that "neither of the parties made the Responses, and that there was no person present but Miskler and his wife." That Brown emphasized that no rings were exchanged and that the vows were not repeated indicates that he criticized the contract under the old rules that had been used to gauge informal marriages and recalls the questions of the ecclesiastical courts to test the validity of a marriage in the 1560s. Clearly, Brown had some sense of the rules that governed informal contracts as well as formal ones (banns, license).[60]

Parental consent was most accepted under the Puritans in Old and New England. While the Revolution limited parental power over their children's marriages to when their children were under age twenty-one, it also consolidated the legal basis of parental power over minor children. The full set of assumptions that underlay the Revolution, which argued that true liberty and power should accompany the development of the understanding, upheld parental power until a child had reached maturity and developed a fullness of judgment. The only relaxation was that parental power was increasingly restricted to the time in children's life before they had reached an age of emancipation. The critical questions surrounded when such judgment was obtained and what limits could exist on parents' power. The disputes over marriage reveal the ambiguities on this question within contract theory as it was becoming more widely accepted in both England and America in the eighteenth century. They also point to the ways that these dilemmas were shaped by the Reformation emphasis on both parental power and individual choice. The debates over marriage both parallel and recall the debates over church membership and reveal the common ground accepted by both patriarchal and consent-based political ideology.[61]

In early Virginia, especially, the power of masters was much stronger than that of parents over their children. The draconian laws, which allowed masters to add significant time to the contracts of their servants if they married or, even briefly, to void such marriages, not only severely restricted the marriages of servants but also must have profoundly affected the illegitimacy rates. (Indeed, note that for a time the incentives encouraged illegitimacy: if a

60. Snead case quoted in Morgan, *Virginians at Home*, 35; Walsh, " 'Till Death Us Do Part,' " in Tate and Ammerman, eds., *Chesapeake in the Seventeenth Century*, 130 n. 9. (The Brown case was discussed in detail in Chapter 5, above.) Such cases are difficult to find during the colonial period: because the marriages were informal, they rarely appear in the records. We know of Brown's case only because the father wrote a legislative petition.

61. On the decline in enforcement, see Bloch, "Women and the Law of Courtship," in Bloch, *Gender and Morality in Anglo-American Culture*, 88–89.

servant girl had an illegitimate child, she would serve less time for her master, only one to two years and whipping, whereas marrying doubled the time of her original contract.) The powers given to masters to restrain such marriages increased servants' vulnerability and dependence at the same time as it increased masters' control over their labor.[62]

Throughout the colonial and early national period, the marriage vows of slaves were not generally seen as legally binding, which gave masters even more control over their status than over white servants. Slave marriages in Virginia and Maryland in the colonial period were mostly informal, although even there some masters considered slave marriages seriously enough that they provided a moral restraint on masters' selling them separately. Whereas earlier this disability was clearly linked to the fact that most people of African origin were not baptized, by the early nineteenth century courts justified denying enslaved people the right to contract marriage by comparing them to children in their ability to contract. Throughout, denying slaves the ability to form binding vows—regardless of their age—increased masters' control over them. Massachusetts, from the eighteenth century, on the other hand, legally recognized both slave marriages and divorces, indicating that enslaved people there had a status more similar to servants'.[63]

What do these changes really mean for the rest of society in England and America, those whom the laws permitted to marry? As informed consent became more important, younger marriages became more unusual, and real choice arguably increased. Did one have more choice over one's partner if one married at nine and could refuse the marriage at twelve or fourteen (and choose another partner)? Or when one could choose to marry the father's butler or the mother's maid at fifteen, only to be denied by one's mother or father (in one's best interest)? Or, with a father's consent, in particular, finding someone of one's own equal status (or higher)? The answer must partly depend on how common it was for prepubertal children to marry in the

62. My interpretation here both draws on and fits closely with that of Brown, *Good Wives, Nasty Wenches.*

63. For the early-nineteenth-century court cases on slave marriages, see Margaret A. Burnham, "An Impossible Marriage: Slave Law and Family Law," *Law and Inequality Journal,* V (1987), 187–225, esp. 207–214. Burnham also has material on Massachusetts courts' recognizing slave marriages as binding in the eighteenth century. Also see, especially, Brown, *Good Wives, Nasty Wenches,* 276–277, 358–361; Lorena S. Walsh, *From Calabar to Carter's Grove: The History of a Virginia Slave Community* (Charlottesville, Va., 1997), esp. 288 n. 12. On punishment for white-black relationships, see, among others, Philip D. Morgan, *Slave Counterpoint: Black Life in the Eighteenth-Century Chesapeake and Lowcountry* (Chapel Hill, N.C., 1998), esp. 398–412; Brown, *Good Wives, Nasty Wenches,* esp. chap. 6.

seventeenth century and before. And on whether one was the butler or the maid. Before the eighteenth century, teenagers without masters probably had greater control over their marriage choices. Yet inheritance played a more important role, then, as well, since land and property were critical for status and for support of a family (so that parental control over inheritance translated into influence). For daughters, especially, dowry was almost always at the discretion of the family, although sometimes it could be fixed by wills or other sources. For sons, the certainty of inheritance under entails (and the exclusion of younger sons) must certainly have limited fathers' powers more markedly, at least where such institutions existed, in England and Virginia. In colonial New England and Pennsylvania, fathers influenced their sons' marriage choices via inheritance.

A broad perspective on change over several centuries shows that the *minimum* age for marriage rose significantly. The evidence about prepubertal marriages in the sixteenth century is especially striking when compared to an early-twentieth-century American study of state norms on young marriages. Of 250 cases of "child marriage" examined in the early 1920s, 5 of the children (girls) were eleven, and only 61 were under fourteen.[64] On the other

64. Richmond and Hall, *Child Marriages,* 71. Fluctuations in average real marriage age, about which there have been many demographic studies and broad speculation, obviously relate to legislative restrictions on marriage age, but it is difficult to base arguments about parental control or the lack thereof on marriage age itself. Many factors play into such issues besides parental control over marriage, including mortality rates (of potential spouses and fathers during wars, for example), the availability of land, and the beginning of industrialization. Without question, industrialization, including protoindustrialization broadly defined as well as the availability of land in America, gave children more power to control their own marriages in that it enabled them to have income, independent of their parents' wishes, without their father's death. Still, industrialization itself inspired conflicting values: women's labor was more valuable when women were not at the same time rearing children, but the labor of the children was important as well. Particularly see Wally Seccombe, "The Western European Marriage Pattern in Historical Perspective: A Response to David Levine," *Journal of Historical Sociology,* III (1990), 50–74.

Teenage marriages, according to several modern studies, were the norm during the Middle Ages. On average age at marriage during the Middle Ages, see, especially, Walker, "Free Consent and Marriage of Feudal Wards," *Jour. Med. Hist.,* VIII (1982), 125, who cites other studies. On the average ages for marriage in New England, for which women's ages rose while men's fell, see Daniel Scott Smith, "The Demographic History of Colonial New England," in Michael Gordon, ed., *The American Family in Social-Historical Perspective* (New York, 1973), 397–415, esp. 406. On England's demographic statistics related to marriage age and bastardy, see, on marriage, Wrigley and Schofield, *The Population History of England,* 255; on bastardy, E. A. Wrigley, "Marriage, Fertility,

hand, the ecclesiastical court records for the 1560s involved girls under age twelve and boys under age fourteen. Many of these children were only eight or nine when they married. The youngest couple were two and three years old, respectively. Seen in a grand panorama, since the marriages in the sixteenth and the twentieth century were both occurring within the guidelines of the common law broadly defined (since the "common law" in the eighteenth century simply adopted ecclesiastical law), this shift illustrates how the common law, while keeping reference to the ages of twelve for girls and fourteen for boys, could shift its meaning. The change is especially dramatic when we realize that the authors of this study recommended that legislated minimum ages for consent to marriage increase even more. The minimum ages for marriage had already been raised in most states above the eighteenth-century level of twelve for girls and fourteen for boys by 1925. In fact, of the forty-eight states and the District of Columbia in 1925, only fourteen retained the minimum age of twelve for girls; nine had raised it to fourteen; eight had raised it to fifteen; seventeen had raised it to sixteen; and one had raised it to eighteen. The single most common age requirement for females was sixteen. "Ripe age" to marry, in short, rose from seven to sixteen.[65]

The developments in children's ability to consent to marriage contracts can be categorized into three rough stages. In the sixteenth century, all contracts by those children over age seven were valid. They could seek a divorce if they had not ratified the marriage by consummation or words, and, past twelve and fourteen, the marriage contract was generally binding. Between the seventeenth and nineteenth centuries, owing to an increasing sense that valid contracts should be based on intentional choice and that those under age twenty-one, especially, could not exercise such choice, these earlier norms were moderated. Twelve and fourteen gradually became the minimum ages to contract marriage, and parents began to serve as a kind of guarantor of the validity and the beneficial nature of the marriage contract. Legally, individual choice by young people was weakened and undermined over time in favor of parental guidance during a lengthened "minority." The minimum ages for completely binding marriages, once linked to puberty, shifted upward, and parental consent for marriages began to be enforced until these sons and daughters reached age eighteen or twenty-one, depending on the state. Partly due to this emphasis on judgment, which did not completely capture the

and Population Growth in Eighteenth Century England," in R. B. Outhwaite, ed., *Marriage and Society: Studies in the Social History of Marriage* (New York, 1981), 157. Also see David Levine, "Industrialization and the Proletarian Family in England," *Past and Present*, no. 107 (May 1985), 168–203.

65. Richmond, *Child Marriages*, 20, 45.

human attributes necessary for a good marriage, these reforms spawned their own reactions. Should not other human attributes, such as passion or affection, which usually were distinguished from judgment by the late eighteenth century, play a role in the choice of a marriage partner, much more of a role than they would play in other types of contracts? Yes was the answer, certainly, of many novelists by the early nineteenth century.[66]

The last stage, which cannot fully be explored here, is indicated by the minimum marriage ages of the early twentieth century given above, which were higher than those at the beginning of the nineteenth century. Parents' ability to guarantee and approve had been partly dispensed with, and, instead, legislators began to hold that, under age sixteen, for example, a girl could not contract any valid marriage, regardless of who helped her to approve the contract. In some states, the minimum age for marriage began to match the maximum age requiring parental consent, thus effectively eliminating parental consent; given the expectation that a marriage contract is permanent, this position more closely matched that of Locke or Blackstone.

Children's ability to choose was most limited when they were seen legally to be property. The idea of children's being property seems to have been most developed with patriarchal ideology, although even there it was hedged and not necessarily common. Filmer did not say it specifically, but he did grant parents power even over their children's lives and put no limits on that power. "The father of a family governs by no other law than by his own will, not by the laws or wills of his son or servant."[67] Protestants emphasized parental, particularly father's power in a way that clearly fed into patriarchal ideology; at the same time, they emphasized individual consent in a way that challenged that authority. So some Protestants and Puritans sometimes used a language implying that children were property too, in terms, for example, of parents' rights to choose whom their children should marry. But most democratic-republican contract theory, inasmuch as it addressed this question, did not consider children as property, and placed various limits on parents' powers, which corresponded to their children's attaining maturity of judgment. It is in this sense that we should see, for example, Locke's insistence that parents had neither the power of life and death over children nor

66. Among others, see Stone, *Family, Sex, and Marriage*; Degler, *At Odds*; Ellen K. Rothman, *Hands and Hearts: A History of Courtship in America* (New York, 1984); Karen Lystra, *Searching the Heart: Women, Men, and Romantic Love in Nineteenth-Century America* (New York, 1989); Nancy F. Cott, *The Bonds of Womanhood: "Woman's Sphere" in New England, 1780–1835* (New Haven, Conn., 1977).

67. Robert Filmer, *Patriarcha; or, The Natural Power of Kings* (London, 1680), in Johann P. Somerville, ed., *Patriarcha and Other Writings* (Cambridge, 1991), 35.

the right to make contracts for them that extended beyond their minority (and even then could not bind them into contracts that violated some of their fundamental rights). Equating persons with property was more of a patriarchal argument, one with older roots in the law of feudalism. (Consider Littleton's fifteenth-century treatise on land law, for example. Littleton spoke of the heritability of villeins and the heritability of lands in the same breath; because they were of the same type, they could go together. According to the most important fifteenth-century treatise on land law in England, people could be property.) But earlier this relation had been about station or rank (as relations between lord and villein), not about parents and children.[68]

Why did these changes happen? One might attribute them, as did the editor of a volume on child marriages in English ecclesiastical courts, to changes in the laws about wards after 1660. Because marriage avoided wardship altogether (which was a kind of tax on the estate), the very institution of the court of wards encouraged parents to marry their children off young. Once married, they were seen as adults in the eyes of the law. Changes in mortality probably also contributed to this change—if parents wanted to see their children married before they died, then those children would have to marry somewhat younger. So the fact that average mortality (for richer and poorer) was closer then to forty than to our own seventy-plus undoubtedly accounts in some part for these changes. But the changes in these laws were not stimulated by demographic transformations; the most dramatic shifts in longevity have come in the twentieth century, a century with few corresponding changes in marriage law (with the exception, notably, of divorce). So did they result from shifting ideas about status? Partly. But these shifting ideas about status were themselves embedded in a complex logic of contract. The most important roots of these changes originate in changing ideas—religious and philosophical and political—about the right to consent and what that meant. The Roman Catholic Church had always made consent to marriage important. But the meaning of that consent changed over time.

The Reformation both placed more emphasis on parental consent and tried to give marriage a more permanent footing, one to which the husband and wife had more personal commitment (and from which they were less willing to stray). Marriages arranged among children (and indeed arranged marriages generally) were seen as more likely to result in infidelity. At the same time, many Protestants sought to desacralize marriage. Doing so indicates that they were more accepting of divorce. Puritans in Connecticut, in

68. Edw[ard] Coke, *The First Part of the Institutes of the Lawes of England*, 2d ed. (London, 1629), e.g. 121b.

particular, were also more open to divorce (as Americans would become after the Revolution). And perhaps this is one of the most important changes in marriage law after the Revolution; the inchoate judgment of children could lead them to the wrong choice. Therefore, they (and others equally misled) should be able to unmake that choice. But the change in divorce law was also fundamentally about other questions related to contract: specifically, if the other person has broken one side of the contract (in this case through infidelity), should not the wronged person be able to dissolve the contract? Questions about the ability to dissolve contracts were also at the core of contract theory and clearly underlay the American Revolution itself: Witness, to give the most obvious example, the crimes laid at the feet of George III as evidence that he had broken his covenant with the people in the colonies, giving them liberty, thereby, to also dissolve theirs.[69]

The increasing attempts to equate marriage contracts with other types of contracts during the seventeenth and eighteenth centuries, seen especially in the debates surrounding the English Marriage Act and enshrined in legal treatises, almost certainly aroused their own response, since marriage contracts are more permanent and surrounded by different issues than, for example, contracts for goods. Voidability had entirely different consequences for marriage contracts than for other contracts: what would happen to children born to such a union? The idea that valid contracts of all types depended upon the full development of the understanding in those contracting gave parents, and their superior judgment, legal control over the marriages of minor children.

Some began to characterize teenagers, in particular, as ruled by passion, whereas adults were guided by reason. The earlier link between puberty and the ability to choose a mate was sharply dissociated. Just as a girl or boy needed to develop prudence and judgment in order to manage financial affairs, that one must wait to marry, or gain the approval of one's parents, until one had the same abilities to manage one's matrimonial contract. As one of the authors of a pamphlet on the 1753 English Marriage Act wrote: "Men and Women grown to Maturity, must be left to judge in this Matter for themselves; because nobody can, in common Sense, be appointed by Law to think for the rest of the Nation. But Infants or Minors, may and ought to be

69. On the dramatic changes in divorce law after the American Revolution, see Richard H. Chused, *Private Acts in Public Places: A Social History of Divorce in the Formative Era of American Family Law* (Philadelphia, 1994); Norma Basch, *Framing American Divorce: From the Revolutionary Generation to the Victorians* (Berkeley, Calif., 2001).

restrained, as wanting the degree of Judgment necessary to discern the Consequences of their Actions." These ideas originated in a rough form with the Reformation and developed during the political and epistemological debates of the seventeenth and eighteenth centuries. The dilemmas raised as they were put in practice had no easy answers, but they shaped the lives of everyone, rich and poor, white and black, old and young. Marriage is at the core of society, and the law's ability to recognize it as valid (or not) can determine where one lives, with whom, and under what conditions.[70]

In 1797, about two hundred years after the disastrous marriage of Frances to Sir John and Romeo to Juliet, and about one hundred years years after Mary Hathaway married and divorced William Williams, Jane Austen captured the immense shift in English marriage norms in her novel *Pride and Prejudice*. While semiarranged marriages were less common among the elite and child marriages had become legally weak, their specter still haunted the main characters. Lady Catherine wished Mr. Darcy, her nephew, to marry his cousin, her daughter Anne, to preserve the lineage of both, a marriage she and Darcy's mother had planned when Darcy and Anne were children. Although they did not marry as children, as they might have done a century or two before, Lady Catherine was still planning in the old manner: she actually referred to them as "engaged." While *Pride and Prejudice* criticizes both arranged marriages and young marriages, it also captures the continuities with the past, even if without their older legal basis, in late-eighteenth-century England. The novel builds on a tension between marriage based on status and one based on romantic love. When Darcy proposes to Elizabeth Bennet the first time, he admits his reluctance to form any attachment to her because of her social inferiority. When she is offended, he asks her, "Could you expect me to rejoice in the inferiority of your connections?—to congratulate myself on the hope of relations, whose condition in life is so decidedly beneath my own?" Lady Catherine, representative of the established order, later orders Elizabeth to leave Darcy alone, for the good of both of them:. "If you were sensible of your own good, you would not wish to quit the sphere in which you have been brought up." Ultimately, Elizabeth agrees to marry Darcy because her judgment and her heart are in harmony, as, Darcy makes clear, are his own.[71]

70. *A Letter to the Public for the Better Preventing of Clandestine Marriages*, 33–35.

71. Jane Austen, *Pride and Prejudice* (1813), ed. Anna Quindlen (New York, 1996), 140, 257: "My daughter and my nephew are formed for each other. They are descended, on the maternal side, from the same noble line; and, on the fathers', from respectable, honourable, and ancient, though untitled families."

Marriage seems to be something with permanent norms. Yet it became increasingly regulated and supervised during the seventeenth and eighteenth centuries. The basis of choice (and the meaning of that choice) shifted fundamentally, at least as those norms were legally circumscribed. In the process, these shifts shaped the choices (and shut doors and opened others) for real people like Mary Hathaway, William Fitzhugh, and Susannah Brown.

THE EMPIRE OF THE FATHERS
FROM BIRTH TO THE CONSENT OF WHOM?

*"It is said that our holding the Philippines is a violation
of the Declaration of Independence, in that that instrument declares
that all just rights of government depend upon the consent of the governed. . . .
If the literal interpretation of the [Declaration] is the true one, then nothing but
universal suffrage, by men, women, and children, could constitute a just
government. The instrument is to be restrained to the fitness and the reason
of things. All people are not capable of self-government."*
William H. Taft, August 26, 1904

When he encountered Blackstone's admission that "some of our common lawyers have held that an infant of any age (even four years old) might make a testament," the eminent legal scholar William Holdsworth wrote, "This is clearly a misprint for fourteen." Those who have stumbled across evidence of age limits of fourteen for jurors or of no age limits on voters before the late seventeenth century have usually hidden that information in statements to the effect that "there were always age limits" or assumed that de facto age limits existed even if not written into law. To see the mark of a young child on a labor contract or to run across evidence that a child of four or nine married makes us think that something must be wrong with the evidence. I was astonished, even after extensive work on these subjects, to discover that an "executor" of an estate could be a young child—even, as the treatises stated, one in its mother's womb.[1]

---

1. W. S. Holdsworth, *A History of English Law*, 3d ed., rewritten (Boston, 1923), III, 545n. This "misprint," however, went through at least fourteen editions of John Perkins's sixteenth-century legal treatise and through every edition of Blackstone's *Commentaries on the Laws of England* published during his lifetime, even though Blackstone revised his book in other ways. Since Perkins also justified this age, it was not a typographical error. (Although Perkins's book had slightly different titles, the passage remains the same, whether in law French or English. See, for example, *A Profitable Booke . . . Treating of the Lawes of Englande* [in law French] [London, 1565], 97; *A Profitable Booke . . . Treating of the Lawes of England* [1st English ed.] [London, 1642], 220, par. 503; *Treatise of the Laws of England in the Various Branches of Conveyancing* [14th ed.] [London, 1757], par. 503.)

"The qualities required for jury service were several. . . . Of these the most important

The common law itself is partly responsible for this inability to recognize how children's status has changed. With its reliance on custom, it has been seen by lawyers and judges themselves as having stable central concepts, especially the concept of meaningful consent. Yet, as Blackstone and Coke said so clearly, anything that is not reasonable is not precedent, an axiom that leaves open flexibility to new norms that ignore old practices when those no longer seem "reasonable." Statutes also influenced the common law. We should not be misled by the myth of the unchanging common law into trying to see all evidence that does not suit our assumptions as misprints.

Another explanation for why these differences in children's status and competence have been so easily dismissed is our strong assumptions about children's abilities and fathers' authority historically. It seems ridiculous to us that a four-year-old could make a will, or even that a fourteen-year-old could sit on a jury. Likewise, historians have tended to naturalize fatherly power, often equating it simply with "patriarchal power" and claiming that it has always been the norm, that fathers have always governed their children. But we historians make a critical error in thus naturalizing "patriarchal power." Patriarchal power has had different meanings over time, and those meanings were often at odds. In the seventeenth century, it was more about the power of lords than of fathers. Those like Sir Robert Filmer and James I who justified patriarchal power in the wake of the Reformation were trying to increase the authority of lords and lineage, to reify medieval, feudal norms. What fatherly power meant was critical to the debates over monarchy and lordship throughout the seventeenth century.[2]

If there is anything ancient about patriarchal power in England, it con-

---

were the age qualification. . . . The juror was to be an adult but not in his dotage": see P. G. Lawson, "Lawless Juries? The Composition and Behavior of Hertfordshire Juries, 1573–1624," in J. S. Cockburn and Thomas A. Green, eds., *Twelve Good Men and True: The Criminal Trial Jury in England, 1200–1800* (Princeton, N.J., 1988), 117–157, esp. 121. Of Lawson's sources (William Lambarde's *Eirenarcha*, Michael Dalton's *Officium Vice-comitum*, and Matthew Hale's *Pleas of the Crown*), however, the two who mentioned age (Lambarde and Dalton) excluded only "infants" under "14," a very different age than would be required of later jurors, and not "adult" in our modern sense. Albert Edward McKinley articulated the kinds of assumptions about age that have persisted in the modern historiography on suffrage in *The Suffrage Franchise in the Thirteen English Colonies in America* (Philadelphia, 1905), 35.

2. Gordon S. Wood, *The Radicalism of the American Revolution* (New York, 1992), for example, speaks of "ancient patriarchal absolutism" (147). Also see Peter Laslett, *The World We Have Lost* (New York, 1965), 3: "The patriarchal arrangements which we have begun to explore were not new in the England of Shakespeare and Elizabeth. They were as old as the Greeks, as old as European history, and not confined to Europe."

cerned the privileges of the lord, not the father. To understand how the authority of the lord was stronger than that of the father, consider the following passage from Sir Edward Coke's *Complete Copyholder*. "If a copyholder dieth, his Heir under the age of fourteen, . . . this Privilege of appointing the Heir a Guardian for the Copyhold Land (until he accomplish the age of fourteen) *de jure* appertaineth unto the Lord." Copyhold land was under a long-term lease, which could last up to "three lives": the lease descended from father to son for three generations. As feudalism declined in England, these leases became a replacement that retained their feudal roots. Such long-term leases were common practice in England and in Virginia and other colonies. The agreement to rent land from a lord meant that the father also bound his heirs into that obligation. The landlord would even have "custody" of his tenant's son and heir under age fourteen after his death. Only the son who was heir received a guardian, one appointed by the lord, and only until he turned fourteen. Even after turning fourteen the heir continued to be bound as his tenant. A father's action over land—over which he probably had little real choice—also bound his child's person such that the lord had authority over the child. Likewise, rules governing the binding of apprentices and servants privileged masters over fathers. The institution of "custody," so far as it existed, was primarily about the powers of lords and masters.[3]

By the late eighteenth century, however, fathers' legal authority over their own children was in most cases stronger than lords' or masters'. Blackstone's treatise fits much better with our preconceptions about what the common law of custody was—because he framed that law. "The legal power of a father (for a mother, as such, is entitled to no power, but only to reverence and respect) the power of a father, I say, over the persons of his children ceases at the age of twenty one, for they are then enfranchised by arriving at years of discretion, or that point which the law has established . . . when the empire of the father, or other guardian, gives place to the empire of reason. Yet, till that age arrives, this empire of the father continues even after his death; for he may by his will appoint a guardian to his children." The age for custody has increased to twenty-one with an argument that not until then can children attain reason. Fathers can name guardians for all of their children, not only the heir, and can do so even during their own lives. And lords no longer have privileges. Mothers, meanwhile, are mentioned, but only to exclude them. In the earlier

3. Edward Coke, *The Complete Copyholder* . . . (1641?), in Coke, *The First Part of the Institutes of the Laws of England* . . . , 11th ed. (London, 1719), 34. For details on inheritance law and long-term leases (which occurred frequently when land was entailed, for example), see my "Entailing Aristocracy in Colonial Virginia: 'Ancient Feudal Restraints' and Revolutionary Reform," *William and Mary Quarterly*, 3d Ser., LIV (1997), 307–346.

system, the rules of inheritance demarcated the lord's power; in the latter, a child's lack of reason and dependence demarcated the father's.[4]

These passages from Coke and Blackstone, then, capture the central transition in the nature of power and custody, from the power of the lord—to the empire of the father. During the earlier period, status, especially in terms of the power of lords, was embedded into the law. While their youth made it more likely that children had lower status, rank outweighed age in allocating power. Children could have power over others if they inherited young. Likewise, when poor, they were heir to their father's rental agreement (servant, in a sense, to a lord) or could be forcibly bound to a master. The struggle over the legal status of children thus was more than a struggle over simple custody. It was a struggle over the basis of power itself and whether that power should belong to lords or to fathers: to an aristocracy or to all men.

Or to all people, all men and all women? Therein lay the larger dilemma. These justifications and legal consolidations affected everyone, to varying degrees, in that they were about the fundamental ordering of society and about justice itself. The American Revolution applied an ax to ideas of inherited authority and the rights of blood and lineage. At the same time it helped to consolidate newer justifications of parental authority, which gave fathers, in particular, much more legal authority over children under twenty-one. Children became subjects incapable of consent, because they did not have reason. But the emphasis on their informed consent provided an excuse to deny equality and consent to others on the same grounds. Comparing women, blacks, and other groups to children in their reasoning abilities would become common in the wake of the Revolution for those who sought to legitimate elements of the older order.

We cannot understand the Age of Reason—the transformations in power and justice that emerged from its "democraticall" revolutions—unless we pay attention to the changing status of children. Grasping the differences in how childhood was understood and how children were treated yields us much greater insight, above all, into the struggles over consent and equality during this era of upheaval. "Consent" has not had an unchanging meaning. The new principle that consent must be "informed" and reasonable, which led to the exclusion of children, was part of what made democratic political ideology viable, acceptable, and, above all, legitimate. It became the marrow of the law. The principle that responsibility was necessary for both criminal matters and voting became established as consent became more important to the law, at the same time as birth and perpetual status became less important.

4. William Blackstone, *Commentaries on the Laws of England* (1765–1769; rpt. Chicago, 1979), I, 441, 450.

The transformation in children's status provides an index to the transformation in political authority during this period, from authority based on birthright to authority based on consent. Focusing on it reveals how fundamental that shift was, especially in America. The debates were not simply about overt political power: they were about legal identity itself. How the courts began to recognize individuals and their rights is so closely interwoven with these debates that understanding changes in attitudes—about custody, reason, responsibility, rights, equality—is integral to understanding the larger political shift. Status and inheritance, the rise of contract in the law, and the emergence of rules of evidence, to give some examples, were all intertwined with the political debates over whether the power of a government should originate in the consent of the people or in the hereditary and divine authority of a monarchy and aristocracy.

Yet, in the broadest sense, excluding children (and deciding who are children in their ability to reason) is highly contested terrain and does not necessarily lead to democracy. On the one hand, without a definition of meaningful consent we would have no democracy. If, as Hobbes maintained, consent can be forced (he held that children could and did consent) and inherited (a father's consent bound the child and grandchild and so on, with no right of resistance), then consent loses all meaning. On the other hand, does it therefore follow that the definition settled on in the eighteenth and early nineteenth centuries is the only one? The boundaries of "democracy" vary dramatically depending on how one defines meaningful consent: Who can consent? When? The boundaries of personal responsibility vary likewise.

The various changes in children's authority form a coherent pattern as distinctive as a blocked quilt. In the earlier period, teenagers could be on juries and in parliament and could manage estates. Younger children could testify, offer judgment, and have a civil identity. Their legal authority and status depended more on their rank than on their age. During the late eighteenth and early nineteenth centuries, from the restriction that one had to be thirty years old to hold a seat in the United States Senate to the new limits on children's liability for crime or the now powerful concept of custody, young persons could not legally make informed decisions—could not be held responsible for their actions and had no right to offer legitimate consent and to exercise authority over themselves or others. The pattern of age trumping rank repeats itself throughout the different categories of legal identity.

At the same time and in response to the same Revolutionary ideologies, children as a group gained legal provisions and protections with respect to their education and nurture. Indeed, the period after the American Revolution marked the origins of public education as a system for broad learning available to most children. This connected to Revolutionary ideals in two respects: as citizens they needed education to help them qualify for their future political roles and to fulfill the promises of equality of opportunity. Likewise, in response to the emphasis on paternal custody, protecting the nuclear family became more of a goal of social policy so that families were more likely to be permitted to stay together. Children, ideally at least, gained time to play as well as to learn. All children could potentially gain equality when they acquired reason.

The origins of this pattern of changes lay in the seventeenth-century democratic-republican reformers who argued for "reasonable" consent. They sought to make consent a viable basis for authority that could challenge and defeat feudal norms and patriarchal, hereditary authority and obligation. The reformers denied that blind or coerced obedience to a hereditary monarchy constituted legitimate consent. Consent was not hereditary, forced consent was meaningless, and even influenced consent should be invalid.

Their arguments for excluding children from consenting on the grounds that their consent was either forced or influenced grew out of the entwined religious and political struggles in seventeenth-century Britain over the basis of church membership and authority. Baptism soon after birth should not determine one's permanent religious identity. One's assent should embody faith, which required some understanding. Thus many men from Dissenting backgrounds, including John Locke, James Harrington, Algernon Sidney, and John Trenchard, began to use the language and ideology of religious radicals to delineate alternative grounds for political power. Patriarchal ideology, to the extent that it sought to justify older feudal norms about birthright, had allowed children to exercise power—indeed it had to. The reformers' strategy of attacking inherited birthright (and arguing that authority should instead rest on the "reason" and "virtue" that enabled judicious consent) made children with authority a primary target of their criticism. Age became a primary marker of just authority.

The transformations in the basis of political authority and the meanings of consent and equality sketched here suggest how religious reformers' ideas about legal and political consent shaped Enlightenment definitions. The interwoven church and state in England made the religious debates over church membership resonate in the debates over civil membership and authority. Puritans were thus critical reformers. The Reformation's emphasis on personal choice in religious matters was linked closely with a theory of governmental authority that made individual consent central.

Indeed, while Puritan New England did not adopt the most radical Protestantism, and was not democratic in the modern sense, it did put significant effort into framing when consent could and should create legitimate membership and accountability—whether to church, to government, or to more personal relations and exchanges such as marriage. New England thus established new and higher norms for competency in terms of age and laid out the basis for a radical philosophy of government.

These epistemological debates of the seventeenth century were not merely over abstractions but were about the fundamental ordering of society. In rationalizing, clarifying, and reforming English law, Edward Coke, Matthew Hale, and William Blackstone were encoding new norms from the theoretical debate about the nature and roots of political authority. Just as many "republican" political tracts sought to replace inherited authority with authority based on reason, merit, and virtue, these legal reformers extended their arguments beyond public figures to the exercise of private authority, such as children's ability to testify in court. This emphasis on reason and virtue thus became personal, subtle, and pervasive.

Some changes in the legal status of childhood emerged gradually (following common law reformers such as Coke and Hale), but many arose directly from statutes passed following England's two revolutions of the seventeenth century and the American Revolution in the eighteenth century. Especially during the seventeenth century, Pennsylvania and Massachusetts, Dissenter colonies, sought to break with English tradition more than did Virginia. The Revolutionary reforms were thus most dramatic in Virginia, which had adhered most closely to the English model.

These changes in children's legal status that drew respectively from Puritan and republican writings reveal deeper connections between those two strains of thought. Many post-Revolutionary commentators, from John and Abigail Adams to Alexis de Tocqueville, connected democratic thought with Puritan ideas, differentiating between the social systems that had developed in New England and Virginia by the late eighteenth and early nineteenth centuries based on their religious affiliation in the seventeenth. In his "Dissertation on the Canon and the Feudal Law," for example, John Adams equated the hierarchies of Anglicanism with political tyranny: both could exclude consent and reasoned thought. Abigail Adams compared Virginia's form of government and ideology to England's former feudal system, where children were born to a status: "Are not the Gentery Lords and the common people vassals?" Such a connection between Puritanism and "democratic and republican theories" was traced through historical sources and observation by Alexis de Tocqueville (after his tour of 1831–1832) in his *Democracy in America:* "Puritanism was not merely a religious doctrine, but corresponded in many points with the most absolute democratic and republican theories. It was this tendency that had aroused its most dangerous adversaries." He saw Puritanism as shaping different societies in the North and the South, with the North more favorable to equality and consent and so less attached to the privileges of hereditary status.[5]

To say that Massachusetts paid more attention to consent and sought to make consent more meaningful than either Virginia or England is not to say that Massachusetts achieved anything close to an ideal democracy. George Fox, the founder of Quakerism, railed against the hierarchies in New England and what he believed to be the failure of their reforming vision. The Massachusetts town meetings limited democracy in that they sought consensus and excluded the voices of religious dissidents in particular. In short, consent was often influenced. Many limits continued to exist within Puritan thought, and within New England legal institutions more broadly about who had the ability to consent. Choice was not equal to democracy.[6] Nor was the distribution of land or power as equal by the late eighteenth century as it had been during the seventeenth. Changes in political structure (seen most dramatically in the new charter forced on them in 1692, which replaced an annually elected governor with one appointed by the king), economic changes, and population growth had created quite a different society. Massachusetts, thus, both in laws and in social structure, became more anglicized during the eighteenth century. At the same time, Virginia was not as rigid a hierarchy as England itself, at least in terms of the hereditary power of the monarch and the lords in England. Yet, as Abigail Adams pointed out, the presence of so many slaves and the very unequal division of property and power even among whites made it more of an aristocratic system, where status depended on one's birth. Lord Dunmore could justifiably call forth the contradictions in Virginians' claims to authority based on equality and lack of representa-

5. [John Adams], "A Dissertation on the Canon and the Feudal Law" (1765), in *The True Sentiments of America* . . . (London, 1768), 111–143; L. H. Butterfield, Marc Friedlaender, and Mary-Jo Kline, eds., *The Book of Abigail and John: Selected Letters of the Adams Family, 1762–1784* (Cambridge, Mass., 1975), 112, 120; Alexis de Tocqueville, *Democracy in America,* trans. Henry Reeve (New York, 1985), I, 30–32, 35. Also see J. R. Pole, "Historians and the Problem of Early American Democracy," *American Historical Review,* LXVII (1961–1962), esp. 633–634; J. C. D. Clark, *The Language of Liberty, 1660–1832: Political Discourse and Social Dynamics in the Anglo-American World* (Cambridge, 1994), esp. chap. 2; Isaac Kramnick, *Republicanism and Bourgeois Radicalism: Political Ideology in Late Eighteenth-Century England and America* (Ithaca, N.Y., 1990).

6. B. Katherine Brown, "A Note on the Puritan Concept of Aristocracy," *Mississippi Valley Historical Review,* XLI (1954–1955), 105–112; George Fox, *Cain against Abel, Representing New England's Church-Hirarchy, in Opposition to Her Christian Protestant Dissenters* ([London?], 1675); Michael Zuckerman, "The Social Context of Democracy in Massachusetts," *WMQ,* 3d Ser., XXV (1968), 523–544.

tion when he issued his proclamation freeing slaves who would fight for the British. Virginia's system rested on that hierarchy. Thus the democratic-republican ideology of the American Revolution offered a more profound challenge to Virginia than to Pennsylvania or Massachusetts.[7]

Religious and political ideas continued to be connected in the eighteenth century but were not so interwoven as in the seventeenth. Factors weakening the connection included Anglican latitudinarianism (a broader acceptance of different kinds of faith and worship under the umbrella of the Church of England during the eighteenth century) and the fact that much of democratic-republican political theory was not explicitly religious. It was possible for Thomas Jefferson to read and be influenced by Locke and Sidney without focusing either on the origins of their principles or on their religious dimensions.

Likewise, by the late eighteenth century, the extent to which the judges and the legal system in various locales adopted Puritan or democratic-republican–inspired legal changes did not necessarily reveal their religious or even political ideology. That was because the sources that had once seemed radical had become neutral and established. Thus Sir Mathew Hale, while himself originally a Puritan reformer and head of Cromwell's commission to revise the code of English laws, had ceased to be seen as either a Puritan or a reformer by the late eighteenth century and had become an established authority who seemed innocuous. He was one of the most-cited common lawyers in eighteenth-century treatises. So a judge in late-eighteenth-century Virginia without Puritan or even republican sympathies might make a ruling that built on Hale's precedent.

Yet while religious ideas and political thought were increasingly separated, they were not wholly so. Thomas Paine's *Common Sense* is full of biblical appeals, many of them references to individual judgment. Congregational ministers were more likely to side with rebels than were Anglican. Baptists in Virginia in the 1770s were a threat to both the political and religious order. Many English supporters of the American Revolution were Dissenters. Indeed, their religious stance might have constituted the single most important determinant in their support for the Revolution. Even titles of many of the most popular republican political texts, such as *Cato's Letters; or, Essays on Liberty, Civil and Religious,* invoked religious toleration and political liberty in the same breath. For men such as John Adams, "the canon and the feudal

7. Jackson Turner Main, "The Distribution of Property in Post-Revolutionary Virginia," *MHVR*, XLI (1954–1955), 241–258; Brewer, "Entailing Aristocracy in Colonial Virginia," *WMQ*, 3d Ser., LIV (1997), 307–346.

law" were twin bastions of hierarchy and inequality, in church and in state. But choosing Revolution was not simply related to religious affiliation.[8]

The many strands of the Dissenting tradition and the fact that in some colonies Dissenters had become the establishment also shaped how religious ideas interacted with political ones. The Great Awakening of the eighteenth century, which spurred the development of a variety of New Light groups, Baptists, and Methodists, can be seen as one of the causes of the Revolution. The fact that the Great Awakening was characterized by its opponents—many of them Congregationalist ministers in New England, along with Anglican ministers in Virginia—as appealing to the "enthusiasm" of the people might seem to challenge the contention that religion which emphasizes reason encourages democracy. But the awakening did not appeal only to emotions. In a real way, across a variety of spectrums of belief, it was choice as opposed to inherited church membership that the Great Awakening was all about. While appeals to join a faith relied on a deep-seated emotional piety, most ministers also recalled the Protestant principle that faith should rest to some degree on reason. The Great Awakening thus awoke the questions and political radicalism of the seventeenth century.

The Discovery of Childhood

More than a generation of scholars have debated whether "the discovery of childhood" (as Philippe Ariès called it) occurred during the seventeenth and eighteenth centuries. But rather than a "discovery" of the innate nature of childhood, this book contends that definitions of what it means to be a child and an adult were changing in response to fundamental religious and political debates. Connecting the discussion of children to broad shifts in ideology

8. Rhys Isaac, *The Transformation of Virginia, 1740–1790* (Chapel Hill, N.C., 1982), chaps. 8, 11; [Adams], "Dissertation on the Canon and the Feudal Law," in *The True Sentiments of America*, 111–143; James E. Bradley, *Religion, Revolution, and English Radicalism: Nonconformity in Eighteenth-Century Politics and Society* (Cambridge, 1990), esp. chaps. 6, 9; Bradley, "The Religious Origins of Radical Reform in England, Scotland, and Ireland, 1662–1800," in Bradley and Dale K. Van Kley, eds., *Religion and Politics in Enlightenment Europe* (Notre Dame, Ind., 2001), chap. 5. On this question also see Ruth H. Bloch, *Visionary Republic: Millennial Themes in American Thought, 1756–1800* (Cambridge, 1985); Robert A. Gross, *The Minutemen and Their World* (New York, 1976); Robert M. Calhoon, *Dominion and Liberty: Ideology and the Anglo-American World, 1660–1801* (Arlington Heights, Ill., 1994); Bernard Bailyn, *The Ideological Origins of the American Revolution* (Cambridge, Mass., 1967); Patricia U. Bonomi, *Under the Cope of Heaven: Religion, Society, and Politics in Colonial America* (New York, 1986); Jon Butler, *Awash in a Sea of Faith: Christianizing the American People* (Cambridge, Mass., 1990).

not only explains origins but helps to delineate the nature of the changes more clearly. Modern childhood is a by-product of the Age of Reason, which designated children as those without reason. While changing attitudes toward children are of course reflected in art and literature, they are perhaps most profound in the law.

Indeed, only once we take the ideological debates into account and see the broad legal changes can we fully understand the changing perception of children in other venues. It is not, for example, that artists suddenly began to paint children accurately, as Ariès contends, but that the purpose of painting children changed. In the sixteenth and seventeenth and through much of the eighteenth century, most children who were painted or drawn represented elite emblems of authority. Thus these children were not simply children; their faces were made to bear great wisdom. A striking example of this is a drawing of the baby Henry VI as king (see Plate 1). He is portrayed as a wise monarch, even though he is so young that he has to be carried.

Just so, the face of Henry Darnall III, painted in Maryland about 1710, is drawn as wise and noble and mature, even though he is probably only eight years old (see Plate 2). He is given symbols of authority—the bow and arrow, the cape. Meanwhile, the boy who is his slave is clearly taller and older but is made to kneel and to gaze up adoringly at his master, showing reverence, submission, and dependence. He wears a silver collar to signify his servile status. This image idealizes what it means to be born to a status.

Acknowledging profound changes in our perception of children does not mean that earlier English and European societies had no conceptions of childhood. There are still many continuities between ourselves and sixteenth-century England in attitudes toward children, continuities framed, to some extent, by human biology. Obviously, an infant human will always be dependent on someone else for care, dependent on someone else, by physical necessity, to make most decisions on his or her behalf. Shakespeare's *As You Like It* (circa 1599) ascribed seven stages to life: "At first the Infant, / Mewling, and puking in the Nurses arms: / And then the whining Schoole-boy" (2.7.143–145). The first stage is the only one of complete dependence. Childhood, of a sort, is there, albeit, in this case, of a boy of a higher status in society who quickly assumes various responsibilities.

No historian would deny (and no medieval historian, especially, would think of it) that ideas about childhood existed in premodern England and Europe. Nor would they deny that the roots of the ideas about an age of reason lay to some extent within medieval canon and the older Roman civil laws of Justinian (and are represented in the thinking of Aquinas, Augustine, and Aristotle, among others). It also seems clear, as other scholars have shown,

Plate 1. Henry VI.
Circa 1422. Rous Roll Add. Ms. 48976.
Permission British Library, London

Plate 2. Henry Darnall III (as a Child).
By Justus Engelhardt Kühn. Circa 1710.
Courtesy Maryland Historical Society, Baltimore

that parents have usually loved their children—have displayed concern for their pain as well as their prospects, have grieved at their deaths, have enjoyed their presence, and have rejoiced in their successes. But some change was crystallizing around the ways in which childhood becomes distinguished from adulthood and in the nature of the boundaries accorded to different stages of life.[9]

This conceptual shift occurred within our ideas of justice but also within identity itself, within how we think about ourselves. Identity is constructed in many ways, not all of them mediated by culture, so that there are certain biological boundaries to the possibilities of change. A baby, whether described as mewling or cooing, cannot speak the same language as an adult. Yet even within culture and highly formalized systems of justice, broad variations can exist in how both identity and justice are constructed. The shift within principles of justice described here both put much more emphasis on reaching and passing an age of reason and defined childhood as characterized most significantly by an almost complete inability to exercise judgment. In doing so, it elevated reason beyond all other human attributes. It put perhaps too much weight on this sudden transformation, on the difference between a child and an adult.

What was once a new emphasis is still fundamental to our law and to our ideas about human development. John Locke's ideas about stages of child development, as in his *Essay Concerning Human Understanding*, have had a powerful long-term influence. The attainment of degrees of reasoning largely

9. As David Herlihy (*Medieval Households* [Cambridge, Mass., 1985], 158) summarized so beautifully after more than a decade of research by medieval historians: "The medieval family was never dead to sentiment; it is only poor in sources." Also see Frances Gies and Joseph Gies, *Marriage and the Family in the Middle Ages* (New York, 1987), 295–299; Linda A. Pollock, *Forgotten Children: Parent-Child Relations from 1500 to 1900* (Cambridge, 1983); Philippe Ariès, *L'enfant et la vie familiale sous l'ancien regime* (Paris, 1960); John Demos, *A Little Commonwealth: Family Life in Plymouth Colony* (New York, 1970); Ross W. Beales, Jr., "In Search of the Historical Child: Miniature Adulthood and Youth in Colonial New England," *American Quarterly*, XXVII (1975), 379–398; Edward Shorter, *The Making of the Modern Family* (London, 1976); Philip J. Greven, Jr., *The Protestant Temperament: Patterns of Childrearing, Religious Experience, and the Self in Early America* (New York, 1977); Lawrence Stone, *The Family, Sex, and Marriage in England, 1500–1800* (London, 1977); Karin Calvert, *Children in the House: The Material Culture of Early Childhood, 1600–1900* (Boston, 1992).

A few scholars have examined some of the laws about children. These include Beales, "The Historical Child," *Am. Qtly.*, XXVII (1975), 379–398; Ivy Pinchbeck and Margaret Hewitt, *Children in English Society*, I, *From Tudor Times to the Eighteenth Century* (London, 1969); Robert H. Bremner, ed., *Children and Youth in America: A Documentary History*, I, *1660–1865* (Cambridge, Mass., 1970).

defines the stages of childhood for twentieth-century thinkers, from Jean Piaget onward. Other, non-English European philosophers of the Enlightenment, whether influenced by Locke or by other natural law theorists (or by the Reformation more directly), would make some of the same connections between childhood, lack of reason, and dependence. Kant's essay "Was ist Aufklarung? [What Is Enlightenment]" defined it as a man's coming of age. Locke and other natural law theorists were critical characters in connecting the Reformation with the Enlightenment and democratic-republican-liberal political theory, part of an ideological web of influence that crossed national boundaries. Enlightenment thinkers across a wide spectrum—from Cesare Beccaria, Jean-Jacques Rousseau, and Voltaire to members of the Scottish Common Sense school such as Thomas Reid and Francis Hutcheson—accepted many of his ideas about reason and childhood.[10]

Slavery in the Empire of the Father

This transformation in the basis of authority and the status of children helps to answer questions about the connection between American slavery and freedom that have haunted American historians. The laws surrounding American slavery depended on the principle that one was born to a status that permanently circumscribed one's life. One could not choose not to be a slave, just as one could not choose to be a prince. Slavery was part of a patriarchal, neofeudal ideology where property and status were, ideally, fixed by lineage, within which people inherited their status, whether as villeins, tenants, or servants—and could also be property. As shown in this study, democratic-republican ideology challenged that older system of birth status. Should the child have the status of the father—or the mother? Can the status or the actions of the father or mother bind the child permanently, and all their posterity? The answer for the democratic-republican political theorists of the seventeenth century was a resounding no.[11]

Locke, for example, developed his opposition to hereditary status and his support for consent only gradually, but it was central to his later thought. Several pieces of evidence show that Locke was not opposed to hereditary right and slavery between 1669 and 1675, and might even have supported

10. Jean Piaget, *The Moral Judgment of the Child*, trans. Marjorie Gabain (New York, 1965); Samuel F. Pickering, Jr., *John Locke and Children's Books in Eighteenth-Century England* (Knoxville, Tenn., 1981), 14.

11. Edmund S. Morgan, *American Slavery, American Freedom: The Ordeal of Colonial Virginia* (New York, 1975), esp. 322, was the first to make the claim that American freedom rested on American slavery, a claim that has proven very influential.

both practices. But his views were changing over time in response to his involvement in religious and political controversies. His two essays on toleration, for example, written almost twenty years apart, in 1667 and 1685, were very different. The first advocated only limited toleration and supported hierarchy. The latter argued for significant toleration and advocated free consent in religious matters. His drafting of the Fundamental Constitutions of Carolina in 1669 (which set up a hereditary system of authority) and his buying shares in the Royal African Company in 1671 preceded the writing of his *Two Treatises of Government* by more than a decade. Perhaps they even helped to shape his arguments there against hereditary right and status.[12]

By 1685, he had very different opinions on the question of hereditary status: he was strongly opposed to hereditary slavery in particular. His *Two Treatises of Government* contended that, even in the case where a father has made war in an unjust manner and agrees to serve another in exchange for his life (the only case where Locke allowed any semblance of slavery), the father could never bind the child and the child could never be born into slavery. "I say, this concerns not their Children who are in their Minority. For since a Father hath not, in himself, a Power over the Life or Liberty of his Child; no act of his can possibly forfeit it: So that the Children . . . are Freemen." He continued to argue for the inherently free and equal status of children at length. Parents have authority over children only for their own benefit, and only for a limited time. A father cannot transfer his authority over his child to his master.[13]

Locke thus offered a resounding critique of slavery on the grounds that status cannot be inherited. One cannot be born into perpetual slavery, but can choose one's status when one is an adult. Even in childhood, the master of the father has no authority over the son.

12. Ibid., esp. chaps. 15, 16. On the extent of Locke's authorship of the Fundamental Constitutions of Carolina, see K. H. D. Haley, *The First Earl of Shaftesbury* (Oxford, 1968), 242–248. On Locke's involvement in the Royal African Company, see K. G. Davies, *The Royal African Company* (London, 1957), chap. 2, esp. 58, 62, 65, 65n. On slave imports: David W. Galenson, *Traders, Planters, and Slaves: English Market Behavior in Early English America* (Cambridge, 1986), table A-1. On Locke's increasing radicalism: Richard Ashcraft, *Revolutionary Politics and Locke's "Two Treatises of Government"* (Princeton, N.J., 1986), esp. 409n, 413n, and chap. 3. For more on this issue, including how the debate over inherited status played into the origins of slavery in the New World, see Holly Brewer, "Power and Authority in the Colonial South: The English Legacy and Its Contradictions," in Joseph P. Ward, ed., *Britain and the American South: From Colonialism to Rock and Roll* (Jackson, Miss., 2003), 27–51.

13. John Locke, *Two Treatises of Government*, ed. Peter Laslett (Cambridge, 1988), 393 ("Second Treatise," pars. 188, 189).

The Absolute Power of the *Conquerour* reaches no farther than the Persons of the Men, that were subdued by him, and dies with them; and should he Govern them as Slaves, subjected to his Absolute, Arbitrary Power, he *has no* such *Right of Dominion over their Children*. He can have no Power over them, but by their own consent, whatever he may drive them to say, or do; and he has no lawful Authority, whilst Force, and not Choice, compels them to Submission.[14]

"He can have no Power over them, but by their own consent" gets at the heart of the political system that Locke was constructing. One is not born to a status. This ringing indictment of slavery as it was then developing in England's empire was unequivocal. The only bound labor that Locke condoned was in fact a kind of indentured servitude that was punishment for the crime of levying an "unjust war," within which the servant had significant rights. Throughout his treatise, he developed ideas about what free choice means: in the case of labor contracts, as others, valid consent should be free from influence and force. The person agreeing to labor retains certain rights that he cannot grant to another person, that he cannot alien, including the responsibility of providing first for himself and his family. The implication of Locke's extended meditation on contracts is that unjust contracts, whether political contracts or for one's labor, can be broken (are voidable).

While some scholars have been captivated by Locke's limited justification of servitude, have indeed used it as a basis to contend that Locke supported slavery, they have failed to see how narrow that justification was within the seventeenth-century context in which he was writing. Both parts of his *Two Treatises of Government* were in essence a disputation against hereditary status. His careful case against slavery as it existed and was justified by patriarchal and feudal theory was part of his larger quarrel with birthright and birth status. Indeed, his position was virtually identical to—and indeed probably indirectly influenced—that expressed almost two hundred years later in the thirteenth amendment to the United States Constitution, which abolished slavery except as punishment for a crime. "Neither slavery nor involuntary servitude, except as punishment for crime whereof the party shall have been duly convicted, shall exist within the United States." For both Locke and the thirteenth amendment, such servitude could not be hereditary. Not to acknowledge Locke's dramatic criticism of hereditary slavery—in a world where slavery and perpetual status were so easily justified by the reigning authorities—is to profoundly misunderstand his legacy and the meaning of

14. Ibid., 393 (par. 189).

democratic-republican ideology. It is to ignore the way that dependency and inherited status were fiercely debated during the seventeenth century.

Thus if we take Locke on the basis of his later writings, through which Jefferson and other American Revolutionaries knew him, his position on slavery itself was consistent opposition. Likewise, those resonant words from the Declaration of Independence that all men are created equal—upon which Locke's ideas were so influential—insidiously undermined the basis for slavery. However, while Locke's emphasis on equality and reason challenged the legitimacy of slavery, he left (as this book has traced) a way to justify authority temporarily over children and arguably over all dependents. For those who sought to legitimize slavery under democratic-republican theory, this justification of temporary authority over children provided a means to do so that Locke did not in fact himself take: by comparing enslaved people to children. In the formative period of slavery, rationalizations for the practice had rested on assumptions about the naturalness of inherited status (for everyone) or on claims that Africans were heathens or savages or subjects. Africans were compared to children occasionally, as were all subjects within patriarchal theory. Now this comparison assumed a new power and relevance.[15]

From this perspective, Jefferson's position on slavery (and its interaction with Revolutionary ideology) becomes clearer. While Jefferson accepted that the basic Revolutionary principles, as embodied in his own draft of the Declaration of Independence, should apply to blacks, he took steps toward justifying slavery that Locke did not. On the grounds that people were created equal and the necessity of consent, he accepted that slavery was wrong: black slaves were born into an unequal status, and had not agreed to it. He wrote that keeping blacks enslaved and excluding them from any role in a government based on consent and equality would undermine republican government. He even suggested that God would side with the enslaved if they started their own revolution. However, as the years passed (perhaps because he could not relinquish the comforts his slaves brought him), he began to compare enslaved adults to children in their reasoning abilities. This, of course, would

15. In 1726 William Byrd II of Westover used general (prerepublican) patriarchal and biblical language to describe his role on the plantation and the place of his slaves in relation to himself. "I have a large family of my own." "Like one of the patriarchs, I have my flocks and my herds, my bond-men, and bond-women." But he referred to them as his "people." And the comparison of himself to a father went along with only an unspecific analogy comparing his bondmen and -women to children (as all inferiors were in a very general way under patriarchal theory). Byrd to Charles Boyle, earl of Orrery, July 5, 1726, in Marion Tinling, ed., *The Correspondence of the Three William Byrds of Westover, Virginia, 1684–1776* (Charlottesville, Va., 1977), I, 355.

provide a basis for arguing that they could not function on their own and could not consent to slavery or freedom.

Jefferson was thus attempting to define how inequality could be justified for adults within the new theory of equality: If those adults remain children in their reasoning ability, then hereditary inferior status might be acceptable in their case. He speculated "that they [African-Americans] are inferior in the faculties of reason and imagination," though "with great diffidence." He later compared the abilities of slaves explicitly with those of children. In 1788 he wrote, "I can judge from the experiments which have been made, to give liberty to, or rather, to abandon persons whose habits have been formed in slavery is like abandoning children." Twenty-six years later, he was still using this comparison of African-Americans to children as an excuse against taking immediate action to emancipate them: "For, men, probably of any colour, but of this color we know, brought from their infancy without necessity for thought or forecast, are by their habits rendered as incapable as children of taking care of themselves." In this way Jefferson invoked the inequality for children within democratic-republican theory to rationalize inherited racial slavery. In doing so, he helped to create a new kind of racism.[16]

Jefferson's argument that African-Americans might be perpetual children had all the more resonance as a justification for slavery because of the way common lawyers interpreted parental rights in the late eighteenth and early nineteenth centuries. Blackstone's definition of parental custody rights resembled the former rights of lords: he gave fathers, in particular, a kind of property in their children, one he explicitly compared to masters' powers over their servants or villeins in the older common law. Blackstone's definitions would continue into the new Republic, strengthened rather than weakened by influential common lawyers on the American scene such as James Kent. Custody itself became a kind of property right, though one that recognized the humanity of the ward. There were more limits on parents' powers over children than masters had traditionally been held to have over servants. Still, the custodial rights given to parents increased as the perception grew that children were unable to make their own decisions. Thus, oddly, the new arguments for slavery were justified, via the circuitous route of the new custody law, by reference to some of the same old powers of lords over villeins.

James Madison, proprietor of more than one hundred slaves, also strug-

16. Thomas Jefferson, *Notes on the State of Virginia*, ed. William Peden (Chapel Hill, N.C., 1954), 143, 163; Jefferson to Edward Bancroft, Jan. 26, 1788, in Julian P. Boyd et al., eds., *The Papers of Thomas Jefferson* (Princeton, N.J., 1950–), XIV, 492; Jefferson to Edward Coles, Aug. 25, 1814, in John P. Kaminski, ed., *A Necessary Evil? Slavery and the Debate over the Constitution* (Madison, Wis., 1995), 260.

gled with the contradiction between slavery and Revolutionary ideology, yet arrived at different answers from Jefferson's. Madison chose to disagree with Locke and the very premises of the new republican theory: he upheld hereditary status for the children of slaves even after they became adults, and he argued that the property rights of the masters were of higher value than the personal rights of the slaves. He twisted the logic of the theory to argue that in order to free a slave, "to be equitable and satisfactory, the consent of both the Master and the slave should be obtained." Purposely ignoring the question of slaves' right to consent to their status in the first place, he rejected Locke's dictum, "He can have no Power over them, but by their own consent." He thus accepted, fundamentally, that the child could be born into a status as a slave, not equal, with no right to consent even as an adult, contrary to Locke and to other republican theorists. He thus also privileged the rights of masters over those of fathers or mothers. Only by repudiating the central tenet of democratic-republican theory could slave status be thus justified. Thus in both his privileging of property over persons and his acceptance of inherited status, Madison was acknowledging the limits of his attachment to the new theory and his remaining attachment to the old theory of inherited status, however inconsistent and uncomfortable. Although he regarded slavery as a "great evil," he also justified it.[17]

Perhaps we should say that Jefferson's and Madison's discomfort does not matter. But this discomfort was not only within them. It was within the whole of southern society, which continued to grasp onto slavery despite the promises of the new Republic. That discomfort grew into something deeper: a cancer that gnawed at the vitals of American identity.

That the ideological shift represented by the Revolution created deep problems with slavery can be most easily seen in the northern response to the Revolution (in the North's emancipation plans) and in the response of many abolitionists, who used the language of the Revolution to oppose slavery. The older comparison of slaves to subjects, born to a particular status just as was a king or a master, fitted into a coherent logic. But equating people who were enslaved to children was always deeply problematic. Children, after all, do grow up. Laws against educating slaves then gain a more grisly quality: education would not only practically increase slaves' potential to organize rebellions; education leading to reason and understanding would also undermine this critical equation of slaves with children. The fragility of this justification of slavery within democratic-republican theory explains why many elite

17. All cites are from excerpts from Madison's memoranda and letters in Kaminski, ed., *A Necessary Evil?* 268–275.

southerners chose instead to partially reject those principles and to remain attached to older hierarchical principles of status and honor.

Slavery, in other words, was no paradox that existed despite or even because of the Revolutionary emphasis on freedom. It was an explicit contradiction. Isolating the issue of children is fundamental to understanding why. Slavery itself could be fully legitimated only as part of a monarchical order where children had the status of their parents. The inequality of children explains why many of the post-Revolutionary state plans to end slavery (such as Pennsylvania's) offered freedom to those born into slavery only when they reached adulthood—because children were the one group explicitly and consistently excluded from equality by Revolutionary ideology. Most of all, it explains why blacks became so frequently compared to children, even when adults, in the antebellum period, especially in the South.

With the Revolution, those who sought to support hereditary inequality had a strong reason to impute a permanent lack of reason to some adults, because their older justifications of hierarchy among human beings began to be seen as no longer normal. The most common analogy used to defend slavery in the early nineteenth century was the one Jefferson offered: that blacks were children in terms of their ability to reason. The analogy between children and the enslaved African-Americans became commonplace in whites' popular stories, in their political writings, and in their court decisions. Defenders of slavery referred frequently and fondly to slavery as their "Domestic Institution." Most slaves, regardless of their age, became "boys" and "girls." Masters ceased to describe themselves as "kings" and became fathers; they ceased to describe their slaves as "subjects" and began to call them children. Indeed, this kind of description became so pervasive that some historians have interpreted white men's frequent comparison of slaves to children as evidence that African-Americans' natural identities were destroyed by the harshness of slavery, and many nineteenth-century scientists tried to provide teeth to this analogy by proving that African-Americans were naturally inferior. However, the scientists' attempts as well as the use of this language should both be interpreted as rationalizations of slavery and inequality in the face of the Revolutionary principle that all men are created equal.[18]

18. Willie Lee Rose, *Slavery and Freedom*, ed. William W. Freehling (New York), 21–25, argues that referring to slavery as a "domestic institution" became popular by the 1830s but that the origins of its usage began with the Revolution. Philip D. Morgan gives examples of slaves compared to children, savages, and animals in order to justify slavery: see *Slave Counterpoint: Black Culture in the Eighteenth-Century Chesapeake and Low-country* (Chapel Hill, N.C., 1998), 259–262, 271–280. Robert Olwell's study of slavery in South Carolina in the period surrounding the Revolution notes the profound shift in

Jefferson's and Madison's musings about slavery would reach fruition as the nineteenth century progressed: George Fitzhugh's *Sociology for the South,* an important statement of proslavery southern thought first published in 1854, both rejected the principle that all men are created equal and rationalized slavery by comparing the mental abilities of people of African descent to those of children. (Presumably he wanted to meet every possible objection against slavery.)

> Would the abolitionists approve of a system of society that set white children free, and remitted them at the age of fourteen, males and females, to all the rights, both as to person and property, which belong to adults? Would it be criminal or praiseworthy to do so? Criminal, of course. Now, are the average of negroes equal in information, in native intelligence, in prudence or providence, to well-informed white children of fourteen? We . . . think not.

He explained that as children could not "understand" law and could not survive in the "competition" of the real world, neither could "free negroes." If African-Americans were not equal in "native intelligence, in prudence or providence" to "well-informed white children," then they needed someone to take care of them, and slavery was justified. He made the claim most explicitly with respect to women, regardless of their race: "Half of mankind," he declared, "are but grown-up children, and liberty is as fatal to them as it would be to children."[19]

Mothers and Fathers, Girls and Boys

The same ideological debates that changed children's status also helped to shape that of women. During the late sixteenth and seventeenth centuries gender infiltrated its way into the religious and political debates over author-

---

the language that masters used to discuss their slaves' status, whereby they became much more firmly children, with the master as head of a patriarchal family in the wake of the Revolution: "In their masters' metaphors, slaves ceased to be subjects and became children" (*Masters, Slaves, and Subjects: The Culture of Power in the South Carolina Low Country, 1740–1790* [Ithaca, N.Y., 1998], 282–283).

Stanley Elkins shows how pervasive the metaphor of blacks as children was in the nineteenth-century South, in *Slavery: A Problem in American Institutional and Intellectual Life,* 3d ed. (Chicago, 1976), esp. 131–132. Stephen Jay Gould demonstrates how nineteenth-century scientists manipulated their experiments in order to ascribe lower intelligence to blacks: *The Mismeasure of Man* (New York, 1981), e.g., chap. 3, p. 115.

19. George Fitzhugh, *Sociology for the South; or, The Failure of Free Society* (Richmond, Va., 1854), chap. 5, "Negro Slavery," 88, 231, 264.

ity, in some cases becoming the central issue, as in John Knox's 1558 diatribe against the three queens then ruling—two by birthright and one by controlling her son—in England, Scotland, and France. Yet usually reason and age versus hereditary status dominated the discussion over valid authority; only rarely was gender the central question within the struggles over power. But, as the newer political ideologies took hold, they opened questions about women's status: should women be able to offer their consent as well? Were they not reasonable creatures? Despite this ideological opening, women's options tended to be legally foreclosed in the late eighteenth century (at least in the short term). Indeed, women's legal status arguably became worse.[20]

While women in England as a group had less political power and property than men during the sixteenth and seventeenth centuries, many individual women exercised power based on their wealth and lineage. Thus as a queen, as a noble woman (with influence at court or control over who stood for parliamentary election in a borough), or even sometimes as a voter (borough suffrage rules varied dramatically), women had political voices. Indeed, some women might have voted in Virginia before they were specifically excluded, along with children, in 1699. Under the rules of primogeniture women as well as children could become monarchs in their own right. Like age, gender was a component of status, but lineage and wealth mattered more. Women with titles and wealth had more status and power than men of lower station. Gender, by itself, was less of an indicator of legal status than it would be by the late eighteenth century.[21]

Just as children were gaining a more distinct legal identity as children during the eighteenth century but also being placed under the custodial control of fathers, women were being identified more by their gender but also being put under the legal control of their husbands. The common law idea of feme covert (the idea that a husband and wife were legally "one," embodied in the husband) was not invented by Blackstone, but he helped to give it a more universal character, just as he did with paternal custody. Elements of feme covert were present in the earlier law. Yet it had a narrower scope and application in Coke's writings, for example. And, as with custody, Blackstone's ideas on feme covert had broad impact. Perhaps one can see the changes in wom-

20. John Knox, *The First Blast of the Trumpet against the Monstrous Regiment of Women* (1558; rpt. New York, 1972), e.g., 5, 10–11, 39.
21. See, particularly, an old treasure that scholarship has largely ignored: Charlotte Carmichael Stopes, *British Freewomen: Their Historical Privilege* (London, 1894). With regard to the 1699 law restricting women from voting, see William Waller Hening, ed., *The Statutes at Large: Being a Collection of All the Laws of Virginia . . .* (rpt. Charlottesville, Va., 1969), III, 172–175.

en's legal identity and the sharper privileging of the male gender as part of Blackstone's effort to rationalize the law. His triumvirate of the powers of men, as masters, fathers, and husbands, and especially the way that he gave men a property right over servants, children, and wives, incorporated elements of patriarchal ideology under an umbrella of reason. Regardless, during the seventeenth and eighteenth centuries, the common law shifted on this issue in some of the same ways that it was changing with regard to children: with women and children stationed more firmly under the husband's and father's control.[22]

Although such a hierarchy of husband over wife was dictated by neither republican theory nor Enlightenment theory, it was one way of responding to the increasing ideological concerns about consent. However, the basis for the authority of husbands over wives was justified differently (than that of parents over children) within the law. Blackstone, like Locke, acknowledged that women, unlike children, had reason. Blackstone (also like Locke) suggested that marriage was the main way that each woman offered her consent to government. Indeed, according to his treatise, a woman had to have reason in order to contract a valid marriage. Thus Blackstone's logic for women's subordination was, not that women lacked reason, but that, by consenting to her husband in marriage, he (her husband) became her representative, legally and politically. The very concept of feme covert thus partook of Enlightenment theory in a piecemeal way. Married women consented only once—to their husbands—and thereafter only through them.

Outside the law, debate ranged widely during the eighteenth century over whether women had the right to consent. This was partly because the democratic-republican political theorists who justified authority based on

22. Edward Coke, *The First Part of the Institutes of the Laws of England; or, A Commentary upon Littleton* . . . (1628), 11th ed. (London, 1719), 3a, 112a, 132b-133a, 356b; Blackstone, *Commentaries*, I, 430–433. Also see, for example, Tim Stretton, *Women Waging Law in Elizabethan England* (Cambridge, 1998). Blackstone was both retaining some of the older patriarchal status distinctions and also making them fit newer contract-based principles by allying women's status closely with children's. "By marriage, the husband and wife are one person in law: that is, the very being or legal existence of the woman is suspended during the marriage, or at least is incorporated and consolidated into that of the husband: under whose wing, protection, and *cover*, she performs every thing; and is therefore called in our law-french a *feme-covert*" (430). Blackstone will not permit women to form any kind of legal contract after marriage, even with her husband, except for her "necessaries," for which her husband may be liable. Women cannot testify for or against their husbands. Only with respect to criminal liability do women have something of a legal identity. They bear a close similarity to children (and indeed to servants) in Blackstone's analysis of their status under the common law.

consent and pointedly excluded children had much less to say about women. John Locke paid more attention to the issue than did some other authors, but his attitudes toward women's reason and ability to consent were ambiguous. His *Essay Concerning Human Understanding* gives examples of their exercising reason better than some men. His *Two Treatises of Government* has little to say about women, although he allows that mothers deserve the same respect as fathers and that wives deserve respect within marriage. Yet he asserts that, because husbands and wives have "different understandings, [they] will unavoidably sometimes have different wills too; it therefore being necessary, that the last Determination . . . should be placed somewhere, it naturally falls to the Man's share, as the abler and the stronger." Admitting women's full rationality, he gives more power to husbands than to wives, yet hedges this power, ending his discussion by emphasizing women's freedom to break the contract of marriage.[23]

The religious debates of the seventeenth century that spawned the political theories of consent dealt extensively with the status of women. Anne Hutchinson, women's role in witchcraft, whether women could be members of the covenant (since the covenant of the Old Testament was perpetuated by circumcision), women's ability to exercise conscience—all suggest the ways in which women's authority and equality were extensively debated. Indeed, during the eighteenth century, religious ideas about equality and consent and authority continued to intersect with the political debates, and it was probably within religion that these questions about gender received the most attention. Ironically, white women probably had more authority and legal privileges in the South, perhaps because the South remained more attached to an ideal of society in which gender was less important than other hierarchies.[24]

23. Locke, *Two Treatises*, ed. Laslett, 321 ("Second Treatise," par. 82). On the relative absence of women from Enlightenment texts, see Linda K. Kerber, *Toward an Intellectual History of Women* (Chapel Hill, N.C., 1997), 52; Kerber, *Women of the Republic: Intellect and Ideology in Revolutionary America* (Chapel Hill, N.C., 1980), 15. Also see Carole Pateman, "The Disorder of Women: Women, Love, and the Sense of Justice," in Pateman, ed., *The Disorder of Women: Democracy, Feminism, and Political Theory* (Cambridge, 1989), 17–32. Pateman, in *The Sexual Contract* (Stanford, Calif., 1988), shows that several authors who wrote about political authority based on consent made this type of argument. Locke, however, does not develop this argument as much as the later political theorists she discusses. Also see Ellen Carol DuBois, "Outgrowing the Compact of the Fathers: Equal Rights, Woman Suffrage, and the United States Constitution, 1820–1878," *Journal of American History*, LXXIV (1987–1988), 836–862. Kerber rightly points out that Locke paid more attention to women than most others, though it does not seem to me "extensive" (*Intellectual History of Women*, 43).

24. Some very rich studies have addressed the status of women within different

Within the mainstream political debates, women were also sometimes compared to children in their reasoning abilities. Yet the relative absence of explicit discussion of the political place of women in republican political thought is striking, especially after the earlier religious debates about conscience and reason, which often allocated women equal reason with men. The many proponents of education in the late eighteenth century disagreed about whether education should be granted equally to boys and girls. Excluding women from education might be justified on grounds that women did not need as much education for a trade or to exercise citizenship; granting it to them, however, opened the possibility of arguing that women could be equally reasonable. Denying women education was akin to denying education to slaves: if uneducated, they could then more convincingly be compared to children in their inability to reason. Thus Mary Wollstonecraft condemned some Enlightenment political thought, particularly Rousseau's *Émile*, on the grounds that it assigned women to a state of "perpetual childhood." Yet she generally seemed to appreciate Locke (indeed, Rousseau was writing in reaction to the earlier egalitarian elements of Locke's thought). Judith Sargent Murray's 1790 essay "On the Equality of the Sexes" followed an argument implicit within much Enlightenment political writing when she contended that women had equal potential to reason and to understand and thus to have many rights: "I know that to both sexes elevated understandings, and the reverse, are common. . . . Are we deficient in reason? We can only reason from what we know, and if opportunity of acquiring knowledge hath been denied us, the inferiority of our sex cannot fairly be deduced from thence."[25]

---

religious groups during these two centuries and have connected these debates, in many cases, to political membership and power. See Amy Schrager Lang, *Prophetic Woman: Anne Hutchinson and the Problem of Dissent in the Literature of New England* (Berkeley, Calif., 1987); Carla Gardina Pestana, *Quakers and Baptists in Colonial Massachusetts* (Cambridge, 1991); Carol F. Karlsen, *The Devil in the Shape of a Woman: Witchcraft in Colonial New England* (New York, 1987); Susan Juster, *Disorderly Women: Sexual Politics and Evangelicism in Revolutionary New England* (Ithaca, N.Y., 1994), esp. 142–143; Jane Kamensky, *Governing the Tongue: The Politics of Speech in Early New England* (New York, 1997). Also see Laurel Thatcher Ulrich, *Good Wives: Image and Reality in the Lives of Women in Northern New England, 1650–1750* (New York, 1982).

25. Mary Wollstonecraft, *A Vindication of the Rights of Woman* (1792), ed. Miriam Brody Kramnick (London, 1975), 81, and chap. 5, "Animadversions on Some of the Writers Who Have Rendered Women Objects of Pity, Bordering on Contempt." "My own sex, I hope, will excuse me, if I treat them like rational creatures, instead of flattering their *fascinating* graces, and viewing them as if they were in a state of perpetual childhood, unable to stand alone." And see Constantia [Judith Sargent Murray], "On the

Women's status was also addressed in one further way by democratic-republican political theory and legal writings of the eighteenth century: in their role as mothers. The logic of custody embedded in republicanism stressed not only the importance of nurture and education (which could logically give mothers an important role) but also that custody rights for parents depended on parents' providing that nurture. While Blackstone acknowledged this, he contended that mothers had no right to power, only to respect. Yet the principles he laid out (following Locke and other natural law theorists) left the door open to justifying custody rights for mothers. The American commentator James Kent would give women potentially yet more authority, in that he emphasized parental love in addition to nurture as the basis for authority. Although he kept the focus on a father's custodial right, his argument allowed authority for mothers. Custody rights required obligations in order to deserve the authority. Thus, logically, neither could be limited solely to fathers, unless they also provided sole care of their children. By granting mothers custody, the law also acknowledged their ability to exercise judgment and reason, such that this debate influenced the broader discussion of women's status.

The logic of the Revolution thus provided a contradictory legacy. In emphasizing that only those who have reason should be able to exercise choice, it made it possible to exclude women and free blacks from the suffrage by denying their ability to reason "independently." But it was also potentially empowering for many. The Revolutionary ideals of equality and consent provided a radical precedent. If they could prove their ability to reason (perhaps even through the importance of their role as caregivers), they could provide a powerful claim for political and civil rights.

The states of the new Republic thus debated where the Revolutionary ideas should lead for adult white women and black men who owned property, shifting and weaving over the boundaries of equality and who had enough reason to vote. Women who owned property could vote in New Jersey between 1776 and 1807. Black men who met the other requirements for suffrage voted in most states after the Revolution. In North Carolina, for example, free black adult men were deemed citizens with voting rights until 1835.[26] A window of opportunity opened briefly during the Revolution, and shut in the decades that followed. Those in power often accused others—women and blacks—of having insufficient reason to participate, thereby equating them

Equality of the Sexes," *Massachusetts Magazine; or, Monthly Magazine of Knowledge and Rational Entertainment*, II (1790), 132–133.

26. Alexander Keyssar, *The Right to Vote: The Contested History of Democracy in the United States* (New York, 2000), 55.

with children. The same logic of inequality lay behind the literacy tests selectively imposed on black voters in many southern and midwestern states in the wake of Civil War. These tests sought to circumvent the fifteenth amendment, which guaranteed the right to vote regardless of race, by imposing a so-called intelligence requirement instead.

Reason, Consent, and American Democracy

Comparing other groups of people to children would form a powerful argument to legitimate American imperialism in the nineteenth and twentieth centuries. President Andrew Jackson, for example, justified political authority over native Americans by comparing them to children who lacked reason.[27] William Howard Taft illuminates the enduring legacy of the political equation between reason and full citizenship. In 1904, while secretary of war, Taft justified American rule over the Philippines without the Filipinos' consent by claiming that the Filipinos, like women and children at the time of the American Revolution, did not have sufficient reason or fitness to choose their own government. "It is said that our holding the Philippines is a violation of the Declaration of Independence, in that that instrument declares that all just rights of government depend upon the consent of the governed. [But at that time] . . . Women and children were governed, slaves were governed . . . , and the many excluded from voting by property and educational qualifications were governed, and were not consulted in that government and did not consent to it. If the literal interpretation of the instrument is the true one, then nothing but universal suffrage, by men, women, and children, could constitute a just government. The instrument is to be restrained to the fitness and the reason of things. All people are not capable of self-government." Comparing other peoples to children became the paramount justification for American imperialism by the early twentieth century.[28]

The transition from authority based on inherited status toward authority based on consent has promised equality to all persons so long as they can give

27. See, for example, Michael Paul Rogin, *Fathers and Children: Andrew Jackson and the Subjugation of the American Indian* (New York, 1975). While Rogin approaches the use of this metaphor from a psychological point of view (which is different from the point I make here), he does reflect the widespread use of the comparison of white rulers with fathers and Indians with children.

28. Taft quote is from Aug. 26, 1904, U.S., National Archives, Record Group 350, file 141-10. My thanks to Michael Salmon for this reference. On the pervasive infantalizing of people of other nations as a justification for United States imperialism in the twentieth century, see Michael H. Hunt, *Ideology and U.S. Foreign Policy* (New Haven, Conn., 1987).

"informed consent." As different groups have proven their ability to exercise reason, they have exposed the weakness of these arguments that compared grown people to children in order to subordinate them. They have been able to appeal to the beliefs of those in power to legitimate their own claims for inclusion. Poorer white adult men were the first to do so. Initially excluded from voting by property qualifications in all colonies, by 1825 most states—with the exception of a few southern states such as South Carolina and Virginia—allowed even propertyless free white adult males (who were also residents and not felons) to vote. In the monarchical, status-based argument, the exclusion of those without property was logical. They continued to be excluded from voting after the Revolution with arguments such as John Adams's, who claimed that poor men, like children, were dependent on others' wills. But propertyless men could claim, in response, that their dependence on others (paying rent, working for others) did not affect their ability to exercise reason, especially if they were allowed an education. The arguments of poorer adult white males gained more persuasive power with the secret ballot, which ensured that one's vote could not be overtly influenced by those to whom one owed money, a job, or rent.

The proponents of free public education in the years after the Revolution made exactly these points: education would teach reason to citizens so they could make their own informed choices, free of influence. In 1799, for example, the "laborer" William Manning argued that the reason republics fall is that the "Few" have too much influence over the "Many." Why? "The first [reason] is the want of knowledge among the Many and their readiness to hear and follow the schemes of great men without examining and seeing for themselves." The solution, for Manning, was education. Workingmen's parties in the 1820s and 1830s demanded better access to education. Free public education followed the Revolution in many states; in others, unremarkably those where the Revolutionary ideologies were challenged, it was delayed. There is a clear link between expansion of adult male suffrage and free public education in both arguments and practical policy during the antebellum period. South Carolina did not offer free public education until after the Civil War—at roughly the same time as it allowed, for the first time, all adult men to vote. After World War I, such arguments about women's education helped to undergird support for the nineteenth amendment, which gave women the vote.[29]

29. Michael Merrill and Sean Wilentz, eds., *The Key of Liberty: The Life and Democratic Writings of William Manning, "A Laborer," 1747–1814* (Cambridge, Mass., 1993), 154, 182. Also see Ellwood P. Cubberly, *Public Education in the United States: A Study and Interpretation of American Educational History* (1919), rev. ed. (Boston, 1934), esp. chap. 4;

While other groups marshaled the logic of democratic-republican ideology to argue for their own inclusion among the ranks of the rational and the equal, the possibility of justifying inequality by comparing individuals to children remains integral to our system of law and justice. The assumptions about the link between reason and control over one's own political—and personal—destiny have deep roots in our political and legal culture. Only a keen awareness of this centrality can prevent its misuse. Authority based on personal consent is an empowering concept, but it can be used just as powerfully to subordinate groups who can be defined as incapable of responsibility.

What about children themselves? Did any of the seventeenth- and eighteenth-century political and legal thinkers fully perceive the implications of their arguments for children? Are fourteen or eighteen or twenty-one such magical ages that they should grant, with the passing of a day, the difference between dependence and choice? How much power should parents be given over children, if children are denied the right to choose for themselves? And for how long? On what basis should we decide who is the best custodian for a child? What "unalienable rights" do children have? What blend of issues should determine the transition between childhood and adulthood? And have these assumptions about children's nonreasonable nature gone, in fact, too far in infantalizing them, in both freeing them from blame in criminal decisions and denying them critical choices in their own young lives? If we include emotions, such as love, in our allocation of parents' custodial right, cannot children feel those too? Perhaps legal silence should not answer for them. Although their voices should not stand alone, we need to listen.

Lawrence A. Cremin, *American Education: The National Experience, 1783–1876* (New York, 1980), esp. chap. 5; Frederick Rudolph, ed., *Essays on Education in the Early Republic* (Cambridge, Mass., 1965), especially essays by Benjamin Rush, Noah Webster, and Robert Coram. On the struggle over the Virginia suffrage in 1830 and how education was an important part of that debate, see Robert P. Sutton, *Revolution to Secession: Constitution Making in the Old Dominion* (Charlottesville, Va., 1989), 76, 118–120.

APPENDIX

LEGAL TREATISES USED BY AMERICANS
BEFORE THE NINETEENTH CENTURY

Most judges in colonial America, particularly local, received no formal training and relied on legal manuals and practical experience to learn the law. Although we cannot hear the proceedings inside a seventeenth- or eighteenth-
century courtroom, the manuals and their contents are a critical, albeit
imperfect, means of decoding the extant court records. What assumptions
did they have? After working extensively with many local court records and
before I discovered these treatises, I remember wishing desperately that I
could talk to a judge who lived then. If I could just ask a few questions. . . . In
discovering and reading these legal guides, I have felt that I could. Those
strange terms, the code words, the abbreviations, the writs—all became much
clearer with the aid of these treatises. These seemingly magical treatises,
however, varied in their opinions and conclusions. It is thus important to
have a rough map of their usage.

The manuals that judges used varied over time and by colony. For the early
seventeenth century there was only a handful of such guides available, and
choices were limited. In 1647, the General Court of Massachusetts requested
copies of the following legal books, "to the end we may have the better light
for making and proceeding about laws, that there shalbe these books following procured for the use of the Courte from time to time." Aside from a
dictionary and a manual of forms, Sir Edward Coke (spelled here "Cooke")
and Michael Dalton are the only two writers mentioned.

Two of Sir Edward Cooke upon Littleton;
Two of the Books of Entryes;
Two of Sir Edward Cooke upon Magna Charta;
Two of the Newe Tearmes of the Lawe;
Two Daltons Justice of Peace;
Two of Sir Edward Cooks Reports.[1]

1. Cited by Edwin Powers, *Crime and Punishment in Early Massachusetts, 1620–1692:
A Documentary History* (Boston, 1966), 433. The four volumes of Coke's *Institutes*
were published between 1628 and 1644, and Dalton's *Countrey Justice* was published in

"Cooke upon Littleton" is volume I of the *Institutes;* "Cooke upon Magna Charta" is volume II. The court might well not have known yet about the last two volumes, which had only just appeared. Coke also published a book of "Entryes," a manual of printed forms, so that might have been his as well. The court thus relied on Coke especially, and to a lesser degree on Dalton. Some judges in Massachusetts also came with prior judicial experience, such as John Winthrop, who had been a justice of the peace in England (and had also served as a member of Parliament with Coke).

We have fewer clues about very early Virginia, partly because most of the general court records burned during the Civil War. Clearly, Virginia was following English laws and procedures to some degree. As shown in Chapter 6, a servant who killed his master was convicted of petit treason. The court confiscated objects that caused a person's death as deodand, following English norms. It did so without passing a comprehensive criminal code to cover these matters, relying, apparently, on Virginia's general charters of 1606 and 1621. "Wee requier the said gennerall Assembly, as also the said Counsell of State to imitate and followe the policy of the forme of goverment, Lawes Custome manners of loyall and other administracion of Justice used in the Realme of England." Some judges probably came to Virginia with some formal training. Otherwise, they probably relied on the handful of books they could get, many of them in law French (such as John Perkins's *Profitable Booke . . . Treating of the Lawes of Englande* and various guides for justices of the peace, such as William Lambarde's *Eirenarcha* or William Stanford's *Les plees del coron*). So much is guesswork, but they had few such treatises to choose from. A Virginia law of 1666 recommended Michael Dalton's *Countrey Justice* or similar, unnamed English guides for local justices of the peace in an act for "the better conformity of the proceedings of the courts of this country."[2]

No laws recommended specific manuals for justices of the peace or other judges in Pennsylvania. However, in 1722 in Philadelphia, *Conductor Generalis* was published, a blending of English guides for justices of the peace, which relied heavily on Dalton's *Countrey Justice* as well as William Nelson's

---

1618. There were few "Books of Entryes" published in England before 1650. The most likely candidate for this list was also written by Coke: *A Booke of Entries: Containing Perfect and Approved Presidents of Counts . . .* (London, 1614). Another collection of forms was William Rastell, *A Colleccion of Entrees of Declaracions, Barres, Replicacions, Rejoinders . . .* (London, 1566).

2. Susan Myra Kingsbury, ed., *The Records of the Virginia Company of London* (Washington, D.C., 1906–1935), III, 484; William Waller Hening, ed., *The Statutes at Large: Being a Collection of All the Laws of Virginia . . .* (rpt. Charlottesville, Va., 1969), I, 69, 112, II, 246.

Office and Authority of a Justice of Peace. Conductor Generalis was reprinted in 1749 and 1750 in the same form, and a new version, influenced by Richard Burn's English *Justice of the Peace, and Parish Officer*, appeared in 1743.[3]

Other colonies published their own guides as well. A short handbook for constables, *The Constables Pocket-Book* (1710), appeared in Massachusetts as well as a summary of Massachusetts laws, *The County and Town Officer* (1768), but no full guide to justices of the peace appeared there until *An Abridgment of Burn's Justice of the Peace*, a modification of the most popular English guide, in 1773. The first guide written by a colonial justice appeared in Virginia in 1736, George Webb's *Office and Authority of a Justice of Peace*, followed by a similarly titled treatise by Richard Starke in 1774.[4]

Wealthy Virginians, especially, sent their sons to England to learn the law formally at the Inns of Court. William Fitzhugh, who played an important role in crafting the Virginia law code of 1705, read deeply in older, pre-Coke common law and continually cited sources in law French and Latin. He claimed that the common law was "only to be learned out of ancient authors (for out of the old fields must come the new corn) contrary to the opinion of the generality of our judges and practicers of the law here." He also cited Coke frequently. His contemporaries probably used more of the guides in English (Coke and Dalton are the most notable), which were more accessible.[5]

Beyond legal treatises actually printed in the colonies or those specifically recommended, the contents of lawyers' libraries during the eighteenth century are helpful in determining usage. Herbert A. Johnson examined twenty-two libraries of the most prominent men. (Normal justices of the peace did not own such extensive collections but were likely to own the most popular

3. *Conductor Generalis; or, The Office, Duty, and Authority of Justices of the Peace . . .* (Philadelphia, 1722); Richard Burn, *The Justice of the Peace, and Parish Officer*, 4 vols. (London, 1743). (P. B., *Conductor Generalis; or, A Guide for Justices of the Peace . . .* [New York, 1711], is markedly different from the Philadelphia, 1722, volume.)

4. N[icholas] B[oone], *The Constables Pocket-Book; or, A Dialogue between an Old Constable and a New . . .* (Boston, 1710) (reprinted in 1727); *The County and Town Officer; or, An Abridgment of the Laws of the Province of the Massachusetts-Bay, relative to County and Town Officers* (Boston, 1768); *An Abridgment of Burn's Justice of the Peace and Parish Officer . . .* (Boston, 1773); George Webb, *Office and Authority of a Justice of Peace, and Also the Duty of Sheriffs . . .* (Williamsburg, Va., 1736); Richard Starke, *Office and Authority of a Justice of Peace, Explained and Digested . . .* (Williamsburg, Va., 1774).

A good, although incomplete, guide to the publication of legal books in America until 1801 is Eldon Revare James, "A List of Legal Treatises Printed in the British Colonies and the American States before 1801," in Morton Carlisle Campbell et al., *Harvard Legal Essays . . .* (Cambridge, Mass., 1934), 159–211.

5. Richard Beale Davis, ed., *William Fitzhugh and His Chesapeake World, 1676–1701: The Fitzhugh Letters and Other Documents* (Chapel Hill, N.C., 1963), 26.

and readable of these guides.) Volumes published late in the eighteenth century, of course, could not have appeared in the libraries of men who died before they were published. From those libraries, the following stand out in their popularity.[6]

William Blackstone's *Commentaries on the Laws of England* (1765–1769) appeared in the libraries of eight of ten lawyers who lived past the date of its publication. Reprinted in Philadelphia in 1772 from the first London edition, this first American edition contains a list of more than six hundred "subscribers." By the 1790s, Blackstone's influence was unparalleled in political as well as legal circles: his name was mentioned more than any other in political pamphlets and newspapers of the 1790s.[7]

The most popular guide for justices of the peace in those libraries was *Officium Clerici Pacis* (nine libraries). Since this was only partly a guide for justices of the peace and was in Latin (except for introduction partly in English), it was probably less popular among the less prominent justices and those not formally trained. The next most popular guide for justices of the peace among these libraries was Richard Burn's *Justice of the Peace* (six), followed by Dalton's *Countrey Justice* (four), still used more than a century after its initial publication. The most popular abridgments of the law were Knightley D'Anvers, *A General Abridgment of the Common Law* (twelve), and Matthew Bacon, *A New Abridgment of the Law* (nine). (The first American edition of Bacon, which included American precedents, would be published

6. Herbert A. Johnson, *Imported Eighteenth-Century Law Treatises in American Libraries, 1700–1799* (Knoxville, Tenn., 1978). The law libraries that Johnson examined belonged to the following twenty-two men.

Connecticut: John McClellan (1767–1858).

Massachusetts: John Adams (1735–1826), Francis Dana (1743–1811), Robert Treat Paine (1731–1814), Theophilus Parsons (1750–1813).

New York: James Alexander (1691–1756), John Jay (1745–1829), Joseph Murray (ca. 1694–1757), William Smith, Sr. (1697–1769).

Pennsylvania: Ralph Assheton (1695–1746), Benjamin Chew (1722–1810), John Guest (ca. 1650–1707), James Logan (1671–1751), Jasper Yeates (1745–1817).

South Carolina: James Grindlay (d. 1765), Peter Leigh (d. 1759), Benet Oldham (d. 1768).

Virginia: William Byrd II (1674–1744), Robert "King" Carter (1663–1732), Thomas Jefferson (1743–1826), John Mercer (1704–1768), St. George Tucker (1752–1827).

7. William Blackstone, *Commentaries on the Laws of England* (Philadelphia, 1771–1772). The list of subscribers includes their addresses and professions. The list reveals that Blackstone was popular in all the colonies and with many men besides lawyers. And see Donald S. Lutz, "The Relative Influence of European Writers on Late Eigtheenth-Century American Political Thought," *American Political Science Review*, LXXIII (1984), 189–197.

in Philadelphia in 1813.) The most popular commentaries and institutes besides Blackstone were Thomas Wood, *An Institute of the Laws of England* (eight), Christopher Saint-German, *Doctor and Student* (seven), and Matthew Hale, *History of the Common Law* (six).[8]

Criminal law formed its own particular genre. Matthew Hale's *History of Pleas of the Crown* and William Hawkins's *Treatise of the Pleas of the Crown* (which drew on Hale: apparently Hawkins was familiar with Hale's manuscript) were the most popular in that field, both appearing in eleven libraries. The most popular treatises on procedure and evidence were Giles Duncombe, *Tryals per Pais* (nine); Francis Buller, *Introduction to the Law relative to Trials at Nisi Prius* (seven), Geoffrey Gilbert, *The Law of Evidence* (five); and Michael Dalton, *Officium Vicecomitum* (five). (The volumes by Buller and Gilbert were also published in New York and Philadelphia, respectively, in 1788.)[9]

Coke upon Littleton (volume I of his *Institutes*) was the single most common treatise on land law, appearing in eleven libraries. With regard to natural law, Samuel von Pufendorf, *Law of Nature and Nations*, appeared in ten libraries (in French only in one of them). A volume relating to children, *The Infants Lawyer*, appeared in three libraries.[10]

These clues were supplemented by the cases themselves. Higher court decisions, especially, cited the authorities whose precedents they were following. Tracking down those authorities was revealing. They cited English

8. J. W., *Officium Clerici Pacis: A Book of Indictments, Informations, Appeals, and Inquisitions*... (London, 1675) (chiefly forms rather than procedures, so not as helpful for understanding policy as Burn and others); Burn, *The Justice of the Peace*; Michael Dalton, *The Countrey Justice*... (London, 1618); Knightley D'Anvers, *A General Abridgment of the Common Law*, 3 vols. (London, 1705–1737); [Matthew Bacon], *A New Abridgment of the Law*, 5 vols. (London, 1736–1766); Thomas Wood, *An Institute of the Laws of England*... (London, 1720); [Christopher Saint-German], *The Dialogue in English, betweene a Doctor of Divinity, and a Student in the Laws of England* (London, 1638); [Matthew Hale], *The History of the Common Law of England* (London, 1713).

9. Sir Matthew Hale, *Historia Placitorum Coronae: The History of Pleas of the Crown*..., 2 vols. (London, 1736); William Hawkins, *A Treatise of the Pleas of the Crown*..., 2 vols. (London, 1716–1721); Giles Duncombe, *Tryals per Pais; or, The Law of England concerning Juries by Nisi Prius*... (London, 1702); Francis Buller, *An Introduction to the Law relative to Trials at Nisi Prius* (Dublin, 1768); [Geoffrey] Gilbert, *The Law of Evidence*, 5th ed. (Philadelphia, 1788); Michael Dalton, *Officium Vicecomitum: The Office and Authority of Sheriffs*... (London, 1700).

10. Samuel von Pufendorf, *Of the Law of Nature and Nations*, trans. Basil Kennett and William Percivale (Oxford, 1703); *The Infants Lawyer; or, The Law (Both Ancient and Modern) Relating to Infants, Setting Forth Their Priviledges, Their Several Ages for Divers Purposes*... (London, 1697).

cases, starting with Coke's *Reports*. Judges also cited English precedent in the Virginia General Court during the early eighteenth century (in crafting their own reports in the 1730s—the only records we have left), and the Massachusetts Superior Court during the mid-eighteenth century frequently cited English cases. Americans began to publish their own reports generally after the Revolution, which also cited authorities, both legal treatises and cases, many of them English.[11]

More local, informal manuals for justices of the peace appeared after the Revolution. The most important of these for Virginia was William Waller Hening's *New Virginia Justice*, which first appeared in 1795 and went through numerous editions in the early nineteenth century. Samuel Freeman's *Massachusetts Justice*, which appeared in Boston in 1795, relied much more on just Massachusetts law, and less on English precedent and the common law, than such guides as Webb's or Hening's in Virginia or *Conductor Generalis* in Pennsylvania. A new version of *Conductor Generalis*, "revised and adapted to the United States of America," compiled by James Parker, appeared in Philadelphia in 1792 and was reprinted in 1793.[12]

As a partial consequence of the Revolution, several comprehensive American treatises would appear in the nineteenth century, all of them much indebted to Blackstone: in particular, St. George Tucker's Virginia version of *Blackstone's Commentaries* (1803); Tapping Reeve, *The Law of Baron and Femme* (1816); and James Kent, *Commentaries on American Law* (1826–1830). The influence of Blackstone can be seen in Kent's nickname, the "American Blackstone."[13]

11. R. T. Barton, ed., *Virginia Colonial Decisions: The Reports by Sir John Randolph and by Edward Barradall of Decisions of the General Court of Virginia, 1728–1741*, 2 vols. (Boston, 1909); Josiah Quincy, Jr., comp., *Reports of Cases Argued and Judged in the Superior Court of Judicature of the Province of Massachusetts Bay, between 1761 and 1772*, ed. Samuel M. Quincy (Boston, 1865). Both contain the earliest reports of American cases. For a complete list of reports of mostly early-nineteenth-century decisions in the supreme courts of each state, see John William Wallace, *The Reporters: Arranged and Characterized with Incidental Remarks*, 4th ed. (Boston, 1882).

12. William Waller Hening, *The New Virginia Justice, Comprising the Office and Authority of a Justice of the Peace* . . . (Richmond, Va., 1795); Samuel Freeman, ed., *The Massachusetts Justice: Being a Collection of the Laws of the Commonwealth of Massachusetts, relative to the Power and Duty of Justices of the Peace* . . . (Boston, 1795); James Parker, comp., *The Conductor Generalis* . . . (Philadelphia, 1792). Freeman also wrote *Town Officer*, published in Portland in 1791 and reprinted in Boston in 1793 and 1794. Also, in 1794, a slim volume that contained almost only forms appeared: Collinson Read, *Precedents in the Office of a Justice of Peace* . . . (Philadelphia, 1794).

13. Tapping Reeve, *The Law of Baron and Femme* . . . (New Haven, Conn., 1816); James

What emerged from all this was that the single most popular law books from the seventeenth century were Coke's and Dalton's. Indeed, Coke's *Institutes* remained the most popular guide to the common law until the publication of Blackstone's *Commentaries* in the 1760s. Jefferson, for example, learned the law by poring, painfully, over Coke's *Institutes* (a task I understand only too well). Hale's guides, though written in the late seventeenth century, were widely published, used, and cited only in the eighteenth. Blackstone, like Coke, became an immediate authority and was widely read. Above all, what became clear, however, is that Blackstone and later legal commentators relied mostly on Coke and Hale. Evidence law as it developed in the eighteenth century (as discussed in Chapter 5, on witnesses) owed a great debt to Hale in particular.

These guides and reports were indispensable to my study. Many seventeenth- and eighteenth-century legal terms are either no longer used or have changed in meaning; thus it was not enough to have studied modern law. Only with the aid of these treatises is it possible to crack the codes, and the silences, of early American law.

Kent, *Commentaries on American Law*, 4 vols. (New York, 1826–1830); St. George Tucker, *Blackstone's Commentaries: With Notes of Reference, to the Constitution and Laws, of the Federal Government of the United States; and of the Commonwealth of Virginia*, 5 vols. (Philadelphia, 1803). Also, there were less detailed, more general publications, such as James Wilson, *An Introductory Lecture to a Course of Law Lectures* (Philadelphia, 1791).

INDEX

legal reform, 250; on indentured
servants, 274; and arranged mar-
riage, 293
Chauncy, Charles, 112
Childhood: redefined, 8; development
of, 347, 348, 351, 352
Chitty, Joseph, 159, 166, 171
Church, failure to attend, 193, 229
Church membership, 68–75; and con-
sent, 48, 49, 52; and Protestants,
49, 50, 52, 85; and infant baptism,
50, 68; and Puritans, 68, 72, 73; and
conversion, 69, 70, 85; and Catholic
Church, 85–86; and Quakers, 86
Churchwardens, 230, 244, 256, 272,
276
Citizenship, 125–126, 131, 133–137,
139, 342
Civil law. See Roman law
Civil prosecution of children, 160, 161,
202
Clergy: and jury service, 143; and marriage, 298, 308–310, 315, 326, 328,
329. See also Benefit of clergy
Clothes: wearing improper, 193
Coke, Edward, 11, 284, 360; on age restrictions for office holding, 31, 249;
on oath taking, 133; on children and
court proceedings, 161–163, 173,
196; and legal reform, 174–177, 237,
238, 344; influence of, 174–176,
369, 370, 372, 375; on deodand, 188,
189; on guardianship, 235, 236, 247,
248, 261, 340; on children and land,
240, 247–249; on children's necessities, 266; and marriage, 301–303;
on reason and precedent, 339
Coke, Frances, 302, 303
Coke upon Littleton (Coke), 179, 369,
370, 373
Commentaries on the Laws of England
(Blackstone), 153, 208, 210, 217,
259–261, 322, 372, 375
Common law, 10, 11, 339. See also
Blackstone, William; Coke, Edward;
Hale, Matthew

Commons, House of, 26, 27, 31, 314,
316, 326
Common Sense (Paine), 109, 110, 346
Competency, 3, 4, 91–93, 111, 287; and
witness testimony, 154, 157–161,
165, 167, 171. See also Consent:
meaningful; Culpability; Reason:
and self-determination
Comyn, Samuel, 267, 268, 283
Conciliarists, 47
Conductor Generalis . . . (anon.), 205,
206, 259, 370–371; on jury service,
143, 144
Confirmation, 65–69
Congregationalists, 346, 347
Connecticut, 222, 270, 278, 279, 334,
335
Consent: and age of reason, 8; meaningful, 8, 12, 127, 232, 268, 280,
297, 339, 342, 345; and suffrage,
42–44; informed, 47, 341, 366; and
church membership, 48, 49, 52;
and political authority, 83, 86; coerced, 90, 272, 280, 283, 292, 307,
343, 345; and women, 103, 361; and
laws, 114–115; and representation,
114–119, 365; and military service,
129, 138, 139; and citizenship, 133,
134; and criminal culpability, 216;
and legal reform, 237, 238; and contractual agreements, 239, 243, 246,
285, 286, 320; and indentured servitude, 273–276; and apprenticeships, 278, 279; and labor contracts,
279, 354; implied, 283; and marriage, 288–292, 295–298, 300–
302, 304, 306–311, 313–315, 319,
320, 322–325, 328, 330, 332–334,
361; and slavery, 357. See also Competency; Government: by consent
Constables, 144
Constitution, United States, 34, 36;
ammendments to, 354, 365, 366
Contracts: and children, 7, 238–246,
248, 249, 265–271, 276, 283, 284,
318–322, 325; in the Middle Ages,

Contracts (*cont.*)
238, 239; types of, 238, 240; and coercion, 239, 241–245, 277, 280;
voidability of, 239–241, 243, 245,
246, 248, 265, 267–271, 277, 291,
298, 319, 335, 354; and parental obligation, 260, 261; and liability, 266–
271, 342; and assumpsit actions,
285; for marriage, 293; permanent
and temporary, 321, 325, 335. *See also*
Marriage
Contributing to delinquency of minor,
221, 222
Conversion experience, 45, 64, 69, 70,
85
Copyhold, 234, 245, 258, 340
Cotton, John, 55, 59–61, 70, 80
Councillors, 24, 25, 33
Council of Trent, 52, 308
Countrey Justice, The (Dalton), 163,
184, 195, 236, 259, 369, 370, 372
Covenant of grace, 53, 55, 73, 81
Criminal intent, 182, 194, 195, 206–
208, 210, 211, 221–224, 227
Criminal prosecution: and children, 1,
5, 150–161, 163–168, 171–174, 181,
182, 184–186, 194–207, 210–215,
220–225, 228, 342; age limits for,
132, 182, 184, 187, 190, 193, 198,
199, 206–208, 225, 226, 228; in
Virginia, 150–154, 156, 159, 167,
172, 173, 184, 204, 220, 225; and
women, 153–154, 159, 172, 228; in
Massachusetts, 156, 157, 160, 172,
184, 202, 203, 219–221; in Pennsylvania, 158, 165, 172, 205, 206, 220;
in New England, 159; in Tennessee,
159, 220, 221; in New Jersey, 160,
222; and blacks, 200, 222–228; and
Connecticut, 222; and Native Americans, 222
Criminal reform and children, 183,
215, 216, 227, 229
Crompton, Richard, 163
Cromwell, Oliver, 30, 32, 88, 313
Culpability, 182, 187–189, 191, 192,

194, 195, 199, 202; and age, 204,
206–209, 215, 216, 220–224, 226,
227
Custody, 231, 250, 251; and estate administration, 253, 254, 340; as property right, 356; and women, 364
Custom, 150, 170, 178, 179

Dalton, Michael: on jury service, 143,
146; on witness testimony, 163; on
children and crime, 184, 195, 199,
206; influence of, 201, 369, 370,
372, 373, 375; on parental rights,
236, 259
Daniel, Azariah, 275
Daniel, William, 186
D'Anvers, Knightley, 372
Darnall, Henry, III, 348, 350
Davis, John, 194
Dean, John, 182, 184
Death penalty, 5, 54, 152, 158, 163, 168,
190, 192, 197, 199–201, 203, 210,
211, 213–215, 224, 225, 229, 259,
306
Declaration of Independence, 123, 355,
365
Deeds, 238–241, 248, 249, 265
Dell, Annis, 155, 156
Democratic political theory, 13, 14, 341
Democratic-republican political the-
ory, 13, 14, 49; on equality and edu-
cation, 127; and political authority,
131; and consent, 280, 320, 333, 343,
346, 361, 362; as nonreligious, 346;
on inherited status and dependency,
355, 356; and slavery, 357, 358; and
women, 361, 362, 364
Deodand, 188, 191, 205, 370
*Dialogue between a Southern Delegate
and His Spouse, . . .* (V.), 118, 119
Discourses concerning Government
(Sidney), 98, 99, 107
Discretion. *See* Age of discretion
Dissenters: and age of reason, 8; influence of, 49; and voluntary society,
72; and consensual authority, 83,

343; and political theory, 87–90; and legal reform, 169, 171; and American Revolution, 346

"Dissertation on the Canon and the Feudal Law" (Adams), 110, 115, 116, 344

Divorce, 288–290, 300, 332, 334, 335. *See also* Annulment

Doggett, Simeon, 126

Doherty, Mary, 220, 221

Dominium, 19, 46–47, 128

Dowries, 247, 303, 331

Drake, George K., 222–224

Drawing and quartering, 131, 190, 205

Dueling, 191

Dulany, Daniel, 116, 117

Duncombe, Giles, 165, 373

Dunster, Henry, 55

Ecclesiastical courts, 298, 308, 312

Education: religious, 20, 21; public, 124–127, 342, 366

Edward VI, 25

Edwards, Jonathan, 64, 69, 70

Elections: parliamentary, 26, 27, 47, 48; and influence of nobles, 27, 28; of children, 32–35

Elizabeth I, 48

Ellsworth, Oliver, 135

English Liberties; or, The Freeborn Subject's Inheritance (Care), 32, 33, 35

Entail, 37–39, 303, 331. *See also* Land: entailed

Epistemology and legal reform, 168–172, 344

Equality: and government by consent, 102, 122, 123, 365, 366; and reason, 341, 343

Essay concerning Human Understanding (Locke), 92–94, 108, 125, 351, 362

Essay upon the Law of Contracts and Agreements (Powell), 280

Essential Rights of Protestants (Williams), 111

Evans, Arise, 32

Evidence: rules of, 147, 160, 164, 165; hearsay, 156, 164, 166, 171, 172, 174

Executors and executrices, 253, 254. *See also* Inheritance

Family: and apprenticeships, 230; and social rank, 230, 231, 246, 296, 297; and parental custody, 232, 282; and guardianship, 233, 234, 340; and inheritance, 235–237, 253, 254, 258, 292, 301, 303, 305–308, 331, 340; and labor agreements, 244, 263, 274–276, 278–280; and poor relief, 257; protection of, 343

Farmer, A. W. (Samuel Seabury), 121

Federalist Papers, 35, 122

Felony, 1, 158, 160, 163, 168, 199, 206

Feme covert, 134, 135, 360, 361

Feudalism, 104–106

Filmer, Robert: on monarchical authority, 22–24, 29, 48, 130, 339; on Parliament, 46; responses to, 88, 91, 98, 99, 103; on parental authority, 92, 98, 333

Finch, Thomas, 114, 115

Fines, 206, 214, 220, 273, 292, 296, 309, 310, 312, 313, 315, 326, 328

Fitzhugh, George, 359

Fitzhugh, William, 173, 290, 337, 371

Forced entry, 206

Forfeiture: of inheritance, 152, 305–306; of property, 190, 191, 313, 314

Forgery, 310

Fortescue, John, 47

Fox, Charles James, 316

Fox, George, 65, 85, 345

Freeman, Samuel, 374

French, Thaddeus P., 221, 222

Gawdy, Francis, 184–186

Gawdy, Thomas, 184–186

George II, 211

George III, 335

Gerson, Jean, 47

Gibson, John Bannister, 327

Gilbert, Geoffrey, 164, 165, 373

Howard, John, 215, 216
Hutcheson, Francis, 127, 352

Ibbetson, James, 320, 321
Illegitimacy, 329, 330
Imperialism, 365
Imprisonment, 152, 182, 183, 185, 186,
    203, 214, 215, 218, 219, 228, 229,
    243, 244, 259, 273, 306, 313, 314
Incest, 159
Indentured servitude, 309–311, 315,
    329, 330, 340
Indentures, 238, 239, 243, 273, 277
Indians. *See* Native Americans
Infant baptism, 65–67, 343; and
    church membership, 50, 68; dis-
    pute over, 51–56, 60–61, 71, 72, 80,
    81; restrictions on, 57–59, 63, 64; of
    grandchildren, 61, 63, 64
Infidelity, 334, 335
Inheritance: and entail, 37–39, 245–
    247, 253, 303, 307, 308, 331; and in-
    testacy, 38, 39; forfeiture of, 152,
    305, 306; and administrator, 253;
    and executor and executrix, 253,
    254; and succession, 340; and estate
    management, 342. *See also* Heredi-
    tary status; Primogeniture; Wills
Institute of the Laws of England (Wood),
    167, 208, 265, 373
Institutes of the Laws of England (Coke),
    31, 162, 169, 176, 179, 246, 247,
    249, 369, 370, 373, 375
Interregnum, 30, 176; and legal re-
    form, 86, 142, 168, 169, 178, 250,
    316; and marriage, 313
Intestacy, 38–39

Jackson, Andrew, 365
James I: on monarchical authority, 21,
    22, 339; on age limits for political of-
    fice, 32; on transported children,
    272; and marriage, 302
James II, 14, 88, 90, 274
Janeway, James, 45, 69
Jefferson, Thomas, 125, 346, 375; on

entail and inheritance, 39; on rea-
    son and political inclusion, 122–
    124; on religious freedom, 123; on
    public education, 126, 127; on cit-
    izenship, 135, 136; on military ser-
    vice and suffrage, 139; on underage
    marriage, 326; on slavery, 355, 356,
    358
Jingle, Bob (pseud.), 119
Johnson, George, 298
Johnson, Herbert A., 371, 372
Judges: and witness testimony, 156–
    159, 172; and legal reform, 170, 174,
    178, 179; and parental authority,
    247–249
Jurors: instructions to, 147, 148, 160,
    172, 199, 221, 223, 224; service as,
    132, 141–148, 169, 338, 339, 342
Justice of the Peace . . . , The (Burn), 167,
    371, 372
Justices of the peace: and criminal in-
    tent, 194; and labor contracts, 244,
    255, 272, 274, 276; and marriage,
    312, 313, 315, 326, 328
Justinian, 164, 165, 196

Kant, Immanuel, 352
Kent, James, 356; on paternal custody,
    262, 263, 282, 284, 285, 364; on
    contracts and children, 266, 268,
    269; on common law marriage,
    327; on women and authority, 364;
    influence of, 374
Kenyon, Lloyd, 266, 267
Kidnapping, 273–275. *See also* Abduc-
    tion
King, Peter, 213
Knight's service, 233, 234, 245, 247,
    258, 295, 306
Knox, John, 360

Labor agreements and contracts, 230,
    244, 256, 263, 271–274, 276–280
Lambarde, William, 370; on jury ser-
    vice, 143; on witness testimony, 163;
    on punishment for crime, 193; on

Lambarde, William (*cont.*)
  understanding and crime, 195, 196, 226
Land: and candidacy, 26; and knight's service, 233, 234, 245, 247; and so-cage, 234, 235, 247, 248, 251, 253; in copyhold, 234, 245, 340; and guardianship, 235, 247, 248, 251; conveyance of, 238–240; preservation of, 245, 246; entailed, 245–247, 253, 303, 307, 308; rented, 249
Language, 147; of the law, 169, 175, 178
Larceny. *See* Theft
Latitudinarianism, 346
Law of Evidence . . . , The (Nelson), 164, 165
Laws
—colonial: on age restrictions for office holding, 17, 18, 30, 31; on religious education, 20; on suffrage and elections, 41, 42; on infant baptism, 56; on military service, 138, 139; on jury service, 144; on marriage, 152, 309–311, 313–315, 324, 328; on witness testimony, 172, 173; on jurisprudence, 184; on lying, 202; on culpability for crime, 202; on slavery, 204; on rioting, 206; on forced entry, 206; on guardianship, 251, 252, 255; on children, 259; on wills, 265; on kidnapping, 273; on indentured servitude, 273, 309, 310; on abduction, 310; on courtship, 312, 313
—federal: on citizenship, 135; on military service, 138
—state: on jury service, 145, 146; on culpability for crime, 220; on labor contracts, 278; on marriage, 324
Legal references: books and manuals, 9, 10, 159, 167, 243, 369–375; for justices of the peace, 142–144, 146, 163, 165, 167, 172, 184, 199, 202, 205, 206, 310, 370, 372, 374
Legal reform: and Whigs, 32, 33, 218; and American Revolution, 37, 219,

220; and Levellers, 41, 169; and Puritan theology, 49, 169, 175; and Interregnum, 86, 142, 168, 169, 178, 250, 316; and Glorious Revolution, 108, 142; Hale and, 168–170, 174, 176–178, 182, 183, 206, 207, 227, 344; epistemology and, 168–172, 344; and Dissenters, 169, 171; and judges, 170, 174, 178, 179; Blackstone and, 174, 178, 179, 215, 344; Coke and, 174–177, 237, 238, 344; and consent, 237, 238; and Charles II, 250
Legh, Peter, 27
Letter to the Public . . . for the Better Preventing Clandestine Marriages, A (anon.), 317, 318
Levellers, 41, 79, 169
Leverett, John, 82, 83
Leviathan (Hobbes), 90
Liability, 342; criminal, 183, 184, 202; contractual, 266–271. *See also* Culpability
Libraries, 371–373
Literacy, 142, 184
Littleton, Thomas, 247, 268, 334; on homage and fealty, 133, 134; on guardianship, 236, 247; on land, 240, 248, 249
Locke, John, 3, 4, 14, 15, 88, 107, 108, 126, 320, 343, 346; on church membership, 72, 73; on child rearing, 79, 80; on government by consent, 91, 92, 226; on parental authority, 92, 93, 130, 226, 281, 283, 321, 333, 334; on slavery, 93; on consent and reason, 93–97, 127, 281; on women, 96, 97, 103, 362; and education of children, 97, 98, 124, 351; influence of, 97, 108, 110, 111, 113, 125, 136, 171, 226, 320, 321, 351, 352; on 1689 settlement, 106; and language, 147; on hereditary status and slavery, 352–355
London, City of, 235, 241, 272

Lords, House of: and young members, 26, 31; and marriage, 314, 316, 326

Lordship, 339–341

Lovejoy, Arthur O., 75

Ludwell, Jane, 28

Ludwell, Philip, 28

Luther, Martin, 301

Lying, 202

Maccarty, John, 197, 198, 200

Madison, James, 35, 122, 356, 357

Maine, Henry, 6, 7, 231, 232

Manslaughter, 190–192, 204

Marriage, 1, 168, 169, 196, 233, 234, 247, 290; coerced, 150–154, 292, 298, 300–302, 305–307; clandestine, 152, 294, 297, 298, 301, 308–310, 313, 314, 316, 317, 327–329; vows in, 238, 239, 288, 292, 297–301, 313, 327–330; unconsummated, 288, 289, 300; voidability of, 291, 298, 299, 301, 314, 316, 322, 324, 325, 335; as contract, 291, 298, 318–320, 322, 325, 330, 332, 333, 335; and county court, 288–290; arranged, 292, 293, 295, 296, 299, 302, 334; and attraction, 292, 293, 301, 311, 318, 333; in literature, 293, 294, 336; and banns, 298, 308, 309, 323, 329; illegal, 308–310, 313, 315, 326; licenses for, 309, 310, 314, 323, 328, 329; common law, 327

Marriage acts. See Parliament: Acts of, on marriage

Marshall, John, 270

Marshall, Stephen, 71

Martin, James, 134, 135

Martin, Joseph Plumb, 129

Martin v Massachusetts, 134

Martyrs, Book of (John Foxe), 50

Mary I, 89, 90, 308

Maryland, 212, 328, 330

Mason, George, 34, 43

Massachusetts, 1, 30, 134, 135, 344, 346; and estate law, 38; and suffrage, 41, 42, 44; and infant baptism, 56; and military service, 129, 138, 148; and jury service, 144, 145, 148; criminal prosecution in, 156, 157, 160, 172, 184, 202, 203, 219–221; and families, 251, 252, 257, 258; and labor contracts, 256, 271, 278, 279; and disciplining children, 259; and contracts for land, 265; and kidnapped children, 273; and patriarchalism, 305; marriage in, 305, 309, 312, 313, 324, 326–328, 330; and abduction, 311; and slavery, 330; and democracy, 345; General Court of, 369, 370; and legal texts, 369–371, 374

Massachusetts Body of Liberties, 202, 251, 252

Mather, Cotton, 82

Mather, Increase, 80, 81

Mather, Richard, 58, 59, 80

Mayhew, Jonathan, 112

Maynwaring, Roger, 22

Military service, 129, 131, 132, 134, 137, 148; for convicted criminals, 5, 211, 212; and parental consent, 129, 138, 139; coerced, 137, 138; and suffrage, 139, 140; failure to prepare for, 193

Milk for Babes Drawn out of the Breasts of Both Testaments . . . (Cotton), 80

Milton, John, 101, 102

Minow, Martha, 287

Misadventure, death by, 187, 190, 191, 227

Monck, Christopher, 26–28, 197, 198

Montesquieu, 108, 125, 179, 218, 261

Moore, Peter, 181

Morris, Gouverneur, 42, 43, 121, 128, 237

Mulattos, 172, 173

Murder, 5, 155, 156, 159, 190–199, 204, 220, 224, 225, 227, 229

Murray, Judith Sargent, 363

Murray, William, Lord Mansfield, 282

Native Americans, 172, 173, 222, 365

Natural law, 75, 76, 171, 177, 179, 261,

Natural law (*cont.*)
262, 280, 287. *See also* Grotius,
Hugo; Locke, John; Pufendorf, Samuel von; Suárez, Francisco
Nelson, William, 164, 370, 371
New England: and infant baptism, 54–57, 64; and conversion of children, 69; and criminal prosecution, 159; and paternal control, 303, 331; and social change, 343, 344; and Congregationalists, 347. *See also* Massachusetts
New Hampshire, 159
New Jersey, 160, 222, 269, 364
New York, 259, 326, 327
Nobility, 26, 27
Norcott, John, 55
North Carolina, 364

Oaths, 132–134, 148, 154, 157–160, 163, 166, 167, 172, 173, 220, 222
Obedience, 2, 19, 20
Oceana (Harrington), 32, 98
Office and Authority of a Justice of Peace (Webb), 143, 153, 167, 173, 259, 371
Office holding by children, 1, 17, 18, 26–28, 342
Of the Laws of Ecclesiastical Polity (Hooker), 76, 77
Otis, James, 113, 117, 118
Owen, John, 77
Oxenbridge, John, 62

Paine, Thomas, 29, 109, 110, 122, 218, 346
Pardon, 186, 191, 194, 198, 201, 206, 207, 209–211, 225
Parents: authority of, 84, 92, 93, 98, 103, 104, 111, 119, 130, 226, 236, 247–249, 261–262, 281, 283, 321, 333, 334; consent of, 129, 138, 139; punishment by, 202, 203, 258–260; and custody, 232, 282; obligations of, 260, 261; and parental rights of slaves, 263–269; concern of, for children, 351

Parke, Daniel, 17, 28
Parker, James, 374
Parker, Samuel, 77
Parliament, 1, 342; age restrictions for, 30, 31; and consent, 46–48. *See also* Commons, House of; Lords, House of
—Acts of: on age restrictions for office holding, 18, 30; repeal of, 31, 178, 314; on suffrage, 41; on religious uniformity, 66, 177; on jury service, 142; on abduction, 152, 153, 306, 307, 310; on rape, 155; on English in court proceedings, 178; on exempting children from prosecution, 193; on transportation of criminals, 211, 212; on criminal statistics of children, 215; on penitentiaries, 215, 218; on apprenticeships, 243, 244, 251, 260; on paternal authority, 250, 261, 262; on kidnapping, 274; on marriage, 313, 314, 316, 317, 319, 321–323, 325, 326, 335
Parsons, Theophilus, 289, 328
Patriarchalism, 16, 21–24, 103; and status relationships, 4, 29; Allestree on, 84, 304, 305, 311; and American Revolution, 112, 113; and marriage, 305
Patriots of North-America . . . , The (anon.), 120
Penitentiaries, 183, 215, 218, 219, 229
Penn, William, 33, 42
Pennsylvania, 1, 33, 344, 346; and entail, 38, 303; and suffrage, 41, 42, 44, 139; and oath taking, 134; and military service, 134, 138, 139, 148; jury service in, 143–146; criminal prosecution in, 158, 165, 172, 205, 206, 220; criminal reform in, 216, 229; and estate administration, 254; and guardianship, 254, 255; and families, 258; and disciplining children, 259; and labor contracts, 263, 275–277, 279; and kidnapped children, 273; and apprenticeships, 278; and

Roman law, 164, 171, 176, 196, 261, 348

Romeo and Juliet (Shakespeare), 293, 294

Rousseau, Jean-Jacques, 108, 127, 352, 363

Rule from Heaven (Evans), 32

Rush, Benjamin, 125, 216, 218

Rye House Plot (1683), 14, 88

Saint-German, Christopher, 194, 196, 373

Salem witch trials, 156, 184, 202, 203

Savoy Declaration of Faith, 63, 64

Sayer, Joseph, 320

Seabury, Samuel, 112, 121

Sedition, 225, 229

Selden, John, 176

Shakespeare, William, 24, 25, 293, 294, 348

Shapiro, Barbara, 171

Sharp, Samuel, 254, 255

Sharpe, Thomas, 185, 186

Shepe, John, 185, 186

Sheriffs, 143, 146

Shooter, Charles, 211

Sibthorp, Robert, 22

Sidney, Algernon, 3, 13–15, 42, 88, 107, 108, 343, 346; on primogeniture, 29, 99; on women, 103

Slaves and slavery: hereditary, 5, 353, 354, 357; and oath taking, 134; and witness testimony, 172, 173; and criminal prosecution, 225, 228; and white labor contracts, 231; and parental rights, 263, 264; and marriage, 311, 330; depiction of, 348, 350; as punishment, 353–354; and equation with children, 355–359; and ability to reason, 355, 356, 358, 359; and education, 357

Smith, Thomas, 242, 296

Socage, 234, 235, 247, 248, 251, 253, 254, 260

Sociology for the South (Fitzhugh), 359

Somers, John, 100, 101

Somerset, Charles, 27

Some Thoughts concerning Education (Locke), 97

Southard, Samuel, 269

South Carolina, 263, 264, 366

Spelman, Henry, 105

Stanford, William, 163, 195, 370

Status, 6; and primogeniture, 23; and political office, 26–28, 36; and political inclusion, 119, 120; and punishment for crime, 186, 193, 197, 198, 227; and guardianship, 236, 237; and contracts, 243–246, 272, 276, 277; and land ownership, 245; and marriage, 293, 295, 296, 299, 300, 302, 303, 306, 307, 311–313, 316, 325, 326, 331, 336; and authority, 341. *See also* Hereditary status

Stebbing, Henry, 319–322

Stocks, 205, 220

Stoddard, Solomon, 64

Story, Joseph, 269, 282

Stuart, Phoebe, 1

Stubbes, Philip, 296, 297

Suárez, Francisco, 16

Subjectship, 131–133

Suffrage, 1, 366; qualification for, 40–44, 139, 140; and criminal responsibility, 183; for free blacks, 364

Suicide, 189–191, 205

Supreme Court of the United States, 147, 148, 270

Supreme courts, state, 147, 148

Swearing, 205, 220

Swinburne, Henry, 241, 248, 253

Taft, William Howard, 365

Taylor, Jeremy, 147

Ten Commandments, 19, 20, 85, 103, 107, 108

Tennessee, 159, 220, 221

Testimony. *See* Witness testimony

Theft, 185, 186, 193, 196–201, 206, 211, 212, 221, 244, 304

Titles and political office, 26, 36

Tocqueville, Alexis de, 344, 345